MW00642145

"If theology is the study of God and all other things in relation to God, then the focus of a doctrine of creation is 'all other things.' This is a tall order and one reason why it is difficult to come up with a list of masterpieces on the subject. This book ranges widely, covering topics from food to philosophy, but always in relation to the goodness of God, the created order, and its implications for humanity. The authors show convincingly that there is nothing in the world to which God the Creator cannot rightly declare, 'Mine, and for my glory!'"

Kevin J. Vanhoozer, research professor of systematic theology at Trinity Evangelical Divinity School

"This book is dazzling in its sources and range, and it is rigorous and provocative in its judgments. Grounded in a solidly Reformed outlook derived primarily from Barth and Kuyper, the authors evaluate the doctrine of creation and related realities such as sin, providence, and eschatology with attention to biblical texts and scholarship, to the whole of the theological tradition, and to philosophy from Plato to the French phenomenologists. They defend Christian faith in creation with power and panache."

Matthew Levering, James N. and Mary D. Perry Jr. Chair of Theology at Mundelein Seminary

"Here is a faithfully Reformed yet distinctly contemporary work on the doctrine of creation. It is a welcome addition to the badly needed, and now happily emerging, literature applying the giants of the neo-Calvinist tradition to issues of doctrine for the English-speaking world. But it is no sleepy doctrinal tome. This is a book of theology that answers questions the church is actually asking. Widely read, richly cited, and ecumenically minded, Ashford and Bartholomew mine the Reformed tradition at its best and place its treasures before the church and the academy to correct, challenge, and continue our work in the theater of God's glory."

Jessica Joustra, Redeemer University

"Learned, erudite, and comprehensive, this monumental dogmatic exploration follows the contours of the Christian creeds to formulate a neo-Kuyperian dogmatic account of creation. This work has the capacity to be a theological classic. Through close engagement with ancient and modern Christian thought, Ashford and Bartholomew retrieve the past, assess the present, and offer a fresh, constructive, and thoroughly biblical presentation of God and the totality of the created order. Some may disagree with their presentation of the doctrine, but no one will be able to ignore it. I pray this work establishes a renaissance of the doctrine of creation for our day."

Heath A. Thomas, president and professor of Old Testament at Oklahoma Baptist University

"A fresh, in-depth presentation of the biblical doctrine of creation. Ashford and Bartholomew write from the perspective of Kuyperian thought, with a commitment to exegetical warrant and catholic sympathy. This is the kind of theology we need more of!"

Timothy George, distinguished professor of divinity at Beeson Divinity School of Samford University and general editor of the twenty-eight-volume Reformation Commentary on Scripture

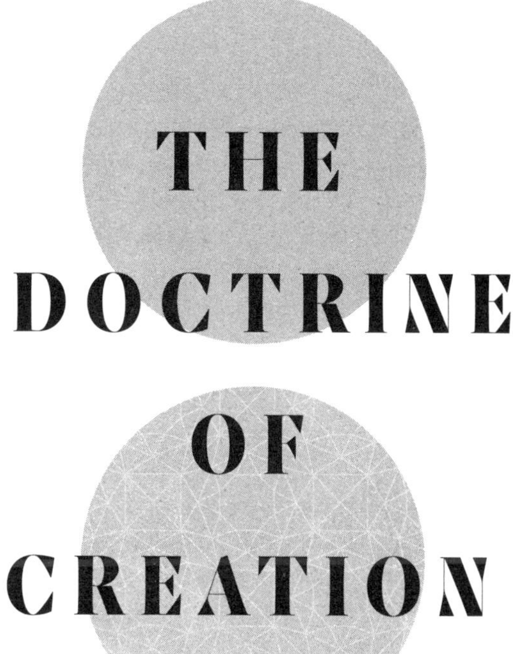

THE DOCTRINE OF CREATION

A CONSTRUCTIVE KUYPERIAN APPROACH

Bruce Riley Ashford and

Craig G. Bartholomew

An imprint of InterVarsity Press
Downers Grove, Illinois

InterVarsity Press
P.O. Box 1400, Downers Grove, IL 60515-1426
ivpress.com
email@ivpress.com

InterVarsity Press® is the book-publishing division of InterVarsity Christian Fellowship/USA®, a movement of students and faculty active on campus at hundreds of universities, colleges, and schools of nursing in the United States of America, and a member movement of the International Fellowship of Evangelical Students. For information about local and regional activities, visit intervarsity.org.

Figure 8.1. Hans Holbein, The Ambassadors, *National Gallery, London / Wikimedia Commons*

Cover design and image composite: David Fassett
Interior design: Daniel van Loon
Image: kraft paper texture: © Getty Images

ISBN 978-0-8308-5490-5 (print)
ISBN 978-0-8308-5491-2 (digital)

Printed in the United States of America ♾

InterVarsity Press is committed to ecological stewardship and to the conservation of natural resources in all our operations. This book was printed using sustainably sourced paper.

Library of Congress Cataloging-in-Publication Data
A catalog record for this book is available from the Library of Congress.

P *25 24 23 22 21 20 19 18 17 16 15 14 13 12 11 10 9 8 7 6 5 4 3 2 1*

Y *39 38 37 36 35 34 33 32 31 30 29 28 27 26 25 24 23 22 21 20*

Dedicated with thanks and hope to the Kirby Laing Foundation in the UK

for their generous and ongoing support of our work.

CONTENTS

PREFACE

In recent decades Western culture has undergone radical changes, while in the Majority World we are witnessing an astonishing revival of religion. Given the contextual nature of the theological task, Christian dogmatics must therefore now refresh its interface with Western and global culture. In so doing, it must maintain continuity with the faith "once for all delivered to the saints." And, as Alasdair MacIntyre has argued, all such scholarship necessarily operates out of a tradition and develops from and in this tradition. Clifford Anderson notes that Abraham Kuyper and Karl Barth may have been "the greatest Reformed minds of the nineteenth and the twentieth century respectively."[1] As will be apparent, we have great respect for Karl Barth, and his work is a major dialogue partner in this volume. However, the tradition in which we work and in which this book is positioned is that of Dutch neo-Calvinism, or what is commonly called the Kuyperian tradition, named after Abraham Kuyper (1837–1920).[2]

The Kuyperian tradition is an orthodox Christian tradition that we see as entirely congruent with our evangelicalism. Craig is an Anglican and Bruce a Baptist. Both of us discovered the Kuyperian tradition as evangelicals and have found it to be incredibly enriching and relevant for today. We have never experienced the Kuyperian tradition as restrictive and have found it to be a fertile place from which to engage fully with other traditions and to learn all we can from them. We hope that is clear in this volume, in which we lean on the rich tradition of reflection on creation down through the ages. In recent decades the Kuyperian tradition has made immense strides in philosophy, but far less so in theology. The only recent English systematic theology in the Kuyperian (Dooyeweerdian) tradition is the one-volume

[1]Clifford Blake Anderson, "Jesus and the 'Christian Worldview': A Comparative Analysis of Abraham Kuyper and Karl Barth," *Cultural Encounters* 2, no. 2 (2006): 61.

[2]Michael Goheen and Craig developed a one-page outline of the core elements of this tradition, and you can find that in the appendix. Cf. also Craig. G. Bartholomew, *Contours of the Kuyperian Tradition: A Systematic Introduction* (Downers Grove, IL: InterVarsity Press, 2017).

work by Gordon Spykman, *Reformational Theology: A New Paradigm for Doing Dogmatics*.[3]

This book (along with further volumes possibly to follow) is thus designed to explore and develop the rich resources of the Kuyperian tradition for contemporary systematic theology. The doctrine of creation is central to the Kuyperian tradition, but remarkably the tradition has not produced a major doctrine of creation. Thus, we are delighted to contribute toward filling this gap.

Above we quoted Anderson's comparison of Barth and Kuyper. Of course, as Anderson notes, there are important differences between them. One vital thing they have in common is their engagement with Scripture. Nowadays it is rare to find theologians like Karl Barth, who, as his theological framework takes hold, does more and not less exegesis. Kuyper, too, is exemplary in this respect. His three-volume classic, *Common Grace*, published in English by Lexham Press, devotes the first volume to common grace *in Scripture*, before he moves on to theology and its application. Our aim here is to do theology in deep engagement with Scripture, as do Kuyper and Barth. This is exceptionally hard work, and readers will often find detailed exegesis in subsections, much like in Barth's *Church Dogmatics*. Scripture, and not our or any other tradition, has final authority when it comes to theology. Barth is in many ways the father of contemporary theological interpretation, and we welcome this renaissance and seek to embody its springtime in biblical interpretation in our work.[4]

Indeed, we learned from Calvin that a role of theology is to help Christians read their Bibles better. This, after all, is why he wrote his *Institutes*. In our view this is particularly true of the doctrine of creation. As the first act in the great drama of Scripture,[5] creation is fundamental to all that follows, and our reading of the Bible will inevitably be deficient without a robust, biblical doctrine of creation. Our hope is that a doctrine of creation that engages deeply with Scripture will similarly enrich contemporary biblical interpretation.

The Kuyperian tradition is known for being wonderfully trinitarian and Christocentric.[6] Another distinctive of the tradition is the way it carries

---

[3]Gordon J. Spykman, *Reformational Theology: A New Paradigm for Doing Dogmatics* (Grand Rapids, MI: Eerdmans, 1992). However, we are glad to report that Cornelis van der Kooi and Gijsbert van den Brink's one-volume *Christian Dogmatics: An Introduction* (Grand Rapids, MI: Eerdmans, 2017) is now available in English.

[4]See Craig G. Bartholomew and Heath A. Thomas, eds., *A Manifesto for Theological Interpretation* (Grand Rapids, MI: Baker Academic, 2016).

[5]See Craig G. Bartholomew and Michael W. Goheen, *The Drama of Scripture: Finding Our Place in the Biblical Story*, 2nd ed. (Grand Rapids, MI: Baker Academic, 2014).

[6]David Bosch notes, for example, that Kuyper was the first to root mission in the doctrine of the Trinity (Bartholomew, *Contours of the Kuyperian Tradition*, 182).

through the comprehensive range of creation in its work and vision. This is one reason we regard this tradition as so important for today. Especially in our final chapter, readers will get a sense of how the doctrine of creation opens out into area after area of contemporary life. It was for good reasons that Barth situated ethics under the doctrine of creation in his *Church Dogmatics*. In our view, if we are to facilitate a depth of engagement of the gospel with contemporary culture, as Lesslie Newbigin called for repeatedly, then something like the Kuyperian tradition is urgently needed.

Theology is vital for the life of the church. Theologians reflect on Scripture and seek to articulate and develop the core beliefs of Scripture and thus of the church in dialogue with their contexts. Every generation needs to do this afresh as new challenges and questions arise, drawing on Scripture and the great tradition of Christian thought. Our hope is that this volume will contribute to a renewed appreciation for and appropriation of the doctrine of creation. There is much at stake in this regard. Indeed, it is hard to see how Christians today will rise to the many challenges for public theology and ethics without a robust, biblical doctrine of creation.

It should be noted that unlike much contemporary work on creation, we have resisted making contemporary science our major dialogue partner. We do turn to science in the final chapter but only briefly. Our goal is the development of a constructive, biblical doctrine of creation, and in our view a next step would be deep engagement with science.

We are grateful to acknowledge the help of Craig's research assistants, Keegan Lodder and Mark Standish, and Bruce's research assistant, Dennis Greeson. We are delighted to dedicate this book to the Kirby Laing Foundation. They generously funded Craig's postdoctoral work and continue to support our work through the Kirby Laing Institute for Christian Ethics with remarkable grace.

ACKNOWLEDGMENTS

THIS BOOK HAS its origins in an informal gathering of scholar-friends at Craig's former home in Hamilton, Ontario, where we identified the need for constructive theology as a priority. We are grateful to Michael Goheen, Heath Thomas, and David Beldman, who joined us for that weekend. A donor kindly funded a small gathering of like-minded scholars in Princeton, at which we were able to share an early version of some of our work. The KLICE Scripture Collective provides an incredibly rich context in which to do our work, for which we remain so grateful. In 2019 Bruce was granted a sabbatical by SEBTS, and in 2019–2020 Craig was a senior research fellow at the Carl Henry Center at Trinity International University. We are grateful to both institutions for their support in this work. IVP Academic has been a joy to work with. This book was commissioned when Dan Reid and David Congdon were at IVP; it has been brought to completion under Jon Boyd and the sterling work of Rebecca Carhart, Ryan Davis, Elissa Schauer, Sheila Urban, Dan van Loon, and their teams. Community is at the heart of the KLICE Scripture Collective, and this work has emerged out of a deep friendship within that context, for which we both give thanks.

ABBREVIATIONS

ANF	*Ante-Nicene Fathers*
CD	Karl Barth, *Church Dogmatics*. Edited by G. W. Bromiley and T. F. Torrance. Translated by G. W. Bromiley et al. 4 vols. Edinburgh: T&T Clark, 1958.
CTJ	*Calvin Theological Journal*
ESV	English Standard Version
IJST	*International Journal of Systematic Theology*
JETS	*Journal of the Evangelical Theological Society*
JSOT	*Journal for the Study of the Old Testament*
LXX	Septuagint
MT	Masoretic Text
NICNT	New International Commentary on the New Testament
NICOT	New International Commentary on the Old Testament
NIGTC	New International Greek Testament Commentary
NIV	New International Version
NRSV	New Revised Standard Version
NPNF[1]	*Nicene and Post-Nicene Fathers*, Series 1
NPNF[2]	*Nicene and Post-Nicene Fathers*, Series 2
PNTC	Pillar New Testament Commentary
ST	Thomas Aquinas, *Summa Theologiae*
WBC	Word Biblical Commentary

INTRODUCTION

We begin at an unusual place in Scripture for a doctrine of creation—namely, the well-known story of Peter's disowning of Jesus in Mark 14:66-72. What, you might wonder, could this searing account of Peter's betrayal of Jesus possibly have to do with the doctrine of creation? A great deal, as it turns out. In his extraordinary work *Mimesis*, written while in exile in Istanbul, Erich Auerbach (1892–1957) uses *this* story to illustrate, by comparison with extracts from Petronius's (AD 27–66) *Satyricon* and Tacitus's (AD 56–117) *Annals*, the limits of realism in antiquity, limits overcome by Jewish-Christian literature, of which Mark 14 is his major example.[1]

Auerbach argues that "a scene like Peter's denial fits into no antique genre. It is too serious for comedy, too contemporary and everyday for tragedy, politically too insignificant for history—and the form which was given it is one of such immediacy that its like does not exist in the literature of antiquity."[2] The representation of Peter is entirely realistic; it is filled with tension and heart-breaking betrayal and presents us, through the experience of this humble fisherman, with the image of the human person in the deepest, highest, and most tragic sense. Such realism is incompatible with the style of antiquity, in which it could only be thought of as farce or comedy but is in fact neither. As Auerbach notes, "It portrays something which neither the poets nor the historians of antiquity ever set out to portray: the birth of a spiritual movement in the depths of the common people, from within the everyday occurrences of contemporary life, which thus assumes an importance it could never have assumed in antique literature."[3]

And this feature is not unique to the story of Peter's disavowal of Jesus. Peter and the other characters in the New Testament are caught up in a

---

[1]Erich Auerbach, *Mimesis: The Representation of Reality in Western Literature*, 50th anniversary ed. (Princeton, NJ: Princeton University Press, 2003), 24-76.

[2]Ibid., 45.

[3]Ibid., 42-43.

universal movement that gradually emerges into the foreground of history. What the New Testament shows is the unfolding of historical forces:

> What we see here is a world which on the one hand is entirely real, average, identifiable as to place, time, and circumstances, but which on the other hand is shaken in its very foundations, is transforming and renewing itself before our eyes. For the New Testament authors who are their contemporaries, these occurrences on the plane of everyday life assume the importance of world-revolutionary events, as later on they will for everyone.[4]

How, one is compelled to ask, did the authors of the Gospels capture this ethos and thereby transform realism in literature? Remarkably—for, as Auerbach noted, "I am a Prussian and of the Jewish faith"[5]—he locates the source of this major shift in representation in the incarnation:

> It was graphically and harshly dramatized through God's incarnation in a human being of the humblest social station, through his existence on earth amid humble everyday people and conditions, and through his Passion which, judged by earthly standards, was ignominious; and it naturally came to have . . . a most decisive bearing upon man's conception of the tragic and the sublime.[6]

Not surprisingly, there has been considerable discussion of Auerbach's work in literary circles.[a] His work is part of the "romance philology" of the early and mid-twentieth century, and the sort of realism it advocates has not always fared well amidst the changes in literary studies since then. However, as A. D. Nuttall observes, "Auerbach's book survives. When a writer is honest and learned and intelligent, he deserves to survive. Since 1946 criticism has deviated from lines laid down by Auerbach and has contested many of his assertions. Again and again he emerges from the dust and confusion in somewhat better shape than his attackers."[b]

Robert Doran notes that *Mimesis* can be read alongside modern histories of religion such as Marcel Gauchet's *The Disenchantment of the World: A Political History of Religion*.[c] For Gauchet, Christianity contains the seed of the modern secular state. By bringing transcendence down to earth, Christianity allowed the state to emerge, which then gradually divests itself of otherworldly reference, leading to secularism. Doran suggests that Auerbach can be read similarly, but in our view this is not the case and certainly

---

[4]Ibid., 43.

[5]Quoted by Edward Said, introduction to Auerbach, *Mimesis*, xvii.

[6]Auerbach, *Mimesis*, 41. Ian A. McFarland argues that "the doctrine of the incarnation . . . is arguably the key to a specifically Christian understanding of creation from nothing." *From Nothing: A Theology of Creation* (Louisville, KY: Westminster John Knox, 2014), 107.

not true of Christianity. Suffice it to note that the way in which in the Gospels "low-born, anonymous individuals are represented with dignity and nobility, in effect performing aesthetically the religious ideas expounded in the text,"[d] leads logically in the opposite direction to secularism—namely, to a world "charged with the grandeur of God."[e]

[a]E.g., A. D. Nuttall, "Auerbach's Mimesis," *Essays in Criticism* 54, no. 1 (2004): 60-74; Galili Shahar, "Auerbach's Scars: Judaism and the Question of Literature," *Jewish Quarterly Review* 101, no. 4 (2011): 604-30; Robert Doran, "Literary History and the Sublime in Erich Auerbach's 'Mimesis,'" *New Literary History* 38, no. 2 (2007): 353-69.
[b]Nuttall, "Auerbach's Mimesis," 72.
[c]Doran, "Literary History," 361.
[d]Ibid., 362.
[e]Gerard Manley Hopkins, *The Major Works, Including All the Poems and Selected Prose* (Oxford: Oxford University Press, 1986, 2002), 128.

The incarnation is inextricably intertwined with the doctrine of creation, as, for example, John's prologue to his Gospel makes clear. Early on in his classic *On the Incarnation*, Athanasius likewise observes that "as we give an account of this [the incarnation], it is first necessary to speak about the creation of the universe and its maker, God, so that one may thus worthily reflect that its recreation was accomplished by the Word who created it in the beginning. For it will appear not at all contradictory if the Father works its salvation in the same one by whom he created it."[7] It is the biblical doctrine of creation and its extraordinary correlate in the incarnation that links the particular and the universal, that infuses the ordinary and the concrete with the presence of the divine, that unleashes historical forces with eternal significance, that creates the context for a drama of this earthy, visceral, concrete, everyday world in which God is the chief actor and in which we are invited to participate.

Auerbach's work helps to defamiliarize us with the doctrine of creation, which we too often take for granted. Approaching our world through the lens of creation is radical in our late modern context and provides fresh perspectives on area after area of life. For example, we would not quickly associate creation with a revolution in representation in literature, and yet that is precisely what, according to Auerbach, we find in the Gospels, indeed in the whole Bible. Much recent work on Christian spirituality has likewise recognized the role of the ordinary, the everyday, and this too is rooted in creation.

From this fresh perspective we can see how right Karl Barth was when he wrote, "But it is a great and special thing to have and to confess the belief: *credo in Deum . . . creatorem coeli et terrae.*"[8] The doctrine of creation is like

[7]Athanasius, *On the Incarnation*, trans. John Behr (Yonkers, NY: St. Vladimir's Seminary Press, 2011), 53.
[8]Barth, *CD* III/1, 8.

Moses and the burning bush; it is one before which we should take off our shoes, for we stand on holy ground. Appropriated by faith in "the One who, according to the Easter story, goes through closed doors,"[9] this doctrine enables us to break through the closed doors of a jaded, mute secularism and of a sub-Christian sacred-secular dualism in order to begin to see the world for what it really is—namely, the creation in which, as Gerard Manley Hopkins pointed out, Christ plays in ten thousand places.[10] The doctrine of creation should be approached in a spirit of worship and awe because thereby we enter the spirit in which it will be celebrated for all eternity:

> You are worthy, our Lord and God,
>   to receive glory and honor and power,
> for you created all things,
>   and by your will they existed and were created. (Rev 4:11)

Our Approach

The doctrine of creation is something we appropriate by faith and thus confess rather than reason toward. Accordingly, we begin in chapter one with an examination of the confession of creation in the Apostles' and Nicene Creeds and the central issues that emerge from this confession. The doctrine of creation has a long history in the life of the church through the ages, for better and for worse, and in chapters two and three we trace key moments and theologians in this history, one that we describe as both travail and glory.

In chapter four we attend to the source of creation in God as the *Father Almighty* and to the one attribute identified by the creeds, his omnipotence. God creates heaven and earth, two primary places, and chapters five through seven focus on the furnishing of the earth (chap. 5), the diverse "inhabitants" and places of the earthly realm (chap. 6), and the heavenly realm (chap. 7).

Genesis 1:1–2:3 has two peaks, the creation of humankind and God's resting on the seventh day. Chapter eight attends to that second peak, focusing on Sabbath, as well as the fall and what we call "misdirection." Part of humankind's vocation is to develop the potentials built into the creation to the glory of God, what we call the creation mandate, and we attend to creation and that delightful work of culture making in chapter nine. God's work with his creation does not cease once it has come into existence, and in chapter ten we

---

[9]Barth, *CD* III/1, 4.
[10]Hopkins, *Major Works*, 129.

deal with providence. This is intimately related to God's economy, his goal or telos for his creation, and we focus on this in chapter eleven.

Creation is utterly comprehensive and therefore has implications for all of life as God has made it. Much of this cannot be dealt with in this volume. Nevertheless, in chapter twelve we provide a series of caveats, exploring the doctrine in various directions to show its fertility and relevance.

I/WE BELIEVE

THE DOCTRINE OF CREATION AS AN ARTICLE OF FAITH

THE CREEDS ARE WONDERFUL, compressed statements that need to be recovered, celebrated, and appropriated afresh today. Consider an analogy with a large-scale map. If you love your country, then you will understand the value of a such a map enabling you to see the overarching shape of the land in which you live. Similarly, the creeds map for us the great and indispensable landmarks of the geography of Christian belief.

Their indispensability is revealed in the pages of church history. J. N. D. Kelly's *Early Christian Creeds* probably remains the standard work in English on the history of the early creeds. Reading Kelly, it is fascinating to navigate the origins of the creeds in the Old Testament and New Testament and developments among the early church fathers and on toward the medieval era. Kelly rightly notes that "the creeds of Christendom have never been dry-as-dust documents. . . . They have been theological manifestos, shot through with doctrinal significance and sometimes deeply stained with the marks of controversy."[1]

Luke Timothy Johnson alerts us to the importance of the creed for today. "I think that the Christian creed enunciates a powerful and provocative understanding of the world, one that ought to scandalize a world that runs on the accepted truths of Modernity."[2] He notes that at least from the mid-nineteenth century onward, part of being an intellectual has involved a distaste for creeds, especially those of Christianity. Indeed, "for Modernity, belief in a creed is a sign of intellectual failure."[3] Johnson rightly notes that

[1]J. N. D. Kelly, *Early Christian Creeds*, 3rd ed. (1972; repr., London: Routledge, 2014), 131.
[2]Luke Timothy Johnson, *The Creed: What Christians Believe and Why It Matters* (New York: Doubleday, 2005), 7.
[3]Ibid., 2.

when we reflect on the creed, we ought to bear such cultured despisers of the faith in mind because we live in modernity, and even many believers who recite the creeds weekly espouse the worldview of modernity without realizing it.

Johnson helpfully discerns three functions of the creed: it is a personal and communal profession of faith, it is a rule of faith, and it provides a definition of faith. As he asserts, the provision of a definition of faith remains vital today. When Christians say the creed, we affirm certain truths and commit ourselves to live by them. In so doing we reject other beliefs that many of our contemporaries believe to be true. Being a Christian means consciously espousing a specific worldview and the concomitant practices of the church as one seeks to embody that worldview in daily life.

Faith is a way of knowing reality, and Christians ought to insist on the realism entailed in our confession. Faith connects us with the true shape of the world and is not "less real" than the limited but impressive "ways of knowing by which the wheels of the world's empirical engine are kept spinning."[4] We need formative practices that establish us again and again in a view of the world that includes "all that is, seen and unseen."

As we begin our immersion into the doctrine of creation, the creeds thus position us within the heart of the one, holy, catholic, and apostolic church. They provide us with a large-scale map of the geography of Christian doctrine, and it is no mistake that they begin immediately with creation. The Apostles' Creed begins,

> I believe in God, the Father almighty,
> creator of heaven and earth.

The Nicene-Constantinopolitan Creed begins,

> We believe in one God,
> the Father, the Almighty,
> maker of heaven and earth,
> of all that is, seen and unseen.

Our concern in this volume is that act of creation with which the creeds begin. Donald Wood points out that the first article of the Nicene Creed draws three relations to our attention:

[4]Ibid., 101.

- the relation between the Father, "the maker of all things," and the Son, "through whom all things came to be"
- the relation between God and creation
- the relation between heaven and earth[5]

To the relationship between Father and Son, we would add the equally significant relation between them *and the Spirit* as the source and giver of life. Implicitly the Apostles' Creed and explicitly the Nicene Creed see the act of creation as that of the triune God. In chapter four—and throughout—we will attend to the trinitarian nature of God as creator. The third relation is dealt with in chapter seven. Here we will focus on the second relation.

The Nicene Creed originated in the fourth century AD out of the Council of Nicaea and the Council of Constantinople. A delightful tradition arose of linking the Apostles' Creed directly to the apostles,[a] but it is in fact later than the Nicene Creed, originating in the eighth century. However, the Apostles' Creed is a descendant of the much earlier Roman Creed or Symbol.

Creedal language has its origins in both Old Testament and New. Gerhard von Rad drew attention to creedal statements in the Hexateuch (Deut 26:5-10; 6:12-24; Josh 24:2-13) as the basis from which the larger narratives were developed. Von Rad noted that there is no mention in these creeds of the Sinai event, nor of creation, both of which he argued were added later. He found similar, albeit later, historical summaries in Psalms 78, 105, and 136, of which he observed, "These historical summaries in hymn form are still thoroughly confessional in kind."[b]

Von Rad did us a disservice in making creation subsidiary and secondary to redemption. He also failed to refer to one of the most significant creedal statements in the Old Testament—namely, the Shema in Deuteronomy 6:4. With its emphasis on God as "one"—the only God and the only one to whom Israel owes allegiance—the Shema's influence on the Nicene Creed may be seen in the opening line and in "one Lord." Just as creation is implicit in the one-clause christological creedal statements we find in the New Testament, such as "Jesus is Lord," so too is it implicit in the Old Testament creedal statements.

We cannot here discuss the development of creedal statements in any detail, and readers are referred to the major works in this area.[c] Suffice it to note that in the New Testament creation is implicit in the one-clause christological creedal statements but explicit in some of the two-clause ones. Particularly noteworthy are the following: "Yet for us there is one God, the Father, from whom are all things and for whom we exist, and one Lord, Jesus Christ, through whom are all things and through whom we

[5]Donald Wood, "Maker of Heaven and Earth," *IJST* 14, no. 4 (2012): 381-95.

exist" (1 Cor 8:6), and "In the presence of God, who gives life to all things, and of Christ Jesus, who in his testimony before Pontius Pilate made the good confession, I charge you . . ." (1 Tim 6:13).

The same foundational emphasis on creation is found throughout the church fathers, a study of whose doctrines of creation makes for a research feast. Creedal language among the Fathers has its origins in baptismal formulae and in catechetical instruction. One of the earliest and most famous is found in *Shepherd of Hermas* 2: "First of all, believe that God is one, Who created and fashioned all things, and made all things come into existence out of non-existence." J. N. D. Kelly notes that Hermas was familiar with the Father, Son, and Holy Spirit triad, so that "First of all" suggests a trinitarian pattern for the catechesis of which this is a fragment.[d]

Both the Nicene and the Apostles' Creeds refer to creation as the first divine action, and both refer to "heaven and earth," a merism for everything. The Nicene Creed adds "of all that is, seen and unseen." In our view this addition is more of an unpacking of "heaven and earth" than a significant addition. A legacy of Greek philosophy and of the Platonic tradition in particular was to privilege the unseen over the seen. The Nicene Creed makes clear that both are part of God's good creation. As Luke Timothy Johnson observes, we tend to be in the reverse situation today, one in which the reality of the unseen needs to be emphasized.[e] The Nicene Creed also includes references to creation in its reference to Christ as the one "by whom all things were made" and to the Holy Spirit as "the Lord and giver of life." Its doctrine of creation is thus more strongly and overtly trinitarian than that of the Apostles' Creed.

---

[a]Cf. Kelly, *Early Christian Creeds*.

[b]Gerhard von Rad, *Old Testament Theology*, vol. 1, *The Theology of Israel's Historical Traditions* (Louisville, KY: Westminster John Knox, 2001), 123.

[c]See Jaroslav Pelikan, *Credo: Historical and Theological Guide to Creeds and Confessions of Faith in the Christian Tradition* (New Haven, CT: Yale University Press, 2003); Wolfram Kinzig, ed., *Faith in Formulae: A Collection of Early Christian Creeds and Creed-Related Texts*, 4 vols. (Oxford: Oxford University Press, 2017); Liuwe Westra, *The Apostles' Creed: Origin, History and Some Early Commentaries*, Research on the Inheritance of Early and Medieval Christianity 43 (Turnhout: Brepols, 2002); etc.

[d]Kelly, *Early Christian Creeds*, 67.

[e]Johnson, *Creed*, 99.

The Nicene Creed speaks of the Son as "eternally begotten" but of heaven and earth as made by the Father and through the Son. The language of "begotten" points to the *necessary* relation between the Son and the Father, whereas "maker of heaven and earth" evokes the contingency of the creation and its utter dependency on God's resolve to create.[6] Wood rightly reiterates this in Robert Sokolowski's "now-familiar counterfactual terms":

---

[6]Ibid., 385.

> In the Christian understanding, if the world had not been, God would still be. Furthermore, God would not be diminished in any way, in his goodness and perfection, if the world were not. While the world is understood as possibly not having been, God is understood as not being perfected in any way, as not increasing in goodness, by virtue of the actual existence of the world.[7]

At base the doctrine of creation means that apart from God everything that exists owes its existence to God's free act of ushering the world into existence and sustaining it as such. This receives added emphasis in the Nicene Creed's "seen and unseen." Both creeds affirm *creatio ex nihilo*. Among the church fathers there was some disagreement about this, so that Justin Martyr, for example, believed that God created from formless matter;[8] "seen and unseen" rules out such a view if it means that such matter is uncreated.

The first clause of the creeds thus presents us with the contingency of creation, *creatio ex nihilo*, and internal differentiation within the creation between heaven and earth and between things seen and unseen. Chapters four, five, and six deal with this differentiation within creation, or what we call "creation order."

Creation as a Doctrine of Faith

What is involved in the creeds is a *confession*, a declaration from the core of our being, that commits the person or persons making this declaration to a particular view of life and of the world.[9] As with the Lord's Prayer, the confession positions the one or ones making the confession within the circle of believers. The result is that such confession is far more than mental assent to a set of propositions; it includes a strong cognitive dimension but always as part of the disposition of the whole person. Belief or faith emerges from the deepest recesses of the human person, from what Old Testament Wisdom literature calls "the heart," as do reason and emotion, so that what is confessed in the creeds is arrived at not *first* or *finally* via logic or rational analysis of our world but through faith in Jesus Christ.

Within the circle of believers this doctrine often seems obvious, so that one might conclude that any rational person would espouse it. However, Hebrews 11:3 is clear that it is only "by faith" that we understand that the world

---

[7]Ibid., 386.

[8]Justin Martyr, *1 Apology* 10.2.

[9]See Donald Evans's *The Logic of Self-Involvement* (London: SCM Press, 1963) for a fine exploration of the language of self-involvement when it comes to creation. Cf. Pelikan, *Credo*, 35-63.

was made by the word of God, a reference to Genesis 1, in which the creation emerges through divine fiat.

Faith always finds expression in worship, and thus it is not surprising that in the scenes of worship in Revelation creation is often mentioned. In Hebrews 11 faith is trust in what we cannot see, and this finds an analogy in Revelation 4:1, in which John sees a door standing open in heaven. The voice like a trumpet (cf. Rev 1:10) beckons John to "come up here," and so he enters heaven through the open door and is granted to see what is not normally available to faith. He sees God on his throne surrounded by twenty-four elders on their thrones, the seven torches of fire, and the four living creatures.

The position of ἐστίν at the start of Hebrews 11:1 is emphatic: Ἔστιν δὲ πίστις ἐλπιζομένων ὑπόστασις, πραγμάτων ἔλεγχος οὐ βλεπομένων. Hebrews is classical in its tendency to omit the copula, and where ἐστίν occurs, as here, it is exceptional or indicates that it functions in another way.[a] Turner translates ἐστίν as "represents"; Lane as "celebrates."[b] The meaning of ὕποστασις is also disputed. The linguistic evidence of the meaning at the time Hebrews was written indicates objective, tangible reality in contrast to appearances.[c] Hence Lane translates ὕποστασις as "objective reality," Spicq as "objective guarantee,"[d] and Bruce as "firm foundation," although he leans toward the more subjective meaning of "assurance."[e] Lane notes that the second clause is in apposition to the first and proposes that ἔλεγχος be translated as "demonstration."[f] The use of the negative οὐ with a participle is unusual in the New Testament and indicates that the negation is decisive; "it stresses the fact that the events cannot be perceived through objective sense perception."[g] This is confirmed by the Old Testament examples of faith given in this section, of believers who often had nothing to depend on other than the promises of God. As is common in Hebrews, "faith" in the opening verse of this new section links back to Hebrews 10:38-39 in the previous section, reminding us of the committed nature of faith. Käsemann thus rightly notes that "faith arises when a person lets himself be convinced by God, and so attains a certainty which is objectively grounded and which transcends all human possibilities in its reliability."[h]

Hebrews 11:3 is the first in a chain of examples—anaphora—all beginning with Πιστει, best translated as "By faith . . .": πίστει νοοῦμεν κατηρτίσθαι τοὺς αἰῶνας ῥήματι θεοῦ, εἰς τὸ μὴ ἐκ φαινομένων τὸ βλεπόμενον γεγονέναι. Hebrews 11:3a clearly refers to Genesis 1. Κατηρτισθαι means "put in proper order"[i] and is used in the Septuagint with the meanings "to establish, create, order." Thus NIV's "formed" is preferable to NRSV's "prepared." Such ordering by fiat is precisely what we find in Genesis 1. The word νοειν evokes Romans 1:20 and Wisdom 13:1-5. Importantly, the author notes that such understanding is "by faith"; it is a gift that comes with faith. Faith is more than cognitive but not less. Hebrews 11:3b is couched in Hellenistic language, and some have discerned the influence of Platonism here, but Platonism is here rejected since for Plato and Plotinus the world was made out of a *visible* mass.

Hebrews 11:1-3 is rich in creation doctrine. Creation is to be celebrated (cf. Job 38:7); it is truly doxological. Bruce translates Hebrews 11:6, "Now without faith it is impossible *to give him pleasure* . . ."[j] As we celebrate the world in all its God-given dimensions as creation, we give God pleasure! By faith our world is seen objectively and with certainty *as creation*. The doctrine of creation can only be grasped by faith and not through that which can be seen. By means of its anti-Platonism, Hebrews 11:3 expresses implicitly a doctrine of *creatio ex nihilo*.[k]

---

[a]Cf. Nigel Turner, *A Grammar of New Testament Greek*, vol. 3, *Syntax* (Edinburgh: T&T Clark, 1963), 307.
[b]William L. Lane, *Hebrews 9–13*, WBC 47b (Dallas: Word, 1991), 325.
[c]Ibid.
[d]Ceslas Spicq, *L'Épître aux Hébreux*, vol. 2, *Etudes Bibliques* (Paris: Gabalda, 1952), 337-38.
[e]F. F. Bruce, *The Epistle to the Hebrews*, rev. ed., NICNT (Grand Rapids, MI: Eerdmans, 1990), 276-67.
[f]Lane, *Hebrews 9–13*, 326.
[g]Ibid.
[h]Ernst Käsemann, *Das wandernde Gottesvolk: Eine Untersuchung zum Hebräerbrief*, 4th ed., Forschungen zur Religion und Literatur des Alten und Neuen Testaments 37 (Göttingen: Vandenhoeck & Ruprecht, 1961), 22.
[i]Lane, *Hebrews 9–13*, 331.
[j]Bruce, *Epistle to the Hebrews*, 281.
[k]See ibid., 279-80; Arnold Erhardt, *The Framework of the New Testament Stories* (Cambridge, MA: Harvard University Press, 1964), 200-233.

The living creatures never cease to declare God's holiness, and whenever they worship, the twenty-four elders fall down and declare:

> You are worthy, our Lord and God,
>   to receive glory and honor and power,
> for you created all things,
>   and by your will they existed and were created. (Rev 4:11)

We learn from this that the doctrine of creation is a doxological truth as well as an eschatological one. The twenty-four elders represent the one, catholic people of God, and it is as they are before God that they worship God *for his act of creation* and for his sustaining the creation in existence. The living creatures symbolize all animate life, and in their worship they do what all of creation is meant to do! John is told to come up through the door "and I will show you what must take place after this." His vision is thus of what is to come, in the sense of the last days inaugurated by Christ, and thereby alerts us to the inextricable link between the doctrine of creation, Christology, and eschatology.

Beale notes, "The circular constructions around the throne symbolically enhance God's cosmic, universal kingship, a symbolic configuration attested elsewhere in the ancient world."[a] The three stones mentioned in Revelation 4:3 (cf. Ex 28; Ezek 28) evoke God's glory and anticipate the fuller list of precious stones in Revelation 21, where God's glory is manifested not only in heaven but throughout the new creation.[b] Many proposals have been made about the identities of the elders.[c] In our view the number twenty-four indicates that they represent the twelve tribes of the Old Testament and the twelve apostles of the New Testament, thereby representing the one, catholic people of God. The seven torches in front of the throne are described as the seven spirits of God. There is a clear reference here and in Revelation 5:6 to the vision in Zechariah 4:1-14. The seven torches represent the Spirit of God; in Revelation 4 they are in heaven, but in Revelation 5, as a result of Christ's work, they are sent out as agents of God "into all the earth." The identity of the four living creatures—one like a lion, one like an ox, one like a human, and one like a flying eagle—has also occasioned dispute. Beale concludes that they represent the "whole created order of animate life" as well as representing the creator, as indicated by their omniscient seeing.[d] Revelation 4:11 finds its closest Old Testament parallel in Daniel 4:37, in Nebuchadnezzar's concluding hymn of praise, a reminder, inter alia, of the journey that can be required to come to this confession! In Revelation 4:11b we find *creatio continua* and *creatio ex nihilo* mentioned, assuming "they were" to mean something like "they continually exist";[e] intriguingly, the former occurs first, presumably because this would be a major encouragement to John's readers.

[a]G. K. Beale, *The Book of Revelation: A Commentary on the Greek Text*, NIGTC (Grand Rapids, MI: Eerdmans, 1999), 320.
[b]Ibid., 321.
[c]See A. Feuillet, *Johannine Studies* (New York: Alba House, 1964), 183-214; Charles Brütsch, *Die Offenbarung Jesu Christi: Zürcher Bibelkommentare* (Zurich: Zwingli, 1970), 220-24.
[d]Beale, *Book of Revelation*, 329; cf. Brütsch, *Die Offenbarung Jesu Christi*, 230-33.
[e]Cf. Beale, *Book of Revelation*, 335; A. F. Johnson, "Revelation," in *The Expositor's Bible Commentary*, ed. Frank E. Gaebelein (Grand Rapids, MI: Zondervan, 1981), 12:464.

Why is this doctrine doxological *and* eschatological? Because it is only clear in the light of God and his good purposes for the creation. The doctrine of creation implies that this is indeed the best of all possible worlds, as Leibniz asserted.[10] However, this side of the fall and amidst the often dark forces of history, it is easy to sympathize with Voltaire, who ruthlessly satirized Leibniz's view in his novel *Candide*. The effect of what has gone wrong in God's "very good" (Gen 1:31) creation is that, as Hebrews alerts us, we do not now naturally see that the world was created by the word of God. Belief in creation is "by faith." It is only as we encounter the living God in worship

[10]On Leibniz, see Barth, *CD* III/1, 388-414. See chap. 10 below, on providence, for more detail on this issue.

and learn of his purpose for his creation, particularly as revealed in Christ, that we are able to embrace the doctrine of creation as the glorious truth that it is. It *is* glorious and ought to call forth the sort of response illustrated in Revelation 4:9-11.

Hebrews 11:3 is part of Hebrews 11:1-3, the introductory statement about the nature of faith that precedes the roll call of that great crowd of witnesses who achieved greatness through trusting God's promise, often against great odds. This reminds us that just as faith is often far from easy, so too is belief in the doctrine of creation. Job is not part of the roll call of faith in Hebrews 11, but he would be a worthy addition. Belief in God as creator and God's just ordering of his world is central to Job but also at the heart of his questioning and crisis.

It is perhaps in Job 3 that Job's problem with the doctrine of creation emerges most personally and clearly. Job's soliloquy/lament is very personal; he uses the creation language of Genesis 1 in particular to express his agony and in the process, as several scholars have noted, extends his curse to destroy not just himself but the entire creation.[a] In Job 3:8 Job calls on the magicians who are able to unleash the Sea and Leviathan, the great monsters of chaos "who presumably would devour not only Job's night of conception but also the cosmos itself."[b] In Genesis 1 and Psalm 33 we find creation by divine decree (see chap. 5). Job subverts this tradition by beginning in Job 3:3-10 with seven curses directed against *the day* of his birth and *the night* of his conception. The dominant metaphors in Job 3 are the binary poles of light and darkness, which are found in day one of the creation account in Genesis 1. The seven curses recall the seven days of creation in Genesis 1:1–2:3. Perdue notes that "'Day' and 'Night,' the temporal order of creation and history, are assaulted in what can only be described as a blasphemous effort to return to primordial chaos, prior to the time of beginnings."[c] Furthermore, Genesis 1:1–2:3 uses fifteen jussives to accomplish creation, whereas Job's curses in 3:3-10 contain sixteen jussives and prohibitions, adding one to counter the view of Genesis 1:1–2:3.[d] Genesis 1:1–2:3 ends in "rest" (*šābat*), and Job also seeks "rest" (3:17, 26) but he uses the alternative word *nûaḥ*, perhaps an ironic denial of Sabbath rest. Job's problem with creation is focused on himself in chapter three: "Why were there knees to receive me, or breasts for me to suck?" (Job 3:12). He rails in particular against his creation, but, of course, as part of creation his curse must also extinguish the knees and breasts that received him and ultimately the entire creation.

McGrath asserts, "Job 38:1–42:6 sets out what is unquestionably the most comprehensive understanding of God as creator to be found in the Old Testament, stressing the role of God as creator and sustainer of the world."[e] This neglected text will be referred to in several chapters since it deals with a variety of issues related to creation. For now it is important to note the emphasis on epistemology in 38:4-5, in which the words *understanding* and *know* occur. As others have recognized, Job 38–42 contains myriad questions, all designed to decenter Job and to foreground Yahweh as creator and sustainer of the universe. Not surprisingly, therefore, the dominant interrogative is "Who?" These chapters stress Yahweh's deity and Job's creatureliness and thus his limitations. He was not there when Yahweh laid the foundation of the earth (Job 38:4); he does not comprehend the mysteries of light and darkness and of the elements, nor does he oversee the animal world, which often operates far from human sight and existence; and he certainly cannot control Behemoth and Leviathan, figures that probably symbolize dangerous and potentially uncontrollable elements in the creation, including evil. Job is not a book about the epistemology of creation, but it does bear strongly on this and alerts us, inter alia, to the ontological gap between God and the human. Creation implies a view of the whole, and this is only available to God, so that a relationship with him is indispensable to grasping this doctrine.

[a]Michael A. Fishbane, "Jeremiah 4:23-6 and Job 3:3-13: A Recovered Use of the Creation Pattern," *Vetus Testamentum* 21, no. 2 (1971): 151-67; Dermot Cox, "The Desire for Oblivion in Job 3," *Studii Biblici Franciscani Liber Annus* 23 (1973): 37-49; Leo G. Perdue, "Job's Assault on Creation," *Hebrew Annual Review* 10 (1987): 295-315; Perdue, *Wisdom Literature: A Theological History* (Louisville, KY: Westminster John Knox, 2007), 98-102.
[b]Perdue, *Wisdom Literature*, 99.
[c]Ibid., 100.
[d]Ibid.
[e]Alister E. McGrath, *Christian Theology: An Introduction*, 5th ed. (Oxford: Wiley-Blackwell, 2011), 216.

Amidst his suffering it is only through his encounter with God and his tour of the creation that Job is able to find again the solid ground of belief in God and thus in creation. Clearly, therefore, the doctrine of creation is an article of faith, as Barth insists.[11] Belief in creation is utterly foundational to Christian belief, as its occurrence in the first clause of the creeds makes crystal clear. As Johnson observes, "The designation of God as creator, or as 'the one who makes' (*ho poiētēs*), grounds all other statements of the creed. It is because God, the one, all-powerful Father, is the source of all things that God can be revealer, savior, sanctifier, and judge of all."[12]

The Doctrine of Creation and the *Sensus Divinitatis*

Barth rightly insists that belief in creation issues from faith, but one wonders whether Barth does not go too far when he maintains that the doctrine of creation "is neither native to him [the human person] nor accessible by way of observation and logical thinking; for which he has no organ and no ability."[13]

[11]Barth, *CD* III/1, 3-41.
[12]Johnson, *Creed*, 93.
[13]Barth, *CD* III/1, 3.

Calvin would certainly argue otherwise. He maintains that "there exists in the human minds and indeed by natural instinct, some sense of Deity."[14] God has so endowed humans that all are aware that there is a God *and that he is their maker*. Calvin invokes the universality of religion in support of his view, and while he acknowledges that humans try to efface this knowledge, "all men of sound Judgment will therefore hold, that a sense of Deity is indelibly engraved on the human heart. And that this belief is naturally engendered in all, and thoroughly fixed as it were in our very bones."[15]

Thus, for Calvin, belief in God *and in him as creator* is indeed native to humankind, who naturally possess a sense of the divine (*sensus divinitatis*). However, it is equally important to note Calvin's awareness that humans in their rebellion against God seek to evade and suppress this knowledge. Calvin, of course, lived long before the Enlightenment and the widespread atheism of the post-Enlightenment era. Schopenhauer (1788–1860), with his overwhelming sense of the misery and brokenness of life—he strongly disagreed with Leibniz that this is the best of all worlds—was the first modern philosopher to openly embrace atheism. Since then atheism has become standard fare in Western academic circles so that it is harder nowadays to argue, like Calvin, from the universality of religion. Indeed, to a significant extent modernity, with its diverse institutions, has been built on the premise of a-theism (away from theism) so that a rejection of God is no longer just an individual matter but one that seeps through the major public institutions of our day. However, just as the secularization hypothesis was receiving widespread affirmation in the twentieth century, by the end of that same century sociologists such as Peter Berger were revising their theories to take account of the huge renaissance of religion worldwide and speaking of *desecularization*.[16]

What is important to note is that even the phenomenon of widespread atheism is not a defeater for the *sensus divinitatis*. Paul's argument in Romans 1:18-32 supports Calvin's view, albeit from a different angle.

---

[14]John Calvin, *Institutes* 1.3.1, trans. Ford Lewis Battles (Philadelphia: Westminster, 1960).

[15]Calvin, *Institutes* 1.3.3 (Battles).

[16]Linda Woodhead, Paul Heelas, and David Martin, eds., *Peter Berger and the Study of Religion* (London: Routledge, 2001); Peter L. Berger, ed., *The Desecularization of the World: The Resurgence of Religion in World Politics* (Grand Rapids, MI: Eerdmans, 1999); Peter L. Berger and Samuel Huntington, eds., *Many Globalizations: Cultural Diversity in the Contemporary World* (Oxford: Oxford University Press, 2002); Peter L. Berger and Thomas Luckmann, *The Social Construction of Reality: A Treatise in the Sociology of Knowledge* (New York: Knopf Doubleday, 1967).

Romans 1:18 refers to all ἀσέβειαν (sin as an attack on God's majesty) and ἀδικία (sin as a violation of the just order of God).[a] Sin manifests itself as a refusal to acknowledge God's majesty and results in a violation of creation order. Κατέχω has here the meaning of "suppress, hold down." As Cranfield notes,

> Sin is always (cf. v. 25) an assault upon the truth (that is, the fundamental truth of God "as Creator, Judge, and Redeemer," which, because it is the truth, must be taken into account and come to terms with, if man is not to live in vain), the attempt to suppress it, bury it out of sight, obliterate it from the memory; but it is of the essence of sin that it can never be more than an *attempt* to suppress the truth, an attempt which is always bound in the end to prove futile.[b]

Τὸ γνωστὸν τοῦ θεοῦ preserves the hiddenness of God (cf. Luther's *deus absconditus*), but it does indicate that God is knowable because God has revealed it ἐν αὐτοῖς, "in their midst."[c] As Cranfield notes, "In their midst and all around them and also in their own creaturely existence . . . God is objectively manifest: His whole creation declares Him."[d] In our view ἀπὸ κτίσεως κόσμου should be understood as referring to both *since* the creation of the world and *from* the creation.[e] Romans 1:20 expresses the idea that although God is invisible, his eternal power and divine nature are known and seen through what he has made—namely, the creation. Δύναμις is common in the New Testament and is even used as a periphrasis for the name of God (Mt 26:64 = Mk 14:62). Θειότης, however, is first found in Biblical Greek in Wisdom 18:9 and occurs only here in the New Testament. It is a Hellenistic term referring to the divine nature and attributes.

The crux of Paul's argument comes, of course, in Romans 1:20-25. God's revelation of himself in creation renders humankind without excuse. So present is God in his creation that "they knew God" but became futile (the verb used is ματαιόω) in their thinking and their hearts (καρδία) were darkened. Here we see the problem with natural theology. It is not that the knowledge of God is unavailable from his revelation in creation; the problem is that the very core of humans has become darkened so that every attempt is made to suppress this knowledge. Cranfield rightly notes that this "implies no contempt for reason. . . . But it is a sober acknowledgement of the fact that the καρδια as the inner self of man shares fully in the fallenness of the whole man, that the intellect is not a part of human nature somehow exempted from the general corruption."[f] Folly (Rom 1:22) and God's judgment in handing humans over to the "lusts of their hearts" (Rom 1:24) are the problem, not the revelation of creation. And as Augustine astutely observes,

> Eternal Wisdom, of course, is the origin or beginning of the intelligent creation; this beginning, while abiding unchangeably in itself, would certainly never cease to speak to the creature for which it is the beginning and summon it by some hidden inspiration to turn to that from which it derived its being, because in no other way could it possibly be formed and perfected.[g]

This should not, however, obscure the darkening effect of distorted human practices in cultural development, as we note below in relation to modernity. Intriguingly, ματαιόω is from the same root as ματαιότης, the noun used in the Septuagint to translate *hebel* in Ecclesiastes. Ecclesiastes 7:23-29 is a turning point in the book in which Qohelet acknowledges that his quest for "wisdom" has landed him in the arms of Dame Folly and he cannot find Lady Wisdom.[h] Epistemologically, what Qohelet calls "wisdom" is very different from wisdom in Proverbs; it is dependent on experience, reason, and observation alone and does not start with the fear of the Lord. In this way Ecclesiastes provides us with a fascinating portrait of futility and how to emerge from it—namely, by finding one's way back to "Remember your creator . . ."

Not surprisingly, in the Catholic Church an interpretation of Romans 1:20 more along the lines of natural theology prevails. At the end of chapter one, *Dei Verbum* cites Vatican I:

> As a sacred synod has affirmed, *God, the beginning and end of all things, can be known with certainty from created reality by the light of human reason* (see Rom. 1:20); but teaches that it is through His revelation that those religious truths which are by their nature accessible to human reason can be known by all men with ease, with solid certitude and with no trace of error, even in this present state of the human race. (emphasis added)

As will be clear from our discussion above, we do think that God as origin (creator) and telos can be known from creation but differ over the capacity and will of (fallen) human reason to discern this. We find Bonaventure's comment helpful in this respect: "The world was like a damaged book which God brought to perspicacity (*illuminavit*) and rectified by the book of Scripture."[i] For Bonaventure, that the world was created freely by God, in time and *ex nihilo*, is a truth in principle accessible to human reason. However, in fact people have recognized this only through Scripture and revelation.

---

[a]C. E. B. Cranfield, *A Critical and Exegetical Commentary on the Epistle to the Romans: An Introduction and Commentary on Romans I–VIII*, vol. 1, International Critical Commentary (London: T&T Clark, 1975), 112.

[b]Ibid.

[c]Ibid., 113.

[d]Ibid., 114.

[e]Contra Cranfield; ibid.

[f]Ibid., 118.

[g]Augustine, *Literal Meaning of Genesis* 1.5.10. In Augustine, *On Genesis: A Refutation of the Manichees, Unfinished Literal Commentary on Genesis, the Literal Meaning of Genesis*, ed. John E. Rotelle, trans. Edmund Hill (Hyde Park, NY: New City Press, 2005), 172.

[h]Cf. Craig G. Bartholomew, *Ecclesiastes*, Baker Commentary on the Old Testament Wisdom and Psalms (Grand Rapids, MI: Baker Academic, 2009).

[i]Bonaventure, *Collationes in Hexameron* 3.1.12.

Paul argues that God's invisible attributes—what cannot be seen—namely, his power and "divine nature," are clearly seen in "the things he has made," namely, in the creation. As in Psalm 19:1-4, Paul envisages the creation so clearly bearing the mark of the master craftsman that no one has an adequate excuse for not worshiping God. Paul's language—"power," "things that have been made"—points clearly to a recognition of God and God as creator.

However, and here we connect back to Barth's view, Paul is equally clear that humans in their "unrighteousness suppress the truth" (Rom 1:18 ESV). Humans are made for God so that belief in him and in him as creator is indeed native to them; the creation bears continual testimony to God's deity and power. And yet in our depravity we hold down this knowledge and worship images and the creature rather than the Creator. According to Paul, part of the judgment resulting from such idolatry is that God hands humans over to their depravity, "to a debased mind to do what ought not to be done" (Rom 1:28 ESV). This handing over bespeaks a settled condition of rebellion in which suppression of the *sensus divinitatis* becomes habitual so as to appear normal.

From this perspective modern atheism should be seen not as irreligious but as a form of the worship of the creature in which humankind usurps the place of God. This is clearly evident in the major emphasis on human autonomy in modern thought and not least in Kant's notion that *we ourselves* generate the moral law, which is absolute. However, since the human being is a creature and not the creator, this is always a tense position to occupy, to which the tensions in Kant's moral philosophy and his view of evil bear eloquent testimony.[17] Indeed, as G. C. Berkouwer notes, the whole of life—whether acknowledged or not—is a response to God so that the sort of suppression of God we find in modern atheism is ultimately unsustainable and exceedingly hard work since it goes against our native, created condition.[18] The difference between atheism in Calvin's day and atheism in our own is that it has taken on a wide-ranging cultural embodiment in the West so that, as Charles Taylor notes, the conditions for belief in God are not propitious. From this angle modernity can be seen as a massive, Babel-like attempt to suppress the knowledge of God, making it far harder to hear the witness of the creation and to recover one's "native" condition.[19]

One might wonder, therefore, whether the difference between Calvin and Barth on this issue matters. In our opinion it does. An example is the fertile

[17]See Richard Kroner, *Kant's Weltanschauung* (Charleston, SC: Nabu Press, 2011), on the tensions in Kant's ethical philosophy, and Gordon E. Michalson (*Fallen Freedom: Kant on Radical Evil and Moral Regeneration* [Cambridge: Cambridge University Press, 1990]) on the ways in which Kant's view of evil resurfaces the issue of God.

[18]C. G. Berkouwer, *Man: The Image of God*, Studies in Dogmatics (Grand Rapids, MI: Eerdmans, 1962), 59.

[19]Charles Taylor, *A Secular Age* (Cambridge, MA: Belknap Press, 2007).

use made by Alvin Plantinga of the *sensus divinitatis* in the development of his epistemology of warrant.[20] The *sensus divinitatis* is a central feature in Plantinga's externalist epistemology and in his advanced Aquinas/Calvin model. It is precisely the *sensus divinitatis* that enables Plantinga to develop a distinctively Reformed epistemology in philosophy, a move that Barth would oppose.

This recalls the debate between Barth and Emil Brunner over natural theology, which reached its high point in 1934.[21] Central to the debate was whether or not there are grounds for speaking of a "point of contact" in human nature for the saving action of God. Barth denied this emphatically as the slippery slope to the dangers of natural theology and not least as this beckoned in Nazi Germany. Brunner evokes Scripture (Rom 1:18-20; 2:14-15) and the Reformers to argue that God is indeed revealed in creation and that this revelation precedes his revelation of himself in Jesus. He distinguishes between the formal and material image of God in humankind. The formal image remains unaltered by the fall. Humans remain humans! Materially, however, the image is lost since humankind is sinful through and through and there is nothing in humans that is not defiled by sin (the doctrine that is traditionally called total depravity, which does not mean that humans are as bad as possible but that every aspect of their lives is tainted deeply by sin).

In our view—although we would articulate it differently—Brunner is right on this issue. His approach is akin to the very useful Kuyperian distinction between *structure* and *direction*.[22] This approach identifies the good creation order with the structures that come with creation, as opposed to the direction given to them by human beings. The capacity for family life (structure), for example, is given with creation, but the fall opens up the possibility for sinful humans to radically misdirect this structure toward abuse and oppression or to direct it toward rich, relational family life and thus toward God. The capacity for imagination and creativity (structure) comes with creation; sin opens up the possibility of misdirecting this gift as, for example, we see in the

---

[20]See Craig G. Bartholomew and Michael W. Goheen, *Christian Philosophy: A Systematic and Narrative Introduction* (Grand Rapids, MI: Baker Academic, 2013), 220-24.

[21]See Heinz Zahrnt, *The Question of God: Protestant Theology in the Twentieth Century* (New York: Harcourt, Brace & World, 1969), 55-83. Brunner's "Nature and Grace: A Contribution to the Discussion with Karl Barth," and Barth's reply, "Nein! Answer to Emil Brunner," both appeared in 1934. They are published together in Karl Barth and Emil Brunner, *Natural Theology: Comprising "Nature and Grace" by Emil Brunner and the Reply "No!" by Karl Barth*, trans. Peter Fraenkel (1946; Eugene, OR: Wipf & Stock, 2002).

[22]Albert M. Wolters, *Creation Regained: Biblical Basics for a Reformational Worldview*, 2nd ed. (Grand Rapids, MI: Eerdmans, 2005), 87-114.

pervasive "creative" development of pornography today. Humans are made for God so that, in one sense, relationship with God is the most natural thing in all the world. Barth is so concerned—understandably perhaps in his context—to protect the sovereignty and initiative of God that he is in danger of subverting the very doctrine of creation that he insists is known by faith alone. Heinz Zahrnt notes, by comparison, how Brunner's approach enabled him to attend to politics, philosophy, other religions, and social justice, all from the perspective of the gospel.[23]

In his fascinating work *I Am the Truth: Toward a Philosophy of Christianity*, the Catholic philosopher Michel Henry addresses the same issues but with a different vocabulary. Central to his argument is the distinction between "Life" (God) and "life." With this distinction he links reception of the Word with the doctrine of creation: "The original compatibility between the Word and the person who must carry inside the possibility of hearing it is the relation of Life to the person."[a] For Henry,

> the possibility of hearing the Word of life is itself for each person and for each living Self contemporaneous with his birth and consubstantial with his condition of Son. I hear forever the sound of my birth, which is the sound of Life, the unbreakable silence in which the Word of Life does not stop speaking my own life to me, in which my own life, if I hear that word speaking within it, does not stop speaking the Word of God to me.[b]

Henry stresses the foundational aspect of creation in redemption:

> But it is not the word of Scripture that lets us hear the Word of Life. Rather it is the latter, by engendering us at each instant, by making us Sons, that reveals within its own truth that truth recognized by the Word of Scripture, to which it testifies. The one who listens to this word of Scripture knows that it speaks true, *since inside him the Word that establishes him in Life listens to itself.*[c]

How valuable, then, are arguments for creation? In the history of theology diverse views are taken on this issue. As is well known, Aristotle argued for a First Cause underlying the order of the world, and Thomas Aquinas made use of this element in Aristotle's philosophy in his Five Ways of demonstrating the existence of God. Melanchthon, for example, moves easily from articulating the biblical doctrine of creation to nine signs and proofs "which testify that this world does not exist by accident, but that God is an eternal mind, the Creator of all things." These include the arguments that "there is a God, as all by nature confess," and "therefore this knowledge of Him is true"; the order of society; the proof from final causes; and so on.[d] Similarly, today we have

---

[23]Zahrnt, *Question of God*, 69-83.

seen the emergence of the argument for design in opposition to Darwinian evolution, an argument that *could* be extrapolated to a Designer.

As noted above, it is far harder in our context to make such arguments. Bavinck is understandably far more aware of the challenges to belief in creation and rightly, in our view, discerns religion as the root of different views of the world.[e] He asserts, "The doctrine of creation is known only from revelation and is understood by faith (Heb. 11:3)."[f] Evidentialism remains a popular approach to apologetics with its view that if reason functions properly and objectively, then one will arrive at the truth that accords with Scripture. In our view the Reformed epistemologists (Kelly James Clark, Alvin Plantinga, Nicholas Wolterstorff) are in line with Paul in Romans 1 in rejecting such an approach. There is no neutral ground in the creation, and the darkened heart needs to be illuminated by the gospel in order for one's eyes to be opened to see *what is all around one*. As Psalm 119 recognizes—"open my eyes, so that I may behold"—the problem is not with the evidence but with our eyes, with our hearts. Does this mean that arguments for creation are of no value? No. They are useful in showing that belief in creation is not irrational, in shoring up the faith of believers, and they may be invaluable in evangelism, provided one is aware that intellectual persuasion may be a landmark en route to conversion but will not itself convert. Even if one could prove a First Cause, such a First Cause or a Designer is a long way from the biblical creator. Of course, God is the "cause" of the creation, and it owes its order or design to him, but we acknowledge, as Pascal did in a note sown into his coat, discovered after his death, "the God of Abraham, Isaac, and Jacob; not the God of the philosophers."

[a]Michel Henry, *I Am the Truth: Toward a Philosophy of Christianity*, trans. Susan Emanuel, Cultural Memory in the Present (Stanford, CA: Stanford University Press, 2003), 225.
[b]Ibid., 226.
[c]Ibid., 230.
[d]Philip Melanchthon and J. A. O. Preus, *The Chief Theological Topics: Loci Praecipui Theologici 1559*, 2nd ed. (St. Louis: Concordia, 2011), 43-45, quotations from 43 and 44.
[e]Herman Bavinck, *In the Beginning: Foundations of Creation Theology*, ed. John Bolt, trans. John Vriend (Grand Rapids, MI: Baker, 1999), 23-60.
[f]Ibid., 25.

The Doctrine of Creation and Scripture

While we agree that creation is only fully understood as such in the light of the Christ event so that a biblical doctrine of creation will be trinitarian,[24] it cannot be stressed too strongly just how fundamental creation is to the entire drama of Scripture. Herman Bavinck rightly speaks in this respect of a "creation-based worldview."[25] The doctrine of the Trinity is an abstraction

[24]See Herman Bavinck, *In the Beginning: Foundations of Creation Theology*, ed. John Bolt, trans. John Vriend (Grand Rapids, MI: Baker, 1999), 39-45.
[25]Bavinck, *In the Beginning*, 56.

from or development of the data found especially in the New Testament in relation to Jesus Christ. Undoubtedly, as the fulfillment of the Old Testament and the center of history, Christ casts his light on the entire spectrum from creation to new creation. And yet, in terms of the biblical story, there would be no Jesus (if we can put it in such a provocative way) without creation, since the incarnation itself requires the creation.[26] As Barth himself notes, "What else is the proclamation of Jesus and the New Testament but the establishment, revelation and execution of this long-awaited right of the Creator to His creature?"[27] "Creation sets the stage for the story of the covenant of grace. The story requires a stage corresponding to it; the existence of man and his whole world."[28]

In twentieth-century biblical and theological studies, the doctrine of creation did not fare well.[29] Paul Ricoeur rightly says, "For the past few decades, one problem has dominated the exegesis and theology of the Old Testament: what degree of independence is to be accorded the doctrine of creation in relation to the fundamental soteriological affirmation that is assumed to run through both testaments of the Bible. . . . Within Christian communities, then, the stakes of this discussion are high."[30]

In a move comparable to Barth's fear of natural theology, Gerhard von Rad maintained that Israel's belief in creation was secondary to its belief in redemption and that Old Testament insights into the shape of the world are irrelevant for Old Testament theology.[31] The wariness of a perversion of creation order is understandable, but the downplaying of creation is not.[32] Stories of creation were widespread in the ancient Near East and make it highly unlikely that Israel would come to the worship of Yahweh without some doctrine of creation. Indeed, as has often been noted, one of the thrusts of Genesis 1:1–2:3 is its polemic against alternative ancient Near Eastern views of the world, such as the Enuma Elish. As Rolf P. Knierim perceptively notes, "More than anything else, there is a compelling

[26]Barth argues that the second person of the Trinity is Jesus Christ in eternity. We disagree.

[27]Barth, *CD* III/1, 38.

[28]Barth, *CD* III/1, 44.

[29]See Rolf P. Knierim, *The Task of Old Testament Theology: Substance, Method, and Cases* (Grand Rapids, MI: Eerdmans, 1995), 176-85.

[30]André LaCocque and Paul Ricoeur, *Thinking Biblically: Exegetical and Hermeneutical Studies*, trans. David Pellauer (Chicago: University of Chicago Press, 1998), 31.

[31]Gerhard von Rad, *Old Testament Theology*, vol. 1, *The Theology of Israel's Historical Traditions*, trans. D. M. G. Stalker (Edinburgh: Oliver and Boyd, 1962), 152.

[32]See Othmar Keel and Silvia Schroer, *Creation: Biblical Theologies in the Context of the Ancient Near East*, trans. Peter T. Daniels (Winona Lake, IN: Eisenbrauns, 2015), 1-15.

ground for why Israel had to see cosmic order and Yahweh as related to one another: Israel's agrarian existence in Palestine over centuries from the time of the settlement onward. This fact is fundamental. . . . Israel had to accept a worldview that was concerned with cosmic and natural order and with cyclic reality."[33] In this respect it is worth noting how Ellen Davis's creative dialogue between the Old Testament and the new agrarianism, especially that of Wendell Berry, foregrounds precisely the issue of creation order.[34]

Clearly, in its canonical shape Scripture begins with creation and ends with a new heaven and a new earth, a renewed creation. However, some influential historical criticism resisted seeing creation as fundamental to the entire Old Testament, and some New Testament scholarship has argued that in the New Testament land is Christified and spiritualized.[35]

The influence of such views lingers, albeit in different forms. As we will see in our discussion of *creatio ex nihilo*, many of the Old Testament and New Testament texts traditionally thought to support, at least in substance, this doctrine are now regarded rather differently. And so we need to point out the overwhelming biblical evidence for creation as a presupposition of the entire drama of Scripture.

> Westermann's work on Genesis is full of rich insights. However, he argues that "chs. 1–11 of Genesis must be regarded as a separate element of the Pentateuch, that is, as a relatively self-contained unity, and not primarily as a part of 'Genesis.'" He asserts, "One cannot therefore refer what is said about God's saving acts in history to God's creative action without more ado. The Old Testament does not speak of faith in the Creator; there is no 'creation faith.'"[a] Knierim by comparison notes in the Psalms "the indisputable fact that the object of faith is the creator."[b] Westermann seems to be concerned to protect creation from being made subordinate to salvation history, a concern we share, but in the process he ends up with a contradictory position, as the following passage indicates:
>
>> It is not possible to regard Gen 1 directly and without reservation as the beginning of salvation history or even as its preparation. The reason why this chapter is at the beginning of the Bible is so that all of God's subsequent actions—his dealings with

[33]Knierim, *Task of Old Testament Theology*, 177.

[34]Ellen F. Davis, *Scripture, Culture, and Agriculture: An Agrarian Reading of the Bible* (New York: Cambridge University Press, 2009).

[35]See Craig G. Bartholomew's *Where Mortals Dwell: A Christian View of Place for Today* (Grand Rapids, MI: Baker Academic, 2011) for discussion and critique.

> humankind, the history of his people, the election and the covenant—may be seen against the broader canvas of his work in creation.[c]

In our view the second sentence does precisely what the first says one cannot do! If Genesis 1 is not the preparation for (salvation) history, then how can it be the broader canvas against which to see (salvation) history?

Von Rad also expresses different emphases in his writings.[d] We have referred above to his subordination of creation to redemption and his disparaging of Old Testament insights into the shape of the world for Old Testament theology. However, in his *Wisdom in Israel* his insights on creation, wisdom, and epistemology are profound, and in his popular *God at Work in Israel* he is quite clear that "to understand Israel correctly, one must begin with the creation of the world; for Israel has its place in God's plan for the world. It is for that reason that the book of Genesis begins with the creation. . . . One misunderstands Israel, her faith and her worship, unless one sees it all from the vantage point of the creation of the world."[e]

---

[a]Claus Westermann, *Creation* (Philadelphia: Fortress, 1974), 2, 175.

[b]Rolf P. Knierim, *The Task of Old Testament Theology: Substance, Method, and Cases* (Grand Rapids, MI: Eerdmans, 1995), 186.

[c]Westermann, *Creation*, 175.

[d]Othmar Keel and Silvia Schroer, *Creation: Biblical Theologies in the Context of the Ancient Near East*, trans. Peter T. Daniels (Winona Lake, IN: Eisenbrauns, 2015), 11.

[e]Gerhard von Rad, *God at Work in Israel*, trans. John H. Marks (Nashville: Abingdon, 1980), 98-99.

Because Genesis 1 has been assigned to the Priestly writer by source critics, fertile work has been done on cultic texts in the Old Testament, demonstrating again and again the link between cultus and creation. Although one need not affirm the source criticism, the insight that in Genesis 1 God forms creation as a temple in which to dwell is a welcome discovery. In the twentieth century a renaissance of interest in Old Testament wisdom developed once it was realized that it embodies a theology of creation, an insight that continues to yield significant fruit. But it is not only cultic and wisdom texts in the Old Testament that develop a theology of creation, but also Old Testament narrative, the legal collections, and the prophets, to say nothing of the Psalter. In Genesis 12:1-3, for example, a form of the word translated "bless" occurs five times in parallel to the fivefold use of "curse" in Genesis 1–11. The theology of blessing is rooted in creation, and the covenant with Abraham evokes a recovery of God's purpose of blessing for all nations. Westermann notes of blessing in Genesis 1:1–2:3 that "the connection between blessing and creation remains basic to all further uses of the word. When God blesses, it is the creator who blesses and the blessing itself works itself out effectively in the life of what is blessed or of the one asking the blessing. Blessing implies creation and is effective as the work of the creator."[36] Creation is fundamental to the writing of the prophets, as, for example, the hymn fragments in Amos demonstrate.[37] As intertextuality has taken hold in biblical studies, it is far easier to see the myriad ways in which creation theology underlies and informs all the genres of the Old Testament.

The major theme of Jesus' teaching in the Synoptics is the kingdom of God/heaven,[38] with alternative but synonymous vocabulary in John. The kingdom is about the recovery of God's purposes for his entire creation through his Son. The breaking in of the kingdom in Jesus opens up the eschatological space between the coming of the kingdom in Jesus and its final consummation with his return and the ushering in of the new heavens and the new earth. Not surprisingly, therefore, we find throughout Paul's letters important creation passages, such as in Romans 8, Ephesians 1, and Colossians 1. The same New Testament eschatology is found in the General Epistles, and Revelation is extraordinary in its vision of a new creation, of that day when "the kingdom of the world has become the kingdom of our Lord and of his Messiah" (Rev 11:15).[39]

All orthodox Christianity confesses the doctrine of creation, but as we will see in chapter two, the danger of an eclipse of this fundamental doctrine has recurred again and again throughout history beginning with the Gnostic threat so ably repudiated by Irenaeus. A major contribution of Dutch Calvinism has been to repeatedly foreground creation and its utterly integral role in relation to all other doctrines. As Barth poignantly notes, "Faith in Jesus Christ is a life in the presence of the Creator."[40]

The Doctrine of Creation and God

Genesis 1:1 literally begins, "In the beginning—he created—God [Elohim]." Biblically, the doctrine of creation is an extension of and utterly subordinate to the doctrine of God. One way to understand Genesis 1 is to think of it like

[36] Claus Westermann, *Creation* (Philadelphia: Fortress, 1974), 140.

[37] Craig G. Bartholomew and Heath A. Thomas, *The Minor Prophets: A Theological Introduction* (Downers Grove, IL: IVP Academic, forthcoming).

[38] For the vast literature on the kingdom of God in the twentieth century see Lesław D. Chrupcała, *The Kingdom of God: A Bibliography of 20th Century Research* (Jerusalem: Franciscan Printing Press, 2007).

[39] On creation in the New Testament see Sean M. McDonough, *Christ as Creator: Origins of a New Testament Doctrine* (Oxford: Oxford University Press, 2009).

[40] Barth, *CD* III/1, 32.

being taken on a tour of an exhibition and then being asked whether you would like to meet the artist. God is the central character in Genesis 1, in which he is represented in royal terms as the all-powerful one who ushers creation into existence as an act of his own free will. As Revelation 4:11 says, "By *your will* they existed and were created."

Genesis 1 uses the generic term for God, *Elohim*, which would have been understood across the ancient Near East. The juxtaposition of Genesis 1:1–2:3 with 2:4–3:24 is important in this respect. While some scholars argue that there are different sources underlying these sections, in their literary and canonical shape they form part of an ongoing narrative with a clear logic. Genesis 1:1–2:3 deals with the creation of the whole—namely, heaven and earth, a trope for the totality of creation. Genesis 2:4–3:24 moves on to the first couple and the particular place in which they dwell on earth amidst the vast creation, as we will see in chapter five. The diverse relationships in which humans live, and not least that with God, come into focus. Thus, it is significant that whereas in Genesis 1 God is referred to as Elohim, in Genesis 2:4–3:24 we find the unusual juxtaposition of "Yahweh Elohim." The theology of Yahweh is found in Exodus 3 and Exodus 6 and evokes God as the one who rescues Israel from slavery and brings it to himself—that is, as the covenant God. This juxtaposition following Genesis 1 serves as a powerful reminder that Elohim is Yahweh, the particular God of Israel and not a generic "God."

Since the doctrine of creation is an extension of the doctrine of God, our view of creation will inevitably be deeply shaped by how we view God. Biblically, God as creator is clearly presented in the following ways.

Radically other than the creation. Genesis and the rest of the Bible do not, of course, present us with a systematic doctrine of God. In Genesis the narrative simply unfolds before us with God as the central character. However, as we follow the narration, we can abstract truths about this God. A perennial temptation in the history of thought has been to see something immanent within the creation as divine, what we can call pagan thought. This was common in the ancient Near East but is overtly rejected in Genesis 1 and elsewhere:

> When we read in Psalm 19 that "the heavens declare the glory of God; and the firmament sheweth his handiwork," we hear a voice which mocks the beliefs of Egyptians and Babylonians. The heavens, which were to the psalmist but a witness of God's greatness, were to the Mesopotamians the very majesty of godhead, the highest ruler Anu. To the Egyptians the heavens signified the

> mystery of the divine mother through whom man was reborn. In Egypt and Mesopotamia the divine was comprehended as immanent: the gods were in nature. The Egyptians saw in the sun all that a man may know of the Creator; the Mesopotamians viewed the sun as the god Shamash, the guarantor of justice. But to the psalmist the sun was God's devoted servant who "is a bridegroom coming out of his chamber, and rejoices as a strong man to run a race." The God of the psalmists and the prophets was not in nature. He transcended nature—and transcended, likewise, the realm of mythopoeic thought. It would seem that the Hebrews, no less than the Greeks, broke with the mode of speculation which had prevailed up to their time.[41]

The royal king. The Apostles' Creed singles out God as "*almighty* . . . creator of heaven and earth." This is entirely in line with what we find in Genesis 1, in which God is portrayed in supremely royal terms. The whole of creation—"heaven and earth"—is created (*bārā'*) by God, and his royalty is portrayed throughout Genesis 1 by his exercise of divine fiat, but here in unprecedented terms by ushering creation into existence by mere command. As king, God *speaks* and *sees* repeatedly in this opening salvo of the Bible and in the process demonstrates his complete sovereignty over the creation, ushering it into existence, discerning its nature, and ordering it into a differentiated, "very good" whole. Indirectly God's kingship is foregrounded in Genesis 1:26-28 with the creation of humankind. Humankind is given dominion/rule over the creatures occupying the three major places in the creation—namely, sea, sky, and earth. In this way humankind is portrayed as royal, but, as with the dignity of the authorities in Romans 13, we see in Genesis 1:29-30 that everything humans have and are is "given" by God, the true and absolute king. The creed is thus right to refer to God's character as Almighty before referring to his creation of heaven and earth.

Immanently involved with his creation. Clearly God the creator transcends the creation and ontologically is radically other than it. It is his workmanship and comes into existence as a free act of his will. However, it is equally obvious from the opening chapters of the Bible that God is immanently involved with his creation and especially with humankind, one of two peaks of the creation narrative in Genesis 1.

The Apostles' Creed confesses, "I believe in God, the *Father* almighty, creator of heaven and earth." In this way it expresses a trinitarian doctrine

[41]Henri Frankfort and H. A. Frankfort, conclusion to *The Intellectual Adventure of Ancient Man: An Essay on Speculative Thought in the Ancient Near East*, by Henri Frankfort, H. A. Frankfort, John A. Wilson, Thorkild Jacobsen, and William A. Irwin (Chicago: University of Chicago Press, 1946), 363.

of creation in which the work of creation is that of the One whom Christ revealed to us as the Father. There is thus truth in Barth's point that the doctrine of creation follows Christology, in that we are only in a position to make this confession once we have come to faith in Jesus. Indeed, the incarnation is the reality par excellence that alerts us to God's involvement with his creation. However, in order to understand Jesus we have to read about him in the light of the Old Testament, and then he in return illumines the whole of the Bible. There is thus a forward and backward movement that is unavoidable.

What the confession of the creator as "Father" does alert us to is the deep, deep involvement of God with his creation. At Jesus' baptism, for example, when he identifies himself with sinners and emerges from the waters, the heavens break open and the Father's voice is heard affirming Jesus as Son and as the beloved, instructing all who would hear to listen to him. There are strong creation motifs at work in the narratives of Jesus' baptism, and the depiction of the Father in these narratives bespeaks the heavenly One who remains deeply engaged with his creation. The reference to the beloved can legitimately be reversed with Jesus, as it were, alerting us to his beloved Father. John 1:18 tells us, "No one has ever seen God. It is God the only Son, who is close to the Father's heart, who has made him known." Just as the Father reveals the Son to us in his baptism, so the whole life of Jesus is an exposé of the beloved Father. His life is, as it were, one long revelation of the Father, calling us to return home so as also to become one of the beloved. And it is this Father, as John memorably tells us, who so loved *the world* that he gave his only begotten Son (Jn 3:16).

"Father" evokes a relationship of intimacy and care, as the context and content of the Lord's Prayer makes clear. This intimate involvement of God with his creation is clearly evident in the opening chapters of the Bible, in which God is portrayed as personal, if not more than personal. God speaks and sees. In Genesis 1:26 he addresses the heavenly court as fellow persons and intelligent beings: "Let us . . ." He creates humankind as creatures whom he can address (Gen 1:28-30; 2:15-17), implying that both God and humans are linguistic beings. Humankind names the animals in reflection of God's naming in Genesis 1. Perhaps the most personal of all indicators of the immanent involvement of God in the creation is found in Genesis 1:2, in which the Spirit of God hovers over the unformed universe like a mother bird. In stark contrast to ancient Near East creation stories, God is portrayed as radically other-person centered in his production of the perfect home for humankind.

The Doctrine of Creation and Realism

Nowadays most people have little trouble believing in the reality of the world but often considerable trouble in believing in the creator God. As Barth notes, in general we rightly assume being and not appearance or nonbeing.[42] Intriguingly, however, Barth asserts that belief in the reality of our world is *as* challenging as belief in God as creator. At the outset of his first volume on creation he notes,

> It is only too easy to suggest that, while the reality of God as the Creator is uncertain, and therefore needs proof or revelation, the reality of the creature is all the more certain, so that the one is to be treated as a factor which is not given but has still to be sought, whereas the other may be presupposed *rocher de bronce*. . . . In preoccupation with only one side of the question, there has been a dangerous failure to realise that the question of creation is not less but even more concerned with the reality of the creature rather than that of the Creator.[43]

Barth himself is clear that "if the world is not created by God, it is not. If we do not recognise that it has been created by God, we do not recognise that it is."[44] For Barth this issue is of sufficient weight to devote an entire section to it in his *Church Dogmatics*, titled "Creation as Actualisation."[45] He insists on the link between God as creator and the reality of the world: "God's creation is affirmed by Him because it is real, and it is real because it is affirmed by Him."[46] The reality of God, who stands protectively behind and above the creation, affirms the reality of the creation. "God is real. His creature is actualisation. Hence his creature is real."[47]

Ontologically this implies a type of realism: "We are forbidden to doubt existence and ourselves."[48] And this "realism" has epistemological implications:

> This self-disclosure of the Creator . . . is the living confrontation which meets the creaturely consciousness and in virtue of which knowledge of existence, reality and being is possible and real even outside of God, in the order of the creature which is distinct from Him. This knowledge begins with knowledge of the existence of God, and then, descending from this its primary and proper object, it becomes knowledge of the existence of the knower and his

[42]Barth, *CD* III/1, 345.
[43]Barth, *CD* III/1, 6.
[44]Barth, *CD* III/1, 6.
[45]Barth, *CD* III/1, 344-65.
[46]Barth, *CD* III/1, 345.
[47]Barth, *CD* III/1, 350.
[48]Barth, *CD* III/1, 346.

> environment. For the primary content of the divine self-disclosure, and therefore the primary object of the knowledge based upon it, is God Himself and His own existence. But this content and object include the knower and his world, and assure him of the existence of the same. For God Himself . . . is the ground of the existence of that which is distinct from Him and outside Him.[49]

The major shift from the medieval period to the modern was the shift in focus from starting with God and ontology to starting with humanity and epistemology. Barth perceptively notes, in our terms, that an implication of the doctrine of creation is that the medieval view is the right one.

The doctrine of creation also implies that we can know the world to a significant extent and know it truly. In *Real Presences* George Steiner argues similarly for a view according to which there is substance (i.e., real presence) underlying our experiences of beauty, love, pain, friendship, wonder, and so on.[50] Steiner's language of real presences alludes to the Eucharist, and he argues that to sustain belief in real presences we need *a grammar of creation*. As with Barth, the link between a reality that is real and can be known is made with the world as creation.

One might, however, wonder whether Barth is right that without the Creator the existence of the world is thrown into doubt. This sounds extreme but is certainly supported by the exigencies of modern philosophy. As is well known, Enlightenment and post-Enlightenment philosophy found less and less room for God as it focused more and more exclusively on humanity, epistemology, and the world. A great irony is that as modern philosophy sought epistemological certainty grounded in the human being as knower, the reality of the world started to recede. Descartes sought to doubt everything and thereby to find solid ground in his *cogito*, ground that, on looking back, can only appear as sinking sand. Hume headed off in the direction of radical skepticism so that even causality could not be known with certainty. It was Hume's skepticism that awoke Kant from his dogmatic slumbers. Kant sought to establish firm grounds for true knowledge—not of the world as it is (the noumenon) but only of the world as it appears to us phenomenally. Kant's system is riddled with tensions, and skepticism soon reared its ugly head again with multiple attempts to counter it. Husserl's phenomenology was a last-ditch attempt to secure solid epistemological grounds for scientific knowledge, but his major pupil, Heidegger, turned his phenomenology in a

---

49Barth, *CD* III/1, 348-49.

50George Steiner, *Real Presences* (Chicago: University of Chicago Press, 1989).

hermeneutic direction in which all knowledge emerges out of our thrownness into the world, out of *Dasein*.

Nietzsche, with his radical critique of the Enlightenment, is the precursor of postmodernism, much of which leaves us adrift in the flux and play of history without any hope of true knowledge of the world. Such radical historicism may seem refreshing after the straitjackets of modernity, but in reality it is merely the DNA of modernity working itself out to its logical conclusion of nihilism. As Steiner so perceptively remarks, it is to the credit of Derrida that he confronts us with either nihilism or "In the beginning was the Word"![51] Similarly, Barth notes that "Jesus Christ is the Word by which the knowledge of creation is mediated to us because He is the Word by which God has fulfilled creation and continually maintains and rules it."[52]

Not only has modern thought ended up in doubt about the reality of the world, but it has also engaged in highly destructive *reductionism* in its quest for certain knowledge. It is common among modern thinkers to find the view that only a limited number of aspects of reality are real, since they can be known by science, whereas other aspects such as beauty, truth, delight, and wonder are subjective and not truly part of knowledge.

In his extraordinary *A Guide for the Perplexed*, E. F. Schumacher weighs in against such reductionism and provides a superb illustration of what it involves. While visiting Leningrad, he noticed that while he could see several large churches, they were nowhere on his map. An interpreter explained that in Russia—of that time—they did not show churches on maps. Schumacher, however, pointed out a church on his map. Ah, responded his interpreter, that was a museum and not what they called a "living church." It was only the living churches that were not shown! Schumacher comments,

> It then occurred to me that this was not the first time I had been given a map that failed to show many of the things I could see right in front of my eyes. All through school and university I had been given maps of life and knowledge on which there was hardly a trace of many of the things that I most cared about and that seemed to me to be of the greatest possible importance for the conduct of my life.[53]

As he notes, "The maps produced by modern materialistic scientism leave all the questions that really matter unanswered."[54]

---

[51]Ibid., 138.

[52]Barth, *CD* III/1, 28.

[53]E. F. Schumacher, *A Guide for the Perplexed* (New York: Harper Colophon, 1977), 11.

[54]Ibid., 14.

The doctrine of creation resists reductionism and any attempt to absolutize a particular aspect of the creation from which the rest purportedly can be explained. Alas, the history of philosophy is littered with just such attempts. It is to the credit of the Dutch philosopher Herman Dooyeweerd (1894–1977) that he attempts to articulate a Christian philosophy that avoids such reductionism. Dooyeweerd discerns fifteen modal aspects in which all entities function, and these range from the arithmetic to the pistic via such modes as the aesthetic, the lingual, and the social. In the context of such an approach, aesthetic experience is as real as numerical and logical analysis. The creation is a rich diversity and calls for an epistemology that does justice to all its many dimensions.[55]

Although Barth recognizes that the doctrine of creation has serious ontological and epistemological implications, he is remarkably reticent to allow these play in philosophy. We will have more to say about this in chapters ten and eleven. For now it should be noted that the clearest articulation for the sort of epistemology that flows from this doctrine is that articulated by Oliver O'Donovan in his magisterial *Resurrection and Moral Order*.[56] For O'Donovan the resurrection of Christ reaffirms the order of creation, but this order is only known correctly "in Christ." In this way the realism implied by the doctrine of creation is retained, but it is clearly no naive realism but rather a *critical* realism rooted in the fear of the Lord, as Proverbs reminds us.

The Act of Creation as Sui Generis

By its very nature there is no comparable act for humans to that of creation. It is by God's act of creation that the world as we know it is ushered into existence so that creation is altogether sui generis. We confess it, experience it, and understand it in part, but it remains a mystery that recedes into the very God from whom creation comes. Barth suggests that the only adequate analogy to creation is the eternal begetting of the Son by the Father: "In contrast to everything that we know of origination and causation, creation denotes the divine action which has a real analogy, a genuine point of comparison, only in the eternal begetting of the Son by the Father, and therefore only in the inner life of God Himself, and not at all in the life of the

[55]It is a worthwhile exercise to compare Schumacher's analysis of reality with that of Dooyeweerd. On Dooyeweerd see Bartholomew and Goheen, *Christian Philosophy*, 243-67.

[56]Oliver O'Donovan, *Resurrection and Moral Order: An Outline for Evangelical Ethics* (Leicester, UK: Apollos, 1986).

creature."[57] Both "events" have no parallel in our experience, and both are sui generis; thus, while we welcome Barth's desire to preserve the sui generis nature of the act of creation, we find this parallel with the inner life of the Trinity unconvincing since, if anything, the eternal begetting of the Son is even more mysterious than the act of creation.

Christoph Schwöbel more helpfully draws attention to the relationship between the act of creation, divine agency, and human agency. Schwöbel rightly observes that divine agency is central to Christian belief and worship but has become problematic in modern thought and theology.[58] Just as the *imago Dei* implies a similarity between humans and God but also a radical difference, so too there is a similarity between divine and human agency but also a radical difference.[59] Nowhere is this clearer than with the act of creation. According to Schwöbel, God's agency as the creator differs from intra-creation agency in that it is comprehensive and makes possible all agency within the creation. He concludes that divine agency cannot therefore be used to explain agency within the creation, or vice versa.

The radical difference between God's agency and ours is expressed in the traditional divine attributes of omnipotence, omnipresence, and omniscience. Schwöbel rightly attends to *creatio ex nihilo* with its implication that God is the ultimate agent who, through creation, makes possible all other agency. In this respect God is the supremely perfect agent, and this world is the world God intended to bring into being, hence the repeated description of it as "good" in Genesis 1:1–2:3. In terms of God's omnipotence (see chap. 4), God's agency in creation implies a self-imposed limitation in order to facilitate genuine, creaturely freedom for humans. In relation to God's self-limiting, Schwöbel quotes the rich insight of Simone Weil: "Not only the Passion but Creation itself is a renunciation and sacrifice on the part of God. The Passion is simply its consummation."[60] Creation not only is inseparable from God's omnipotence but also implies his omnipresence "insofar as God is seen as universally present to creation as its creative power of being."[61]

That God's universal agency in creation makes all other agency possible does not mean, in our view, that certain events cannot be interpreted as

---

[57]Barth, *CD* III/1, 13-14.

[58]Christoph Schwöbel, *God: Action and Revelation* (Kampen: Kok Pharos, 1992), 23-28.

[59]Cf. ibid., 58.

[60]Simone Weil, *Gateway to God*, ed. David Raper (London: Fontana, 1974), 80.

[61]Schwöbel, *God*, 39.

examples of "special divine action."[62] God's universal agency in creation and his particular action in certain events are complementary. Approaching divine agency through the lens of the Trinity and the full humanity of Christ, Schwöbel rightly asserts that "in Jesus Christ God reveals his faithfulness in sustaining the created universe in spite of the human contradiction against the order God had created. If this is true, God's creative agency and his redemptive agency cannot be incompatible. Rather they must be *complementary*."[63]

This discussion alerts us to a point noted above—namely, that creation is an extension of, and utterly subordinate to, the doctrine of God. Indeed, our discussion of creation and divine agency moves us into a hornet's nest of issues in contemporary analytical theology and philosophy. An example of this is found in Brian D. Sommer's *Revelation and Authority: Sinai in Jewish Scripture and Tradition*. Sommer refers to Maimonides, who, he claims, argues that at Sinai God could not have spoken or conveyed a thought, "for if God acted at a given moment to think a specific thought or to express a particular wish . . . then God is not eternal and unchanging."[64] Clearly such a view of God as a "perfect being" severely problematizes a Christian doctrine of creation. Maimonides is concerned to bring Jewish thought in line with Greek philosophy, whereas in our view, valuable as Greek concepts have been in articulating a doctrine of God, we need to be sure that they are shaped by Scripture rather than the other way around.[65] Schwöbel proposes, for example, that the personal and metaphysical attributes of God should be understood as relational predicates.[66] A host of philosophers and theologians are now attending to such issues.[67] In our view it is crucial that our doctrine of God emerges from Scripture and is normed by Scripture,[68] and elaborated on by a Christian philosophy, itself normed by Scripture. Colin Gunton provocatively argues, "It is when Christian theology becomes dependent on the

[62]Cf. Paul Gwynne, *Special Divine Action: Key Issues in Contemporary Debate* (Rome: Gregorian & Biblical Press, 1996).

[63]Christoph Schwöbel, "Divine Agency and Providence," *Modern Theology* 3 (1987): 234.

[64]Brian D. Sommer, *Revelation and Authority: Sinai in Jewish Scripture and Tradition* (New Haven, CT: Yale University Press, 2015), 83.

[65]Michael D. Williams, "Systematic Theology as a Biblical Discipline," in *All for Jesus: A Celebration of the 50th Anniversary of Covenant Theological Seminary*, ed. Robert A. Peterson and Sean Michael Lucas (Fearn, UK: Mentor, 2006), 167-96.

[66]Schwöbel, *God*, 60.

[67]See writings by Alvin Plantinga, Eleonore Stump, William Lane Craig, Oliver Crisp, Alan Torrance, etc.

[68]See Craig G. Bartholomew, *The God Who Acts in History: The Significance of Sinai* (Grand Rapids, MI: Eerdmans, 2020).

philosophers' speculations rather than on the equivalent Old Testament polemics against paganism that the troubles begin."[69]

The sui generis nature of creation raises the issue of the *analogia entis*. As Brunner rightly observes, the problem is not with the *analogia entis* but with a doctrine of the *analogia entis* premised on natural theology.[70] The latter approach must assume a philosophy—generally Aristotelian—and then extrapolate from there. Ironically, this ends up making our doctrine of God dependent on immanent insight, not rooted in Scripture.

Brunner evocatively notes, "As Man represents the maximum of freedom in the sphere of the visible creation, so also his whole being represents a maximum of parabolic similarity, which exists in spite of the absolute dissimilarity between creaturely being and the Being of God."[71] Based on revelation, the *analogia entis* thus flows from the doctrine of creation, and in this context Scripture rightly alerts us to the fact that, like humans, God thinks, speaks, acts, wills, and so on. Such analogy needs careful development in any doctrine of God and philosophy of religion.

The Goodness and Comprehensiveness of Creation

A legacy of Neoplatonism in Christianity is the perennial temptation to doubt the goodness of creation. The gravitational pull of Platonism is upward and away from the creation. There is, as we will see in chapter six, a legitimate and indispensable *vertical* orientation to human life, since the doctrine of creation clearly articulates a two-realms theology of heaven and earth, with heaven as the abode of God. It is not for nothing that Jesus teaches his disciples to pray, "Our Father *in heaven* . . ." It is this legitimate vertical dimension that has always made Platonism seem so compatible with Christianity, and indeed a genuine insight of Platonism is that we need a reference point outside the earthly, concrete world to anchor our understanding of this world. However, in the process Platonism denigrates this world, making, for example, the body the prison of the soul. In contrast, while Christianity refuses to deify this world and makes it utterly subordinate to God and his abode, as his handiwork and as his "footstool" it has extraordinary dignity and inherent, creaturely value.

[69]Colin Gunton, *Act and Being: Towards a Doctrine of the Divine Attributes* (Grand Rapids, MI: Eerdmans, 2002), 6.

[70]Emil Brunner, *Dogmatics*, vol. 1, *The Christian Doctrine of God*, trans. by Olive Wyon (Philadelphia: Westminster Press, 1950), 175-82.

[71]Emil Brunner, *Dogmatics*, vol. 2, *The Christian Doctrine of Creation and Redemption*, trans. Olive Wyon (Philadelphia: Westminster Press, 1952), 22.

The goodness of the whole of creation is clearly enunciated in Genesis 1 with its repeated "God saw . . . was good." God does not need to look to see whether his handiwork is good, but he delights in doing so. And how, as readers and listeners, can we deny the goodness of light, earth, sky, sea, the planets and the stars and the sun, the animals of the world, and humankind if God reflects on them as they appear and declares them "good"? Lest there should be any doubt about this at all, Genesis 1:31 concludes that God saw *all that he had made* and "indeed, it was very good." Within the divine economy, God's resounding "Yes!" to creation is found in the incarnation, as we will see in the next chapter with Irenaeus and Athanasius.

There are many dimensions to the goodness of creation. It means that it fulfills God's intention. It means that in its creaturely mode it shares in the goodness of God: "the creature's goodness is its capability to respond to the Creator's goodness"; "it expresses the vocational capacity of the creature to fulfill the expectation of its Creator."[72] It means that we too should look and see and acknowledge of all that God has made that it is good. It means that all of creation is inherently valuable and to be taken seriously and cared for. As Barth notes, "Creaturely goodness is the benefit of creation."[73]

Even as we write this, we are well aware that this side of the fall it is often only by faith in what we cannot see (cf. Heb 11:3) that we affirm the goodness of creation. In chapter eight we discuss the mysterious yet real fall of humankind with catastrophic effects on the entire creation. Amidst the collateral damage of the fall and sin, we sometimes find ourselves in Job-like situations in which it is nigh impossible to see a world charged with the grandeur of God's glory, as Gerald Manley Hopkins so eloquently put it. Hopkins himself was no stranger to deep depression,[74] and yet out of that darkness he was able to write of Christ playing in ten thousand places.

Indeed, the doctrine of creation implies that in some sense Leibniz was right to argue that *this is* the best of all possible worlds. As Barth notes, "In the order of created existence as such there can be nothing better than what it is."[75] Barth rightly says toward the end of a nuanced interaction with Leibniz and his followers, "He must be taken seriously in dogmatics because he too, although in a very different way, tried to sing, and in his own way did

[72]LaCocque in LaCocque and Ricoeur, *Thinking Biblically*, 10, 6.
[73]Barth, *CD* III/1, 366.
[74]Frederick Buechner, *Speak What We Feel (Not What We Ought to Say): Reflections on Literature and Faith* (New York: HarperOne, 2001), 1-43.
[75]Barth, *CD* III/1, 366.

in fact sing, the unqualified praise of God the Creator in His relationship to the creature."[76]

The goodness and the comprehensiveness of creation go together. By the comprehensiveness of creation, we draw attention to the multifaceted and rich diversity of the creation, including its inbuilt dynamic potential for development. It is in the divine speeches in the latter part of Job that one receives the strongest sense of the rich diversity of creation. In Job 38–42 we hear of

- the foundation of the earth;
- the boundaries of the sea, its great depths, and its garment, the clouds;
- the mysteries of light and darkness and the newness of the dawn each morning;
- the varieties of weather, including snow, hail, rain, lightning, and wind;
- desert places where no human lives;
- the constellations of stars;
- the wonderful diversity of animal life; and
- Behemoth and Leviathan.

If the divine speeches emphasize the "natural" world, we should not forget the celebration of culture making in Job 28, with its use of the metaphor of mining.

By definition the doctrine of creation relates to *all that is*—apart from evil, which is a parasite on the good creation. Barth notes, therefore, that "it is our duty—and this is what we are taught by the self-revelation of God in Jesus Christ—to love and praise the created order because, as is made manifest in Jesus Christ, it is so mysteriously well-pleasing to God."[77]

Evangelicalism, in particular, has been dogged by various forms of a sacred-secular dualism. A manifestation of this is the vocational pyramid with the most "spiritual" vocations being those dealing with the "soul"—namely, those of pastors and missionaries. Such work is erroneously referred to as full-time service in contrast to Christians in other vocations, who are, presumably, part-time servants of Christ! Here we witness the reemergence of a Neoplatonism that the doctrine of creation utterly resists. As Eugene Peterson declares, "We are all in holy orders!"[78] The only question is where and how, amidst the rich diversity of God's creation, we are called to serve.

---

[76]Barth, *CD* III/1, 405.

[77]Barth, *CD* III/1, 370.

[78]Eugene Peterson, *Leap over a Wall: Earthly Spirituality for Everyday Christians* (New York: HarperCollins, 1997), 32.

The doctrine of creation is radical in that it goes to the deepest roots of everything that has been created and leaves no area of life in the world untouched. In chapter twelve we will explore multiple examples of ways in which major areas of life are profoundly affected by one's doctrine of creation. This doctrine is indeed the common property of orthodox Christians, but mere possession does not necessarily mean adequate engagement! Schumacher, to whom we referred earlier, says of his school and university years, "It was still possible, on suitable occasions, to refer to God the Creator, although every educated person knew that there was not really a God, certainly not one capable of creating anything, and that the things around us had come into existence by a process of mindless evolution, that is by chance and natural selection."[79]

By contrast, the biblical doctrine of creation asserts unequivocally that there really is a God and that he is, as C. S. Lewis evocatively puts it, the hunter, the warrior, the king, the God who approaches at infinite speed.[80] As Paul says, he is the living and true God. And we ourselves, and everything around us, are his creation! We urgently need to recover this doctrine as "the presupposition which has to precede all other presuppositions, axioms and convictions, and the effectiveness of which can be counted on in every conceivable connexion."[81] This is true not least in dogmatics. We should expect to find the "thread" of creation woven into the fabric of every other doctrine because it is so utterly and pervasively significant. Alas, this has not always been the case, and in the next chapter we explore some of the many ways in which historically and today the doctrine of creation has been eclipsed.

---

[79]Schumacher, *Guide for the Perplexed*, 12.
[80]C. S. Lewis, *Miracles: A Preliminary Study* (Glasgow: Geoffrey Bles, 1947), 114.
[81]Barth, *CD* III/1, 23.

TWO

THE TRAVAILS AND GLORIES OF THE DOCTRINE OF CREATION

EARLY CHURCH TO POST-REFORMATION

ALL ORTHODOX CHRISTIANS uphold and affirm the doctrine of creation. It is enshrined forever in the catholic creeds, as we saw in chapter one, and the biblical data for it are pervasive throughout both Testaments. Doctrine, however, is something that develops in the life of the church through history.[1] For example, the doctrine of the person of Christ was hammered out over centuries in the early church.[2] No such process, however, has ever occurred in quite the same way for the doctrine of creation. It remains the case that the church historically, and today, has often struggled to articulate and embrace a full-orbed doctrine of creation.[3] Thus the history of the doctrine of creation is one of travail and glory. The travail continues, and there is much at stake in recovery of a full, biblical doctrine of creation. This chapter traces the doctrine of creation's travail and glory from the early church through the Reformation and post-Reformation periods, and chapter three will bring the history up to our current time and debates.

[1]E.g., Hastings Rashdall, *Doctrine and Development: University Sermons* (London: Methuen, 1898); John Henry Newman, *Essay on the Development of Christian Doctrine*, 6th ed. (Notre Dame, IN: University of Notre Dame Press, 1989); Peter Toon, *The Development of Doctrine in the Church* (Grand Rapids, MI: Eerdmans, 1979); Jaroslav Pelikan, *The Christian Tradition: A History of the Development of Doctrine*, 5 vols. (Chicago: University of Chicago Press, 1975–1989); Alister McGrath, *The Genesis of Doctrine* (Grand Rapids, MI: Eerdmans, 1997).

[2]See Alois Grillmeier, *Christ in Christian Tradition: From the Apostolic Age to Chalcedon (451)* (London: Mowbray, 1965).

[3]A useful reader is Ian A. McFarland, ed., *Creation and Humanity: The Sources of Christian Theology* (Louisville, KY: Westminster John Knox, 2009).

In this chapter the patristic period deserves special attention, as the church fathers' conversation with Gnostic heresies is the ground from which the doctrine grows. As the conversation continues, a gnostic thread runs throughout church history and remains today, threatening the glory of the doctrine of creation with the travails of heresy. Gnosticism seems to sing an especially alluring siren song and can be successfully countered only with a full-orbed doctrine of creation. When this full-orbed doctrine of creation shines brightest, it

- begins with the trinitarian creator God;
- affirms the goodness of God's creation without hierarchy between material and spiritual;
- celebrates humanity as God's image bearers called to develop God's good creation despite the prevalence of sin in the world; and
- looks forward to God's restoring, elevating, and enhancing creation's original form in the eschaton.

Gnosticism in its various forms and offshoots denies each of these, leading to a distorted view of our world and potentially to a denial of the God who created all things through Christ and his Spirit. Tracing the history of this doctrine is instructive in keeping us along paths that God has laid for us in Scripture as we seek to articulate the glory of creation and its creator in our own time. To that history we now turn.

Our argument in this section is *not* that the doctrine of creation is the major doctrine of the church. The doctrine of creation is subsidiary to the doctrine of God. At the same time, it alerts us to the fact that our knowledge of God is made possible and constrained by his act of creation "in the beginning." We only know God as he shows himself to us—revelation to creatures—*within* the creation. Indeed, we will have a reduced doctrine of God if we do not fully appropriate God as creator. It is only through God's revelation of himself in Jesus that we come to know God as Father, and so, as Barth, for example, has argued, there is a sense in which the doctrine of the person and work of Christ is the door through which we must enter in order to obtain a Christian doctrine of God. Barth asserts, "By becoming man in Jesus Christ, the fact has also become plain and credible that God is the Creator of the world."[a] However, as noted elsewhere in this volume, contra Barth, we would argue that without creation there could be no Jesus. As God's first act in relation to our world, creation is fundamental to everything that follows.

All of this alerts us to the fact that perichoresis—the interwovenness of the acts of Father, Son, and Spirit—applies not only to the acts of the persons of the Trinity but also to the doctrines of the faith. These doctrines are irretrievably intertwined; distortion in one inevitably and negatively affects others. In our view this interpenetration of the doctrines comes to light especially clearly with the doctrine of creation. Though subsidiary to the doctrine of God, as his first act it is fundamental to all that follows, so that failure to take full account of the first act in the great drama of Scripture will lead to reductionistic and distorted doctrine if we abstract—as one must—from other parts of the story in order to develop systematic doctrines without taking full account of the first act of the drama. Many examples of this could be given; suffice it to mention a few. Take ecclesiology, for example. A robust doctrine of creation would prevent us from ever making the mistake of equating the kingdom of God with the institutional church, and yet in practice this confusion is far too common. And the effects are debilitating. Worship becomes confined to what we do when we gather as "church" rather than, as in Romans 12:1-2, being our total life response to the gospel as we offer *our bodies*—the totality of our personhood—as living sacrifices. The sermon, rather than enabling us to hear God's life-giving word for *all of life*, becomes narrowed down to our spiritual lives and how we can contribute to the building of the institutional church. A second example is the doctrine of the ascension.[b] Many churches either fail to celebrate this as a feast day or have little idea precisely what to celebrate on such an occasion. Such failure is not new; Davies, for example, finds a dearth of intelligent references to the ascension through the whole millennium following Origen and Augustine.[c] Both problems stem from a deficient doctrine of creation, thus a deficient doctrine of salvation, and thus a failure to see that Christ's ascension to the place of kingship over the entire creation is the culmination of his redemptive life and work.

[a]Karl Barth, *Dogmatics in Outline*, trans. G. T. Thomson (London: SCM Press, 1966), 52.

[b]Cf. Douglas Farrow, *Ascension and Ecclesia: On the Significance of the Doctrine of the Ascension for Ecclesiology and Christian Cosmology* (Grand Rapids, MI: Eerdmans, 1999).

[c]J. G. Davies, *He Ascended into Heaven: A Study in the History of Doctrine* (London: Lutterworth, 1958), 147; Farrow, *Ascension and Ecclesia*, 129.

The Patristic Period: Fertile Ground for a Doctrine of Creation

The early church never treated the doctrine of creation in isolation or systematically as a modern theologian might do, but dealt with it in a variety of genres and debates. Paul M. Blowers observes,

> The early church took its cues from the Bible's own thorough integration of creation and redemption in the divine economy. Well beyond the apostolic era, patristic exegetes continued to expound on the New Testament's witness to the "cosmic Christ," and, especially from Irenaeus of Lyons onward, to articulate the role of Jesus Christ—pre-incarnate, incarnate, and post-incarnate—as himself Creator and not simply the mediating agent of the

> Father in his creative work. The Son's hominization as the Second Adam in Jesus of Nazareth, a particular human being in history, was conceived as the ultimate ratification of God's commitment to the *material* creation and as the definitive outworking of God's original plan for the world. . . . The conviction of many patristic interpreters was that the advent of Christ inaugurates the new, eschatological creation.[4]

This is rich territory indeed. The works of Irenaeus, Tertullian, Origen, Athanasius, Basil of Caesarea, Augustine, and Maximus the Confessor all played major roles in these initial stages of articulating a Christian doctrine of creation and the ensuing conversation over the next couple of millennia. While each of these made major contributions, they were also influenced negatively at times by Greek philosophies and their resulting theologies. In order to trace the travail and glory of the doctrine of creation, therefore, one must be attuned to how theologians not only counter certain philosophies but also are influenced by them. Thus, we begin with philosophical and historical influences on biblical interpretation before diving into the church fathers themselves.

Greek influences: Plato, Plotinus, and Philo. Many Christian theologians formed their understanding of creation in conversation with Greek philosophy. This should not be surprising, for theology is inherently contextual and dialogical. For better and for worse, philosophy often provides the conceptual apparatus, and for early Christians it was the Greek philosophers who did so. The Greek philosophical tradition asked many of the same questions about the cosmos, provided some of the conceptual apparatus for grappling with those questions, and provided answers to those questions that some Christian theologians found helpful. Greek philosophical cosmologies were attempts to demythologize the Greek worldview by rationally critiquing its polytheism. It was the Greek dualists whose ideas exerted a corrupting influence on many patristic theologians. Although Parmenides provided an initial instance of dualism, it is Plato's dualism that has remained influential in the history of the Christian doctrine of creation. Plato modified Parmenides by positing a hierarchy of being in which the world is divided into two realms. The upper realm is immaterial and invisible. It is the most "real" and is accessible only to the intellect. The lower realm is material and visible. It is less "real" than the upper realm and is accessible by the senses. The upper

[4]Paul M. Blowers, *Drama of the Divine Economy: Creator and Creation in Early Christian Theology and Piety* (Oxford: Oxford University Press, 2012), 2.

realm consists of ideal "Forms" that provide the templates out of which the material things of the lower realm are made. So everything in the material world is a decaying and inferior copy of its ideal Form, which exists in the immaterial upper realm. Plato came to consider the ideal Forms as divine, because they are perfect, unchanging, and eternal.[5] The concept of a hierarchy between an upper and lower realm is a key ingredient to what would become one of the most significant challenges to the Christian doctrine of creation—Gnosticism.

In his *Timaeus* Plato depicts a Craftsman ("Demiurge"[a]) who created the world by copying and multiplying the Forms. He argues that the universe is the product of intelligent and beneficent agency. While we appreciate Plato's *Timaeus* for its recognition that the universe is beautiful and that it is the product of intelligent and beneficent agency, it is important to note that Plato's conception of the universe is flawed and contradictory. Lovejoy notes that there is in Plato an otherworldly and a this-worldly motif.[b] His philosophy of the realm of Forms and Ideas is the one through which "the conception of an unseen eternal world, of which the visible world is but a pale copy, gains a permanent foothold in the West."[c] However, as Lovejoy notes, Plato "also gave the characteristic form and phraseology and dialectic to precisely the contrary tendency—to a peculiarly exuberant kind of this-worldliness" expressed particularly in his *Timaeus*.[d]

Even on the most integrative reading of Plato, a tension remains between the Forms and the preexisting matter out of which the Craftsman created. Furthermore, Plato's conception does not call forth worship of the Craftsman/Creator, nor does it recognize the creation as "good" or "very good." Indeed, the universe—an ordered and majestic *material* world—must necessarily be a lower and lesser reality than the immaterial realm of the Forms.

[a]*Plato's Timaeus: Translation, Glossary, Appendices and Introductory Essay*, trans. Peter Kalkavage (Newburyport, MA: Focus, 2001), §28a6.
[b]Arthur O. Lovejoy, *The Great Chain of Being: A Study of the History of an Idea* (1936; Cambridge, MA: Harvard University Press, 1964).
[c]William R. Inge, *The Platonic Tradition in English Religious Thought* (1926; Whitefish, MT: Kessinger, 2003), 9.
[d]Lovejoy, *Great Chain of Being*, 45.

Plato's dualism set the course for his successors, who, even when they departed from Plato on particular points, operated within a philosophical environment suffused with Platonic influence. Plotinus modified Plato's dualism, influencing Origen, Augustine, and other Christian theologians. Plotinus posited a hierarchical view of reality, a great chain of being, at the lower end of which is the material world. At the top of Plotinus's hierarchy is the One

[5]Nicholas P. White, *Plato on Knowledge and Reality* (Indianapolis: Hackett, 1976).

(Nous), which contains the ideal Forms. Below the One is Soul (Psyche), which serves as the mediating link between the upper realm and the lower realm. The lower realm is inferior to the upper realm and in fact emanates from the upper realm. The lower realm is less "real" than the upper realm and receives only as much reality as can be mediated to it by the great chain of being. We should not underestimate the challenge the Fathers faced: "Thus by way of *Greek concepts* is sought the intelligence of truth the most *anti-Greek*. Such is the contradiction in which the Fathers and Councils are taken up more than once."[6] The melding of Greek philosophy and biblical theology had already taken place in Jewish thinking prior to the church fathers. Philo serves as a good example.

Philo of Alexandria (20 BC–AD 50) was a Hellenistic Jewish philosopher who used allegorical exegesis to harmonize Greek philosophy with Jewish biblical interpretation. In the process he influenced several church fathers. Philo rightly believed that the world was created rather than eternal, but, as Gunton notes, his interpretation of the Genesis account unfortunately "is combined with certain platonic assumptions which override essential aspects of the text, particularly its celebration of the goodness of the whole of the created order, material and 'spiritual' alike."[7] Gunton notes two specific instances. In *On the Creation*, Philo interprets the "heaven and earth" of Genesis 1:1 to imply a two-step creative process in which God creates heavenly Forms first and earthly material second.[8] He further interprets the "image of God" in Genesis 1:26-27 to exclude the human body. Philo writes, "Let no one represent the likeness as one to a bodily form for neither is God in human form, nor is the human body God-like. No, it is in respect of the mind, the sovereign element of the soul, that the word 'image' is used."[9] Philo rejects Plato's divinization of the Forms and affirms, against Platonism, that material creation is "good." However, his Platonic assumptions about the inferiority of the material

---

[6]Michel Henry, quoted in Emmanuel Falque, *God, the Flesh, and the Other: From Irenaeus to Duns Scotus*, trans. William C. Hackett (Evanston, IL: Northwestern University Press, 2015), 118. Michel Henry alerts us repeatedly to the contrast between the Greek and Christian view of the body: "The violence of this confrontation between the Greek conception of the body and the Christian conception of flesh will thus explode on the scene from the first propagation in the antique world of the new religion, whose essential content is the affirmation of the coming of God in the human condition in the form of his incarnation." *Incarnation: A Philosophy of Flesh*, trans. Karl Hefty (Evanston, IL: Northwestern University Press, 2015), 126.

[7]Colin E. Gunton, *The Triune Creator: A Historical and Systematic Study* (Grand Rapids, MI: Eerdmans, 1998), 46.

[8]Philo, *On the Creation* 4.16. (Philo, *On the Creation of the Cosmos According to Moses*, trans. David T. Runia [Boston: Brill, 2001]).

[9]Philo, *On the Creation* 23.69.

world warp his interpretation of the Genesis account, causing him to affirm a creation in which immaterial reality is "more good" than material reality. Even though his view of creation was disconnected from Christ and thus sub-Christian, Philo sets the stage for building unity between the Bible and Greek philosophy later exhibited by the church fathers. As we will see in the church fathers, this "yes" and "no" to Greek philosophy takes several forms, beginning with Irenaeus.

Irenaeus—the founding father. Irenaeus of Lyons (AD 130–202) was a presbyter among Christian emigrants to France in the early second century and was most likely martyred during a massacre of Christians in AD 202. His writings are occasional, marked by the challenges the church faced. That situation was Gnosticism and its inroads among the Christian community in Lyons and throughout the Roman Empire. Gnostic theologies—for there is no single Gnostic theology—are philosophico-religious worldview complexes marked by beliefs that (1) the world is a hierarchy in which there are at least two gods, including a supreme deity who is the source of the spiritual realm and a lesser deity who created the material realm; (2) spirit is good, but matter is evil; (3) the supreme deity did not create the world, because that would implicate him in the creation of evil; (4) the supreme deity saves us from this inferior material world and does so by means of secret knowledge, or *gnosis*; (5) the New Testament is associated with the superior deity, while the Old Testament is associated with the lesser god; (6) a group of agents mediate between god and the world, between the spiritual and material; (7) ethical systems are based on the inherent badness of embodied life in this world and therefore lead either to ascetic or licentious ethics; and (8) the cosmos will finally be annihilated.

Irenaeus considered Gnosticism not only foolish but dangerous and sought to expose its corruption of the Christian gospel and break its back so that it no longer held influence in the Christian community. Irenaeus countered these Gnostic theologies by asserting creation as an act of divine love from a triune God and thus the nonhierarchical goodness of all creation, the necessity of the Old Testament for rightly understanding God, and the redemption of all things as the culmination of God's purposes for creation. In Irenaeus one can find the beginnings of articulating a more fully orbed doctrine of creation. Douglas Farrow notes that "Christian dogmatics makes its first appearance in the second-century struggle with Gnosticism."[10] Central

[10]Douglas Farrow, *Ascension and Ecclesia: On the Significance of the Doctrine of the Ascension for Ecclesiology and Christian Cosmology* (Grand Rapids, MI: Eerdmans, 1999), 43-44.

to this struggle was the relationship between redemption and creation. "In other words, was redemption the antithesis of creation or its fulfillment? . . . This question, already a cosmological one, virtually created the discipline of dogmatics."[11] In this creation, one can hardly underestimate the importance of Irenaeus's engagement with Gnosticism.

For the Gnostics, "the universe, the domain of the Archons, is like a vast prison whose innermost dungeon is the earth, the scene of man's life."[12] However, a spark of the divine is contained within the human soul, which sets humankind radically apart from the evil creation. Through a savior who descends from above, humans are provided with what they need for salvation—namely, *gnosis*. As Hans Jonas describes the Gnostic view, "Equipped with this *gnosis*, the soul after death travels upwards, leaving behind at each sphere the psychical 'vestment' contributed by it: thus the spirit stripped of all foreign accretions reaches the God beyond the world and becomes reunited with the divine substance."[13] Salvation thus liberates us to escape the material world and travel upward to our true home in God. H. Paul Santmire notes, "Gnosticism is perhaps the most extreme example in Western history of a world view shaped by the metaphor of ascent—by that metaphor, indeed, and no other."[14]

As such, Gnosticism subverts everything Christians hold dear—the creation that God called "good," the incarnation in which Christ took on human flesh, and our hope of dwelling together with the Lord in a new heaven and earth. "In sum," Gunton writes,

> Gnosticism was—and, indeed, remains—a Christian heresy which fed upon Greek philosophical suspicions of the goodness and reality of the material world. Like many heresies, however, it provided the spur to efforts to counter it, and in the process gave the church one of its greatest theological achievements. For Irenaeus' doctrine of creation was forged in opposition to [it].[15]

Irenaeus rejected the Gnostics' denial of the creator God, the Old Testament, and their view of God as distant and removed from concrete, everyday life.[16]

---

[11]Ibid., 44.

[12]Hans Jonas, *The Gnostic Religion: The Message of the Alien God and the Beginnings of Christianity* (Boston: Beacon, 1958), 43.

[13]Ibid., 45.

[14]H. Paul Santmire, *The Travail of Nature: The Ambiguous Ecological Promise of Christian Theology* (Philadelphia: Fortress, 1985), 34.

[15]Gunton, *Triune Creator*, 49-50.

[16]The twentieth century saw a revival in scholarly commentary on Irenaeus's theology in general and his doctrine of creation in particular. Gustaf Wingren (*Man and the Incarnation: A Study in*

He saw creation as humanity's God-given home and of great value to the God who became incarnate to redeem fallen humanity and thereby to renew the entire creation. In his struggle with Marcion (ca. AD 85–160[17]) and the Gnostics over the unity of the Bible, Irenaeus articulates the unity of the Bible as a single story,[18] as Robert Louis Wilken explains:

> Two histories converge in the biblical account, the history of Israel and the life of Christ, but because they are also the history of God's actions in and for the world, they are part of a larger narrative that begins at creation and ends in a vision of a new, more splendid city in which the "Lord God will be their light." The Bible begins, as it were, with the beginning and ends with an end that is no end, life with God, in Irenaeus's charming expression, a life in which one is "always conversing with God in new ways." Nothing falls outside of its scope.[19]

Irenaeus accused the Gnostics of failing to interpret biblical texts within the context of the entire canon. "They disregard the order and the connection of the Scriptures, and so far as in them lies, dismember and destroy the truth."[20] Through his focus on Scripture's unity Irenaeus was able to reject the anthropomorphic theology of his opponents and the rationalist epistemology from which it came.[21] Irenaeus rejects natural theology and insists that "if we have specific and definite knowledge of Him [God]—and we do—it is a gift. God addresses himself to us through his Word, and his Word is himself."[22] Unlike his opponents, Irenaeus developed his theology not on an opposition between the one and the many but on the freedom of God to be deeply involved with

---

the Biblical Theology of Irenaeus, trans. R. MacKenzie [Eugene, OR: Wipf & Stock, 1959], 3) asserts that Irenaeus's doctrine of creation is where one must begin in order to understand Irenaeus's broader theology, and his approach is now standard.

[17]Cf. Judith M. Lieu, *Marcion and the Making of a Heretic: God and Scripture in the Second Century* (Cambridge: Cambridge University Press, 2015).

[18]Nathan MacDonald ("Israel and the Old Testament Story in Irenaeus' Presentation of the Rule of Faith", *Journal of Theological Interpretation* 3 [2009]: 267-84) argues that it is too simplistic to to see Irenaeus's *Demonstration of the Apostolic Preaching* as a summary of the Rule of Faith organized around the plot movements of the biblical narrative. He bases his argument on a heretofore untranslated work appearing in the Armenian language that MacDonald says reveals Irenaeus's interest in articulating the basis of the Rule in Old Testament prophecy and prefiguration rather than his supposed interest in Scripture's overarching narrative. We respond that MacDonald may be correct about Irenaeus's primary purpose, but it does not follow that Irenaeus does not have a secondary purpose or secondary effect—namely, an exposition of the Bible's narrative coherence.

[19]Robert Louis Wilken, *The Spirit of Early Christian Thought: Seeking the Face of God* (New Haven, CT: Yale University Press, 2003), 63.

[20]Irenaeus, *Against Heresies* 1.8.1 (*ANF* 14:326).

[21]Farrow, *Ascension and Ecclesia*, 47.

[22]Ibid., 48.

his creatures. "He [God] is wholly other and genuinely accessible at the same time."[23] True *gnosis* is not just rational but relational.

Irenaeus understood that Christian salvation cannot be conceived except on the backdrop of a good creation, created *ex nihilo*, as an act of divine love. Ian McKenzie writes that "creation is an act of the love of God. . . . It is this love of God which means that creation and redemption are so closely bound for Irenaeus. Creation and incarnation are but the two sides of the one act of the love of God towards what he makes."[24] God creates out of the overflow of his goodness, a goodness that has a Christocentric reference and a redemptive telos.[25] Irenaeus argues that God created *ex nihilo*. "He is the only God, the only Lord, the only Creator, the only Father, alone containing all things, and himself commanding all things into existence."[26]

Irenaeus further argues that the incarnation demonstrates the goodness of material reality. "For if the flesh were not in a position to be saved," he writes, "the Word of God would in no wise have become flesh."[27] The Gnostics asserted that salvation came via knowledge, but Irenaeus responded that salvation came via the incarnation and atonement, which are embodied actions. The problem with the world—its frailty—is not materiality but sin and distortion, and it is this with which Christ came to deal.

For Irenaeus, the world is not a hierarchical chain of being with immaterial reality at the top and material reality at the bottom. Instead, it is a seamlessly good world created by the one and only good God. For this reason he rejected Gnostic teaching about the necessity of intermediary agents and in its place affirmed the Christian doctrine of the Trinity. "For God did not stand in need of these [intermediary beings], in order to the accomplishing of what He had Himself determined with Himself beforehand should be done, as if He did not possess His own hands. For with Him were always present the Word and Wisdom, the Son and the Spirit, by whom and in whom, freely and spontaneously, He made all things."[28]

In contrast to the Gnostic metaphor of ascent, Santmire discerns migration to the good land as the root metaphor operative in Irenaeus's thought.[29] God's

---

[23]Ibid., 48.

[24]Iain MacKenzie, *Irenaeus's Demonstration of the Apostolic Preaching: A Theological Commentary and Translation* (Burlington, VT: Ashgate, 2002), 94.

[25]Gunton, *Triune Creator*, 52-55.

[26]Irenaeus, *Against Heresies* 2.1.1 (*ANF* 14:359). On Justin, Basilides, Theophilus, and Irenaeus on *creatio ex nihilo*, see Eric Osborn, *Irenaeus of Lyons* (Cambridge: Cambridge University Press, 2001), 69-73.

[27]Irenaeus, *Against Heresies* 5.14.1 (*ANF* 14:541).

[28]Irenaeus, *Against Heresies* 4.20.1 (*ANF* 14:487).

[29]Santmire, *Travail of Nature*, 38.

original intention for creation was dynamic; God intended to lead it from its original state to final fulfillment. Hence the incarnation is aimed not just at redeeming humanity but at leading the creation to its telos. Christ *recapitulates* in himself what has preceded him in human history and thereby overcomes sin and leads the whole of human history to its consummation. Alois Grillmeier writes, "Creation, the incarnation of Christ, redemption, and resurrection, belong together as different parts of one all-embracing saving work of God."[30]

Santmire further notes how Irenaeus's unified, universalized theology of creation history, articulated above, influences his view of the present; the God of the eschaton now blesses creation, now renews it, now cares for and is intimately involved in his creation.[31] In his explication of the economic Trinity, Irenaeus uses the delightful image of hands: God's hands refer to the work of the Word and the Spirit in his creation. Irenaeus acknowledges the curse of the earth following humankind's fall but rejects the notion of a cosmic fall. Creation retains its created goodness, and humans are intended to be at home in the world.

The concept of recapitulation dominated second-century theology, being found in Ignatius, Justin Martyr, Tertullian, Irenaeus in particular, Clement of Alexandria, and Athanasius. Osborn says of recapitulation in Irenaeus, "The complexity of the concept is formidable. At least eleven ideas—unification, repetition, redemption, perfection, inauguration and consummation, totality, the triumph of Christus Victor, ontology, epistemology and ethics (or being, truth and goodness)—are combined in different permutations."[a] After a lengthy discussion of recapitulation Osborn asks,

> What then is recapitulation? Who is the agent? It is the work of the incarnate Christ. What is summed up? The totality of humanity and the universe is recapitulated in Christ. What happens in recapitulation? First, the whole history of salvation is resumed, so that beginning, middle and end are brought together. . . . Secondly, the sovereignty of Christ over all things is assumed; just as he reigns over the unseen world, so he is lord of the visible world, which he supports by the axis of his cross. Thirdly, all things are recreated, restored, renewed and set free. Lastly, all things achieve the purpose for which they were made; they are not merely repaired but are brought to perfection in Christ.[b]

Hick leverages Irenaeus's writings on creation in order to support his theodicy.[c] Farrow, however, observes,

[30]Grillmeier, *Christ in Christian Tradition*, 101.
[31]Santmire, *Travail of Nature*, 44.

The "imperfection" is this: the love for God which is the life of man cannot emerge *ex nihilo* in full bloom; it requires to grow with experience. But that in turn is what makes the fall, however unsurprising, such a devastating affair. In the fall, man is "turned backwards." He does not grow up in love of God as he is intended to. The course of his time, his so-called progress, is set in the wrong direction.[d]

[a]Eric Osborn, *Irenaeus of Lyons* (Cambridge: Cambridge University Press, 2001), 97. Osborn identifies three motifs in recapitulation: "Christ corrects and perfects all that is; as Christus Victor he is the climax of the economy of saving history; and as the perfection of being, goodness and truth, he gives life to the dying, righteousness to sinners and truth to those in error." *Tertullian: First Theologian of the West* (Cambridge: Cambridge University Press, 1997), 17.

[b]Osborn, *Irenaeus of Lyons*, 117.

[c]John Hick, *Evil and the God of Love* (San Francisco: Harper & Row, 1978).

[d]Douglas Farrow, "St. Irenaeus of Lyons: The Church and the West," *Pro Ecclesia* 4, no. 3 (1995): 348.

Thus, Irenaeus's eschatology is restorationist. The good creation is one that God built so that it would mature, refine, and develop, and such maturation occurs finally in the eschaton. Irenaeus writes, "[Christ] will himself renew the inheritance of the earth . . . in which the new fruit of the vine is drunk, and the resurrection of His disciples in the flesh. For the new flesh which rises again is the same which also received the new cup."[32] From passages such as this, M. C. Steenberg concludes, "The chiliastic kingdom is perceived not as a destruction of the current economy and initiation of a new, but the fulfillment, restoration and renewal of that which God originally began in creating 'the heavens and the earth' (Gen 1.1)."[33] Irenaeus's eschatology therefore bears on his protology, and vice versa, such that each is revelatory of the other, with both being related to the incarnate Son.[34]

Irenaeus's efforts were not for naught. His argument not only won the day but in the end won the era. The sort of Gnostic dualisms refuted by Irenaeus were soon officially excluded by church councils. For instance, the Council of Nicaea (325) implicitly rejects dualism by affirming that God is "creator of all that is, visible and invisible," while the Synod of Toledo (400) explicitly rejected dualism by stating, "If anyone says and believes that this world and all its instruments have not been created by the almighty God, let him be anathema. . . . If anyone says or believes that the world has been made by a god other than the one of whom it is written, 'In the beginning, God created

[32]Irenaeus, *Against Heresies* 5.33.1 (*ANF* 14:562).

[33]M. C. Steenberg, *Irenaeus on Creation: The Cosmic Christ and the Saga of Redemption*, Supplements to Vigiliae Christianae (Boston: Brill, 2008), 55.

[34]Ibid.

heaven and earth' (Gen 1:1), let him be anathema." But the church's battle with Gnosticism would not end there.

The gnostic impulse has remained a perennial temptation in Christian thought, as we will see with Origen and, to a far lesser extent, with Augustine. As Farrow observes, "Now if it is largely to the credit of Irenaeus that a deliberately docetic approach to Christology—*viz.*, one which openly severed the link between creation and redemption at the expense of the human Jesus—could never again be taken seriously, it is nonetheless true that dualist tendencies were far from being fully vanquished in the church."[35] Furthermore, as we will explore below, major parts of modern and postmodern thought represent a resurgent gnosticism in our day. Tertullian would take up the battle against Gnosticism with regard to Marcion.

Tertullian—glory continued. Tertullian (AD 160–220), the first theologian of the West, who wrote in Latin, was a gifted theologian who used his considerable intellectual powers to defend and articulate the gospel. He understood the power of words, and Osborn playfully observes of his thought, "At creation, God who had always been rational became verbal and the place had never been quiet since."[36] With Irenaeus, Tertullian played a major role in taking on the Gnostics and Marcion. Tertullian exemplifies what Brunner describes: "For the preservation of the Christian doctrine of Creation the Old Testament was of immeasurable importance. The Church had to meet the difficulties raised by Gnosticism on two fronts. She defended both at the same time, the Old Testament and the doctrine of Creation, and in so doing, the unity of God as Creator and Redeemer."[37] Tertullian's lengthiest dispute was with Marcion, who distinguished the God of the Old Testament from the God of the New. Tertullian saw and responded to the threat this represented: "Dualism was the foremost threat to emerging Christian theology."[38]

Tertullian is clear that the world is not divine, but it is worthy of God:

> Goodness spake the word; Goodness formed man of the dust of the ground into so great a substance of the flesh, built up out of one material with so many qualities; Goodness breathed into him a soul, not dead, but living. Goodness gave him dominion over all things, which he was to enjoy and rule over, and

[35]Farrow, *Ascension and Ecclesia*, 87.

[36]Eric Osborn, *Tertullian: First Theologian of the West* (Cambridge: Cambridge University Press, 1997), xiv.

[37]Emil Brunner, *Dogmatics*, vol. 2, *The Christian Doctrine of Creation and Redemption*, trans. Olive Wyon (Philadelphia: Westminster Press, 1952), 36.

[38]Osborn, *Tertullian*, 88.

> even give names to. In addition to this, Goodness annexed pleasures to man; so that, while master of the whole world, he might tarry among higher delights, being translated into paradise, out of the world into the Church. The self-same Goodness provided also a help meet for him, that there might be nothing in his lot that was not good.[39]

For Tertullian, God "holds the universe in His hand as if it were a bird's nest."[40]

Furthermore, Tertullian is aware of the potential for development in God's good creation: "Meanwhile the world consisted of all things good, plainly foreshowing how much good was preparing for him for whom all this was provided."[41] Tertullian affirms strongly the unity of God as creator and redeemer, as Osborn notes: "Creation proves God's existence; redemption proves his nature."[42] His doctrine of creation, like that of Irenaeus, is Christocentric: "The golden thread which runs through his thought is the recapitulation of all things in Christ."[43]

It is fascinating to see how Tertullian develops his ethics in relation to the doctrine of creation.[44] He asserts,

> We do not forget the debt of gratitude we owe to God, our Lord and Creator; we reject no creature of His hands, though certainly we exercise restraint upon ourselves, lest of any gift of His we make an immoderate or sinful use. So we sojourn with you in the world, abjuring neither forum, nor shambles, nor bath, nor booth, nor workshop, nor inn, nor weekly market, nor any other places of commerce. We sail with you, and fight with you, and till the ground with you; and in like manner we unite with you in your traffickings—even in the various arts we make public property of our works for your benefit.[45]

As Osborn observes, we find in Tertullian a realism that manifests nothing of Plato's devaluation of matter.[46]

Origen—the travail of hierarchy between material and immaterial. Origen (AD 185–254) writes in the next generation after Irenaeus and takes a troubling turn away from Irenaeus's and Tertullian's path-setting work on creation. Origen posited a hierarchical chain of being, similar to the

---

[39]Tertullian, *Against Marcion* 2.4 (*ANF* 3:300).
[40]Tertullian, *Against Marcion* 2.25 (*ANF* 3:317).
[41]Tertullian, *Against Marcion* 2.4 (*ANF* 3:300).
[42]Osborn, *Tertullian*, 94.
[43]Ibid., 8.
[44]Note that Karl Barth deals with ethics under the doctrine of creation.
[45]Tertullian, *Apology* 42 (*ANF* 3:49).
[46]Osborn, *Tertullian*, 7.

conceptions of Plato and the Gnostics, in which some beings are higher (and therefore more real) than others. He believed in a dual process in which God created that which is primal (the organizing principles for the empirical world) apart from that which is visible (the material world). When Genesis 1 calls God's creation "good" and "very good," Origen concludes that it is referring to the primal stage rather than the creation of the visible, material world. For him, the material world is not evil, although it is relegated to tertiary status as a mere instrument to educate humanity, whose true destiny is to transcend spiritually the material and physical state.

Origen affirms the resurrection of the body, but his eschatology is one that leads to disembodied existence in God. He writes, "If you do not wish to fall in the wilderness, but to have attained the promised land of the fathers, you should have no portion in the land nor should you have anything in common with the earth."[47] Panayiotis Tzamalikos describes Origen's view as one in which humans are sojourners whose temporary station in this world is left behind as the human being enters through Christ into God's timeless being.[48] After this jump, the world will cease to exist, as it is no longer needed. Origen's eschatology is one in which God's creation comes to nothing.

Origen's writings make clear that he has retrofitted the biblical narrative with a Neoplatonic worldview that denigrates God's good creation. He rightly affirms the goodness of creation but wrongly posits a hierarchical chain of being and a salvific metaphor of ascent from the material to the immaterial. As theologians are tempted to do, Origen reinterprets Scripture to fit the philosophical system he prefers. Athanasius would recover the holistic view of creation, denying any hierarchy of being within creation, while insisting on a hierarchy of being between God and his creation.

Athanasius—the glories of the divine Christ. Athanasius's (AD 296–373) theology in general, and his rebuttal of the Arians in particular, played a decisive role in the history and development of Christian doctrine. Irenaeus had framed his opposition to the Gnostics in terms of God granting creation its existence as a good gift and had emphasized the immediacy of relation between God and creation. Athanasius similarly emphasizes God's immediate presence to this world, as well as related themes such as God's creation of humanity as fundamentally receptive to the divine, and redemption as the restoration of that receptivity. "Irenaeus," writes Khaled Anatolios,

[47]Origen, *Homily XXVII on Numbers* 4, in *Origen: An Exhortation to Martyrdom, Prayer, and Selected Works*, trans. Rowan A. Greer (New York: Paulist Press, 1979).

[48]Panayiotis Tzamalikos, *Origen: Philosophy of History and Eschatology* (Leiden: Brill, 2007), 272.

> played a significant role in the development of the Christian conception of the relation between God and world, by breaking away from the tendency to dissociate divine transcendence and divine immanence. The work of Athanasius underscores the significance of this Irenaean breakthrough and gives it a fuller systematic expression with reference to the whole nexus of Christian doctrine.[49]

For Athanasius, like Irenaeus, there is no hierarchy of being. God is present immediately to his image bearers.

As Thomas Weinandy notes, Athanasius's seminal work, *On the Incarnation*, is crafted in such a way that it subverts three errant views of creation.[50] Against the Epicureans, who believed that things came into being by themselves and are not guided by God's providence, Athanasius affirms creation and providence. Against Plato, who believed that God shaped creation out of previously existing matter, he affirms creation *ex nihilo*. Against the Gnostics, who posited an elaborate hierarchy of being that renders the material world inferior or even evil, he asserts that God created all things out of nothing and therefore creation is good.

Athanasius's cosmology serves as a continuation of his doctrine of God as he expounds on the way that creation's structure serves to reveal God's providence and power. He writes, "God by his own Word gave the Universe the Order it has, in order that since He is by nature invisible, men might be enabled to know Him at any rate by His works."[51] For Athanasius, creation is imprinted with God's character; it manifests God's intelligence and beauty. It reveals God through its order and harmony, characteristics that point toward an intelligent agent. Athanasius draws on the Platonic tradition by speaking of God's involvement with the world in terms of *participation*. Created things are external to the Father, but they participate in God, depending on his power for their vitality and stability.

The goodness of creation in general is made manifest by the goodness of human creation specifically. "Athanasius's anthropology," Anatolios writes, "is . . . one in which the whole structure of the human being is conceived as properly ordained toward God."[52] While the Gnostics considered the body ontologically bad, Athanasius does not. He is very clear about the goodness of creation, even, for example, of bodily fluids and

---

[49]Khaled Anatolios, *Athanasius: The Coherence of His Thought* (New York: Routledge, 1998), 23-24.
[50]Thomas G. Weinandy, *Athanasius: A Theological Introduction* (Burlington, VT: Ashgate, 2007), 28-30.
[51]Athanasius, *Against the Pagans* 3.35 (*NPNF*^{2} 4:22).
[52]Anatolios, *Athanasius*, 64.

processes.[53] For him, the body is structurally good because it is God's creation, but it is directionally yet to be determined because in a fallen world humanity exercises its freedom either in service of God or against him. If individuals orient themselves toward God, the body fulfills a good and doxological function. If, however, individuals orient themselves primarily toward themselves and their own bodies, the body accordingly becomes an idolatrous obstruction to doxology.

In response to the Arians, Athanasius argued that the Son's agency in creation proves exactly the opposite point: the Son is divine. "The outcome," Gunton writes, "is to sharpen the distinction between God and the world, so that Athanasius placed the Son of God firmly on the side of God."[54] This ontological distinction had the positive effect of strengthening Christian teaching on God's independence from his creation and therefore his free personal relationship to the world through the Son. Thus, creation was central to Athanasius's refutation of the Arians. In fact, Peter Leithart argues that the doctrine is "arguably as central to Athanasius's theology as his formulations of Trinitarian theology or Christology."[55] As Leithart delightfully states, Athanasius evangelized metaphysics by drawing upon the doctrine of creation.[56]

However, the discontinuity Athanasius posited had a negative effect. Gunton writes, "There are objections to Athanasius' rather exaggerated stress on the discontinuity between God and the creation, and indeed with all such conceptions. Unless it is allied with an equally strong—and Irenaean—stress on the affirmation of the material world, there is always the danger of taking away with the platonic left hand what has been given by the Trinitarian right."[57] Athanasius tended to stress Christ's divinity to such an extent that his humanity is left by the wayside. Basil of Caesarea, however, focused on the material nature of creation proclaiming the glory of God.

Basil of Caesarea—creation proclaims the glory of God.[58] Basil of Caesarea (Basil the Great, AD 330–379) was a staunch and eloquent defender of Nicaean Christianity, preparing the way for the Council of Constantinople with his articulation and defense of the doctrine of the Trinity. Less well

[53]Athanasius, *Against the Pagans* 3.35 (*NPNF*^{2} 4:22).

[54]Gunton, *Triune Creator*, 67.

[55]Peter J. Leithart, *Athanasius* (Grand Rapids, MI: Baker Academic, 2011), 89.

[56]Leithart, *Athanasius*, 1-26.

[57]Gunton, *Triune Creator*, 68.

[58]Sigurd Bergman, *Creation Set Free: The Spirit as Liberator of Nature*, trans. D. Stott (Grand Rapids, MI: Eerdmans, 2005), develops an environmental doctrine of the Spirit and creation in dialogue with Gregory of Nazianzus, another of the three Cappadocian Fathers.

known is the fact that the doctrine of creation was central to his thought. Essential for Basil was that all creation, including the beautiful diversity of material creation, pointed to the glory of its creator. Philip Rousseau observes that for Basil "human identity is at root the identity of a hearer or reader (albeit inspired by the Spirit and alert to the presence of Christ)."[59] Thus, for Basil, "this whole world is as it were a book that proclaims the glory of God."[60] In order to hear God, we must read both Scripture and creation. And Basil did indeed attend to both, rigorously.

Basil preached to a crowded church on Genesis, and his sermons are fascinating in the detail with which they discuss plants, birds, fish, and animals.[61] At a point in *Homily 8*, Basil asks, "How shall we make an exact review of all the peculiarities of the life of birds?"[62] Doubtless to his hearers' (and to our) astonishment, he goes on to describe the features of a variety of birds! Basil poses the question, Why has the elephant a trunk? and proceeds to discuss the elephant in some detail.[63] The doctrine of creation compelled Christian thinkers such as Basil to take the creation with utmost seriousness, and such close observations are woven in with exhortations to honor the creator. In his renowned *Traces on the Rhodian Shore*, Clarence Glacken says of Basil's descriptions of the natural world that it "is the best of its kind until the works of Ray and Derham[64] in the late seventeenth and early eighteenth centuries before the heady discoveries of Galileo, Descartes, and Newton."[65] Whereas Basil emphasized the goodness and beauty of the material creation, this would be Augustine's chief struggle.

Augustine—the danger of a limited dualism. The greatest of the Latin Fathers, Augustine's (AD 354–430) influence on Western Christianity is unmatched. In relation to the doctrine of creation, his influence is significant and not entirely positive. In the shadow of Neoplatonism and in the wake of his rejection of Manichaeism, Augustine returned to the opening chapters of

---

[59]Philip Rousseau, "Human Nature and Its Material Setting," *The Heythrop Journal* 49, no. 2 (March 2008): 222-39.

[60]Basil, *Hexaëmeron* 11.4.51, quoted in Stephen M. Hildebrand, *Basil of Caesarea* (Grand Rapids, MI: Baker Academic, 2014), 37. On the authenticity of chaps. 10 and 11 of Basil's *Hexaëmeron*, see Hildebrand, *Basil of Caesarea*, 171n3.

[61]Cf. Robert Louis Wilken, "The Beauty of Centipedes and Toads," in *On Earth as It Is in Heaven: Cultivating a Contemporary Theology of Creation*, ed. David Vincent Meconi, Catholic Theological Formation Series (Grand Rapids, MI: Eerdmans, 2016), 17-26.

[62]Basil, *Homily 8*, 5 (*NPNF*^{2} 8:98).

[63]Basil, *Hexaëmeron* 9.5.

[64]Both were Christians.

[65]Clarence J. Glacken, *Traces on the Rhodian Shore: Nature and Culture in Western Thought from Ancient Times to the End of the Eighteenth Century* (Berkeley: University of California Press, 1963), 194. We are indebted to Wilken ("Beauty," 22) for this quote.

Genesis some five times as an author, recognizing their centrality but also their mysterious depths.

> As Hill notes, "The effort to think through the mystery of creation runs like a leitmotif through Augustine's work."[a] Over nearly thirty years Augustine wrote five commentaries on Genesis 1–2. For Augustine, the fact of creation was undeniable: "Earth and the heavens are before our eyes. The very fact that they are there proclaims that they were created."[b] The challenge for him was how to understand this: "Let me hear and understand the meaning of the words: In the Beginning you made heaven and earth."[c] Augustine never ceased listening so as to understand these words. He worked on *The Literal Meaning of Genesis* for some fifteen years; it was finally published in AD 416 and represents his mature thought.
>
> [a]Edmund Hill, introduction to *On Genesis*, by Augustine, ed. John E. Rotelle (Hyde Park, NY: New City Press, 2002), 13.
> [b]Augustine, *Confessions* 11.4 (trans. R. S. Pine-Coffin [New York: Penguin, 1961]).
> [c]Augustine, *Confessions* 11.3 (Pine-Coffin).

Positively, creation history begins *ex nihilo*, ends in new creation, and has its midpoint in the incarnation. Because creation is *ex nihilo*, any form of generation or emanation is excluded. Like Irenaeus before him, Augustine affirmed God as the sole creator to whom all things owe their existence. All of God's material creation is therefore "good." The fact of evil cannot be used as a counterpoint by the pagans, because evil is not a "thing" and is not created by God. Evil is a privation of the goodness God created. Evil finds its source not in God but in humanity's use of its God-given freedom. And like Irenaeus, Augustine affirms that the creator is the triune God. "By the Trinity, thus supremely and equally and unchangeably good, all things were created," such that "the whole Trinity is revealed to us in the creation."[66]

Significantly, Augustine's theology is one in which God's creation comes to something rather than nothing.

> Then shall the [form] of this world pass away in a conflagration of universal fire. . . . And by this universal conflagration . . . our substance shall receive such qualities as shall, by a wonderful transmutation, harmonize with our immortal bodies, so that, as the world itself is renewed to some better thing, it is fitly accommodated to men, themselves renewed in their flesh to some better thing.[67]

[66]Augustine, *Enchiridion* 10 (*NPNF*[1] 3:240); *City of God* 11.24 (trans. Gerald G. Walsh, ed. Vernon J. Bourke [Garden City, NY: Image Books, 1958]).

[67]Augustine, *City of God* 20.16 (Walsh).

History finds its culmination in a new heavens and earth. In his original creative act, God's goal was a beautiful creation that glorified him; likewise, in his eschatological renewal of creation, God will weave together every strand of creation to produce a beautiful tapestry to his glory.[68] Like Athanasius's contribution, however, Augustine's legacy is mixed.

Augustine's writings are not an entirely trustworthy guide to the biblical teaching on creation. Although the older Augustine rejected decisively his early Manichaeism, he drew on the Neoplatonists in his rejection of Manichaeism's absolute dualism. Unfortunately, Neoplatonism itself treats the material world as inferior, and Augustine never was able to divest himself entirely of Neoplatonic residue. As Gunton and others have noted, Augustine continued throughout his career to treat the material world as less good than the immaterial realm.[69] Yet, as Bradley Green avers, "Perhaps one of the first things that should be said in response to Gunton is that in Augustine's theology the created order is good, *even if it is a lesser good than ultimate spiritual realities*. That is, in Augustine there appears to be *limited* dualism, where the created order (especially the physical realm) is viewed as somewhat less than higher, spiritual realities."[70]

Commenting on Genesis 1, Augustine writes, "So when we hear . . . *And God saw that it was good*, we understand . . . that in that same goodness [and kindness and courtesy of his Spirit] where it had pleased him that it should be made, it pleased him that it should remain made."[71] Later, in commenting on Genesis 3, he affirms the goodness of the created order even after the fall: "Those things, however, which lose their proper comeliness by sinning, do not in the least for all that bring it about that they too are not good when rightly coordinated with the whole, with the universe."[72] So we admire Augustine for retrieving the Christian doctrine of creation's goodness in the aftermath of his Manichaeism and in an intellectual era marked by Neoplatonism, and yet

---

[68]Augustine treats the eternal state in some depth and breadth in *City of God*, describing the embodied and material nature of the eternal state and speculating about how our physical bodies contribute to its blessedness (*City of God* 22). He even argues that Plato and Varro would have taught the resurrection of the body if their best insights had been combined. For a concise summary, see Matthew Levering, *The Theology of Augustine: An Introductory Guide to His Most Important Works* (Grand Rapids, MI: Baker Academic, 2013), 147-49.

[69]Gunton, *Triune Creator*, 74.

[70]Bradley G. Green, *Colin Gunton and the Failure of Augustine: The Theology of Colin Gunton in Light of Augustine* (Eugene, OR: Pickwick, 2011), 174.

[71]Augustine, *On Genesis* 2.6.14 (trans. Edmund Hill, ed. John E. Rotelle [Hyde Park, NY: New City Press, 2002]).

[72]Augustine, *On Genesis* 3.24.36 (Hill).

we diverge from Augustine's limited dualism that lessens the goodness of the material creation.

This (limited) dualist framework kept Augustine from ever reading the Genesis account on its own terms. When he read the biblical writer's account, he interpreted God's creation of "heaven and earth" as a two-stage creation, with the first and superior creation being heaven and the second and inferior creation being earth. He writes, "Out of nothing didst Thou create heaven and earth,—a great thing and a small,—two such things, one near unto Thee, the other near to nothing,—one to which Thou shouldest be superior, the other to which nothing should be inferior."[73] Likewise, when he could not bring himself to believe that the "be fruitful and multiply" of Genesis 1:28 really and truly refers to physical reproduction, he interpreted it to mean spiritual fecundity, which after the fall was corrupted and changed into carnal fecundity. Augustine affirmed that God's creation is "very good," but for him the material part of it is somehow less good than the immaterial.

Maximus the Confessor—incarnation and the goodness of the material world. Whereas Augustine is the most influential Western father, Maximus the Confessor (AD 580–662) is often recognized as the greatest theologian and philosopher of the Byzantine tradition. Although he has been underappreciated in contemporary Western theological discourse, Hans Urs von Balthasar, in his *Cosmic Liturgy*, resurrects Maximus for the purpose of affirming the goodness of the material world.[74] Maximus distinguishes clearly between God and his creation and rejects any concept of being that seeks to unite the two. The goal of creation is union with God, but this union does not demand the loss of its materiality. The goodness of the material world is in fact reestablished through the Son's incarnation, resurrection, ascension, and return. "Because our earth was no longer, for [the Son], a different reality from Paradise, he appeared to his disciples on it once again, after his Resurrection, and associated with them, so showing that from now on the earth was one, united with itself."[75]

Maximus's ontology of creation is affirmed by contemporary Eastern theologians such as Alexander Schmemann, who recognizes creation's goodness

---

[73]Augustine, *The Confession and Letters of St. Augustine, with a Sketch of His Life and Work* 12.7, trans. J. G. Pilkington (Grand Rapids, MI: Eerdmans, 2001); *NPNF*[1] 1:177.

[74]Hans Urs von Balthasar, *Cosmic Liturgy: The Universe According to Maximus the Confessor* (San Francisco: Ignatius, 2003), 61.

[75]Maximus, *Ambigua* (*PG* 91:1309a, b).

being reestablished by the incarnation and resurrection and affirmed through the church's liturgy and sacraments.[76] Through the liturgy and sacraments, the church serves as the presence of God's kingdom in this world, a presence that is thoroughly creational and material. In a telling passage in his journals, entered toward the end of his life, Schmemann writes,

> I realized that "theologically" I have one idea—the eschatological content of Christianity, and of the Church as the presence in *this* world of the Kingdom, of the age to come—this presence as the salvation *of* the world and not escape *from* it. . . . Once you love [the Kingdom], you cannot avoid loving all creation, created to reveal and announce the Kingdom. This love is already transfigured. Without . . . the world, the Kingdom of God is incomprehensible, abstract and in some way absurd.[77]

Thus, Maximus's affirmation of creation's ontological goodness has proven influential in contemporary discourse, especially through von Balthasar in the West and Schmemann in the East.

Thomas Aquinas—the Middle Ages, Aristotelian philosophy, and creation. The Middle Ages provides a confused testimony to the biblical doctrine of creation. On the one hand, Christians seek God through his material creation; on the other hand, they seek God through renouncing the material world. "In general in the Middle Ages," Gunton writes, "the Platonic forms or Aristotelian and Stoic *rationes* tend to displace Christ as the framework of creation. The effect is to replace something oriented to materiality with something at best ambivalent about it."[78]

Thomas Aquinas (1225–1274) is the central theologian in medieval theology, and his legacy illustrates this medieval ambivalence. On the one hand, Aquinas rightly affirmed that God created the world freely and that he created it "good." Commenting on John 1:10, Aquinas distinguishes between three Johannine uses of the word *world*. The first two uses are positive, uses in which John refers to the world as created and the world as renewed by Christ. Only in the final sense of the word—the world deformed by sin after the fall—does John speak negatively.[79] "To detract from the perfection of

[76]Alexander Schmemann, *For the Life of the World: Sacraments and Orthodoxy*, 2nd ed. (Crestwood, NY: St. Vladimir's Seminary Press, 1973); Schmemann, *The Eucharist: Sacrament of the Kingdom* (Crestwood, NY: St. Vladimir's Seminary Press, 2003).

[77]Alexander Schmemann, *The Journals of Father Alexander Schmemann, 1973–1983* (Crestwood, NY: St. Vladimir's Seminary Press, 2000), 174.

[78]Gunton, *Triune Creator*, 102.

[79]Thomas Aquinas, *Commentary on the Gospel of John*, trans. Fabian R. Larcher and James A. Weisheipl (Washington, DC: Catholic University of America Press, 2010), 54.

creatures," Aquinas writes, "is to detract from the perfection of the divine power."[80] He further affirmed the created world on the basis of the incarnation, the reality of a future bodily resurrection, and the sacraments, all of which affirm creation's goodness.[81]

On the other hand, he unfortunately tied creation to a God who is a First Cause, whose Being is participated in by all others,[82] and to a creation with a hierarchical chain of being.[83] Thus, Aquinas's schema is a "christianized neoplatonism."[84] Mind takes priority over matter, and the (immaterial) mind seeks to rise beyond the material world. Ever present in Aquinas's writings are the twin influences of Augustine and Aristotle, both of whom contributed to his hierarchical model. Augustine's theology pushed Aquinas up and away toward the heavenly realm, while Aristotle's philosophy pulled him downward to this material world. Aquinas attempted to forge a legitimate biblically grounded synthesis between Augustine and Aristotle and between the heavenly and earthly realms.

Aquinas's two-realm hierarchy carried with it a unique view of the relationship between creation, the fall, and redemption: grace perfects and completes nature. The problem with this paradigm is that it implies that the lower (natural) story is simply incomplete, rather than—as Scripture teaches—being thoroughly twisted and distorted by sin and idolatry. As we will see, the emerging medieval nature-grace framework proved unsustainable as Duns Scotus and Ockham split them apart, a split that was solidified in modernity. Prior to modernity, however, the Reformation sought to recover the goodness of creation.

---

[80]Thomas Aquinas, *Summa Contra Gentiles: Book Three: Providence*, trans. Vernon J. Bourke (South Bend, IN: University of Notre Dame Press, 1975), 230.

[81]Concerning bodily resurrection, Aquinas refused to entertain the notion that the "I" can survive death unless eventually it is reunited with its body (*Summa Contra Gentiles: Book Four: Salvation*, chap. 79). For a helpful, concise summary, see Brian Davies, *Aquinas* (New York: Continuum, 2002), 93-95.

[82]Aquinas, *Summa Theologiae* 1a.6.4, 1a.8.1.

[83]Etienne Gilson, *The Christian Philosophy of St. Thomas Aquinas* (Notre Dame, IN: University of Notre Dame Press, 1956), 160-73. Gilson notes that Thomas's treatment of angels "is the culminating point of a long development in which there converge heterogeneous elements of both religious and philosophical origin," in which Aquinas attempts a synthesis of biblical material with astronomical theories and metaphysical speculation. Gilson's evaluation is that Thomas's synthesis is highly original and coherent. Robert Jenson similarly recognizes hierarchical ontology in Aquinas's Five Ways but is less positive than Gilson toward Aquinas's "Christianized Platonism." See Robert W. Jenson, *The Knowledge of Things Hoped For: The Sense of Theological Discourse* (Oxford: Oxford University Press, 1969), chap. 3.

[84]Gunton, *Triune Creator*, 100.

The Reformation and Post-Reformation Era

The Reformers helped renew the doctrine of creation by speaking of God's creative and providential work in trinitarian and personal terms rather than the causal conceptions generated by medieval theologians, and by affirming the goodness of ordinary material life.[85] In *Sources of the Self*, Charles Taylor addresses this subject in a wonderful section titled "God Loveth Adverbs," arguing that the Judeo-Christian tradition uniquely affirms ordinary life and this affirmation in the modern era comes primarily from the Reformers. "The crucial potentiality," Taylor writes, "was that of conceiving the hallowing of life not as something which takes place only at the limits, as it were, but as a change which can penetrate the full extent of mundane life."[86] This connects, of course, to our discussion of Auerbach in the introduction. But the full extent of ordinary life could be affirmed only by denying a long-standing medieval distinction between the sacred and the profane—a distinction rooted in dualism and a hierarchical conception of reality—and instead affirming the interpenetration of the sacred and the profane. While Luther, Calvin, and the Puritans work to recover the goodness of material creation, some Anabaptist theologians adopt hierarchical pattern of thought, placing the spiritual realm over against the material.

Martin Luther—the masks of God. Luther (1483–1526) departed from medieval theological method as he addressed the topic in its home environment, the biblical narrative, rather than foregrounding Aristotelian cosmology or causation. In *Lectures on Genesis*, Luther gives a trinitarian interpretation of Genesis 1, and in various other writings he affirms creation *ex nihilo*.[87] "All things must be God's," Luther writes, "since nothing can be or become, if he would not bring it into existence; and when he stops, nothing can continue to exist."[88] He vigorously affirmed the inherent goodness of God's creation, and in so doing he broke with Neoplatonist theologies that viewed matter as inferior. The material world is good, and furthermore out of the effulgence of its goodness it reveals God. "Now the whole creation," Luther writes, "is a face or mask of God."[89] As

---

[85]Ibid., 146-54.

[86]Charles Taylor, *Sources of the Self: The Making of the Modern Identity* (Cambridge: Cambridge University Press, 1989), 221.

[87]Luther scholar Regin Prenter concludes, "Luther always speaks about creation in terms of the Trinity." *Spiritus Creator: Luther's Concept of the Holy Spirit* (Philadelphia: Muhlenberg, 1953), 192. We owe this citation to Gunton, *Triune Creator*, 148.

[88]Paul Althaus, *The Theology of Martin Luther* (Philadelphia: Fortress, 1966), 105.

[89]Martin Luther, *Luther's Works*, vol. 26, ed. Jaroslav Pelikan, trans. Walter A. Hansen (St. Louis: Concordia, 1963), 95.

creation reveals God, God in turn enters into relationship with his creation. The perceptive reader of Luther's work will note that he writes about the God-creature relationship in terms of personal dependence, unlike medieval theologians, who sometimes spoke in terms of absolute dependence.[90] Indeed, as we depend on God, he reveals himself to us and in fact sends us out into the physical and material world to worship and serve him there in the midst of our ordinary lives.

Oswald Bayer notes that Luther's career as an Augustinian monk was marked by a concept of "imitative discipleship" in which Luther was concerned with nature and the world only to the extent that they related to some otherworldly moral imperative. After his theological reformation, however, "Luther's way led him from this world-denying ethic of discipleship to that explicit affirmation of world and nature which radiates from his writings with increasing intensity."[91] Dietrich Bonhoeffer notes that "Luther's return from the monastery to the world, to the 'calling,' is, in the true New Testament sense, the fiercest attack and assault to be launched against the world since primitive Christianity."[92]

John Calvin—God's handiwork. Like Luther, Calvin (1509–1564) tended to use personal language to speak of God's relation to his creation, usually bypassing the medieval tendency to speak in terms of Aristotelian cosmology or causation. In his commentary on Genesis, he affirms that God created out of nothing and that the material creation celebrates God's glory.[93] He emphasized human delight in created beauty and argued against any sort of asceticism that restricts one from enjoying and contemplating God's good creation. "We may have no reluctance," Calvin writes, "to devote our whole lives to the contemplation of it."[94] Further, the contemplation of creation ought to lead one to delight in God. Creation in fact reveals God so clearly that humans are without excuse for rejecting him. Humans themselves are a "microcosm" of God's handiwork and as such are the highest proof of God's wisdom. And yet, despite this lucid and compelling revelation of God in creation, humans turn

[90]Brian Davies, *Thomas Aquinas on God and Evil* (Oxford: Oxford University Press, 2011), 44; Mary T. Clark, introduction to *An Aquinas Reader*, rev. ed., ed. Mary T. Clark (New York: Fordham University Press, 2000), 1-29.

[91]Oswald Bayer, *Freedom in Response: Lutheran Ethics; Sources and Controversies*, trans. Jeffrey F. Cayzer (Oxford: Oxford University Press, 2007), 98.

[92]Dietrich Bonhoeffer, *Ethics*, trans. Eberhard Bethge (London: SCM Press, 1955), 223.

[93]Gunton, *Triune Creator*, 152-54.

[94]Calvin, *Institutes* 1.14.2 (*Institutes of the Christian Religion*, trans. Henry Beveridge [Peabody, MA: Hendrickson, 2008]).

away from God, confusing creation's glory with God's glory and worshiping the creation instead of God. Calvin writes,

> But upon [God's] individual works he has engraved unmistakable marks of his glory, so clear and so prominent that even unlettered and stupid folk cannot plead the excuse of ignorance. . . . Wherever you cast your eyes, there is no spot in the universe wherein you cannot discern at least some sparks of his glory. . . . This skillful ordering of the universe is for us a sort of mirror in which we can contemplate God, who is otherwise invisible.[95]

Luther and Calvin together renewed and retrieved the doctrine of creation by providing robust affirmations of its goodness, by arguing that the material creation reveals God's glory, and by conceiving God's creative activity in the concrete language of personal action rather than in the abstract language of causality. The result of affirming the goodness of creation and God's glory found therein is the recovery of the central glories of creation first articulated in Irenaeus. The radical wing of the Reformation, however, was decidedly more ambiguous in its affirmation of God's good creation.

The Anabaptists—mistaking earthly for wordly. The Radical Reformers differed significantly from Luther and Calvin and tend to represent a regression in the history of the doctrine of creation. Their manner of preaching the "new creation" first of all moved "creation" to the periphery, relegating it to relative insignificance in God's redemptive plan. But it also created an unhealthy dualism between the material and immaterial aspects of God's creation. Robert Friedmann writes, "We recognize in Anabaptist writings the acceptance of a fundamental New Testament dualism, that is, an uncompromising ontological dualism in which Christian values are held in sharp contrast to the values of the 'world' in its corrupt state."[96] Contemporary Anabaptist Thomas Finger likewise acknowledges, "Historic Anabaptists . . . often overplayed Spirit and downgraded matter."[97] Consider the language of the anonymous Great Article Book of the Hutterites: "Between the Christian and the world there exists a vast difference like that between heaven and earth. The world is the world, always remains the world, behaves like the world and all the world is nothing but the world."[98] This Hutterite tract, likely written by

---

[95]Calvin, *Institutes* 1.5.1 (Beveridge).

[96]Robert Friedmann, *The Theology of Anabaptism: An Interpretation* (Eugene, OR: Wipf & Stock, 1998), 38.

[97]Thomas N. Finger, *A Contemporary Anabaptist Theology: Biblical, Historical, Constructive* (Downers Grove, IL: InterVarsity Press, 2004), 563.

[98]Ibid., 39.

Bishop Peter Walpot around 1577, conflates "worldly" with "earthly." Just as the ethereal heavens are good and the material earth is bad, the argument goes, so Christians must evidence holiness, while unbelievers will manifest sin.

This example is representative of some Anabaptist theologians who failed to distinguish between the structures of creation and the moral direction of creation, and between the rebellious human "world" and the natural nonhuman "world." Such ontological dualism, combined with an expectation of the immanent coming of Christ, led to cultural separatism. This ontological dualism that leads to separatism carries with it the scent of gnosticism. The experience of sin's corruption on creation leads to belief in its ontological condemnation. In this way of thinking, God's salvation takes us "up and away" from the world, and thus the Christian life is envisioned as one that is in a significant way "separate" from the material world. The Anabaptists' doctrine of creation explains their withdrawal into remote locations such as Moravia, Russia, and even Paraguay, where they could serve the Lord with less compromise.[99]

> Contemporary Anabaptists do not necessarily follow their heritage in that respect. Neo-Anabaptist Stanley Hauerwas draws on Thomas Aquinas, Karl Barth, Ludwig Wittgenstein, and others to affirm the embodied nature of the Christian life. Repeatedly throughout his writings—following Wittgenstein—he seeks to subvert aberrant theologies that are antipathetic toward the body. These gnostic antipathies manifest themselves in epistemology (in attempts to get out of our own skin in order to know the world in an absolute or comprehensive manner), philosophy of language (in "picture" theories of language), anthropology (in Cartesian "ghost in the machine" dualisms), and theology and philosophy (in every attempt at "system-building," which in effect assumes that we can step back from the world in order to build grand theories about it).
>
> Hauerwas affirms the creational nature of the Christian life by arguing that the sacraments are central to it. For him, the bodily actions and physical gestures of the church are of great importance, and none of them are more important than baptism and the Eucharist. "These [baptism and Eucharist] are essential gestures of the church," he writes, and "we cannot be church without them. . . . Without them, we are constantly tempted to turn God into an ideology to supply our wants and needs rather than have our needs and wants transformed by God's capturing our attention through the mundane life of Jesus of Nazareth."[a]
>
> He likewise affirms the physical and material in his ethics of embodiment. The body is not a peripheral garment to be discarded by the soul after death. Nor should it be discarded before birth (abortion) or at the end of life (euthanasia or suicide). Again,

[99]Ibid., 41.

in order to make his point he appropriates Wittgenstein both by drawing on his arguments against (the general problem of) Cartesian dualism and by quoting Wittgenstein's statements against (the particular issue of) suicide. He begins one article on suicide with a quote from Wittgenstein: "If suicide is allowed then everything is allowed. If anything is not allowed then suicide is not allowed. This throws a light on the nature of ethics, for suicide is, so to speak, the elementary sin." Hauerwas explains it shortly thereafter: "Everyone seems to agree that if anything is a moral problem suicide and euthanasia are prime examples and thus ready grist for the ethicist's mill. As Wittgenstein suggests, we seem to be on fundamentally moral grounds when dealing with the taking of one's own life."[b]

However, it remains an open question as to whether Hauerwas has successfully appropriated a full, biblical doctrine of creation. Hays notes Hauerwas's lack of detailed biblical engagement in his writings, and Hauerwas seems wary of affirming creation order.[c] In defense of marriage, for example, Hauerwas does not, like Jesus (Mt 19:4-6), refer back to creation but argues that "Christians do not believe marriage and the family exist for themselves, but rather serve the ends of the more determinative community called church. The assumption that the family is an end in itself can only make the family and marriage more personally destructive."[d]

[a]Stanley Hauerwas, *Christian Existence Today: Essays on Church, World, and Living in Between* (Durham, NC: Labyrinth, 1988), 107.

[b]Stanley Hauerwas, *The Hauerwas Reader*, ed. John Berkman and Michael G. Cartwright (Durham, NC: Duke University Press, 2001), 577.

[c]Richard B. Hays, *The Moral Vision of the New Testament: A Contemporary Introduction to New Testament Ethics* (San Francisco: HarperCollins, 1996), 259.

[d]Stanley Hauerwas, *After Christendom? How the Church Is to Behave If Freedom, Justice, and a Christian Nation Are Bad Ideas* (Nashville: Abingdon, 1991), 127.

The Puritans—the glory of vocation. The Puritans are often accused of caring little for creation, valuing it as instrumental for their own existence and sanctification. Santmire's castigation of them is representative when he writes, "The way for the ethic of exploitation was . . . prepared by the earlier Puritan doctrine of the dominion of man over nature."[100] But leading scholars such as Nicholas Wolterstorff, Leland Ryken, and T. M. Moore actually appeal to the Puritans to support their affirmation of creational and cultural life.[101] Jonathan

[100]H. Paul Santmire, *Brother Earth: Nature, God and Ecology in Time of Crisis* (New York: Nelson, 1976), 30-31.

[101]Nicholas Wolterstorff, *Until Justice and Peace Embrace* (Grand Rapids, MI: Eerdmans, 1983), 8-10; Leland Ryken, *Redeeming the Time: A Christian Approach to Work and Leisure* (Grand Rapids, MI: Baker, 1995), 95-126; T. M. Moore, *Consider the Lilies: A Plea for Creational Theology* (Phillipsburg, NJ: P&R, 2005). Moore's book expounds Jonathan Edwards's theological framework for creational theology; he surfaces not only Edwards's theological affirmation of creational life but also the depth of Edwards's existential appreciation for nature.

Edwards's writings and sermons are noteworthy for often including elaborate and passionate treatments of the goodness and beauty of God's creation.[102] Take, for example, his sermon on Psalm 94:8-11, where he writes,

> The brute creatures, birds, beasts, fishes, and insects, though there be innumerable kinds of them, yet all seem to have such a degree of perception and perfection given them, as best suits their place in the creation, their manner of living, and the ends for which they were made. There is no defect visible in them; they are perfect in their kind; there seems to be nothing wanting, in order to their filling up their allotted place in the world.[103]

Many New England Puritans not only recognized the splendor of God's creation but also sought to reverse the effects of sin on it. Edward Johnson declared, "This is the place where the Lord will create a new heaven and earth in, new churches, and a new commonwealth together."[104] His statement is no doubt misguided, but it does reveal the Puritans' value for creation and their desire to shape God's good world into conformity with his original intentions.

The Puritans tied their affirmation of creation to an affirmation of cultural work. "The whole life of a Christian," Richard Sibbes writes, "is a service to God. There is nothing that we do but it may be a 'service to God.' . . . We should not thrust religion into a corner, into a narrow room, and limit it to some days, and times, and actions, and places. . . . To 'serve' God is to carry ourselves as the children of God wheresoever we are: so that our whole life is a service to God."[105] Similarly, John Cotton writes, "Not only my spiritual life but even my civil life in this world, all the life I live, is by the faith of the Son of God."[106] Likewise William Perkins:

> Now if we compare worke to worke, there is a difference betwixt washing of dishes, and preaching of the word of God: but as touching to please God none at all. . . . So . . . he is spirituall which is renewed in Christ, and all his works which spring from faith seeme they never so grosse. . . . Yea deedes of

---

[102]Moore, *Consider the Lilies*, 133. On Edwards's Platonism and his view of divine participation, see Wolter Huttinga, *Participation and Communicability: Herman Bavinck and John Milbank on the Relation Between God and the World* (Amsterdam: Buijten & Schipperheijn, 2014), 69-70.

[103]Jonathan Edwards, *The Works of Jonathan Edwards*, ed. Sereno E. Dwight and Edward Hickman (Carlisle, PA: Banner of Truth Trust, 1974), 2:253.

[104]Edward Johnson, "Wonder-Working Providence of Sion's Savior in New England (c. 1650)," in *The Puritans in America: A Narrative Anthology*, ed. Alan Heimert and Andrew Delbanco (Cambridge, MA: Harvard University Press, 1985), 115.

[105]Richard Sibbes, "King David's Epitaph," in *The Complete Works of Richard Sibbes*, ed. Alexander Balloch Grosart (Edinburgh: Nichol, 1863), 6:507.

[106]Quoted in Ryken, *Redeeming the Time*, 218.

> matrimonie are pure and spirituall . . . and . . . the wiping of shoes and such like, howsoever grosse they appeare outwardly, yet are they sanctified.[107]

The Puritans' goal was to find God in everyday life—not only in creation itself but also in creationally based vocation and cultural labor. Of equal significance, the Puritans expected creation to come to something in the form of a new heavens and earth. William Dyrness argues that the Puritans "lived and died" in expectation of God's restorative work in the new creation.[108]

Conclusion: Travail and Glory in the Premodern Period

The Christian tradition up to the modern era is uneven in its affirmation of the goodness of God's creation. Von Balthasar notes that the Greek fathers exhibited a tendency that "proceeds unambiguously away from the material to the spiritual. . . . Spiritualization, presented in a thousand different colorations, is the basic tendency of the patristic epoch."[109] Some theologians, such as Origen, do indeed entice us away from our better selves; others, such as Athanasius or Augustine, leave us a positive but ambiguous heritage; a few, such as Irenaeus, point the way forward clearly and without ambiguity. Indeed, Irenaeus's engagement with Gnostic heresies in the second century set the stage for the development of the doctrine of creation over the next millennium and a half of church history. Those who followed would continue to argue for the glories of the doctrine of creation in the triune God as creator of all things, the goodness of material and spiritual creation, and God's restoring, elevating, and enhancing creation's original form in the eschaton through the incarnate Son. Furthermore, the Reformers and the Puritans rightly emphasized the impact of the doctrine of creation on all of life, especially our daily work.

Despite these glories, the poisonous fruit of a hierarchy between the material and the immaterial creation would continue to grow from its Gnostic roots throughout church history. Even when both the material and the immaterial were affirmed as good, often the material creation was understood as "less good." One must reject this notion while also sympathizing with why this aspect of Gnosticism is so alluring. When one experiences the effects of

---

[107]Quoted in Charles H. George and Katherine George, *The Protestant Mind of the English Reformation, 1570–1640* (Princeton, NJ: Princeton University Press, 1961), 139.

[108]William A. Dyrness, *Reformed Theology and Visual Culture: The Protestant Imagination from Calvin to Edwards* (Cambridge: Cambridge University Press, 2004), 213-15.

[109]Hans Urs von Balthasar, "The Fathers, the Scholastics, and Ourselves," trans. Edward T. Oakes, *Communio* 24 (1997): 375.

sin's curse in the decay, pain, and death around and within us, one can easily understand how even the giants of church history understood salvation as freedom from material creation rather than freedom to a restored material creation. The glory of the biblical narrative, however, affirms the ontological goodness of creation while affirming the devastating nature of sin's effects on our current experience of God's world. In redemption, therefore, God does not cast aside material creation as shackles from which we must be freed, but restores the material creation, including the redemption of our bodies, so that we might enjoy the fullness of the world free from the shackles of sin and death.

THREE

THE TRAVAILS AND GLORIES OF THE DOCTRINE OF CREATION

THE MODERN PERIOD

MODERNITY WAS A PERIOD OF SECULARIZATION, including the secularization of nature. By the modern period, even the Reformation tradition, which had played a part in recovering the doctrine of God's good creation, now contributed to the secularization of nature. Santmire writes, "We may legitimately speak of the secularization of nature in the Reformation tradition in the nineteenth and twentieth centuries. . . . Nature came to be viewed by many modern Protestant thinkers as a mere thing, a world of objects . . . and therefore a world which humans must constantly transcend if they are to be rightly related to God."[1] At the same time, as we will note in this chapter, neither can a faithful doctrine of creation thrive when the creator and creation are collapsed into each other, as will be seen in the theologies of this chapter. Thus, this chapter concludes the history of the doctrine of creation by following these trends in the doctrine of creation from the eighteenth to the twenty-first century, attending closely to the glories and travails that often grow together and respond to one another.

In the eighteenth century, a neo-gnostic philosophy emerged that separated the higher and lower realms of our experience in this world with little connection between the two. This separation resulted in two seemingly opposite travails. One impulse was to exalt the life of the mind above the

[1]H. Paul Santmire, *The Travail of Nature: The Ambiguous Ecological Promise of Christian Theology* (Philadelphia: Fortress, 1985), 133.

material world, continuing the gnostic thread that gave supremacy to the immaterial realm. The seemingly opposing impulse—to value the material as supreme over the immaterial—also emerged, leading to the supremacy of the natural sciences and empirical data as the source and arbiter of all truth. Yet both of these were grounded in a similar epistemological quest: What can *I* know to be true of the world? Thus, even empiricism grounded itself in the (neo-)gnostic soil of the supremacy of the mind over matter. Following a brief discussion of this philosophical grounding, this chapter works through the glories and travails of the doctrine of creation from the glories of Johann Georg Hamann's christological hermeneutics, French Catholic phenomenology, and the anti-dualism found in Bonhoeffer and Wittgenstein to the travails of Schleiermacher's religious experience, Moltmann's panentheism, process theology's dipolar God, and the current debates in modern evangelicalism. We conclude by placing the Dutch Reformed tradition in this history, suggesting that this tradition can move us forward in hope for the doctrine of creation in our age.

Modernity's (Neo-)Gnostic Philosophical Grounding

While Aquinas had sought to forge a careful, biblically grounded synthesis between the heavenly and earthly realms, between grace and nature, John Duns Scotus and William of Ockham pulled these apart.[2] Ordinary human life belonged simply to the lower realm of nature and therefore became severed from God and the gospel. Grace no longer perfected nature. Human reason likewise belonged to the lower realm; it was increasingly viewed as autonomous and independent of Scripture. Enlightenment philosophers went further and posited an antithetical relationship between the two spheres, seeking to apply scientific reason rather than biblical revelation to all spheres of human society, including religion. The post-Enlightenment worldview increasingly clashed with a Christian worldview, and, sadly, many Christians relinquished the gospel's claims to universal validity, succumbing to the privatization of religion. For them the lower realms (marked by autonomous reason) laid claim to truth, while the upper realm (informed by biblical revelation) could lay claim only to value. Science was the master of the public realm of reason, while Christianity possessed only the realm of private taste.

[2]This development is complex and has been attended to in detail by many theologians. See, e.g., Louis Dupré, *Passage to Modernity: An Essay in the Hermeneutics of Nature and Culture* (New Haven, CT: Yale University Press, 1993), and his several other works related to this theme.

The Dutch philosopher Herman Dooyeweerd recognized the instability of the modern view of nature and argued that it was underlain by a tense bipolar religious motivation that he called the "nature-freedom ground motive." The nature-freedom ground motive is one that oscillates back and forth between an emphasis on natural (and deterministic) laws and human freedom (and moral responsibility). This ground motive, as Dooyeweerd understood it, had dominated Western culture from the time of the Renaissance up through the twentieth century. Renaissance humanists for the most part emphasized humanity's freedom and dignity, while modern scientists tended to emphasize the mechanistic and deterministic laws of nature. The history of modern philosophy can be interpreted as a struggle to reconcile the two motifs.

In *The Roots of Western Culture*, Dooyeweerd gives a unique and compelling interpretation of Western civilization from the perspective of Reformational Christianity. He argues that a civilization or culture expresses communal rather than individual thought and practice, that communal thought always and necessarily is religiously based, that non-Christian religious frameworks are inherently unstable, and that therefore a fully Christian worldview is the only one that can bring stability. Dooyeweerd's method consists of a polemical contrast between Christian and non-Christian religious "ground motives" and their role in the rise and development of Western culture. For Dooyeweerd, a ground motive is a "spiritual force that acts as the absolutely central mainspring of human society" and that arises from "either the spirit of God or that of an idol."[a] He argues that Western culture has been influenced by four ground motives: form-matter (Greek), nature-grace (Thomist), nature-freedom (modernist), and creation-fall-redemption (biblical-Christian). In the form-matter ground motive, one sees a combination of the older nature religions (in which formless matter is governed by blind fate) and the newer Greek religions (in which form is deified). The nature-grace ground motive combines the old form-matter motive with Christian thought to form a syncretistic blend. Ultimately, the Greek dualisms are incorporated into Christian thought, thus corrupting it. The nature-grace dualism splits creation into natural and supernatural, thus exempting nature from the deleterious effects of the fall and restricting the power and scope of redemptive grace to the supernatural realm. Philosophy, science, and other disciplines need to be perfected and completed by revelation, but they do not need to be infused, reformed, or restored by that revelation. The third non-Christian ground motive is nature-freedom.

[a]Herman Dooyeweerd, *Roots of Western Culture: Pagan, Secular, and Christian Options*, trans. John Kraay, Collected Works, Series B, vol. 15 (Ancaster, ON: Paideia, 2012), 9.

Descartes, for example, tried to bring resolution to the tension by locating the mechanistic aspect of the human person in the human body while locating the freedom of the person in the soul. By contrast, Kant located the rationally knowable aspect of reality in phenomenal nature while locating freedom and moral responsibility in the noumenal realm. Hobbes, Locke, and a host of others likewise tried to resolve the tension, but the tension is irresoluble, Dooyeweerd argued, because the nature-freedom ground motive ignored biblical teaching about the nature of created reality. In the biblical teaching, the created order reveals God as the "integral origin" of all things, as the One who resolves dialectical tension inherent in the nature-grace ground motive. Indeed, God is the author of both nature and grace.[3]

The Eighteenth and Nineteenth Centuries: Of Mind, Matter, and the Self

The success of the project of this "radical Enlightenment"[4] depended on marginalizing and eradicating the doctrine of creation. We see this in the shift from starting with ontology—the nature of reality as God's creation—to starting with epistemology and how *I/we* know truthfully about—indeed, constitute—the world. Such a shift is seen clearly in Kant's idealism, as mentioned above. What is remarkable, but largely unknown, is that a major Christian philosopher-theologian, Johann Hamann, challenged this turn in Kant at its outset, and a robust doctrine of creation is central to his thought. Hamann also profoundly influenced Kierkegaard's view of creation and the creatureliness of humanity. Schleiermacher stands between them as seeking a different way forward by locating the essence of Christianity in human experience, clearly grounding his theology in Enlightenment rationalism. We begin with the oft-forgotten Hamann and his response to Kant.

Johann Georg Hamann—a christological hermeneutic of the doctrine of creation. Although recognized in Germany, where he was known as "the Magus of the North,"[5] Johann Georg Hamann (1730–1788) has been largely ignored in the Anglo-American world.[6] In lists of great philosophers, his

[3]Herman Dooyeweerd, *Roots of Western Culture: Pagan, Secular, and Christian Options*, trans. John Kraay, Collected Works, Series B, vol. 15 (Ancaster, ON: Paideia, 2012), 29.

[4]Jonathan I. Israel, *Radical Enlightenment: Philosophy and the Making of Modernity 1650–1750* (Oxford: Oxford University Press, 2001).

[5]A sobriquet given to Hamann by Carl von Moser, which alludes to the wise men who followed the star to find Jesus (Mt 2:1-12).

[6]For an introduction to Hamann, see Craig G. Bartholomew and Michael W. Goheen, *Christian Philosophy: A Systematic and Narrative Introduction* (Grand Rapids, MI: Baker Academic, 2013);

name is almost always omitted, and much the same goes for theology.[7] Karl Barth rightly describes Hamann as an "irregular dogmatician" in that his writings are occasional, and he is certainly no systematician.[8] However, as Graham Ward points out, "Barth stands in the tradition of Hamann (and Kierkegaard)—a theological conservatism opposed to the metaphysics of modernity as the gospel itself is opposed to the metaphysics of modernity."[9] Von Balthasar devotes a full chapter to Hamann in his *Glory of the Lord*,[10] and the missiologist Hendrik Kraemer describes Hamann as "arguably the most profound Christian thinker of the eighteenth century."[11] Hamann himself was well aware that he was unlike most theologians; alluding to Amos 7:14, he notes, "I am no theologian, but a herdsman who picks wild figs."[12] For Hamann, the Scriptures provide the lens through which one understands the world around one as well as the "I" in oneself. Hamann thus provides a beacon of light within the overwhelming shadow of Kant and Descartes.

Hamann attended the University of Königsberg, where he imbibed and appropriated the spirit of the Enlightenment. After university he worked for the business of a friend's family and was sent on a diplomatic mission to London. The mission was a disaster, and Hamann's life steadily fell apart. He bought a Bible and, on the second time of trying to read it, was thoroughly converted, the effect of which in the space of a few months was his "London Writings," which Oswald Bayer and Bernd Weissenborn see as comparable to Augustine's *Confessions*.[13] The Behrens family welcomed Hamann back to Königsberg but were distressed by his conversion and sought to reconvert him to the Enlightenment tradition. Their strategy was to introduce Hamann to a philosopher at the University of Königsberg, Immanuel Kant!

Frederick Beiser, *The Fate of Reason: German Philosophy from Kant to Fichte* (Cambridge, MA: Harvard University Press, 1993); Oswald Bayer, *A Contemporary in Dissent: Johann Georg Hamann as Radical Enlightener* (Grand Rapids, MI: Eerdmans, 2012); and esp. John R. Betz, *After Enlightenment: The Post-Secular Vision of J. G. Hamann* (Oxford: Wiley-Blackwell, 2012).

[7]Cf. Betz, *After Enlightenment*, 18.

[8]Barth, *CD* I/1, 277-78; cf. Bayer, *Contemporary in Dissent*, 3.

[9]Graham Ward, "Barth, Modernity and Postmodernity," in *The Cambridge Companion to Karl Barth*, ed. John Webster (Cambridge: Cambridge University Press, 2000), 277.

[10]Hans Urs von Balthasar, *The Glory of the Lord: A Theological Aesthetics*, vol. 3, *Studies in Theological Style: Lay Styles* (Edinburgh: T&T Clark, 1986).

[11]Hendrik Kraemer, *The Christian Message in a Non-Christian World* (London: Harper and Brothers, 1938), 117.

[12]Johann Georg Hamann, *Londoner Schriften*, ed. Oswald Bayer and Bernd Weissenborn (Munich: Beck, 1993), 115.

[13]Betz, *After Enlightenment*, 39. For the important difference between Hamann and Augustine, see Bayer, *Contemporary in Dissent*, 65.

Hamann wrote to Kant after their first meeting, a letter that is considered to be the origin of the *Sturm und Drang* (Storm and Stress) movement. His letter most likely also introduced Kant to Hume, whom Kant famously said woke him from his dogmatic slumbers and led to his philosophical idealism for which he is so well known. In his correspondence with Kant, Hamann argues that faith provides a particular and indispensable kind of knowledge. Faith shows us the limits of reason; indeed, our existence, and that of those things that are external to us, must be believed and cannot be proven to exist.

What is remarkable about Hamann is that once converted he saw that Scripture interprets ourselves to ourselves[14] and provides us with a lens for understanding the world as creation. "Since Hamann allows the Bible to be his concrete historical a priori, he is led into an inexhaustibly spacious area of existence."[15] Oliver Davies, who foregrounds the theological fecundity of Hamann in his *Creativity of God*, notes,

> It is already evident in the early *Biblical Reflections*, however, that Hamann was linking nature with creation through divine speech, and embedding knowledge within the life of the senses: two themes which take on a particular importance for his distinctively scriptural cosmological thought on the one hand and his contestation of Enlightenment thought on the other.[16]

Hamann's articulation of the links between conversion, Scripture, nature, and history are akin to the concerns of philosophical hermeneutics, so that Hamann occupies a central place in this area, prior to Schleiermacher, and in anticipation of many of the concerns of Gadamer.[17] Indeed, through his lens of creation Hamann articulates a hermeneutic antithetical to that of the modern subject. As Bayer says, "Scripture interprets me and not I Scripture."[18] Similarly with the books of nature and history—they remain sealed until opened by the illumination of the Spirit and Scripture. The heavens do indeed declare the glory of God, and nature and history are drenched with such speech: "Speak, that I may see you!—This wish was fulfilled by creation, which is a speech to creatures through creatures;[19] for day unto day utters speech,

---

[14]"He leads me . . . into the hell of self-knowledge and out of it again." Bayer, *Contemporary in Dissent*, 61.

[15]Ibid., xvi.

[16]Oliver Davies, *The Creativity of God: World, Eucharist, and Reason* (Cambridge: Cambridge University Press, 2004), 67-68.

[17]Ibid., 69.

[18]Quoted in Betz, *After Enlightenment*, 41.

[19]Bayer notes that Hamann's expression "a speech to creatures through creatures" is "the terse formula of a Christian doctrine of creation as such" (*Contemporary in Dissent*, 75).

and night unto night shows knowledge. Its watchword traverses every clime to the end of the world, and its voice can be heard in every dialect."[20] The problem is that "the human ear is stopped. It must be opened. A miracle of salvation must first take place. Only in this way can nature be heard as creation."[21] This miracle takes place through Christ so that Hamann's doctrine of creation is no "worldly mediation in general"[22] but thoroughly Christocentric. Hamann's hermeneutic enables him to take all of life seriously as part of God's good creation and to adopt an approach akin to what Kramer and J. H. Bavinck call "subversive fulfillment" in relation to non-Christian cultural contributions. Michael Goheen describes this as the gospel fulfilling or seizing the creational insight or longing or structure while at the same time rejecting the idolatrous distortion.[23] "But Hamann's primary source is Scripture itself, which—according to a theology of creation—becomes the key to our understanding of the world."[24]

Indeed, one of Hamann's arguments against the Enlightenment is that it is inherently reductionistic and cannot do justice to the rich, visceral nature of the creation. As Hamann says, "All the colors of this most beautiful world grow pale once you extinguish its light, the firstborn of creation."[25] John Betz notes that "it is now clear that the key to a full-blooded aesthetics is Christ. . . . Whereas without Christ we can neither fully see nor fully feel, with Christ 'the more we are able to see and taste and behold and touch His loving condescension . . . in his creatures.'"[26]

Davies observes, "If the Kantian system served to secularize reason by loosening its connection with the metaphysical and the religious, then Hamann's contribution was to embed reason again in the divinely created world order."[27] Of humankind as made in the *imago Dei* Hamman says,

> This analogy of man to the Creator endows all creatures with their substance and their stamp, on which depends fidelity and faith in all nature. The more vividly this idea of the image of the invisible GOD dwells in our heart, the more

---

[20]Johann Georg Hamann, "Aesthetica in Nuce (1762)," in *Writings on Philosophy and Language*, ed. Kenneth Haynes, Cambridge Texts in the History of Philosophy (Cambridge: Cambridge University Press, 2007), 65.

[21]Bayer, *Contemporary in Dissent*, 71.

[22]Ibid., 77.

[23]Personal communication. See Michael W. Goheen, *Introducing Christian Mission Today: Scripture, History and Issues* (Downers Grove, IL: IVP Academic, 2014).

[24]Davies, *Creativity of God*, 69.

[25]Hamann, "Aesthetica in Nuce," 78.

[26]Betz, *After Enlightenment*, 133.

[27]Davies, *Creativity of God*, 71.

> we are able to see and taste his loving-kindness in creatures, observe it and grasp it with our hands. . . . Every reaction of man unto created things is an epistle and seal that we partake of the divine nature, and that we are his offspring.[28]

An enduring emphasis of Hamann's is God's condescension, including his condescension in creation and in his inspiration of Scripture.[29] Betz locates Hamann's "profoundly anti-Gnostic sensibility" in this motif.[30] This sensibility sets Hamann in direct opposition to Kant and the Enlightenment tradition. For Kant, it is to the "tribunal" of reason and criticism that everything must submit.[31] For Hamann, it is to God's word in Scripture and in the world and God's eschatological judgment in Christ that "all must submit,"[32] thus turning Kant on his head.

Hamann's corpus is notoriously dense, allusive, and challenging. It is deliberately so, as he sought to show those who thought they were enlightened (in the light) that they first needed to enter the darkness before they could truly enter the light, the light that enlightens every person coming into the world. Hamann's corpus still requires major excavation for our day. For our purposes, one gets a taste of his relevance to the doctrine of creation in the chapter in Davies's *The Creativity of God*, titled "Speech Revealed," that follows on from his discussion of Hamann.[33] Hamann uses the metaphor of divine speech for both Scripture and creation,[34] and Davies similarly expands on the etymological connection between "YHWH" (Ex 3; 6) and the "Let there be's" of Genesis 1:1–2:3, rightly suggesting that the name of God resonates with Genesis 1.[35] Davies concludes,

> This linguistic-creative process of the Old Testament culminates in the conversation, or "speaking with," that takes place on Mount Sinai between God

---

[28]Hamman, "Aesthetica in Nuce," 78-79.

[29]Hamann begins his *London Writings* with amazement at God's condescension in being an author. Cf. Kevin Vanhoozer's use of this metaphor (*Remythologizing Theology: Divine Action, Passion, and Authorship* [Cambridge: Cambridge University Press, 2010]) and Vernon White's affirmation of Vanhoozer's approach (*Purpose and Providence: Taking Soundings in Western Thought, Literature and Theology* [London: T&T Clark, 2015], 115-18).

[30]Betz, *After Enlightenment*, 38.

[31]Immanuel Kant, *Critique of Pure Reason*, trans. Norman Kemp Smith (New York: Modern Library, 1958), 7.

[32]Betz, *After Enlightenment*, 20.

[33]Davies, *Creativity of God*, 75-94. For Hamann on being human, on history, reason, social life, marriage, sexuality, and time, see Bayer, *Contemporary in Dissent*, chaps. 8–12.

[34]Barth (*CD* III/1, 83) references Hamann in support of his view of the creation stories in Genesis as saga or divinatory poetry. For God as "the Poet of the World" and for how Hamann differs from Whitehead, see Bayer, *Contemporary in Dissent*, 54-55.

[35]Davies, *Creativity of God*, 78-80.

> and Moses, who is to be God's agent in his intervention for the sake of his people. Divine presence here is not exercised from outside language, by some sovereign and independent agent, but is rather enfolded within language which acquires revelatory functions. Such an active penetration by God into the heart of human history implies a particular structure of revelation, grounded in the mutuality which inheres in language as such. . . . As a God whose speaking is originary and creative of the world, God too must enter the realm of human speaking, acting and knowing. This kenotic, revelatory movement is necessarily a saving moment, for the divine presence of itself redeems and liberates as it enters and shapes the human condition in a deepening creativity.[36]

It is hard not to hear overtones of Hamann in this extract from Davies. Hamann was very influential in his day and not least on Søren Kierkegaard. Schleiermacher, however, would turn to our experience as the means by which we discern the divine.

Friedrich Schleiermacher and the liberal tradition. Friedrich Schleiermacher (1768–1834) sought to provide a middle way between pre-Enlightenment orthodoxy and Enlightenment rationalism by locating the essence of Christianity in human experience. On the one hand, pre-Enlightenment theologians did theology from above (viewing it as a response to divine revelation), which Schleiermacher thought stifled humanity and confused dogma with God. On the other hand, Enlightenment theology (deism) did theology from below (viewing it as a construction of human reason), which Schleiermacher thought led to sterile natural religion reduced to religious philosophy. In place of these approaches, Schleiermacher viewed theology as reflection on Christian religious experience, the attempt to present Christian piety in human language.

According to Schleiermacher, the doctrine of creation therefore should not be constructed as a response to cosmological curiosity, because curiosity has little or nothing to do with piety.[37] Nor should it be a recapitulation of the traditional Christian beliefs about creation. "We need have no scruples," writes Schleiermacher, "in completely abandoning the creedal expression."[38] Instead

---

[36]Ibid., 83.

[37]Schleiermacher writes, "In general the question of the origin of all finite being is raised not in the interest of piety but in that of curiosity, hence it can only be answered by such means as curiosity offers." *The Christian Faith*, ed. H. R. Mackintosh and James S. Stewart (Berkeley, CA: The Apocryphile Press, 2011), 149.

[38]Schleiermacher, *Christian Faith*, 145. One should note that Schleiermacher views himself as carefully handling the confessions. He wanted to be a responsible interpreter of the church's faith and

of curiosity or recapitulation, he wants to treat the doctrine of creation as a pious confession of our dependence on God. The doctrine of creation *ex nihilo* is a rejection of dualism and an assertion that nothing in the world exists independently of God's sovereignty. Because God brought the world into existence and because he preserves it, we are absolutely dependent on him.

Schleiermacher exhibits a platonizing tendency to see God's relationship to the world in terms of the dependence of the temporal world on the timeless. This tendency is rooted in an insufficient concept of God's providence. In this way, Schleiermacher deprives creation of its rightful integrity, value, and independence, reducing it to a secondary role facilitating the Christian community's experience of absolute dependence.

Søren Kierkegaard—the glory of creatureliness. Søren Kierkegaard (1813–1855) is known for his philosophical and theological corpus and for a life filled with personal tragedy and loneliness, but what is not well known is the delight Kierkegaard found in the wonders of creation. His corpus is a fecund reservoir of reflection in relation to creation, but it remains underresourced, probably because of the unsystematic nature of Kierkegaard's treatment of the doctrine. We note here four key points from Kierkegaard's doctrine of creation derived from his disparate writings.

First, Kierkegaard believes, against the gnostic dualisms, that faith leads us to the recovery of the finite and material. This recovery is illustrated in *Fear and Trembling*, where Kierkegaard imagines a "knight of faith," a knight who is not ethereal or otherworldly but in fact is a fully embodied human being.[39] This knight is a solidly physical man, one whose walk is vigorous, who takes delight in creative and cultural aspects of life, who enjoys nature walks, who smokes his pipe, and who takes an interest in the goings-on surrounding him.

Second, as Charles Bellinger notes, Kierkegaard's notion of continuing creation is the key entry point for exploring a Kierkegaardian doctrine of creation:

> I propose that there is a key in Kierkegaard's idea of continuing creation, as found in *The Concept of Anxiety*. This is suggested by Kierkegaard's decision to begin the book with a consideration of the creation story in Genesis. The crucial difference between human beings and the lower animals is that we have the ability to be conscious of the ongoing process of creation which is occurring

sought to retain the language of the creeds whenever it was possible.

[39]Søren Kierkegaard, *Fear and Trembling*, ed. C. Stephen Evans and Sylvia Walsh (Cambridge: Cambridge University Press, 2006), 32-33.

> within our souls. This ability produces anxiety, which makes sin possible; yet anxiety is also a sign of our relationship to our Creator and thus points toward the possibility of redemption and growth into maturity.[40]

In a delightful chapter on humans as creatures, titled "Out There with the Lilies and the Birds," Kierkegaard scholar George Pattison says, "Kierkegaard, I suggest, never forgets that the doctrine of creation is one of the great poles of Christian teaching. We can find traces and expressions of this awareness at many points in his authorship, but it is never more consistently thematized than in the many discourses he wrote on the lilies and the birds referred to in the Sermon on the Mount."[41]

Third, Kierkegaard's analysis of the temptation toward human autonomy as a denial of the doctrine of creation is acute. He artfully sums up this sentiment, writing, "To be dependent on God, utterly dependent, is to be independent."[42] Berkouwer regularly noted that all of life is a response to God, an insight rooted in the doctrine of creation. Similarly, Pattison says of Kierkegaard's thought, "While we must actively desire God, we are already within the God-relationship by virtue of our being created. Without God we would not be at all. Without God we would cease to be."[43]

Fourth, Kierkegaard articulates a profound view of the human person as becoming, but never at the expense of the realism of creation. He warns against the aesthetic fantasy of self-invention in which our fantasies and longings are prioritized over reality. In the light of postmodern ideologies of self-creation and the disturbing doctrines of gender fluidity, according to which "children are being told that gender is 'fluid' and that the biggest clue to gender is not found in the shape of your body but in the state of your mind,"[44] the relevance of Kierkegaard's understanding of human creatureliness should not be underestimated. Pattison notes of Kierkegaard's doctrine of the *imago Dei*,

> In an article that argues persuasively for the essentially Irenaean structure of Kierkegaard's teaching, Niels-Jørgen Cappelørn makes the point with exemplary succinctness: "Yet what is at issue is not that God creates human beings anew

---

[40]Charles K. Bellinger, "The Crowd Is Untruth: A Comparison of Kierkegaard and Girard," *Contagion* 3 (1996): 114.

[41]George Pattison, *Kierkegaard and the Theology of the Nineteenth Century: The Paradox and the "Point of Contact"* (Cambridge: Cambridge University Press, 2012), 102.

[42]Quoted in ibid., 111.

[43]Ibid., 103.

[44]Glynn Harrison, *A Better Story: God, Sex, and Human Flourishing* (London: Inter-Varsity Press, 2017), 120. Harrison is a British psychiatrist, and his book is nuanced and pastoral.

but that he creates a new person in the person. In the perspective of a theology of creation it is the same person, but in that of soteriology it is a new being."[45]

At the outset of this chapter we noted that the doctrine of creation is something quite wonderful. Kierkegaard captures this: being creaturely is a cause for thanksgiving, a cause for wonder at God's love in creating this world and humans with their capacity to be "independent" of God, a cause to celebrate work as a means by which we are God's coworkers.

The Twentieth Century: Of God's Relationship to His Creation

The twentieth century is a significant period for theology in general. The theologies that emerged from this century hold great sway over theology in our current time. Household theological names such as Barth and Bonhoeffer, as well as schools of thought such as process theology and French Catholic phenomenology, emerged over the course of this period, offering rich glories and dangerous travails with regard to the doctrine of creation. At times we experience glory and travail together in the work of a contemporary theologian. For example, Barth rightfully focuses on Jesus of Nazareth as the Word become flesh, but this focus leads Barth to an unfortunate wholesale rejection of natural theology and diminishing of the creation itself. Wittgenstein and Bonhoeffer follow, both of whom recover a measure of creation's glory in their fights against dualism. The travails of Moltmann's (1926–) panentheistic view of "God with us" and process theology's dipolar God follow the glory of Wittgenstein and Bonhoeffer. We end with the tremendous work in French phenomenology to recover the glory of creation, particularly in its anthropology that highlights two "arks of creation," bodies and speech. But we begin with Barth, the theologian who emphasized the Word of God enfleshed in Jesus of Nazareth.

Karl Barth—the Word became flesh. Over against Schleiermacher and subsequent liberal-revisionist theologians, Karl Barth (1886–1968) wanted to build an account of creation that was specifically Christian, one that was not merely an account of the origins of reality or of God as an abstract First Cause. He made the Trinity central to the doctrine, speaking of the Father as the source of creation, with Son and Spirit as the executors or mediators of his creative activity. Barth affirmed creation's goodness and saw the crucifixion and resurrection as the place where its goodness is brought into sharpest focus. Only at the place where creation's goodness is threatened and finally

[45]Pattison, *Kierkegaard*, 115.

overcome can creation's goodness be understood unambiguously. Barth consistently treats creation in relation to redemption and treats both of them under the rubric of covenant. From eternity, God purposes to elect humanity into reconciled relationship with him. As a result, he makes a historical covenant to elect Christ, and in him all of humanity.

Covenant and creation, therefore, are related in two manners. First, creation is the external basis of the covenant.[46] In other words, if God will enact his covenant love for his people, there must be a place in which he does it. Creation is that place. Creation is like a temple that exists not for itself but for liturgical consummation. Second, covenant is the internal basis of the creation.[47] In other words, creation has no meaning apart from God's covenant. Creation exists for the purpose of realizing God's plan.

Essentially, for Barth, creation does not exist for itself, nor does it exist primarily for God's glory. Creation serves as a stage on which redemption plays out. For Calvin and most Reformed theologians, including Abraham Kuyper and Herman Bavinck, God creates in order to glorify himself, but, as Kathryn Tanner has argued, Barth views God's ultimate end in creation as reconciliation rather than self-glorification.[48] God created the world so that he could send his Son to give us grace. Barth's conception ultimately demotes creation to secondary status. Heinz Zahrnt is harsh in his appraisal, calling Barth's polemic "unrestrained" and "unwilling to understand" in his forcing of the created order into a "Christological pattern that deprives creation of its own meaning and status."[49] Gunton is less harsh but clear still that "the weakness of Barth's theology of creation . . . is . . . his repetition . . . of the Western tendency so to subordinate creation to redemption that the status of the material world as a whole is endangered."[50]

Barth rejected any form of natural theology, which he argued was at the root of many gospel subversions, such as Roman Catholic theology, liberal

---

[46]Barth, *CD* III/1, 41. This recognition that Gen 1 is the major covenantal text has since been confirmed by the close exegesis of William J. Dumbrell in *Creation and Covenant: An Old Testament Covenant Theology*, 2nd ed. (Milton Keynes, UK: Paternoster, 2013).

[47]Barth, *CD* III/1, 41.

[48]Oliver Crisp, "Karl Barth on Creation," in *Karl Barth and Evangelical Theology: Convergences and Divergences*, ed. Sung Wook Chung (Grand Rapids, MI: Baker Academic, 2006), 81. See Kathryn Tanner, "Creation and Providence," in *The Cambridge Companion to Karl Barth*, ed. John Webster (Cambridge: Cambridge University Press, 2000), 111-26.

[49]Heinz Zahrnt, *The Question of God: Protestant Theology in the Twentieth Century* (New York: Harcourt, Brace & World, 1969), 55-68.

[50]Colin E. Gunton, *The Triune Creator: A Historical and Systematic Study* (Grand Rapids, MI: Eerdmans, 1998), 165.

Protestant theology, and Nazi ideology. Barth writes that "the logic of the matter demands that, even if we only lend our little finger to natural theology, there necessarily follows the denial of the revelation of God in Jesus Christ."[51] One can only know God through his incarnate Word, Jesus Christ. We know that it is true because of our confession of it, and this is self-authenticating.

Barth's rejection of natural theology was a decisive rejection of the liberal tradition, which viewed humanity's relationship to God as something of a given in nature and history. But his rejection of natural theology was also a decisive rejection of his erstwhile theological ally, Emil Brunner. In his 1934 work, *Nature and Grace*, Brunner allowed a limited and biblically disciplined place for natural theology. Barth's response to Brunner was titled "*Nein!*" (*No!*). This represents Barth at his most unrestrained, calling natural theology the "great temptation and source of error" in Christian theology.[52] "The 'No' which Barth hurled at Brunner," Zahrnt writes, "was a symbol of his uncompromising attitude to the struggle within the Church. In the 'mediating theology' Barth saw the cause of all the misfortune of the Protestant Church in Germany."[53] In just a few years, Barth's "No" would provide the Confessing Church in Germany with its battle cry. Under Barth's guidance, the Confessing Church formulated the Barmen Declaration, which declared in its first thesis that Jesus Christ is the one and only Word of God.

As discussed in chapter one, with Oliver O'Donovan we affirm the reality of creation order and that it holds for all creation and human beings. With Barth—and O'Donovan—we affirm that it can only be known truly in its interrelationship in Christ.

Ludwig Wittgenstein—rejecting Descartes's "I." The later writings of Ludwig Wittgenstein (1889–1951), arguably the most influential philosopher of the twentieth century, and not least in theology,[54] were animated by his affirmation of the bodily nature of human being and by his rejection of philosophical approaches that reveal an antipathy toward the body. Although Wittgenstein's Christianity is of an ambiguous nature, it seems clear that his Christian belief influenced his philosophy at significant points,[55] not the least of which is his anthropology.

---

[51]Barth, *CD* II/1, 173.

[52]Karl Barth and Emil Brunner, *Natural Theology: Comprising "Nature and Grace" by Emil Brunner and the Reply "No!" by Karl Barth*, trans. Peter Fraenkel (1946; Eugene, OR: Wipf & Stock, 2002), 75.

[53]Zahnrt, *Question of God*, 67.

[54]Bruce Riley Ashford, "Wittgenstein's Theologians: A Survey of Ludwig Wittgenstein's Impact on Theology," *JETS* 50, no. 2 (2007): 357-75.

[55]James W. McClendon Jr. and Brad J. Kallenberg, "Ludwig Wittgenstein: A Christian in Philosophy," *Scottish Journal of Theology* 51, no. 2 (1998): 131-61.

Early in his career, Wittgenstein remarked that he had lost his faith, but what he really seems to have lost is a belief in the rationalist Catholic apologetics of his day. Upon entering the Austro-Hungarian War, Wittgenstein faced regularly the reality of death and soon began praying and writing about God in his diaries. More importantly, he bought Tolstoy's *Gospels in Brief*, read it several times, and recommended it to everyone he met. Brian McGuinness says that Wittgenstein became an evangelist at this point and was known among the soldiers as "the one with the gospels."[56] Further, Wittgenstein's life changed from the reading of it. "The Christianity that he found in Tolstoy seemed to him the only sure way to happiness, but it was not an easy way. Man must renounce the flesh, the gratification of his own will, must make himself independent of outward circumstances, in order to serve the spirit which is in himself and in all men."[57]

Later in his career, however, Wittgenstein developed an approach to philosophy that subverts the bodily antipathy exemplified by his years as a Tolstoyan evangelist. This approach reveals an affirmation of the creational nature of human existence. Wittgenstein's rejection of traditional philosophical method is premised on his rejection of mind-body dualism. "I have tried to convince you," he writes, "of just the opposite of Descartes' emphasis on 'I.'"[58] Against Plato, Descartes, and the whole Western tradition, Wittgenstein rejects the philosophical method that views the mind as being able to separate itself from the body. He argues that mind is inextricably intertwined with the body, that interiority is bound up with the public and physical. The public and physical foster the inner and mental, rather than vice versa. Wittgenstein's holist anthropology had implications for epistemology and philosophy of language, as he rejected any philosophy that sought for the human mind or human language to be able to step back from the world in order to "capture" reality. For him, our knowing and speaking are inextricably bound up with our bodies and our social and linguistic contexts.[59] In short, Wittgenstein's later philosophy is one that emphasized the *embodied* nature of life and

---

[56]Brian McGuinness, *Wittgenstein, a Life: Young Ludwig, 1889–1921* (Berkeley: University of California Press, 1988), 220-21; cf. Ray Monk, *Ludwig Wittgenstein: The Duty of Genius* (New York: Free Press, 1990), 115-16.

[57]Monk, *Ludwig Wittgenstein*, 116.

[58]Ludwig Wittgenstein, *Wittgenstein's Lectures, Cambridge 1932–1935*, ed. Alice Ambrose (Oxford: Blackwell, 1979), 63.

[59]For an exploration of Wittgenstein's thought related to these issues, see Fergus Kerr, *Theology After Wittgenstein*, 2nd ed. (London: SPCK, 1997). For a concise summary, see Ashford, "Wittgenstein's Theologians."

rejected gnostic tendencies in modern philosophy. Likewise, Bonhoeffer rejected any dualism in God's good creation.

Dietrich Bonhoeffer—God's deeply loved world. In Dietrich Bonhoeffer's (1906–1945) day, dualisms between matter and spirit and between Old Testament and New had been used by some Christians to reinforce Nazi anti-Semitism. In this context Bonhoeffer wrote *Creation and Fall*, a theological exposition of Genesis 1–3 that affirms the goodness of God's creation, a goodness that continues after the fall. "Because the world is God's world," Bonhoeffer writes, "it is good. God, the Creator and Lord of the world, wills a good world, a good work. The flight from the created work to bodiless spirit, or to the internal spiritual disposition [*die Gesinnung*], is prohibited. God wills to look upon God's work, to love it, call it good, and uphold it."[60]

In his *Ethics*, Bonhoeffer argues that we must get rid of the sacred-secular divide and immerse ourselves as Christians in the totality of this fallen world. For Bonhoeffer, "the 'world' is . . . the sphere of concrete and therefore limited responsibility which knows the world as being created, loved, condemned, and reconciled by God and which acts within the world in accordance with this knowledge."[61] As embodied beings, we must necessarily live out our faith within this world. "Any attempt," Bonhoeffer writes, "to escape from the world must sooner or later be paid for with a sinful surrender to the world."[62] The Christian therefore is one who lives his or her holistic existence in the world: "It is not the religious act that makes us Christian, but participation in the sufferings of God in the secular life."[63] By living holistically in the secular world, the Christian becomes a person "for others," a person who is both more fully human and more fully Christian. "The difference between the Christian hope of resurrection and a mythological hope," writes Bonhoeffer, "is that the Christian hope sends a man back to his life on earth in a wholly new way."[64]

Within the Lutheran tradition, Bonhoeffer is clearly a fertile node for development of a doctrine of creation. His doctrine of divine mandates is not as strong as the Kuyperian doctrine of creation order, but it is nevertheless helpful.[65] Bonhoeffer especially draws on Ecclesiastes to affirm the mundane.

---

[60]Dietrich Bonhoeffer, *Creation and Fall: A Theological Exposition of Genesis 1–3*, ed. John W. De Gruchy, trans. Douglas S. Bax, Dietrich Bonhoeffer Works 3 (Minneapolis: Fortress, 1997), 45-46.

[61]Dietrich Bonhoeffer, *Ethics*, trans. Eberhard Bethge (London: SCM Press, 1955), 202.

[62]Ibid., 66.

[63]Dietrich Bonhoeffer, *Letters and Papers from Prison*, ed. Eberhard Bethge and Frank Clarke, trans. Reginald Horace Fuller, 3rd ed. (New York: Macmillan, 1972), 361.

[64]Ibid., 336-37.

[65]Dietrich Bonhoeffer, *Ethics*, 282-87.

And, of course, in his life and martyrdom he embodied that vocation to which Hauerwas loves to refer—namely, that we must keep reminding the world, that world that causes us so much pain, that it is in fact God's deeply loved world. Moltmann would also affirm God's love for his creation.

Jürgen Moltmann—God with us. Jürgen Moltmann's (1926–) doctrine of creation comes into focus only when one examines his whole theological corpus in light of his concern for the ecological crisis. Richard Bauckham summarizes Moltmann's approach in a four-point outline that begins with his *ecological doctrine of creation*.[66] Moltmann wants to subvert historic Christian views that give any form of exploitative "dominion" pride of place in the creation account. Rather than viewing God primarily as king, and humans primarily as vice regents exercising dominion, he views God as three persons in perichoretic relation and humans as persons in community with one another and with the rest of creation. This *trinitarian doctrine of creation* pictures creational life as a pattern of reciprocal relationships. "All living things," Moltmann writes, "live in one another and with one another, from one another and for one another."[67] Moltmann's model is panentheistic, as God relates to his creation through mutual indwelling. The trinitarian nature of creation issues forth in a *messianic doctrine of creation* in which creation is not merely protological but fundamentally eschatological. The telos of the cosmos is the coming kingdom of God. "Redemption and eschatology do not, therefore, serve to lift humanity out of the material world, but confirm humanity's solidarity with the rest of God's creation in its longing for eschatological liberation."[68] Finally, Moltmann proscribes a *sabbatical doctrine of creation*, in which the Sabbath is the eschatological goal of creation. This sabbatical theme converges with the messianic theme to highlight the teleological nature of the doctrine of creation. One can find resonance between Moltmann's theology and the deity of process philosophy and theology.

Process philosophy and theology—the God who changes. Alfred North Whitehead (1861–1947) developed process philosophy and influenced a number of Christian theologians to adapt the process philosophy model to theology. In Whitehead's model, God is dipolar. His primordial/potential pole is the world of eternal and unchanging potential. This pole is abstract and potential, and therefore stable and unchanging. God's consequent/actual pole

---

[66]Richard Bauckham, *The Theology of Jürgen Moltmann* (Edinburgh: T&T Clark, 1995), 183-90.

[67]Jürgen Moltmann, *God in Creation: A New Theology of Creation and the Spirit of God* (Minneapolis: Fortress, 1993), 17.

[68]Bauckham, *Theology of Jürgen Moltmann*, 188.

is the cosmos, his lived reality. This pole is consequently changing as God *prehends* (feels) experiences and entities. So God is both unchanging and changing. Further separating Whitehead's thought from traditional Christian theism is his panentheism and his belief that God works (even in his creative acts) through persuasion.

He is hesitant to speak about God as "creator" because such a description generally carries with it an idea of God as "controller." Whitehead rejects any attempt to make God controller, because he refuses to make God responsible for evil. This notion of a "transcendent creator, at whose fiat the world came into being, and whose imposed will it obeys, is the fallacy which has infused tragedy into the histories of Christianity and of Mahometanism."[69] Additionally, Whitehead hesitates to call God "creator" unless it is realized that God himself is also created. "It is as true," he writes, "to say that God creates the World, as the World creates God."[70] God is an "accident" of creativity, the "primordial creature," and the "outcome of creativity."[71] And yet, with those and other caveats, Whitehead does call God "creator."

Charles Hartshorne (1897–2000), John Cobb (1925–), David Ray Griffin (1939–), and others adopted Whitehead's model for their own purposes in creating a fuller process theology. Like Whitehead, they view God as dipolar rather than monopolar. He is a finite, changing, and ever-perfecting being who should be seen as dependent on the world and collaboratively working with the world instead of independent of the world and sovereign over it. Significantly, instead of creating out of nothing, God created out of chaos. For Cobb, the doctrine of creation *ex nihilo* "is part and parcel of the doctrine of God as absolute controller" and is a doctrine that Cobb rejects.[72] Cobb, like Whitehead, builds his doctrine of creation in conversation with evolutionary science. He argues that the world has developed from simple to complex and correspondingly has increased in value. "Complex actualities," he writes, "enjoy more value than simple ones. The direction of the evolutionary process on the whole is toward more complex actualities, resulting from God's basic creative purpose, which is the evocation of actualities with greater and greater enjoyment."[73] This inexorable drive toward greater complexity and enjoyment

[69]Alfred North Whitehead, *Process and Reality: An Essay in Cosmology*, ed. David Ray Griffin and Donald W. Sherburne, corrected ed. (New York: Free Press, 1978), 342.

[70]Ibid., 348.

[71]Ibid., 7, 31, 38.

[72]John B. Cobb and David Ray Griffin, *Process Theology: An Introductory Exposition* (Philadelphia: Westminster Press, 1976), 65.

[73]Ibid., 64.

is in harmony with God's character. "The evolutionary development of our world propounded by modern science can be interpreted in harmony with the character and purpose of God. The creatively and responsively loving God is incarnately active in the present, bringing about . . . a greater good that will involve a fuller incarnation of the divine reality itself."[74]

The doctrine of creation presented by process philosophers and theologians is not Christian in any meaningful sense of the word. It is a pantheistic vision that undermines the "God the Father almighty" of the creeds and that cannot conceive of God apart from the world, thereby being unable to conceive of God apart from the evil that stains our world. In other words, process theology suffers from the travail so common in gnostic ways of thinking. Furthermore, such a God as the process theologians construct is coeternal with the natural world. Thus, there is no account of the origins of "creation" beyond the preexistent chaos from which God produces order. Over against these travails, a remarkable recovery of the doctrine has appeared in the French phenomenologists.[75]

French Catholic phenomenology—the ark of creation. The phenomenological approach to philosophy and theology focuses on the study of consciousness and on objects of direct experience. Initially, in Edmund Husserl's (1859–1938) philosophy, phenomenology was a major attempt to provide a secure foundation for the Enlightenment project. Later, a galaxy of French Catholic phenomenologists, indebted to theologians such as Henri de Lubac, opened up phenomenology from the inside out to deliver a rich theological/philosophical development in this tradition. These philosophers include Jean Luc Marion (1946–), Jean-Yves Lacoste (1953–), Jean-Louis Chrétien (1952– 2019), Michel Henry (1922–2002), and Emmanuel Falque (1963–). They have produced a rich body of literature that is Augustinian in its roving across the borderline between philosophy and theology. Falque notes that the type of "philosophy of the threshold" practiced by philosophers such as Paul Ricoeur, which always restrained itself at the entranceway to theology, is over.[76] "It has at last become possible, at least in certain places and in certain circumstances, to describe oneself as 'at the same time' philosopher and theologian."[77]

---

[74]Ibid., 68.

[75]Dominique Janicaud et al., *Phenomenology and the "Theological Turn": The French Debate* (New York: Fordham University Press, 2001).

[76]Emmanuel Falque, *The Metamorphosis of Finitude: An Essay on Birth and Resurrection*, trans. George Hughes (New York: Fordham University Press, 2012), x.

[77]Ibid., x.

The merging of philosopher and theologian signals the merging once again of nature and grace. And the results are noteworthy. In our reading of these French scholars, which is far from exhaustive, it is rare to find the language of creation explicitly present, but implicitly it is all over the place and wonderful to behold. Below, we focus on the insights of Chrétien, Lacoste, Henry, and Falque.

Jean-Louis Chrétien. Chrétien has, for example, produced a remarkable philosophy of language in his *The Ark of Speech*, and creation is central to it. As we will see in our discussion of Adam naming the animals in chapter five, "the ark" is a metaphor taken from Noah's ark and used to exquisite effect. At the very outset of this work, Chrétien notes, "When he speaks for the first time, man does not enter language: he must already inhabit it. Indeed, as the very letter of the story puts it, God has already addressed man, has already spoken to him before man starts to speak, so that he will start to speak in his turn."[78] Chrétien's creation-based account of language forms a stark contrast with the postmodernism that tends to see language as a form of violence, thus—in theological terms—collapsing creation into fall along gnostic lines. Chrétien says, for example, of Maurice Blanchot's postmodern approach to language that "his basic thesis makes of Adam's speech, not the first ark, but the first flood."[79]

Jean-Yves Lacoste. Lacoste provides us with a rich liturgical "anthropology."[80] He chooses "liturgical" over "religious" because of Schleiermacher's reduction of the religious to feeling. Liturgy means here "the logic that presides over the encounter between man and God writ large," and Lacoste coins the phrase "liturgical reason."[81] Heidegger is a major dialogue partner for Lacoste in this work, but, intriguingly, Lacoste tends to acknowledges his debts to Bonhoeffer and St. John of the Cross but not to Heidegger.

As we will see in chapter six, a theology of place flows out of the doctrine of creation, and part one of Lacoste's *Experience and the Absolute* is titled "Man and His Place." Lacoste insightfully argues that liturgy will redirect our view of place from being-there to being-toward, thus making relation central.[82] Lacoste notes, "It falls to liturgy to do justice to the complexity of the

---

[78]Jean-Louis Chrétien, *The Ark of Speech*, trans. Andrew Brown (New York: Routledge, 2004), 1.

[79]Ibid., 6.

[80]Jean-Yves Lacoste, *Experience and the Absolute: Disputed Questions in the Humanity of Man*, trans. Mark Raftery-Skehan (New York: Fordham University Press, 2004). The word *anthropology* is in quotes because Lacoste does not favor the term.

[81]Ibid., 2, 53.

[82]Ibid., 25.

question of place in a way that a phenomenology in which world and earth constitute the ultimate or the intranscendable par excellence cannot."[83] Because of this doing of justice, and drawing deeply from Bonhoeffer, Lacoste insists that the Absolute's eschatological claims must take precedence over the historical claims of the world, without for a moment denying the particularity of existence.[84] For Heidegger, *Dasein* is characterized by being-toward-death, whereas "liturgy proposes a mode of experience in which death is no longer the secret of life."[85] Lacoste writes, "We must, finally, dare to say that liturgy enables us to dwell in the world and on the earth by superimposing on our facticity the order of an ethical vocation that alone authorizes us to let the Kingdom invest itself in world and earth in advance."[86] Far from such an approach detracting from human life, "liturgy, understood in its broadest sense, is the most human mode in which we can exist in the world or on the earth."[87]

Michel Henry. Henry has similarly done extraordinary work on what it means to be human. We noted in our introduction the inseparable connection between the incarnation and creation, and one of Henry's books is *Incarnation: A Philosophy of Flesh*. Part three of this work is titled "Salvation in the Christian Sense." We noted in the previous chapter the importance of Irenaeus for a doctrine of creation, and Henry engages substantially and positively with Irenaeus. He notes that "we are now witnesses to the true reversal of the Gnostic positions. Gnosticism did not want a real flesh like ours for the Christ, an earthly, material flesh, which was too trivial for its liking. . . . It is that life, the Life of God self-revealed in its Word, that was made flesh. . . . The flesh in which the Word comes comes from the Word itself, in other words, from Life."[88] Lacoste points out that Henry's "Life/life" distinction "quite simply points out to phenomenology that, when it concerns itself with the words (and works) of Christ, it finally arrives at the arch-phenomenon that gives meaning to all other phenomena."[89] Henry specifically advocates a trinitarian anthropology:

---

[83]Ibid., 39.

[84]Ibid., 61.

[85]Ibid., 66.

[86]Ibid., 74.

[87]Ibid., 98.

[88]Michel Henry, *Incarnation: A Philosophy of Flesh*, trans. Karl Hefty (Evanston, IL: Northwestern University Press, 2015), 170-71.

[89]Jean-Yves Lacoste, foreword to *Words of Christ*, by Michel Henry, trans. Christina M. Gschwandtner, Interventions (Grand Rapids, MI: Eerdmans, 2012), x.

> Because I who live did not bring myself into life myself . . . this living being, this Self, and this flesh do not arrive in themselves except in the proceeding of absolute Life, which arrives in itself in its Word, and experiences itself in this Word, which experiences itself in it, in the reciprocal phenomenological interiority of their common Spirit. Thus in contrast to the formal God of monotheism, the Trinitarian God of Christianity is the real God who lives in each living Self, without which no living being would live, and to which every living being bears witness to in its very condition as living.[90]

The creation reflects the trinitarian nature of the creator.[91]

Emmanuel Falque. How to think about humanity is central to Falque's works, as is the doctrine of the resurrection. We have titled this section "The Ark of Creation" because Falque develops Chrétien's use of the metaphor of the ark for language to that of the "ark of flesh."

> But before the *ark of speech* there is the *ark of flesh*. . . . "Doing" comes before "speaking;" or even better, before "saying" is discovered the "pre-saying," in the sense of a pre-predicative formation by which God gives man the existence and activity of his flesh itself as the original place of his first dwelling. Such is in fact the teaching of Irenaeus, which we are today strongly encouraged to reappropriate.[92]

Both arks connect us deeply into creation, and thus we find it evocative to think of creation as "the first ark," wonderfully designed as the home for humans and all the other creatures of God.

We cannot begin to engage these rich works in the detail they call for; suffice it to say that the French Catholic phenomenologists provide the reader with a feast, one closely aligned to and explicative of the doctrine of creation. As authors writing in the Kuyperian tradition, we are particularly delighted to see the rapprochement of theology, philosophy, and Scripture in their writings.

The Twenty-First Century: Continuing to Strive for Creation's Glory

The twenty-first century is still young and not far removed from the twentieth century, and some of the previous century's most influential theologians remain alive today. Thus, we are still realizing the full impact and significance

---

[90]Henry, *Incarnation*, 170-71.

[91]We focus on the positive aspects of Henry's work in this section, but see Joseph Rivera, *The Contemplative Self After Michel Henry: A Phenomenological Theology* (Notre Dame, IN: University of Notre Dame Press, 2015), for a strong critique of aspects of Henry's view of creation.

[92]Emmanuel Falque, *God, the Flesh, and the Other: From Irenaeus to Duns Scotus*, trans. William C. Hackett (Evanston, IL: Northwestern University Press, 2015), 120.

of the twentieth century's creation theologies. Yet it is worth noting the rise of Radical Orthodoxy at the turn of the twenty-first century and the issues within modern evangelicalism that exert their force within the church and in the broader culture. We believe that as we work out the impact of older theologies and encounter new ones, the Dutch Reformed tradition has much to offer for us to avoid common travails and magnify oft-neglected glories. We therefore end this section, this chapter, and this survey of history by outlining the contours of the Kuyperian tradition and the potential for its doctrine of creation to chart a way forward in our time.

Radical Orthodoxy. The theological "school"[93] known as Radical Orthodoxy (RO) emerged at the turn of the twenty-first century through the efforts of theologians such as John Milbank (1952–), Catherine Pickstock (1970–), Graham Ward (1955–), and several of their students.[94] RO theologians hold a unique view of the created world.

> RO theologians are influenced by philosophers as diverse as Plato, Hamann, and Alasdair MacIntyre and theologians as diverse as Augustine, Aquinas, Kierkegaard, and Hauerwas. At the bottom of their agenda is the conviction that modern and postmodern society is sick and that Christianity is the only remedy for that sickness. "Today," write Milbank, Pickstock, and Ward, "the logic of secularism is imploding. Speaking with a microphoned and digitally simulated voice, it proclaims—uneasily, or else increasingly unashamedly—its own lack of values and lack of meaning. In its cyberspaces and theme-parks it promotes a materialism which is soulless, aggressive, nonchalant and nihilistic."[a] Christians therefore should confront it with the Christian story and should do so through word and deed. It cannot be cured by theologies infected by the "secular" (e.g., liberation theology, eco-theology), but only by truly Christian theology.
>
> [a]John Milbank, Catherine Pickstock, and Graham Ward, eds., *Radical Orthodoxy: A New Theology* (New York: Routledge, 1999), 1.

In Christian theology there is no neutral ground and therefore no "secular" realm. The entirety of the created order "participates" in God's being. "The central theological framework of radical orthodoxy," write Milbank, Pickstock, and Ward, "is 'participation' as developed by Plato and

[93]Graham Ward describes RO as a "theological sensibility," Catherine Pickstock as a "loose tendency." See Wolter Huttinga, *Participation and Communicability: Herman Bavinck and John Milbank on the Relation Between God and the World* (Amsterdam: Buijten & Schipperheijn, 2014), 19.

[94]Several of these, such as Philip Blond and Peter Leithart, are now established scholars in their own right.

reworked by Christianity, because any alternative configuration perforce reserves a territory independent of God. The latter can lead only to nihilism (though in different guises). Participation, however, refuses any reserve of created territory, while allowing finite things their own integrity."[95] For RO, participation is not identity, but it is in fact real relationship. Reason, therefore, is not neutral, precisely because it is participation in the divine life. Therefore, reason is "rational" only if it is reasoning within the framework of Christian theology.

RO theologians speak of "suspending the material." In so speaking, they communicate that God interrupts or suspends our material reality and gives it back to us as a gift. Because our material reality is a gift from God, we recognize that creational reality is enchanted with the divine and we value it accordingly. Thus Christians should affirm the value and interconnectedness of the various dimensions of human society and culture (e.g., social, ecclesial, political) and bring their Christian convictions to bear on those same dimensions.

Critics of RO argue that their suspension of the material actually undermines Christian theology in general and the doctrine of creation in particular. James K. A. Smith addresses RO's Platonic doctrine of participation: "I continue to be confused by RO's central claim that Plato's ontology—and, in particular, Plato's doctrine of participation (*methexis*)—offers a (necessary?) framework for articulating theology."[96] Smith notes RO's explicit affirmations of the goodness of creation and shows the ways in which it has modified the Platonic doctrine, but concludes that there is an antithesis between Platonic "participation" and "suspension of the material" on the one hand and Christian teaching on the ontological goodness of creation on the other.

Wolter Huttinga compares Milbank's and Herman Bavinck's views of the relationship between God and the world. He notes that it was RO's critique of secular society that resonated with his neo-Calvinist tradition[97] but that it also "articulated a lost sense of mystery we had been longing for."[98] As Huttinga observes, "participation" is not alien to the Reformed tradition. For

---

[95]John Milbank, Catherine Pickstock, and Graham Ward, eds., *Radical Orthodoxy: A New Theology* (New York: Routledge, 1999), 3.

[96]James K. A. Smith, *Introducing Radical Orthodoxy: Mapping a Post-Secular Theology* (Grand Rapids, MI: Baker Academic, 2004), 198.

[97]Smith (ibid., 15) suggests that Milbank's *Theology and Social Theory* echoed themes in Abraham Kuyper's thought nearly a century earlier.

[98]Huttinga, *Participation and Communicability*, 18-19.

example, participation is an important theme in Calvin.[99] Both RO and the Reformed tradition are concerned to protect the difference between God and the world while allowing for maximal engagement with God, with sharing in his life. Huttinga discerns a parallel to RO's participation motif in Bavinck's doctrine of God's communicability.[100] Both Bavinck and Milbank lay great stress on the incarnation. Bavinck, however, rightly relates the incarnation far more strongly to sin than does Milbank, although with Milbank he sees the incarnation as exceeding it as a response to sin in relation to God's magnificent gift and the opening of his life to the world. Huttinga concludes that Bavinck is more nuanced than Milbank and that "it is Bavinck's view that captures all of the decisive elements within the patristic tradition."[101] In our view the far stronger engagement with Scripture in Bavinck is vital to note, as well as Bavinck's refusal to see theology alone as the Christian "science."[102] There is little sign of RO taking root in other disciplines, whereas central to the Kuyperian tradition is the notion of the inner reformation of the academic disciplines along Christian lines. In these respects, the Kuyperian tradition embodies a more holistic doctrine of creation as well as a profound honoring of the Christ event as an explosion of good news that illumines the whole of creation and history.

Modern evangelical issues—the beginning and the end. During the modern period, there has been considerable debate about the creation "days" in the Genesis account.[103] One view is that creation took place in six twenty-four-hour days. Some theologians representative of this view, such as Ken Ham, argue for a young earth on the basis of a count of the years represented in various genealogies and the assumption that days of creation were literal days as we understand them today.[104]

Several other views have emerged with the rise in the nineteenth century of modern scientific disciplines of geology and evolutionary biology. These

---

[99]See J. Todd Billings, *Calvin, Participation, and the Gift: The Activity of Believers in Union with Christ* (Oxford: Oxford University Press, 2007); Julie Canlis, *Calvin's Ladder: A Spiritual Theology of Ascent and Ascension* (Grand Rapids, MI: Eerdmans, 2010); Hans Boersma, *Heavenly Participation: The Weaving of a Sacramental Tapestry* (Grand Rapids, MI: Eerdmans, 2011).

[100]Huttinga, *Participation and Communicability*, 24.

[101]Ibid., 226.

[102]Ibid., 224.

[103]For a concise view of the debate about the "days" of Gen 1, see J. Daryl Charles, ed., *Reading Genesis 1–2: An Evangelical Conversation* (Peabody, MA: Hendrickson, 2013), and David G. Hagopian, *The Genesis Debate: Three Views on the Days of Creation* (Mission Viejo, CA: Crux Press, 2001).

[104]Ken Ham, "Young Earth Creationism," in *Four Views on Creation, Evolution, and Intelligent Design*, ed. J. B. Stump and Stanley N. Gundry (Grand Rapids, MI: Zondervan Academic, 2017), 17-48.

views attempt to reconcile scientific theories of the earth's age with what seems to be Scripture's insistence on a historical Adam. The oldest of these theories is the "gap theory." Proponents of this view, such as Thomas Chalmers and G. H. Pember, hold that because the fossil record reveals that the earth is much older than Scripture's genealogies that date back to Adam seem to suggest, and because these fossils reveal evidence of death, disease, and decay, the pre-Adamic world was no paradise, as Scripture suggests is true of the pre-fall world. In this view, therefore, God is seen to have created an originally perfect world millions of years ago populated by Stone Age humans before the historic Adam. At some point Lucifer rebelled against God and led the pre-Adamic humans into sin, causing God to create a new human race, beginning with Adam and Eve around six thousand years ago.[105]

Another view that attempts to reconcile Scripture with modern scientific analysis of the age of the earth is the revelation-day theory. The proponents of this view, such as P. J. Wiseman and James M. Houston, argue that though creation was revealed to Moses to have been created in six twenty-four-hour days, there is a difference between what God revealed and what he actually performed in creation. The reason for this discrepancy, they argue, is that God's revelation was not intended to detail how creation came about in the particulars concerning God's actions, but rather to instruct that all creation came about from God, which ought to lead to glorification and worship of him.[106]

Another view that reconciles Scripture and science is the day-age theory, whose proponents argue each day in the Genesis narrative is symbolic of separate eras and not indicative of literal twenty-four hour days.[107] One representative of this view, Bernard Ramm, argues that the Scriptures give us the "*who* of creation," while science tells us "the *how* and the *when*," and he considers his day-age proposal a *via media* between fiat creationism and theistic evolutionism.[108] Other proponents of this view make more exegetical arguments for its validity, looking to Psalm 90:4 and 2 Peter 3:8, in which "with the Lord one day is as a thousand years."[109]

---

[105]Kenneth D. Keathley and Mark F. Rooker, *40 Questions About Creation and Evolution* (Grand Rapids, MI: Kregel Academic, 2014), 111-18.

[106]Gordon R. Lewis and Bruce A. Demarest, *Integrative Theology* (Grand Rapids, MI: Zondervan, 1987–1994), 2:24.

[107]Keathley and Rooker, *40 Questions About Creation and Evolution*, 119-26.

[108]Lewis and Demarest, *Integrative Theology*, 2:25; cf. Bernard Ramm, *The Christian View of Science and Scripture* (Grand Rapids, MI: Eerdmans, 1956), 113-15.

[109]Keathley and Rooker, *40 Questions About Creation and Evolution*, 122.

One more view that attempts to reconcile the Genesis narrative with science is the analogical day theory. Proponents argue that the days of Genesis 1 are God's workdays, analogous to human workdays. These days are periods of unspecified duration that may overlap partially or may be grouped logically instead of chronologically. A prominent proponent of this view is C. John Collins.[110]

So far the previous five views articulate their positions in conscious dependence on the conclusions of modern science. One final view to consider is the literary framework theory, whose proponents may or may not look to science to set the parameters of the discussion. Those who hold to this view are instead interested in the doctrinal or kerygmatic function of the literary genre of the Genesis account. In this view, proponents argue that "Genesis 1 presents a topical, nonsequential order for the days of creation, rather than a literal and sequential order."[111] Although differences exist among proponents of this view, Lee Irons and Meredith Kline's explication is broadly representative. Irons and Kline argue that the six days form two triads (or panels). The first triad, days one through three, reveals three creation kingdoms, while the second triad, days four through six, reveals three creation kings. Each of these kingdoms and kings is subordinate to God, who establishes himself as King on the Sabbath.[112] Besides Irons and Kline, other proponents of this view include Mark Ross, Henri Blocher, and Gordon Wenham, and, as will become apparent, it is the one we espouse.

During the twentieth century and continuing today, a number of contemporary evangelicals view the apocalyptic imagery of 2 Peter 3:12-13 as referring to a substantial annihilation of the present cosmos. This interpretation of the text, which posits discontinuity between the old earth and the new, fits with the general tenor of popular twentieth-century American fundamentalism, which tended to view the present material world as ontologically corrupted by the fall. Contemporary evangelicals are not alone among modern theologians, however, in their promotion of cosmic annihilationism. Reformation and post-Reformation theologians debated this question, with Lutheran theologians tending to favor an entirely new creation and Reformed theologians preferring a renewal of the present creation. Eduard Böhl, for example, argued that the universe will be annihilated entirely, at which time God will create

---

[110]C. John Collins, *Genesis 1–4: A Linguistic, Literary, and Theological Commentary* (Phillipsburg, NJ: P&R, 2006) 124.

[111]Keathley and Rooker, *40 Questions About Creation and Evolution*, 127.

[112]Lee Irons and Meredith Kline, "The Framework View," in Hagopian, *Genesis Debate*, 217-56.

ex nihilo a new world entirely discontinuous with the first.[113] In the midst of the competing voices of modern evangelicalism, we believe the Dutch Reformed tradition offers hope for the doctrine of creation moving forward in the twenty-first century.

The Dutch Reformed tradition—a way forward. In the twenty-first century, a full-orbed Irenaean doctrine of creation presents itself as a salient remedy for the ills of our modern and postmodern eras, both of which have succumbed to (neo-)gnosticism in potentially disastrous ways.[114] We must regain the doctrine of creation, delivering it from its travails and allowing it to fulfill its rich potential. Among Christian traditions in the modern period, the Dutch neo-Calvinist tradition is, in our opinion, particularly fruitful in providing resources for a recovery and renewal of the Irenaean doctrine of creation's goodness.[115] Abraham Kuyper, Herman Bavinck, and their successors set forth a robust doctrine of creation's goodness that is world-affirming. For them, the doctrine of creation is indispensable for understanding reality, foundational to the formation of other Christian doctrines, and possessive of radical and far-reaching consequences for the Christian life. As we note in the preface, this is the tradition in which we write and in which this book is positioned. For now we outline the broad contours of the neo-Calvinist view of creation in seven propositions as follows.

First, the creator is the triune God. Bavinck notes that God the Father created the world through the Son and in the Spirit. "In this context," he writes, "the Son and the Spirit are not viewed as secondary forces but as independent agents or 'principles' (*principia*), as authors (*auctores*) who with the Father carry out the work of creation, as with him they also constitute the one true God."[116] The doctrine of creation is a work of the whole Trinity. Similarly, the new creation will be a work of the whole Trinity, as at that time creation will return to the Father in the Spirit and through the Son.[117]

113Eduard Böhl, *Dogmatik: Darstellung der Christlichen Glaubenslehre auf Reformirt-Kirchlicher Grundlage* (Amersterdam: Von Scheffer, 1887), 610.

114See Eric Voegelin, *Science, Politics, and Gnosticism*, trans. William J. Fitzpatrick (1968; repr., Washington, DC: Regnery, 1997); Augusto Del Noce, *The Crisis of Modernity* (Montreal: McGill-Queen's University Press, 2014).

115For an introduction to the Kuyperian tradition see Bartholomew, *Contours of the Kuyperian Tradition*.

116Herman Bavinck, *Reformed Dogmatics*, ed. John Bolt, trans. J. Vriend (Grand Rapids, MI: Baker Academic, 2003–2008), 2:421.

117Ibid., 2:426. The fertility of the Kuyperian doctrine of the Trinity should not be underestimated. Kuyper, for example, was one of the very first to anchor mission in the doctrine of the Trinity, as David Bosch recognizes (Bartholomew, *Contours of the Kuyperian Tradition*, 182).

Second, God's creation is ontologically good. "The doctrine of creation," Bavinck writes, "maintains the divinity, the goodness and sacredness of all created things."[118] Creation is an act of the triune God whereby he created all things and did so for his own glory. "It is God's good pleasure to bring the excellencies of His triune being into manifestation in His creatures, and so to prepare glory and honor for Himself in those creatures."[119] God's revelation in Christ "joins itself to the revelation, which nature itself makes known to us; it elevates this to its fullest right, and maintains it in its real value, and by its doctrine of creation cuts all polytheism and all dualism up by the roots. Not only mind but also matter, not only man but also nature, is of divine origin, and has lain in the thought of God before it came into being."[120] God's creation is comprehensively good, in both its material and its immaterial aspects.

Third, God's creation is a coherently ordered diversity. God took the dark and unformed creation and gave it deep structure with splendid diversity and solid regularity. Kuyper argued that God's creation is (potentially) divided into various spheres (e.g., religion, art, politics), which, each according to its God-given purpose, are independent of one another as spheres of creational life but are never independent of God as Lord. "There are in life," Kuyper writes, "as many spheres as there are constellations in the sky and that the circumference of each has been drawn on a fixed radius from the center of a unique principle, namely, the apostolic injunction *hekastos en toi idioi tagmati* ["each in its own order": 1 Cor 15:23]."[121] This led Kuyper to assert that all of life—life under each of these spheres—must be brought under submission to Christ's lordship. "Because God has fully ordained such laws and ordinances for all life, therefore . . . all life [must] be consecrated to His service, in strict obedience."[122] Indeed, the social and cultural mandate of Genesis 1:26-27 instructs us to do our cultural work to God's glory.

Kuyper often extolled the diversity of God's good creation, reminding his readers and congregants that God told life to multiply after its kind. "Raise your eyes," Kuyper writes,

> look up at the starry heavens, and you will see not just a single beam of light but an undulating, scintillating sea of light coming from myriads of

[118]Herman Bavinck, *The Philosophy of Revelation* (Eugene, OR: Wipf & Stock, 2003), 107.
[119]Herman Bavinck, *Our Reasonable Faith* (Grand Rapids, MI: Eerdmans, 1956), 169.
[120]Bavinck, *Philosophy of Revelation*, 107.
[121]Abraham Kuyper, "Sphere Sovereignty," in *Abraham Kuyper: A Centennial Reader*, ed. James Bratt (Grand Rapids, MI: Eerdmans, 1998), 467.
[122]Abraham Kuyper, *Lectures on Calvinism* (Grand Rapids, MI: Eerdmans, 1931), 53.

> bright-shining stars, each of which the Lord calls "by name" for the simple reason that each has a name, a nature, and a substance of its own. They all differ in the speed of the light they emit and each of them sparkles along its own path. Uniformity in God's creation! No. . . . Where in God's entire creation do you encounter life that does not display the unmistakable hallmark of life precisely in the multiplicity of its colors and dimensions, in the capriciousness of its ever-changing forms?[123]

Often Kuyper notes the fact that our eternal state in the new creation will include doxologies from a humanity diversified by tribes, tongues, peoples, and nations (Rev 5).[124] Creation is a rich and integrated whole consisting of well-ordered particulars, each of which God endows with divine meaning and significance, and each of which is held together by Christ (Col 1:17).

Fourth, God intends for his image bearers to develop his good creation. For the neo-Calvinist, creation has built-in potentialities that God intends for his imagers to bring to fruition. In other words, God created his world "very good," but he did not create it "perfect." Indeed, Kuyper viewed the created order as being equipped by God, endowed, from the very beginning, with all the powers needed to be cultivated and developed to higher levels of perfection. Thus, in the political realm, for example, all the givens that govern that sphere were present from the very start.[125] In other words, God's creation is a "very good" environment in which his imagers can "be fruitful and multiply," "till the soil," and "name the animals," activities that each represent the human culture-making enterprise. The "cultural mandate" of Genesis 1 is the original (pre-fall) Great Commission. God intends for his imagers to take what he has given them and make something of it for his glory.

Fifth, since the fall, God's good creation is twisted toward wrong ends. In the aftermath of the fall, Kuyper argued, there is now a great battle between the kingdom of God and the kingdom of darkness. In this battle, the Evil One continually speaks a word against God's Word, an antithesis in opposition to God's thesis for the world. The Kuyperian tradition is clear that the antithesis runs through the heart of *every* person, believer and unbeliever alike. Christians are—or should be—conscious of this and seek to obey the cultural mandate by bringing all their activities in each sphere under Christ's lordship,

---

[123]Abraham Kuyper, "Uniformity: The Curse of Modern Life," in Bratt, *Abraham Kuyper*, 34.
[124]Ibid., 35.
[125]Abraham Kuyper, *Our Program: A Christian Political Manifesto*, trans. Harry van Dyke (Bellingham, WA: Lexham Press, 2015), 29-41.

such that they are able not only to proclaim Christ with their lips but also to promote him with their (cultural) lives. Non-Christians remain in the *imago Dei* but pay allegiance to different religious imperatives as they work out their humanity. Thus, the spiritual struggle operates to some extent in every human heart, sphere of culture, and era of history. Its reality impinges on life holistically and cannot be relegated to some ethereal realm.

Sixth, sin and evil cannot corrupt God's good creation structurally or substantially. The triune God created the cosmos, and therefore sin or evil cannot be a part of the substance, or structures, of creation. Sin and evil can deform the creation, misdirecting it away from Christ's glory, but they do not change it substantially. "Sin," Bavinck writes,

> is not a substance, but a quality; not *materia*, but *forma*; it is not the essence of things, but rather adheres to the essence; it is a *privatio*, though a *privatio actuosa*, and to that extent contingent, an alien intruder like death. It can therefore be isolated from the essence and removed from it. The world is and remains susceptible to purification and deliverance. Its essence can be saved, and its original state can return.[126]

Since God's creation is marred not in its substance but in its direction, God's grace does not annihilate creation or add to creation but instead redirects it toward Christ. Bavinck writes, "The essence of the Christian religion consists in the reality that the creation of the Father, ruined by sin, is restored in the death of the Son of God and re-created by the grace of the Holy Spirit into a Kingdom of God."[127] Christ's gracious redemption brings about a reformation of human life and will one day bring about a restoration of God's creation.

Seventh, God's restoration of creation will be an elevation and enhancement of creation in its original form. God will one day restore his good creation. This means that he will not annihilate it. Bavinck writes, "[Christ] presupposes the work of the Father in creation and in providence. . . . He cannot have come to annihilate the work of the Father, or his own work in creation and providence, but rather to save it from the destruction which has been brought about by sin."[128] The doctrine of restoration further entails that, rather than returning creation to its original Edenic state (a view referred to

[126]Herman Bavinck, *De Algemeene Genade* (Kampen: Zalsman, 1894), 45-46; English translation from Jan Veenhof, *Nature and Grace in Herman Bavinck*, trans. Albert M. Wolters (Sioux Center, IA: Dordt College Press, 2006), 22.

[127]Bavinck, *Reformed Dogmatics*, 1:112.

[128]Bavinck, *Philosophy of Revelation*, 267.

as repristination), God will elevate his good creation beyond its original state. There is a movement that "proceeds from creation through redemption to sanctification and glorification. The end returns to the beginning and yet is at the same time the apex which is exalted high above the point of origin. The deeds of God form a circle which mounts upward in the form of a spiral."[129]

For the neo-Calvinist tradition, the doctrine of creation's goodness serves as bookends to the great dramatic narrative of Christian Scripture, casting its shadow over, and holding together, everything between. In the beginning, God created the heavens and earth and pronounced them "very good" (Gen 1:31). After the fall, creation groans and awaits God's restoration in the form of a renewed creation, in which "nothing unclean will enter" (Rev 21:27). Gordon Spykman, a proponent of the neo-Calvinist tradition, summarizes well: "It is religiously and theologically of utmost importance to allow our thinking to be normatively shaped by the biblical witness to a good creation, both as an original state of affairs and as an eschatological hope."[130] If not, how can God be good?

Conclusion: What Now?

As we have seen in this chapter and the previous one, the doctrine of God's good creation has developed unevenly and with many setbacks. Time after time, theologians have succumbed to a dualism that draws a line between the material and the immaterial aspects of God's creation and views the latter as superior to the former. However, as Scripture makes clear, and as theologians such as Irenaeus affirm, the line to be drawn is between God and his creation rather than between two aspects of his creation such as spirit and matter. Both the material and immaterial aspects of God's creation are good, indeed very good, and a faithfully Christian understanding will not only affirm creation's goodness but work out its implications for other doctrines and for the Christian life.

This internal undermining of creation throughout history is now matched and indeed exceeded by external forces such that the church finds itself needing to regain the doctrine in order not only to safeguard the faith once for all delivered but also to promote the common good and safeguard the public interest. The work of the Jewish sociologist Philip Rieff is especially helpful in surfacing the de-creative forces at work in our late modern era. In

---

[129]Bavinck, *Our Reasonable Faith*, 114.

[130]Gordon J. Spykman, *Reformational Theology: A New Paradigm for Doing Dogmatics* (Grand Rapids, MI: Eerdmans, 1992), 143.

a trilogy published at the beginning of the century, Rieff argues that our Western societies are in the midst of an unprecedented attempt to do away with sacred order. Sacred orders have always underlain social orders, and culture has always served as the mediator of sacred order to social order. In our era, however, the cultural elite are seeking to do away with sacred order, leaving social order to float in midair.

Rieff speaks of our present era as "an unprecedented . . . age without moralities and religions." In our era, the cultural elite produce "deathworks," cultural products that are "an all-out assault upon something vital to the established culture."[131] He calls these elite "virtuosi of de-creation of fictions where once commanding truths were."[132] These virtuosi include Nietzsche, Joyce, Picasso, Derrida, and others—artists and culture-makers and intellectuals who promulgate "a doctrine of de-creation in which the new world is a series of more or less horrible or at least horribly clever pastiches and negations of the complete and ever completing world of the older symbolists who saw in what there is that which is."[133] Whereas true culture expresses and celebrates creation and re-creation, these virtuosi promote the perversity of destruction that finds pleasure in suffering and death. Their "creative" acts are really de-creative, deathworks of the self.

> Derrida's role as a perpetrator of de-creativity is illumined in Brian Ingraffia's *Postmodern Theory and Biblical Theology.* Ingraffia compares and contrasts Derrida with Nietzsche and Heidegger, with all three serving as agents of the deconstruction of the ontotheological character of metaphysics. For Derrida, this deconstruction includes not only the overturning of an existing ontotheological hierarchy but also the atheistic elevation of a new "concept." Derrida leans on Saussure to posit the arbitrary nature of the sign, wherein arbitrariness signals that there is not a natural relationship between the sign and thing or the signifier and signified. Linguistic meaning is constituted through the play of differences, the structure of the trace, between a sign and other signs. Ultimately, this understanding of linguistic meaning subverts the notion of divine intention and even divine presence. As Ingraffia describes it,
>
> > The trace names the process whereby both the signified and the thing itself are infinitely deferred from absolute presence. Traditional semiotics has always defined the sign as the absence of the thing, the signifier as the absence of the

[131]Philip Rieff, *My Life Among the Deathworks: Illustrations of the Aesthetics of Authority*, ed. Kenneth S. Piver, Sacred Order/Social Order 1 (Charlottesville: University of Virginia Press, 2006), 7.

[132]Ibid., 4.

[133]Ibid., 26.

signified, but it presupposed that the sign was conceivable only on the basis of the deferred presence which would be reappropriated in the logos. But . . . Derrida concludes that the sign can no longer be defined by presence but rather by the trace.[a]

Before Derrida, Heidegger had considered Being as never "present" in metaphysics, as only leaving the trace of its absence, but Derrida goes further, arguing that trace is more primal than Being itself. In *Of Grammatology* Derrida writes, "The trace is not only the disappearance of origin. . . . It means that the origin did not even disappear, that it was never constituted except reciprocally by a nonorigin, the trace, which thus become the origin of the origin."[b] We agree with Derrida on one point: the god of rationalist metaphysics can be deconstructed in such a manner, but, as Ingraffia writes, "the God written about in the Bible is completely different from this man-made god. . . . The God of the Bible destroys humanity's pretensions to a realm and life of one's 'own' and labels any efforts to claim one's own life as one's own sin."[c] Derrida displaces the rationalist God of ontotheology, posited by Descartes, Hegel, and others, but his critique does not touch on the God of the Bible, the creator who remains present to us. "Derrida has deconstructed the metaphysical belief in a truth proceeding from and present in our own consciousness, our 'own cisterns.' He has shown cracks in this cistern, that it cannot hold water. But although humanity's cistern has been broken, the water of life, the spring of living water, remains untasted, forgotten."[d]

[a]Brian D. Ingraffia, *Postmodern Theory and Biblical Theology: Vanquishing God's Shadow* (Cambridge: Cambridge University Press, 1995), 216-17.

[b]Jacques Derrida, *Of Grammatology*, trans. Gayatri Chakravorty Spivak (Baltimore: Johns Hopkins University Press, 1998), 61.

[c]Ingraffia, *Postmodern Theory*, 222.

[d]Ibid., 224.

With Rieff, we recognize our present era as one—at least in part—of de-creation, one in which God's creational design for human creativity and culture making is being twisted such that many works of culture are de-creative assaults on the creation order. "The contemporary *kulturkampf* is unique because it is not between sacred orders but between great abolitionist movements directed against all sacred orders in any of their historical or theoretical manifestations."[134] Among the de-creating virtuosi, Rieff singles out Derrida as one whose strategy for undermining sacred order includes mocking the "policing character" of eternal truth. In response to Derrida, Rieff argues that it is teachers—upholders of the reading discipline—who must function as police.

[134]Ibid., 14.

> As teaching agents of sacred order, and inescapably within it, the moral demands we must teach, if we are teachers, are those eternal truths by which all social orders endure. The unprecedented historical task of our real police is to so magnify the downward direction of change, by which the present third world war against all sacred orders is being conducted, that the higher illiteracy of it no longer lures [us] to defeat by a massive decline in [our] own reading ability.[135]

Following Rieff, we argue that it is incumbent on biblical scholars, pastors, teachers, and professors of all types to resist the de-creative tendencies of our late modern era.[136] In the face of de-creation, we point to God the creator, who called the world into existence by means of his word, who through his word ordered his profusely diverse creation, and who remains present to creation by means of his word. We invite the world to take note, not only of creation, but of the creative task given to us at the time of creation—the cultural mandate—a task that enables us to image God by taking what he has created and making something more of it. And we undertake that task in submission to and by the enabling grace of the Son, through whom God created the world and by whom the created world will one day be renewed and restored.

---

[135]Ibid., 15.

[136]Bruce R. Ashford, "A Theological Sickness unto Death: Philip Rieff's Prophetic Analysis of Our Secular Age," *Themelios* 43, no. 1 (2018): 34-44.

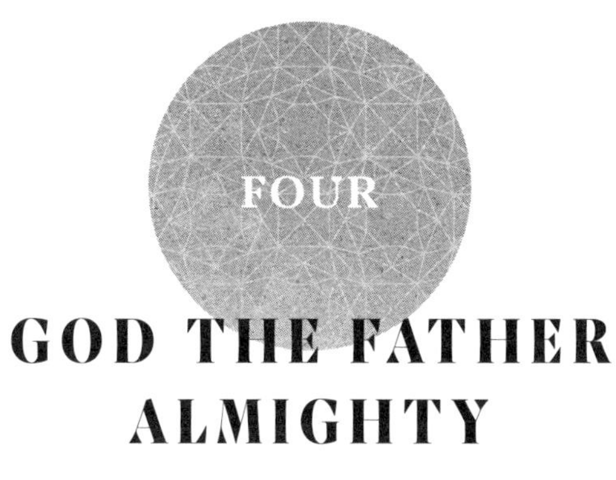

FOUR

GOD THE FATHER ALMIGHTY

The doctrine of God's omnipotence—or, as I prefer to say, almightiness—is not a matter of course but a matter of faith. It belongs to the very core of Christian faith to believe that God, *the sole source of all truth, goodness and beauty, is almighty, rather than the forces of falsehood, evil and ugliness.*

Gijsbert van den Brink

In His omnipotence He stands over the reality which He has created as its Lord, and revealing Himself He is exalted in its midst. In His omnipotence He is the source of all created life and its preservation. It has its life in and by His.

Karl Barth

No worse falsehood was ever perpetrated than the traditional concept of omnipotence. It is a piece of unconscious blasphemy, condemning God to a dead world, probably not distinguishable from no world at all.

Charles Hartshorne

These two attributes of goodness and justice do together make up the proper fullness of the Divine Being as omnipotent.

Tertullian

The early church understandably made use of Greek philosophical vocabulary to articulate what they believed. Apart from inventing a whole new vocabulary, this was a necessary and important move. At the same time it was fraught with danger, the danger of importing non-Christian ideology into the Christian faith. This was particularly so with the doctrine of God and of creation, and thus theologians and philosophers continue to debate the pros and cons of Greek terminology, of terms such as *aseity*, *unity*, *immutability*, and *simplicity*, for example, in relation to God.[1]

Theological conceptions of God's might in terms of "omnipotence" are no exception. Although the Christian tradition is rightly unanimous in describing God as "almighty" and connecting his might inseparably with him as creator, we must be careful to track the development of our language, especially the language of omnipotence, and evaluate its fidelity to Scripture. P. T. Geach, for example, asserts that "'almighty' is the familiar word that comes in the creeds of the Church; 'omnipotent' is at home rather in formal theological discussions and controversies."[2] "Almighty" speaks of God having power *over* all things, whereas omnipotent is generally taken to mean the power to do anything. For Geach, "almightiness . . . must be ascribed to God if we are to retain anything like traditional Christian belief in God," but it is a different matter with omnipotence. "When people have tried to read into 'God can do everything' a signification not of Pious Intention but of Philosophical Truth, they have only landed themselves in intractable problems and hopeless confusions."[3]

FATHER ALMIGHTY

An issue raised by the words "I believe in God the *Father almighty*" concerns the relationship of *Father* and *almighty* to each other and to *God*. Modern exegetes of the creed generally treat "Father almighty" as a single title. Against this modern view Kelly points out that there is no evidence for such an honorific periphrasis for God either in the Septuagint or in the New Testament.[a] The words *Father* and *almighty* are first linked together in *The Martyrdom of Polycarp* 19.2 and in Justin's *Dialogue with Trypho* 139 (*ANF* 1:139). Kelly thus concludes that

---

[1]See, e.g., Gijsbert van den Brink and Marcel Sarot, eds., *Understanding the Attributes of God* (New York: Lang, 1999); Michael D. Williams, "Systematic Theology as a Biblical Discipline," in *All for Jesus: A Celebration of the 50th Anniversary of Covenant Theological Seminary*, ed. Robert A. Peterson and Sean Michael Lucas (Fearn, UK: Mentor, 2006), 167-96; Christopher R. J. Holmes, *Revisiting the Doctrine of the Divine Attributes: In Dialogue with Karl Barth, Eberhard Jüngel, and Wolf Krötke*, Issues in Systematic Theology (New York: Lang, 2007); James F. Keating and Thomas Joseph White, eds., *Divine Impassibility and the Mystery of Human Suffering* (Grand Rapids, MI: Eerdmans, 2009); Isaak August Dorner, *Divine Immutability*, Fortress Texts in Modern Theology (Minneapolis: Augsburg Fortress, 1994); Hendrikus Berkhof, *The Christian Faith: An Introduction to the Study of Faith*, trans. S. Woudstra (Grand Rapids, MI: Eerdmans, 1979), 107-11, 133; Wolfhart Pannenberg, *Basic Questions in Theology: Collected Essays*, trans. George H. Kehm (Minneapolis: Fortress, 1971), 119-83.

[2]P. T. Geach, *Providence and Evil: The Stanton Lectures 1971–2* (New York: Cambridge University Press, 1977), 3.

[3]Ibid., 4.

> of the two descriptive predicates FATHER and ALMIGHTY, the one which is associated the more closely with God is FATHER. The basic, primordial verity in which belief is proclaimed is GOD THE FATHER. . . . The further title ALMIGHTY must have been conflated with it very early, as a result no doubt of the influence of the language of the Septuagint on Christian theological usage.[b]

In the formative period of the creed's development, *Father* referred to God as Father and creator of the universe. Thus, in terms of its earlier usage *Father* and *almighty* are close to being synonyms. We cannot be sure why *almighty* was added, but our suggestion is that as the trinitarian aspect of *Father* took hold, it became valuable to add *almighty* as a way of retaining the original meaning of *Father.*

---

[a]J. N. D. Kelly, *Early Christian Creeds*, 3rd ed. (1972; repr., London: Routledge, 2014), 132.
[b]Ibid., 133-34.

ALMIGHTY

The Apostles' and Nicene Creeds refer to only one attribute of God—namely, his omnipotence. The Latin *omnipotens* probably translates the Greek *pantokratōr.* In the Septuagint *pantokratōr* occurs some 170 times for the translation of "(Lord of) Hosts" and, less frequently, *Shaddai*, both names of God. The precise meaning of these names is contested. "Hosts" most probably refers to the armies of heaven.[a] Alternatively, some see it as a reference to the stars and planets (i.e., the hosts of heaven). In our view it most likely refers to the armies of heaven, but either way it evokes power and the ability to do everything God wills in history.

Kelly observes,

> There was nothing controversial about describing God as Father and as Almighty. The underlying meaning of παντοκράτωρ in Greek, however, and the meaning taken for granted in the second-century Church, was by no means identical with that of "Almighty" in English or *omnipotens* in Latin. The exact equivalent of these would have been παντοδύναμος. Παντοκράτωρ is in the first place an active word, conveying the idea not just of capacity but of the actualization of capacity. More important, the basic conception involved is wider than that contained in "Almighty." Παντοκράτωρ has the meaning "all-ruling," "all-sovereign." This is brought out in numberless patristic contexts, but with particular force in the first few chapters of the second book of St Irenaeus's *Adversus haereses.*[b]

The alternative meaning, that underlying παντοδύναμος, and now present in the English translation "almighty," soon made itself felt. In Origen's *Contra Celsum*, for example, we see that the pagan philosopher Celsus thought that Christians taught that God could do anything. Origen replies, "Now in our judgment God can do everything which it is possible for Him to do without ceasing to be God, and good, and wise." [c]

An important point in relation to omnipotence is that *it was not* a term the church took over from Greek thought as an attribute of the divine already loaded with philosophy. Neither among the Greek gods nor with Plato's Forms nor with Aristotle's unmoved Mover was omnipotence an attribute. As van den Brink shows, "The idea that God is omnipotent does not owe its enduring popularity in Christian theology to the influence of Greek thought, since omnipotence is simply not a Greek category."[d] He rightly notes that "this biblical conception of God's powerful activity is a far cry from the Greek idea of divine impotence and inertia, but . . . on the other hand it cannot simply be identified with our pre-conceived notion of literal omnipotence."[e]

Since the early medieval period, a discussion developed about whether God can only do the things he wants to do, so that his power is bound to his will. Is God unable to do things other than what he does, and if so, does this not limit God and detract from his perfection? In this context the medieval distinction between God's absolute and ordained power developed. The distinction first clearly developed in the report of a dinner discussion between Bishop Peter Damian and his friend Abbot Desiderius, probably in 1067.[f] At this dinner a difference of opinion emerged over Jerome's statement that "although God can do all things, He cannot raise up a virgin after she has fallen."[g] Damian agreed with Jerome; Desiderius rejected Jerome's view because he thought it restricted God's freedom and perfection. "To put it in the later terminology: we should not conceive of God's power only as *potentia ordinata*, i.e. from the point of view of what He has willed and ordained to do, but also as *potentia absoluta*, i.e. in an absolute sense."[h]

This dinner debate anticipated later positions. Anselm (*Proslogion*) and Abelard opted for Desiderius's view, whereas the later Anselm (*Cur Deus Homo?*), the Victorines, the Cistercians, and Peter Lombard all took Damian's view. It is vital to note that none of these theologians thought of God has having two powers; rather, what is at issue is that there are two ways to speak of the single power of God, without regard to God's revealed will or from the perspective of God's will as revealed in the actual creation and history. "The only reason for distinguishing a *potentia absoluta* in God is to conceptualize the conviction that the realm of God's possibilities did not coincide with the number of possibilities in fact realized by Him."[i] This emphasis on the *potentia absoluta* provided a key bulwark against Greek-Arabic necessitarianism, so that creation is not necessary but contingent.

However, soon all sorts of misunderstandings of the distinction developed. A major shift is evident in John Duns Scotus, who appeals to a legal parallel so that God can make *de potentia absoluta* what he cannot make *de potentia ordinata*.[j] Scotus does not view God's freedom to suspend the creation order established by him as only hypothetical. Thus, he paved the way for a skeptical reading of the distinction.[k] The skepticism emerged, for example, in the serious consideration among Occamist circles in Oxford around 1330 that God could lie.[l] Because of the arbitrariness and shadow the distinction came to cast over God, it was resolutely rejected by the Reformers, although they would have upheld the original distinction. As Case-Winters notes of Calvin, "His reason for doing so seems to have been his concern to maintain that God's power is not independent of God's moral character; rather it expresses it."[m]

[a]H.-J. Zobel, "Seba'ot," in *Theological Dictionary of the Old Testament*, trans. Douglas W. Stott, ed. G. Johannes Botterweck, Helmer Ringgren, and Heinz-Josef Fabry, (Grand Rapids, MI: Eerdmans, 2003) 12:215-32.

[b]J. N. D. Kelly, *Early Christian Creeds*, 3rd ed. (1972; repr., London: Routledge, 2014), 137.

[c]Origen, *Origen Against Celsus* 3.70, in *Fathers of the Third Century: Tertullian, Part Fourth; Minucius Felix; Commodian; Origen, Parts First and Second*, trans. F. Crombie, ed. A. Roberts, J. Donaldson and A. C. Coxe (Buffalo, NY: Christian Literature Company, 1885).

[d]Gijsbert van den Brink, *Almighty God: A Study of the Doctrine of Divine Omnipotence* (Kampen: Peeters, 1993), 173; cf. 172-76.

[e]Ibid., 184.

[f]Ibid., 69.

[g]*Select Letters of St. Jerome*, trans. F. A. Wright (Cambridge, MA: Harvard University Press, 1933), 62.

[h]Van den Brink, *Almighty God*, 70.

[i]Ibid., 72.

[j]Ibid., 78-79.

[k]Cf. ibid., 78-83.

[l]Ibid., 85-86.

[m]Anna Case-Winters, *God's Power: Traditional Understandings and Contemporary Challenges* (Louisville, KY: Westminster John Knox, 1990), 45.

This chapter draws us on to the terrain of the doctrine of God more strongly, especially in relation to God's omnipotence, for if there is one thing that creation reveals about God, it is that he is almighty. Intriguingly, the language of God as almighty is not nearly as common in the Bible as one might expect, and it occurs particularly in Job and Revelation. Nevertheless, as Bavinck notes, "Scripture nowhere sets bounds to God's power" and in myriad ways portrays God as the Almighty One.[4]

Indeed, in addressing the question of God's power in relation to omnipotence, Barth asserts that "the revelation of God the Father is itself the revelation of the divine omnipotence. This is the source from which we have to learn basically what power and omnipotence is, in opposition to every preconception."[5] Thus, in line with the overarching trinitarian shape of the Apostles' Creed and the title of this chapter, Barth sees God's nature as almighty as woven throughout the biblical testimony.

Not only in theology but also in philosophy, power is an important theme, and so it becomes doubly important that we develop a view of God as almighty from Scripture. This will enable us to assess the value of traditional

[4]Herman Bavinck, *Reformed Dogmatics*, vol. 2, *God and Creation* (Grand Rapids, MI: Baker Academic, 2004), 245-46.

[5]Barth, *CD* II/1, 525.

descriptions of God as omnipotent, as well as to engage critically with contemporary views of power in both theology and philosophy. There are many roads into a discussion of power from Scripture, but we will begin with three psalms that explore God's power in relation to creation before going on to examine the Elijah narratives and then to explore some of the key areas in the New Testament, all of which will enable us to round out a biblical view of God as Father almighty.

The Incomparableness of God

Othmar Keel rightly notes that "Israel brought with it from the desert experiences and conceptions of God which could not be easily harmonized with the various conceptions of God prevalent in the new environment."[6] Israel emerged in a context full of gods, and consequently there is a strong apophatic or polemical dimension to its faith as it comes to expression in the Old Testament. Israel's positive view of Yahweh often emerges through declaring what Yahweh is not. "Incomparable" is a negative quality and one that surfaces repeatedly in the Old Testament and not least in the psalms, to which we now turn.

Psalms 29, 82, 93, and 104. Taken together, Psalms 29, 82, 93, and 104 provide a holistic view of God as the one who rules over all things. Psalm 29 is an Old Testament hymn that celebrates God's sovereignty. It consists of the usual hymnic elements of (1) a call to praise (Ps 29:1-2), (2) the content of praise (Ps 29:3-10), and (3) a prayer based on the praise (Ps 29:11). However, apart from its form, it is most unusual. The call is addressed to the בְּנֵי אֵלִים, literally "the sons of the gods." The content of praise consists of a sevenfold proclamation of what the voice of Yahweh achieves. The proclamation reaches a climax in the description of Yahweh as king in Psalm 29:10.

There is a reference to the temple/Zion in Psalm 29:9, in which all say, "Glory!" However, as a whole, the psalm focuses on the creation, using the theophany of a storm to evoke Yahweh's character. Psalm 29 thus "looks to the heavenly realm and imagines the cosmic palace of God. There the Lord is enthroned as sovereign of the universe. His throne is above the flood, the cosmic ocean that was thought in the cosmology of the ancient east to surround the world. Around the throne are the heavenly host, the divine beings who make up the heavenly court and council."[7] As in Psalm 82, it is likely that

[6]Othmar Keel, *The Symbolism of the Biblical World: Ancient Near Eastern Iconography and the Book of Psalms*, trans. Timothy J. Hallett (Winona Lake, IN: Eisenbrauns, 1997), 178.

[7]James Luther Mays, *The Lord Reigns: A Theological Handbook to the Psalms* (Louisville, KY: Westminster John Knox, 1994), 135.

the imagery here is of the assembly of the "gods," an assembly chaired by Yahweh.[8] In the ancient Near East the gods were nothing if not powerful, but remarkably here they are called on to ascribe glory and strength *to Yahweh*, to worship him in holy splendor.

כָּבוֹד (glory) is "a summary term for the attributes of the Lord as king. . . . The strength and power, holy splendor and majesty of the Lord are his glory. . . . Glory is a term for the manifestation, the display of the Lord's divine royalty in the world."[9] עֹז (strength) is the same word that occurs in Psalm 46:1. Clinton McCann says of this verse,

> The word *strength* underscores the conviction of God's sovereignty. It occurs twice in the Song of Moses and Miriam (Exod. 15:2, 13), which culminates in the affirmation that "the Lord will reign forever and ever" (15:18). The word also occurs frequently in the enthronement psalms that celebrate Yahweh's rule (29:1; 93:1; 96:7; 99:4). In short, Psalm 46:1 establishes the conviction that Yahweh rules the world.[10]

Part of the background to Psalm 29 is the association of the thunderstorm with the Canaanite god Baal, whose voice was thought to be heard in the thunder.[11] Through its sevenfold use of "The voice of the Lord" and its use of "Yahweh" sixteen times, Psalm 29 declares unequivocally that it is Yahweh, not Baal, who is almighty and rules the world. Whereas in Psalm 46:1-2 "trouble" is portrayed in the strongest terms of the very foundations of the creation being shaken, trouble to which Yahweh's "strength" is the answer, here in Psalm 29 it is the voice of Yahweh alone that can shake the creation, as the evocative imagery in Psalm 29:5-9 makes clear.

Psalm 29 is unusual in its exclusive focus on God's power in nature. From the temple comes the cry "Glory!" but clearly Yahweh's power extends way beyond his reign over his people. Psalm 29 is unequivocal in its poetic affirmation of the greatness of God's power, power that is appropriate to Yahweh who sits enthroned as king forever.

If Psalm 29 celebrates Yahweh's incomparable power, which the gods are called to ascribe to him, the prayer in Psalm 29:11 asks that he give "strength"

---

[8]The Old Testament clearly enunces a doctrine of the heavenly council. Here and below the "sons of the gods" could refer literally to angels, or it could be a metaphorical subversion of the ancient Near Eastern motif of the council of the gods, without affirming the existence of the gods. The Old Testament is clear that there is one God, Yahweh.

[9]Mays, *Lord Reigns*, 136.

[10]Clinton J. McCann Jr., *A Theological Introduction to the Book of Psalms: The Psalms as Torah* (Nashville: Abingdon, 1993), 137.

[11]Cf. Leah Bronner, *The Stories of Elijah and Elisha* (Leiden: Brill, 1968), 62.

to his people and bless them with peace (שָׁלוֹם). God's extraordinary power is not alien to peace but is in fact its very condition. McCann identifies a probable allusion to Psalm 29 in Luke 2:8-12 and rightly notes that "the proclamation of the heavenly beings in Luke 2 is essentially the same as that in Psalm 29—glory to God, the correlate of which is peace among God's people."[12] James Luther Mays observes that Psalm 29 is often used liturgically for the first Sunday after Epiphany in association with the baptism of Jesus. "The storm says: 'This is my cosmos'; the baptism, 'This is my Christ.' The two go inseparably together. The Christology is not adequate unless its setting in cosmology is maintained."[13]

Patrick Miller notes of Psalm 82, "It is not a psalm that has been significant in the history of piety or worship."[14] Adrio König, however, makes it central to his discussion of the motif of "mocking the gods" in the Old Testament.[15] In Canaanite mythology El convened the council of the gods, but in Psalm 82:1 Yahweh (God) has replaced El as the chair! Astonishingly, the gods are put on trial and found guilty because they have not provided justice, and this especially for the weak and the needy. Such injustice threatens the very foundations of the creation (Ps 82:5). The psalm concludes with an appeal to God to bring justice to the earth, "for all the nations belong to you!" (Ps 82:8). Thus, what might at first appear to be an acknowledgment of the existence of other gods turns out to be a strong statement of exclusivism:

> The Lord took over the presidency of the council of gods, and did it in such a way that El was eliminated and no longer appeared in the picture. Other Old Testament traditions, in which the Lord takes over the name El, should be interpreted in this light. It is not the merging of the Lord with one or another god named El, but an elimination of El, with the Lord taking over his place and functions.[16]

As in Psalm 29, Yahweh's incomparableness is not alien to justice but its very condition.

Psalm 93 is one of the kingship psalms at the center of the Psalter. Psalm 93:1 depicts Yahweh as girded with "strength," the same word referred to above. His strength is shown in his *establishing* the world, just as his throne is *established*. "The two are coordinate because in the way the psalm thinks about reality, the

---

[12]McCann, *Theological Introduction*, 164.
[13]Mays, *Lord Reigns*, 138.
[14]Patrick D. Miller, *Interpreting the Psalms* (Philadelphia: Augsburg Fortress, 1986), 120.
[15]Adrio König, *Here Am I! A Christian Reflection on God* (Grand Rapids, MI: Eerdmans, 1982), 11-13.
[16]Ibid., 12.

establishment of the world was the deed by which the Lord gained kingship, and his kingship is guarantee of the stability of the ordered, inhabitable world."[17] An implication of Yahweh's strength and establishment of the creation is that his "decrees are very sure" (Psalm 93:5). "Decrees" probably refers to Yahweh's ordinances for religious and social life: "In the view of the psalmist, the commandments that order human life are the decrees of the sovereign of the universe."[18] As we have seen above, Yahweh's strength or power is a wonderful attribute of his that guarantees the stability of creational life.

Psalm 104 is a hymn that celebrates Yahweh's greatness and glory (Ps 104:1, 31) in his creation and his provision for his creatures. As in Psalm 29, the voice of Yahweh is likened to thunder (Ps 104:7). This is an exquisite psalm full of Yahweh's power and goodness. Psalm 104:1-9 is based on a pattern of divine activity well attested in the ancient Near East. However, "in the adaptation, the other gods are eliminated; the victory establishing the reliability of earth is permanent and need not be repeated in annual cycle or crisis times; and resulting creation is unified ontologically with no remnant of cosmic dualism."[19] The antiphon used during Pentecost, "Lord, send out your Spirit and renew the face of the earth," stems from Psalm 104:30. In the prayer (Ps 104:31-35) the psalmist prays, "May the Lord rejoice in his works" (ESV). At Jesus' baptism the Father declares of the author of the new creation, "This is my Son, the Beloved, with whom I am well pleased" (Mt 3:17).

Together, these four psalms give us a sense of the theology of Yahweh's power that so pervades the Old Testament. It is the power of the creator, of the king, of the incomparable one.

Elijah, a prophet like fire, and the God before whom we stand.[20] If the Psalms declare and celebrate Yahweh's power, the historical narratives *depict* that same power in action. And nowhere is it more strikingly depicted than the Elijah-Elisha narratives in Kings. Since the discovery of the Ras Shamra tablets in 1929 onward, we have learned a great deal about the god Baal and how the ministries of Elijah and Elisha are directed against Baal, showing that Yahweh and not Baal is the one with power. We know very little about Elijah the Tishbite other than that he was hairy and wore a leather belt around his waist (2 Kings 1:8)! Elijah lived and prophesied during the reigns of Kings Ahab and Ahaziah in the Northern Kingdom. During this time the Northern

---

[17]Mays, *Lord Reigns*, 301.

[18]Ibid.

[19]Ibid., 333.

[20]Sirach 48:1 describes Elijah as a "prophet like fire."

Kingdom was succumbing to Baal worship, a direction supported in particular by Queen Jezebel, Ahab's foreign wife (1 Kings 16:29-33). Ahab built a temple for Baal in Samaria, erected an altar there, and made a sacred pole, the symbol of Asherah, the wife of El.

The god Baal was all about power. His name means "to own, to rule, to possess." Baal dominated the Ugaritic pantheon and is associated with rain and thus the fertility of land and animals, with oil and corn, with fire and lightning, with control over life, and with ascent as the "rider of the clouds." Baal was a warring god and fought against other gods such as the Prince of the Sea and Mot, the god of the underworld.

Leah Bronner has shown how, in almost every episode in the narratives of Elijah and Elisha, the goal is to show that Yahweh and not Baal is the one with real power, the one to whom the powers attributed to Baal really belong.[21] This is most clear in the celebrated clash between Elijah and the prophets of Baal on Mount Carmel. Baal controlled fire and lightning and is often depicted with a thunderbolt in ancient Near Eastern iconography. The palace in which he lived is described as formed by fire.[22] In the Old Testament "the fire of God" is a common expression. Fire is employed as a symbol of God and his presence (Ezek 1:4; Zech 2:5); it can represent his holiness (Deut 4:24), his righteous judgment (Zech 12:9; Mal 3:2), and his wrath against sin (Jer 21:12).

The clash on Mount Carmel is thus about who really possesses the powers associated with Baal. The contest is set up such that "the god who answers by fire is indeed God" (1 Kings 18:24). Despite the best efforts of the prophets of Baal there is "no voice, no answer, and no response" (1 Kings 18:29). When Elijah prays, "the fire of Yahweh" falls and consumes the offering and the altar. In 2 Kings 1, when King Ahaziah sends messengers to inquire of Baal-zebub as to whether he will recover from his fall, Elijah intervenes and fire twice consumes the fifty men sent twice by Ahaziah to Elijah. Elijah is furthermore transported to heaven by a chariot of fire and horses of fire (2 Kings 2:11-12). Bronner discerns in Elijah's ascent a polemic against Baal as rider of the clouds. Yahweh's *servant* is able to do what Baal claims to do. Intriguingly, in 1 Kings 19, when Elijah flees and encounters Yahweh at Horeb, Yahweh is described as *not in the fire* (1 Kings 19:12). Bronner suggests that this is a reminder that Yahweh is not part of nature but transcends it.[23]

---

[21]Bronner, *Stories of Elijah and Elisha.*

[22]Ibid., 61.

[23]Ibid., 63.

Rain and famine are central motifs in the Elijah narratives, and here too Yahweh is clearly presented as in control of them. So too is he in control of oil and corn, of having children, of healing, and of resurrection, all capacities associated with Baal. It is important to note that some of the episodes take place outside Israel, indicating that Elijah and Elisha by no means restricted Yahweh's power to Israel; they were, at least in practice, monotheists. "But Elijah's lofty conception of God virtually excludes all other objects of worship and makes all the gods idols."[24]

At the outset of this chapter we quoted Barth, who says of God, "In His omnipotence He stands over the reality which He has created as its Lord, and revealing Himself He is exalted in its midst." Elijah and Elisha, these two great prophets of God's power, both use the expression "Before whom I stand," אֲשֶׁר עָמַדְתִּי לְפָנָיו (1 Kings 17:1; 18:15; 2 Kings 3:14) to describe their relationship to Yahweh. "It is an expression apparently peculiar to Elijah and Elisha and disappeared after their age from prophetic speech."[25] In each case it is accompanied with a description of Yahweh "who lives," the true and living God, as Paul might say.

The Elijah-Elisha narratives reveal Yahweh unequivocally as all-powerful. His power is dangerous and explosive and yet always directed toward leading his people back to him. There are, of course, many other places in the Old Testament to which we could turn for a theology of the power of God. The plagues and the exodus are the obvious example, demonstrating Yahweh's power over Pharaoh and once again a mocking of the gods (cf. Ex 15:11). God's power is celebrated in the Song of Moses (Ex 15:1-18) and in the Song of Miriam (Ex 15:21). Exodus 15:6 describes Yahweh's right hand as "glorious in power [כֹּחַ]." If we need reminding, the exodus would have alerted any Israelite to the fact that Yahweh's sovereignty and power are not confined to Israel but extend over the great empires and emperors of the day. The Song of Moses ends appropriately, "Yahweh will reign for ever and ever." Alan Richardson notes that "in the Old Testament the historically decisive event, which became for the Hebrew mind the symbol and type of all God's comings in history, is the Miracle of the Red Sea."[26] With the Elijah-Elisha narratives and the exodus we are dealing with Yahweh as Lord of history, but this inevitably backs up into him as creator. *As creator* he is the originator of history and its lord and king. Indeed, in the sections of the Old Testament we have explored, the

---

[24]Ibid., 25.

[25]Ibid., 29-30.

[26]Alan Richardson, *The Miracle Stories of the Gospels* (New York: Harper & Brothers, 1941), 3-4.

blurring of the boundary between creation and history is noteworthy. It is in his acts in history that Yahweh mocks the gods, thus revealing himself alone as God and as the creator.

Since we focus on Genesis 1–2 in detail in other parts of this book, we have not attended to them here. Suffice it to note that in the creation narratives we also have a clear depiction of Yahweh as all-powerful. He speaks by divine fiat the world into existence and forms (יָצַר) humankind from the dust of the ground.[27] Keel notes, "The experience of the utter contingency of the world is expressed most strongly in those passages which describe the processes of creation in terms of command and execution."[28] Michael Horton says evocatively that "God speaks the world into existence, and the world answers back in a symphony of praise, each species chirping, barking, bellowing, or otherwise communicating its delight and dependence on God and each other. Yet it is human beings who are created as communicative partners in covenant."[29]

The reverse side of the creation's contingency and utter dependency on God is, of course, God's power. It is because he is almighty that God is able to create the world. As inhabitants within his creation, we discover him as the creator and thus as almighty and hear the invitation to "answer back" as his creatures.

Jesus and the New Testament

"Christ is to the New Testament writers the manifestation of the power of God in the world, and His mighty deeds are the signs of the effectual working of that power. But in this age the power of God is veiled; revelation is by the gift of faith."[30]

In our examination of key texts in the Old Testament, we have seen again and again how the power of God is integrally related to his kingship, which looks back to creation and forward over history. This flows over into the main theme of Jesus' teaching—namely, the kingdom of God/heaven. This theme does and should evoke all the connotations of God's reign and power that we have seen so clearly in the Old Testament. König, for example, suggests that the centrality of Jesus' opposition to Satan and the demonic in his ministry is an extension of the motif of the mockery of the gods in the Old Testament:

---

[27]On God as *Deus Faber*, see Keel, *Symbolism*, 204-5.

[28]Keel, *Symbolism*, 205.

[29]Michael Horton, "Let the Earth Bring Forth . . . ," in *Sanctification: Explorations in Theology and Practice*, ed. Kelly Kapic (Downers Grove, IL: IVP Academic, 2014), 132.

[30]Richardson, *Miracle Stories*, 126.

"The gods of the Old Testament are classified quite clearly with Satan and his followers . . . and so become part of that total host of supernatural beings which under Satan are in opposition to Jesus Christ—and which through him are dethroned and made into a laughing stock."[31]

The theme of power emerges at the outset of Jesus' ministry in his temptations in the wilderness. Among other things, Jesus is tempted to attain power over the kingdoms of the world through worshiping Satan (Mt 4:8-10). Central to the three temptations is the great temptation to achieve his mission *apart from the cross.* In this way the temptations alert us to the fact that while Jesus is king, and thus the kingdom has come, his power and glory are veiled and put aside to a large extent in order to fulfill his cruciform mission and to create the space in the world for reconciliation to God.

Nevertheless, repeatedly there are occasions in which the veil is temporarily drawn aside so that through cracks, as it were, we glimpse his glory and power. Jesus' so-called nature miracles are examples,[32] and the calming of the storm is one such case (Mk 4:35-41). Scholars have noted the intertextual links with Jonah 1:4. In reply to the disciples' question, "Who then is this, that even the wind and the sea obey him?" (Mk 4:41), Jonah 1:9 provides the answer: "the Lord, the God of heaven, who made the sea and the dry land."

There are so many places in which we catch glimpses of Jesus' power. Mark 9:14-29 is another such place, where Jesus rebukes his disciples when he is asked *whether* he is able to heal a demon-possessed boy; the dialogue evokes Jesus' power over evil. And *the* place in Jesus' public ministry in which the veil is drawn aside is in his transfiguration, in which his clothes become a dazzling white, producing terror among his disciples.

In the New Testament the resurrection is the monumental example of God's power, of "the God of peace, who brought back from the dead our Lord Jesus, the great shepherd of the sheep" (Heb 13:20). Paul (Rom 1:4) asserts that it was by the resurrection that Jesus was declared to be the Son of God with power. Jesus' ascension is the symbol of his kingship over everything. In Mark 14:62 he says, "I am; and 'you will see the Son of Man seated at the right hand of the Power,' and 'coming with the clouds of heaven.'"

"Son of Man" is Jesus' preferred self-designation. It is deliberately cryptic, enabling him to identify himself without catalyzing final opposition to him,

---

[31]König, *Here Am I!*, 16.

[32]Cf. Richardson, *Miracle Stories*.

as would be and was caused by publicly declaring himself to be the Messiah. The background to the Son of Man sayings is Daniel 7:13-14, in which one like a son of man receives kingship over all, a vision of tremendous power. Intriguingly, in Jesus' answer to the high priest in Mark 14:62, such is the nature of God that τῆς δυνάμεως (the Power) is used as a circumlocution for God.

The theme of power is thus central to Jesus' ministry, but it is John who clearly draws the connection between Jesus and creation (Jn 1:1-3). In his incarnation Jesus, the Word of God, came to "what was his own" (Jn 1:11), and to those who received him he gave *power* to become children of God. Acts is the indispensable bridge between the Gospels and the Epistles and has much to say about power. However, it is in the Epistles that the theology of Jesus as king and creator is clearly explicated. In 1 Corinthians 1:24 Paul describes Christ as "the power of God and the wisdom of God." It is in Colossians in particular that the theology of Christ as creator and redeemer is most clearly set forth (Col 1:15-20). All things were created through him and for him, and he is the head of his body, the church. In Ephesians Paul prays that his readers might know something of God's resurrection power (Eph 1:15-23).

As we noted above, God is referred to as almighty particularly in Job and Revelation. In Revelation, written to churches suffering persecution, God's power is closely linked to his being creator, and he is worshiped as the almighty creator (Rev 1:8; 4:8, 11; 5:12; 7:12; 11:16; 14:7; 15:3; 16:7; 18:8; 19:6). The term παντοκράτωρ (the Almighty) is used in 2 Corinthians 6:16 and also in Revelation 1:8; 4:8; 11:17; 15:3; 16:7, 14; 19:6, 15; 21:22. The biblical data thus confirms Geach's point discussed at the outset that "almighty" refers to God's rule over the creation rather than his ability to do anything.

Father almighty. From the biblical data there can be no question that God is almighty. This is revealed especially in his act of creation but also in his ongoing involvement with his creation. Indeed, as we have seen, it is hard to separate these aspects in the biblical data we have examined. This is insightful because as we confess in the creed, "I believe in God, *the Father* almighty, creator of heaven and earth." While we accept that "Father" means more than "Father of the Son," it remains true that the creed overall articulates the doctrine of creation and God's omnipotence *within the doctrine of the Trinity*. Creation is especially the work of the Father but also that of the Son and the Spirit, as is expressed theologically in the doctrine of perichoresis.

What is vital to note here is that it is *as the Father* that God is almighty. When it comes to God's omnipotence, we are deep within the realm of mystery and God's incomparableness. God is unique, and so too is his omnipotence.

This means that we have to emerge into a closer understanding of his omnipotence from within his revelation. Philosophical questions remain important, as we have seen, but to try to start with an analysis of power as humans experience it and then extrapolate this to God is going to be of very limited help. Thomas Oden rightly observes that "Christian teaching does not deal merely with 'God in himself' as if God could be viewed abstractly apart from God's works or historical activity. God is known through what God does. God's essence is beheld only indirectly through the outworking of God's energies, the working (*energia*) of God in and through God's creatures."[33]

Creation confronts us with power on an unprecedented scale, but we need to remember that the power with which it confronts us is the power *of God*, the power of Elohim (Gen 1:1–2:3), and more significantly the power of Yahweh Elohim (Gen 2–3). We say more significantly because the unusual conflation of "Yahweh" and "Elohim" in Genesis 2–3 alerts us clearly to the fact that the almighty creator God is the redeemer God of the covenant.

God's omnipotence thus has to be seen as absolutely real and fully part of who God is. As Barth notes, "God is able, able to do everything; everything, that is, which as His possibility is real possibility."[34] Barth wisely deals with God's *constancy* and *omnipotence* together. He asserts rightly that God's omnipotence is never simply a *potentia*, a physical possibility, but always also a *potestas*, a legal and moral possibility: "God's might never at any place precedes right, but is always and everywhere associated with it. Like all true might, it is in itself and from the beginning legitimate power, the power of holiness, righteousness, and wisdom which is grounded in itself, in the love and freedom of the divine person."[35]

A helpful biblical emphasis in this respect is that we learn about God from his works, and not least from his work of creation. In Paul's well-known statement in Romans 1:20 we read, "Ever since the creation of the world his [God's] *eternal power* and divine nature, invisible though they are, have been understood and seen through the things he has made." In this respect it is worth reflecting on that small Hebrew word that occurs repeatedly in Genesis 1:1–2:3—namely, טוֹב. There is much to be said about this word, but here we draw attention to how it reflects back on God as almighty

[33]Thomas C. Oden, *The Living God*, vol. 1 of *Systematic Theology* (New York: HarperCollins, 1987), 228. Oden cites John Chrysostom for support on this point (*Concerning the Statutes*, homily 10.8, 9 [*NPNF*[1] 9:410-11]) as well as Irenaeus (*Against Heresies* 4.20 [*ANF* 1:487-92]).

[34]Barth, *CD* II/1, 522.

[35]Barth, *CD* II/1, 526.

creator. If we turn the telescope around, as it were, we are confronted with an almighty God who is altogether good and who exercises his power in concert with his goodness.

This emphasis on God's power as entirely in concert with his many other attributes is found throughout Scripture. As we have seen above in our examination of four psalms, you learn a great deal about a person's worldview from how they worship. You also learn much from how people pray. Jesus taught his disciples to pray, "Our Father in heaven . . ." "Father" speaks both of the redemptive power of God as shown in the exodus and of the love and intimacy of the relationship between God and his people;[36] "in heaven" reminds us of the transcendence, otherness, and power of God. Both power and love are essential elements in any doctrine of God.

Although God's power is manifested in creation, it is by no means exhausted in the creation, as the medieval debate between *potentia absoluta* and *potentia ordinata* indicates. And if this assertion seems obvious, the reader should note the unhelpful tendency in modern theology, climaxing in Schleiermacher, to identify God's omnipotence with his omnicausality. In the summary at the head of section fifty-four of his *Christian Faith*, Schleiermacher asserts,

> In the conception of the divine omnipotence two ideas are contained: first, that the entire system of nature, comprehending all times and spaces, is founded upon divine causality, which, as eternal and omnipresent, is in contrast to all finite causality; and second, that the divine causality, as affirmed in our feeling of absolute dependence, is completely presented in the totality of finite being, and hence everything happens and occurs for which there is a causality in God.[37]

Barth notes in this respect that "this existence is of such a nature that the totality of finite being is the complete and exhaustive presentation of the divine causality. Thus there is no divine causality or omnipotence which does not have its corresponding development or occurrence in the totality of finite being."[38] Such a view leads into a pantheist and/or deist direction and mistakenly abandons the distinction between what God can do and what he actually does. As Barth observes, "Creation, reconciliation and redemption

[36]N. T. Wright, "The Lord's Prayer as a Paradigm for Christian Prayer," in *Into God's Presence: Prayer in the New Testament*, ed. Richard N. Longenecker (Grand Rapids, MI: Eerdmans, 2001), 132-54; Brant Pitre, "The Lord's Prayer and the New Exodus," *Letter and Spirit* 2 (2006): 69-96.

[37]Friedrich Schleiermacher, *The Christian Faith*, ed. H. R. Mackintosh and J. S. Stewart (Edinburgh: T&T Clark, 1989), 211.

[38]Barth, *CD* II/1, 529.

are the work, really the work of His omnipotence. He is omnipotent in this work."[39] However, creation is not a *necessary* work of God but one executed in his freedom, and his rule over the creation remains in place.

In philosophy, especially in analytical philosophy, questions are raised about God's omnipotence as to whether God can do anything conceivable. For example, can an omnipotent being create a boulder that is too heavy for the being itself to lift?

> In philosophy the nature of omnipotence is controverted. One understanding of omnipotence is the ability to cause any state of affairs whatsoever. Descartes (*Meditations*, section 1), for example, appears to have held such a view, whereas Aquinas and Maimonides argue that such a view of omnipotence is incoherent. Among contemporary philosophers, Conee defends the view that an omnipotent being would have the power to bring about any state of affairs whatsoever.[a]
>
> [a]Earl Conee, "The Possibility of Power Beyond Possibility," in *Philosophical Perspectives*, 5th ed. (Atascadero, CA: Ridgeview, 1991), 447-73.

In our view it is important to note in relation to God that where logic can wade, faith can and must swim—and swim deeply into the mystery of God as revealed in Scripture. As Barth notes, "This does not mean the collapse but the true and proper establishment of that reliability and confidence."[40] There is doubtless value in logically exploring the character of God, but it is an enterprise fraught with danger. In this respect, Barth is right to affirm the role of logical analysis while insisting that theologians must distinguish between the limits of creaturely logic and the revealed God. He asserts,

> The system or the various systems within which the ideas of what is creaturely possible have their place as we can know it, and within which this or that can be labelled as impossible either by definition or in itself, are to be understood only as relative systems, related to creaturely reality and power as a whole, and devised in what is itself the creaturely power and reality of human reason. . . . But as such this confidence can only be relative.[41]

Barth says insightfully of God's omnipotence that God has the power as Father, Son, and Holy Spirit to be *fully himself*: "He is fully Himself in the world and in man."[42] To be able to do anything, as some define omnipotence,

[39]Barth, *CD* II/1, 527.
[40]Barth, *CD* II/1, 536.
[41]Barth, *CD* II/1, 535.
[42]Barth, *CD* II/1, 532.

would in fact be a limitation and is not true of God. As Barth says, God himself is the standard and criterion of what is possible so that "every meaningful statement about God's omnipotence must be able to base itself on God's Word." The alternative is to generate "the irruption of a Third Reich of madness."[43] God himself is master over his power, and he alone decides what is possible and impossible for himself. "We are forced to say that God is omnipotent in the fact that He can do everything that is in His power."[44]

The issue of the relationship between "universals" and creation is an intriguing one, and one over which much ink has been spilt. The Scholastics successfully fought the battle over the eternity of matter, but what of universals? Intriguingly, it was Descartes who argued for the creation of eternal truths.[a] He held that necessary truths are as dependent on God's power as contingent ones. There is, however, considerable debate about how to read Descartes on this subject. Central to Descartes's view—and helpful—is that we cannot explain God's power in a way that we can fully understand. Also, it is important to note that Descartes was reacting against the view of Francisco Suárez that eternal truths are necessarily independent of God's will and intellect.

Van den Brink argues that "from a historical point of view the position that God's power ranges over the eternal truths as well as over created reality marks the first step of the secularization of the European mind, rather than being part and parcel of the Christian tradition."[b] But how then should we conceive of the relationship between God's power and universals? Inherent in this discussion is the vexed question of how to define *omnipotence*. In his exploration of the philosophical arguments, van den Brink notes that the context, the "conceptual network" in which the subject is examined, is crucial and that the theological context frames the discussion in a different way.

According to van den Brink, an inductive approach to omnipotence in religion is limited; we need to proceed from what we are shown about God's omnipotence within the Christian tradition. God has revealed himself as omnipotent in his actions; this is clear, for example, in Genesis 17:1 and sets an Abrahamic approach apart from an Anselmian one in the following ways:

- With Abraham we have to do with a commissive (cf. the liturgical setting in Revelation) rather than a constative approach to omnipotence.
- God's "loss of power" in the Bible is a voluntary one; indeed "this biblical portrayal offers us an unambiguous solution to the paradoxes of omnipotence."[c] "A Christian account of divine power could hardly omit the Pauline emphasis, but it could

[43]Barth, *CD* III/1, 537.
[44]Barth, *CD* II/1, 535.

well be omitted by perfect being theology; perhaps perfect being theology must discount it."[d]

- There is no need to insist that God must possess a form of literal omnipotence unqualified by his character. "It is precisely the wish to maintain that it is possible for God to do literally everything, including what is contrary to His nature and perhaps even what seems logically impossible for Him to do, which gives rise to some of the antinomies and hairsplitting discussions."[e]

As regards the laws of logic and creation, van den Brink identifies five positions held by philosophers:

- universal possibilism, according to which God can make true logical contradictions at any time he chooses
- universal creationism,[f] according to which God is unable to change the modal status of propositions but free to determine the modal status as well as their truth value at the moment of creation
- theistic activism (Karl Barth and Thomas V. Morris), according to which all abstract objects are necessary objects but created by God
- standard independentism, according to which universals exist uncaused and necessarily, independent of God (Ockham and Wittgenstein)
- universals as part of the mind of God (Augustine; Van den Brink argues for this view)[g]

[a]Gijsbert van den Brink, *Almighty God: A Study of the Doctrine of Divine Omnipotence* (Kampen: Peeters, 1993), 93-112.
[b]Ibid., 113.
[c]Ibid., 181.
[d]Ibid., 182; a quote from an unpublished paper by Paul Helm.
[e]Ibid., 182-83.
[f]E.g., Roy Clouser, "Religious Language: A New Look at an Old Problem," in *Rationality in the Calvinian Tradition*, ed. Hendrik Hart (Lanham, MD: University Press of America, 1983), 395-401.
[g]Van den Brink, *Almighty God*, 202-3.

While it is clear in the biblical discussions of creation that the creaturely is contingent, utterly dependent at every moment of its existence on the sustaining power of God, it is also clear that God delegates or endows real power to his creation.[45] Creaturely power is real only in terms of its basis in God's power, but it is real power and, insofar as it remains positively rooted in God's power, is fundamentally good. The challenge is not to relinquish power but to direct it along the lines of love and justice.

[45]For a helpful treatment of the debate among philosophers about God's omnipotence and its compatibility with human freedom, see Gijsbert van den Brink, *Almighty God: A Study of the Doctrine of Divine Omnipotence* (Kampen: Peeters, 1993), 206-26.

A Defenseless Superior God or a Hospitable One?

Hendrikus Berkhof argues that the influence of Greek philosophy on the doctrine of God's omnipotence led to a one-sided emphasis on God's transcendence.

> Berkhof argues that under the influence of Greek philosophy the early church stressed the majesty and transcendence of God but not his condescendence, what we below will call God's *hospitality*. In the Middle Ages, as we have seen, a distinction was made between God's *potentia absoluta* and his *potentia ordinate*, but little attention was given to his condescension. The Jesuit Molina proposed his *scientia media*, according to which "God has knowledge of metaphysically necessary states of affairs via natural knowledge, of what He intends to do via free knowledge, and in addition, of what free creatures would do if they were instantiated (via middle knowledge)."[a] During the Enlightenment a renewed emphasis was placed on God's kenosis to create room for humankind's autonomy. Barth's theology is a major attempt to inject biblical theology back into the doctrine of God's omnipotence, but work remains to be done in this area.
>
> [a]John D. Laing, "Middle Knowledge," *Internet Encyclopedia of Philosophy*, accessed March 10, 2020, www.iep.utm.edu/middlekn/.

Berkhof rightly seeks to balance such an emphasis on God's majesty with that of his *condescendence*, and yet he goes too far in referring to God's "defenseless superior power."[46] He argues that, contrary to popular opinion, "the first impression one gets from the biblical account of revelation is that of God's impotence, of how man has taken the initiative away from him, of what we shall call here his 'defenselessness.'"[47] Berkhof, however, goes on to reject any description of God as "impotent" and argues that what is at stake is *how* God exercises his power.

We concur with the need to relate God's power and condescendence but propose that instead of "defenselessness" we connect God's omnipotence with his *hospitality*. This, after all, is a major theme in Genesis 1–2. Unlike the gods in other creation accounts, God directs his power lovingly toward creating a good creation and the perfect home for human beings. God exercises his power in an other-centered way. He brings into being and creates the space apart from himself for the creation and in particular for the human person, who has the freedom to respond to God as a covenant partner or not. Berkhof rightly notes, "How drastic this surrender of power is, also for God, is shown

[46]Hendrikus Berkhof, *The Christian Faith: An Introduction to the Study of Faith*, trans. S. Woudstra (Grand Rapids, MI: Eerdmans, 1979), 146.
[47]Ibid., 134.

when man prefers to use his freedom to withdraw from the intended encounter and fellowship with God."[48] Berkhof says that here a definite limit is set to God's power, but what must be noted is that it is God himself who, in his power, sets this limit. It takes great strength—one could say "power"—to remain hospitable in the face of rebellion and opposition. As Barth notes, "It is by His power that He creates or at any rate tolerates other powers. In this His power is always power in and over them, and He is always first and last the only one who is full of power."[49]

The extent of God's hospitality becomes exquisitely apparent in Jesus. We have noted above the indications in Jesus' public ministry of his power and authority, but this is veiled and deliberately so, as Paul notes in his marvelous hymn in Philippians 2. In Jesus, as Barth so poignantly notes, God's Son goes off into the far country in order that we might come home. Unlike what so often happens among humans, with God omnipotence and self-sacrifice are not antithetical but marvelous expressions of God's freedom to be fully himself—that is, omnipotent. Berkhof observes that this condescension is also true of the Spirit; he too "goes the way of the cross, because everywhere he is resisted and grieved."[50]

Berkhof maintains that God's defenselessness "does not as such exclude an active exercise of power; it does exclude a forcible exercise of power which wipes out the power of the opposite."[51] In terms of biblical support, Berkhof refers, inter alia, to the "continual and usually futile calling and pleading of the prophets."[52] However, a cursory reading of the prophets and the story of Israel would call into question any sense that God's condescension means that he does not exercise forcible power and wipe out his opposition. The threat of the day of Yahweh in the prophets turned out to be very real for Israel as first the Northern and then the Southern Kingdom was dragged off into exile. Our examination of the Elijah-Elisha narratives above provides multiple examples of God's willingness to exercise his power in history forcibly. Within the Minor Prophets we have both Jonah, standing for God's compassion for and patience with Nineveh, and Nahum, with its declaration of terrible judgment on Nineveh.

In the midst of our good but fallen world, it will often seem to us as though God is defenseless, but Scripture assures us he is not. Hospitable, yes,

---

[48]Ibid., 135.

[49]Barth, *CD* II/1, 538.

[50]Berkhof, *Christian Faith*, 135.

[51]Ibid., 134.

[52]Ibid., 136.

remarkably so, but defenseless, no. We noted above that the description of God as "almighty" occurs particularly in Job and Revelation, both books dealing with suffering and struggle. Amidst the human experience of being defenseless, Scripture assures God's people that God is almighty!

God's exercise of his power on occasion to wipe out opposition to him bears witness to the fact that his patient hospitality will not last forever. The day of the Lord will come when his power will be unveiled against all sin and opposition to him. Far from his condescension limiting his power, it serves as a reminder of the God with whom we have to do. As Barth says, "There is no being not subject to the will of God."[53]

God's Omnipotence and Evil

It is precisely the integrality of God's omnipotence and love and goodness that creates the problem of theodicy.

THEODICY

A great deal has been written about theodicy. The term itself comes from the German philosopher Leibniz (1710 in his work *Theodicy*), who aimed to demonstrate that evil in the world does not conflict with God's goodness.[a] Indeed, for Leibniz, this is the best of all possible worlds. It is the core Christian beliefs in monotheism, creation, God's omnipotence, and God as personal and good that bring the challenge of evil into clear relief.[b] David Hume articulates the problem: "Is he [God] willing to prevent evil, but not able? Then he is impotent. Is he able, but not willing? Then he is malevolent. Is he both able and willing? Whence then is evil?"[c] A variety of solutions to theodicy have been proposed:[d]

The denial of omnipotence. In David Ray Griffin's *process theodicy* he denies *creatio ex nihilo* and states, "My solution dissolves the problem of evil by denying the doctrine of omnipotence fundamental to it. . . . There has always been a plurality of actualities having some power of their own."[e]

A recent example of such a theodicy is that of John Caputo in *The Weakness of God: A Theology of the Event*. According to Caputo, the problem with the theological account of power is that it is itself "too much in love with power, constantly selling its body to the interests of power, constantly sitting down to table with power in a discouraging contradiction of its own good news."[f] Caputo proposes that we "stop thinking about God as a massive ontological power line that provides power to the world."[g] Instead he suggests taking the concept of power as force and turning it on its head: thinking of power as "something that short-circuits such power and provides a provocation to the

---

[53]Barth, *CD* II/1, 555.

world that is otherwise than power."[h] Caputo calls such alternative conceptions of power a "weak force" and likens it to a call (Latin *vocare*) or an invitation in which we see God's power as an active weakness in the world. Caputo reenvisions the

> power of the kingdom [of God as] the powerless power to melt hearts that have hardened, to keep hope alive when life is hopeless, to revive the spirits of the dispirited and the despairing, to pray for something otherwise than the world that is closing in around us on every side, to pray for the possibility of something coming, in short, in a paradigmatically religious expression, the possibility of the impossible (Derrida), for with God all things are possible.[i]

For Caputo, God's weakness is *in fact weak*, not a variation or perfection of human force. It is victorious over human force not because God's weakness is more powerful or stronger than human force but because God's weakness confounds, disturbs, evades, and unsettles human force, showing it to be anti-real, anti-creational.

The denial of God's comprehensive goodness. According to Frederick Sontag's anthropodicy, we should begin with the problem of evil rather than starting with God as good and all-powerful, and then move toward our view of God. "It is the status of evil in God's nature which forces us to reconceive divinity. Some faults in our world can be explained by claiming that they are not seen as evil in God's sight but only in ours. However, such an event as a holocaust surely does not appear 'good' to God in any sense of the word."[j] Sontag loosens theism's hold on God as wholly good and calls on mystery at such points.

The Irenaean theodicy. This is associated with John Hick, who finds in Irenaeus's thought a framework for developing a theodicy.[k] Hick writes, "In this Irenaean theodicy our mortality, frailty and vulnerability, within a natural order which is not built so much to comfort us as to challenge us, are not a punishment for Adam's sin but a divinely appointed situation within which moral responsibility and personal growth are possible."[l] Indeed, in Hick's "Irenaean" theodicy, "God, as the sole Creator and Ruler of the universe, bears the ultimate responsibility for it."[m] Humans were initially created through the evolutionary process as morally and spiritually immature. Moral and natural evil are necessary parts of the creation through which God is forming perfect creatures.

The free-will defense. From this perspective evil is a result of God giving humans free will.[n] In response to J. L. Mackie, the Kuyperian philosopher Alvin Plantinga develops a rigorous defense of this approach.[o] Evil is not inconsistent with a wholly good omnipotent God because there are certain things that even an all-powerful God cannot do. In the context of his "counterfactuals of freedom" and "transworld depravity," Plantinga argues that God cannot change free decisions. This world is the best one God could create if he is to respect the free will of humans. Natural evil may result from the demonic realm (Plantinga's "luciferous defense").

Richard Swinburne also argues for a free-will defense. He asserts that "a generous God . . . will seek to give us great responsibility for ourselves, each other, and the world, and thus a share in his own creative activity of determining what sort of world it is to be."[p] A theodicy, Swinburne says, should be based on a "free-will defense [that] claims that it is a great good that humans have a certain sort of free will which I shall call free and responsible choice. . . . Necessarily there will be the natural [not predetermined] possibility of moral evil."[q]

The theodicy of protest or the anti-theodicy. John Roth, who articulates a protest theodicy, agrees with Hegel that history is "the slaughter-bench at which the happiness of peoples, the wisdom of states, and the virtue of individuals have been sacrificed."[r] Roth calls us to acknowledge evil for what it is and to hold God accountable. The danger in such an approach is that one relinquishes the belief that God is wholly good.

John Howard Yoder discussed theodicy in his "Trinity Versus Theodicy: Hebraic Realism and the Temptation to Judge God." He opposes the narrow meaning of theodicy, understood as justifying God.[s] Zachary Braiterman, writing amidst post-Holocaust theology, coined the phrase "antitheodicy," which means "refusing to justify, explain, or accept [the relationship between] God (or some other form of ultimate reality), evil, and suffering."[t] Yoder refers to—and affirms—such an approach as the Jewish case against God, updated since Auschwitz. The faithful continue to pray, after having denounced God for what he has let happen.

In Job we find an approach to terrible suffering that resonates with Yoder's type of anti-theodicy. Theodicy is here resolved not intellectually but only through deep encounter with God, especially God as creator. Certainly Job's journey toward resolution is full of protest. Ecclesiastes, by comparison, provides support for an intellectual analysis of evil. Qohelet's journey involves protest as well as recognition that God made the world straight but humans have twisted it.

---

[a]Cf. Larry M. Jorgensen and Samuel Newlands, *New Essays on Leibniz's Theodicy* (Oxford: Oxford University Press, 2014).

[b]Cf. Stephen T. Davis, ed., *Encountering Evil: Live Options in Theodicy* (Louisville, KY: John Knox, 1981), ix.

[c]David Hume, *Dialogues Concerning Natural Religion* (London: Penguin Classics, 1990), 198.

[d]Cf. Chad Meister and James K. Dew Jr., eds., *God and Evil: The Case for God in a World Filled with Pain* (Downers Grove, IL: InterVarsity Press, 2013).

[e]David Ray Griffin, "Creation Out of Nothing, Creation Out of Chaos, and the Problem of Evil," in Davis, *Encountering Evil*, 105.

[f]John D. Caputo, *The Weakness of God: A Theology of the Event* (Bloomington: Indiana University Press, 2006), 8.

[g]Ibid., 13.

[h]Ibid.

[i]Ibid., 16.

[j]Frederick Sontag, "Anthropodicy and the Return of God," in Davis, *Encountering Evil*, 148.

[k]John Hick, "An Irenaean Theodicy," in Davis, *Encountering Evil*, 39-52.

[l]John Hick, *Evil and the God of Love* (San Francisco: Harper & Row, 1978), 86.

[m]Ibid., 90.

[n]Alvin Plantinga, "The Free Will Defense," in *The Analytic Theist: An Alvin Plantinga Reader*, ed. J. F. Sennett (Grand Rapids, MI: Eerdmans, 1998), 22-49. For a useful treatment, see Gijsbert van den Brink, *Almighty God: A Study of the Doctrine of Divine Omnipotence* (Kampen: Peeters, 1993), 240-73.
[o]J. L. Mackie, "Evil and Omnipotence," *Mind* 64 (1955): 200-212. Repr. in *Philosophy of Religion*, ed. B. Mitchell (London: Oxford University Press, 1971), 92-104.
[p]Richard Swinburne, *Is There a God?* (New York: Oxford University Press, 1996), 96.
[q]Ibid., 98.
[r]John K. Roth, "A Theodicy of Protest," in Davis, *Encountering Evil*, 10.
[s]John Howard Yoder, "Trinity Versus Theodicy: Hebraic Realism and the Temptation to Judge God," in *The Trinity and Theodicy: The Trinitarian Theology of von Balthasar and the Problem of Evil* (Farnham, UK: Ashgate, 2013). An important discussion of theodicy in the Yoder tradition is that of Stanley Hauerwas, *Naming the Silences: God, Medicine, and Suffering* (Grand Rapids, MI: Eerdmans, 1990). Hauerwas notes how theodicy generally occurs amidst unacceptable enlightenment presuppositions. Historically speaking, he asserts, "Christians have not had a 'solution' to the problem of evil. Rather, they have had a community of care that has made it possible for them to absorb the destructive terror of evil that constantly threatens to destroy all human relations" (ibid., 53).
[t]Zachary Braiterman, *(God) After Auschwitz: Tradition and Change in Post-Holocaust Jewish Thought* (Princeton, NJ: Princeton University Press, 1998), 4.

Doubtless philosophical discussions of theodicy will continue. One thing that should be clear from our discussion in this chapter is that biblically it simply will not do to relinquish God's omnipotence along the lines proposed by John Caputo and others.[54] To take one example, Caputo's view that God does not have an army to reinforce his decisions is simply flatly contradicted by Scripture. Just before the siege of Jericho, Joshua encounters a mighty angel and asks whether he is with the Israelites or one of their enemies. The angel replies, "Neither; but as commander of the army of the LORD I have now come" (Josh 5:14). There is much of theological interest in this reply. But our point here is that God does indeed have the hosts of heaven at his disposal. As Geach rightly notes, belief in God as almighty is not a piece of old metaphysical baggage that can easily be relinquished but is at the heart of biblical faith.[55] Denying it brings the entire theological edifice, including the doctrine of creation, crashing down. Here again it is to Scripture that we must turn. The Bible is profoundly in touch with the brokenness of the world and the reality of evil. The cross is the most profound revelation of evil as it turns its power against the Son of God. Ironically, it is this very event that manifests God's power and wisdom in Christ, who is the power and wisdom of God.

Scripture never provides a full explanation for the reality of evil. It provides parameters within which to understand and live this reality, parameters such as the effect of sin, the reality of Satan and evil forces, and so on, subjects dealt

[54]Bonhoeffer also overstates the case for God's weakness. See the quote in Berkhof, *Christian Faith*, 137-38.
[55]P. T. Geach, *Providence and Evil: The Stanton Lectures 1971–2* (Cambridge: Cambridge University Press, 1977), 8.

with in chapter six. What is clear, however, is that again and again Scripture finds in God's power as creator the resource for living with evil in the present and, ultimately, for dealing with it in the future. Psalm 82, for example, which we examined above, ends with a prayer for God to rise up and judge the earth, "for all the nations belong to you." Psalm 104 ends with the request: "Let sinners be consumed from the earth, and let the wicked be no more." The psalmists look to God to act in his power and to eradicate evil from his creation. Similarly in the New Testament evil is seen as the great problem and the coming of the kingdom the answer. Jesus will return *in power* to usher in the new creation, cleansed and purged of evil. In Scripture, far from God's being the omnipotent creator problematizing evil, it is the resource for living through evil and overcoming it.

God's Omnipotence and *Creatio Ex Nihilo*

God's power in creation is manifest particularly in that he creates *ex nihilo.* "The claim that *creation from nothing* means *nothing*—absolutely nothing—*apart from God* is certainly an affirmation of divine omnipotence, but once again, it need not imply a tyrannical or arbitrary deity."[56] The heart of this doctrine is expressed in Genesis 1:1 and in John 1:3: "All things came into being through him, and without him not one thing came into being." John 1:1-5 is a renarration of the opening verses of Genesis 1.[57] Scholars continue to doubt whether the Old Testament, and Genesis 1:1 in particular, actually teaches directly or implicitly this doctrine. Othmar Keel and Silvia Schroer express a common view when they write,

> The highly philosophical construct of a *creatio ex nihilo*, which appears in the historical record for the first time only in the second century AD, arising in the early church, cannot be found in the Hebrew Bible. It developed from the ontological perspective that had its origins in the time of Aristotle and leads, in regard to understanding Genesis 1 and other passages, to error.[58]

---

[56]Ian A. McFarland, *From Nothing: A Theology of Creation* (Louisville, KY: Westminster John Knox, 2014), 94.

[57]Richard Bauckham, "Monotheism and Christology in the Gospel of John," in *Contours of Christology in the New Testament*, ed. Richard N. Longenecker (Grand Rapids, MI: Eerdmans, 2005), 149-50. McFarland writes, "John does not speak explicitly of creation from nothing any more than does Genesis, but the evangelist does offer a rescript of Genesis 1 that points toward a theological resolution of its grammatical and ontological ambiguities in much the same way that the New Testament identification of Jesus as the image of God (2 Cor. 4:4; Col. 1:15; cf. Heb. 1:5) gives definite content to Genesis's suggestive but undefined category of the divine image" (*From Nothing*, 88).

[58]Othmar Keel and Silvia Schroer, *Creation: Biblical Theologies in the Context of the Ancient Near East*, trans. Peter T. Daniels (Winona Lake, IN: Eisenbrauns, 2015), 139.

Even 2 Maccabees 7:28 is no longer regarded as a sure indicator of belief in *creatio ex nihilo*.[59]

There has been renewed attention to the doctrine of *creatio ex nihilo* in recent years.[a] Genesis 1:1 is a critical text for our understanding of creation and of *creatio ex nihilo*, despite protestations to the contrary, but how to translate Genesis 1:1-3 is contested.

Wenham points out four possible ways to translate verses 1-3:[b]

a. Genesis 1:1 is a temporal clause that is subordinate to the main clause in v. 2, leading to a translation "In the beginning, when God created. . . . , the earth was without form and void . . ."

b. Genesis 1:1 is a temporal clause subordinate to the main clause in v. 3, with v. 2 as a parenthetic comment, leading to the translation "In the beginning when God created . . . (now the earth was formless and void) God said . . ."

c. Genesis 1:1 is a main clause summarizing all of Genesis 1:2-31. This approach reads v. 1 as a title, which leads to a translation "In the beginning God was the creator of heaven and earth."[c]

d. Genesis 1:1 is a main clause describing the first act of creation, leading to the traditional translation "In the beginning God created the heavens and the earth."

View a was first put forward by Ibn Ezra but has received minimal support.

View b was first put forward by Rashi.

As we will see below, Gary Anderson refers to b as the *consensus* view today. Arguments for this view are as follows:

בְּרֵאשִׁית does not have the definite article, and it may thus be a construct rendering a translation "In the beginning of God's creating. . . ." In such a sentence the verb is usually in the infinitive, but here it is a perfect בָּרָא; but this is not without parallel (Hos 1:2). Furthermore, רֵאשִׁית rarely has the absolute sense, which the traditional translation requires. Genesis 2:4b, which is usually seen as the start of the second account of creation, begins בְּיוֹם עֲשׂוֹת יְהוָה אֱלֹהִים אֶרֶץ וְשָׁמָיִם, "in the day of the making by the Lord God of earth and heaven," confirming the temporal rendering of 1:1.

The Enuma Elish and the Atrahasis Epic[d] both begin with comparable dependent temporal clauses. Anderson argues that "reading Genesis 1:1 in light of the Enuma Elish suggests that God is both confronted with and limited by the state of the universe prior to creation."[e]

Wenham discerns several problems with this view. First, the absence of an article with בְּרֵאשִׁית does not mean it is necessarily in the construct case. Second, as other verses in the Old Testament indicate, it may well have an absolute sense (cf. Is 46:10;[f] 40:21; 41:4, 26; Gen 3:22; 6:3, 4; cf. the analogous expression in Prov 8:23). Third, if, as Wenham and we think, the second section in Genesis begins with Genesis 2:4a, the

[59]Cf. ibid., 139; Gerhard May, *Creatio Ex Nihilo: The Doctrine of "Creation Out of Nothing" in Early Christian Thought*, trans. A. S. Worrall (London: T&T Clark, 1994).

parallel between 2:4b and 1:1 disappears. Fourth, the context of בְּרֵאשִׁית in 1:1 at the outset of the Bible means an absolute sense is highly likely here.

Genesis 1:1, according to approach c above, is seen as a title in chiastic correspondence to Genesis 2:4a; an *inclusio* that frames the intervening narrative. However, the end of Genesis 2:3, אֲשֶׁר־בָּרָא, would also make an *inclusio* with 1:1, as Wenham notes. In 1:1 heaven and earth is a merism for the whole, thus "everything."

Of approach d, Wenham observes that the versions and Masoretic pointing imply this was the standard view from the third century BC (LXX) through to the tenth century AD (MT). Hasel, furthermore, points out that Genesis 1:2-3 is not a straight borrowing of extrabiblical ideas; it is composed and not just borrowed.[g] Wenham concludes that the traditional translation is the correct one and that verse 1 should thus be seen as the first creative act of God.

Recently, the doctrine of *creatio ex nihilo* has received fresh attention. Gary Anderson notes that the relationship of *creatio ex nihilo* to the Bible has been a vexed issue since the emergence of historical criticism.[h] In his view, "all of the standard prooftexts for the doctrine have been shown to lack the clarity and precision that they were once thought to possess."[i] He says of Genesis 1:1–2:4a that "the consensus among scholars (with which I agree) is that the first three verses depict God forming the world out of preexistent matter."[j] Genesis 1:1-2 comprises a set of subordinate clauses that set up the main clause in verse 3; verse 2 thus describes the "chaotic substrate" that preceded God's first creative act. Anderson acknowledges that the Septuagint and John 1:1 point toward *creatio ex nihilo* but argues that we should not therefore abandon the Hebrew.

In order to make sense of Genesis 1:1-3, Anderson appeals to Childs's distinction between the discrete witness of a text and its underlying subject matter. Genesis 1:1-3 does draw on ancient Near Eastern creation narratives, but with regard to the Enuma Elish, for example, the differences are as significant as the similarities. Remarkably, in Genesis 1 creation proceeds without opposition; the sea monsters are created by God and controlled by him. Anderson quotes Levenson with approval: "In fact, rather than *creatio ex nihilo*, 'creation without opposition' is the more accurate nutshell statement of the theology underlying our passage."[k]

Anderson makes much of the fact that *creatio ex nihilo* arose in a Greco-Roman philosophical environment in which the eternity of matter constrained and limited the gods. It was this view that the early fathers of the church struggled against. "But this particular problem is not something that the biblical writer ever faced or could even imagine."[l] But Anderson is reluctant to argue that Genesis 1:1 "refutes" *creatio ex nihilo*. It is better to say that in his creation God encounters no opposition, which, for Anderson, is very different from the Greco-Roman world's view of creation. Doubtless the author of Genesis 1 used sources in which God has first to destroy the forces of chaos—the well-known *Chaoskampf* texts—but the author rejects this view. Darkness in Genesis 1 is part of the chaos substrate, but by the seventh day all trace of it has vanished.

Anderson quotes Levenson to the effect that that which the Sabbath (day seven) represents will only be available in the eschaton.[m]

Anderson says, "The only conclusion I think we can draw from the Bible's final canonical form is that the existence of darkness at creation must have been something God permits rather than confronts by necessity."[n] Genesis 2:1-3 provides something of an aporia in relation to the rest of Genesis 1:1–2:4a. The close of 1:1–2:4a stands in tension with its opening. Part of Anderson's solution is to move the focus of the doctrine to how the world is governed by God rather than how it originated.

How compelling is Anderson's account? In our view, not very. Above we have noted Wenham's case for the traditional reading, and other authors such as Sarna, Childs, von Rad, and Hamilton could be invoked at this point.[o] It is hard to know what a "consensus" means when such authors remain outside the analysis. Furthermore, the dependence of Genesis 1 on the Enuma Elish and the role of a *Chaoskampf* motif in Genesis 1:1–2:3 is by no means certain.[p] Also, Anderson's aporia looks more like a contradiction, with Genesis 2:1-3 presenting a very different view to Genesis 1:1-31. Taking the seventh day as forward-looking leaves us with a creation that originally was really not "very good."

Anderson makes much of the fact that the doctrine of *creatio ex nihilo* only emerged in confrontation with Greek philosophy. Now, it may well be true that as a precise theory this is the case, but it seems to imply that Greek philosophy triggered a whole new element of precision and hard thinking. If we take Alvin Plantinga's definition of philosophy as thinking hard about something, then, as Yoram Hazony has recently reminded us, the Hebrew Bible is full of such "philosophy."[q] We should not be anachronistic in thinking that the ancient Near Eastern world lacked sophisticated views of preexisting matter. Kaufmann reminds us, "In pagan myth . . . the primordial realm is the necessary presupposition for theogony. Divine beings and powers must have a derivation—in the spirit of the later philosophic formula, *ex nihilo nihil fit*. Lacking a theogony, the Bible has no need of a pre-existent realm."[r]

Anderson's movement of the focus of *creatio ex nihilo* to God's governance of the world is a helpful reminder of what the doctrine entails, but, one has to ask, governance *over what*? As Bauckham points out, origin and sovereignty or governance are inseparable: "In the Jewish definition of the one God's exclusive divinity, as well as being the sole Creator of all things, God is also understood as the sole sovereign Ruler of all things."[s] Similarly, Webster says, "God's acts of creating and governing are inseparable."[t]

We agree that there is no explicit doctrine of *creatio ex nihilo* in the Bible, in the sense of a carefully articulated theory/doctrine. But in our view John 1:1-3 and many other texts line up with Genesis 1 in proclaiming such a doctrine in substance. Kaufmann thus rightly observes that

> Nowhere do we find that the cosmic elements—e.g., earth, heavens, sun—were fashioned out of pre-existent stuff. Hence, it is reasonable to suppose that the

obscure passage, Gen 1:1-2, means: God first created the tōhū wāḇōhū, i.e., upper spaces, darkness, water, and earth which was covered by water. . . . The notion of a pre-existent stuff thus lurks in the background of biblical cosmologies as a vestigial idea which has no meaningful role in the accounts themselves. . . . The monotheism of these stories is, thus, not the outcome of an artificial adaption of pagan materials. It permeates their every aspect and finds expression even in passages of artless naivete.[u]

---

[a]E.g., David B. Burrell et al., eds., *Creation and the God of Abraham* (Cambridge: Cambridge University Press), 2010; Ian A. McFarland, *From Nothing: A Theology of Creation* (Louisville, KY: Westminster John Knox, 2014); Gary A. Anderson and Markus Bockmuehl, eds., *Creation* ex nihilo*: Origins, Development, Contemporary Challenges* (Notre Dame, IN: University of Notre Dame Press, 2018).

[b]Gordon J. Wenham, *Genesis 1–15*, WBC 1 (Waco, TX: Word, 1987), 11-12.

[c]For this type of interpretation, see Othmar Keel and Silvia Schroer, *Creation: Biblical Theologies in the Context of the Ancient Near East*, trans. Peter T. Daniels (Winona Lake, IN: Eisenbrauns, 2015), 140-41.

[d]On this issue, see Victor P. Hamilton, *Book of Genesis: Chapters 1–17*, NICOT (Grand Rapids, MI: Eerdmans, 1990), 107.

[e]Gary A. Anderson, "*Creatio ex nihilo* and the Bible," in Anderson and Bockmuehl, *Creation* ex nihilo, 22.

[f]On the relevance of Is 46:9-10, see Hamilton, *Book of Genesis*, 106.

[g]Cf. Gerhard F. Hasel, "The Significance of the Cosmology in Gen 1 in Relation to Ancient Near Eastern Parallels," *Andrews University Seminary Studies* 10 (1972): 1-120; "The Polemic Nature of the Genesis Cosmology," *Evangelical Quarterly* 46 (1974): 81-102.

[h]Anderson, "*Creatio ex nihilo*," 15.

[i]Ibid., 15.

[j]Ibid., 16.

[k]Ibid., 18; Jon D. Levenson, *Creation and the Persistence of Evil: The Jewish Drama of Divine Omnipotence* (Princeton, NJ: Princeton University Press, 1994), 122.

[l]Anderson, "*Creatio ex nihilo*," 19.

[m]Ibid., 20.

[n]Ibid., 21.

[o]Nahum M. Sarna, *The JPS Torah Commentary: Genesis* (New York: Jewish Publication Society, 1989). Sarna's commentary follows the JPS translation, which follows what Anderson considers the consensus view today, but Sarna differs from it and argues for the traditional view: "Precisely because of the indispensable importance of pre-existing matter in the pagan cosmologies, the very absence of such mention here is highly significant. This conclusion is reinforced by the idea of creation by divine fiat without reference to any inert matter being present. Also, the repeated biblical emphasis upon God as the exclusive Creator would seem to rule out the possibility of pre-existent matter" (ibid., 5).

Brevard S. Childs, *Myth and Reality in the Old Testament*, Studies in Biblical Theology 27 (London: SCM Press, 1960), 32: "This verse can be interpreted grammatically in two different ways. . . . While there is a choice grammatically, the theology of P excludes the latter possibility [viz., that 1:1 is a dependent temporal clause subordinated to v. 3]. . . . We have seen the effort of the Priestly writer to emphasize the absolute transcendence of God over his material."

Gerhard von Rad, *Genesis: A Commentary*, Old Testament Library (Philadelphia: Westminster John Knox, 1972), 48: "Syntactically perhaps both translations are possible, but not theologically. . . . God, in the freedom of his will, creatively established for 'heaven and earth,' i.e., for absolutely everything, a beginning of subsequent existence."

[p]Cf. the essays in Joann Scurlock and Richard H. Beal, eds., *Creation and Chaos: A Reconsideration of Hermann Gunkel's* Chaoskampf *Hypothesis* (Winona Lake, IN: Eisenbrauns, 2013). Bernard F. Batto (*In the Beginning: Essays on Creation Motifs in the Ancient Near East and the Bible* [University Park, PA: Eisenbrauns, 2013], 218) says, "Reversing an opinion common among critical biblical scholars of the last century, recent biblical scholars increasingly find that Genesis 1 is not literarily dependent on its Babylonian counterpart." Joann Scurlock ("*Chaoskampf* Lost—*Chaoskampf* Regained: The Gunkel Hypothesis Revisited," in Scurlock and Beal, *Creation and Chaos*, 258) says, "What **is** a noticeable contrast is the omission in Gen 1:1–2:4a of any mention of the Chaoskampf in connection with creation." For a theological interpretation of Gen 1:2 that engages with these issues, see Craig G. Bartholomew, "Genesis 1:2 and the Doctrine of Creation," in *Acts of Interpretation: Scripture, Theology, and Culture*, ed. Stephen A. Cummins and Jens Zimmerman (Grand Rapids, MI: Eerdmans, 2018), 83-99.

[q]Yoram Hazony, *The Philosophy of Hebrew Scripture* (Cambridge: Cambridge University Press, 2012).
[r]Yehezkel Kaufmann, *The Religion of Israel: From Its Beginnings to the Babylonian Exile* (Chicago: University of Chicago Press, 1960), 68.
[s]Richard Bauckham, "Monotheism and Christology in the Gospel of John," in *Contours of Christology in the New Testament*, ed. Richard N. Longenecker (Grand Rapids, MI: Eerdmans, 2005), 152.
[t]John Webster, "On the Theology of Providence," in *The Providence of God: Deus Habet Consilium*, ed. Francesca Aran Murphy and Philip G. Ziegler (London: T&T Clark, 2009), 166.
[u]Kaufmann, *Religion of Israel*, 68.

In our view Genesis 1:1 affirms what is at the heart of *creatio ex nihilo*. As Westermann observes, the creation account is distinct because "there can be only one creator and . . . all else that is or can be, can never be anything but a creature."[60] However, refutations of *ex nihilo* keep appearing;[61] indeed, there is a sustained attempt to say this doctrine is imposed on the biblical texts by alien metaphysics. Caputo sees this metaphysical turn as disastrous; rather than being enthralled by the idea that God has absolute power over creation and nonbeing, we should believe in a weaker god who brings forth creation from the chaotic "deep."[62] *Ex nihilo*, in his view, suppresses chaos and indeterminacy, but we should embrace creation's chaotic indeterminacy as a "beautiful risk."[63] The fear here seems to be of *creatio ex nihilo* as involving the imposition of a tyrannical and arbitrary divine will. McFarland rebuts this claim by noting that creation is an extension of the doctrine of God, understood as the Trinity. Although we think that Genesis 1:1 and John 1:1-3 are clearer on *creatio ex nihilo* than does McFarland, we find his grounding of *creatio ex nihilo* in Christology helpful and insightful. He argues that John's use of "the Word" in John 1 is significant because it evokes difference within God that precludes any reduction of creation to brute will.[64]

In terms of this chapter it should be noted that any affirmation of preexisting matter out of which God created subverts the incomparableness of God, the major biblical theme explored above. Bavinck rightly notes, "The expression *ex nihilo* was eagerly preserved in Christian theology only

[60]Claus Westermann, *Genesis 1–11: A Commentary*, trans. John J. Scullion (Minneapolis: Augsburg, 1984), 124.
[61]For a discussion of Ricoeur, LaCocque, and those who deny *ex nihilo*, see Brian D. Robinette, "The Difference Nothing Makes: Creation Ex Nihilo, Resurrection, and Divine Gratuity," *Theological Studies* 72 (2011): 525-57.
[62]John D. Caputo, *The Weakness of God: A Theology of the Event* (Bloomington: Indiana University Press, 2006).
[63]Ibid., 64. Caputo's approach should be clearly distinguished from views that see the doctrine of *creatio ex nihilo* developing, presumably normatively, over centuries among God's people. Cf., e.g., Ernan McMullin, "Creation *ex nihilo*: Early History," in *Creation and the God of Abraham*, ed. David B. Burrell et al. (New York: Cambridge University Press, 2010), 11-23.
[64]McFarland, *From Nothing*, 90.

because it was admirably suited for cutting off all sorts of errors at the root."[65] Berkhof reminds us of the importance of *creatio ex nihilo* for our assurance that God and his creation are good: "For that reason the confession of our creation, both in the Bible and in the church's hymns, so often takes the form of a hymn of praise. If created reality, which can enrapture but also frighten us, has its sole source of being in the initiative of the Father of Jesus Christ, then, in spite of everything, it must be a good thing. Creation is good because the creator is good."[66] Anderson's point, noted above, that *creatio ex nihilo* is about more than origins is well taken. Indeed, in the doctrine of creation, *creatio ex nihilo* connects into divine governance and many other themes, thus reminding us of the close connection between creation and *creatio continua*. The theme of governance will be explored in chapter ten on providence.

God's Omnipotence and Monotheism

In an older work William Newton Clarke rightly asserts, "Companion to omnipresence and omniscience is Omnipotence. As in those attributes, so in this, the unity and soleness of God is asserted, and the doctrine is that of monotheism; for omnipotence is not other than unipotence, the adequacy and control of the One, in relation to all that is not himself. . . . God is master of the universe, and holds it in control."[67] The emergence of monotheism in Israel is contested, with many arguing that it emerged slowly.[68] What is clear is that canonically monotheism is affirmed,[69] and it is central to the doctrine of creation and the worldview of Israel, the Old Testament, and the Bible as a whole. Monotheism is implied in the motif of the mocking of the gods, as we have seen above. Its centrality to the Bible is also evident in biblical wisdom, according to which wisdom is available to humans in the creation because it stems from one source—namely, Yahweh (cf.

---

[65]Herman Bavinck, *Reformed Dogmatics: God and Creation*, ed. John Bolt, trans. J. Vriend (Grand Rapids, MI: Baker Academic, 2003–2008), 2:418.

[66]Berkhof, *Christian Faith*, 159.

[67]William Newton Clarke, *The Christian Doctrine of God* (Edinburgh: T&T Clark, 1912), 351.

[68]Cf. Patrick D. Miller, *The Religion of Ancient Israel* (Louisville, KY: Westminster John Knox, 2000); Johannes Cornelis de Moor, *The Rise of Yahwism: The Roots of Israelite Monotheism* (Leuven: Leuven University Press, 1997); Mark S. Smith, *The Origins of Biblical Monotheism: Israel's Polytheistic Background and the Ugaritic Texts* (New York: Oxford University Press, 2001); Smith, *The Early History of God: Yahweh and the Other Deities in Ancient Israel*, 2nd ed. (Grand Rapids, MI: Eerdmans, 2002); Smith, *The Memoirs of God* (Minneapolis: Fortress, 2004).

[69]Cf. Christoph Schwöbel's fine article "Radical Monotheism and the Trinity," *Neue Zeitschrift für Systematische Theologie und Religionsphilosophie* 43, no. 1 (2001): 54-74.

Prov 3:19-20).[70] Christoph Schwöbel explores the critiques of monotheism, H. Richard Niebuhr's defense of it, and the relationship between monotheism and the Trinity. He argues, "Far from undermining the concept of monotheism the doctrine of the Trinity secures a radical monotheism that can claim ontological universality and not only the quasi-universal particularity of a social faith or tribal religion."[71]

Among philosophers there has been a debate about whether more than one entity could be omnipotent. Swinburne argues that it is possible for more than one omnipotent being to exist.[72] Much depends here on whether "omnipotence" is defined as necessary or contingent.[73] However one resolves this philosophically, it is clear biblically and theologically that only one being is omnipotent—namely, the biblical God.

A debate also continues about the cultural and historical implications of monotheism, with some arguing that polytheism is far more helpful for our pluralistic cultures.[74] Rodney Stark, however, argues that Christian monotheism is fundamental to the rise of science in the West, with its concomitant notions of the omnipotent creator, an ordered universe, and humans with (limited) power to discover God's ways in his world.[75] This framework allows one to affirm the positive aspects of modernity while recontextualizing it within God-ordained limits and purposes.[76]

God's Omnipotence and the Trinity

If the omnipotent God is one, he is also triune. The creeds make this clear, and as Barth rightly says, "The omnipotence of which the creed speaks is the omnipotence of God the Father, the omnipotence of the God and Father who reveals Himself to be God and Father in accordance with the remaining content of the creed, and is therefore of one essence with the Son and the Holy Spirit."[77] Father, Son, and Spirit are all omnipotent. However, the Apostles'

---

[70]Craig G. Bartholomew and Ryan P. O'Dowd, *Old Testament Wisdom Literature: A Theological Introduction* (Downers Grove, IL: IVP Academic, 2011); cf. Schwöbel, "Radical Monotheism."

[71]Schwöbel, "Radical Monotheism," 74.

[72]Richard Swinburne, *The Christian God* (Oxford: Clarendon, 1994), 170.

[73]Cf. Van den Brink, *Almighty God*, 138-40.

[74]Cf. Jan Assmann, *Of God and Gods: Egypt, Israel, and the Rise of Monotheism* (Madison: University of Wisconsin Press, 2008); Schwöbel, "Radical Monotheism"; Rodney Stark, *One True God: Historical Consequences of Monotheism* (Princeton, NJ: Princeton University Press, 2001).

[75]Rodney Stark, *The Victory of Reason: How Christianity Led to Freedom, Capitalism, and Western Success* (New York: Random House, 2007).

[76]Cf. Bob Goudzwaard and Craig G. Bartholomew, *Beyond the Modern Age: An Archeology of Contemporary Culture* (Downers Grove, IL: IVP Academic, 2017).

[77]Barth, *CD* II/1, 524.

and Nicene Creeds particularly associate the Father's omnipotence with creation, although from the doctrine of the Trinity and perichoresis we know that the Son and the Spirit are also involved in the act of creation. Where trinitarian doctrine is vital is in compelling us to hold together God's power with his love and grace. As Newbigin rightly notes, "The power that controls all the visible world, and the power at work in the human soul, is one with the man who went his way from Bethlehem to Calvary."[78]

Modernity and Power

A theological exploration of God's power, and thus of derivative powers, is not a merely academic exercise. In fact, a right understanding of God's power is utterly central to an understanding of our modern world. For better and for worse, modernity is defined by the unleashing of unprecedented power. Romano Guardini rightly notes, "The modern age, with intellect and technique in hitherto unknown proximity to material reality, grasps at the world. What determines its sense of existence is power over nature."[79] In many cases this has been for good, as, for example, in advances in health care, but far too often it has been damaging, indeed demonic. The danger of power in modernity has been widely analyzed. One wonders, for example, whether Guardini, in his reference to "technique," is thinking of the acute analysis of technique by the French sociologist Jacques Ellul. The twentieth century, regarded by many as the most brutal in history, was *the* century in which humankind's power manifested itself. Advanced technology was used by Nazi Germany to gas millions of Jews and many others to death.

Similarly, the nuclear threat emerging on the technological heels of World War II alerted us to the potential for humankind to destroy itself and large parts of the creation. Our grasping at the world has put us in a situation in which the very biosphere is threatened by climate change that is fueled by our desire for a lifestyle of consumption of cheap goods that we have the power to produce.[80] The armaments industry has become a massive enterprise making huge amounts of money on the back of war and corruption. We in the West live constantly under the threat of terrorists gaining possession of nuclear armaments. Drones can now drop bombs under the control of a

[78]Lesslie Newbigin, *Truth to Tell: The Gospel as Public Truth* (London: SPCK, 1991), 37. Cf. McFarland's helpful work *From Nothing*, which grounds creation in Christology.

[79]Romano Guardini, *The End of the Modern World* (Wilmington, DE: ISI Books, 1998), 117.

[80]Cf. Naomi Klein, *This Changes Everything: Capitalism vs. the Climate* (New York: Simon & Schuster, 2014).

person sitting comfortably at his or her computer thousands of miles away from the area affected. Little wonder that the Canadian engineer Bill Vanderburg titled his fourth book on technology *Our War on Ourselves*.[81]

In this context the doctrine of creation and of God's omnipotence has a vital role to play. It reminds us that we, as creatures, have real power, but that power is not limitless and can be radically misdirected. The doctrine alerts us to the importance of limits that we need to respect if we wish to flourish. It also serves notice that, as with the Tower of Babel, the omnipotent God will not stand by forever as we casually ignore his norms for his creation. Judgment will come, in one form or another.

[81]Willem H. Vanderburg, *Our War on Ourselves: Rethinking Science, Technology, and Economic Growth* (Toronto: University of Toronto Press, 2012).

LAYING THE FOUNDATIONS

THE FURNISHING OF THE CREATION

My hand laid the foundation of the earth,
and my right hand spread out the heavens;
when I summon them,
they stand at attention.

Isaiah 48:13

The special aspect of the theological significance of the structure of the world has received little attention.

Rolf P. Knierim

In a theater production it is possible to change the stage setting for a different act of the drama, as many of us have experienced. In the biblical grand narrative this is decidedly not the case. Creation is the opening act, and as such it sets the stage for the entire scriptural narrative. History and redemption operate out of this act; they take place in the creation and with creation as the backdrop at every point. It is hard, therefore, to overstress the importance of the doctrine of creation. As Ola Tjørhom notes, "The Father is the creator, the Son is the ultimate liberator of creation, and the Holy Spirit conveys life to all created beings. Surely, a misplaced confusion of creation and redemption must be avoided." He adds, "Actually, without creation there is nothing to save—creation is the 'stuff' of salvation."[1]

Barth gets at the fundamental nature of this doctrine with his poignant insight that creation is the external basis of the covenant and that covenant

[1]Ola Tjørhom, *Embodied Faith: Reflections on a Materialist Spirituality* (Grand Rapids, MI: Eerdmans, 2009), 33, 36.

is the internal basis of creation.[2] Genesis 1 is indeed *the* foundational covenantal text, to which the biblical covenants look back and from which they develop. Covenant in this respect is a thick concept dealing with God's purpose in history, with his creation, and with redemption. The drama of Scripture unfolds from the opening act, and we will continually misrepresent the other acts if we do not attend comprehensively to God's ordering of creation.

The setting of the stage of creation is particularly clear in Genesis 1:1–2:3, although Genesis 2 and many other passages have important insights to contribute. Genesis 1 deals with the forming and ordering of creation and its *furnishing*, as Augustine puts it, as it comes into existence.[3]

> Augustine translates Genesis 2:1: "And heaven and earth and all their furniture [*ornatus*] were finished." Augustine uses "furnishing" (*ornatus, ornandum*) to refer to populating the spaces created. In this he is in line with the patristic tradition, which Thomas describes at the start of his discussion of the days of creation:[a] first, creation; second, the work of distinction;[b] and third, the work of adornment.
>
> [a]*ST* Ia, 65.
> [b]See *ST* Ia, 66-67.

In Barth's terms Genesis 1 deals with creation as the external basis of the covenant.[4] He writes, "The first biblical creation story (Gen. 1:1–2:4a) . . . describes creation as it were externally as the work of the powerful but thoroughly planned and thought-out and perfectly supervised preparation, comparable to the building of a temple, the arrangement and construction of which is determined both in detail and as a whole by the liturgy which it is to serve." The patristic and Augustinian notion of the furnishing of the world in Genesis 1 has proven evocative and helpful, as demonstrated by the number of scholars who invoke the metaphors of architecture and the home when referring to creation. Edmond Jacob, for example, describes creation in Genesis 1 as "an architect intending to build a house inside which new inhabitants should be entirely at their ease; this house must be substantial, sheltered from dangers, pleasant, with a measure of luxury not forbidden there. . . . The architect is not confused with the creation."[5]

[2]This insight occurs repeatedly. See, for e.g., Barth, *CD* III/1, 97.
[3]Augustine, *Literal Meaning of Genesis* 2.13.27, 4.1.1. Barth, *CD* III/1, 143, 156, also uses the metaphor of furnishing.
[4]Barth, *CD* III/1, 98.
[5]Edmond Jacob, *Theology of the Old Testament* (New York: Harper & Row, 1958), 136-37.

Although the major dimensions of covenantal theology are clearly present in Genesis 1,[6] the change of God's name from Elohim in Genesis 1:1–2:3 to the uncommon Yahweh Elohim in Genesis 2:4–3:24 indicates an intentional covenantal focus. Genesis 2:4–4:26, the second section in Genesis, narrows the focus to the first couple in Eden and concludes in Genesis 4:26 with the statement that "at that time people began to invoke the name of the LORD [Yahweh]." We will use Genesis 1:1–2:3 as the basis for our discussion of the formation of the creation in this chapter, and Genesis 2–3 will be attended to closely in chapter six.

THE GENRE AND STRUCTURE OF GENESIS 1:1–2:3

Creation is a sui generis event, and thus it is not surprising that scholars struggle to define the genre of this opening salvo in the scriptural narrative.[7] Genesis 1:1–2:3 has, of course, been the focus of debate about its genre and content, and not just in the modern age. In the shadow of Neoplatonism, Augustine returned to the opening chapters of Genesis some five times as an author, recognizing their centrality but also their mysterious depths.

> As Fiedorowicz notes, "The effort to think through the mystery of creation runs like a leitmotif through Augustine's work."[a] Over nearly thirty years Augustine wrote five commentaries on Genesis 1–2. For Augustine, the fact of creation was undeniable: "Earth and the heavens are before our eyes. The very fact that they are there proclaims that they were created."[b] The challenge for him was how to understand this: "Let me hear and understand the meaning of the words: In the Beginning you made heaven and earth."[c] Augustine never ceased listening so as to understand these words. He worked on *The Literal Meaning of Genesis* for some fifteen years; it was finally published in 416 and represents his mature thought.
>
> Fiedorowicz notes of Augustine's *Literal Meaning*, "A milestone was reached in the interpretation of Genesis when Augustine recognized that the spreading of God's work over six days was simply a literary garb and that the author did not intend to give a scientific description of the act of creation."[d] In his mature work Augustine argues that

[6]Palmer Robertson defines a covenant as "a bond in blood sovereignly administered" (*The Christ of the Covenants* [Phillipsburg, NJ: P&R, 1980], 4; emphasis removed). The blood aspect is, of course, not present in Gen 1 since it is prefall. However, the bond and sovereign administration are clearly present.

[7]See Gordon J. Wenham, *Genesis 1-15*, WBC 1 (Dallas: Word, 1987), 5-10; J. L'Hour, *Génesis 1-11: Los pasos de la humanidad sobre la tierra*, Cuaderno bíblico 161 (Estella, Spain: Editorial Verbo Divino, 2013).

God's act of creation is simultaneous and the days are not time periods but categories for teaching purposes.

[a]H. Fiedorowicz, "General Introduction," in *On Genesis*, by Augustine, trans. Edmund Hill, ed. John E. Rotelle (Hyde Park, NY: New City Press, 2002), 13.
[b]Augustine, *Confessions* 11.4.
[c]Augustine, *Confessions* 11.3.
[d]Fiedorowicz, "General Introduction," 166.

In recent decades scholars have ranged in assessing the genre of Genesis 1 from that of wisdom (Blocher),[8] to a poetic narrative shaped for liturgical use (Brueggemann),[9] to "not a narrative, but a didactic poem" (Ricoeur),[10] and so on. Barth classifies it as *saga*, "in the sense of an intuitive and poetic picture of a pre-historical reality of history which is enacted once and for all within the confines of time and space."[11] In our view it is probably impossible to be precise about the genre, not least because of its unique kerygma. As one approaches Genesis 1, the following elements need to be taken into account.

First, most importantly, Genesis 1 must be seen as the first act in the drama of Scripture, in which the stage is set for all that follows. In this respect "creation is the beginning of history, its initial event."[12] Genesis 1 tells of the coming into existence of the creation and therefore is clearly *narrative*. Westermann, contra Ricoeur above, rightly says, "Gen 1:1–2:4a is a narrative. Even if this description needs to be modified quite a bit, it must nevertheless be the starting point."[13]

Second, we should recognize that Genesis 1 was written by an Israelite for the Old Testament people of God, and therefore we need to read it, at least initially, in their context.

Third, as many scholars including Barth have recognized, Israel was exposed through its history to a variety of creation stories, and its story is told in the context of these other stories. There are areas of agreement, but, more importantly, at many points Genesis 1 is polemical against other ancient Near Eastern views of creation and of the world, as we will see.

[8]Henri Blocher, *In the Beginning: The Opening Chapters of Genesis*, trans. David G. Preston (Leicester, UK: Inter-Varsity Press, 1984).
[9]Walter Brueggemann, *Genesis*, Interpretation (Atlanta: Westminster John Knox, 1982), 22.
[10]Ricoeur in André LaCocque and Paul Ricoeur, *Thinking Biblically: Exegetical and Hermeneutical Studies*, trans. David Pellauer (Chicago: University of Chicago Press, 1998), 36.
[11]Barth, *CD* III/1, 81.
[12]LaCocque and Ricoeur, *Thinking Biblically*, 5.
[13]Claus Westermann, *Genesis 1–11: A Commentary*, trans. John J. Scullion (Minneapolis: Augsburg, 1984), 80.

Fourth, it needs to be recognized that Genesis 1 is carefully crafted Hebrew *literature*,[14] and we will hear its powerful message as we attend to its literary shape and poetics rather than by starting with our twenty-first-century scientific questions, which it does indeed address indirectly but was certainly not designed to answer by its human author. Genesis as a book is divided up by its תלדות headings, and it is important to note that Genesis 1:1–2:3, in our view, stands outside these "historical" markers as the introduction to Genesis and the Pentateuch, indeed to the entire Bible. The first occurrence of תלדות is in Genesis 2:4, and we read this as the heading *for what follows*.[15]

Fifth, Genesis 1 is not only the first act in the drama of Scripture but also the first act in the annals of history. God called forth something from nothing, thereby creating not only an ordered world of humans, animals, and inanimate matter but also history itself. Genesis 1, rightly understood, is thus also *historical*.

Genesis 1:1–2:3 divides up naturally into eight sections, with Genesis 1:1-2 as the introduction. The refrain "And there was evening and there was morning, the *x* day" divides up the rest of the section into seven parts or days. The refrain is not found in day seven, on which God rested (Gen 2:1-3).

Genesis 1:1: Heading, Summary, First Act?

Genesis 1:1 continues to generate debate as to how best to translate it, as discussed above, where we argued for the traditional translation. Familiarity should not prevent us from reflecting on the radicality of this verse. In the Hebrew the first word is "In the beginning."[16] Contrary to the thought of Aristotle and many others, matter is not eternal. This verse takes us back to the point of origin of the entire creation; unlike God, who has no beginning, the creation is ushered into existence by God. Part of this beginning is the creation of time, as we will see, so that *this* "beginning" is absolute and "utterly unique,"[17] pregnant with mystery. It pushes us back into the life and will of God, who sovereignly and freely decided to bring the creation into existence. Dietrich Bonhoeffer rightly notes, "The place where the Bible begins is one where our own most impassioned waves of thinking break, are thrown back upon themselves, and lose their

---

[14]Cf. L'Hour, *Génesis 1–11*, chap. 3.

[15]Cf. Wenham, *Genesis 1–15*, 49.

[16]Barth notes of "in the beginning" that it tells us that "with this beginning it also looks to an end" (*CD* III/1, 99).

[17]Dietrich Bonhoeffer, *Creation and Fall: A Theological Exposition of Genesis 1–3*, ed. John W. De Gruchy, trans. Douglas S. Bax, Dietrich Bonhoeffer Works 3 (Minneapolis: Fortress, 1997), 32.

strength in spray and foam."[18] Bonhoeffer, as well as Russell R. Reno, note, therefore, that we must be cautious of thinking of creation *temporally*—as Bonhoeffer says, "We can always go back behind a temporal beginning"—and rather conceive of it *substantively* in terms of source and basis.[19]

Ricoeur resists the idea that Genesis 1–2 teaches an absolute beginning, and he prefers to speak of "multiple beginnings."[a] Ricoeur acknowledges that Genesis 1 appears to point in this direction but maintains that the distinction between absolute and relative is alien to Hebraic culture, as it was to other ancient Near Eastern cultures. According to Ricoeur,

> This paradox of a multiplicity of founding events confirms my initial comment concerning the prejudices belied by the biblical Creation narratives. It is never a question of a Creation *ex nihilo*, the beginning is not unique by definition, and a first event cannot be represented by a point in a line. These events have a temporal thickness that calls for the unfolding of a narrative.[b]

Ricoeur's discussion is wonderfully stimulating, but it rests on the documentary hypothesis and subverts the central role of Genesis 1 in teaching an absolute beginning. We will look more closely at *creatio ex nihilo* below; suffice it here to note that we affirm that the doctrine of creation requires a narrative, and one, indeed, that embodies a "temporal thickness," but in our view Genesis 1:1–2:3 teaches, *through narrative*, an absolute beginning.

[a]André LaCocque and Paul Ricoeur, *Thinking Biblically: Exegetical and Hermeneutical Studies*, trans. David Pellauer (Chicago: University of Chicago Press, 1998), 35.
[b]Ibid., 49.

The second word in Genesis 1:1 is "he created" (ברא), indicating that creation is a free act of the divine will.

ברא has been thought to indicate *creatio ex nihilo*. This is not necessarily the case, although in our view *creatio ex nihilo* is implied in Genesis 1:1. ברא in the Old Testament always has God as its subject. The products of ברא are humankind (Gen 1:27), unexpected novelties (Num 16:30; Is 65:17), the sea monsters (Gen 1:21), mountains (Amos 4:13), animals (Ps 104:30), and Israel (Is 43:15). As Numbers 16:30, for example, clearly demonstrates, ברא does not necessarily connote *creatio ex nihilo*. Stek concludes his judicious examination of ברא as follows: "While *bara'* had evidently come to be a specialized term in that it was used exclusively of God and refers to bringing something 'new' into being, *it is silent as to the utilization of pre-existent materials or the time . . . or the means involved*. In biblical language, *bara'* affirms of some existent reality *only that God conceived, willed and effected it*."[a]

[18]Ibid., 25.
[19]Ibid., 32; Russell R. Reno, *Genesis* (Grand Rapids, MI: Baker Academic, 2010), 35, 38.

Stek relates this range of usage to the Old Testament's holding of *creatio* and *creatio continua* closely together.[b] Schmidt more positively points out that while ברא does not explicitly denote *creatio ex nihilo*, it retains the same idea—namely, "God's effortless, totally free and unbound creating, his sovereignty."[c]

Ricoeur is adamant that "before the Hellenistic era, the notion of Creation *ex nihilo* was unknown. Or, rather, the question to which this answer corresponds had not yet been posed."[d] Some find in 2 Maccabees 7:28 the first clear articulation of the doctrine, but this is contested. In his examination of its history, May says, "To be sure, it corresponds factually with the Old Testament proclamation about creation, but as a theory it is not yet present in the Old Testament."[e] May argues that *creatio ex nihilo* was forged in the second century AD in the confrontation between the church fathers and Gnosticism. A crucial question is whether *creatio ex nihilo* does indeed correspond factually with the Old Testament.

Intertextuality may help here. Fishbane rightly notes the close links between Isaiah's theology of creation and Genesis 1:1–2:3.[f] However, for Fishbane, "Deutero-Isaiah provides a spiritualizing polemic against a variety of notions embedded in the creation account of Gen 1:1–2:4."[g] On this reading, a central concern of Deutero-Isaiah, in the context of Persian influence, was the status of preexistent matter such as "waste and void" and "darkness." Intriguingly, Fishbane argues, contra Ricoeur, that in the context of Persian influence the ontological status of preexistent matter would have been of concern. "The God of Israel is, the prophet argues in language targeted toward Gen. 1, the only god; and primal matter was utilized in a structured form: it never had the status of a restive or unformed chaos."[h] In our view Isaiah is in line with Genesis 1 rather than polemically set against it. Isaiah 45:7 alerts us to the good character of darkness as created, and Isaiah 45:18 fits with God's forming "waste and void" into a habitable environment. Furthermore, in our view, Isaiah severely undercuts any view of creation from preexisting matter. Isaiah 45:7, for example, is quite clear that God creates darkness.

[a]Howard J. Van Till et al., *Portraits of Creation: Biblical and Scientific Perspectives on the World's Formation* (Grand Rapids, MI: Eerdmans, 1990), 207-13, here 213.
[b]Ibid., 211.
[c]H. H. Schmid, *Gerechtigkeit als Weltordnung*, Beitraega zur Historischen Theologie 40 (Tübingen: J. C. B. Mohr, 1968), 166-67.
[d]André LaCocque and Paul Ricoeur, *Thinking Biblically: Exegetical and Hermeneutical Studies*, trans. David Pellauer (Chicago: University of Chicago Press, 1998), 34.
[e]Gerhard May, *Creatio Ex Nihilo: The Doctrine of "Creation Out of Nothing" in Early Christian Thought*, trans. A. S. Worrall (London: T&T Clark, 2004), xi.
[f]Michael A. Fishbane, *Biblical Interpretation in Ancient Israel* (New York: Oxford University Press, 1985), 325-26.
[g]Ibid., 325.
[h]Ibid.

Barth rightly notes,

As the subject *Elohim* points to the sum and Lord of all divine powers, so the predicate *bara'* points to the creative act whose subject can only be this *Elohim*

> and whose nature that which corresponds to this *Elohim*, i.e., a pure act of creativity, unhindered by any opposition, unlimited by any presupposition, not requiring the co-operation of any other agent and excluding any idea either of the co-operation of a pre-existent reality or of conflict against it.[20]

The object of God's creation is "the heavens and the earth." There is debate as to whether this is God's first act of creation or whether it is a summary of all that follows in Genesis 1:1–2:3. In our opinion it functions *in both ways*, as a summary of the whole *and* as the lead-in to Genesis 1:2. In this opening section of Genesis, 1:1 is the only place we find the word "heavens" (*haššāmayim*) until Genesis 2:1. "Earth" occurs several times, although as a differentiated place it only appears on the third day (Gen 1:9). "The heavens and the earth" is a spatial expression in which the two extremes of creation—heaven and earth—are invoked to refer to the totality of the creation. In this sense Genesis 1:1 is indeed a summary of the whole.

Augustine poses the question, "And why is it put like this: *In the beginning God made heaven and earth*, and not like this: *In the beginning God said, Let heaven and earth be made; and heaven and earth were made*, in the same way as the account of light is given: *God said, Let light be made; and light was made*?"[a] Augustine suggests various reasons for this and prefers the view that creation by the Word would not fit with the incompleteness and imperfection of Genesis 1:2. However, by asking the question in this way, he alerts us to the vital difference between Genesis 1:1 and the following sentences, all beginning with *wĕ* (and). Wenham suggests that "earth" may have different meanings in verses 1 and 2.[b] In our view the meaning is the same but the function different. In verse 1 "earth" as the lower extremity functions within a merism, whereas in verse 2 the lower extremity itself is the focus.

[a]Augustine, *Literal Meaning* 1.3.8, in Augustine, *On Genesis: A Refutation of the Manichees, Unfinished Literal Commentary on Genesis, the Literal Meaning of Genesis*, ed. John E. Rotelle, trans. Edmund Hill (Hyde Park, NY: New City Press, 2005).
[b]Gordon J. Wenham, *Genesis 1–15*, WBC 1 (Dallas: Word, 1987), 15.

In the Old Testament "heaven(s)" can refer to the abode of God as well as to the sky.[21] Barth is adamant that "the heavens" is the abode of God, "this highest and proper heaven," although he acknowledges that there is no further

[20]Barth, *CD* III/1, 99-100.
[21]For a detailed discussion of "Der Himmel" in the Old Testament, see Cornelis Houtman, *Der Himmel im Alten Testament: Israels Weltbild und Weltanschauung*, Oudtestamentische studiën 30 (Leiden: Brill, 1993). Houtman proposes seeing "heaven and earth" as a dynamic bipolarity with humankind at one end and God at the other, and with God as dominant.

reference to it in what follows.[22] In this view "the heavens" refers to the invisible realm including the abode of God, all of which is created at this point. Thus Genesis 1:1 would refer to the origin of the angelic realm as well as the earthly realm. Rather than "the heavens," Genesis 1 uses "the sky" in the rest of the chapter, and this supports Barth's view.

Additional support for this view is found in the parallels between the cosmology of Genesis 1:1–2:3 and ancient Near Eastern cosmology, in which Yahweh reigns from above the upper waters. In the Bible it is common to refer to God's abode as heaven, so that, as elsewhere in the Bible, Genesis 1:1 teaches a two-realms theology—namely, that of heaven (the upper realm) and that of the earth (the lower realm). "The heavens" functions with "the earth" as a spatial expression for the whole of creation, including God's abode.

Genesis 1:1 thus introduces us to creation as *ordered into particular places*, here at its most basic level, *heaven and earth*. Knierim refers to this as "creation as structured by cosmic space."[23] He rightly notes that the idea of creation as *structured place* (he uses the word *space*) is found not only in Genesis 1 but also in the Wisdom literature, in the prophetic literature, and particularly in the Psalter. Knierim notes that the Old Testament vocabulary of חק (statute), חכמה (wisdom), and צדק / צדקה (righteousness) also speaks of Yahweh's world order.[24]

The bipartite differentiation of creation is deeply embedded in the Yahweh-traditions; indeed, "we must assert that Israel perceived creation as a structured unity because of Yahweh the creator, and not apart from or in spite of him. It saw Yahweh and the structure of the world as being related in an ultimate way in which the unity of creation was just as important for the creator as the oneness of the creator was for the creation."[25]

> Genesis 1:1–2:3 raises the issue of Israel's world picture (*Weltbild*). Certainly in this opening salvo of the biblical narrative, Israel's cosmology shares much in common with ancient Near Eastern accounts, as Keel and Schroer have shown.[a] Keel and Schroer reconstruct the Israelite image of the world—"no complete iconographic Israelite image of the world, like those of Egypt and Mesopotamia, has survived."[b]

---

[22]Barth, *CD* III/1, 101. Augustine (*Literal Meaning* 1.1.2) agrees; cf. *Confessions* 12.13: "Heaven here means the Heaven of Heavens—that is, the intellectual heaven" (trans. R. S. Pine-Coffin [New York: Penguin, 1961]).

[23]Rolf P. Knierim, *The Task of Old Testament Theology: Substance, Method, and Cases* (Grand Rapids, MI: Eerdmans, 1995), 186.

[24]Ibid., 199-202.

[25]Ibid., 187.

Yahweh inhabits the heavens above the waters, as well as the temple. "God's action and order dominate the space between heaven and earth."[c] However, Keel and Schroer are adamant that

> people in the ancient Near East did not conceive of the earth as a disk floating on water with the firmament inverted over it like a bell jar, with the stars hanging from it. They knew from observation and experience with handicrafts that the lifting capacity of water is limited and that gigantic vaults generate problems in terms of their ability to carry dead weight. The textbook images that keep being reprinted of the "ancient Near Eastern world picture" are based on typical modern misunderstandings that fail to take into account the religious components of ancient Near Eastern conceptions and representations.[d]

Houtman argues that Israel had no one *Weltbild*, since its various descriptions of the cosmos cannot be harmonized into a single picture, but it did have a worldview (*Weltanschauung*) in that it ascribed the origin and existence of the world to Yahweh.[e]

---

[a]Othmar Keel, *The Symbolism of the Biblical World: Ancient Near Eastern Iconography and the Book of Psalms*, trans. Timothy J. Hallett (Winona Lake, IN: Eisenbrauns, 1997), 15-60; Othmar Keel and Silvia Schroer, *Creation: Biblical Theologies in the Context of the Ancient Near East*, trans. Peter T. Daniels (Winona Lake, IN: Eisenbrauns, 2015), 78-84.
[b]Keel and Schroer, *Creation*, 83.
[c]Keel, *Symbolism*, 27.
[d]Keel and Schroer, *Creation*, 78.
[e]Cornelis Houtman, *Der Himmel im Alten Testament: Israels Weltbild und Weltanschauung*, Oudtestamentische studiën 30 (Leiden: Brill, 1993).

Knierim says the following of the phrase "heaven and earth":[26]

- It always implies a spatial view of our world and implies a basic need to distinguish heaven from earth. This need arises because earth receives its order in relation to heaven.
- Earth is viewed as the abode of humans, whereas heaven is the place of God.
- "The cosmological polarity of heaven and earth provides the spatial realms for the tension between Yahweh's universal kingdom and universal human history. . . . It expresses in nuclear form the foundational concern of the Old Testament . . . the concern for the meaning of God's creation as universal cosmic order, especially in view of the acute threat to this order arising from humans on earth."[27]

We asserted above that Genesis 1:1 is a heading and summary of Genesis 1:1–2:3 as well as the lead-in to Genesis 1:2 and following. The link

---

[26]Ibid., 187-91.
[27]Ibid., 191.

between verse 1 and verse 2 is "the earth," clearly referring back to verse 1. It should be noted that after verse 1 every subsequent verse in this section begins with the conjunction *wĕ*, indicating the flow of the narrative. The common meaning of *wĕ* is "and," although Hebrew scholars rightly recognize that it can have a variety of nuances such as "but" (adversative *wĕ*) and "now." As Walter Ong has pointed out, however, in a literary-oral culture such as Israel was, it is unlikely that some of the detailed nuances attributed to *wĕ* in Genesis 1 would ever have occurred to Israelites listening to this narrative.[28] In Genesis 1:2 *wĕ* indicates a link with Genesis 1:1, to be translated either as "and" or "now," but in terms of the relationship "the earth" is the connecting element. In our view, verse 2 should thus be understood as referring to the initial creation—not preexisting matter—before it went through the process of formation to become our recognizable world. As Luther notes, "He [God] first creates the rudiments of heaven and earth, but these as yet unfashioned, and waste and void, with no life or growth or shape or form."[29]

Barth adamantly rejects this interpretation. Inter alia, he appeals to Isaiah 45:18, which does indeed state that God did not create the earth *tōhû*, the latter being the same word used in Genesis 1:2. However, the parallel expression in Isaiah 45:18 is instructive in this respect—namely, "he [God] formed it to be inhabited." There is thus no contradiction between our reading of Genesis 1:2 and Isaiah 45:18, since from our perspective the *tōhû* and *bōhû* of verse 2 refer to the pre-*habitable* creation—that is, the initial creation before it was ordered and formed by God.

> In his *Confessions* Augustine says, "For you, O Lord, made the world from formless matter, which you created out of nothing."[a] Augustine argues that this "formless matter" was prior as a source but not prior in time, since creation was simultaneous.[b] Thomas Aquinas notes that the Fathers differ on this issue, and central to the differences is how "formless" is understood. He notes Augustine's view but then says, "But the other holy writers understand by formlessness, not the exclusion of all form, but the absence of that beauty and comeliness which are now apparent in the corporeal creation."[c] From this perspective "the earth was void" or *invisible* in that the waters covered it, and *empty* in that it was unadorned.
>
> [a]Augustine, *Confessions* 12.8, trans. R. S. Pine-Coffin.
> [b]Augustine, *Literal Meaning* 1.14.28.
> [c]Thomas Aquinas, *ST* Ia, 66.

[28]Walter Ong, *Orality and Literacy*, 2nd ed. (New York: Routledge, 2002), 37-38.

[29]Luther, *Sermon on Genesis*, 1527, in *D. Martin Luthers Werke: Kritische Gesammtausgabe*, 24, 25, 24, quoted in Barth, *CD* III/1, 103.

Barth, however, argues,

> Our only option is to consider v. 2 as a portrait, deliberately taken from myth, of the world which according to His revelation was negated, rejected, ignored and left behind in His actual creation, i.e., in the utterance of His Word; and to which there necessarily belongs also the "Spirit of *Elohim*" who is not known in His reality and therefore hovers and broods over it impotently because wordlessly.[30]

For Barth, Genesis 1:2 presents a world over which the Word of God has not been uttered, a monstrous chaos, which represents the shadow side of creation to which God says, "No!" The Spirit of God[31]—"a divine power which is not that of the creative Word"[32]—hovers over the waters but cannot rectify this lack, but only serves to foreground it more clearly: "It belongs to the very nature and essence of such a sphere that in it even the Spirit of *Elohim* is condemned to the complete impotence of a bird hovering or brooding over shoreless or sterile waters."[33] In this way verse 2 alerts us to the risk God takes in creating.[34]

In our view Barth's is a creative but unconvincing interpretation.[35] The *wĕ* with which Genesis 1:2 begins links it into the narrative chain that extends to the end of Genesis 2:3, and there is nothing that demarcates it as the sort of aside we find in Barth's reading. We agree with Barth that the *ruah Elohim* is the Spirit of God but resist the view that this is a divine power *not that of the Word*. Irons and Kline rightly note, "The Spirit is hovering over the formless void to fashion it into an orderly cosmos."[36] Indeed, in our view Barth's reading raises the unhelpful possibility of a dualism of evil and good present in the beginning. Barth, of course, denies this, but it is a fair implication of his reading.

> Augustine learned from a Syrian Christian, probably Saint Ephrem (d. 373), that מרחפת in Genesis 1:2 could mean "brooding over the water in the way birds brood over their

[30]Barth, *CD* III/1, 108.

[31]Barth, *CD* III/1, 107. Barth rightly argues that the *ruah Elohim* is not just a mighty wind but the Spirit of God.

[32]Barth, *CD* III/1, 108.

[33]Barth, *CD* III/1, 107.

[34]Barth, *CD* III/1, 109.

[35]Cf. Craig G. Bartholomew, "Genesis 1:2 and the Doctrine of Creation," in *Acts of Interpretation: Scripture, Theology, and Culture*, ed. Stephen A. Cummins and Jens Zimmerman (Grand Rapids, MI: Eerdmans, 2018), 83-99.

[36]Lee Irons and Meredith G. Kline, "The Framework View," in *The Genesis Debate: Three Views on the Days of Creation*, ed. David G. Hagopian (Mission Viejo, CA: Crux Press, 2001), 242. Cf. Barth, *CD* III/1, 240.

eggs, where that warmth of the mother's body in some way also supports the forming of the chicks through a kind of influence of her own kind of love."[a] He connects this with Luke 13:34, in which Jesus expresses his longing to gather Jerusalem under his wings as a hen gathers her chicks. Kuyper adopts a similar view and asserts, "The figure implies that not only the earth existed but also the germs of life within it; and that the Holy Spirit impregnating these germs caused the life to come forth in order to lead it to its destiny."[b]

Many modern interpreters see Genesis 1:2 as a description of the primeval chaos and translate רוח אלהים as "a mighty wind" (so von Rad, Speiser, Schmidt, Westermann). Wenham opts for "the Wind of God" as a vivid image of the Spirit of God.[c] As Wenham notes, reading אלהים as a superlative is unlikely in this chapter, and nowhere else in the Old Testament does רוח אלהים mean a "mighty wind."[d] רוח אלהים must refer to some attribute or action of אלהים. But which one? Deuteronomy 32:11 is the only other place in the Old Testament where the Piel stem of רחף (hover and tremble) is used, here of an eagle hovering over its young as a picture of God's care and guidance of Israel in the wilderness. Intriguingly, in the description of the wilderness the word תהו is found in Deuteronomy 32:10, one of the two words used in Genesis 1:2 for the state of the earth. NRSV translates, "He sustained him . . . in a howling wilderness waste." One cannot be certain, but in our view this image from Deuteronomy 32 fits well with Genesis 1:2. God is present by his Spirit in his courteous and living way, and the Spirit hovers creatively over the formless earth in preparation for God's formative work in turning the "wilderness" into a habitable environment. There is also the possibility of an intertextual allusion to Genesis 1:2 in Deuteronomy 32, implying that God's formation of Israel is related to and akin to a new creation.

[a]Augustine, *Literal Meaning* 1.18.36, in Augustine, *On Genesis: A Refutation of the Manichees, Unfinished Literal Commentary on Genesis, the Literal Meaning of Genesis*, ed. John E. Rotelle, trans. Edmund Hill (Hyde Park, NY: New City Press, 2005).

[b]Abraham Kuyper, *The Work of the Holy Spirit*, trans. H. De Vries (Grand Rapids, MI: Eerdmans, 1900), 30.

[c]Gordon J. Wenham, *Genesis 1–15*, WBC 1 (Dallas: Word, 1987), 2.

[d]Ibid., 17.

Table 5.1. The days of creation

DAY 1 *Light—day/night*	DAY 4 *Lights in the sky*
DAY 2 *Waters, dome—sky*	DAY 5 *Sea creatures, birds*
DAY 3 *Waters gathered, dry land, plants*	DAY 6 *Animals, humankind*
DAY 7 *God rests*	

As table 5.1 indicates, there is clearly a correlation between days one and four, two and five, and three and six. Augustine already recognized some kind of correlation between the days.[37] Indeed, the correlation is sufficiently strong to provide support for the so-called framework hypothesis.[38] It was the Dutch theologian Arie Noordzij who introduced the triad approach,[39] which has since been developed by Kline and others into the framework approach. According to Noordzij,

- Days one to three deal with the creation kingdoms (light; sky/seas; land/vegetation)
- Days four to six deal with the creature kings (luminaries; sea creatures/winged creatures; land animals/men)

Whether or not it is right to call the main characters of days four through six "creature kings," there is clearly a relationship between the creation of light on day one and the luminaries of day four; between the two places of the waters and the sky (day two) and their inhabitants, the sea creatures and the birds (day five); and between land and plants (day three) and animals and humankind (day six). We will explore this in more detail below.

The days—creation of our time. We have already noted how the refrain "there was evening and there was morning, the *x* day" structures Genesis 1:1–2:3 and noted the correlation between days one through three and four through six. At one level, as Barth rightly insists, twenty-four-hour days are clearly in view, as expressed in typically Jewish fashion: "it was evening and it was morning." But on another level, the point of the "days" is not to teach us that God ushered the world into existence in six consecutive periods of twenty-four hours. As we will see throughout this chapter, the point of the days is to teach us about creation's order and about humanity's role under God's kingship. Genesis 1 literally and truthfully teaches that God created time and did so before the appearance of humans, but its point is not to provide modern scientific data about the time frame within which God created the world. God's creation of time precedes humans, who are therefore always timed creatures, and this alerts us to the validity in Heidegger's concept

---

[37]Augustine, *Literal Meaning* 2.13.26; cf. 4.1.1-5, 14 on his number symbolism.

[38]Cf. Irons and Kline, "Framework View."

[39]Arie Noordzij, *God's Word en der Eeuwen Getuigenis: Het Oude Testament in het Licht der Oostersche Opgravingen* (Kampen: University of Utrecht, 1924). N. H. Ridderbos translated parts of Noordzij's work in *Is There a Conflict Between Genesis 1 and Natural Science?* (Grand Rapids, MI: Eerdmans, 1957).

of *Dasein*, his way of articulating that humans are always already thrown into the world and find themselves amidst history. Of course, for Heidegger there is a shadow side to this, with death always beckoning as the outer boundary of *Dasein*, whereas here in Genesis 1, time—we are reminded repeatedly—is fundamentally a good thing.

Augustine recognizes the *narrative* genre of Genesis 1 and says that because of this genre "one thing had to be mentioned before the other, although God made each of them, as we have said, simultaneously."[a]

> So then, God did not in fact say, "Let this or that creature be made" every single time that the phrase is repeated in this book, *And God said*. It was one Word, after all, that he begot, in which he said all things before they were made singly; but the scriptural style comes down to the level of the little ones and adjusts itself to their capacity by putting before them each single kind of creature one by one, and then looking back at the eternal formula of each kind in the Word of God.[b]

He argues that "evening" indicates a finished work.[c]

In Genesis 1 the creation of place/space precedes the introduction of time, although time is implied by "in the beginning." Clearly history, and more particularly the history of God's involvement with Israel, is central to the entire Bible, but how do we recover the integrality of creation order and history? Few biblical scholars have wrestled with this as closely as Knierim.[d] Knierim says, "The totality of reality was not perceived by Israel under the category of history alone."[e] Indeed, "one may question whether an appropriate understanding of Israel's concept of history is possible without a sufficient understanding of Israel's concept of reality."[f] Yahweh is the criterion for history and not history the criterion for Yahweh's presence in the world. Knierim maintains that Israel "encountered Yahweh as the crisis of history," and history is not the theater for the revelation of God's glory but "the realm in which the struggle for the meaning of creation is waged."[g]

History is notoriously difficult to define, as is time, as Augustine noted. A way into this discussion is to begin with history writing as a form of narrative. In history writing events and actions are plotted within a narrative in order to makes sense of a period, an event, and so on. Ricoeur helpfully distinguishes three forms of mimesis involved in narrative emplotment.[h] For our purposes, Mimesis 1 is the most interesting, for this is the prenarrative grounding of Mimesis 2 (narrative emplotment) in reality. Does reality itself have a narrative shape, or is that imposed on it by narrators? In practice, of course, humans continually impose their narratives on the creation; nevertheless, it is clear from the whole of the Bible that there is a narrative dimension built into the creation so that creation order is far from static but contains within it the potential for historical development. There is, in other words, order *for history,* for development, for unfolding, and so on. The possibility and actuality of history is *part of* God's good order for creation.

Westermann alerts us to the importance of Genesis 5 in this respect.[i] He reads Genesis 5 as the continuation of the account in Genesis 1:1–2:4a. Readers may wonder what a *genealogical* chapter such as this has to do with history; for Westermann, rightly, a great deal. The two basic elements in Genesis 5 are the recurrence of the same vocabulary and the variable, the names and numbers. Westermann notes,

> By presenting the very beginning of the history of humankind within this framework, P is pointing out that at its roots and in all its phases and forms the constant and the variable are there and intermeshed. The person's state as a creature and its consequences form the constant, the names and the numbers the variable.
>
> This is basic and decisive for the understanding of history. The western view of history considers only the variables to be constitutive. . . . P . . . is saying that history never consists merely in historically demonstrable processes, developments and an apparently unique course of events. Rather, there are at work in every event elements of the stable, always and everywhere the same, which are common to all humankind at all times and which render questionable a science of history that prescinds from these constants.[j]

Although we would not assign these texts to a separate author or source (P), Westermann rightly notes that what we call the cultural mandate is being carried out in Genesis 5. "P is saying here that the plan of God in creating human beings is spelling itself out. . . . The power of the blessing shows itself effective in the relentless rhythm and steady succession of generations that stretch out across time."[k]

---

[a]Augustine, *Literal Meaning* 1.15.29, in Augustine, *On Genesis: A Refutation of the Manichees, Unfinished Literal Commentary on Genesis, the Literal Meaning of Genesis*, ed. John E. Rotelle, trans. Edmund Hill (Hyde Park, NY: New City Press, 2005).
[b]Augustine, *Literal Meaning* 2.6.13.
[c]Augustine, *Literal Meaning* 1.17.35.
[d]Rolf P. Knierim, *The Task of Old Testament Theology: Substance, Method, and Cases* (Grand Rapids, MI: Eerdmans, 1995), 171-75, 185-213.
[e]Ibid., 172.
[f]Ibid., 173.
[g]Ibid., 175.
[h]Paul Ricoeur, *Time and Narrative*, 3 vols., trans. Kathleen McLaughlin and David Pellauer (Chicago: University of Chicago Press, 1984–1988).
[i]Claus Westermann, *Genesis 1–11: A Commentary*, trans. John J. Scullion (Minneapolis: Augsburg, 1984), 347-48.
[j]Ibid., 347.
[k]Ibid., 348.

Creation by Word: The Let There Be's

Throughout Genesis 1 we find repeated "And God said . . ." and "Let there be . . ." This alerts us, at least in Genesis 1, to the primacy of creation by word. Of course there are other verbs used for God's creative activity (*bara'*, *'asah*, *natan*, *hibdil*, etc.), but Barth notes that when the author uses these other words, "he is not describing actions which have to be distinguished from *'amar* [he said], but paraphrasing *'amar* in the efficacy proper to it only at this point."[40] "Paraphrasing" might be a bit strong, but the point is that creation by word and divine fiat is central to Genesis 1 and is picked up elsewhere in the Bible (Ps 33:6, 9; 148:5; Amos 9:6; Is 41:4; Heb 11:3; etc.). In Isaiah 48, quoted at the outset of this chapter, we find together the metaphors of laying, spreading out, and summoning. Where we need to be cautious is in discerning a verbal and thus ontological connection between creation by word and creation by *the Word* as in John 1. Augustine pursues this route, arguing that by "*Let it be made*, we should understand an incorporeal utterance of God in the substance of his co-eternal Word."[41] There is, however, nothing magical or ontological about creation by "word," and it is rare in the New Testament for Christ to be referred to as "the Word." The point of creation by fiat in the ancient Near Eastern context is that the world is not created *from* God but *by* God,[42] and the divine fiat reflects his majesty and omnipotence: "Nowhere is the real power of a master so fully apparent as in his commandment which is obeyed."[43]

The royal authority of God evident in the power of his word is a central covenantal theme in Genesis 1. Of course, God's royal authority far exceeds that of any treaty king. He speaks, and the creation takes shape before him. The point of the "Let there be's" is that the emerging shape or structure of the creation corresponds precisely to God's design for it. In Genesis 1:1 we see an initial fundamental ordering in the distinction between heaven and earth. In the rest of Genesis 1 we have a *progressive differentiation* of the creation,[44] albeit with new elements such as light introduced. This differentiation is particularly evident in the works of "separation" (*hibdil*),

---

[40]Barth, *CD* III/1, 111.

[41]Augustine, *Literal Meaning* 1.4.9, in Augustine, *On Genesis: A Refutation of the Manichees, Unfinished Literal Commentary on Genesis, the Literal Meaning of Genesis*, ed. John E. Rotelle, trans. Edmund Hill (Hyde Park, NY: New City Press, 2005).

[42]Barth, *CD* III/1, 114.

[43]Walther Zimmerli, quoted in Barth, *CD* III/1, 111. Cf. the self-descriptions of Elijah and Elijah as standing before Yahweh, an image for being called and obeying.

[44]Cf. Edward S. Casey, *Getting Back into Place: Toward a Renewed Understanding of the Place-World* (Bloomington: Indiana University Press, 1993), and Craig G. Bartholomew, *Where Mortals Dwell: A Christian View of Place for Today* (Grand Rapids, MI: Baker Academic, 2011), 10-12.

specifically mentioned in Genesis 1:4, 6, 14, 18, but also implied in many other parts of the chapter.[45]

Philosophically we encounter here a form of *realism*. The world is given a discernible shape by God, a shape that he finds good and finally very good. This is worth stressing amidst some of the extremes to which social constructivism has gone in our day. Humans have significant freedom, as we will see, but only as creatures within the creation. Berkouwer thus rightly observes that all of human life is a response to God in one way or another.[46] Genesis 1 repeatedly stresses that "God saw" and "it was good." This encourages the reader to see the world similarly.

> Augustine discerns in God's activity of creation "a supreme and holy and just courtesy and a kind of love in his activity which comes not from any need on his part but from generosity."[a] God's seeing that what he made is good signifies that he takes pleasure in his creation and that it pleased him that it should be made. We should follow God's example.
>
> [a]Augustine, *Literal Meaning* 1.5.10-12, in Augustine, *On Genesis: A Refutation of the Manichees, Unfinished Literal Commentary on Genesis, the Literal Meaning of Genesis*, ed. John E. Rotelle, trans. Edmund Hill (Hyde Park, NY: New City Press, 2005).

The "Let there be" and "It was so" phrases also provide the basis for the doctrine of creation order of which humans form a part. The world is shaped in accordance with God's word and is held in shape in this way. Within the Kuyperian tradition we speak in this respect of creational law and order, according to which life is normed by God. Some laws we simply *have to* obey, such as gravity. Other norms, such as not eating from the tree of the knowledge of good and evil, we are free to obey or disobey.

Days one and four: Light and luminaries. In retrospect, it is not surprising that God first creates light, since this forms a contrast with *the darkness* covering the face of the deep. Barth rightly says that what is referred to here is natural light and natural darkness, but he regards the darkness as "that which declares the reality which was rejected," relating this back to his reading of Genesis 1:2.[47] He makes much of the fact that only the light and not the darkness is called "good" in Genesis 1:4. In our view this is a mistake. Darkness already exists in verse 2, and hence it is not something new that is now created,

[45]On this theme, see Paul Beauchamp, *Création et Séparation: Étude Exégélique du Chapitre Premier de La Genèse* (Paris: Desclée, 1969).
[46]Berkouwer, *Man: The Image of God*, 59.
[47]Barth, *CD* III/1, 117.

whereas light *is* new. Furthermore, God calls the light "day" and the darkness "night," thus ushering time into existence, and there is no indication that darkness and night are somehow less than good.[48]

On day one we also witness the polemical nature of Genesis 1. Light is not an emanation from God but his creation, and neither is it the property of the sun or moon, since it preexists them. "We have only to be able to read it with the ears of an ancient Egyptian, with his deep-rooted tradition of the inestimable glory and majesty and divinity of the sun, to gauge how profound is the change undertaken in this verse—that light is put before the sun and all the constellations!"[49] If this polemic is more implicit with day one, it is explicit with day four. The writer deliberately eschews the Hebrew words for sun and moon, instead referring to them as the "greater light" and the "lesser light."

God has already separated light from darkness on day one, but now the lights in the sky are assigned this task. The sun is *to rule* (literally "for dominion") the day, while the moon is to rule the night.[50] This is a different word from that used of human dominion (*yārad*), but the relationship is instructive nevertheless. The sun and moon are not gods who lord it over the earth.[51] Instead, their rule is one of service; they function for signs, seasons, days, and years. Barth notes that with the fourth day there begins "the furnishing of the cosmos."[52] Time already exists, but that does not mean humans will be able to know it properly. The lights are created not in order to be served but to serve, and to serve humankind in particular. God does not need these lights, but animals and humankind do. As Barth notes,

> There could be time, there could be natural history and human history, even without these luminaries. But without them there could not be the time and history in which man, surrounded by the animal kingdom, can play a conscious and active part as a partner of the Creator. . . . The office of these lights, the heavenly bodies, is to summon him in relation to his Maker to sight, consciousness and activity. If he lived in a world which lacked this presupposition,

[48]Gerhard von Rad asserts, "Night is a survival of the darkness of chaos, now however kept in bounds by a protective order." *Old Testament Theology*, vol. 1, *The Theology of Israel's Historical Traditions* (Louisville, KY: Westminster John Knox, 2001), 144.

[49]Barth, *CD* III/1, 120-21.

[50]This language supports Noordzij's view of creature kings.

[51]Barth (*CD* III/1, 159) notes that the Old Testament does ascribe to the heavenly host "a kind of personal being and activity." In our view this is to confuse the function of metaphors such as "rule."

[52]Barth, *CD* III/1, 156.

> he could not have been created in the image of God nor called to be a partner in the divine covenant of grace.[53]

Augustine creatively asserts, "This night, however, was not to remain without its own décor, but with the light of moon and stars was to give both comfort to people who are often obliged to work at night, and sufficient time to meet the needs of animals which cannot bear the light of the sun."[54]

Days two and five. Genesis 1:2 refers to the deep and the waters, and this theme is picked up again in Genesis 1:6-8. The imagery is that of a dome being introduced so as to separate the waters below from the waters above. God names the dome "sky." Lights, as we have seen, are placed in the dome on day four, and on day five sea creatures to fill the waters and birds of every kind to fly above the earth across the dome are created by God's divine fiat. It is intriguing, as Barth notes, that God chooses to fill first the spheres that are by nature more distant or alien to humankind—namely, the seas and the sky.[55] For Barth, the fact that these spheres are filled by God should serve as an encouragement to humankind that they too can flourish in their sphere—that is, on the earth. In this respect it is noteworthy that Genesis 1:21 mentions first the *tannînim* (the great sea monsters). In the Old Testament the *tannînim* often symbolize the enemy that God conquered (Job 7:13; Ps 74:13; Is 27:1; 51:9). Barth says,

> By mentioning the *tanninim* first and foremost as if they were merely a special noteworthy species among the other aquatic animals, the creation saga has in some special sense taken the bull by the horns. . . . It means precisely that the sinister sea hides no monsters of chaos. . . . There is no species in these spheres that is not created by God; no species that, far from questioning, does not confirm the habitable condition of the earth for man.[56]

Unlike on day four with the sun and moon, the sea creatures and birds are not said to be created to rule over the oceans and the sky, so that in this respect Noordzij's thesis is less persuasive. Even less convincing is Barth's view of the waters in Genesis 1:6-8. His view relates back to his interpretation of Genesis 1:2, and in the light of that verse he argues that the delimitation of the waters involves the "radical crushing of the sovereignty of the element of chaos."[57] For

[53]Barth, *CD* III/1, 157.
[54]Augustine, *Literal Meaning* 2.14.28.
[55]Barth, *CD* III/1, 169.
[56]Barth, *CD* III/1, 173.
[57]Barth, *CD* III/1, 133.

Barth, "the reference can only be to the primal flood of chaos."[58] In our view this makes no sense since the oceans are one of the places that God fills, and he sees that this filling is good and blesses the sea creatures and birds, giving them a mandate akin to that given to humankind (Gen 1:22; cf. Gen 1:28).

In terms of the waters above and the waters below, clearly some form of ancient Near Eastern cosmological imagery is at work here, imagery also found elsewhere in the Old Testament, such as in the flood narrative in Genesis 6–9 (cf. Gen 8:2).[59] However, in our view this is not a matter for concern; indeed, how else are ancient authors supposed to communicate the great theological truths we find in Genesis 1 and elsewhere? In this respect it is important to note that the Bible uses a variety of metaphysical metaphors to communicate the truth of creation, as, already, Augustine recognized.[60]

Days three and six. Day three sees the emergence of the dry land (earth, *ʾereṣ*) and of plants of every kind, including fruit trees. Day six witnesses the creation of wild and domestic animals—cattle, creeping things, wild animals—and of humankind, the occupants of earth. On day six the plants are given to the land animals and the birds and to humans for food. With day three, the three major places of the world have emerged—namely, sea, sky, and land. By day five the creatures of the sea and sky have been created, and now it is the turn of the earth creatures.

It is intriguing that animals and humankind are created on the same day, highlighting the kinship between humankind and the animal world. In Genesis 1 the animals are said to come forth from the earth, but this is not said of humankind. In Genesis 2, however, humankind is indeed formed from the earth. Barth says of "the beast,"

> At every point it is inferior to man and yet his companion and even forerunner. It is inferior, for man alone is created in the image of God. He alone will hear and obey the Creator. He alone is honoured to be God's partner in

[58] Barth, *CD* III/1, 136.

[59] Othmar Keel, *The Symbolism of the Biblical World: Ancient Near Eastern Iconography in the Book of Psalms*, trans. Timothy J. Hallett (Winona Lake, IN: Eisenbrauns, 1997), 35-47; Othmar Keel and Silvia Schroer, *Creation: Biblical Theologies in the Context of the Ancient Near East*, trans. Peter T. Daniels (Winona Lake, IN: Eisenbrauns, 2015), 78-84; Howard J. Van Till et al., *Portraits of Creation: Biblical and Scientific Perspectives on the World's Formation* (Grand Rapids, MI: Eerdmans, 1990), 226-29.

[60] Cf., e.g., Is 40–55. Note the variety of metaphors for creation in, e.g., Is 40:12, 22; 45:18; 48:13. Augustine, *Literal Meaning* 2.9.21.

> the covenant of grace.[61] With him alone will there be an independent history. But in all these things the beast will be a constant companion.[62] Everything which will take place between God and himself is to be significantly accompanied by what takes place, by life and death, in the animal kingdom; and in these events it will have witnesses which cannot be silenced even where human witnesses fail, and which will often speak more forcefully and impressively than all human witnesses. Man's salvation and perdition, his joy and sorrow, will be reflected in the weal and woe of this animal environment and company.[63]

Barth is way ahead of his time with these comments, recognizing, as he does, the interwovenness of animals and humans, to say nothing of sea creatures and birds and the land, sky, and sea. There is no suggestion in Genesis 1 that nonhuman creation derives its validity only in relation to humankind. It has its own integrity in relation to God. Animals and humans are presented in Genesis 1:29-30 as herbivores—itself evocative—but what is noteworthy is that God grants *permission* to animals, birds, and humans to eat the plants as food. Plants are a gift from God and not something that can or should just be taken for granted. "As He gives man everything—light, the firmament, dry land, animal companions and finally existence—so now He gives the necessary food. He and His gift will never fail when man is in need. God's table will always be abundantly spread for all."[64] Genesis 1:29-30 follows on immediately from God's granting of dominion to humans, and, as Davis has perceptively noted, the implication is that in the exercise of their dominion humans will be responsible to make sure that plants are available to birds and land animals for food.[65] Here, for example, is an imperative toward the indigenous garden, which comes alive with birds, butterflies, and other creatures as the garden is filled with species of plants suited to and desired by local animal inhabitants.

> Augustine has an interesting discussion of the creation of dangerous and poisonous animals. He refers to Daniel in the lions' den and the viper on Paul's hand in Acts 28:3-5

[61]However, as we will see in chap. 9, animals *are* included in the covenant with Noah and recur in surprising places such as Jonah in the Scriptures.

[62]Cf. Brian Fagan, *The Intimate Bond: How Amimals Shaped Human History* (London: Bloomsbury, 2016).

[63]Barth, *CD* III/1, 178.

[64]Barth, *CD* III/1, 207.

[65]Ellen F. Davis, *Scripture, Culture, and Agriculture: An Agrarian Reading of the Bible* (Cambridge: Cambridge University Press, 2009), 57-58.

and concludes, "So it would have been quite possible for these creatures to do no harm when they were created." Nevertheless, he argues regarding carnivorous animals that "some are the proper diet of others."[a]

[a]Augustine, *Literal Meaning* 3.15.24, in Augustine, *On Genesis: A Refutation of the Manichees, Unfinished Literal Commentary on Genesis, the Literal Meaning of Genesis*, ed. John E. Rotelle, trans. Edmund Hill (Hyde Park, NY: New City Press, 2005).

Leon Kass asserts that eating is "no trivial matter. It is the first and most urgent activity of all animal and human life: We are only because we eat."[66] One would think that the food chain would feature large in Christian theology because food and eating is so central to humans' and animals' well-being. Alas, this has rarely been the case. It is instructive to note that it was the same group in the United Kingdom in the nineteenth century who fought for the abolition of slavery who also fought for the prevention of cruelty to animals. In nineteenth-century Britain, cruelty to animals was public and easily verified. Nowadays it is hidden behind the sanitary walls of factory farms and driven by maximum financial gain irrespective of the cost to animals or humans. Suffice it to note here that Genesis 1 provides us with an incipient *theology of food*, and not just for humans but for animals too.

Furthermore, day six is fascinating in identifying both wild and domestic animals as created simultaneously by God. Evolutionists would argue that domestic animals were first wild animals and that the "natural" state for animals is wild. It is surely true that some "domestic" animals were wild and have been domesticated, but Genesis 1 suggests that domestication is given with creation. Especially in the light of the herbivorous nature of animals and humankind, this speaks of a very intimate relationship between animals and humankind.

This brings us to the creation of humankind, following the creation of the animals. "Let us" occurs only at this point in the narrative and alerts the reader to the magnitude of what is now to take place. In our view the much-debated plural "us" refers to the council of Yahweh in heaven, contra Barth, who discerns in this divine soliloquy "a summons to intra-divine unanimity of intention and decision."[67] It is as though God pauses reflectively at this point in order to draw attention in the heavenly council to what is now to

[66]Leon R. Kass, *The Hungry Soul: Eating and the Perfecting of Our Nature* (New York: Maxwell Macmillan International, 1994), 2.

[67]Barth, *CD* III/1, 182; see Wenham, *Genesis 1–15*, 27-28, for the variety of views.

come. Gerhard von Rad suggests that "unlike the rest of Creation, he [humankind] was not created by the word; but in creating him God was actuated by a unique, solemn resolve in the depths of his heart."[68]

Image and *likeness* are synonyms, with *likeness* adding the nuance of similarity without exact repetition. "*Our* image" could indicate that humankind shares a commonality not only with God but also with the angelic host, who form the council of Yahweh, but in Genesis 1:27 the focus is exclusively on "in the image of God *he* created them." Thus, we are cautious of von Rad's view that God took the pattern for humankind from the heavenly world.[69]

Kelsey resists approaching theological anthropology through Genesis 1:26-28, choosing instead to use Old Testament Wisdom literature as his entrance.[a] In our view this is a mistake and embodies a false dichotomy between wisdom and narrative. The book of James, for example, is full of wisdom motifs, and in James 3:9 James references Genesis 1:26. McFarland follows Kelsey in this respect.[b] Both lean on Westermann, but his view is far from convincing and contradictory. For Westermann, Genesis 1:26-28 is about a process and an event rather than about the nature of human being, and it only has meaning in its context.[c] However, it is also important for him that Genesis 1:26-30 originated in an independent narrative. He argues that the meaning of Genesis 1:26-28 is that "humanity as a whole . . . is created as the counterpart of God; the intention is to render possible a happening between creator and creature."[d] Clearly the creation of humankind *is* an event that facilitates a relationship, but there is no reason at all that this should be contrary to Genesis 1:26-28, which provides insight into what it means to be human, both functionally and ontologically.

McConville notes how in Genesis 5:1-3 the following generation inherits the *imago Dei*, and its further occurrence in Genesis 9:5-6 "says something about the very identity of the human."[e] Psalm 8 is closely related to Genesis 1, and O'Donovan notes, "The theological doctrine of mankind, offered us with supreme poetic magnificence in the eighth Psalm, shows him set within an order which he did not make, joyfully accepting his privileged place within it."[f] While the precise language of humans in the *imago Dei* is sparse in the Old Testament, the broader intertextual links are overwhelming. For example, if Barth and Dumbrell are correct that Genesis 1 is *the* covenantal text in the Old Testament, then the other major covenants look back to it. In our view the same sort of work that Stordalen has done with Genesis 2–3 can be done with Genesis 1:1–2:3, demonstrating that intertextually the links to Genesis 1 in the Old Testament and the New Testament are far stronger than is often recognized.[g]

---

[68]Von Rad, *Old Testament Theology*, 1:144.
[69]Ibid.

Related to this is the relationship between Genesis 1 and Genesis 2–3, which we explore in chapter six. McConville argues that "the first narrative development of the concept [*imago Dei*] comes immediately, in Genesis 2:4b–3:24."[h] In the New Testament the *imago Dei* is clearly referred to in Colossians 3:10, 1 Corinthians 15:48, and James 3:9. Of course, the emphasis of the New Testament is that Jesus is *the* image of God, which we will discuss below.

---

[a]David H. Kelsey, *Eccentric Existence: A Theological Anthropology* (Louisville, KY: Westminster John Knox, 2009), 1:176-89.

[b]Ian A. McFarland, *The Divine Image: Envisioning the Invisible God* (Minneapolis: Fortress, 2005).

[c]Claus Westermann, *Genesis 1–11: A Commentary*, trans. John J. Scullion (Minneapolis: Augsburg, 1984), 155-58.

[d]Ibid., 158.

[e]J. Gordon McConville, *Being Human in God's World: An Old Testament Theology of Humanity* (Grand Rapids, MI: Baker Academic, 2016), 21-22.

[f]Oliver O'Donovan, *Resurrection and Moral Order: An Outline for Evangelical Ethics* (Leicester, UK: Apollos, 1986), 38.

[g]T. Stordalen, *Echoes of Eden: Genesis 2–3 and Symbolism of the Eden Garden in Biblical Hebrew Literature*, Contributions to Biblical Exegesis and Theology 25 (Leuven: Peeters, 2000).

[h]McConville, *Being Human*, 31.

As readers will be aware, much has been written about what precisely constitutes the image and likeness. "Image" is, in our view, a striking and unexpected metaphor pointing to an important, constitutive similarity but also to difference. As a multi-vocal image, it has multiple references. The Kuyperian tradition has rightly recognized that a central aspect of the image is the *functional* aspect of exercising dominion over the earth ("subdue it") as well as the creatures of the three major places of the world. The Kuyperian tradition refers to this cultural aspect as *the cultural mandate* (see chap. 7). Von Rad similarly remarks, "What is crucial about man's image is his function in the non-human world. Thus, through the image of God in man Creation, in addition to coming from God, receives a particular ordering towards God."[70] André LaCocque perceptively notes that "the first words of God to the human couple are commandments, commandments to proliferate and to rule over the universe; that is, to relate most closely to each other and to the world."[71]

We agree with this but suggest that there is more to the image. Barth has rightly foregrounded the "male and female" of Genesis 1:27, an aspect of this text that is routinely ignored. As he notes, we only ever encounter humans as gendered, as male or female, and *somehow* this is an integral part of the *imago*

---

[70]Ibid., 1:147.

[71]LaCocque and Ricoeur, *Thinking Biblically*, 10.

Dei: "Men are simply male and female."[72] Barth specifically identifies this with sexual intercourse: "This is the particular dignity ascribed to the sex relationship. It is wholly creaturely, and common to man and beast. But as the only real principle of differentiation and relationship, as the original form not only of man's confrontation of God but also of all intercourse between man and man, it is the true *humanum* and therefore the true creaturely image of God."[73] We are less sure than Barth about this, not least because any idea of sexuality in Yahweh was alien to Israel,[74] but agree that in some way gender and its interrelationship is part of the image, perhaps as the evocation of *sociality*, particularly as manifested in marriage. Colossians 1:15 tells us that Christ is the image of the invisible God, and in Ephesians 5:32 Paul says of the two becoming one flesh in marriage, "This is a great mystery, and I am applying it to Christ and the church."

This alerts us to the *ontological aspect* of the image, and indeed, for humans to exercise stewardship over God's good creation, they will need to be thinking, linguistic, creative, imaginative, social, gendered beings. In terms of language it becomes apparent that linguisticality is part of the image in Genesis 2, but already here in Genesis 1 it is only to the humans that Genesis 1:28 records, "God blessed them, and God *said to them* . . ." The sea creatures and birds are similarly addressed (Gen 1:22) but indirectly.

In the New Testament, Christ is described as the image of God (2 Cor 4:4; Col 1:15; Heb 1:3), and we are said to be being conformed to his image (Rom 8:29; 2 Cor 3:18; Col 3:10). Barth and McFarland make Jesus *the* entranceway into theological anthropology. For Barth, anthropology must be based solely on Christology: "As the man Jesus is Himself the revealing Word of God, He is the source of our knowledge of the nature of man as created by God."[75] Similarly, McFarland asserts that "the *imago dei* is not a property or characteristic of Jesus' existence as a human being; it *is* that existence in its entirety."[76] Only once we have moved from "in Adam" to "in Christ" does our creation in the *imago Dei* become "theologically significant."[77]

In our view Barth's and McFarland's overly christological lenses are in danger of succumbing to a reductionistic anthropology. Suffice it here to note

---

[72]Barth, *CD* III/1, 186.
[73]Barth, *CD* III/1, 186.
[74]Rad, *Old Testament Theology*, 1:146.
[75]Barth, *CD* III/2, 41.
[76]Ian A. McFarland, *The Divine Image: Envisioning the Invisible God* (Minneapolis: Fortress, 2005), 60; cf. Barth, *CD* III/2, 55.
[77]McFarland, *Divine Image*, 58.

two dimensions of the image of God in Christ. First, this expression points to the uniqueness of Christ, who reveals God to us in the way that only the Son can (Jn 1:18). Thus Ridderbos asserts that "the Son is always the Image of (invisible) God (2 Cor. 4:4; Col. 1:15), whereby again we must not in the first place seek a universal *religionsgeschichtliche* or Old Testament parallel, or other points of contact, but in the first place must think of the tremendous revelatory reality of the divine glory in Jesus Christ."[78]

Second, Christ fulfills Genesis 1:26-28 as the true man, the second Adam, and thus reveals to us what it means to be fully human. Gustaf Wingren notes the importance of Colossians 3:10 for Irenaeus, with its emphasis on the "new self, which is being renewed in knowledge according to the image of its creator."[79] In this sense sanctification involves being conformed to the image of Christ, or becoming what God always intended us to be. O'Donovan articulates the relationship between Christ and creation as regards the *imago Dei* as follows:

> In his conquest over death and in his glorification at the Father's right hand we see man as he was made to be, not subject to the angelic forces of sin and mortality which presently oppress him, but able for the first time to take his place in the cosmos as its lord. . . . It fulfills and vindicates the primal order in a way that was always implied, but which could not be realized in the fallen state of man and the universe.[80]

Day seven. There is no doubt that as Genesis 1 gathers momentum, it moves toward the creation of human beings. This is especially true from day four onward. In contrast to the Enuma Elish, Genesis 1 is largely—but not exclusively—all about creating the world as a perfect home for humans. It is after the creation of animals and then humans that God sees all that he has made and declares it "very good." Barth says of the creation of humankind,

> Only with the positing of this new beginning is the whole of the work of creation concluded and made ready for its completion on the day of the divine rest. With all its manifold presuppositions, consequences and reservations, this whole has aimed and moved towards man as the true occupant of the house founded and prepared by God, the central creature on the ground and in space and in the midst of all the others, the one being capable of and participating in

[78]Ridderbos, *Conflict*, 127-28.

[79]Gustaf Wingren, *Man and the Incarnation: A Study in the Biblical Theology of Irenaeus*, trans. R. MacKenzie (Eugene, OR: Wipf & Stock, 1959), 24.

[80]Oliver O'Donovan, *Resurrection and Moral Order: An Outline for Evangelical Ethics* (Leicester, UK: Apollos, 1986), 54.

light. It is only when man is created that it can be said that God saw all that He created, and that it was "very good."[81]

However, the goal of Genesis 1 is reached not with the creation of humans, but with Genesis 2:1-3, day seven, as it were, on which God finishes his work and rests. Barth observes, "It is only with reservation that he [humankind] can be described as 'the crown of creation.' Strictly speaking, creation is crowned only when God in His joyful Sabbath rest looks back upon it and down on what He has created. But it is the work concluded and terminated on the sixth day with the creation of man that is the object of this completing divine rest and joy."[82]

An intriguing aspect of Genesis 2:2 is that we are told that it is only on day seven that God *finishes* the work that he has done, but we are not told that he does anything apart from resting![83] Von Rad is helpful in this respect: "But the completion of God's Creation was the resting on the seventh day."[84] Work, we might say, is incomplete without it being contemplated, seen, and enjoyed.

Barth argues that two features of God are revealed by day seven—namely, his freedom and his love. "When," Barth asks, "is He God more truly, or more perfectly Himself in the whole course of His work of creation, than in this rest on the seventh day? Here it is revealed unequivocally that His work cannot have any claim on Him or violate Him; that as the Creator He is always His own Lord."[85] By completing creation in his resting, God associates himself freely and fully with his creation. As von Rad notes, "It would be sheer folly to regard this resting of God's which concluded the Creation as something like a turning away from the world: it is in fact a particularly mysterious gracious turning towards his Creation."[86]

The seventh day also alerts us to the theological distinction between creation and providence. Having ushered his creation into existence, God sustains it and remains fully engaged with it. But the fact that he finished creating on day seven draws a firm boundary between creation and providence. As von Rad notes, the seventh day "implies the drawing of a clear distinction between the work of Creation on the one hand, and the

---

[81]Barth, *CD* III/1, 181.

[82]Barth, *CD* III/1, 181.

[83]But see Wenham, *Genesis 1–15*, 35, for the argument that the verb should be translated as a pluperfect (viz., "had finished").

[84]Rad, *Old Testament Theology*, 1:147.

[85]Barth, *CD* III/1, 215.

[86]Rad, *Old Testament Theology*, 1:148.

sustaining and preserving care with which God accompanies his Creation on the other."[87]

Conclusion

By Genesis 2:1-4 the creation is complete and very good. Light, time and history, day and night, seasons, and the three major places—sky, sea, land—and their inhabitants have all been created. The world has been created and its furnishing is complete. And behind it all stands the royal king, Elohim. As von Rad notes, "The world and its fullness do not find their unity and inner coherence in a cosmological first principle, such as the Ionian natural philosophers tried to discover, but in the completely personal will of Jahweh their creator. . . . At the apex stands the all-comprehensive statement that 'God' created the world."[88] Similarly, LaCocque says that it is incorrect to call the universe a cosmos if "cosmos" implies a "harmony grounded upon reason, whereas the harmony of the world according to Genesis is by decree, by Law, and an equation is established between harmony and obedience."[89]

As the verse from Isaiah quoted at the outset says, God has truly laid the foundation of the earth and stretched out the heavens. When he summons them, they do indeed stand at attention. Scripture confronts us with a dynamic and complex divinely ordered creation, and the rest of the biblical story unfolds from this point.

In our view it is impossible to emerge from Genesis 1 without a doctrine of *creation order*. Knierim provocatively asserts that "world order explicated what it meant for Israel to say 'Yahweh.'"[90] In the New Testament we meet with Jesus particularly in the ecclesia (Col 1:18), but the Jesus we encounter is none other than the Word through whom all things came into existence so that there is no contradiction between creation order and its source. And yet, especially in the twentieth century, theologians became wary of this doctrine. Such wariness is understandable because of the abuse to which it was subjected. Craig grew up in apartheid South Africa, in which the ordering of the nations of Genesis 10 was used to justify the oppression and evil of apartheid. Similar ideologies were used to justify the preeminence of the Aryan race and National Socialism.

We recognize the danger of the abuse of a doctrine of creation order, but abuse should not justify abandonment. It helps to see this if we consider the

---

[87]Ibid., 1:147.
[88]Ibid., 1:141-42.
[89]LaCocque and Ricoeur, *Thinking Biblically*, 6.
[90]Knierim, *Task of Old Testament Theology*, 199.

alternative not to believe in creation order. Indeed, much postmodernism provides us with a good example of the sort of *historicism* that results if we abandon belief in the discernible shape God has given to the creation. This element in postmodernism is simply an outworking of the DNA of modernity. The political theorist Eric Voegelin identifies the attempt to eradicate the divine order in creation as gnostic:

> The aim of parousiastic Gnosticism is to destroy the order of being, which is experienced as defective and unjust, and through man's creative power to replace it with a perfect and just order. . . . In order, therefore, that the attempt to create a new world may seem to make sense, the givenness of the order of being must be obliterated; the order of being must be interpreted, rather, as essentially under man's control. And taking control of being further requires that the transcendent origin of being be obliterated: it requires the decapitation of being—the murder of God.[91]

It is God's order given to the creation and sustained by him that provides fixity within freedom for human life. Postmodernism, especially in its extreme forms, demonstrates that once we let go of God and his good order for our world, nothing is stable, and ironically humans pride themselves on being able to construct their worlds as they wish. Indeed, very few are prepared, like Nietzsche, to follow postmodernism through to its consistent conclusions. Creation order is writ so deep in the fabric of our world that we inevitably find ourselves returning to it, no matter how much we try to rebel against it. From Genesis 1 we have learned that God's order for creation consists in such things as

- the existence of light;
- the reality of time, days, seasons, years, and history;
- the three great places of our world: sky, sea, and land;
- the distinction between birds, sea creatures, and land animals;
- the extraordinary world of flora and fruit trees and their importance in the food chain;
- humankind as similar to and yet distinct from the other creatures and with unique capacities;
- humankind as called to responsible stewardship of the creation;
- humankind as gendered and inherently relational; and
- humankind as inherently religious—that is, made for God.

---

[91]Eric Voegelin, *Science, Politics, and Gnosticism*, trans. William J. Fitzpatrick (1968; repr., Washington, DC: Regnery, 1997), 35-36.

Every one of these aspects is complex, with depths that are mysterious and able to be studied in great detail without our fully fathoming its entirety. In theory we might (foolishly) resist belief in these realities, but in practice humans take almost all of them for granted. Alas, too many fail to ask how we can account as humans for this fixity to our existence. Scripturally the answer is, of course, creation. Philosophically, as noted already in chapter one, this inevitably commits Christians to some form of realism. While we have significant freedom and power, our power and creativity is *always* exercised in the context of God's dynamic order for his creation. Our world, of which we are part, has a discernible shape, and in our investigation of it we seek to discover what is really there rather than creating it ourselves.

It is in the Kuyperian tradition in particular that this insight has been most fruitfully developed. The Thomist tradition also has a doctrine of creational law, but in Thomas's theology and philosophy this is a form of natural theology in which the law of creation can, to a very significant extent, be understood by unaided human reason. In our view, because the origin of this order is in the personal will of God, it is only in relationship with him that we can begin to know this order aright. "The fear of the Lord is the beginning of wisdom/knowledge." From this perspective the starting point is all-important, and deviation at this point distorts the entire project of knowledge. This does not, of course, mean that all we need or desire to know is contained in the starting point. The starting point is the beginning of a journey of discovery as we explore God's handiwork in all its rich and glorious facets.

Creation order relates to all of reality—to creation—and not just ethics or morality, although it has much to do with such areas of life as well. Physics, biology, psychology, environmental studies, aesthetics, sociology, history, economics, and so on are all explorations of God's creation, its order and its unfolding. What we are not advocating is a static notion of creation order. By definition, there is a fixity to God's order for creation, but that includes all the dynamics involved in God's call to humankind to "subject the earth" and to steward the creation. In this respect the Kuyperian tradition makes a helpful distinction between aspects of God's order or law for creation that we simply have to obey—gravity, the need to eat to stay alive, breathing air to live—and laws or norms that are God-given but that humans can choose to obey or disobey. Such norms are positivized or actualized by humans, and there is generally more than one way to do so depending on the time, the circumstances, and personal choice. From this perspective it is normative for societies to be governed, but the principle of just government has been and can be positivized in a variety of ways. Of course, government can also be developed in a way that distorts rather than actualizes justice.

Creation order is good news! There is a way for us to be and become fully human and to live and develop our world along the grain of its creation so as to contribute to shalom and flourishing.

Ricoeur approaches the idea of creation order or "ordering" with caution.[a] In dialogue with Schmid, Ricoeur proposes several correctives to the idea of creation order:[b]

Creation order must be thought of as contingent. Ricoeur acknowledges helpfully that thinking of the real as a whole—that is, as ordered—subverts the modern tendencies to reduce reality to a mathematical model and thereby remove all its opacity, and to make the thinking subject the center of meaning. On the other hand, Ricoeur prefers to think of creation as *genesis*, as an *event* rather than an order. "If, however, we do join the ideas of necessity and contingency under that of 'ordering,' we may ask whether the idea of order itself does not take on a more dynamic than static sense, particularly when we pass from the cosmic to the human plane of right and justice."[c] In our view Ricoeur is in danger of introducing false dichotomies into the doctrine of creation. Creation is a *unique* "event"; it is about genesis, but about the genesis of an ordered creation. And this order is stable but dynamic and not static. As Augustine sees, "novelties are possible, things which have not happened before and yet are not at variance with the ordering of the world."[d]

The issue of justice problematizes creation order. For Ricoeur, the gap between God's order and injustice in the world disturbs any doctrine of creation order by calling its efficacity into question. "Schmid may well say that the retribution still arises from the thinking of order, which, having been upset, is restored, but the possibility remains that evil appears as inscribed in the ethical structure of Creation."[e] Following Levenson, Ricoeur prefers the motif of mastery and combat over that of order.

> Job's protest indicates the breaking apart of the idea of order as encompassing creation, justice, and salvation. The injustice of the world constitutes such a massive fact that the presumed tie between the idea of justice and that of creation loses almost all its pertinence. Creation may remain the surrounding horizon, but it ceases to be the encompassing idea that would constitute its identification with the idea of order.[f]

Clearly for Ricoeur theodicy problematizes creation order beyond repair. In our view it is only against the backdrop of creation order that injustice comes fully into view and with its dynamic holds out the possibility of final retribution.

Underlying Ricoeur's resistance to creation order appears to be a fear of totalizing.[g] While postmodernism has alerted us to the dangers of metanarratives, in our view some totalizing picture is unavoidable, and some are much better than others! At the heart of the biblical metanarrative stands the cross, which alerts us to the grace of the biblical story and its resistance to violent coercion.

---

[a]Paul Ricoeur, "Thinking Creation," in *Thinking Biblically: Exegetical and Hermeneutical Studies*, by André LaCocque and Paul Ricoeur, trans. David Pellauer (Chicago: University of Chicago Press, 1998), 31-67.

[b]Ibid., 55-64; Hans Heinrich Schmid, "Jahweglaube Und Altorientalisches Weltordungensgedanken," in *Altorientalische Welt in der alttestamentlichen Theologie* (Zurich: Theologischer Verlag, 1974).

[c]LaCocque and Ricoeur, *Thinking Biblically*, 57.

[d]Augustine, *City of God* 12.21 (trans. Bettenson).

[e]LaCocque and Ricoeur, *Thinking Biblically*, 58.

[f]Ibid., 61; Jon D. Levenson, *Creation and the Persistence of Evil: The Jewish Drama of Divine Omnipotence* (San Francisco: Harper & Row, 1985).

[g]LaCocque and Ricoeur, *Thinking Biblically*, 61.

SIX

PLACE, PLANTS, ANIMALS, HUMANS, AND CREATION

No philosophy of human life can be adequate if it concentrates on the relationship in which the individual stands to other human individuals and ignores that in which he stands to the entire universe.

E. L. Mascall

Even on the level of brute experience, the world is not merely squalid, widespread as squalor undoubtedly is. It is a world in which exquisite beauty is to be found, beauty in the things of nature, beauty in the artefacts of man, beauty in human behaviour and human relationships. But this beauty is uniformly imperfect, only understandable in terms of Creation and the Fall.

E. L. Mascall

Ritualizing nature, then, means standing within the cultural world of Christian worship and seeing what one can see as one contemplates the world of nature from that standpoint. . . . Anyone who, in faith, enters into the liturgy and whose mind and heart is shaped by that practice, can have hope for the entire creation.

H. Paul Santmire

The doctrine of creation ought to inspire in us a sense of worship and wonder. It draws our attention to the extraordinary diversity in creation and to the creativity of God in producing such a world as ours. Abraham Heschel asserts, "Wonder or radical amazement is the chief characteristic of the religious man's attitude toward history and nature."[1]

---

[1]Abraham J. Heschel, *God in Search of Man: A Philosophy of Judaism* (New York: Farrar, Straus and Giroux, 1955), 45.

In Genesis 1:1–2:3 the creation as a whole comes into being. In Genesis 2 the spotlight moves to the home of the first couple in the great park of Eden and the relationships that constitute human being. In chapter five we discussed what it means for human beings to be in the *imago Dei*. We also made some preliminary comments about the plants and animals, subjects that we will pursue in more detail here.

Historical criticism identifies two creation narratives in Genesis 1–3, assigned to two sources—namely, P (Gen 1:1–2:4a) and J (Gen 2:4b–3:24). A legacy of this is to read them independently of each other; however, it is not necessary to see two different authors or sources, or to see them as opposed to each other.[a] Instead, they are complementary accounts of God's creative acts. There are important differences between the two, but canonically and in relation to the literary shape of Genesis 1–11 their juxtaposition and the relationship between them should be explored.[b]

As a literary unit, Genesis is structured by the *toledoth* headings. Genesis 1:1–2:3 precedes this literary shaping, with Genesis 2–4 as the first major section within a *toledoth* heading.[c] Genesis 1:1–2:3 should therefore be read as the introduction to Genesis (and the Pentateuch) as a whole, while Genesis 2–3 begins the narrative that will lead on to Abraham and Israel. "The role of the *toledot* formula in 2.4, which introduces the story of mankind, is to connect the creation of the world with the history which follows."[d] Thus, Genesis 2–3 has more of a narrative or historical function within Genesis than does 1:1–2:3.[e]

An important key for the relationship between Genesis 1:1–2:3 and Genesis 2–4 is the theme of *place*. In 1:1–2:3 the earth emerges as the potential, ideal home for humans. However, the differentiation in 1:1–2:3 develops further in chapters 2–4. Genesis 2:4b, with its inversion of "heavens and earth" to "earth and heavens," indicates a shift in focus to the earth.[f] Genesis 2 is consequently more place specific, with its attention to Eden as the park in which Adam and Eve are to live. "P is concerned with the 'world' and man within it, while J shows the construction of man's immediate environment and defines his relationship to it."[g] Casey says,

> When it is added . . . that "a mist went up from the earth and watered the whole face of the ground" (2:6) and that "God planted a garden in Eden, in the east" (2:8), we attain a still more definite degree of place-determination, one that now includes quite particular places (i.e. patches of ground) that have proper names and even cardinal directions. . . . The movement is from less determinate to more determinate places.[h]

Thus the move from Genesis 1 to 2 depicts progressive implacement, culminating in Eden as the particular place where the first couple are to dwell. As Casey notes, "*Implacement* itself, being concretely placed, is intrinsically particular."[i]

There are thus good reasons for reading Genesis 1–2 as a unity. Indeed, Genesis 1:1–2:3 provides indispensable background information for understanding Genesis 2.

[a]Joshua A. Berman's *Inconsistency in the Torah* (Oxford: Oxford University Press, 2017) is helpful for understanding the complexity in identifying different sources and especially for differentiating between modern and ancient expectations of "consistency" in narrative discourse.

[b]Cf. Brevard S. Childs, *Introduction to the Old Testament as Scripture* (Minneapolis: Fortress, 1979), 149-50.

[c]With Gordon J. Wenham (*Genesis 1–15*, WBC 1 [Dallas: Word, 1987], 49, 55, 56), we take Gen 2:4 to be a heading for what follows in Gen 2–4.

[d]Childs, *Old Testament as Scripture*, 146.

[e]See Wenham, *Genesis 1–15*, 53-55.

[f]As Barth notes, "The heavens are not overlooked or denied, but in this saga attention is focused on the earth" (*CD* III/1, 234).

[g]Gerhard von Rad, *Old Testament Theology*, vol. 1, *The Theology of Israel's Historical Traditions*, trans. D. M. G. Stalker (New York: Harper, 1985), 150.

[h]Edward S. Casey, *Getting Back into Place: Toward a Renewed Understanding of the Place-World* (Bloomington: Indiana University Press, 1993), 14.

[i]Ibid., 23.

Places and Creatures

Days two and three in Genesis 1 establish the places that are inhabited by the birds, fish, animals, and humankind on days five and six. With regard to place, this is telling: the birds fly in the sky; the fish swim in the waters; the animals and humankind live on the earth and receive their nutrition from the plants.

That plants are food for humans and animals does not equate to a utilitarian ethic in which the plants (or, later, animals) are only brought into existence as food. At the end of day three, the emergence of vegetation from the earth is seen by God to be "good" in and of itself. Genesis 2:9 specifically foregrounds the nutritive *and* the aesthetic dimensions of the trees in Eden. And when it comes to animals, it needs to be remembered that it is only after the flood that humans are given permission to eat them (Gen 9:3); prior to that humans are portrayed as vegetarian. One might expect that once humans are given permission to eat animals that animals would recede into insignificance. However, God's solemn covenant with Noah includes "every living creature that is with you" (Gen 9:12; cf. Gen 9:17). As Westermann observes, "God binds himself unilaterally and without reservation to the assurance that results from the end of the flood and includes humankind and *all other living beings as well.* The unconditional approval that God gives to his creation is the basis of the history of nature and humanity."[2] The creation emerges progressively as a coherent whole, and part of the role of humans as royal stewards

[2]Claus Westermann, *Genesis 1-11: A Commentary*, trans. John J. Scullion (Minneapolis: Fortress, 1984), 473, emphasis added.

of the creation is to ensure that the earth flourishes so that birds, fish, and animals are also able to flourish in the their contexts alongside humans.

Genesis 1:1–2:3 thus depicts progressive differentiation of places, careful distinctions, and coherent wholeness. Humans differ from animals and birds and trees in that they alone are made in the *imago Dei*. However, this difference is not an excuse for exploitation but a capacity for responsible service. Indeed, the diversity and goodness of birds, fish, and animals, and land, sky, and sea alert us to the respect due them as part of God's creation. Alas, much of human history is an abysmal record of the exploitation of animals. William Wilberforce's and the Clapham Sect's campaign against slavery is well known; less known is the fact that the same group fought for the rights of animals and founded the RSPCA (Royal Society for the Prevention of Cruelty to Animals), which led to its global counterparts. We need to recover such compassion today, a day in which the industrialization and commercialization of the food chain means that abuse of animals has increased.

The goodness of God's creatures evokes the diverse ways in which they reflect God's handiwork. Paul articulates this in 1 Corinthians 15:39: "God has provided variety in nature; **thus not every kind of flesh is the same flesh, but there is one kind for men, another for beasts, another for birds, and another for fish**."[3] As humans we have in common with animals, birds, and fish being "flesh." As such we need to respect the other "flesh" in the creation. Indeed, wisdom opens out on a wonder-filled exploration of the whole creation that is captured in the best natural history. R. J. Berry evocatively refers to Psalm 111 as the research scientist's psalm.[4] Psalm 111:2 says, "Great are the works of the Lord, *studied by all who delight in them*." Henry Spence notes that the verb for "studied" (דָּרַשׁ) means "searched into and carefully studied by all who take an interest in such things. *Derushim*, 'objects of study,' is etymologically connected with *madrasa*, a college, a 'place of study and research.'"[5] Psalms 111 and 112 are acrostic psalms, and both begin "Praise the Lord." Psalm 111 focuses on Yahweh's works and Psalm 112 on the blessedness of those who fear Yahweh. Allen says of Psalm 111 that its "theme is declared at the outset: the great salvation history of ancient Israel to which Israel owed

[3]C. K. Barrett, *The Gospel According to St. John: An Introduction with Commentary and Notes on the Greek Text*, 2nd ed. (Philadelphia: Westminster John Knox, 1978), 371.

[4]R. J. Berry, "The Research Scientist's Psalm," *Science and Christian Belief* 20, no. 2 (2008): 147-61.

[5]Henry D. M. Spence, *The Complete Pulpit Commentary: Psalms to Song of Songs* (Harrington, DE: Delmarva, 2013).

its creation and meaning."[6] This suggests that Psalm 111 focuses on redemption rather than creation, but this is a false dichotomy. Part of God's great work is to provide food (Ps 111:5), and the psalm culminates in the typical wisdom motif that "The fear of the LORD is the beginning of wisdom" (Ps 111:10). The theology of wisdom is rooted in creation. Berry's appropriation of this psalm is appropriate, as is that of the environmentalist Calvin DeWitt, when he says of Psalm 111:2 "This verse from Psalm 111 pretty much sums up my passion in life. . . . And as you and I sing from this integral score, we sing along with the vast variety of creatures and their various kingdoms—plant, animal, protist, and more—that join in myriad ways to bring peculiar honors to our King."[7] The story of natural history is one of wonder, disrespect, use, and abuse.[8] But it is a story of which Christians should be aware if we pray, "hallowed be your name. Your kingdom come. Your will be done, on earth as it is in heaven."

In what follows we will focus on the three great places of creation: the sea, the land, and the sky.

The sea. Our planet is justifiably called *the blue planet*. The oceans constitute 71 percent of our planet's surface, and only recently have they begun to be explored.[9] William Broad notes that "what dominates . . . is the deep, which lies beyond the shallows that border the continents and in total accounts for about 65 percent of the Earth's surface. This domain is so wide and so deep that by some estimates it comprises more than 97 percent of the space inhabited by living things on the globe, dwarfing the thin veneer of life on land."[10]

A Roman Catholic, Jacques Cousteau (1910–1997), led the way in exploration of the depths of the oceans. He defends the Bible against the critique that it encourages the exploitation of nature but rightly asks, "How many of the people rise to their feet or fall to their knees in cathedrals . . . all the while ignoring the living word of God just outside the window? . . . They choose to

---

[6]Leslie C. Allen, *Psalms 101–150*, WBC 21 (Waco, TX: Word, 1983), 92.

[7]Calvin B. Dewitt, *Song of a Scientist: The Harmony of a God-Soaked Creation* (Grand Rapids: MI: Square Inch, 2012), 9-10.

[8]See Craig G. Bartholomew, *Where Mortals Dwell: A Christian View of Place for Today* (Grand Rapids, MI: Baker Academic, 2011).

[9]See William J. Broad, *The Universe Below: Discovering the Secrets of the Deep Sea*, illustrations by Dimitry Schidlovsky (New York: Simon & Schuster, 1997); Robert D. Ballard and Will Hively, *The Eternal Darkness: A Personal History of Deep-Sea Exploration* (Princeton, NJ: Princeton University Press, 2002); Callum Roberts, *The Ocean of Life: The Fate of Man and the Sea* (New York: Viking Penguin, 2012).

[10]Broad, *Universe Below*, 19-20.

believe in a God who has issued divine commands; how many honor His divine commands to safeguard the environment?"[11]

In Genesis 1:9 the waters are divided and the land appears.[12] Some modern translations translate "waters" here as "oceans." The combination of land and water is called "good." On day four the sun and moon are created, which "regulate the tidal cycles and affect creatures from small to large, for example, the daily vertical migration of plankton and the long-distance migration of Nassau grouper to spawning aggregations near the winter full moons."[13] The oceans are filled on day five. In Genesis 1:22 the fish and the birds are commanded to be fruitful and multiply. "It is a picture of how marine life was designed to flourish and reproduce in astounding numbers."[14] R. D. Sluka notes that Job 38–42 is "almost a course in ecology"! "God uses creation—biodiversity, if you like—to reveal his character to Job."[15] While the sea is often a negative symbol in the Bible—certainly the reason why in Revelation there is no sea in the new heavens and earth[16]—in certain psalms God's creation of the sea and its creatures is celebrated. In Psalm 104:25-26 we read,

Yonder is the sea, great and wide,
  creeping things innumerable are there,
  living things both small and great.
There go the ships,
  and Leviathan that you formed to sport in it.

Separation is a central motif in Genesis 1:1–2:3, and on day three we see the separation of waters and land. We have already noted Barth's discernment of a chaos motif in Genesis 1:2, and he also sees in the setting of limits to the waters the holding back of the threat of chaos. In our view, however, there is no indication of this in Genesis 1:9, with the boundaries being a good part of God's development and ordering of his creation. Indeed, we find here a tension in Barth's thought.

---

[11]Jacques Cousteau and Susan Schiefelbein, *The Human, the Orchid, and the Octopus: Exploring and Conserving Our Natural World* (New York: Bloomsbury, 2007), 117.

[12]For an accessible exploration of Scripture and the sea, see Meric Srokosz and Rebecca S. Watson, *Blue Planet, Blue God: The Bible and the Sea* (Norwich, UK: SCM Press, 2017).

[13]R. D. Sluka, *Hope for the Ocean: Marine Biodiversity, Poverty Alleviation and Blessing the Nations* (Cambridge: Grove Books, 2012), 4.

[14]Ibid., 4.

[15]Ibid., 5.

[16]Barth observes, "In the new heaven and the new earth, as we learn from Rev. 21:1, there will be no more sea, i.e., man will be fully and finally freed from each and every threat to his salvation, and God from each and every threat to His glory" (*CD* III/1, 149).

For Barth, water in Genesis 1 is both physical and a sign of danger.[a] He arrives at this view by reading Genesis 1 in relation to the salvation history of Israel and of the exodus in particular. He notes of the waters in the exodus, "Water . . . is a representative of all the evil powers which oppose and resist the salvation intended for the people of Israel, thus trying to resist God Himself."[b] He helpfully observes that "it is thus the more noteworthy that the most striking Messianic deeds of Jesus are His walking on the sea in royal freedom, and His commanding the waves and storm to be still by His Word."[c]

There is no doubt that the seas, oceans, and rivers are used as symbols of evil in the Old Testament, and for a non-seafaring people it is not hard to understand why.[d] However, in our view Barth errs in affixing a kind of metaphysical status to water as a negative image. In Job 40–41, for example, both Behemoth and Leviathan, land and sea animals, are used as symbols of God's creative power. Intriguingly, a large bronze sea was part of the temple furniture (1 Kings 7:13-14, 23-26). Keel and Schroer understand the imagery here as Yahweh preventing the world from sinking into the waters of chaos.[e] Srokosz and Watson, however, identify more than divine control symbolized by this sea: "The sea was from this perspective a sacred space, an essential aspect of God's dwelling-place and equally vital as a source of life."[f] From Ezekiel 28:2 they conclude that in some sense the heart of the seas is viewed as a sacred place.[g] Thus we find it unhelpful to see the fundamentally good nature of water tarnished as almost entirely a negative symbol.

At stake here is the role of myth in the Old Testament. Thiselton points out the value of intertextuality in this respect.[h] The images of Rahab, Leviathan, and the dragon do not function with the unconscious view of myth but as "myth-consciously-used-as-symbol"[i] or as "broken myth." Genesis 1 serves canonically to alert the reader to the fact that all of the creation is good, including water and the oceans. The rest of the Old Testament should be read through this lens rather than the other way around.[j] Recent scholarship questions the connection between *těhôm* in Genesis 1 and Tiamat, but it is worth reading the Enuma Elish to see just how far removed the ethos of Genesis 1 is from that creation account.[k] In our view this is another case in which the Old Testament is distinct while remaining in dialogue with its ancient Near Eastern context.

---

[a]For Barth, "water" is more than a sign; it participates "as an image in a higher order" (*CD* III/1, 148).

[b]Barth, *CD* III/1, 147.

[c]Barth, *CD* III/1, 149.

[d]Cf. Philippe Reymond, *Eau, Sa Vie et Sa Signification Dans l'Ancien Testament* (Leiden: Brill, 1958); James E. Rupp, *The Sea Motif in the Old Testament* (Dallas: Dallas Theological Seminary, 1966); Toshio Tsumura, "Symbolism of the Sea in the Old Testament" (MTh thesis, Ashbury Theological Seminary, 1969); John N. Day, *God's Conflict with the Dragon and the Sea: Echoes of a Canaanite Myth in the Old Testament* (Cambridge: Cambridge University Press, 1985); Carola Kloos, *YHWH's Combat with the Sea: A Canaanite Tradition in the Religion of Ancient Israel* (Amsterdam: Brill, 1986); Othmar Keel, *The Symbolism of the Biblical World: Ancient Near Eastern Iconography and the Book of Psalms*, trans. Timothy J. Hallett (Winona Lake, IN: Eisenbrauns, 1997), 73-76, 136-40; Ehud Ben Zvi and Christoph Levin, eds., *Thinking of Water in the Early Second Temple Period* (Berlin:

de Gruyter, 2014). See in particular the essays by Robert Luyster and Herbert G. May in *Cult and Cosmos: Tilting Toward a Temple-Centered Theology*, ed. L. Michael Morales (Belgium: Peeters, 2014), 249-58 and 259-71

[e]Othmar Keel and Silvia Schroer, *Creation: Biblical Theologies in the Context of the Ancient Near East*, trans. Peter T. Daniels (Winona Lake, IN: Eisenbrauns, 2015), 83.

[f]Meric Srokosz and Rebecca S. Watson, *Blue Planet, Blue God: The Bible and the Sea* (Norwich, UK: SCM Press, 2017), 101.

[g]Ibid., 117.

[h]Anthony C. Thiselton, *New Horizons in Hermeneutics* (Grand Rapids, MI: Zondervan, 1992), 41.

[i]Ibid.

[j]See the excellent article by Bernard Och, "Creation and Redemption: Towards a Theology of Creation," in Morales, *Cult and Cosmos*, 318-30.

[k]See James B. Pritchard, ed., *The Ancient Near East: An Anthology of Texts and Pictures* (Princeton, NJ: Princeton University Press, 2011), 28-39.

Clearly the oceans and their inhabitants are a glorious part of God's creation, so that despoiling the oceans diminishes God's glory and is detrimental to humans. We are increasingly aware of how greed is in fact despoiling the oceans. Bottom trawling, dynamite fishing, and the use of poisons such as cyanide to fish are examples. "Grouper hide in holes and crevices on the bottom and the cyanide is squirted into the hole, stunning the fish and allowing easy removal and subsequent revival. The fish are then transported live to Hong Kong via ship. The problem is that the cyanide kills smaller fish and coral."[17] The cumulative result is that "we are taking more out of the sea than can be replenished. In the UK it is estimated that fishermen have to spend 17 times as much effort today to catch the same amount of fish as they did 120 years ago."[18]

An initiative that is helping to care for the fish of the world is Marine Protected Areas (MPAs). Where these have been established, fish grow larger and repopulate the surrounding areas. Our ecology, however, is *an ecology*, and "it does no good to set up a MPA and then let developers build huge hotels with a golf course that pumps sewage into the ocean and where fertilizers run off with each rainfall."[19]

Sluka suggests three biblical principles to inform our care of the oceans: sabbath, justice, and blessing to the nations. It is fascinating to note how unintentional sabbaths for fish during the two world wars led to vast replenishment of stocks. As Sluka perceptively notes, "If we extend the idea of a Sabbath rest to space, not just time, we can see that MPAs can function to allow populations the chance to return to a healthier state, with larger fish, producing more young, repopulating large areas."[20]

[17]Sluka, *Hope for the Ocean*, 9.

[18]Ibid.

[19]Ibid., 12.

[20]Ibid., 16.

The principles of justice and of blessing the nations are crucial when it comes to the oceans and their creatures. They have intrinsic value and deserve protection, but appropriate care also benefits the poorest of the poor.[21] "The socio-economic aspects of MPAs have received less attention from researchers, but are now becoming much more important and vital to the success of the MPAs themselves."[22] Leviticus 25 and the law of Jubilee are of relevance here: "There is a strong link between the anointed one and the year of Jubilee. The gospel Jesus proclaims includes freedom for the poor, not just spiritual freedom, but hearkening back to Jubilee legislation, freedom to benefit from the abundance of the land (and sea). Marine Protected Areas are a tool for proclaiming the year of the Lord's favour."[23] Nick Spencer and Robert White, paraphrasing David Cameron, note, "The acid test for biblically derived policies (in any area and not just sustainable living) will not be how they affect the better off, but how they protect, help and transform the lives of the vulnerable."[24] Many of the marine biodiversity hotspots are found among the poorest of the poor, and appropriate care for them would honor God and benefit the people.

Psalm 111 ends with the typical wisdom statement that the fear of the Lord is the beginning of wisdom. Susan Power Bratton argues, "Scientific fisheries management has, far too frequently, been overconfident of its knowledge and, in practice, devoid of wisdom."[25] In response she rightly refers to passages such as Job 38.

We noted above the appalling use of cyanide to fish groupers. This leads us to a question that is gaining attention—namely, the relationship between humans and animals, *including* fish. One might think that fish are unable to develop relationships with humans. Cousteau, however, relates the extraordinary story of Ulysses, a grouper of about sixty pounds who attached himself to Cousteau and his team of deep sea divers. Cousteau writes,

> Ulysses became our inseparable friend. He followed us everywhere, sometimes nibbling our fins. After deep dives, when we were decompressing thirty feet

---

[21]Craig Leisher, Pieter van Beukering, and Lea M. Scherl, *Natures Investment Bank: How Marine Protected Areas Contribute to Poverty Reduction* (Arlington, VA: The Nature Conservancy, 2007), www.nature.org/media/science/mpa_report.pdf.

[22]Sluka, *Hope for the Ocean*, 17.

[23]Ibid., 17.

[24]Nick Spencer and Robert White, *Christianity, Climate Change and Sustainable Living* (London: SPCK, 2007), 147.

[25]Susan Power Bratton, "The Precautionary Principle and the Book of Proverbs: Towards an Ethic of Ecological Prudence in Ocean Management," *Worldviews* 7, no. 3 (2003): 270.

down on a weighted and measured cable, the boredom was enlivened by Ulysses' horsing around with us until we went to the ladder. Afterwards he would hang around just under the surface, sitting on his tail, like a boy sadly watching his playmates being called in to supper. Ulysses quickly got on to our diving schedule and would be found early in the morning waiting under the ladder for the day's first sortie. He would go bounding down with us for a round of clumsy mischief and meals from the canvas bag.[26]

The land. The Hebrew word for humankind in Genesis 1:26-28—namely, *ʾādām*—forges the closest possible bond between humankind and the earth, with its connection with *ʾădāmâ* (cultivable ground),[27] although the word used for the earth as a whole in Genesis 1 is *ʾereṣ*. In Genesis 2:7, however, Yahweh Elohim forms *ʾādām* out of the *ʾădāmâ*, and in Eden it is out of the *ʾădāmâ* that Yahweh Elohim causes trees to grow that are nutritionally—and aesthetically—satisfying.

In his discussion of the third day of creation in Genesis 1, Barth notes that it is a day of a new beginning:

> The vegetable kingdom which grows out of the dry land in obedience to the Word of God will not be the only living creature. But it is the first, and the presupposition of all the rest. Every living creature is alive because of that which it has in common with the vegetable kingdom, and it remains alive because it finds food, its spread table, in the vegetable kingdom. This spread table belongs necessarily to the centre of the house built by God. But this relationship is not seen immediately. The plant is undoubtedly created for its own sake as well.[a]

[a]Barth, *CD* III/1, 143.

Throughout Genesis 2:4–3:24 *ʾădāmâ* is used for Eden, and *ʾereṣ* does not occur. "Earthling"[28] is thus an apt name for human beings, evoking our *embodied* nature. Theodore Hiebert says,

> This *ʾădāmâ* or cultivable soil, is presented by the Yahwist as the setting for human society. The relationship between them, between human life and arable land, is described in two ways. In the first place, the first human, *ʾādām*, is

[26]Jacques Yves Cousteau, *The Living Sea* (New York: Harper & Row, 1963), 157. See ibid., 129-30, for photographs of Ulysses.

[27]Theodore Hiebert, *The Yahwist's Landscape: Nature and Religion in Early Israel* (New York: Oxford University Press, 1996), 34-35.

[28]Carol A. Newsom, "Common Ground: An Ecological Reading of Genesis 2–3," in *The Earth Story in Genesis*, ed. Norman C. Habel and Shirley Wurst (Sheffield: Sheffield Academic Press, 2000), 60-72.

> described as the cultivator of *ʾădāmâ*. . . . But the connection between the first human being and the arable land, between *ʾădām* and *ʾădāmâ*, runs even deeper for the Yahwist. Not only does *ʾădām* cultivate *ʾădāmâ*, he is fashioned by God out of the land he farms.[29]

Because humans are embodied, implacement is unavoidable. We see this in the shift from Genesis 1:1–2:3 to Genesis 2:4–3:24. In Genesis 1 the whole world comes into existence as a good, potential home for humans, but human habitation is necessarily particular, and for the first couple we see in Genesis 2, that means Eden. Place names start to multiply in Genesis 2—Eden, Pishon, Havilah, Gihon, Tigris, and Assyria—thereby evoking the differentiation toward a specific place: "Place-names embody this complex collective concreteness despite their considerable brevity."[30]

Genesis 2 thus begins the story of human history with the implacement of Adam and Eve in Eden. We are told little about this "garden" other than that it is fertile with a variety of trees, aesthetically pleasing, and a river flows out of it so that it is well irrigated. Because of this limited information we far too easily read into Eden our own experiences of gardens or a Romantic ideal of untamed wilderness. How should we think of Eden?

First, Eden is a specific place. "The biblical witness is speaking of a definite place on earth."[31] Wenham describes the narrative of Eden as "highly symbolic."[32] "The garden of Eden is not viewed by the author of Genesis simply as a piece of Mesopotamian farmland, but as an archetypal sanctuary, that is a place where God dwells and where man should worship him. Many of the features of the garden may also be found in later sanctuaries particularly the tabernacle or Jerusalem temple. These parallels suggest that the garden itself is understood as a sort of sanctuary."[33] However, he notes that "the mention of the rivers and their location in vv 10-14 suggests that the final editor of Genesis 2 thought of Eden as a real place, even if it is beyond the wit of modern writers to locate."[34] This is further implied by the *toledoth* context in which Genesis 2:4–4:26 occurs, signaling the unfolding history of humankind. In addition, the move in Genesis 1–3 is from heavens and

---

[29]Hiebert, *Yahwist's Landscape*, 35.

[30]Edward S. Casey, *Getting Back into Place: Toward a Renewed Understanding of the Place-World* (Bloomington: Indiana University Press, 1993), 23.

[31]Barth, *CD* III/1, 252.

[32]Gordon J. Wenham, "Sanctuary Symbolism in the Garden of Eden Story," in Morales, *Cult and Cosmos*, 161-66.

[33]Ibid., 161.

[34]Wenham, *Genesis 1–15*, 61-62.

earth, to earth, to the garden. The setting in Genesis 2:5-8 implies a Mesopotamian site for Eden.[35]

But what sort of garden is Eden? Intriguingly, the ancient Near Eastern context may imply that Eden is more of an urban phenomenon than a rural one. D. C. Benjamin argues that "it is more likely that the Eden in the story of the Adam is a landscaped garden or urban masterpiece than an undeveloped wilderness or a geological wonder."[36] Tuplin, however, thinks Eden is modest and comparable to the other gardens in the Old Testament.[37] While we cannot be sure of the imagery at work here, gardens constituted an important part of the irrigation economies of Mesopotamia and Egypt. For the wealthy and the influential, the garden could be vast and alongside their residences.

In Ecclesiastes, part of Qohelet's Solomonic quest for wisdom involves "great works": building houses, planting vineyards, making gardens and parks with all kinds of fruit trees, and constructing pools from which to water the trees (Eccl 2:4-6). This alludes to Yahweh Elohim's creation of Eden in Genesis 2, and Qohelet's activities fit with the royal fiction in Ecclesiastes and the projects of kings in the ancient Near East. That it was generally the wealthier who owned and developed such gardens confirms the monarchical dimension, albeit democratized, of the *imago Dei* in Genesis 1. Stordalen suggests that the presence of Yahweh Elohim in the garden indicates continuity between Eden and the royal Assyrian gardens: "Adam in story narration clearly is no conventional king. Still Adam and Eve, in analogy with Mesopotamian rulers, enjoy divine benevolence on behalf of all humankind."[38]

At a minimum Eden would have been a vast area, probably enclosed by walls, beautiful and fertile and ideal for cultivation. It was designed for human habitation. The urban connotations of gardens in the ancient Near East mean that Eden may well have included buildings. God as king, a central image of God in Genesis 1, plants a garden, and as the royal stewards, Adam and Eve dwell in the garden, which is a royal residence.[39]

---

[35]Ibid., 66. Cf. Hiebert, *Yahwist's Landscape*, 52-59, who argues that the Yahwist has in mind the Jordan Valley oasis of the past.

[36]D. C. Benjamin, "Stories of Adam and Eve," in *Problems in Biblical Theology: Essays in Honor of Rolf Knierim*, ed. Henry T. C. Sun (Grand Rapids, MI: Eerdmans, 1997), 43-44.

[37]Christopher Tuplin, *Achaemenid Studies* (Stuttgart: Steiner, 1996), 81.

[38]T. Stordalen, *Echoes of Eden: Genesis 2–3 and Symbolism of the Eden Garden in Biblical Hebrew Literature*, Contributions to Biblical Exegesis and Theology 25 (Leuven: Peeters, 2000), 298.

[39]For an alternate view see Hiebert, *Yahwist's Landscape*, 61.

Eden is a one-off, archetypal garden, and there is no hint of Adam and Eve traveling away from it and back to it. However, reading the Eden narrative alongside 1:28, we can assume that God's intention was for Eden to expand way beyond its borders. Only after the fall is the way to Eden closed. We can thus characterize Eden as a fully fledged dwelling place.

As such, Eden has the specific characteristics of a garden. Historically there are a great variety of gardens, and Edward Casey restricts his analysis to three types: early enclosed gardens, informal landscape gardens, and formal gardens. He identifies the following characteristics of gardens:

- Mood is an intrinsic feature.
- Gardens instruct us as to the expanded building potential of certain material elements—ground, wood, water, rock.
- Gardens offer dwelling of some sort.[40]

For Casey, gardens do not normally include permanent dwellings, but clearly Eden does, so that in this sense it is hestial, to use Casey's term, developed from Hestia, the Greek goddess of the hearth.[41]

Gardens are *cultivated* places,[42] which fits with Yahweh Elohim placing Adam and Eve into Eden to "till it and keep it" (Gen 2:15). Indeed, Hiebert suggests that the animals are created to assist Adam with the task of cultivation. He also argues that Eve's being created to be a helper *like Adam* means that the family unit, the nucleus of agricultural society, is established.[43] A translation of *'bd* (NRSV "till") is "to serve,"[44] and this undermines any sense of brutal mastery. "In tilling the soil we care for it by ploughing and planting in ways useful to the growing of food. . . . We must question the presumption that building is an exclusively Promethean activity of brawny aggression and forceful imposition."[45] Barth observes that in the light of humankind's dependence on plants, the human is the most "necessitous" of all creatures, and Barth asks, "Will his sovereignty over plants and beasts consist in anything but the fact that he has more to be grateful for than these other earthly creatures, not only for his own existence, but for that of the whole earthly sphere which is the indispensable presupposition of his own?"[46]

---

[40]Casey, *Getting Back into Place*, 168-70.

[41]Ibid., 140. Casey distinguishes between hermetic and hestial dwelling. Hestial relates to the "intimacy and memorability of domestic space."

[42]Ibid., 155.

[43]Hiebert, *Yahwist's Landscape*, 60.

[44]Wenham, *Genesis 1–15*, 67.

[45]Casey, *Getting Back into Place*, 173.

[46]Barth, *CD* III/1, 143.

Casey says of gardens, "Even if we pause from time to time, for the most part we perambulate in gardens."[47] Apart from being places of hard work, gardens evoke a mood of sociality, contemplation, and reflection. This relates to Genesis 3:8, in which Adam and Eve "heard the sound of the LORD God walking in the garden at the time of the evening breeze." The garden is not just a place for production but is also one of "intimacy, meditation, and family solidarity."[48] The sanctuary symbolism of Eden fits with the intimate relationship depicted here between Adam and Eve and God.[49] The unusual use of "Yahweh Elohim" alerts us to the relationship with God in which Adam and Eve participate,[50] and undermines any dichotomy between creation/nature and redemption/history.[51] The mood of reflection and sociality extends beyond that between Adam and Eve and God to include the plants and the animals. In his classic *Natural History of Selborne*, Gilbert White observes that "There is a wonderful spirit of sociality in the brute creation, independent of sexual attachment." He tells the story of a person who kept one horse and one hen: "By degrees an apparent regard began to take place between these two sequestered individuals. The fowl would approach the quadruped with notes of complacency, rubbing herself gently against his legs: while the horse would look down with satisfaction, and move with the greatest caution and circumspection, lest he should trample on his diminutive companion."[52] In Eden, we can imagine this sociality to include Adam and Eve and God.

Genesis 1–2 thus provides us with a *theology* of place; Eden is the garden of Yahweh (cf. Gen 13:10). The "tree of life is an essential mark of a perfect garden in which God dwells."[53] Barth says, "While He gives man the enjoyment of the whole Garden and all its trees, by the planting of the tree of life in its midst God declares that his primary, central and decisive will is to give him Himself."[54]

In contemporary theology the earth has been given the most sustained attention, and we will not explore it further other than to note that the doctrine

---

[47]Casey, *Getting Back into Place*, 155.

[48]Ibid., 158.

[49]Wenham, "Sanctuary Symbolism in the Garden of Eden Story."

[50]L'Hour, "Yahweh Elohim." 1974.

[51]See Hiebert, *Yahwist's Landscape*, 3-22.

[52]Gilbert White, *The Illustrated Natural History of Selborne* (London: Thames and Hudson, 1981), 164-65. White's *Natural History* was first published in 1789.

[53]Wenham, *Genesis 1–15*, 62.

[54]Barth, *CD* III/1, 282.

of creation calls us to explore agriculture, cities, gardens, wilderness, and indeed all aspects of life that develop the potentials built into the creation.[55]

Our argument in this section assumes that Genesis 2–3 is a decisive text in the Bible as a whole. Brueggemann, by comparison, says of Genesis 2–3, "It has been assumed that this is a decisive text for the Bible and that it states the premises for all that follows. In fact, this is an exceedingly marginal text. No clear subsequent reference to it is made in the Old Testament, though there are perhaps links in Ezek. 28."[a] In his *Echoes of Eden* Stordalen explores the possibility that the major motifs of Genesis 2–3 "could be contexted in a wider symbolic web" in the Old Testament.[b] Through a detailed analysis of Eden (garden) symbolism in the ancient Near East and the Old Testament, Stordalen concludes,

> The investigation indicated that the Eden symbol might have been more vital to ancient Yahwistic culture than the Eden story—although there were passages presupposing a story similar to the one now found in Genesis 2–3. Eden symbolism was applied to religiously vital institutions, such as the Temple, the Gihon source, Wisdom and Torah. These appear as "echoes" of Eden in the everyday world. Also, the Eden story was applicable in ways that are theologically concordant with what appear to be central passages and notions in biblical Yahwism. So the symbol of the Eden Garden would not have been particularly "marginal" . . . to a Persian Age biblical audience.[c]

In fact there are several clear references to the garden of Eden in the Old Testament (Gen 13:10; Is 51:3;[d] Ezek 28:11-19; 31:1-18; 36:35; Joel 2:3; Prov 3:18; 11:30; 13:12; 15:4). In his discussion of allusions and intertextuality, Stordalen deals with the relationship between Eden and depictions of Zion, as well as the motif of seeing people as inhabitants of Eden. In an influential article, Wenham develops a compelling and detailed case for seeing Eden symbolically as an "archetypal sanctuary" with multiple parallels to Zion.[e] He also notes that such a view accounts for a smooth transition from Genesis 1:1–2:3 to Genesis 2:4-24.[f]

Ecclesiastes 2:1-11 also seems to be intertextually related to Genesis 2.[g] Zakowitch refers to a narrative technique in the Bible that he calls "inverted reflection stories."[h] In such stories the author develops the character as the antithesis of a character in another story. With Verheij and contra Stordalen,[i] we think that here Qohelet attempts to be like God in creating an Eden, but, of course, his attempt fails miserably.

Stordalen also explores the motif of animal peace and that of a long, healthy life in the Old Testament (Is 65:17-25; Num 22–24; Gen 9:20-27; Job 15:7-10; Lev 26:3-13) and possible resonances with Genesis 2–3.[j] Inverted symbolism may also be at work

[55]Cf. Bartholomew, *Where Mortals Dwell*. For environmental theology readers are referred, in particular, to the fine corpus of works produced over a lifetime by the Lutheran theologian Paul Santmire.

in the Balaam story since, as Savran notes, the only two animals who speak in the Bible are the serpent and Balaam's donkey.[k] Of course, Balaam's mistake is not to listen to the donkey, whereas Eve is unwise in listening to the serpent and following his advice.

Wenham notes that the description of the tree of the knowledge of good and evil in Genesis 2:9; 3:6 as pleasant to the sight, good for food, and to be desired to make one wise is echoed in Psalm 19:8-9.[l] In our view this is correct; it is the tree of the knowledge of good and evil that is in view, ironically set against obedience to the law, which fits (cf. Ps 19:1-6) with how God has made the world. A deficient doctrine of creation has led scholars to see Psalm 19:1-6 as originally separate from Psalm 19:7-14, whereas God's torah reflects the grain of his creation.

Several scholars, including N. T. Wright, have astutely observed the intertextuality between Genesis 3:7 ("Then the eyes of both were opened") and Luke 24:31 ("Then their eyes were opened").[m] However, there may also be an ironic allusion to Genesis 3:7 in Psalm 19:8's "enlightening the eyes." McDowell has explored the relationship between the making of humankind in Genesis 2–3 and certain Mesopotamian and ancient Egyptian rituals. She discerns a strong contrast between Babylon and Genesis 2–3 as regards the motif of the opening of the eyes: "In each case, the opening of the eyes was not only an act of animation, but of divinization, or, in Gen 3:5-6, an attempt by Adam and Eve at divinization."[n] Obedience to the torah is the path of true sight and enlightenment, not the quest for autonomy. Mettinger similarly says of Genesis 2–3, "The Eden Narrative functions to validate and to explain. It validates the loyal observance of the divine commandment as the very foundation of the value system. It also explains the hardships of the human condition: suffering, vicissitudes, and death."[o]

There is thus ample reason for seeing Genesis 2–3 as part of a "wider symbolic net" in the Old Testament. McConville perceptively notes that Genesis 2–3 is the "first narrative development" of the concept of the *imago Dei*.[p] Indeed, in our view, the links between Genesis 1–3 and the rest of the canon are far stronger than is often realized. In Genesis 5:1 we find a reference back to the *imago Dei*. The covenant with Noah, as we argue elsewhere, is grounded in Genesis 1:1–2:3. The juxtaposition of Yahweh with Elohim in Genesis 2–3, although not on the lips of the serpent, identifies the creator God as Yahweh, Israel's redeemer. Clines observes that the promises to the patriarchs reaffirm the divine ideals for humankind set out in Genesis 1–2.[q] Comparably, Rogerson finds in the creation narratives a critique of life as we experience it in the actual world.[r] And so we could continue. In the New Testament Jesus refers back to Genesis 2 when asked about divorce, and Revelation is replete with motifs from Genesis 2–3. Thus, the wider symbolic net is far bigger than often supposed.

---

[a]Walter Brueggemann, *Genesis*, Interpretation (Atlanta: Westminster John Knox, 1982), 41. Cf. Claus Westermann, *Genesis 1-11: A Commentary*, trans. John J. Scullion (Minneapolis: Augsburg, 1984), 276; Robert P. Gordon, "The Ethics of Eden: Truth-Telling in Genesis 2–3," in *Ethical and Unethical in the Old Testament: God and Humans in*

Dialogue, ed. Katherine Dell (London: T&T Clark, 2010), 11-33, for similar comments in an otherwise fine article. There is an extensive literature on Gen 2–3 apart from the commentaries.

[b]T. Stordalen, *Echoes of Eden: Genesis 2–3 and Symbolism of the Eden Garden in Biblical Hebrew Literature*, Contributions to Biblical Exegesis and Theology 25 (Leuven: Peeters, 2000), 30.

[c]Ibid., 474.

[d]Brevard S. Childs notes that this imagery of Eden in Is 51 reverberates with God's promises in Is 41:17-20 and Is 35. *Isaiah: A Commentary* (Louisville, KY: Westminster John Knox, 2001), 402.

[e]Gordon J. Wenham, "Sanctuary Symbolism in the Garden of Eden Story."

[f]Ibid., 165.

[g]A. J. C. Verheij, "Paradise Retried: On Qohelet 2:4-6," *JSOT* 50 (1991): 113-15; Craig G. Bartholomew, *Ecclesiastes*, Baker Commentary on the Old Testament Wisdom and Psalms (Grand Rapids, MI: Baker Academic, 2009).

[h]Yair Zakowitch, "Reflection Story—Another Dimension of the Evaluation of Characters in Biblical Narrative," *Tarbit* 54, no. 2 (1985): 165-76 (in Hebrew).

[i]Verheij, "Paradise Retried"; Stordalen, *Echoes of Eden*, 403-6.

[j]Ibid., 437-49.

[k]George Savran, "Beastly Speech: Balaam's Ass and the Garden of Eden," *JSOT* 64 (1994): 33-55.

[l]Wenham, "Sanctuary Symbolism," 165; cf. Stordalen, *Echoes of Eden*, 428-30.

[m]See Christopher A. Graham, *The Church as Paradise and the Way Therein: Early Christian Appropriation of Genesis 3:22-24* (Leiden: Brill, 2017), 83-87.

[n]Catherine L. McDowell, *The Image of God in the Garden of Eden*, Siphrut 15 (Winona Lake, IN: Eisenbrauns, 2015), 235.

[o]Tryggve N. D. Mettinger, *The Eden Narrative: A Literary and Religio-historical Study of Genesis 2–3* (Winona Lake, IN: Eisenbrauns, 2007), 84.

[p]J. Gordon McConville, *Being Human in God's World: An Old Testament Theology of Humanity* (Grand Rapids, MI: Baker Academic, 2016), 31.

[q]David J. A. Clines, *Job 1–20*, WBC 17 (Dallas: Word, 1989), 78-79.

[r]J. W. Rogerson, *A Theology of the Old Testament: Cultural Memory, Communication and Being Human* (London: SPCK, 2009), 48.

The sky. "Let birds multiply on the earth" (Gen 1:22). The sky is the third major place identified in Genesis 1. We now understand just how vast is the sky, and it remains a relatively unexplored territory. The first landing on the moon occurred on July 20, 1969, and now if you are gazing at the stars you can often see satellites moving steadily across the sky. Alas, the sky has become yet another dumping ground as expired equipment is left to roam around space.

In this section we will concentrate on birds, those creatures that occupy the sky. Part of the wonder of wisdom is attention to birds. In Psalm 50:11 God declares, "I know all the birds of the air," and part of imaging God will involve seeking comparable knowledge. Proverbs 30:18-19 declares:

Three things are too wonderful for me;
    four I do not understand:
the way of an eagle in the sky,
    the way of a serpent on a rock,
the way of a ship on the high seas,
    and the way of a man with a girl.

Solomon was renowned for his wisdom, and this included knowledge of birds (1 Kings 4:33).

In his magnificent *Birdscapes*, Jeremy Mynott notes that "any evocation of a place may miss a crucial aspect if it does not include in the account of its natural setting some reference to its characteristic bird life."[56] This charge cannot be laid against the Bible. Many passages, especially in the Psalter, speak of God's concern for birds;[57] and significantly, a sign of judgment on a place,[58] especially in Jeremiah, is the absence of birds and birdsong. In the New Testament birds play a not insignificant role. Alluding to Matthew 6:22, Wallace Stegner says of the prairies, "This is a land to mark the sparrow's fall."[59] And in his delightful book about the grassland birds of North America, Trevor Herriot observes,

> The summer-ending song of a bird that very likely failed to raise any young this year cries out to a more perfect fidelity dwelling in this land that marks the sparrow's fall. In the gospel of Stegner's allusion, Jesus tells peasants of Galilee that not a single sparrow falls to the ground without God's knowing and caring. . . . The power of Stegner's adaptation is in the shift it makes from God to land. Not only God, but the land itself keeps watch, keeps faith—for in prairie we sense an abiding awareness and attention that may be more obscure in other landscapes. God knows the sparrow. The land knows the sparrow. The trick of remaining here is to become a people who know the sparrow too, who will not give up on creatures who ask only for a place in the grass.[60]

The main theme of Jesus' teaching was the kingdom of God or heaven, and in one of his parables Jesus compares the kingdom to the way in which the small black mustard seed becomes "the greatest of shrubs," in which the birds come and make their nests (Mt 13:31-32; Mk 4:30-32; Lk 13:18-19).[61] The parable evokes the development of the kingdom in the creation,[62] and the

---

[56]Jeremy Mynott, *Birdscapes: Birds in Our Imagination and Experience* (Princeton, NJ: Princeton University Press, 2009), 204. Daniel Hillel's useful *The Natural History of the Bible: An Environmental Exploration of the Hebrew Bible* (New York: Columbia University Press, 2006) is an example in this respect; birds are not listed in his index.

[57]Ps 50:11; 104:12, 16–17; 148:10; Is 31:5; Dan 2:38; 4:21; Hos 2:18; Ezek 17:23; 31:6.

[58]Eccl 12:4; Hos 4:3; Zeph 1:3; Jer 4:25; 9:10; 12:4.

[59]Wallace Stegner, *Wolf Willow: A History, a Story, and a Memory of the Last Plains Frontier* (New York: Penguin Putnam, 1990), 8.

[60]Trevor Herriot, *Grass, Sky, Song: Promise and Peril in the World of Grassland Birds* (Toronto: HarperCollins Canada, 2012), 69.

[61]On this parable, see Klyne R. Snodgrass, *Stories with Intent: A Comprehensive Guide to the Parables of Jesus* (Grand Rapids, MI: Eerdmans, 2008), 216-28.

[62]For important Old Testament background, see Ezek 31, in which Egypt is compared to a great tree in which the birds of the air make their nests (v. 6). There are also Eden motifs in this chapter (vv. 8-9, 18).

"birds" are generally taken to represent the Gentiles.[63] However, a more literal interpretation would mean that the kingdom will bring harmony to the entire creation so that even the birds of the sky will dwell in peace.

In his *Wisdom of Birds: An Illustrated History of Ornithology*, Tim Birkhead argues that the Englishman John Ray (1627–1705) was the most influential ornithologist of all time:

> Ray spearheaded a new vision of the natural world, and he did so with a gentle modesty that belied a brilliant mind and wonderful clarity of vision. . . . Ray's God was responsible for the natural world in all its beauty and in particular the wonderful fit between an animal and its environment—something he called physico-theology (later known as natural theology) and what we today call adaptation. The culmination of his life's work, *The Wisdom of God*, published in 1691, laid out Ray's ideas in brilliant, readable style. In its day, physico-theology was as significant as Darwin's natural selection would be one hundred and fifty years later.[64]

A devout Christian, Ray exhorts his readers in the *Wisdom of God*, "Let it not suffice us to be Book-learned, to read what others have written and take upon trust more Falsehood than Truth: but let us our selves examine things as we have opportunity, and converse with Nature as well as Books." Ray initiated a nomenclature by developing a definition of a species, which inspired Linnaeus some sixty years later. Ray's physico-theology provided a conceptual framework for ornithology, and his *Wisdom* initiated the study of birds in their natural environments.[65]

Birds play a dominant role in Gilbert White's *Natural History*. White was a priest and deeply influenced by Ray's physico-theology. Maybey observes, "Although he lived at a time when the rule of reason and the supremacy of man were accepted almost as gospel, White contrived to portray the daily business of lesser creatures as a source not just of interest, but of delight and inspiration. To that extent the book is a glimpse of a place of sanctuary."[66] James R. Lowell delights in White's *Natural History* and says, "His volumes are the journal of Adam in Paradise."[67] Allen says of it, "For it is, surely, the testament of Static

---

[63]Snodgrass (*Stories with Intent*, 224) thinks this unlikely.

[64]Tim Birkhead, *The Wisdom of Birds: An Illustrated History of Ornithology* (London: Bloomsbury, 2008), 7. However, cf. Birkhead's subsequent book, *The Wonderful Mr Willughby: The First True Ornithologist* (London: Bloomsbury, 2018).

[65]Birkhead, *Wisdom of Birds*, 8-9.

[66]Richard Maybey, *Gilbert White: A Biography of the Author of* The Natural History of Selborne (London: Profile, 1986, 2006), 2.

[67]James R. Lowell, *My Study Windows*, 3rd ed. (London: Samson Low, Son, and Marston, 1871), 1.

Man: at peace with the world and with himself, content with deepening his knowledge of his one small corner of the earth, a being suspended in a perfect mental balance. Selborne is the secret, private parish inside each one of us."[68] White was fascinated by bird migration and loved swallows and martins in particular.

John James Audubon's (1785–1851) name is renowned in birdwatcher circles, especially because of his *Birds of America*. Audubon was a complex character, and his methods would certainly not always fit with our twenty-first-century sensibilities.[69] Significantly, for our purposes, he was "a devout Quaker, he said his prayers out loud every night, kneeling beside his bed, and firmly believed that the natural world, along with all its creatures, had been created by the Almighty. . . . His admiration of nature, in all its forms, was unbounded, and he was haunted by the fear that mankind had already begun to destroy the environment."[70]

In John Ray there was no dualism between wonder and analysis. As science developed, however, it became more and more reductionistic so that a tension developed between wonder and analysis. In Mynott's wonderful *Birdscapes*, a tension is nevertheless felt throughout between his love of birds and his wariness of projecting anthropomorphisms onto birds.[71]

> While we understand Mynott's wariness of projecting human emotions onto birds, we suspect that it is related to the Enlightenment's tendency to produce reductionist ontologies that marginalize wonder. We need an ontology and an epistemology that does justice to our experience of birds without erasing important distinctions.
>
> One such ontology is that of the Dutch philosopher Herman Dooyeweerd, at the heart of which is antireductionism. There are three major building blocks to Dooyeweerd's philosophy: particular entities (this bird); fifteen modal aspects (how entities function); and individuality structures (God's order for entities). Dooyeweerd's philosophy enables our lived experience to be taken with full seriousness. He argues that every entity functions in all fifteen modal aspects. For example, the aesthetic and spiritual aspects of a bird are not imaginary projections but real. They are a genuine part of what it means for a bird to be a bird. Vladimir Nabokov's description of standing among rare butterflies thus fits with reality: "This is ecstasy, and behind the ecstasy is

---

[68]Quoted in Mynott, *Birdscapes*, 191.

[69]On Audubon's life and struggle to publish *The Birds of America*, see Duff Hart-Davis, *Audubon's Elephant: The Story of John James Audubon's Epic Struggle to Publish the "Birds of America"* (London: Orion, 2003).

[70]Ibid., 42.

[71]Mynott, *Birdscapes*, 23-27, 43, 112, 147, 180, 267, 289-96, 301-2.

something else, which is hard to explain. It is like a momentary vacuum into which rushes all that I love. A sense of oneness with sun and stone. A thrill of gratitude to whom it may concern—to the contrapuntal genius of human fate or to tender ghosts humouring a lucky mortal."[b]

Importantly, Dooyeweerd argues that although entities function in all fifteen modes, they may not function as a *subject* in all modes; in some they may function *objectively*.[c] Thus, for Dooyeweerd, a bird functions as a subject in all modes up to and including the sensitive and objectively in the remaining modes. Thus a bird is a living, sensate organism, and its qualifying mode—the sensitive—gives it its distinctive character as an "animal." A bird cannot speak or name other objects, but its function in the lingual mode means that part of creation is the capacity built into creation for humans to name birds. A bird will not admire the beauty of other birds, but its functioning in the aesthetic mode means that its beauty is not imaginary or a human projection; it is real and able to be recognized and enjoyed by humans. This nonreductionistic approach is very helpful as we consider plants and animals.

In his *Arctic Dreams*, Barry Lopez describes the effect of his evening walks among the tundra birds while camped in the western Brooks Range of Alaska: "I took to bowing on these evening walks. I would bow slightly with my hands in my pockets, toward the birds and the evidence of life in their nests—because of their fecundity, unexpected in this remote region, and because of the serene arctic light that came down over the land like breath, like breathing."[d] Dooyeweerd's philosophy allows us to take the reality and richness of this experience seriously.

[a]For the negative significance of Descartes's philosophy for animals, see Kathryn Shevelow, *For the Love of Animals: The Rise of the Animal Protection Movement* (New York: Holt, 2009), 27-32.

[b]Nabokov, *Speak, Memory* (1966), quoted in Mynott, *Birdscapes*, 96.

[c] Bartholomew and Goheen, *Christian Philosophy*, 243-67.

[d]Barry Lopez, *Arctic Dreams: Imagination and Desire in a Northern Landscape* (New York: Bantam Books, 2013), xx.

Suburban life today easily distances us from earthy reality and thus deprives us of the attentiveness the creation requires.[72] Herriot remarks, "It's a fool's dream, but a part of me can't stop imagining that if enough people would discover all that is good and holy in these birds, we might be able to turn things around before it's too late."[73] He says of his drawings and writing, "Each story, argument, species profile, and drawing was conceived within a

[72]For the effects of sprawl and strategies to counteract them, see Elizabeth A. Johnson and Michael W. Klemens, eds., *Nature in Fragments: The Legacy of Sprawl*, New Directions in Biodiversity Conservation (New York: Columbia University Press, 2005).

[73]Herriot, *Grass, Sky, Song*, 3.

longing to reclaim the original spirit of grassland that survives yet in its birds. Beneath that longing lie the deeper human wish we all share: to find out how we might belong to a place, to find a way home."[74]

It is only through such *attentiveness* that we will discover all that is good and holy in "these birds," and the place to start is just where we are. As we make place for birds in our lives, they will call us back into place. In the process we might be surprised by the willingness of wild animals to live with humans. Herriot wonderfully narrates one Edgar's experience of chickadees in Central Butte:

> In the fall of '26 he got to know some chickadees on the property. One was cheekier than the rest, brave enough to come to his outstretched hand and get bread crumbs. Within a week he had five chickadees all over his head and shoulders. They'd ride to the barn with him and in the morning when he went out to do chores he'd give a whistle, imitating their song, and they would come to greet him.
>
> The birds disappeared for a spell, but the next fall he was out with a friend hunting rabbits and the friend said, "Edgar, there's a bird riding on your gun barrel." Edgar gave the whistle and four more chickadees came out of the bush to join the one on his rifle. He hadn't seen them for months and he was half a mile away from the yard where he'd been feeding them, but they still knew Edgar, and responded to his call.[75]

Animals: Partners and Naming

Partners. Like humans, the animals are formed from the ground; the same verb, "formed" (יָצַר), is used of both humans and animals. Both are brought forth from the ground (הָאֲדָמָה), but humans are said to be formed from the dust of the הָאֲדָמָה. This *forming* evokes a degree of similarity and intimacy between animals and humankind, but in Genesis 2:18-24 the narrative highlights the difference. The similarity meant that Adam might have found a "helper as a partner" (עֵזֶר כְּנֶגְדּוֹ; literally, "one who helps as his counterpart") among the animals, but he does not. That partner is found only in Eve. As Leon Kass perceptively notes, "Man's naming of the animals reveals to him his human difference: he names the animals but they cannot name him. Man alone among the animals can name."[76]

---

[74]Ibid., 4.

[75]Ibid., 62-63.

[76]Leon R. Kass, *The Beginning of Wisdom: Reading Genesis* (New York: Free Press, 2003), 76-77.

Genesis 1 alerts us to the fact that man and woman are created in the image of God. In chapter five we noted Barth's insightful views about humans always being gendered. The gendered nature of image bearers suggests the importance of *sociality* in image bearing. Genesis 2 elaborates on the relationship between man and woman through a narrative of the creation of the woman as a suitable counterpart to the man.

Westermann notes, "All human community is centered around the community of man and woman. This is described in two phrases which look first only to the community of man and woman, and then in a broader sense to all human community."[77] In Genesis 2:18 Yahweh Elohim identifies the lack of a "helper as his partner" for the man as "not good" (לֹא־טוֹב), the only place in Genesis 1–2 that this expression is used.

כְּנֶגְדּוֹ literally means "that which is over against him, his counterpart." "Together with the mutual help is the mutual correspondence, the mutual understanding in word and answer as well as in silence, which constitutes life in common."[78] The creation of the woman out of the rib of the man should not be taken literally. It indicates, rather, just how closely the man and the woman belong together. The word for "made," בָּנָה, in Genesis 2:22 literally means "build." It is the common term in Akkadian and Ugaritic to describe the creation of humans by the gods.[79] Only in Amos 9:6 is it again used in the Old Testament for creation.

Genesis 2:23 describes the "jubilant welcome"[80] of the man to the woman! Finally the man has found a suitable helper and counterpart. "Bone of my bones, and flesh of my flesh" is "the formula of relationship."[81] We will explore below the important theme of naming in Genesis 2. Unlike with the animals, here Adam does not have to be asked to name the woman; he does so spontaneously: יִקָּרֵא אִשָּׁה כִּי מֵאִישׁ לֻקֳחָה־זֹּאת, "this one shall be called Woman, for out of Man this one was taken." As is apparent from the Hebrew, there is a play on the names "Man" and "Woman," as in English. Westermann rejects the view that we have here the foundation of monogamy and the institution of marriage.[82] In our view, however, the institution of marriage is clearly established here, as is evident from Genesis 2:24. "One flesh" does not just refer to

[77]Claus Westermann, *Genesis 1–11: A Commentary*, trans. John J. Scullion (Minneapolis: Augsburg, 1984), 227.
[78]Ibid., 227.
[79]Ibid., 230-31.
[80]J. G. Herder in ibid., 231.
[81]W. Reiser, "Die Verwandtschaftsformel in Genesis 2:23," *Theologische Zeitschrift* 16 (1960): 1-4, in ibid., 232.
[82]Ibid., 232.

sexual unity but to "a relation . . . of most intimate, personal, spiritual and corporeal association."[83] In an agrarian society family bonds were understandably strong, so that the "leaving and cleaving" refers to a significant break for the formation of a new social unit.

It is significant that in the Gospels Jesus refers questions about divorce back to the creation narrative. Marriage is a permanent relationship with divorce never a desirable result, however necessary. The creation of man and woman also raises a host of ethical issues, such as the issue of gender, the different roles of men and women, and the theology of sexuality.

From Genesis 1 it is crystal clear that women are just as much image bearers as men and so equally called to be active in the creation in all spheres of life as image bearers. It is just as clear in Genesis 2 that men and women are somehow different and that this is a good difference and not a bad one. Men and women complement each other wonderfully and especially so in marriage. There is, it should be noted, no suggestion here or elsewhere in Scripture that same-sex marriage is permissible or desirable.[84]

Paul's exposition of the family in his letters clearly lends itself to trinitarian theology. Marc Ouellet rightly observes that "Paul sees the relationship between man and woman as being part of the *imago Dei*; the fecundity of this relationship announces Christ who, in union with the Church, will fill the world with his fullness."[85]

> Ouellet recognizes that the theology of the family must be grounded in creation and must also be developed within the context of Scripture and the tradition as a whole.[a] Rooted in creation, the family has inherent value in and of itself. In this sense it needs no justification. At the same time, as Paul makes clear in Ephesians 5, as part of God's creation the family witnesses to the triune nature of its maker. As Ouellet notes,
>
> > In the daily relationships of love in the family, the interlacing Trinitarian relations of fatherhood, sonship, and fruitful unity, which constitute Trinitarian holiness, shine forth. The incarnate Word, shaped by the Holy Spirit through the hands of

[83]Franz Delitzsch, *A New Commentary on Genesis*, trans. Sophia Taylor (Eugene, OR: Wipf & Stock, 2001), 145.

[84]This is, of course, contested. Ian A. McFarland says, "There has been no explicit discussion of the much debated question of same-sex marriage—though the logic of my argument suggests no intrinsic theological barrier to the ecclesial sanctioning of same-sex unions on the same terms as opposite sex-ones" (*The Divine Image: Envisioning the Invisible God* [Minneapolis: Fortress, 2005], 22). In our view this is one of the ways in which McFarland's resistance of Gen 1:26-28 as a/the gateway into theological anthropology manifests itself.

[85]Marc Ouellet, *Divine Likeness: Towards a Trinitarian Anthropology of the Family*, trans. Philip Milligan and Linda M. Cicone (Grand Rapids, MI: Eerdmans, 2006), 29.

> Mary and Joseph, brought forth this mystery in our midst and made possible the sacramental encounter between the Trinity in heaven and that on earth, the family, icon of the Most High.[b]

Catholics are rightly recognizing the indispensable role of the Christian family in the mission of the church. Protestants would do well to do likewise. Bartholomew notes the vital importance of the family for learning how to read Scripture.[c]

[a]Marc Ouellet, *Divine Likeness: Towards a Trinitarian Anthropology of the Family*, trans. Philip Milligan and Linda M. Cicone (Grand Rapids, MI: Eerdmans, 2006).
[b]Ibid., 123.
[c]Craig G. Bartholomew, *Introducing Biblical Hermeneutics: A Comprehensive Framework for Hearing God in Scripture* (Grand Rapids, MI: Baker Academic, 2015).

Naming. We noted in chapter five that humans are lingual creatures. In Genesis 2:18-20 the animals are brought before Adam by Yahweh Elohim for him *to name* them. Contra so much postmodernism, this means that *being is sayable*. This is not to equate human speech with God's, but it is to insist that in principle being is sayable.

Notably, the fish are not mentioned, and Gunkel suggests that they are overlooked.[86] However, as Westermann rightly points out, "But that is not the case. He [the author] is thinking of the animals from the viewpoint of human beings."[87] This relates to the unusual name of God in Genesis 2—namely, Yahweh Elohim, the God who is also Yahweh (i.e., the covenant God). Thus Westermann's helpful point should be further nuanced; the author is indeed thinking of the animals from the viewpoint of humans but also from the viewpoint of humans and animals in relation to God. Yahweh Elohim brings every animal and every bird to the man to see what he will name them.

According to Westermann, "man gives the animals their names and thereby puts them into a place in his world."[88] In our view the more complex relationality in operation leads to a more helpful view of the naming. The spirit of this *naming* is well captured in Herriot's experience: "The thought of creatures being endemic to the place I lived stirred something to life in my brain. I began to see that learning the names of things mattered, not so much in the possession it afforded as in its capacity to call things forth from generality into a particularity that allowed for admiration, familiarity, even wonder."[89]

[86]Herman Gunkel, *Genesis* Herders Theologischer Kommentar zum Alten Testament 1/1, 6th ed. (Göttingen: Vandenhoeck and Ruprecht, 1963).
[87]Westermann, *Genesis 1-11*, 227.
[88]Ibid., 228.
[89]Herriot, *Grass, Sky, Song*, 12.

In the Christian tradition a remarkable recovery of *being as sayable* is found in Chrétien's *The Ark of Speech*.[90] Chrétien takes the image of the ark from Noah's ark. His reflection on Adam's naming of the animals is acute and representative of his view of language as hospitality.

> Much more essential, and worthy of consideration, is the fact that this story makes human speech into the *first ark*. The animals have been gathered for human speech and brought together in this speech, which names them long before they are brought together . . . in Noah's ark to be saved from the flood and the destruction it brings. . . . Their first guardian, their first safeguard, is that of speech, which shelters their being and their diversity. This is true for more than just the animals. No protective gesture could take responsibility for the least being if the latter had not been taken up into speech.[91]

Contrary to Westermann's view, naming does not place animals in the man's world but protects their God-given identity within the creation. Chrétien notes that the naming of the animals is humankind's first test. Will the man use language as an "ark" in which to protect the otherness of the animals, or will he impose his desire on them?

Like George Steiner, Chrétien relates his view of language to creation: "In the account of creation given in the first chapter of Genesis we see brought into play, so that the game of the world can be played, a word and a gaze—and they are inseparable."[92] Paul Celan noted the common root of *denken* (think) and *danken* (thank), and, as Chrétien notes, "To think is to thank, but for this to be true, to thank must be to think really and truly, in other words to see."[93] For Chrétien,

> The world itself is heavy with speech, it calls on speech and on our speech in response, and it calls only by responding itself, already, to the Speech that created it. How could it be foreign to the word, when it subsists, through faith, only by the Word? . . . The speech we utter about the world does not come from beyond the world, it is no more a stranger to the world than we are.[94]

In the Christian tradition the world has often been likened to a book, and Chrétien observes that "within the book, God has created readers: us."[95]

---

[90]See esp. his chapter "The Offering of the World," in Jean-Louis Chrétien, *The Ark of Speech*, trans. Andrew Brown (New York: Routledge, 2004), 111-48.

[91]Ibid., 2.

[92]Ibid., 115.

[93]Ibid., 119.

[94]Ibid., 129.

[95]Ibid., 141. Cf. our comments on Basil of Caesarea in chap. 2.

Reading must be learned, and requires, certainly in our present condition, effort and patience; the fact remains that this book is not written in an unintelligible language. By virtue of the way God has made the world, including human beings, being is sayable.

Barry Lopez and Debra Gwartney edited *Home Ground: Language for an American Landscape*, an alphabetical resource created by a group of writers aimed at recovering our vocabulary for land. Lopez notes in his introduction,

> We put a geometry to the land—backcountry, front range, high desert—and pick out patterns in it: pool and riffle, swale and rise, basin and range. We make it remote (north forty), vivid (bird-foot delta), and humorous (detroit riprap).
>
> It is a language that keeps us from slipping off into abstract space.[96]

Conclusion

Amidst a life of much suffering, the Welsh Jesuit Gerard Manley Hopkins captured the wonder of creation better than most. He speaks of a world "charged with the grandeur of God," and in his poem "As Kingfishers Catch Fire" he speaks of Christ, who "plays in ten thousand places."[97]

Such poetry moves us close to the vision of this chapter. God's creation is an intricate network of relations, of which humans are part. We have a unique role to play in this network, but only insofar as we honor it, and live and work to grant it space to grow and flourish, so that more and more the whole creation becomes a grand symphony to the glory of God.

[96]Barry Lopez and Debra Gwartney, *Home Ground: Language for an American Landscape* (San Antonio: Trinity University Press, 2006), xxii-xxiii.

[97]Hopkins, *Major Works*, 129.

THE HEAVENLY REALM

The only tenet which can be established as a doctrine concerning angels is this: that the question whether the angels exist or not ought to have no influence upon our conduct, and that revelations of their existence are now no longer to be expected. . . . The idea of the Devil, as developed among us, is so unstable that we cannot expect anyone to be convinced of its truth; but, besides, our Church has never made doctrinal use of the idea.

FRIEDRICH SCHLEIERMACHER

God's action in Jesus Christ, and therefore his lordship over his creature, is called the "kingdom of heaven" because first and supremely it claims for itself the upper world. From this God selects and sends his messengers, the angels, who precede the revelation and doing of his will on earth as objective and authentic witnesses, who accompany it as faithful servants of God and man, and who victoriously ward off the opposing forms and forces of chaos.

KARL BARTH

The most important truth about the Devil is this:
Jesus Christ has conquered him.

EMIL BRUNNER

IN COLOSSIANS 1:15-20 we encounter an early hymn that celebrates the fact that by Christ "all things in heaven and on earth were created, things visible and invisible," that "in him all things hold together," and that "through him God was pleased to reconcile to himself all things, whether on earth or in heaven." This doxological masterpiece recognizes two distinct realms in the created order—heaven and earth, or visible and invisible. Christ created both realms, holds both realms together, and reconciles both realms. Scripture teaches that there is a boundary between our present world of experience and another "world" that lies beyond our experience. The Bible portrays a heavenly realm replete with a host of spiritual beings. Jesus and the apostles spoke often about the spirits (e.g., Mt 11:10; Lk 20:36), and so did the prophets and apostles. Indeed, Scripture says so much about the heavenly realm and its host, and ascribes to them such important functions and actions in providence and history, that we would be remiss not to reflect on God's unique purpose for them in his economy.

Before reflecting on the biblical evidence and theological implications of an invisible realm, we must first look at modernity's rejection of this invisible realm. In modernity the world became simply a machine that operates according to a set of rules. Although this mechanistic view of creation has fallen out of favor, the metaphysical implications remain. Thus, the belief in an invisible realm is no longer assumed by many today, as it was in previous times. Into this void of belief, the present chapter articulates the heavenly realm as a created place where God's presence is more immediate than our normal experience. It is a place in which angels dwell and perform their ministry before God. As spirits and persons, angels have been given a ministry to serve God and humanity toward the end of reconciling all things back to God in Christ. Hence, from this heavenly realm, angels traverse heaven and earth to serve humanity in God's redemptive purposes. Fallen angels, by virtue of their rebellion against God, have a kind of anti-ministry that seeks to unravel God's design and work against his good purposes in redemption. Ultimately, however, the outcome of this redemptive drama is not in doubt. Christ has conquered the principalities and powers in the heavenly realms. Thus, with a sure hope we look forward to a renewed and reconciled heaven and earth. Indeed, we look forward to the time that they will meet, becoming the place where we will dwell with God forever.

Modernity's Rejection of the Invisible Realm

While belief in an invisible realm has been the norm across the eras of world history and remains so today globally, modernity has created serious doubts regarding a world imperceptible by scientific observation. Modernity has brought with it huge benefits and progress in so many areas that we would be fools not to acknowledge them. Modern science has led us into an unprecedented understanding of the inner logic of many aspects of the universe. However, as David Hart points out, "The new picture of the world came into being as a unified whole, in which—as is always the case—truth and error, established knowledge and baseless prejudice, were inseparably mingled."[1] The breakthroughs in science required a thorough revision of how science works, but "the new anti-metaphysical method soon hypertrophied into a metaphysics of its own," envisioning the world as a machine.[2] This opened what Hart calls an "imaginative chasm" between the premodern and modern worlds.[3] Whereas in the premodern world the universe was seen as a kind of theophany of God, now deism and then atheism triumphed. Belief in angels and in demons were immediate casualties of this shift.

Jonathan Israel argues that the European Enlightenment was a "single highly integrated intellectual and cultural movement" and that "a close reading of the primary material strongly suggests . . . that Spinoza and Spinozism were in fact the intellectual backbone of the European Radical Enlightenment everywhere."[4] Spinoza equated God with nature, and his determinist system left no room for miracles, providence, angels, demons, and the immortal soul.

Israel tracks in detail the myriad ways in which Spinoza's naturalism influenced thinker after thinker, inevitably causing them to conclude that belief in angels and demons was a relic of a primitive past. In the early modern period such views were extremely controversial, and several major philosophers, such as Descartes, Malebranche, Boyle, Berkeley, and Locke, opted for a more moderate approach that left space for belief in angels and demons. With the triumph of the radical Enlightenment, such debates disappeared, although now, with the unprecedented revival of religion globally, it is possible they will be back on scholarly agendas.

Science has long since moved on from the mechanical model, but "the mechanical philosophy's great metaphysical master narrative . . . remains the frame within which we now organize our expectations of science and, consequently, of reality."[5] A picture, Wittgenstein might say, holds us captive, and it has no room for demons and angels, let alone the living God. Hart argues that current debates about belief in God that view the debates as a clash between religion and science are an inexcusable conceit: in fact such debates

---

[1]David Bentley Hart, *The Experience of God: Being, Consciousness, Bliss* (New Haven, CT: Yale University Press, 2013), 50.

[2]Ibid., 57.

[3]Ibid., 58.

[4]Jonathan I. Israel, *Radical Enlightenment: Philosophy and the Making of Modernity 1650–1750* (Oxford: Oxford University Press, 2001), v-vi.

[5]Hart, *Experience of God*, 64.

represent a clash between theism and naturalism, "and the latter is by far the less rationally defensible of the two."[6]

Theologians inevitably interact with their context, and some modern theologians responded differently than others to the naturalism and materialism of the radical Enlightenment. Some minimized Christian teaching concerning a heavenly realm with spiritual beings who act and interact in the same places and spaces where we live and work and play. Schleiermacher's view, as quoted above, is illustrative of this sort of reductionism. Schleiermacher thought Christ spoke about angels and demons in the same way that we today might speak of elves and fairies. If the spirit world exists, it has no real relevance. Similarly, Bultmann relegates belief in a "heavenly host" to a primitive world of myth.[7]

However, other modern theologians find a significant place for the heavenly realm and host. Pannenberg, for example, discerns a resurgence in the doctrine of angels and demons. He writes,

> Paul Tillich linked them to the archetypes of depth psychology and to a new awareness of the suprahuman power of the demonic in literature. Gerhard Ebeling related them to the experience that forces are at work in our relation to God and the world that are hidden from us but nonetheless active. Paul Althaus said that the reality of angels was a matter not merely of faith but also of experience. Hans-Georg Fritzsche used the term "field of force" in this connection, though without clarifying the link to scientific usage. We stand, he said, in a field of force that embraces the ego, which is where angels and demons belong.[8]

Many modern theologians revive the doctrine of angels and demons but tend toward viewing those "spirits" as impersonal forces or societal structures rather than as personal beings.

> During the twentieth century, an increasing number of scholars interpreted Paul's "principalities and powers" impersonally. Berkhof argued that Paul borrowed these terms from Jewish apocalyptic literature but demythologized them for appropriation by the church: Paul viewed the principalities and powers as societal structures rather than invisible spirits.[a] Yoder followed Berkhof and equated the principalities and powers with societal structures—intellectual, political, religious—that have absolutized

---

[6]Ibid., 76-77.

[7]Rudolf Bultmann, *Jesus Christ and Mythology* (New York: Charles Scribner's Sons, 1958), 14-15.

[8]Wolfhart Pannenberg, *Systematic Theology*, trans. Geoffrey W. Bromiley (Grand Rapids, MI: Eerdmans, 1994), 2:105-6.

themselves and thereby usurped Christ's rightful place as Lord.[b] Wink demythologized the principalities and powers, transposing them into oppressive human rulers and political structures.[c] Newbigin drew on Berkhof and Wink to argue that Paul's use of "principalities and powers" exists in relation to physical reality. Just as Paul identified Jewish law and the Roman Empire as examples of powers, Newbigin argued, we are justified in referring to number, change, ideology, or even the invisible forces of the free market as "powers."[d]

While we affirm the need to push back against reductionist Western individualism, and while we agree that "powers" have a hand in distorting and misdirecting social, cultural, and political institutions, we reaffirm the powers' personal and invisible nature. Following Peter O'Brien, we should note first that Christ confronts the principalities and powers "in the heavenly places" (Eph 1:20). Second, we recognize that Paul instructs the Christian that our warfare is with principalities and powers *rather than* with flesh and blood (Eph 6:12). Finally, Jesus himself believed in personal spirits and in the exorcism of demonic spirits.[e] O'Brien writes, in relation to Ephesians,

> Against Walter Wink the powers are not to be demythologized or collapsed into human rulers or political structures which oppress people. Paul believes that the powers are spiritual agencies *in the heavenly realms* which stand behind earthly and human institutions (cf. 6:12). All things are subject to Christ's present rule (1:22, 23), and this includes specifically the principalities and authorities over whom Christ is exalted in the heavenly realm. There seems to be no doubt that such spiritual powers can and do work through earthly structures; but to identify them with the structures is reductionistic.[f]

Similarly, Wolters argues for a "Reformational" perspective that is anchored in creation.[g] He distinguishes between normative principles and human positivization. What Newbigin refers to as "structural elements" Wolters refers to as "normative principles" and understands them as part of God's good created order. These normative principles structure our existence, but "human positivizations," such as social and cultural institutions, are always and invariably twisted and misdirected by human sin and idolatry. The structure remains good, but the misdirection of the structures is bad. Evil spirits are involved in this twisting and misdirecting but are not to be conflated with the twisted and misdirected social institutions themselves. Christ came to redeem human existence in its totality and thus one day will redirect social and cultural institutions, realigning them according to his will. We find O'Brien's and Wolter's perspective compelling, in that it recognizes that spiritual warfare affects social, cultural, and political realities but at the same time does not allow the principalities and powers to be conflated with, or reduced to, those same realities.

---

[a]Hendrikus Berkhof, *Christ and the Powers* (Scottsdale, PA: Herald Press, 1977), 14-59.
[b]John Howard Yoder, *The Politics of Jesus*, 2nd ed. (Grand Rapids: Eerdmans, 1994), 134-61.

[c]Walter Wink, *Naming the Powers: The Language of Power in the New Testament* (Philadelphia: Fortress, 1984), 3-140; Wink, *Unmasking the Powers: The Invisible Forces That Determine Human Existence* (Philadelphia: Fortress, 1986), 128-52.
[d]Lesslie Newbigin, *The Gospel in a Pluralist Society* (Grand Rapids, MI: Eerdmans, 1989), 198-210.
[e]Peter T. O'Brien, "Principalities and Powers and Their Relationship to the Structures," *Reformed Theological Review* 40 (1981): 1-10.
[f]Peter T. O'Brien, *The Letter to the Ephesians*, PNTC (Grand Rapids, MI: Eerdmans, 1999), 144.
[g]Albert M. Wolters, "Creation and the 'Powers': A Dialogue with Lesslie Newbigin," *Trinity Journal for Theology and Ministry* 4 (2010): 85-98.

Despite modernity's pervasive skepticism about the heavenly realm, the Enlightenment rejection of the Judeo-Christian worldview did not close down interest in the "other side." John Fleming observes that "the period of the Enlightenment witnessed, among other things, a remarkable efflorescence of occultism and mysticism."[9] In his book on angels Peter Kreeft observes, "The book's father was my unhappiness about the quality of angel books currently flooding the market and my surprised happiness about their quantity. There is a huge hunger out there, but it's being fed with fast food."[10] Similarly, David Jones in his *Angels: A Very Short Introduction* observes, "At the time of writing, an Internet search for 'angel' registered 287,000,000 hits, which was, for example, five times as many as 'Christianity' and six times as many as 'astronomy.'"[11] The lack of quality resources can create practical and powerful problems that need sound theological remedies.

The twentieth century, which so celebrated science and reason, turned out to be what many regard as the most brutal in history. In his commentary on Mark, C. E. B. Cranfield notes perceptively in his treatment of Mark 1:21-28, in which Jesus casts out an unclean spirit,

> Here we are up against something that presents many difficulties to the modern mind, which is apt to dismiss the whole subject as outgrown superstition. . . . To suggest that there might be more truth here in the N.T. picture than has sometimes been allowed is not to wish to turn the clock back on scientific progress or to open the flood-gates to obscurantism. The question whether the spread of a confident certainty of the demons' non-existence has not been their greatest triumph[12] gets tragic urgency from such twentieth-century features as Nazism, McCarthyism, and Apartheid. And lest we should

[9]John V. Fleming, *The Dark Side of the Enlightenment: Wizards, Alchemists, and Spiritual Seekers in the Age of Reason* (New York: Norton, 2013), 3. Cf. John Gray, *The Immortalization Commission: Science and the Strange Quest to Cheat Death* (Toronto: Anchor Canada, 2012).
[10]Peter Kreeft, *Angels (and Demons): What Do We Really Know About Them?* (San Francisco: Ignatius, 1995), 14.
[11]David A. Jones, *Angels: A Very Short Introduction* (Oxford: Oxford University Press, 2011), xvi.
[12]Cf. C. S. Lewis's *Screwtape Letters* in this respect.

> be prejudiced by the memory of such horrors as the burning of witches, it must be said that they were due, not to taking the N.T. too seriously, but to failing to take it seriously enough.[13]

Christians have not always helped their case for heaven by trivializing the invisible world and reducing the demonic to the sort of manifestations one finds in the movie *Ghostbusters* or the children's series Harry Potter, while ignoring the battle that rages across creation and in politics, economics, education, family life, and so on. We are now living amidst a major resurgence of religion across the globe and especially in the developing world. Theories of secularization, the beliefs that underlie the sort of view articulated by Schleiermacher above, are being replaced by theories of desecularization, and thus the time is ripe to reassess Christian belief in heaven.

The heavenly realm as created "place." Donald Guthrie writes of the New Testament portrayal of heaven, "We shall not expect . . . to find a description of a place, so much as the presence of a person."[14] However, the Bible portrays heaven not only as the *presence* of God but also as a *place* where his presence is most immediate. We are told that Jesus, at his ascension, was taken into heaven (Acts 1:11) and that Stephen "gazed into heaven," where he saw Jesus located at the right hand of God the Father (Acts 7:55-56). The biblical doctrine of resurrection speaks to the subject analogously: Jesus was raised and given a glorified body as he entered a place (heaven) just as we will be given glorified bodies in order to inhabit a place (the new heavens and earth).

Barth completes the doctrine of providence with a section on the kingdom of heaven, which includes a treatment of the heavenly host. He writes,

> God's action in Jesus Christ, and therefore his lordship over his creature, is called the "kingdom of heaven" because first and supremely it claims for itself the upper world. From this God selects and sends his messengers, the angels, who precede the revelation and doing of his will on earth as objective and authentic witnesses, who accompany it as faithful servants of God and man, and who victoriously ward off the opposing forms and forces of chaos.[15]

Barth goes on to argue that heaven is a *place* within creation that, like the rest of creation, stands in covenant relationship with God. It is in fact superior to

---

[13]C. E. B. Cranfield, *The Gospel According to St. Mark: An Introduction and Commentary*, Cambridge Greek Testament Commentaries (Cambridge: Cambridge University Press, 1959), 75. Cf. Emil Brunner, *Dogmatics*, vol. 2, *The Christian Doctrine of Creation and Redemption*, trans. Olive Wyon (Philadelphia: Westminster Press, 1952), 135.

[14]Donald Guthrie, *New Testament Theology* (Downers Grove, IL: InterVarsity Press, 1981), 875.

[15]Barth, *CD* III/3, 369.

earth, as God is nearer to heaven than to earth. God works and speaks from heaven such that we can speak about heaven as the place where God's will is done.[16] Thus, heaven is the place from where God reigns. However, other than that knowledge, the precise way in which heaven is a place is unknown, and indeed unknowable, to us.

Jenson builds on Barth's view, arguing that heaven is not only a place but a *sacramental* place, a place from which God beckons us forward toward his kingdom.[17] Revelation paints a picture in which earth also beckons heaven, a picture in which the Lord brings heaven with him to earth, renewing and restoring his creation. Heaven's future is on earth, and the earth's future is heavenly. "Heaven and earth," writes N. T. Wright, "are not after all poles apart. . . . Nor are they simply different ways of looking at the same thing. . . . No, they are different, radically different, but they are made for each other in the same way (Revelation is suggesting) as male and female."[18] Thus John's vision stands as the antithesis of gnosticism in its many variations, of every philosophy or religion that seeks to escape the earth, the physical, the material. Just as Jesus taught his disciples to pray, God's kingdom will come and his will will be done on earth just as it is done in the heavenly realm. In the meantime, God's church serves as a preview of that day, a place where his people draw near to him and, by doing so, near to heaven, though their feet remain firmly planted on earth.

The angels. Inhabiting the heavenly realm, we are told, are heavenly spirits, or "angels." The Greek *angelos* means "messenger or envoy," as does the Hebrew *mal'āk*. So "angel" is a name that derives from the function of these spiritual beings rather than from their essence. The biblical writers refer to distinct kinds of angels: cherubim, seraphim, principalities, powers, dominions, thrones, hosts, camps, and legions. Some angels are even given names. We are told that Michael is an archangel (Jude 9) who leads the heavenly army (Rev 12:7) and whose name means "Who is like God?" Similarly, we know Gabriel as one who makes announcements at significant points in redemptive history (Lk 1:11-13, 26-33) and whose name means "devoted to God." Lucifer is an adversary of God; he is also called the great dragon, the ancient serpent, or Satan (Rev 12:9). Beyond this rudimentary sketch, however, and traditional speculative systems and maps of celestial hierarchies

[16]Barth, *CD* III/3, 369.

[17]Robert W. Jenson, *Systematic Theology* (Oxford: Oxford University Press, 1999), 2:120-27.

[18]N. T. Wright, *Surprised by Hope: Rethinking Heaven, the Resurrection, and the Mission of the Church* (New York: HarperOne, 2008), 105.

notwithstanding, Scripture does not reveal much about the different kinds of spirits in the heavenly realm.

Angelic nature—angels as spirits and persons. Beyond their functions as messengers, what is the nature of angelic being? In the wake of the medieval era, and especially in the modern era, one notices a marked decrease in interest in this topic among theologians. Abraham Kuyper published a book titled *De Engelen Gods* (The angels of God), and he includes a section titled "Locus de Angelis" in his discussion of the doctrine of creation in his *Dictaten Dogmatiek* (Dictated dogmatics).[19] It was, however, with the resurgence of Barth studies that the heavenly realm and its host once again became a subject of serious theological reflection. Yet even Barth refuses to theologize about the angelic nature. Pannenberg summarizes Barth's view:

> Unlike the tradition, especially Aquinas . . . , Barth refused to examine the nature of angels. He regarded any study leading to a philosophy of angels as an aberration . . . and not sufficiently oriented to what Scripture says about them. Scripture itself, he said, tells us nothing about the nature of angels . . . , focusing instead on their function and ministry, which Barth thought he could define comprehensively as the ministry of witnesses to God and his kingdom.[20]

In our view there is a place for Christian philosophical and theological exploration of the nature of angels, who are part of the created order.

Scripture portrays the angels as *spiritual* and *personal* beings. Indeed, they are *created* as spiritual and personal beings (Heb 1:14). Reflecting on Psalm 148:1-5, Augustine writes, "Here [in v. 5] the angels are most expressly and by divine authority said to have been made by God, for of them among the other heavenly things it is said, He commanded, and they were created."[21] Although they were created by God through Christ and for Christ, some angels chose against God. We are told that they sinned and "did not keep their own position, but left their proper dwelling," and will therefore be "kept in eternal chains in deepest darkness for the judgment" (Jude 6; cf. 2 Pet 2:4).[22]

---

[19]Abraham Kuyper, *De Engelen Gods* (Kampen: Kok, 1923); *Dictaten Dogmatiek van Dr. A. Kuyper*, vol. 2, *Locus de Sacra Scriptura, Creatione, Creaturis* (Grand Rapids, MI: J. B. Hulst, n.d.).

[20]Pannenberg, *Systematic Theology*, 2:103.

[21]Augustine, *The City of God* 11.9 (trans. Marcus Dods [New York: The Modern Library, 1950], 353).

[22]Cf. Augustine, *The City of God* 12.1 (Dods, 381); Aquinas, *ST* I.63.2 (*Summa Theologiae*, trans. Fathers of the English Dominican Province [Allen, TX: Christian Classics, 1981], 313).

Jude has its challenges exegetically but is an important resource for biblical material on angels. God's punishment of the angels in Jude 6 for not keeping their own position—probably a reference to Genesis 6—serves as a warning to the readers.[a] The false teachers who are disturbing Jude's addressees are guilty, inter alia, of slandering the glorious ones—that is, God's good angels who deserve respect. Bauckham asserts,

> Much more plausible is . . . the view that it was the angels as givers and guardians of the law of Moses whom the false teachers slandered . . . and, we may add, the angels as guardians of the created order. . . . According to Jewish belief, the law of Moses was mediated by angels (. . . Acts 7:38, 53; Heb 2:2) and angels watched over its observance. . . . They were also, more generally, the guardians of the created order . . . and (according to the most probable interpretation of 1 Cor 11:10) it is to this function of the angels that Paul refers when he recommends proper conduct in the Christian assembly "because of the angels."[b]

[a] Richard Bauckham, *Jude–2 Peter*, WBC 50 (Dallas: Word, 1983), 50-51.
[b] Ibid., 58.

So the angels are created beings, some of whom are fallen. They are created as *spirits*, which differentiates them from the rest of the animate and inanimate creation (Heb 1:1). Along with the majority tradition, we conceive of angels as incorporeal beings, even though we find it difficult to apprehend the concept metaphysically.[23]

These spirits abide in the heavenly places (1 Kings 22:19; Mt 18:10; Gal 1:8), although they traverse heaven and earth. Their appearance is striking and resplendent. Ezekiel praises the Prince of Tyre for his beauty by comparing him to a cherub (Ezek 28:13-14); Matthew describes the angel at Jesus' tomb as having an appearance like lightning and clothes that are white like snow (Mt 28:3), and Paul tells us Satan masquerades as "an angel of light" (2 Cor 11:14).

As created beings, they are *intelligent*. Both good and bad angels possess intellectual capacities (2 Sam 14:20; Lk 1:13; Eph 6:11; Rev 10:5-6). They are *moral* beings who were created good. Although some of them fell, the remaining angels always do the Lord's will (Mt 6:10; Lk 20:36). They are *emotional* beings who have affection for God (Is 6:3; Rev 4:8-9) and who experience joy when a sinner repents (Lk 15:10). They are powerful beings (Ps 103:20), mightier than humans (2 Pet 2:11) and capable of exerting power over the physical capacities of human beings (Gen 19:10-11).

[23]Thomas C. Oden (*Systematic Theology*, vol. 1, *The Living God* [Peabody, MA: Hendrickson, 2006], 240-41) cites Irenaeus, Athanasius, Aquinas, and others in support of the angels' incorporeality.

Thus we find ourselves substantially in agreement with Kreeft's summary:

> Angelology has data, and its theories are justified by its data. For instance, the traditional theory of angels, which I will try to explain and defend in this book, says that angels are (1) creatures of God, (2) bodiless spirits, (3) with intelligence (4) and will, (5) who live in God's presence in heaven, (6) obey his will, (7) carry his messages (angel means "messenger"), (8) assume bodies as we assume costumes, (9) influence our imagination (10) but not our free will, and (11) move material things supernaturally.[24]

Angelic ministry. In the Bible angels perform multiple tasks. They sing praises to God (Ps 148:2), run errands for him (Mt 1:20-24), constitute the heavenly army, wage war with fallen angels (Eph 6:12; cf. Jude 9). They rejoice over the salvation of sinners (Lk 15:10). They watch over believers (Ps 91:11-12) and minister to them (Heb 1:14), as angels did with Daniel (Dan 6:22), Jesus (Mt 4:11), and the apostles (Acts 5:19-20). The Bible also describes the angels in fascinating and imaginative, metaphorical ways. They shouted for joy when God created (Job 38:7), and the psalmist (Ps 103:21-22) exhorts them to praise and bless Yahweh, just as the seraphs do in Isaiah 6.

We learn some interesting things about angels in Psalm 103. They are addressed as Yahweh's "angels, you mighty ones" (מַלְאָכָיו גִּבֹּרֵי כֹחַ) who "do his bidding, obedient to his spoken word" (עֹשֵׂי דְבָרוֹ לִשְׁמֹעַ בְּקוֹל דְּבָרוֹ; Ps 103:20). They are "his ministers that do his will" (מְשָׁרְתָיו עֹשֵׂי רְצוֹנוֹ; Ps 103:21). Mays discerns the common Old Testament motif of the heavenly court in Psalm 103.[a] White explores this motif of Yahweh's council in detail.[b] One finds the motif of the heavenly council in Job 1–2, Psalm 82, Deuteronomy 32:8, 1 Kings 22:19-22, Zechariah 3:1-5, and elsewhere. White analyzes the structure of Yahweh's council and discerns three tiers among its members:

- God
- The councilors: judicial officials
- Agents: court officers and the commissioned
- Other groups relate to the council who are not members: observers, defendants, etc.

In all this variegated imagery, the picture is of a hierarchy of real creatures who not only worship Yahweh but are deeply involved in his work and move easily between heaven and earth.

[a]James Luther Mays, *The Lord Reigns: A Theological Handbook to the Psalms* (Louisville, KY: Westminster John Knox, 1994), 327.

[b]Ellen White, *Yahweh's Council: Its Structure and Membership*, Forschungen Zum Alten Testament 2/65 (Tübingen: Mohr Siebeck, 2014).

[24]Kreeft, *Angels (and Demons)*, 28-29.

In Scott Hahn's view,

> Scripture suggests to us that angels are the ordinary means by which God gets things done—the way he guides world history, as seen in the Old Testament Book of Daniel and the New Testament Book of Revelation. The ancient rabbis and the Church Fathers believed that angels also maintained the physical laws of the universe. They kept the stars in their courses, and they swelled the rivers when the time was right. Scripture reveals that individual human beings have guardian angels, and so do nations (see Daniel 10: 13, 10: 20, and 12: 1) and churches (see Revelation 2: 1, 8, and 12, for example).[25]

Robert Jenson asserts that angels accompany redemptive history at certain "ontologically perilous junctures."[26] They appear at Jesus' conception and birth, at his resurrection from the dead, and at points in between, such as Jesus' temptation. They appear at similarly perilous junctures in the life of the church, such as when an angel freed Peter from prison (Acts 12:7-9). Kreeft writes, "Angels appear on the brink of chaos, or catastrophe, or at least at the threat of chaos or catastrophe."[27]

Their ministry of praise and accompaniment involves *bearing witness* and *acting on God's behalf*. Unfallen angels bear witness to God's actions as those who are present when he acts, and they act on his behalf as those who serve him without the taint of sin or rebellion. Theirs is a pure witness that confirms the word of Christ and the witness of the prophets and apostles. Barth writes, "Without the angels God himself would not be revealed and perceptible. Without them he would be hopelessly confused with some earthly circumstance, whether in the form of a sublime idea or a golden calf. But by means of his holy angels he sees to it that this dimension is always open and perceptible."[28] Although Barth certainly overstates the epistemological necessity of angelical existence, he is right to emphasize that the angels are a tangible means by which God makes the heavens known to the earth, disrupting reality in ways that unveil the inbreaking of his kingdom.

---

[25]Scott Hahn, *Angels and Saints: A Biblical Guide to Friendship with God's Holy Ones* (New York: Image Books, 2014), 84.

[26]Robert W. Jenson, *Systematic Theology*, vol. 2, *The Works of God* (Oxford: Oxford University Press, 2001), 119.

[27]Kreeft, *Angels (and Demons)*, 19.

[28]Barth, *CD* III/3, 485. But note that a few pages later Barth says, "God is present on earth without the angels" (*CD* III/3, 495).

Jenson describes the angelic ministry similarly:

> As directed to us, the angels' witness counters our unbelief. In our subjectivities, there is indeed conflict between earth's various and, when isolated, purposeless regularities and creation's eschatological plot. We do indeed direct our lives by extrapolating from the past, and we are irresistibly tempted to that doleful sort of interpretation that under the conditions of modernity becomes mechanism. The angels tell us we need not do this, need not live by the past, for "to you is born this day . . . a Savior . . . the Messiah, the Lord." They tell us not to adapt to "Babylon is great" for she is "Fallen, fallen!" As to where we hear the angels speak so, the first answer is straightforward: in Scripture.[29]

Concerning angelic action on God's behalf, Jenson notes that they do not merely witness Babylon's destruction; by God's will they also accomplish its overthrow.

Living amidst secular modernity, it is hard to indwell such a world, but we need to take Scripture's overwhelming witness in this respect seriously, albeit not naively. If angels are as real as Scripture suggests, how are we to relate to them? Should we appeal to or pray to them, for example? As we see in Psalm 103, there is certainly biblical warrant for exhorting the angels. And in Protestant hymns we find expressions such as "angels help us to adore him, you behold him face to face," which certainly has the form of a hymnic appeal or prayer. In our view, however, we are nowhere encouraged in Scripture to pray directly to angels but are taught to pray to "Our Father," always aware that the angels are there to do his bidding in response to our prayers, precisely as with Jesus in Luke 22:42-43.

Angels and humans. The angelic beings are similar to humans in their qualities of spirituality, rationality, and morality, but they differ from humans in their incorporeality. Moreover, the witness of the Bible is that they have a temporary and limited superiority to humans. They are temporarily superior to humans (Heb 2:9) in respect to their greater knowledge and power (Mt 24:36; Gen 19:11), yet it is human beings, not angels, who are created in God's image in likeness and to whom the future age belongs. Bavinck writes,

> Angels may be the mightier spirits, but humans are the richer of the two. In intellect and power angels far surpass humans. But in virtue of the marvelously rich relationships in which humans stand to God, the world, and humanity, they are psychologically deeper and mentally richer. . . . Angels experience God's

---

[29]Jenson, *Systematic Theology*, 2:125.

> power, wisdom, goodness, holiness, and majesty; but the depths of God's compassions only disclose themselves to humans. The full image of God, therefore, is only unfolded in creaturely fashion in humans—better still, in *humanity*.[30]

Indeed, according to Hebrews 1:14 the angelic beings are created not only to glorify God but also to serve humanity. They serve humanity by reminding us to continually praise and glorify God (Job 38:7; Ps 103:20; Rev 5:11-12), providing protection (Acts 5:19; 12:6-11), providing care (Ps 34:7), and taking interest in humanity's spiritual welfare (Lk 15:10; Heb 1:14). Moreover, in the end it is God's image bearers who will help judge the angels (1 Cor 6:3). In the New Testament we find passages that portray the angels as spectators of redemptive history, who wish but are unable to experience it for themselves (Eph 3:10; 1 Pet 1:12).

How then do we receive the witness of Psalm 8:5 and Hebrews 2:5-9 that humankind is lower than the angels? The relationship between the Masoretic Text and the Septuagint, and the use of the Septuagint in Hebrews 2, complicates the issue of the relationship between human beings and angels. Lane notes of the three lines reproduced from the Septuagint of Psalm 8 that they "combine to form a confession of faith that celebrates the three successive moments in the drama of redemption, i.e., the incarnation, the exaltation, and the final victory of Jesus."[a] The crucial question for our discussion becomes the nature of Jesus' humiliation, which made him lower than the angels. In our view it is helpful here to remember that, as Lane notes of Hebrews 2, "in Jesus we see exhibited humanity's true vocation. In an extraordinary way he fulfills God's design for all creation and displays what had always been intended for all humankind, according to Psalm 8. He is the one in whom primal glory and sovereignty are restored."[b] Jesus remains human after his exaltation, and thus his little while of being lower than the angels is related not to his humanity but to the fallen nature of the creation and humankind's fall from being what they were designed to be, God's image bearers. Indeed, Mays draws our attention to the verbs "remember" (תִּזְכְּרֶנּוּ) and "visit" (תִּפְקְדֶנּוּ) in Psalm 8:4, verbs that remind us that the psalmist knows about human life as an Israelite, a member of Yahweh's covenant people.[c] It is from this experience that the psalmist asks his more universal question, "What are human beings?" Mays thus observes, "The psalm speaks its praise of God from the primeval vantage of the original purpose of God, in this like Genesis 1 and 2. This gives the psalm a protological dimension and therefore an eschatological potential."[d] From this perspective Hebrews 2 can be seen as developing the implicit eschatological potential of

[30]Herman Bavinck, *Reformed Dogmatics*, ed. John Bolt, trans. J. Vriend (Grand Rapids, MI: Baker Academic, 2003–2008), 2:462.

the psalm. Thus Hebrews 2:5-9 should not be taken to suggest that humans are lesser than angels.

[a]William L. Lane, *Hebrews 1–8*, WBC 47a (Dallas: Word, 1991), 48.
[b]Ibid.
[c]James Luther Mays, *The Lord Reigns: A Theological Handbook to the Psalms* (Louisville, KY: Westminster John Knox, 1994), 67-68.
[d]Ibid., 69.

Angelic beings and Christ. Christ exists as creator of, and Lord over, the angels. The angels were created through him and for him (Col 1:16). They will accompany him when he comes in glory (Mt 25:31). From the incarnation through to his ascension, he is served and worshiped by angels. The same will be true when he returns in glory.

Whether Christ is the Savior of the angels is contested and somewhat speculative. According to Bavinck, when passages such as Ephesians 1:10 and Colossians 1:15-20 declare that all things relate to Christ as mediator, they are declaring that Christ restores all things to their proper and original relationship, with him as their Lord.[31] His redemption restores him rightfully to the position of Lord, but not by making him the savior of angels with regard to forgiveness of sins. Though we find in the Scriptures a portrayal of a human fall that parallels the fall of certain angels, there is no similar portrayal of an angelic redemption that parallels human redemption.

However, the telos of creation is a new *heaven* and a new earth, raising at least the question of what the renewal of heaven involves. McFarland notes that

> Christians bear witness that glory pertains to creation's present no less than its future when they pray for God's will to be done on earth as it is in heaven. . . . This is not to say that heaven any more than earth has achieved its final glory, for the Christian hope includes the creation of a new heaven not less than new earth (Rev. 21:1). According to Scripture heaven, too, will be shaken at the last day, prior to its final and definitive renewal (Matt. 24:29; Heb. 12:26; cf. Hag. 2:6, 21).[32]

We can only speculate on what this renewal involves.

One might object that, on the basis of 1 Peter 3:19-20, there is reason to believe that redemption is offered to the fallen angels. In this passage Peter says that Christ "went and

[31]Bavinck, *Reformed Dogmatics*, 2:462-63.
[32]Ian A. McFarland, *From Nothing: A Theology of Creation* (Louisville, KY: Westminster John Knox, 2014), 160.

made a proclamation to the spirits in prison, who in former times did not obey, when God waited patiently in the days of Noah, during the building of the ark." Two types of interpretations present themselves. In one interpretation the "spirits" referred to are angelic beings, and in the other they are human beings. We prefer the latter option. Scripture makes clear that demonic beings are condemned (Mt 25:41; Rev 20:9-14). Moreover, Genesis 6:5-13 emphasizes *exclusively* the sin of humanity during this time. Similarly, extrabiblical literature, such as the Babylonian Talmud Sanhedrin (108b), elaborates on human sin, and especially on those persons who mocked Noah for believing God. Peter further writes that Christ "went and made a proclamation" to those spirits. By saying that Christ "went and made a proclamation," he is suggesting that Christ went and preached to humanity via his prophets. Christ did not stay in heaven but instead "went and made a proclamation" through Noah.

Fallen angels (demons). The drama of Scripture includes invisible warfare, as we are reminded in Ephesians 6:10-20. Although God's Word for creation holds and sustains the created order even in the aftermath of the fall, Satan continues to corrupt and misdirect God's good order. Angels are tasked with guarding the creation order, whereas rebellious, fallen angels seek to subvert this order. This antithesis cuts across the invisible realm of creation also, though differently from in the visible realm. In the visible realm, the antithesis runs across all of the material world, including through *each* human heart and manifesting its ugliness also in the hearts and lives of believers. Similar to the visible realm, the invisible heavenly realm experiences the antithesis as it cuts between good angels and bad, but dissimilar to the visible realm, the antithesis does not cut through each angelic being, as some angels never fell and remain innocent and pure.

The nature and origin of fallen angels. We speak of the demons as fallen angels and in so doing concur with the majority tradition in Christian theology. However, Barth sets the stage for his view of the demonic by describing God's creative activity in relation to *das Nichtige*, the lurking possibility of chaos and evil that would mark a graceless world. For Barth, therefore, God's act of creation was already an act of rescue. His "yes" to creation was already and always a "no" to *das Nichtige*. Thus, the act of creation carries within itself already a victory over the powers of darkness. Joseph Mangina summarizes Barth's view:

> God made the world so that, in Jesus, he could "so love" it (Jn 3:16). And this provides us with the clue we need. In deciding for Jesus and his cross, God triumphs over the powers of darkness at a single stroke; thus creation comes

into being with this victory behind it. But what God does all at once and eternally, the creature can only experience in time. That, in effect, is what history is: God's tolerating evil just long enough so that the creature can witness God's victory, and just so participate in it. Death, evil, and the Nihil hold no terrors for us, because God has dealt decisively with these powers once and for all. The creature therefore has no destiny than a life of joyful gratitude for what God has done.[33]

Barth's doctrine of *das Nichtige* has attracted a number of criticisms. One criticism is that it necessitates evil and makes God complicit in it. These critics argue that, because Barth grounds creation itself in God's triumph over evil, it appears that God's permission of evil makes it logically necessary and even amounts to a tacit approval of it.[a] Similarly, Berkouwer argues that, while Barth never intended to minimize the seriousness of sin, his doctrine of *das Nichtige* does nonetheless tend to do so. God's relativizing of humankind's sin

> is not intended by Barth as a denial or a minimizing of the seriousness of sin. It is clearly intended as a divine "relativizing" *in Christ* and through grace, and therefore does *not* involve making sin "harmless." But, for all that, the aprioristic conquest of sin moves over the face of the whole of history. The history of sin coincides, as it were, with the contemporaneous conquest of it by the unchangeable grace of God.[b]

For our part, we agree with Barth that the biblical concept of grace presupposes sin. However, when Barth subsumes humanity's fall into God's eternal decree, he distorts both the doctrine of creation and the nature of grace. He distorts the doctrine of creation by asserting that God's relation to humanity has only and ever been one of grace toward sinners. Yet the biblical account of creation, as we unfold in this volume, is one in which the original creation is good and very good, unblemished by sin or its consequences. We must recognize the fact of God's prelapsarian love for his creation rather than building our doctrine of God's love entirely on his grace toward sinners.

[a]John Hick, *Evil and the God of Love* (San Francisco: Harper & Row, 1977), 138.
[b]Cornelius G. Berkouwer, *The Triumph of Grace in the Theology of Karl Barth: An Introduction and Critical Appraisal*, trans. Harry R. Boer (Grand Rapids, MI: Eerdmans, 1956), 254.

Having dealt with *das Nichtige*, Barth moves on to a discussion of the angels and then, finally, to the demons.[34] Demons, he avers, are not fallen

[33]Joseph L. Mangina, *Karl Barth: Theologian of Christian Witness* (Louisville, KY: Westminster John Knox, 2004), 101.
[34]Barth, *CD* III/3, 519-31.

angels but are manifestations of *das Nichtige*, the chaotic and evil nothingness that has already been defeated by God's "no." On the one hand, they exist, but on the other hand, they are the myth of all myths.[35] They pretend to be angels, but they are not. The power they wield is falsehood, but it is unmasked and slain by God's truth. Barth writes, "It is Jesus Christ, God in his person, who as the Lord and Victor overthrows nothingness and its lying powers. . . . In Jesus Christ himself this triumph is won only in the history of that conflict. And our celebration of it, our liberation from demons, can take place only as we participate in this history."[36] Thus we should not revere or respect the demons, but also we should not ignore them. We are liberated from them as we participate in Christ's triumph over *das Nichtige*. In relation to traditional teaching about the demons being "fallen" angels, Barth argues that Scripture never refers to an angelic fall and that, further, the devil could not have been an angel because he was a liar from the beginning. He argues that the relevant Bible passages have been expounded incorrectly, but as Geoffrey Bromiley and others have noted, Barth never gives a proper exposition himself.[37]

The commendable line of thought running through Barth's treatment of the demons is his emphasis on Christ's victory over the evil powers. Yet, in our opinion, his rejection of the traditional conception of demons as fallen angels is unwarranted exegetically and theologically. God created everything "good," which means that he did not create any sort of evil powers or persons. But somewhere between the creation accounts in Genesis 1–2 and the account of the fall in Genesis 3, some angels rebelled against God. Theirs was the first instance of sin/evil. We infer from Genesis 3 in the context of Scripture as a whole that the serpent who tempted Eve was Satan's mouthpiece and that Satan sinned before the first couple did (Gen 3:1-6). Similarly, 1 John 3:8 says that the devil has sinned "from the beginning." This cannot mean that he sinned at the time of creation, because God created everything good, but that he sinned during the opening act of world history.

Indeed, the nature of the angelic is such that it embodies either pure witness, on the one hand, or pure defiance, on the other. The first act of defiance, accordingly, was an arch-defiance perpetrated by Lucifer and his accomplices among the angels. Because of their rebellion, the rebellious angels

---

[35]Barth, *CD* III/3, 519-31.

[36]Barth, *CD* III/3, 530.

[37]Geoffrey W. Bromiley, *Introduction to the Theology of Karl Barth* (Edinburgh: T&T Clark, 2001), 155.

were removed from God's immediate presence and their activity is restrained (1 Pet 2:4; Jude 6; possibly Is 14:12-15).

The "ministry" of fallen angels—subverting the divine design. Satan's opposition to God is clothed in creational and cultural forms, as he "inhabits" creation but for the purpose of subverting its divine design. Just as God had called Israel to be a light to the nations by embodying a knowledge of Yahweh Elohim as the one true and living God, so Satan beckoned the nations with "gods" who were really demonic forces. Deuteronomy describes Israel's flirtation with these gods: "They made him [God] jealous with strange gods. . . . They sacrificed to demons, not God" (Deut 32:16-17). Similarly, Paul notes concerning the pagans of his day, "What pagans sacrifice, they sacrifice to demons and not to God" (1 Cor 10:20). But the demons not only cloak themselves with false deity; they clothe themselves with humanity. In the Gospels we learn that demons are able to inhabit and control certain persons, to "demonize" them (Mk 1:21-28).

Note the lingual nature of Satan's deception. He tempts by prompting Eve to question God's word (Gen 3:1-7); he is a slanderer (Rev 12:10), the father of lies (Jn 8:44), and the tempter of Christ (Mt 4:1-11). Body language also is significant, as Satan masquerades as a good angel (2 Cor 11:14) and as a false trinity (Rev 16:13). The lingual nature of Satan's ploys is not surprising given the biblical portrayal of God as an inherently communicative triunity.

Job 1–2 is fascinating in this respect. Scholars debate whether "the satan" (*haśāṭān*) mentioned in Job is the same Satan described in later Jewish and Christian literature. Routledge argues convincingly that *haśāṭān* is in fact the enemy of God. He writes, "In the prologue it is difficult to regard the Satan as one of God's loyal servants. He appears as the enemy of God's people, resorting to insinuation to accuse Job and pursuing enthusiastically his task of persecution."[a] We concur with Routledge that Job's *haśāṭān* is indeed an adversary of God and that there is good reason to identify him with Satan of the New Testament writings; Job's *haśāṭān* opposes both God and his people and does so by questioning God's goodness and the goodness of God's order.

In Job 1:6-12 we encounter a scene in which the heavenly beings present themselves before Yahweh, with Satan among them. Satan asks whether Job's righteousness is righteousness at all. Janzen writes,

> The question arises as to whether there could be such a thing as independent and free (*hinnam*) piety on the part of humankind. This question, ostensibly about humankind, is also the implication of a prior question, on which is properly a divine existential question: Is the creator of the world and the divine benefactor of humankind worshipful only by virtue of what deity does for humankind? Or is

> God intrinsically worshipful? . . . In other words, what sort of covenant is possible between God and humankind? In this way of viewing the prologue to Job, we may see how close it stands in its concerns to the story in Genesis 2–3, though with a different outcome.[b]

Further, if this is true, does not this call into question God's order for the world (blessing for obedience, cursing for disobedience)? Thus, Peggy L. Day writes, "The satan is implicitly challenging Yahweh's blueprint for world order; if the righteous always prosper, how can it be ascertained that their behavior is not motivated by material gain? The satan is not accusing Job, or at least not directly. He is attacking the problem at its source, by accusing the creator of perpetrating a perverse world order."[c] This confirms—albeit negatively—the view explored above of angels being responsible for guarding the created order.

The consistent biblical witness is that Satan is an adversary who opposes God by questioning God's order for the world (as he did in the garden), a line of questioning that also effectively questions God's wisdom or goodness. Thus, in *The City of God*, especially in book 14, Augustine argues that the lingual nature of the first deception would be paradigmatic throughout human history, forming the pattern for Satanic rhetoric through the ages. By the crafty use of interrogative and declarative language, Satan was able to persuade the first couple into self-worship and thus self-delusion, culminating in the false promise that they would "be like gods" (Gen 3:5). Because of the twin effects of original sin on the soul—ignorance and weakness—humanity likewise is especially vulnerable to demonic deception, and deceptive discourse is the primary means of such deception. Thus, the first lie is paradigmatic, forming the pattern for Satan's future deceptions and misdirections. Describing Augustine's view, Dodaro writes, "Augustine's insistence upon the fundamental mendacity of Satan's actions is intended to establish the eloquent lie as the cause of social and political disruption characteristic of the earthly city, where he holds sway."[d] At the root of all sin is language. Even Satan ostensibly reasoned with himself at the foundations of the world, when he rejected God's rule and substituted it for his own. Thus, both then and now, "in every sin one detects the contours of a lie."[e]

[a] Robin Routledge, *Old Testament Theology: A Thematic Approach* (Downers Grove, IL: IVP Academic, 2008), 123.
[b] J. Gerald Janzen, *Job*, Interpretation (Louisville, KY: Westminster John Knox, 1985), 41.
[c] Peggy L. Day, *An Adversary in Heaven: śāṭān in the Hebrew Bible*, Harvard Semitic Monographs 43 (Atlanta: Scholars Press, 1988), 80.
[d] Robert Dodaro, *Christ and the Just Society in the Thought of Augustine* (Cambridge: Cambridge University Press, 2004), 68.
[e] Ibid., 69.

And yet Satan and the demons are restrained by God. "As for the discord and strife that we say exists between Satan and God," Calvin writes, "we ought to accept as a fixed certainty the fact that he can do nothing unless God wills and assents to it."[38] The opening chapters of Job make clear that Satan acts only with God's permission and within parameters provided by God. Jude portrays the demons as being held captive in "eternal chains," an allusion to the limitations on their activity (Jude 6). The Gospels make clear that Jesus holds power over the demons and that his displays of power over them were signs of his inbreaking kingdom. The demonic forces have been defeated already in principle, and the day will come when the Lord Christ will consummate his victory over Satan by throwing him into the lake of fire, where he will be tormented forever (Rev 20:10).

The dangers here are similar to those inherent in our study of unfallen angels. We may be tempted to err either by ignoring the forces of darkness or by obsessing over them. We wish to recognize their reality as spiritual beings who oppose Christ and yet cannot escape the reaches of his lordship. We resist the devil by means of our union with Christ. Because we are one with him, we participate in his victory over demonic forces. Because we seek his glory, we resist the one who seeks to usurp his glory. "For if we have God's glory at heart, as we should have, we ought with all our strength to contend against him who is trying to extinguish it. If we are minded to affirm Christ's kingdom as we ought, we must wage irreconcilable war with him who is plotting its ruin."[39]

Conclusion

In the aftermath of modernity's disenchantment of the world, and in spite of modern theology's minimization or even dismissal of the heavenly realm and its host, we affirm that God through Christ created the heavenly and earthly realms, holds them together, and one day will reconcile them both. This doctrine cannot be proven empirically and is based on God's special revelation and on faith. Living as we do in a context in which empirical science functions as the rational ideal and towering cultural authority, our testimony to this doctrine is all the more significant. It reminds us that our lives are part of a grand and sweeping drama, a divine drama, that extends beyond the realm of ordinary experience and includes a heavenly realm that cannot now be seen and a heavenly host that cannot be experienced in the same way as other created things.

---

[38]John Calvin, *Institutes* 1.14.14 (*Institutes of the Christian Religion*, ed. John T. McNeill [Philadelphia: Westminster Press, 1960], 1:175).

[39]Calvin, *Institutes* 1.14.15 (McNeill, 1:174).

EIGHT

SABBATH, FALL, AND MISDIRECTION

God is dead. God remains dead. And we have killed him. How shall we comfort ourselves, the murderers of all murderers? What was holiest and mightiest of all that the world has yet owned has bled to death under our knives: who will wipe this blood off us? What water is there for us to clean ourselves? What festivals of atonement, what sacred games shall we have to invent? Is not the greatness of this deed too great for us? Must we ourselves not become gods simply to appear worthy of it?

FRIEDRICH NIETZSCHE

It is this break of the covenant between word and world which constitutes one of the very few genuine revolutions of spirit in Western history and which defines modernity itself . . . [of which] the vulgarized shibboleth of the "death of God" is a seminal but only partial articulation.

GEORGE STEINER

*This book [*The Crisis of the Officer Class*] is written against those theorists who have sought in vain to liberate us from sacred order by teaching that it does not exist. . . . Authority cannot die. It can only shift up and down its veridical.*

PHILIP RIEFF

THE NINETEENTH-CENTURY PHILOSOPHER Friedrich Nietzsche is known for proclaiming God's death.[1] By this Nietzsche did not mean that the deity had once lived and breathed but now had died. "The murder of God is committed

[1]On Nietzsche's parable of the madman, see Bob Goudzwaard and Craig G. Bartholomew, *Beyond the Modern Age: An Archeology of Contemporary Culture* (Downers Grove, IL: IVP Academic, 2017), 58-62.

speculatively by explaining divine being as the work of man."[2] Nietzsche's prophetic commentary on the situation was that if God is dead, then so is social and moral order as we know it. Without an Author, there is no authority, no order. Nietzsche reached for and grasped a profound truth when he recognized that sacred order underlies social order and that the dissolution of sacred order necessarily eventuates in the disruption and even dissolution of social order as we know it. While Nietzsche celebrated this murder of God, Eric Voegelin sees it as catastrophic and a source of the major ills of modernity.[3] He notes of political science, for example, that "only when the order of being as a whole, unto its origin in transcendent being, comes into view, can the analysis be undertaken with any hope of success; for only then can current opinions about right and wrong be examined as to their agreement with the order of being."[4]

This truth of the inseparability of sacred and social order is revealed in the biblical account of the first couple's fall into sin, and of the disastrous consequences of their quest for autonomy on subsequent society and culture. But any reflection on sin's disruptive history remains superficial unless first one is reminded of what it is that sin has disrupted. Thus, we begin this chapter by looking at the culmination of God's good creation vis-à-vis sin's misdirection of God's good creation order. We then note the paradigmatic nature of Adam and Eve's sin, as well as the all-pervasive presence of sin and the progressive nature of sin in the biblical narrative. In this narrative we see sin's curse worked out as the antithesis of God's blessing of creation and humanity's vocation in the world. We complete the chapter by exploring manifestations of the antithesis in our own culture and arguing for a principled pluralism that can facilitate the reenchantment of the modern world and the republication of God's thesis for the world through the work of his people and the proclamation of the gospel.

---

[2]Eric Voegelin, *Science, Politics, and Gnosticism*, trans. William J. Fitzpatrick (1968; repr., Washington, DC: Regnery, 1997), 36.

[3]Voegelin and Augusto Del Noce discern gnosticism not just at work in postmodernism but at the heart of modernity. Eric Voegelin, *Science, Politics and Gnosticism*, trans. William J. Fitzpatrick, (Washington D.C.: Regnery, 1968, 1997), 16, argues that "Marx is a speculative Gnostic. He construes the order of being as a process of nature complete in itself." Again: "It would be difficult to find another document of modern gnosticism that in power and clarity of expression, in intellectual vigor and ingenious determination, would compare with the manuscript of the young Marx" (ibid., 35). Cf. Augusto Del Noce, *The Crisis of Modernity* (Montreal: McGill-Queen's University Press, 2014), 19-48, 294-99.

[4]Voegelin, *Science, Politics, and Gnosticism*, 12.

The Culmination of God's Good Creation

Henri Blocher notes that Genesis 1:1–2:3 has two peaks—namely, the creation of humankind and the Sabbath. He observes, "The use of the anthropomorphic figure of the week for the creation and of its completion allowed the author to outline a theology of the sabbath."[5] The seventh day is the goal of God's creative work (Gen 2:1-3). God's cessation of creative activity serves as a recognition of creation's completion, its stable order, and its goodness.[6] It is good both structurally (in the way it is ordered) and directionally (in the way all of creation is rightly directed or related to its creator). Further, it serves notice that God wishes to enter into fellowship with humanity. William Dumbrell writes, "The Sabbath day merely provides the ongoing occasion in which the ideal life of the garden as God's intention ('rest,' cf. Jesus in Matt 12:28) for history takes place and is to be perpetuated. God's own cessation is the divine endorsement of creation, and his willingness to enter into fellowship with humanity expresses this."[7]

Barth likewise notes,

> The fact that God rested means quite simply, and significantly enough, that he did not continue His work of creation, i.e., that He was content with the creation of the world and man. He was satisfied to enter into *this* relationship with *this* reality distinct from Himself, to be the Creator of *this* creature, to find in *these* works of His Word the external sphere of His power and grace and the place of His revealed glory.[8]

God's ideal for his image bearers was for them to experience life as unbroken shalom in relationship with himself.

The Corruption and Misdirection of God's Good Creation

Without revelation, we would be left in the dark, not knowing that God brought creation into existence *ex nihilo*, made humanity in his image and likeness, and set us apart as vice regents charged with stewarding his creation under his sovereign guidance. But neither would we know what went so terribly wrong with God's shalomic order. Only God's revealing word can

---

[5]Henri Blocher, *In the Beginning: The Opening Chapters of Genesis*, trans. David G. Preston (Leicester, UK: Inter-Varsity Press, 1984), 57.

[6]For an exposition of Gen 2:1-3 as God's endorsement of his creation and its stable order, see William J. Dumbrell, *Creation and Covenant: An Old Testament Covenant Theology*, 2nd ed. (Milton Keynes, UK: Paternoster, 2013), 33-38.

[7]Dumbrell, *Creation and Covenant*, 35.

[8]Barth, *CD* III/1, 214-15.

bring to surface the abnormality of our present condition and the catalyst for its onslaught.

In chapter six we explored Genesis 2–3 in some detail. It will not surprise readers to hear that the interpretation of Genesis 3 as "the fall" is rejected by many modern exegetes. Westermann rejects the description of this narrative as "the fall" and of original sin.[a] He argues that such a reading has its origins in late Judaism (2 Esdras 7:118 [4 Esdras 7:48]); then in Paul's Adam-Christ typology (cf. Rom 5:12-21), which does not emerge from his encounter with Christ but from late Judaism; and then fully in Augustine. Rabbi Hertz reads Genesis 3 in a traditional way as a story of rebellion and punishment. He asserts that central to the narrative are two themes: the seriousness of rebellion against God and humans' possession of free will. However, of the fall and original sin he writes,

> Judaism rejects these doctrines. Man was mortal from the first, and death did not enter the world through the transgression of Eve. . . . Instead of the Fall of man (in the sense of humanity as a whole), Judaism preaches the Rise of man; and instead of Original Sin, it stresses Original Virtue. . . . Judaism clings to the idea of Progress. The Golden Age of Humanity is not in the past but in the future . . . and all of the children of men are destined to help in the establishment of that Kingdom of God on earth.[b]

Another popular reading, different from Hertz's, is to see humankind's fall as a fall upward to consciousness. Westermann reads Genesis 2–3 as a story of the fallibility and limits of humans, and of the separation from God of sinful humans.

In our view, Genesis 3 is aptly described by Blocher as the "breaking of the covenant."[c] The unusual name for God in Genesis 2–3—Yahweh Elohim—foregrounds covenant in this section and alerts us to the seriousness of rebellion against God, and the motif of death and the narratives that follow on from Genesis 3 demonstrate the catastrophic consequences for humankind.

[a]Claus Westermann, *Genesis 1–11: A Commentary*, trans. John J. Scullion (Minneapolis: Augsburg, 1984), 275-78. Cf. James Barr, who also denies that Gen 3 should be read as "the fall" (*The Garden of Eden and the Hope of Immortality* [Minneapolis: Fortress, 1993], 87-93), and R. W. L. Moberly's critique of Barr and far more constructive reading (*The Theology of the Book of Genesis*, Old Testament Theology [Cambridge: Cambridge University Press, 2009], 70-87). Moberly makes much of "death" as metaphorical. In our view Gen 2–3 as a whole is carefully crafted *literature* with many layers to it, intentionally designed to provoke reflection, for example, on the nature of death. Death is real and literal in Gen 2–3, but the narrative pushes us to explore the precise nature of death, alerting us to the fact that it is far more than physical. We do not think that "metaphor" adequately describes this literary trope.

[b]J. H. Hertz, ed., *The Soncino Edition of the Pentateuch and Haftorahs*, 2nd ed. (London: Soncino Press, 1967), 196.

[c]Henri Blocher, *In the Beginning: The Opening Chapters of Genesis*, trans. David G. Preston (Leicester, UK: Inter-Varsity Press, 1984), 135.

Genesis 3 is a historical *and* a paradigmatic story of crime and punishment that reveals to us the beginning of this world's sickness, the sin and fall of the first couple. The story "behind the story" begins in Genesis 2:4, however. Genesis 2:4–3:23 forms one textual unit and tells a story with four main actors—God, man, woman, and the serpent—and follows a septenary structure.[9] The details of the story are well known, and we will not rehearse them here. Central to the interpretation of Genesis 2–3 is the nature of the forbidden tree, the tree of the knowledge of good and evil.

The forbidden tree represents the wisdom and moral autonomy that God alone possesses. To eat from its fruit is to attempt to grasp the sort of knowledge that is God's prerogative, to grasp at his kingship rather than to remain content with the vice-regency he already had so lovingly bestowed. After eating the fruit, the first couple did indeed gain knowledge, a knowledge of their own nakedness, or personal vulnerability. Dumbrell writes, "Thus poverty of mind, weakness of spirit, and awareness of human limitations by total exposure are also conveyed by the term [naked]. The human couple had accepted this ([Gen] 2:25) without understanding what it could mean. Previously they had known only the good; now they know evil, like God who knows all."[10]

At least five interpretations should be noted concerning the meaning of "the knowledge of good and evil."[a] One of the oldest interpretations of the "knowledge" on offer is that it was sexual knowledge. We agree with Cassuto that "the text in *no way purports* to allude to any aspect of *sexual relationship*; and the multitude of allegorical interpretations with which a number of commentators have embroidered the passage, on the assumption of some such intention, are out of place."[b] A second view suggests that good and evil is a merism for the totality of good and evil; i.e., eating from this tree would provide omniscience. Yet the story does not eventuate in such knowledge. A third view is represented by Blocher, who argues that this knowledge refers to moral autonomy. "By eating, the human couple acquired the ability to determine good and evil without reference or obligation to God."[c] Some commentators criticize this view on the grounds that it is unlikely God will delegate this prerogative to human beings, but these criticisms are mitigated because in the narrative God never does grant such a prerogative since he prohibits eating from this tree in Genesis 2:16-17. A fourth view, represented by Wenham and similar to the third view, argues that the tree gave wisdom: the tree "was forbidden for human consumption because the wisdom acquired through eating it leads to independence from God, whereas true wisdom begins with the 'fear of the Lord' (Pr. 1:7)."[d] A fifth view is that the tree symbolizes moral

[9]Jerome T. Walsh argues for a seven-part structure ("Genesis 2:4b–3:24: A Synchronic Approach," *Journal of Biblical Literature* 96, no. 2 [1977]: 161-77). Dumbrell and others follow his lead.
[10]Dumbrell, *Creation and Covenant*, 49.

discernment. However, humans already possess this. Our view is that the third and fourth views are complementary and that the first couple's sin was a grasping for moral autonomy and wisdom that God alone should have.[e] A key in this respect is the serpent's assertion that "you will be like God, knowing good and evil" (Gen 3:5). Old Testament Wisdom literature recognizes that there is an appropriate human wisdom and a wisdom reserved for God. Human wisdom starts and continues in the fear of the Lord. False wisdom or folly seeks to live on the basis of observation, experience, and analysis alone, apart from the fear of Yahweh. This struggle is embodied in Ecclesiastes.[f]

[a]Cf. Gordon J. Wenham, *Genesis 1–15*, WBC 1 (Dallas: Word, 1987), 63-64.

[b]Umberto Cassuto, *A Commentary on the Book of Genesis*, part 1, *From Adam to Noah (Genesis I–VI)*, trans. Israel Abrahams (Jerusalem: Magnes, 1978), 148.

[c]Henri Blocher, *In the Beginning: The Opening Chapters of Genesis*, trans. David G. Preston (Leicester, UK: Inter-Varsity Press, 1984), 121-34. Cf. M. D. Gow, "The Fall," in *Dictionary of the Old Testament: Pentateuch*, ed. T. Desmond Alexander and David W. Baker (Downers Grove, IL: InterVarsity Press, 2003), 287; Peter J. Gentry and Stephen J. Wellum, *Kingdom Through Covenant: A Biblical-Theological Understanding of the Covenants* (Wheaton, IL: Crossway, 2012), 217.

[d]Gordon J. Wenham, "Genesis," in *New Bible Commentary*, ed. G. J. Wenham et al., 4th ed. (Downers Grove, IL: IVP Academic, 1994), 62.

[e]We are indebted to Grant Taylor for the exegetical and archival research he provided on Genesis 2:4–3:23.

[f]Cf. Craig G. Bartholomew, *Ecclesiastes*, Baker Commentary on the Old Testament Wisdom and Psalms (Grand Rapids, MI: Baker Academic, 2009).

In Genesis 3:9-13 Yahweh takes the stage again and calls to the first couple, who are hiding from him. There is a play in the Hebrew on the words "naked" (Gen 2:25; 3:7) and "serpent." The fall introduces shame, and this manifests itself in a different approach to nakedness. Gregory of Nyssa perceptively comments, "For I imagine that no one who has seriously thought about it will gainsay that one thing alone is by nature shameful, viz. the malady of evil, while no shame attaches to what is alien to evil."[11] The narrative portrays the couple trying to avoid God (Gen 3:10) and then blaming each other for the sin (Gen 3:12-13). "Whereas man had previously delighted in the woman," writes Dumbrell, "now he shifts the blame to her and God. . . . Thus evil, like good, brings its own reward. As the true reward of obedience is personal spiritual growth, so the reward of disobedience is personal spiritual decay, and a kind of dying instantly begins."[12]

In Genesis 3:14-21 Yahweh gives a series of curses that nonetheless have embedded in them the seed of a blessing. He begins by cursing the serpent and declaring that there will be enmity between the serpent and the woman,

[11]Edward R. Hardy, ed., *Christology of the Later Fathers* (Louisville, KY: Westminster John Knox, 1954), 287.

[12]Dumbrell, *Creation and Covenant*, 51-52.

and between the serpent's seed and her seed. This promise is both general and specific. In the general sense it announces the great antithesis that will mark life in a fallen world. In the specific sense it constitutes the *protevangelium*, the first preaching of the gospel: from the seed of woman will be born a Messiah who will provide deliverance from the curse.

Dumbrell notes the ways in which the fall affects the multiple relationships of all the actors.[a] Alienation will now mark the relationship between man and woman, between humanity and animals, and between humanity and the earth. The man will be alienated from the woman, trying to dominate her in a new relational power struggle. She will struggle to find dignity in her roles as wife and mother, all the while experiencing suffering and pain.[b] Similarly, the man will have difficulty finding satisfaction in his work, all the while being frustrated and likewise experiencing pain.[c]

These relational curses must be seen in stark contrast with the blessings God had intended. The Hebrew verb "to curse" is an antonym for "to bless":

> To bless means to endow with potential for life, to give the power to succeed, prosper, reproduce, etc. . . . As opposed, however, to "bless," to "curse" is to alienate, to remove from the benign sphere, to subject to deprivation. The curse of Genesis 3:17 dissolves the former natural relationship between human beings and the earth. The element of pain, sorrow and agonizing effort is emphasized in Genesis 3:18–19 by the reference to thorns and thistles and to the sweat on Adam's brow as effort is expended.[d]

Thus, Dumbrell sees that it was not the ground that was altered as a consequence of the fall, but that "what is impaired as a result of the fall is human beings' control of the ground. . . . The problem after the fall will lie in humans' inability rightly to be able to use creation."[e]

[a]William J. Dumbrell, *Creation and Covenant: An Old Testament Covenant Theology*, 2nd ed. (Milton Keynes, UK: Paternoster, 2013), 51-55.
[b]Ibid., 52.
[c]Ibid., 53.
[d]Ibid., 53.
[e]Ibid., 54.

In Genesis 3:22-23, as in the first part of the story, God once again is the only active character. He turns from the curses to the final penalty: humanity's expulsion from the garden and thus, too, from "reveling in the direct vision of God."[13] God's presence signifies life, and his absence conversely signifies

[13]Gregory of Nyssa in Hardy, *Christology of the Later Fathers*, 280.

death. The first couple and indeed the world have begun to die, and the expulsion pictures this in graphic terms. Genesis 3:24 begins a new scene—life outside the garden. This scene stretches through until the end of the biblical narrative as Christ consummates his kingdom and restores his creation.

The Origins of Sin?

The fall narrative, and Genesis 1–11 as a whole, explains for us what went wrong with the world. It makes a causal connection between the first couple's sin and the sickness and evil we experience in the world. What the narrative does not do, however, is provide a philosophical explanation of the origin of evil. Many explanations have been attempted. Many *naturalists* view the evil aspects of our world as being part of the world as it always has existed. Others, whom we might call *spiritists*, blame sin and evil on the devil, who then takes the ultimate blame. We reject this view because the biblical account makes clear that Adam and Eve actively participated in their own sin and are therefore culpable for it. *Dualists* posit some sort of evil force or evil deity alongside God and blame evil on that deity or force. We reject this view because the biblical account portrays all evil agents (including Satan) as creatures who do not exist alongside God but under his reign. Finally, *monists* posit God as the cause of everything, including evil. When Christian theologians have argued that God ultimately is the cause of evil, usually they have qualified it. Sometimes they qualify it by saying that God never willed a single sin but that he did will sin in general. Other times they say that God's will was merely a permissive will rather than an active and catalyzing will. But we are not willing to say, even in a qualified sense, that God caused original sin. God always has been, and always will be, opposed to sin, even though he tolerates it in this time between the times and redirects it to his glory.

Rather than trying to explain the origin of evil, we are content to affirm what Scripture affirms: Everything God created is good. Nothing that he created was evil. God did not create evil. He is not its author or cause. We agree with Herman Bavinck:

> However they [these philosophical explanations of evil's origin] may differ among each other, they all have this in common that they look for the origin and seat of sin, not in the will of the creature, but in the structure and nature of things, and therefore in the Creator who is the cause of that structure and nature. . . . The wisdom of God is exalted high above this human speculation.

> Scripture is the book which from beginning to end vindicates God and implicates man.[14]

Instead of philosophical explanation for sin's origin, we are given a concrete story about the first couple. In reading this story, and the narrative that extends from it through to the consummated kingdom, we are confronted with the first sin, which lies behind all our sins. This first sin does not corrupt the world in its very structures but corrupts it in its directionality. Sin does not have the power to make bad what God has made good. It can only misdirect God's creation toward bad ends. After the fall, therefore, nothing changes structurally, but everything changes directionally.

Historical and paradigmatic. Wenham helpfully identifies Genesis 2–3 as both protohistorical and paradigmatic. He writes that the story

> is paradigmatic in that it offers a clear and simple analysis of the nature of sin and its consequences, albeit in rich and symbolic language. Disobedience to the law of God brings physical pain and suffering and alienation from him. This is indeed the experience of every man. In this sense the story is paradigmatic. But in all societies, and especially the tightly knit family society of ancient Israel, the behavior of parents has great impact on their children for good or ill. It therefore follows that the disobedience of the first couple from whom Genesis traces the descent of the whole human race must have had great consequences for all mankind. In this sense, then, the story offers a protohistorical account of man's origins and his sin.[15]

Because we recognize the historical and paradigmatic nature of the Genesis account of the fall, we are able to make better sense of later biblical teaching that somehow all of humanity was implicated in Adam's sin and, furthermore, follows in his footsteps as sinner (Ps 51:1-12; Rom 5:12-21). We are confronted with Adam's sin and told that it somehow lies behind our own sins. But in what way does Adam's sin result in us also being sinful? This question is an investigation into the doctrine traditionally known as "original sin."

When Christian theologians refer to "original" sin, they are referring to the fact that our sinful disposition is part of our "original" equipment. We are born with an "original" tendency toward sin. Our tendency to sin is as original in us as a new baby's tendency to breathe or cry. But how and why? Pelagius argued that it is merely a matter of *imitation*. Augustine answers that it is a matter of *natural headship*.[16] Augustine argued that we inherit sin

---

[14]Herman Bavinck, *Our Reasonable Faith* (Grand Rapids, MI: Eerdmans, 1956), 227-28.

[15]Gordon J. Wenham, *Genesis 1–15*, WBC 1 (Dallas: Word, 1987), 91.

[16]Augustine, *City of God* 13.14 (Walsh, 217).

genetically because we are all descendants of Adam. We are genetically guilty; that is, because we all were present in Adam as his "seed," we each inherit Adam's sin through our shared nature that we derive from him. Calvin argued that it is a matter of *representation* rather than merely genetic inheritance.[17] He argued that God's relationship with humanity involved Adam serving as the federal head of humanity. We see this covenant context as the primary lens by which to understand the way we inherit sin. It is imputed rather than imitated (Pelagius) or merely propagated (Augustine). The Pelagian option is ruled out for reasons that shall become clear in the next part of our discussion, but the federal-headship and natural-headship views are both valid attempts to make sense of the mysterious biblical teaching that we all are implicated somehow in Adam's sin. Thus, we wish to retain the best of both views.

The question of federal or natural headship centers on Romans 5:12-19, in which Paul affirms humanity's fallen nature in and through Adam but does not elaborate on the exact nature of that relationship. Thus, there is an element of mystery surrounding this debate, especially two aspects of the debate: original guilt and original pollution. Original guilt is a legal concept referring to fallen humanity's condemnation on account of Adam's sin. Original pollution is an organic and moral term referring to fallen humanity's corruption on account of Adam's sin. Thus, one's view of headship should address original guilt, original pollution, and the relationship between the two.

Natural headship, otherwise known as "realism," on account of its insistence that all humanity was present in or with Adam in a real sense at the fall, holds that individuals inherit both a sinful nature and guilt for a sin they themselves committed. On the positive side, this view is better positioned to defend against the accusation that God is unjust, that he condemns individuals for a sin they did not personally commit. Moreover, as Herman Bavinck notes, the natural-headship view is right to emphasize the organic unity of humanity.[a] And while we deny that sin corrupts human nature ontologically, it does corrupt human nature directionally such that this directional corruption is inherited naturally by all humanity. Similarly, God's work of redemption does not simply touch individuals to affect their eternal destiny, but it also brings healing and redirection to our misdirected nature.

We see several problems with the natural-headship view, however. First, it has difficulty accounting for the nature of our union with Adam. In exactly what way does humanity, in our organic unity, exist in Adam? As Bavinck reminds us, because of the

[17]John Calvin, *Institutes* 2.1.7 (*Institutes of the Christian Religion*, ed. John T. McNeill, trans. Ford Lewis Battles, The Library of Christian Classics 1 [Louisville, KY: Westminster John Knox, 2006], 249-50).

infinite qualitative distinction between the creator and the creature, any fellowship between the two must be covenantal in nature, being composed of God's self-giving condescension, and terms being set for the reception and reciprocation of this self-giving.[b] Creation itself, therefore, bears a covenantal shape. Further, as mentioned, because God's destiny for humanity concerns not merely individuals but the collective whole of humankind, God relates to the whole through an elected head, an individual whose covenant actions serve as paradigmatic for the destiny of the whole. Such seems to be the clear teaching of Romans 5:12-21—an element that finds little stress in the natural-headship view.

Second, the natural-headship (or realist) view, if taken strictly by itself, has difficulty making sense of the analogy Paul draws between Adam and Christ. When federalists assert that Christ is the representative head of humanity, and that he imputes his righteousness to humanity, the analogy with Adam comes easily: Adam is the representative head of humanity and his sin is imputed to us. But for realists to keep the parallelism in the analogy, they must call for a metaphysical participation in or partaking of Christ in order to acquire that which he offers—a view quite at home in Roman Catholic sacramental theology with its hierarchical ontology but foreign to the doctrine of creation we have advocated for here. Thus, Reformed realists must settle for an analogy without such a parallel, positing as they do a "realistic" account of our union with Adam but a "representative" account of our union with Christ.

There are problems also with the federal-headship view. First, most federal-headship proponents hold that on account of God's covenantal arrangement with Adam, after the fall individuals inherit or are credited not only an inability not to sin (*non posse non peccarre*) but also guilt for Adam's sin itself. With Oliver Crisp, we find this assertion problematic for our understanding of God's divine nature and specifically his justice.[c] Second, federalism has difficulty making clear why and how a legal declaration of guilt entails moral corruption. Why does a legal verdict cause a state of moral corruption? Yet, on the positive side, federalists *can* make sense of the parallelism in Paul's analogy, and their view does make sense of the covenantal nature of reality. Thus, we conclude that an account of original sin must draw from the best elements of both federalism and realism.

[a]Herman Bavinck, *Reformed Dogmatics*, ed. John Bolt, trans. J. Vriend (Grand Rapids, MI: Baker Academic, 2003–2008), 3:102.
[b]Ibid., 2:569-70.
[c]Oliver Crisp, "Karl Barth on Creation," in *Karl Barth and Evangelical Theology: Convergences and Divergences*, ed. Sung Wook Chung (Grand Rapids, MI: Baker Academic, 2006), 77-95.

One of the most fetching recent proposals is Marcus Peter Johnson's "Christological realism," in which he draws on the extensive biblical teaching about union with Christ to inform the debate about original sin.[18] Johnson argues that our union with Christ is not only representative but also vital, organic, and personal. Thus, every benefit we receive from being "in Christ" stems from our union with him. Paul's understanding of the union includes forensic imputation (2 Cor 5:21; Phil 3:8-9). "In other words, we are reckoned/regarded as righteous because we have been included in Christ."[19] Similarly, we share in Adam's condemnation on account of the fact that in our organic union with him, he serves as our representative head and his sin is our own. This parallelism, Johnson argues, while perhaps not metaphysically satisfactory, is grounded in a mystery that throughout Paul's writings is portrayed in both forensic and realist categories in our relationship to Christ, and therefore also, by implication, characterizes our relationship to Adam.[20]

Johnson therefore argues that our union with Christ is both legal and transformative. Our union with Christ gives us more than the legal benefit of justification; it also gives us the moral benefit of sanctification. Paul understands that our participation in Christ involves his being our holiness (1 Cor 1:30) and transforming us into his image (2 Cor 3:18; 1 Cor 15:49). Similarly, our union with Adam entails not only our condemnation on account of our participation in Adam's sin but also our corruption. Finally, Johnson argues that "by virtue of our singular, realistic union with Adam, we experience both the guilt and condemnation of his primal trespass, as well as the corrupt condition into which he fell. Guilt and pollution are distinguishable but inseparable dilemmas that issue forth from our union with Adam,"[21] and that find their parallel in the benefits made ours in Christ—namely, justification and sanctification.

Johnson is right to recognize the pervasiveness of biblical teaching on union with Christ and the centrality of this teaching for a broader doctrine of salvation. Further, we affirm his hermeneutical movement to draw on the doctrine of grace in order to help clarify our view of sin. "To speak of grace without sin," Cornelius Plantinga writes, "is to trivialize the cross of Jesus Christ . . . and therefore to cheapen the grace of God that always comes to us with blood on it." Conversely, "to speak of sin by itself, to speak of it apart from the realities of creation and grace, is [not only] to forget the resolve of

[18]Marcus Peter Johnson, *One with Christ: An Evangelical Theology of Salvation* (Wheaton, IL: Crossway, 2013), 69-77.

[19]Ibid., 72.

[20]Ibid., 71.

[21]Ibid., 75.

God [but also] to misunderstand its nature."[22] And although Johnson labels his view christological "realism," the essence of the view is a combination of the best elements of federalism and realism, situated in light of the biblical teaching on union with Christ. Thus, we would likewise situate those elements within the teaching about union with Christ but would emphasize the covenantal nature of reality and situate the center of gravity on the side of a covenantally framed federal headship position.

Holistic depravity. Although *how* we inherit our sinful dispositions from Adam has been a matter of debate throughout church history, the fact *that* we inherit sinful dispositions is set forth in stark terms throughout the pages of Scripture. The apostle Paul, for example, spends the first three chapters of Romans making the case that all human beings—whether Jew or Gentile—are guilty before God because of our sin (Rom 1–3). We suppress the knowledge of God that we do have and choose to worship idols instead of worshiping the one true and living God (Rom 1:18-25). This choice involves us in an ever-widening web of sins (Rom 1:24-32). Our sinful nature controls us (Rom 7:5). It affects our minds (Eph 4:18), our consciences (Heb 9:14), and our hearts (Jer 17:9). It incurs God's wrath (Gen 6:5; Rom 1:18). It is deeply ingrained, located in the depths of our being, thus radiating outward into the whole of our lives. In sum, we are holistically depraved.

To speak of a human being as holistically depraved is not to say that he or she commits every type of sin or sins to the utmost. Nor is it to say that a depraved person cannot perform good actions or that a person's conscience is disabled. Instead, it is to say that human beings cannot do anything to merit saving favor with God.

The doctrine of depravity is vital to the Christian faith, its centrality being seen not only in the biblical testimony, as noted above, but from the writings of the church's greatest theologians. As a doctrine, it was perhaps articulated most fully among the patristic fathers by Augustine, who explored its implications recurrently, and nowhere more significantly than in his two classics. In *City of God*, the doctrine of depravity is everywhere present in the two-cities argument that forms the backbone of the book: there exists a "city of God," whose citizens love God, and a "city of man," whose citizens love earthly goods instead of God and whose disordered love is the cause of all manner of evil in this world. In *Confessions*, Augustine's theological exploration of

[22]Cornelius Plantinga Jr., *Not the Way It's Supposed to Be: A Breviary of Sin* (Grand Rapids, MI: Eerdmans, 1996), 199.

depravity is illumined via autobiographical reflections on his experience of lusting for idols rather than for God. For Augustine, the final and greatest freedom will be freedom from depravity. That freedom, granted by God's gift of adoption, will enable his people to become the kind of "people" that Father, Son, and Spirit are, to enjoy a moral state in which they never again want to sin and, thus, are unable to sin.[23] Augustine is not alone; Calvin, Kuyper, and a host of others join him in recognizing the holistic nature of depravity.

Usurping God's kingship. As David declares in Psalm 51:1-4, we may sin against many people, but ultimately our sin is against God. Cornelius Plantinga writes:

> All sin has first and finally a Godward force. Let us say that *a* sin is any act—any thought, desire, emotion, word, or deed—or its particular absence, that displeases God and deserves blame. Let us add that the disposition to commit sins also displeases God and deserves blame, and let us therefore use the word *sin* to refer to such instances of both act and disposition. Sin is a culpable and personal affront to a personal God.[24]

When we sin, we, like the first couple before us, usurp God's kingship. Dissatisfied with the honor of vice-regency, we aspire to regency. We question God's character and his word, trusting our own wisdom over his. Regarding this usurpation, Barth writes,

> Man only wants to judge. He thinks he sits on a high throne, but in reality he sits only on a child's stool, blowing his little trumpet, cracking his little whip, pointing with frightful seriousness his little finger, while all the time nothing happens that really matters. He can only play the judge. He is only a dilettante, a blunderer, in his attempt to distinguish between good and evil, right and wrong, acting as though he really had the capacity to do it.[25]

Indeed, our sin is an ill-fated mutiny, a misdirected grasp for autonomy, an attempted usurpation of God's kingship. Not only do we usurp God's authority and put ourselves in his place, such as when Eve took on the words of God by declaring the fruit of the tree "good," but we also give to the serpent the authority that rightly belongs to God. In humanity's obeying the serpent's word instead of God's, the serpent becomes our new suzerain, our adopted father. He becomes "the god of this world" (2 Cor 4:4). Hence, although our

---

[23]Augustine, *The City of God* 22.30 (trans. Marcus Dods [New York: The Modern Library, 1950], 406-7).

[24]Plantinga, *Not the Way*, 13.

[25]Barth, *CD* IV/1, 446.

own wisdom may be an attempt to discern between good and evil, it is an unauthorized and blundering attempt, the effects of which are disastrous.

Progressive corruption. As one traces the early chapters of Genesis after the fall, one sees immediately the way in which sin corrupts and misdirects society. Sin corrupts progressively, not limiting itself to the private self but extending to the public self and ultimately to society and culture as a whole. It is like cancer in that it is a dynamic and relentlessly progressive phenomenon that reproduces rapidly and leaves the aroma of death in its wake.

After the Genesis account of the fall and its consequences, we move immediately into a narrative of sin's progression in the line of Cain (Gen 4:1-26). This progressive corruption extends beyond private selves to the whole public realm—social, cultural, and political. Sin does more than deprave individuals in their private selves; it radiates outward into the whole fabric of society and culture.

Dietrich Bonhoeffer writes:

> Cain is the first human being who is born on the ground that is *cursed*. It is with Cain that history begins, the history of death. Adam . . . begets Cain, the *murderer*. The new thing about Cain, the son of Adam, is that as sicut deus ["as God"] he himself lays violent hands on human life. The human being who may not eat from the tree of life grasps all the more greedily at the fruit of death, the destruction of life. Only the Creator can destroy life. Cain usurps for himself this ultimate right of the Creator and becomes the murderer. Why does Cain murder? Out of hatred toward God.[26]

The blood-soaked ground betokens Cain's fate. Rather than repenting, Cain complains that his punishment is more than he can possibly bear (Gen 4:13-14). Instead of fearing God, he fears physical and social exposure (Gen 4:14). So Cain the murderer pities himself instead of repenting, and God in his common grace puts a mark on Cain so that nobody will kill him.

In Genesis 4:17-24 we see further evidence of God's common grace. In this scene, family and society expand even as sin expands. Bruce Waltke observes,

> Cain's family are polygamists and self-avengers, as epitomized by Lamech. Cain's lineage produces the first metallurgy, the first poetry, and the first cities. His lineage is symbolic of human culture with great civilizations and no living God. The ambiguity of godless human culture is portrayed by paralleling advances in civilization with an increase in violence. The earthly city . . . epitomizes the

[26]Dietrich Bonhoeffer, *Creation and Fall: A Theological Exposition of Genesis 1–3*, ed. John W. De Gruchy, trans. Douglas S. Bax, Dietrich Bonhoeffer Works 3 (Minneapolis: Fortress, 1997), 145.

> ambiguity: it provides civilization as a pain reliever for wandering and alienation and as protection against human irrationality and vengeance; it culminates in [Genesis] 11:4 in the building of a city that challenges God's supremacy. . . . Instead of honoring God, the unbeliever honors a human being, naming his city after his son. This reverse direction will give rise to a self-idolizing, Machiavellian state.[27]

Waltke rightly notes that the story of Lamech portrays both the progressive corruption of sin and the generous common grace of God that allows sinful humanity to farm, raise animals (Gen 4:20), and cultivate the arts and sciences (Gen 4:21-24).

Finally, Genesis 4:25-26 serves to contrast Seth's line with Cain's line. Seth's line exemplifies those righteous who worship the one true and living God, Yahweh, rather than grasping for autonomy.

Seth's line produces the spiritual giants Enoch and Noah. Lamech, in the line of Cain, and Enoch, in the line of Seth, represent the seventh generation in the seed of the serpent and in the seed of the woman respectively. The former inflicts death; the latter does not die. In spite of the vicissitudes of history, God keeps his promise to give a seed to destroy the serpent (Gen 3:15).[28]

The Antithesis, Misdirection, and Common Grace

Cain murdered his brother, and his descendant Lamech was a murderer and a polygamist. But Scripture's portrayal of sin's progressive corruption of society and culture does not stop there. Indeed, God "saw that the wickedness of man was great in the earth, and that every intention of the thoughts of his heart was only evil continually" (Gen 6:5 ESV). One notes that God gave the law in part to stem sin's progression in the public realm. The Pentateuch includes numerous social and cultural laws precisely because human sin corrupts the social and cultural order. Similarly, the prophets preach against social ills, against Israel's repeated neglect of widows, orphans, foreigners, and other marginalized and helpless persons. In the New Testament, the apostle Paul's most extended treatise on human sin—the book of Romans—includes a long list of sins, of which most are social in nature (Rom 1:24-32).

Another way of seeing the extent to which sin affects society and culture is to look at the *imago Dei* and the cultural mandate. In the Genesis creation account, God gives humanity social (be fruitful and multiply) and cultural (till the soil)

---

[27]Bruce K. Waltke with Charles Yu, *An Old Testament Theology: An Exegetical, Canonical, and Thematic Approach* (Grand Rapids, MI: Zondervan, 2007), 271-72.

[28]Ibid., 272.

commands. He tells them to practice dominion, to lovingly manage his world under his regency. Implied in these commands is the recognition that God had endowed them with the equipment to obey his charge. These capacities—spiritual, moral, physical, rational, creative, relational, volitional—remain in us after the fall, but indeed remain in a corrupted and misdirected manner.

Even today, this antithesis has sway over every society and culture, and indeed cuts through the heart of every person. With Abraham Kuyper, we use the term *the antithesis* to refer to the radical opposition between God's design for human life and fallen patterns of human life. Kuyper argued that believers and unbelievers have radically different starting points with which they engage the world. He writes,

> [Believers and unbelievers] face the cosmos from different points of view, and are impelled by different impulses. And the fact that there are two kinds of *people* occasions of necessity the fact of two kinds of human *life*, and of two kinds of *science*; for which reason the idea of the *unity of science*, taken in its absolute sense, implies the denial of the fact of palingenesis, and therefore from principle leads to the rejection of the Christian religion.[29]

This view is premised on a certain view of the heart. Scripture refers to the heart over eight hundred times. When Scripture refers to the heart, it is referring to the whole person, to the direction and orientation of a person in his or her fullness. Gordon Spykman writes,

> The heart represents the unifying center of man's entire existence, the spiritual concentration point of our total selfhood, the inner reflective core which sets the direction for all of our life relationships. It is the wellspring of all our willing, thinking, feeling, acting, and every other life utterance. It is the fountainhead from which flows every movement of man's intellect, emotions, and will, as well as any other "faculty" or mode of our existence. In short the heart is the "mini-me."[30]

So the issues of life flow from the heart. The heart is the response side of our relationship with God. Heartfelt religion is comprehensive, reaching the depth dimensions of a person's inner beings and radiating outward to all that a person does. Either we are for God or against God, and that directionality radiates outward into our social and cultural doings.[31] Dooyeweerd writes,

---

[29]Abraham Kuyper, *Principles of Sacred Theology* (Grand Rapids, MI: Eerdmans, 1954), 154.

[30]Gordon J. Spykman, *Reformational Theology: A New Paradigm for Doing Dogmatics* (Grand Rapids, MI: Eerdmans, 1992), 218.

[31]Cf. Michel Henry, *Words of Christ*, trans. Christina M. Gschwandtner, Interventions (Grand Rapids, MI: Eerdmans, 2012), 97: "The illusion which makes the ego its own foundation does not

> The antithesis runs right through Christian life itself. . . . Everywhere . . . in . . . life . . . are manifestations of the turbulent spirit of darkness which wages war against the spirit of Christ in the most reprehensible ways. The antithesis is therefore not a dividing line between Christian and non-Christian groups. It is the unrelenting battle between two spiritual principles that impacts the entire nation and indeed all of humankind.[32]

In the aftermath of the fall, therefore, we find a great struggle between light and darkness, truth and error, the kingdom of darkness and the kingdom of Christ (Col 1:13). This struggle manifests itself in myriad ways in human history and at all levels of social and cultural life. As Christians, we are called to resist the antithesis wherever it is found in social and cultural life. We fight it not only from the pulpit but in every dimension of public life. As God's new people, possessing renewed minds, our social and cultural life—whether religious, scientific, artistic, entrepreneurial, or domestic—looks different from the cultural life of nonbelievers.

And yet the Lord God, in a universal gift to all humanity alike, bestows his common grace, a grace that holds sway across all of society and culture. It appears that the Spirit plays a significant role, one that has both enabling and restraining dimensions. Certain passages of Scripture ascribe human cultural activity to the Spirit's enablement. For example, the Spirit enabled Bezalel and Oholiab to do their work in the tabernacle with excellence (Ex 31:2; 35:30). In another passage, we read of the Spirit's role in restraining sin and its consequences (2 Thess 2:6-7). C. R. Vaughan writes, "[The Spirit] exerts that grand restraining influence without which there can be no such things as home, society, government, civilization, or individual enjoyment anywhere among all the millions of the sinning human race. He restrains both the sinful acts and the natural tendencies of the acts within some tolerable bounds."[33]

In yet other passages the Spirit is associated with aspects of personal character, such as wisdom (Acts 6:3) and faith (Acts 11:24), which are vital

---

merely distort the manner in which humans represent themselves to themselves, and therefore their relationships to the world and to things. It completely subverts the place where we are given to ourselves in absolute Life, namely our 'heart.' If we conceal this internal relationship to the divine Life in which the heart is engendered and in which it remains as long as it lives, then it becomes blind in regard to itself."

[32]Herman Dooyeweerd, *Roots of Western Culture: Pagan, Secular, and Christian Options*, trans. John Kraay, Collected Works, Series B, vol. 15 (Ancaster, ON: Paideia, 2012), 3-4.

[33]C. R. Vaughan, *The Gifts of the Holy Spirit: To Unbelievers and Believers* (Carlisle, PA: Banner of Truth, 1975), 26.

to a Christian's witness and work in the world. The Spirit plays an inevitable role in enabling not only the church but also human society and culture to continue on and even progress and flourish to some extent after the fall; further, the Spirit plays a role in keeping sin and sin's consequences somewhat at bay, so that the world does not become an utter horror. These enabling and restraining roles enable the unregenerate to produce great literature, make breakthroughs in science, or forge positive change in the political realm.

The Antithesis in Western Culture

Modern history reveals the power humans have wielded, over the course of millennia, to shape society and culture. Furthermore, it reveals the disastrous consequences that stem from human attempts to do so apart from God. Consider, for example, Karl Marx's vision for catalyzing social revolutions in which one "clears the decks" of society and culture in order to usher in an idyllic state bereft of God and the church. As Raymond Aron, Mircea Eliade, David Koyzis, and others have shown,[34] Marx's ideology was a totalizing system, an immanent system of salvation with a new god (material equality) who will save the world from evil (material inequality) through a salvation (socialist revolution) that will form a new church (congregations of classless people in the midst of a capitalist world) with a new priesthood (the Communist Party) that lives out a new ethic (with the "good" being defined as that which advances the interests of the revolution) as it marches toward a new eschaton (a Communist utopia in which the state withers away, society is classless, and violence disappears). Marx's vision has exerted an enormous influence historically, affecting the lives of billions of people.

In its historical instantiations, Marxism as an idolatrous ideology and manifestation of the antithesis has had disastrous effects on society. In the Soviet Union, for example, the Communist Party used systematic terror to move the revolution forward. From 1921 to 1953 alone, approximately 1.7 million citizens died in the Gulag, with nearly a million citizens being executed. In Aleksandr Solzhenitsyn's harrowing description, this systematic terror stemmed from the party's atheistic view of humanity. "In the mass and from a distance they [citizens] seem like swarming lice, but they are the crown

[34]E.g., Raymond Aron, *The Opium of the Intellectuals* (New York: Routledge, 2001), 265-94; Mircea Eliade, *The Myth of the Eternal Return* (Princeton, NJ: Princeton University Press, 2005), 141-62; Koyzis, *Political Visions and Illusions*, 168-75.

of creation, right? After all, once upon a time a weak little spark of God was breathed into them too—is it not true? So what has become of it now?"[35]

Indeed, modernity, more than any other period of history, alerts us to humanity's ability to shape the world in which it lives—for better or for worse. Toward the end of the twentieth century and the dawn of the twenty-first, an increasing number of thinkers have analyzed and evaluated what they see as the radical reshaping that is taking place in the modern West. One of the most perceptive is John Carroll in his book *The Wreck of Western Culture*.

John Carroll and secular humanism.[36] Sociologist John Carroll argues that secular humanism has wrecked Western culture by depriving it of the deep insights provided by faith. He begins his analysis by prophesying the universal ruin of Western culture: "We live amidst the ruins of the great, five-hundred-year epoch of humanism. Around us is that 'colossal wreck.' Our culture is a flat expanse of rubble."[37] But diagnosis is not Carroll's primary concern; rather, he is after an intellectual genealogy, and so he investigates how we have arrived at this state of affairs: the West turned away from theism and toward humanism, trying "to create out of nothing something as strong as the faith of the New Testament that could move mountains."[38] To do so meant that one must build an anthropocentric, rather than a theocentric, worldview: "To place the human individual at the center meant that he or she had to become the Archimedean point around which everything revolved."[39]

Carroll's compelling argument traces Western intellectual and spiritual history in general and Western works of art in particular. He focuses on Holbein's *The Ambassadors* and Shakespeare's *Hamlet*. Both of these works illustrate the modern retreat from the theological narratives that have sustained Western society and culture for more than two thousand years. Both works of art center on a skull. Holbein's painting includes a distorted and oblong skull in the foreground of the picture, while Shakespeare's *Hamlet* contains Yorrick's skull.

---

[35]Aleksandr Solzhenitsyn, *The Gulag Archipelago: An Experiment in Literary Investigation* (New York: Harper Perennial, 2007), 300.

[36]In this section material is used from Bruce R. Ashford, "Briefly Noted: The Wreck of Western Culture," *Between the Times*, May 15, 2013, http://betweenthetimes.com/index.php/2013/05/15/briefly-noted-the-wreck-of-western-culture.

[37]John Carroll, *The Wreck of Western Culture: Humanism Revisited*, 2nd ed. (Wilmington, DE: ISI Books, 2008), 1.

[38]Ibid., 3.

[39]Ibid., 2.

Figure 8.1. Hans Holbein, *The Ambassadors*, 1533

In Carroll's narrative, these skulls symbolize Western culture's fear of death; if life and death have been divested of divine meaning, then death becomes the ominous and dominant force in our lives and culture. If death has no more meaning than the Darwinist sense, then life has no meaning cither, and life becomes absurdly horrible, as Nietzsche argued.[40]

Carroll's is an imaginative and especially perceptive interpretation of the intellectual and spiritual history of the West. But it is Philip Rieff's work, which we referred to at the end of chapter three, that we will use to illustrate, via Western civilization, the effects of sin and the fall on social and cultural order. Rieff became famous as a public intellectual in the 1970s because of his

[40]Of course, this is contested, as the recent flurry of literature among analytic philosophers on the meaning of life demonstrates.

work on Sigmund Freud. He viewed Freud as a major cultural figure in the West whose work in the social sciences bequeathed to Western society a new view of humanity, a view Rieff calls "psychological man." Freud perceived that modern people acquired neuroses because they had difficulty finding meaning and purpose in a modern world in which premodern forms of authority are disappearing. Freud employed psychoanalysis to help liberate individuals from religious authority and norms so that they could find meaning and purpose otherwise. Rieff affirms some of the themes present in Freud's work—especially Freud's recognition that religious authority underlay premodern society and that the evaporation of that authority was unnerving for the modern person—but takes them in quite a different direction than Freud would have wanted.

Philip Rieff and sacred order. In Rieff's first major work, *The Mind of the Moralist*, he criticizes Freud for thinking his psychoanalysis freed humankind from religious or mythological authority. Indeed, Freud's "anti-myth" was itself a myth. Rieff writes, "Modern scientific myths are not myths of transcendence but myths of revolt against transcendence."[41] It is Rieff's work in the last years of his life that is most significant for our purposes. Just before he died, Rieff completed a trilogy. In the first volume, *My Life Among the Deathworks*, he argues that sacred order undergirds social order. By "sacred order" he is referring to the world of meaning that gives society the authority needed to uphold its rule internally and defend its vision of the good life externally. Rieff writes, "No culture has ever preserved itself where there is not a registration of sacred order."[42] And again, "Those arbitrary meanings warranted not by any man, but by the one God, are necessary if we are to find some safety in any world." So sacred order is abstract but makes itself concrete in culture and in so doing shapes and maintains social order.[43]

As a "middleman" between sacred order and social order, culture draws on sacred order (and the authority and meaning it endows) in order to uphold social order. Rieff writes, "A culture is the vertical in authority, that space between sacred order and social order which is the world made by world makers."[44] Rieff uses "via" as a shorthand for "vertical in authority" and argues

---

[41]Philip Rieff, *Freud: The Mind of the Moralist*, 3rd ed. (Chicago: University of Chicago Press, 1979), 204.

[42]Philip Rieff, *My Life Among the Deathworks: Illustrations of the Aesthetics of Authority*, ed. Kenneth S. Piver, Sacred Order/Social Order 1 (Charlottesville: University of Virginia Press, 2006), 13.

[43]Ibid., 2.

[44]Ibid., 45.

that healthy societies depend on a strong sense of via. However, culture doesn't always do its job. Instead of upholding the social order, sometimes it undermines it. The cultural works that undermine society are what Rieff refers to as "deathworks." "By deathwork I mean an all-out assault upon something vital to the established culture."[45]

In his Sacred Order/Social Order trilogy, Rieff speaks of four "worlds." The first cultural world was the pagan world, the second was one dominated by monotheisms, and the third is our present world, which wishes to do away with sacred order altogether. The first two worlds regarded their identity as constituted vertically from authority above, while our present third world rejects vertical authority and seeks to operate entirely horizontally from below. In the third world, it is the cultural elites who have tried to get rid of sacred order in the hopes that social order will take care of itself. "The one limiting possibility that the new elites cannot admit, in the world-affirming immanentism of their 'value' conventions, is that of a divine creator and his promised redemptive acts before whom and beside which there is nothing that means anything."[46]

"The contemporary *kulturkampf* is unique," Rieff writes, "because it is not between sacred orders but between great abolitionist movements directed against all sacred orders in any of their historical or theoretical manifestations."[47] He criticizes third-world culture especially for undermining social order by fostering a culture of death (e.g., abortion) and unbridled sexuality (e.g., homosexuality). However, Rieff is not asking Westerners to return to a second-world status. Instead, he argues that we must create a fourth-world culture and do so by recovering the via. "Our own motions in sacred order are locatable once each of us has restored to himself the notion of sacred order. The basic restorative is to understand the purity and inviolate nature of the vertical in authority. Those arbitrary meanings warranted not by any man, but by the one God, are necessary if we are to find some safety in any world."[48]

In his second volume, *The Crisis of the Officer Class*, Rieff notes that the third-world culture is breaking down. As in *Deathworks*, he challenges the West forward toward a fourth-world culture, one that is not premodern but is its own world culture. Rieff is confident that a new world culture will

---

[45]Ibid., 7.
[46]Ibid., 58.
[47]Ibid., 14.
[48]Ibid., 13.

form because sacred order cannot be abolished because the faith instinct cannot be abolished. Rieff writes, "Such an effort in its deadly futility represents a historical ending time, a time just before the faith instinct will show itself again."[49] Sacred order will inevitably resurface, and, as Rieff argues, Judaism and Christianity should be the primary agents in recovering the via.

Although Rieff is not a Christian, he urges us to take God with the utmost seriousness. For him the malady of our age is its atheological bent; likewise, its remedy is theological. In this way, Rieff's work is reminiscent of George Steiner's. While Rieff stalked Nietzsche, Joyce, and Picasso, Steiner's prey was Nietzsche and, ultimately, the deconstructionists. But their evaluations of Western culture and their prognoses are similar. Steiner, like Rieff, argues that a breakdown of the prevalent theistic order has diminished Western culture. He argues that Derrida and the deconstructionists have broken a covenant, as it were, between word and world as they teach their disciples to engage in the arts skeptically and ironically. This broken covenant is a genuine revolution (or, better, devolution), of which "the vulgarized shibboleth of the 'death of God' is a seminal but only partial articulation."[50] In response to Derrida, Steiner urges the Western world to make a "wager on transcendence," so that meaningfulness can be recovered.[51]

Steiner and especially Rieff are helpful for tracing out the way the antithesis has worked itself out in the West, the way it cuts across all of human life, not only corrupting individuals but misdirecting society and culture. Although neither of them is a Christian, both of them are perceptive in identifying the West's malady in its rejection of God and the vital notion of creation order and in offering a theological prescription for its healing. "When there is nothing sacred," Rieff writes, "there is nothing."[52]

Republication and Reenchantment: A Principled Pluralism

In this condition, it is incumbent on the Christian community to continually work for the reordering of that which has been wrecked, the republication

[49]Philip Rieff, *The Crisis of the Officer Class: The Decline of the Tragic Sensibility*, ed. Alan Woolfolk, Sacred Order/Social Order 2 (Charlottesville: University of Virginia Press, 2007), 2.

[50]George Steiner, *Real Presences* (Chicago: University of Chicago Press, 1989), 93.

[51]George Steiner, *Grammars of Creation* (New Haven, CT: Yale University Press, 2002), 214.

[52]Rieff, *Deathworks*, 12.

of God's thesis in light of the antithesis, and the reenchantment of a disenchanted world.[53]

Augustine's *City of God* offers some clues for how we might approach such a republication. Although his context was different from ours, especially significant is that he lived in the midst of a declining empire whose pagan intellectuals wished to subvert the Christian faith. In fact, Augustine wrote *City of God* in the context of the sack of Rome. For the Romans this devastating event needed interpretation. Volusianus and other pagan intellectuals speculated that Christianity caused the downfall of Rome. Rome had been beaten to its knees, they argued, because the Romans had forsaken their gods, their founding political narrative, and their philosophers.

In response to the pagan interpretation of Rome's fall, Augustine counters by exposing the incoherence of the pagan narrative and then offering the biblical narrative as the true story of the whole world. In relation to the pagan *gods*, he shows that the Romans never could decide which deities were actually in control, and that the preeminent Roman historian of religion, Marcus Varro, did not really believe in the gods anyway. In relation to the pagan *philosophers*, Augustine finds common ground in his admiration for Plato and the Neoplatonists but exposes the tragic flaw in the Platonists—their pride—which kept them from believing in the incarnation and resurrection. In relation to their founding *political narrative*, Augustine finds common ground with them in admiring Virgil but exposes the fact that the mythical story of Romulus, Remus, and Rome's founding (as told by Virgil and others) is actually a verdict against Rome. Whereas the pagan intellectuals viewed justice as the unique interpretive key to Rome's glorious history, Augustine argued that Rome had never been just and that its pretention to justice was no more than a veil for its lust for power. Curtis Chang writes, "Augustine . . . presents a political analysis that was stunningly original for its time and for centuries to come. He takes apart an entire civilization's ideologies to reveal them as masks for raw power."[54]

By exposing the inadequacy of their religion, philosophy, and politics, Augustine sought to "take the roof off" the Roman worldview, allowing the

---

[53]In this section material is used from Bruce R. Ashford, "Augustine for the Americans: Lessons on Christianity and Public Life from a Fifth-Century North African Theologian," Ethics and Religious Liberty Commission, April 20, 2015, https://erlc.com/resource-library/articles/augustine-for-the-americans-lessons-on-christianity-and-public-life-from-a-fifth-century-north-african-theologian.

[54]Curtis Chang, *Engaging Unbelief: A Captivating Strategy from Augustine and Aquinas* (Downers Grove, IL: InterVarsity Press, 2000), 74.

realities of the external world to beat in on the Romans as they stood naked and exposed before reality.[55] We too must learn to read our sociocultural context if we wish to speak the gospel with prescience and contribute to the common good. If, as Rieff argues, culture undergirds social order and if, as he argues, we live in a day when many of our culture makers are producing "deathworks," then our (American)[56] service to God includes the necessity of exposing these deathworks for what they are.

After exposing the incoherence of the pagan narrative, Augustine offers the biblical narrative as the true story of the whole world. At the center of Augustine's strategy is his "two cities" argument. For Augustine, all of human society can be divided into two cities—the city of man and the city of God. The citizens of these cities are differentiated respectively by who they love—either God or idols. The two cities take center stage early on in the biblical narrative when Cain murders Abel. The heart of Augustine's argument is that one is drawn toward what one truly loves—either God or idols—and one's chosen love locates one in either the city of man or the city of God. Citizens of the earthly city seek their happiness in temporal things, while those in the city of God seek theirs in an eternal kingdom.

Augustine is not satisfied, however, merely to show the tragic flaws in the competing narratives and the superiority of the biblical narrative. He also wants to make abundantly clear the fact that Christ and his church are not "part of" any other larger narrative. They are not actors on the stage of a grand Roman drama. The truth of the matter is exactly the opposite: Rome itself is only a minor character in the grand sweep of the history of Christ and his people. All of history centers on Christ and his people rather than on Rome and its people. So Augustine puts on display the superior explanatory power of the Christian story and invites the reader to believe on the Christ who stands at the center of the story.

At bottom, Augustine was addressing the ideological and religious pluralism of the Roman Empire, a topic the church must address afresh and anew for each generation and in each cultural context. Our Western democratic societies are no exception. "Western liberal democracies," political scientist Jonathan Chaplin writes, "which hitherto had considered themselves to be stable, confident, and tolerant are increasingly perplexed and disoriented by the presence within them of strong and articulate cultural, religious and

[55]Francis Schaeffer is known for employing the phrase "take the roof off" in order to describe his apologetic strategy of uncovering the inadequacy of false religions and worldviews.
[56]"American" inserted by Bruce Ashford!

other minorities whose claims are disrupting that comfortable self-image."[57] Like Augustine, we must recognize that there is no such thing as a neutral pluralism, and thus we must forgo the claims of secular liberalism and instead promote an authentically Christian view of pluralism.

Pluralism means "manyness," and in striving for a just ordering of society and a faithful Christian witness within that ordering, we must come to grips with the many types of manyness. Richard Mouw and Sander Griffioen distinguish between six types of pluralism, affirming five of the six and promoting a principled pluralism for public life. First, the authors distinguish between normative and descriptive pluralism.[58] A *normative* pluralist is one who advocates diversity, while a *descriptive* pluralist is one who merely acknowledges the existence of diversity. Second, the authors distinguish between directional, associational, and contextual pluralism.[59] *Directional* pluralism acknowledges that within any given society there likely are competing visions of the good life, visions associated with religions, ideologies, or philosophies. *Associational* pluralism acknowledges that within society there exists a variety of associations, such as families, churches, clubs, and corporations. *Contextual* pluralism acknowledges that within society there exists a variety of contexts, such as race, ethnicity, geography, gender, and class.

Third, Mouw and Griffioen draw on the two sets of distinctions above in order to produce six classifications of pluralism.[60] The first type of pluralism, normative directional pluralism, is the only type they reject: a pluralism that affirms false religions, ideologies, and philosophies. The other five types are ones that we recognize as necessary in this time between the times. Together with Mouw and Griffioen we reject normative directional pluralism but affirm descriptive directional pluralism (recognizing the fact that a plurality of religions and ideologies will exist in a fallen world), descriptive associational pluralism (highlighting the fact of many associational patterns) and normative associational pluralism (affirming those associational patterns), descriptive contextual pluralism (highlighting the fact of diverse cultural contexts), and normative contextual pluralism (affirming those cultural contexts).

[57]Jonathan Chaplin, "Rejecting Neutrality, Respecting Diversity: From 'Liberal Pluralism' to 'Christian Pluralism,'" *Christian Scholar's Review* 35, no. 2 (Winter 2006): 143.

[58]Richard J. Mouw and Sander Griffioen, *Pluralisms and Horizons: An Essay in Christian Public Philosophy* (Grand Rapids, MI: Eerdmans, 1993), 14.

[59]Ibid., 16-17.

[60]Ibid., 17-19.

We live in this time between the times, in a fallen world that awaits its renewal.[61] Until that time of renewal and restoration, public life will always and necessarily be to some extent marked by directional pluralism. There will be no ultimate or comprehensive consensus on the nature of justice, the good life, or other issues of significant public import. And yet we must draw on our Christianity forthrightly to work for the common good of our societies. "Christians," Chaplin writes, "should stand ready to declare honestly—and, where appropriate, publicly—that they aspire to reshape the boundaries of legally accepted expressions of directional plurality in their societies in the light of a vision of state and society rooted in Christian faith. Such a declaration . . . is intended . . . to reinvigorate and enrich [democratic debate]."[62] Thus, we wish to gain consensus in the public square whenever and wherever we can for the well-being of all, but without imposing a Christian lifestyle on others. We should employ our Christian beliefs to work for justice and peace, to alleviate injustice and suffering, to gain consensus on significant public issues when we can, and to promote the overall flourishing of society. In so doing, we resist the theocratic impulse toward religious coercion while retaining the Christian imperative to leverage our Christianity for the betterment of society.

Conclusion

Just a few hundred years before Augustine raised his pen, another preacher—Jesus of Nazareth—rose from the dead after having been crucified at the hands of the Roman powers. This Jesus, to whom all authority has been given in heaven and on earth, launched within the created realm the God-in-public-on-earth reality that Scripture calls God's kingdom. He will return one day to consummate his kingdom, reversing the millennia-long vandalizing of his creation and of the shalomic state in which it had been conceived. On that day, the antithesis will be overcome, and the Lord will reign.

---

[61]Material used from Bruce R. Ashford, "Lessons from Father Abraham (Kuyper): Christianity, Politics, & the Public Square," Ethics and Religious Liberty Commission, March 6, 2015, https://erlc.com/resource-library/articles/lessons-from-father-abraham-kuyper-christianity-politics-and-the-public-square.

[62]Chaplin, "Rejecting Neutrality," 174.

NINE

CREATION AND CULTURE

The command of God does not hang ineffectively in the air above man. Its particular aim and concern are with him and his real activity. . . . Man's real activity is always concrete. . . . And the field of his conduct is a tremendously varied sphere of conditions and possibilities determined by time, space, nature and history.

Karl Barth

God is milking the cows through the vocation of the milkmaid.

Martin Luther

All music . . . should have no other end and aim than the glory of God and the recreation of the soul.

Johann Sebastian Bach

God made me fast. And when I run, I feel His pleasure.

Eric Liddell

In his *Art in Action*, Nicholas Wolterstorff's second chapter is titled "The Given with Which the Artist Works." He writes, "It is not only tempting but customary to speak in lofty abstract tones about art—to spiritualize it, etherealize it, de-materialize it. . . . The fundamental fact about the artist is that he or she is a worker in stone, in bronze, in clay, in paint, in acid and plates, in sounds and instruments, in states of affairs."[1] Art combines creativity with the possibilities and limits of the medium with which one works. A particular medium presents both wonderful possibilities and constraints. A good artist will know their medium intimately and align their creativity with the

[1]Nicholas Wolterstorff, *Art in Action* (Grand Rapids, MI: Eerdmans, 1980), 91.

possibilities of the medium in which they work. Similarly, other forms of culture making represent avenues for the development of human creativity and ingenuity. Like the creation of art, human activity in other spheres of culture is carried out with real freedom within the limits of God's call.

This chapter outlines humanity's calling to develop culture under God's authority and according to his creational design. First, we briefly trace the biblical narrative through creation, fall, redemption, and restoration. We participate in the redemption of all things as we heed God's call to develop culture under his rule, patiently waiting for him to restore all things. Integral to our view of developing culture is that God's grace infuses, restores, reorders, and redirects nature to the glory of God. This relationship beckons us to contextualize the gospel in every culture dialogically, putting the biblical narrative in conversation with particular contexts in order to discern the church's faithful witness. The resulting theological practice sends the church into the world, answering the call of God to serve him in every sphere of culture, not only the church.

From Creation to New Creation: A Reflection on Culture

The English word *culture* comes from the Latin word *cultura*, which, in its literal sense, means "cultivation." It was essentially an agricultural term referring to activities such as tilling the soil. Yet Cicero expanded the word's range of meaning by using it metaphorically, asserting that "philosophy is the cultivation of the soul."[2] Building on Cicero, Westerners began to employ the word to refer to artistic, architectural, literary, and intellectual accomplishments of society. Today, among anthropologists, *culture* is used even more expansively, with one influential definition being the "more or less integrated systems of feelings, ideas, and values and their associated patterns of behavior and products shared by a group of people who organize and regulate what they feel, think, and do."[3]

In line with the more expansive meaning, we define *culture* theologically as whatever results from God's image bearers interacting with God's good creation.[4] As God's image bearers interact with God's creation, they cultivate the ground, harvesting goods from the natural world such as vegetables or wood; they produce artifacts from creation's raw materials, such as cloth,

---

[2]Cicero, *On Life and Death*, trans. John Davie (Oxford: Oxford University Press, 2017), 52. *Tusculanae disputationes* 2.5.13.

[3]Paul G. Hiebert, *Anthropological Insights for Missionaries* (Grand Rapids, MI: Baker, 1985), 30.

[4]Bruce Riley Ashford, *Every Square Inch: An Introduction to Cultural Engagement for Christians* (Bellingham, WA: Lexham, 2015), 13.

homes, airplanes; they ponder the relationships of cause and effect and the origins of things, forming worldviews (theism, pantheism, atheism); and they foster ways of life, which include not only belief systems but affective and evaluative grids. Thus, by *culture* we have in mind the ways in which humans shape their lives together. Culture includes such things as housing; the development of towns, cities, and farms; transport; wilderness areas protected through conservation; education; government; art, music, and crafts; and leisure. This notion of culture conforms with biblical teaching that the image of God is the whole person, not seated in one's intellect or will, but encompassing the cognitive, affective, and evaluative aspects of one's being and including patterns of behavior and products produced. The human person, the imager and culture maker, draws on all of who he or she is to shape culture and, in turn, is shaped by the same thing he or she helped produce. Further, in this shaping and being shaped, one interacts extensively across the entire range of nonhuman creation. The concept of culture, therefore, is intimately related to the doctrine of creation.

Creation. In the penultimate act of the creation account, God created humanity in his image, according to his likeness. As Kuyper and Bavinck argued, the whole human, and indeed the whole human race, images God.[5] As Bavinck argues, God is the archetype of creation, and humanity the most complete ectype of his being in creation.[6] Human capacities for spirituality, moral reasoning, interpersonal relations, abstract and concrete reasoning, artistic expression, and linguistic communication are all reflections, however creaturely, of what the creator is like. Our likeness to God, Calvin notes, "extends to the whole excellence by which man's nature towers over all the kinds of living creatures."[7] Because of the way in which these capacities combine to make humanity uniquely in God's image, God could place the man and woman in the garden to be fruitful and multiply, till the soil, and exercise royal stewardship over God's good creation (Gen 1:26 27; 2:15).

Adam's cultivation of the garden serves as a literal activity that foreshadows the metaphorical cultivation that we see throughout the pages of Scripture. Humankind's vice-regency would manifest itself not only in *agri*culture but

[5]Abraham Kuyper, "Common Grace," in *Abraham Kuyper: A Centennial Reader*, ed. James D. Bratt (Grand Rapids, MI: Eerdmans, 1998), 177; Herman Bavinck, *Reformed Dogmatics*, ed. John Bolt, trans. J. Vriend (Grand Rapids, MI: Baker Academic, 2003–2008), 2:576-79.

[6]Bavinck, *Reformed Dogmatics*, 2:554, 561.

[7]*John Calvin, Institutes* 1.15.4 *(Institutes of the Christian Religion*, ed. John T. McNeill, trans. Ford Lewis Battles, The Library of Christian Classics 1 [Louisville, KY: Westminster John Knox, 2006], 188).

in all types of *culture*. Humans would "work the garden" not only by cultivating plant life but also by cultivating art, architecture, music, liturgy, clothing, sport, and entertainment and by forming domestic, religious, social, and political institutions. God did not merely give humanity the *capacity* to make culture; he in fact *commanded* us to use those capacities. As we have noted, the commands given in Genesis 1–2 are often called *the cultural mandate* because they make it imperative for man and woman to bring their influence to bear in every dimension of society and culture. When humans rule, fill, work, and keep, they are shaping culture and in turn being shaped by it. Creation is what God made out of nothing, but culture is what humans make out of God's good creation.

Fall. The second plot movement in the biblical drama involved Adam and Eve rebelling against their creator in a vain attempt for autonomy. Their fall "was not just an isolated act of disobedience but an event of catastrophic significance for creation as a whole."[8] Sin, therefore, has massive and deleterious consequences on humanity's cultural life. "Since humankind's fall," write Michael Goheen and Craig Bartholomew, "the center of each culture is found in some form of communal idolatry that shapes all aspects of social and cultural life and organizes them in rebellions against God."[9] This communal idolatry works itself out through the very imaging capacities that were meant for worshipful culture making. Thus, as far as the image of God extends through human nature and is reflected in the cultural activities of humans in God's creation, so sin pervades every element of it. Nothing is left untouched by sin.

The cultural mandate was not invalidated, however, by the fall corrupting God's creation ontologically. Even though sin and rebellion corrupted the world morally and directionally, it did not corrupt it ontologically or structurally. "Anything in creation," Albert Wolters writes, "can be directed either toward or away from God. . . . This double direction applies not only to individual human beings but also to such cultural phenomena as technology, art, and scholarship, to such societal institutions as labor unions, schools, and corporations, and to such human functions as emotionality, sexuality, and rationality."[10] The directional results of the fall, for human culture, are revealed

[8]Albert M. Wolters, *Creation Regained: Biblical Basics for a Reformational Worldview*, 2nd ed. (Grand Rapids, MI: Eerdmans, 2005), 53.

[9]Michael W. Goheen and Craig G. Bartholomew, *Living at the Crossroads: An Introduction to Christian Worldview* (Grand Rapids, MI: Baker Academic, 2008), 49. This is what Augustine was getting at with his doctrine of two cities, the city of man and the city of God.

[10]Wolters, *Creation Regained*, 59.

in such things as poor reasoning in the realm of philosophy or science, kitsch in the realm of art, and jealousy and slander in the realm of relationships. Anything in creation can be directed toward God or away from him.[11] It is this direction that distinguishes between the good and the bad, rather than some distinction between spiritual and material.

And yet, in spite of sin's disastrous directional effects on the cultural enterprise, things are not as bad as they could be. God graciously restrains the destruction wrought by sin, keeping creation from devolving into complete chaos: "[The Spirit] exerts that grand restraining influence without which there can be no such things as home, society, government, civilization, or individual enjoyment anywhere among all the millions of the sinning human race. He restrains both the sinful acts and the natural tendencies of the acts within some tolerable bounds."[12] One facet of the Spirit's restraining work is the "common" grace he bestows on humanity, which enables his image bearers to use their God-given capacities within the created order. Cornelius Plantinga Jr. writes, "The Holy Spirit preserves much of the original goodness of creation and also inspires new forms of goodness—and not only in those people the Spirit has regenerated. . . . The Spirit also distributes 'common grace,' an array of God's gifts that preserves and enhances human life even when not regenerating it."[13] Because of God's grace through his Spirit, God's good creation continues to be a stage on which we may work out our worship via cultural means.

Redemption and restoration. Immediately after the fall, God promises that the woman's seed will destroy the serpent. Paul recognizes this promise as a prophecy concerning Jesus Christ the promised Messiah, the so-called *protevangelium* or "first gospel." From Irenaeus onward, Genesis 3:15 has been read in this way, but Westermann and many modern exegetes reject this reading.[14] However, Wenham rightly notes, "Once admitted that the serpent symbolizes sin, death, and the power of evil, it becomes much more likely that the curse envisages a long struggle between good and evil, with mankind eventually triumphing."[15] He points out that the oldest Jewish interpretation sees the

---

[11]Ashford, *Every Square Inch*, 29.

[12]C. R. Vaughan, *The Gifts of the Holy Spirit: To Unbelievers and Believers* (Carlisle, PA: Banner of Truth Trust, 1975), 32-33.

[13]Cornelius Plantinga Jr., *Engaging God's World: A Christian Vision of Faith, Learning, and Living* (Grand Rapids, MI: Eerdmans, 2002), 58.

[14]Claus Westermann, *Genesis 1–11: A Commentary*, trans. John J. Scullion (Minneapolis: Augsburg, 1984), 260.

[15]Gordon J. Wenham, *Genesis 1–15*, WBC 1 (Dallas: Word, 1987), 80.

serpent as a symbol of Satan and anticipates his defeat in the days of the Messiah. He also notes that the New Testament alludes to Genesis 3:15 in Romans 16:20, Hebrews 2:14, and Revelation 12.

Here in the opening chapters of Genesis is God's covenant that he will reconcile his image bearers and ultimately the whole creation. This holistic salvation encompasses not only image bearers from among *every* tribe, tongue, people, and nation (Rev 5:9) but extends even further—beyond humanity—to include a restored heavens and earth. "The difference between the Christian hope of resurrection and a mythological hope," writes Bonhoeffer, "is that the Christian hope sends a man back to his life on earth in a wholly new way."[16] This new way includes glorifying God from within our cultural contexts, as a preview of his already-and-not-yet kingdom in which all of creation and culture will praise him. As we engage in cultural life in the arts, the sciences, education, the public square, and so forth, we do so directing those aspects of our life toward Christ, in whom they consist and to whom they should give praise. Rather than destroying his creation, God preserves it in order to heal it. With this recognition comes the imperative to participate in God's work of healing by faithfully redirecting our cultural life and labors in the Spirit toward his creation designs in every context in which we find ourselves.

Nature and Grace: Returning to the Biblical Narrative

Presuppositions about the relationship of nature and grace underlie any view of the relationship between creation and culture. Often theologians do not make explicit their nature-grace presuppositions. In such instances, one must undertake the project of theological excavation because these nature-grace visions have tremendous consequences in the way we view the world. Bernard Zylstra argues that these presuppositions "have exerted a phenomenal impact on the way Christians live in the modern world. For these visions are the human responses to the meaning of the Gospel itself, and they thus shape one's life practice, spirituality, ethic, worldview, and interpretation of Scripture."[17] We can discern four basic views of nature and grace that have shaped the way theologians and traditions have approached creation and culture over the course of the first two millennia of church history.

---

[16]Dietrich Bonhoeffer, *Letters and Papers from Prison*, ed. Eberhard Bethge and Frank Clarke, trans. Reginald Horace Fuller, 3rd ed. (New York: Macmillan, 1972), 176.

[17]Bernard Zylstra, preface to *The Relation of the Bible to Learning*, by H. Evan Runner (Jordan Station, ON: Paideia, 1982), 23.

CHRIST AND CULTURE: NIEBUHR'S CLASSIC TEXT

Our typology of nature versus grace is closely related to H. Richard Niebuhr's classic *Christ and Culture*. Niebuhr develops five views of Christianity and culture. The first view is *Christ against culture*, one that "uncompromisingly affirms the sole authority of Christ over the Christian and resolutely rejects the culture's claims to loyalty."[a] Niebuhr rejects this view for being incoherent (claiming to draw exclusively on revelation but actually also using reason), making false assumptions (that the church is pure, while the culture is full of sin), and being otherwise insufficiently Christian (demoting grace by promoting legalism; being unable to make sense of Jesus as the creator of the natural realm). The second view is *Christ of culture*, one that affirms Christ's lordship over the church but at the same time seems "equally at home in the community of culture."[b] In effect, proponents of this view reconstruct Christ in the image of the culture.[c] These two views lie at opposite ends of the Christ-and-culture spectrum.

The next three views are ones that have in common their rejection of the first two. As Niebuhr sees it, these mediating views constitute the majority of theologians and traditions within church history. Third, therefore, Niebuhr introduces the *Christ above culture* model, one in which its exemplar, Thomas Aquinas, considers that "Christ is far above culture, and he does not try to disguise the gulf that lies between them."[d] Niebuhr rejects this view for being "too neat," for being culturally conditioned anyway, for institutionalizing Christ and the gospel, and for not recognizing fully enough the radically distorting nature of sin on human culture. Fourth, Niebuhr introduces the *Christ and culture in paradox* model, a view that "joins the radical Christian in pronouncing the whole world of human culture to be godless and sick unto death. But there is this difference between them: the dualist knows that he belongs to that culture and cannot get out of it, that God indeed sustains him in it and by it; for if God in His grace did not sustain the world in its sin it would not exist for a moment."[e] Niebuhr criticizes this model for tending toward antinomianism, cultural conservatism, and sociopolitical apathy.

Finally, Niebuhr introduces the *Christ the transformer of culture* model, which grasps the universal and deleterious effects of sin but believes that culture is under Christ's rule and that therefore we must carry on cultural work as a matter of obedience. The factor that distinguishes this model from the previous one is its more optimistic attitude toward the culture project. Niebuhr lists Augustine, Calvin, and Wesley as proponents and offers no criticism of this model.

Aside from quibbles concerning Niebuhr's categories and the historical figures who populate them, the most salient critique of Niebuhr is doctrinal, with no doctrine of Niebuhr's more deficient than his doctrine of creation. Carter demonstrates Niebuhr's weak view of creation and its relation to culture; in fact, Niebuhr never really makes the connection.[f] Carter further criticizes his Christology, arguing that Niebuhr's Christ has feet that "barely touch the earth."[g] His Christ is only barely incarnate, being more mystical and eternal, so that one suspects an ontological dualism between him and the created order. These deficiencies lead in turn to Niebuhr's weak ecclesiology, one in which the church is not really able to bear witness to Christ's lordship collectively on the earth.

[a]H. Richard Niebuhr, *Christ and Culture*, 50th anniversary ed. (San Francisco: Harper & Row, 2001), 45.
[b]Ibid., 83.
[c]Ibid., 19.
[d]Ibid., 129.
[e]Ibid., 156.
[f]Craig A. Carter, *Rethinking Christ and Culture: A Post-Christendom Perspective* (Grand Rapids, MI: Brazos, 2006), 68-69.
[g]Ibid., 64.

Grace above nature. The dominant medieval view, one that can be traced back to Aquinas but that is also held by Protestant theologians, is grace *suspended above nature*. In this view, grace and nature exist in separate realms and are hierarchically related. Aquinas, following Alexander of Hales, held that grace is a "superadded" (*donum superadditum*) quality that elevates the natural above its normal qualities in order that humanity can be led into higher, spiritual "habits" (*gratia habitualis*). For Aquinas, nature must be endowed with grace in order to raise it above its natural potency for its forms to attain to sanctification. Such does not, in Aquinas's eyes, denigrate the ontological status of creation to the realm of profane, but it does reveal the limits of nature. In itself, the realm of nature is incomplete, and grace must be extrinsically applied or infused: "I answer that it must be said that gifts of grace are added to those of nature in such a way that they do not destroy the latter, but rather perfect them; wherefore also the light of faith, which is gratuitously infused into our minds, does not destroy the natural light of cognition, which is in us by nature."[18] The result of such a view is the establishment of an ontological hierarchy of priority, with the realm of grace, with its virtues and saving perfections, set above as fundamentally unconnected to nature. While strictly speaking, in metaphysical terms, grace in this view takes on the characteristic of a quality to be added to nature to fundamentally change something's essence, Bavinck argues that really such a view sees grace as an unearthly substance that, when infused, adds something completely new that was not present before.[19]

Thus, in this view, God's good creation is "nature," and it is relatively autonomous. It remains in good order after the fall and is in no need of redemption. Grace comes alongside creation, complementing it rather than

[18]Thomas Aquinas, *ST* 1.1.8; 2.1.5.
[19]Bavinck, *Reformed Dogmatics*, 3:575-77.

re-forming it. This vision has a distinctive view of the way Christians live in the world. Christians split their time between two realms. In the natural realms, they have families, workplaces, schools, leisure, political interactions, and so forth. In the realm of grace, however, they have church, theology, and devotional lives. The latter realm is higher and more important than the former.

From Bavinck's perspective, Christianity, according to this view, "remains an eternal dualism. . . . [It] does not annihilate the natural, in the manner of the Manichaeans, but devalues it. . . . To be sure . . . it depreciates and depresses the natural; it puts on everything the stamp of contempt and brands it as profane. In [it], the fundamental opposition is not that of holy and unholy, but of consecrated and profane."[20] This view wrongly considers grace something that hovers transcendently above nature, and further wrongly understands nature to be effectively an autonomous realm, relatively unaffected by human rebellion. It does not recognize the twisting power of sin and may not see the cultural mission of the church as the life-and-death battle that it is.

Grace opposed to nature. Alongside the dominant view, some medieval monastics held to a view in which grace is opposed to nature. Finding proponents also among certain Anabaptists, Pietists, Methodists, and contemporary evangelicals, this view sees nature as ontologically corrupted. This view corrects one of the errors of the first view—namely, that nature is some sort of autonomous realm unaffected by sin—but wrongly construes the way in which nature is corrupted by human rebellion. Instead of viewing sin's impact as directional, proponents view it as structural. This leads to dualism and cultural withdrawal. Thus, in the *Great Article Book* of the Hutterites, we find Bishop Peter Walpot writing, "Between the Christian and the world there exists a vast difference like that between heaven and earth. The world is the world, always remains the world, behaves like the world and all the world is nothing but the world. The Christian, on the other hand, has been called away from the world."[21] Christ's redemption delivers us not just from sin and its consequences but also from creation. In this view, "redemption is not a matter of God making all things new but of making all new things."[22]

[20]Herman Bavinck, *De Katholiciteit van Christendom en Kerk* (Kampen: Zalsman, 1888), 21-22, quoted in Jan Veenhof, *Nature and Grace in Herman Bavinck*, trans. Albert M. Wolters (Sioux Center, IA: Dordt College Press, 2006), 11, 34, English translation available as Bavinck, "The Catholicity of Christianity and the Church," trans. John Bolt, *CTJ* 27 (1992): 231.

[21]Robert E. Webber, *The Church in the World: Opposition, Tension, or Transformation?* (Grand Rapids, MI: Zondervan, 1986), 87.

[22]Zylstra, preface, 27.

This vision has a distinctive view of the way Christians live in the world. Because this world itself is fallen, it is not our home and we are permanently in exile. We should focus on building the church *next to* the world instead of doing so *in* the world. Abraham Kuyper describes this view as one that

> concentrated all sanctity in the human soul and dug a deep chasm between this inward-looking spirituality and life all around. Then scholarship becomes unholy; the development of art, trade, and business becomes unholy; unholy also the functions of the government; in short all that is not directly spiritual and aimed at the soul. This way of thinking results in your living in two distinct circles of thought: in the very circumscribed circles of your soul's salvation on the one hand, and in the spacious, life-encompassing sphere of the world on the other. Your Christ is at home in the former but not in the latter.[23]

Grace alongside nature. Built into the Lutheran Reformation was a view of grace as something that exists alongside nature. More than a few contemporary evangelicals, including Michael Horton, David VanDrunen, and D. G. Hart, hold this view, in which nature and grace are parallel realms that each have their own integrity.[24] They speak of two kingdoms that should not be confused. The civil kingdom is ruled by natural law, while the churchly kingdom is ruled by grace. Thus, Lutheran Gene Veith writes, "Christians exercising their vocations in the secular culture must assess their activity in secular terms. . . . There is no need for a distinctively Christian approach to [cultural matters]."[25] We should respect the civil realm as its own autonomous sphere; we should not, and indeed cannot, transform it. VanDrunen and other "two kingdoms" proponents view this model as an extension and development of Augustine's "two cities." But as James K. A. Smith has shown, one should not distort Augustine's city of man by equating it with God's good creation, or likewise transpose Augustine's two cities into a Neo-Scholastic nature-grace dualism.[26] Contemporary proponents of this view rightly lay claim to—at

[23]Kuyper, "Common Grace," 172.

[24]Michael Horton, "The Time Between: Redefining the 'Secular' in Contemporary Debate," in *After Modernity? Secularity, Globalization, and the Re-enchantment of the World*, ed. James K. A. Smith (Waco, TX: Baylor University Press, 2008), 45-66; David VanDrunen, *Natural Law and the Two Kingdoms: A Study in the Development of Reformed Social Thought* (Grand Rapids, MI: Eerdmans, 2010); D. G. Hart, *A Secular Faith: Why Christianity Favors the Separation of Church and State* (New York: Ivan R. Dee, 2006).

[25]Gene Veith, "Two Kingdoms Under One King: Towards a Lutheran Approach to Culture," in *Christ and Culture in Dialogue: Constructive Themes and Practical Applications*, ed. Angus J. L. Menuge (St. Louis: Concordia Academic Press, 1999), 129-44.

[26]James K. A. Smith, "Reforming Public Theology: Two Kingdoms, or Two Cities?," *CTJ* 47 (2012): 122-37.

least part of—Luther's legacy, but not to Augustine's. This view, like the first view, does not sufficiently recognize sin's power to distort and misdirect God's creation. Proponents tend not to see cultural life as part of the church's mission and may not see it as part of a life-and-death battle.

Grace infuses and restores nature. A better alternative to the three views above is to understand grace as something that infuses and restores nature. Many Reformed theologians and some Anabaptists, Catholics, and evangelicals hold this view, in which creation is still God's "good" creation and indeed is the theater of his glory. In the beginning, God established a covenant with his creation that calls the church to a mission as wide as creation. Christ the Savior is the Christ of the creation, and therefore his lordship extends across every square inch of the fabric of creation. "If it is true," Kuyper writes,

> that Christ our Savior has to do not only with our soul but also with our body, that all things in the world belong to Christ and are claimed by him . . . and that in the end Christ will not gather a few separated souls around him . . . but will rule as king on a new earth under a new heaven—then, of course, everything is different. We see immediately that *grace* is inseparably connected with *nature*, that grace and nature belong together.[27]

This view holds that God's Word is the thesis to which human sin is the antithesis. Although sin was able to misdirect God's creation toward wrong ends, it is not as powerful as God's Word and therefore cannot destroy creation. Bavinck argues that sin is "not a substance, but a quality; not *materia*, but *forma*; it is not the essence of things, but rather adheres to the essence; it is a *privatio*, though a *privatio actuosa*, and to that extent contingent, an alien intruder like death."[28] God's common grace sustains the cosmos so that sin does not destroy the fabric of creation, which is structured in such a way as to serve and praise its creator. Likewise, even though human culture is underlain by idolatry, being twisted and directed toward wrong ends, Satan and sin are not able to make the cultural mandate null or void. Culture work remains structurally good and normative, though always twisted and misdirected to some extent by human sin.

God will redeem and restore creation one day to be fully the theater of his glory. God's good creation, misdirected by sin, will be restored and renewed through Christ's death and resurrection. Christ's reformation is not merely a

---

[27]Kuyper, "Common Grace," 173.

[28]Herman Bavinck, *De Algemeene Genade* (Kampen: Zalsman, 1894), 45-46, cited in Veenhof, *Nature and Grace*, 22, 42; English translation available as Bavinck, "Catholicity of Christianity and the Church."

return to the original state (repristination) but an elevation of the original state (restoration). His redemption will give us not only a garden (Eden) but a city (Jerusalem) replete with art, architecture, song, and poem. The final state will be one in which creation's hidden potentials are brought to fruition. God's original creation was "very good," but the new creation will be "even better."

In this view, Christ's redemption brings about a comprehensive reformation of human life. Christians recognize the antithesis, the way in which sin affects absolutely every square inch of the fabric of human life, every dimension of human culture, every nook and cranny of creation. They seek to excavate the idolatrous underpinning of every endeavor and then redirect that endeavor toward Christ and his glory. They do this as a preview of the final restoration, in which Christ will come in power, purifying his good creation and shaping it into its final state.

Only this view takes fully into account Christ's comprehensive lordship and the church's correspondingly comprehensive mission:

> Calvin completed the Reformation and saved Protestantism. Calvin traced the operation of sin to a wider extent than Luther, to a greater depth than Zwingli. But it is for that reason that the grace of God is more restricted in Luther, less rich in Zwingli, than it is in Calvin. In the powerful mind of the French Reformer, re-creation is not a system that supplements creation, as in Catholicism, not a religious reformation that leaves creation intact, as in Luther, much less a new creation, as in Anabaptism, but a joyful tiding of the renewal of all creatures. Here the Gospel comes fully into its own, comes to true catholicity. There is nothing that cannot and ought not be evangelized. Not only the church, but also home, school, society and state are placed under the dominion of the principle of Christianity.[29]

This view of nature and grace, which has roots in Irenaeus and Calvin and influential modern proponents in Kuyper and Bavinck, finds fruitful conversation partners in the *nouvelle théologie* and Radical Orthodoxy with their sharp critiques of nature-grace dualism.[30] Henri de Lubac's work, in particular,

[29]Bavinck, *De Katholiciteit*, 32, cited in Veenhof, *Nature and Grace*, 14-15, 37. Jon Stanley shows how the neo-Calvinist camp is split on whether Bavinck is a restorationist as opposed to a repristinationist ("Restoration and Renewal: The Nature of Grace in the Theology of Herman Bavinck," in *Revelation and Common Grace*, ed. John R. Bowlin, The Kuyper Center Review 2 [Grand Rapids, MI: Eerdmans, 2011], 81-104). Wolters, Spykman, and Veenhof view him as restorationist.

[30]As far back as the middle of the twentieth century, Dutch philosopher Herman Dooyeweerd recognized the *nouvelle théologie* as a potential ally. Dooyeweerd writes, "It is a gladdening symptom of a re-awakening biblical consciousness, that under the influence of Augustinianism an increasing number of Roman Catholic thinkers, belonging to the movement of the so-called *nouvelle théologie*, have begun to oppose this dualistic view. They agree with the Reformed philosophical movement in the Netherlands in advocating the necessity of a Christian philosophy." *In the*

is a fecund vein of the Catholic tradition with which to dialogue, not only because of the inherent value but also in light of his influence on Joseph Ratzinger, John Milbank, and a host of other theologians and ecclesiastical leaders.[31]

Henri de Lubac and the nouvelle theologians. De Lubac and the nouvelle theologians were sharply critical of the received Thomistic tradition because of its dualism that divides the world into separate realms, or stories, of nature and grace. This dualism inferred that the natural realm was a realm of "pure nature," a truly secular realm, devoid of grace. In opposition to this two-realmed or two-storied world, de Lubac employed a strategy of *ressourcement* to argue that nature is both *made for* grace and *fulfilled by* grace. Human nature was created for something that is beyond itself—namely, grace. In line with Augustine, de Lubac recognized that our hearts are restless until they find their rest in God. So the beatific vision is both *above* nature and *in accordance with* nature. Although he avers that the idea of "pure nature" is useful, ultimately he considers it a bad idea because it prepared the soil for modern secularism, which makes nature an autonomous realm with no need for grace. Instead of a pure realm of nature, set apart from grace, de Lubac views nature itself as a gracious gift and indeed a gift that longs for something that exceeds itself. This something—God's new gift of grace—reorders and redirects nature.[32]

The stakes are high in this discussion of nature and grace. The received (dualistic) Thomism paved the way for modern intellectuals to conceive of the world as a purely secular realm, a realm in which God's saving works and word have no import. Similarly, it opened up a way for the accommodationism in Vatican II. As George Lindbeck notes,

> The *ressourcement* [*nouvellle théologie*] and *aggiornamento* people at the Council thought of themselves as collaborators. *Ressourcement* and *aggiornamento* were understood to be two dimensions of the same reality. But the dimension labeled

---

Twilight of Western Thought: Studies in the Pretended Autonomy of Philosophical Thought (Nutley, NJ: Craig Press, 1975), 141.

[31]De Lubac's work on nature in grace can be found in several English volumes, but most importantly in *Surnaturel*, which has not yet been translated into English. See Henri de Lubac, *Surnaturel, Études Historiques*, ed. Michele Sales (Paris: Desclée, 1991); *The Mystery of the Supernatural* (New York: Crossroad, 1998); and *A Brief Catechesis on Nature and Grace* (San Francisco: Ignatius, 1984).

[32]The debate surrounding de Lubac's work is complex. See Nicholas J. Healy, "Henri de Lubac on Nature and Grace: A Note on Some Recent Contributions to the Debate," *Communio* 35 (2008): 535-64; Reinhard Hütter, "Desiderium Naturale Visionis Dei—Est Autem Duplex Hominis Beatitude Sive Felicitas: Some Observations About Lawrence Feingold's and John Milbank's Recent Interventions in the Debate over the Natural Desire to See God," *Nova et Vetera* 5 (2007): 81-131.

> "*aggiornamento*" could be used in a program of accommodation to the modern world, rather than one of an openness to the modern world; and when that happened, *aggiornamento* fell into opposition to *ressourcement*.[33]

Thus, while it might have appeared that the nouvelle theologians had common cause with the theologians of *aggiornamento*, in fact the latter ended up accommodating the Christian faith to modernity rather than vice versa. This unfortunate reversal of conformity was made possible, in our opinion, precisely because of the nature-grace dualism and its attendant secularity.

This is Milbank's point when he contrasts de Lubac and Karl Rahner as symbolizing competing impulses in modern Catholic thought. Referring to them as the "French" and "German" impulses, Milbank writes,

> I shall contend that there is a drastic difference between the two versions of integralism: . . . Whereas the French version "supernaturalizes the natural," the German version "naturalizes the supernatural." The thrust of the latter version is in the direction of a mediating theology, a universal humanism, a *rapprochement* with the Enlightenment and an autonomous secular order. While these themes are not entirely absent from the French version, its main tendencies are in entirely different directions: for the *nouvelle théologie*, towards a recovery of a pre-modern sense of the Christianized person as the fully real person.[34]

Indeed, Milbank argues that for this exact reason—de Lubac's rejection of nature-grace dualism and his consequent ability to guard against autonomous secularity and Christian rapprochement with secular modernity—de Lubac was a "greater theological revolutionary" than Karl Barth.[35] Unlike Barth, de Lubac was able successfully to transcend modernity. Viewing grace as God's gift to infuse, restore, reorder, and redirect nature calls the Christian to pursue culture making as part of God's mission to make all things new.

The Kuyperian Tradition: Building on the Biblical Testimony

Building on its view of grace restoring nature, the Kuyperian tradition has developed a robust theology of culture, the key elements of which are as

---

[33]George A. Lindbeck, "Re-viewing Vatican II: An Interview with George A. Lindbeck," *First Things* 48 (December 1994): 48.

[34]John Milbank, *Theology and Social Theory: Beyond Secular Reason* (Malden, MA: Blackwell, 1993), 207.

[35]John Milbank, "The Programme of Radical Orthodoxy," in *Radical Orthodoxy? A Catholic Enquiry*, ed. Laurence Paul Hemming (Burlington, VT: Ashgate, 2000), 35.

follows.[36] Creation's goodness frames culture's goodness. Kuyper argues that God gives each domain of nature an "infinite diversity" and an "inexhaustible profusion of variations." He writes, "Where in God's entire creation do you encounter life that does not display the unmistakable hallmark of life precisely in the multiplicity of its colors and dimensions, in the capriciousness of its ever-changing forms?"[37] God invests his creation with hidden cultural potential, which he calls his image bearers to actualize. This call is not nullified by the fall. Because of the fall, in which cultural obedience and worship was replaced by cultural disobedience and idolatry, the cultural mandate takes on increased urgency and complexity because the human project of culture making is underlain by a great antithesis.

Culture making is already present pre-fall. This becomes especially clear once we see Eden as a large park rather than an English-style garden or wilderness (cf. Is 28:26). Adam and Eve are engaged in farming, agriculture, and horticulture. Post-fall the Cain-Abel story indicates not that shepherding is good whereas farming crops is not but rather how religion can be misdirected in relation to these good cultural activities. Genesis 4:17-26 is the crucial passage in this respect. Apart from Genesis 2:23—Adam's celebration of the creation of Eve—Lamech's poem in Genesis 4:23-24 is the first poem in the Bible. Comparison between the two illustrates well the above distinction between (good, creational) structure and direction. The capacity for poetry and literature is a good gift that comes with creation but needs to be actualized by humans. Poetry and literature, we would say, is structurally good insofar as it is a given in creation. However, Adam and Lamech direct this gift in radically different ways. Adam's poem evokes wonder and amazement and gratitude. Lamech's, by comparison, reeks with vengeance. What Lamech has done is to take part of the good structure of creation and radically misdirected it toward evil and hubris.

Cain is the first builder of a city, and various types of cultural development take place in the line of Cain: tents and livestock, husbandry, music, tool making and thus technology. Westermann points out that city building arose before Israel's history began. Even in their own land God reminds the Israelites that the land was "a land with fine, large cities that you did not build, houses filled with all sorts of goods that you did not fill, cisterns that you did not hew, vineyards and groves that you did not plant" (Deut 6:10-11). As Westermann observes, "Israel did not regard the foundation of cities and urban civilization as something a priori negative."[a] In his own way Westermann gets at what we call structure and direction.[b]

---

[36]Cf. our discussion of the Kuyperian tradition in chap. 3.

[37]Kuyper, "Uniformity: The Curse of Modern Life," in Bratt, *Abraham Kuyper: A Centennial Reader*, 34.

Thus, in our view, music, tool making, farming, city building, and so forth are part of the development of the potentials built into creation,[c] and their development in the line of Cain a sign of God's common grace. Kuyper, not surprisingly, picks up on this and notes the enormous progress embodied in these inventions.[d] For Kuyper they "supply a strong proof of his [God's] *common grace* given to our race, to emerge not from Seth's line, but from men of Cain's line."[e] Remarkably, Kuyper suggests that this seems to manifest an ordinance governing the entire course of common grace. He is worth quoting at length:

> From these facts we can deduce that God the Lord, far from placing the pagan nations and unbelieving individuals outside his order and plan for the world, rather uses precisely the generation that wanders away from him, and thus cannot serve him in his temple and his sanctuary, to serve him and fulfill his counsel in the material and natural realm, so that later generations that fear him may also profit from these discoveries in the natural realm.[f]

[a]Claus Westermann, *Genesis 1–11: A Commentary*, trans. John J. Scullion (Minneapolis: Augsburg, 1984), 328.
[b]Ibid., 326.
[c]Cf. Craig G. Bartholomew, *Where Mortals Dwell: A Christian View of Place for Today* (Grand Rapids, MI: Baker Academic, 2011).
[d]Abraham Kuyper, *Common Grace*, ed. Jordan J. Ballor and Stephen J. Grabill, trans. Nelson D. Kloosterman and Ed M. Van der Maas, vol. I/2 (Grand Rapids, MI: Christian's Library Press, 2014), 349-52.
[e]Ibid., I/2:349.
[f]Ibid., I/2:350.

This antithesis, as Kuyperians Henry Stob and Herman Dooyeweerd have noted, is not between Christians and non-Christians per se, because it cuts through all of humankind, affecting everybody, including Christians.[38] However, as God's new people, possessing renewed minds, our cultural life—whether religious, scientific, artistic, entrepreneurial, or domestic—should look different from the cultural life of nonbelievers.[39] As Christians, we are called to resist the Evil One in his totalitarian assault on cultural life. We fight it not only from the pulpit but in every dimension of public life.

Common grace. In light of the antithesis and its effects on God's image bearers, the question remains as to why unbelievers often match or even exceed believers in their contributions to human life and culture. The Reformational response is to point to God's universal grace, via the Spirit,

[38]Richard J. Mouw, *He Shines in All That's Fair: Culture and Common Grace; The 2000 Stob Lectures* (Grand Rapids, MI: Eerdmans, 2001), 24-27.

[39]James D. Bratt provides a nice summary of Kuyper's belief that there is some commonality between the two minds, even in the midst of a great rupture. See Bratt, *Abraham Kuyper: Modern Calvinist, Christian Democrat*, Library of Religious Biography (Grand Rapids, MI: Eerdmans, 2013), 210-11, summarizing Kuyper, *Principles of Sacred Theology*, trans. J. Hendrik De Vries (Grand Rapids, MI: Baker, 1980), 150-82.

whereby he restrains sin and enables humanity to continue their lives and even flourish after the fall. Without this "common grace," God's special and saving grace would not have even had the chance to take effect. Mouw writes,

> We proceed with caution, knowing that the rebellious manifesto of our first parents—"We shall be as gods!"—still echoes all around us. But we also know—and this is an important message for common grace theology—that the Spirit of the reigning Lamb is indeed active in our world, not only in gathering the company of the redeemed from the tribes and nations of the earth, but also in working mysteriously to restrain sin in the lives of those who continue in their rebellion, and even in stimulating works of righteousness in surprising places.[40]

Kuyper treated common grace and special saving grace as operations of the same God who sought to remake the world in his image, and rightly argued that the fruits of common grace would one day be assumed into the new heavens and earth after they had been refined and purged. Significantly, this common grace enables nonbelievers to operate and even flourish in the arts, the sciences, and other spheres of life.[41]

Cultural spheres. God's creation order manifests itself in multiple spheres of culture. These spheres—including art, science, religion, government, business, and education—each have their own integrity and function according to unique, God-given principles. The existence of some of these spheres is clear from Scripture—for example, the family, church, and government. Others are identified empirically from how culture developed in history and derive from Kuyper's insight that in order to know creation we have to study it. Kuyper was never clear on the number of spheres and uses different lists in different places in his work. His genius is to recognize that because God is sovereign, no sphere may be absolutized since all utterly depend on the sovereign God and exist under his final authority. "Each sphere," Gordon Spykman writes, "has its own identity, its own unique task, its own God-given prerogatives. On each God has conferred its own peculiar right of existence and reason for existence."[42] The spheres operate under Christ's lordship. They should not assume each other's roles but interact with one another organically. In order for a society to flourish under God's reign, its spheres must be inhabited by a community of persons whose worldview

---

[40]Mouw, *He Shines*, 86.

[41]Abraham Kuyper, *Common Grace*, ed. Jordan J. Ballor and Stephen J. Grabill, trans. Nelson D. Kloosterman and Ed M. Van der Maas, vol. I/2 (Grand Rapids, MI: Christian's Library Press, 2014), 350.

[42]Gordon J. Spykman, "Sphere Sovereignty in John Calvin and the Calvinist Tradition," in *Exploring the Heritage of John Calvin*, ed. David E. Holwerda (Grand Rapids, MI: Baker, 1976), 167.

and moral fabric are sufficient for the mutually beneficial development of these spheres alongside one another.

We undertake our cultural activities seeking to persuade rather than coerce. Kuyper writes,

> We must employ persuasion to the exclusion of coercion in all spiritual matters. Someday there will be coercion, when Christ descends in majesty from the heavens. . . . But [to] us it is only given to fight with spiritual weapons and to bear our cross in joyful discipleship. Therefore, without any craftiness or secret intentions we accept the position of equality before the law along with those who disagree with us and, ask for ourselves no other constitutional liberty than that which makes possible the performance of our Christian duty.[43]

Indeed, alongside his doctrine of sphere sovereignty Kuyper developed a rich theology of public justice whereby, issuing from the state, space is created in a society for diverse worldviews to come to fruition in all spheres of life alongside one another. This view of creation and culture undergirds a genuinely democratic view of government.

These cultural activities make up a large portion of the mission of the church. By "church" we are referring to the church organic, the church as it scatters during the week and enacts its callings in the midst of families, workplaces, and communities. The church institutional serves as the launching point for the church organic, just as the Lord's Day serves as the weekly point of departure for its members' lives throughout the remainder of the week. The (largely cultural) work of the church organic should not be taken lightly or viewed as secondary to the work of the church institutional. The church organic, Kuyper argued, should live as a light that "radiate[s] over the whole world," shining far beyond the confines of a church building, and as a salt that "penetrates in every direction, checking all corruption."[44] In this sense Christian cultural engagement seeks to promote the flourishing of all. These marks encapsulate the Kuyperian view of culture and show the manifold ways in which one's view of culture is affected by one's doctrine of creation.

A persistent criticism of the Kuyperian paradigm is that it is insufficiently biblical.[45] These criticisms often are focused specifically on the "spheres" and ask whether there is any scriptural reason for believing that God's original

---

[43]Kuyper, "Maranatha," in Bratt, *Abraham Kuyper: A Centennial Reader*, 219-21.

[44]Abraham Kuyper, *Lectures on Calvinism* (Grand Rapids, MI: Eerdmans, 1931), 53.

[45]For a critical engagement with Kuyper by a contemporary, see Klaus Schilder, *Christ and Culture*, trans. William Helder and Albert H. Oosterhoff (Hamilton, ON: Lucerna, 2016).

creation design included any sort of spheres. Mouw engages this criticism by noting that Kuyperian theologians "are going beyond the explicit statements of Scripture to explore larger patterns of coherence that can shed light on the patterns of biblically based thought. . . . There is a fit of sorts between the actual biblical passages they allude to and the more speculative claims."[46]

In our view, Mouw is helpful in alerting us to the development involved in theological constructions. However, as we note above, there is clear evidence biblically for the spheres of the family, cultus, law courts, the marketplace, and government. Kuyper, Bavinck, Dooyeweerd, and many others develop this data further from observing history and culture through the lens of Scripture, thereby arriving at the doctrine of sphere sovereignty. In our view, this is a legitimate and necessary move. Wisdom compels us to investigate the whole of the creation from the starting point and foundation of the fear of the Lord. In this light, the Kuyperian approach to culture might be seen in a similar fashion to the early church's approach to the Trinity, an approach that went beyond prooftexts to explore the larger patterns of Scripture.

Contextualization: Theology's Task in the Midst of a Cultural Context

We now turn to a discussion of how to proclaim the gospel amid a particular cultural context, the process known as contextualization. One's doctrine of creation significantly affects one's views of contextualization. For evangelicals, the task is to forge a faithfully biblical message that is meaningful within a given cultural context. The responsibility to be faithful speaks to Scripture's authority. When Scripture is not recognized as authoritative, Christian theologians inevitably reshape the gospel such that it images the culture more truly than it images God. How, therefore, do we go about contextualizing the gospel faithfully and meaningfully? Following Robert John Schreiter, David Clark, and others, we suggest that a dialogical approach yields the most potential for the task of theology.[47]

In a dialogical method, theologians appropriate Scripture to address the questions that are raised in a cultural context, and do so using the language of that context. This initial and provisional "theology" is then taken back to

[46]Richard J. Mouw, "Some Reflections on Sphere Sovereignty," in *Religion, Pluralism, and Public Life: Abraham Kuyper's Legacy for the Twenty-First Century*, ed. Luis E. Lugo (Grand Rapids, MI: Eerdmans, 2000), 98.

[47]Robert John Schreiter, *Constructing Local Theologies* (Maryknoll, NY: Orbis Books, 1985), 6-12; David K. Clark, *To Know and Love God: Method for Theology* (Wheaton, IL: Crossway, 2003), 113-23.

the Scriptures for "cleaning," as the theologian allows Scripture to judge the cultural viewpoint that bequeathed the questions and categories. The theologian also discusses their theology with believers from other eras or cultures in order to help distance themselves from the distorting influences operative in the theologian's own cultural context.

In this manner, questions that are framed in the language and conceptual categories of one culture are brought into conversation with the languages and conceptual categories of other eras and cultures, and at the same time all of it is being brought back to the Scriptures for purification and reformation. This contextualization spiral "recognizes the dialectical movement from thinker to evidence, and from culture to text. But it balances those dialectics with commitment to progressively deeper, richer, and truer understandings. . . . Perfect objectivity is beyond our grasp. But wiser, more informed, and more deeply biblical understandings of God and his will and ways are possible."[48] This view of theology is critically realist in its recognition of human limitations and its attempt, via a dialogical and upwardly spiraling process, to progress ever closer to the goal of theological fidelity.

Barth serves as a good example of this dialogical approach. After Barth finished his theological education, he took an assistant pastorate in Geneva and then a pastorate in a small parish in Safenwil. While he labored in Safenwil, Barth discovered that liberal theology was irrelevant in the pulpit (people want a word from God) and that it was impotent in the public square (ninety-three liberal German intellectuals supported Kaiser Wilhelm's war policy). "An entire world of theological exegesis, ethics, dogmatics, and preaching, which up to that point I had accepted as basically credible," Barth writes, "was thereby shaken to the foundations, and with it everything which flowed at that time from the pens of the German theologians."[49] Later in his career, Barth helped write the Barmen Declaration, which argued that Christ is Lord, rejecting the German elevation of Hitler to messiah status. Barth considered Nazism a false gospel and refused to salute Hitler at the beginning of his lectures or to sign an oath of loyalty to him. In both instances, the liberal German church was unable to critique its own cultural context because it rejected the prophetic and commanding Word of God.

---

[48]Clark, *To Know and Love God*, 119.

[49]Karl Barth, "Concluding Unscientific Postscript on Schleiermacher," in *The Theology of Schleiermacher: Lectures at Göttingen, Winter Semester of 1923–24*, trans. Dietrich Ritschl (Edinburgh: T&T Clark, 1982), 264.

The doctrine of creation underlies this approach as it places value not only on culture but also on cultural diversity. Instead of a creation order that is dull, gray, and monochrome, we have an order that is pulsating with myriad colors, sounds, shapes, and types. In fact, Christ himself is the center around which this diverse creation unfolds (Col 1), and he is the one who will redeem it in all its diverse splendor (Rev 5; 21–22). At the same time the doctrine of creation enables one to avoid cultural relativism since all cultures are subject to the same creation order. This understanding of creation and contextualization naturally leads to a robust understanding of Christian vocation.

Vocatio

To the questions "Are my actions in this world significant? Does my life mean anything?" the Christian tradition answers, "Yes, you are called by God." The English word *vocation* comes from the Latin *vocatio*, which means "calling," and the Reformational tradition argues that one is not only called to salvation in Christ but called also to represent the Lord Christ faithfully in one's family life, church membership, workplace, and community. This web of interconnected callings encompasses the whole of a person's life and is in fact the means by which the Lord God works providentially.

Called to the workplace. Especially significant for our purposes is the calling to a workplace. This calling is a direct extension of the cultural mandate, is exercised in relation to God's good creation, and is a means by which God dramatically conveys his love for the world. In *Of the Work of Monks*, Augustine recognized this, rejecting the excesses of the monastic movement and arguing that God values even the "lower forms" of labor, such as agriculture and labor by hand. Consider God's compassion for the sick and wounded, and the way in which, when God heals, he most often does so through doctors and the vast network of people who support them, such as nurses, orderlies, pharmacists, and physical therapists. These jobs are "callings" that can be undertaken well or badly, and they form a realm in which we can bless others and function as God's arm of providence. Vocation is God's action primarily and our action secondarily. In our view, all (moral) vocations are equal. Doctors, pastors, sewage technicians, professional athletes, even being unemployed—each of these vocations serves its purpose in God's economy and each plays a role in glorifying God and flourishing humanity. It is incumbent on us to undertake our callings, therefore, with an eye toward glorifying God and serving humanity.

In spite of pain and dysfunction now associated with work, the original cultural mandate remains normative. In his encyclical *On Human Work*, John

Paul II captures this tension when he writes, "Man's life is built up every day from work, from work it derives its specific dignity, but at the same time work contains the unceasing measure of human toil and suffering and also of the harm and injustice which penetrate deeply into social life within individual nations and on the international level."[50] This labor is central to imaging God and works itself out though the various modes of cultural existence such as art, science, government, business, and education. Through our work in these spheres, we identify with the cross as we experience the toil involved in our work. At the same time, we identify with the resurrection as our cultural efforts foreshadow the glorified culture of a new heavens and earth.

Indeed, many of Christianity's contributions to our culture have come about through Christian faithfulness and excellence in the workplace. Consider, for example, how Celtic artists and craftsmen played a vital role in reviving European culture during the early medieval period.[51] In the aftermath of Rome's fall, and as darkness settled in on the Western part of the empire, God was working through Celtic art and craftsmanship to plant the seeds of European renewal. Shaped by their Christian faith, informed by Celtic culture, and incorporating elements from other European and Asian cultures with whom their missionary monks had interacted, the artists and craftsmen created a wealth of everyday vessels, religious artifacts, swords, and other artifacts. From this wealth of art and craft emerged at least two new forms—the carved cross and the illustrated manuscript. The carved crosses were adapted from pagan culture, with pagan mythological elements being replaced by elements of the Christian faith. The illuminated manuscripts consisted of highly original pagination, text, script, and color, becoming the standard for manuscripts across Europe for centuries thereafter. Through their artful creations, these artists and craftsmen served the common good, sometimes by the mere beauty or utility of their craft and other times by conveying biblical teaching, expressing their experience of God, and extending an invitation to worship.

Similarly, consider the way Christian scientists have served God and the world through their vocation. As French physicist Pierre Duhem (1913–1959) has demonstrated, the roots of modern science are found in the Christian culture of medieval Europe. Although China and Arabia had produced more

---

[50]John Paul II, *On Human Work* (Washington, DC: U.S. Catholic Conference Office for Publishing and Promotion Services, 1981), 3.

[51]Miranda Green, *Celtic Art: Symbol and Imagery* (New York: Sterling, 1996); Ruth Megaw and Vincent Megaw, *Celtic Art: From Its Beginnings to the Book of Kells* (London: Thames and Hudson, 1991).

advanced technology and higher levels of learning, it was a Christianized Europe that was able to give birth to science as a systematic and self-correcting discipline. Among the aspects of Christian teaching that fostered modern science are the biblical teachings that the physical and material world is both real and good, that the world is ordered and regular, and that God created humans who have both the rational capacity and the spiritual motivation to study the world God created. Moreover, we find Christian influence not only in the roots of the scientific vocation but also in the fruits, with pathbreaking scientific discoveries being made by Kepler, Boyle, Newton, Faraday, Mendel, Pasteur, Maxwell, Ramsey, and numerous other Christians who researched under the presupposition that God created and ordered the natural world.

In our own era, there are countless examples of Christians working faithfully through their vocations to love God and serve the common good. One example is Japanese American artist Makoto Fujimura, whose work has been highlighted at Yale, Duke, Cambridge, and other universities and has been displayed at Dillon Gallery (New York), White Stone Gallery (Philadelphia), and other galleries. He was appointed to the National Council on the Arts (2003) and received the National Council's Chairman's Medal for his arts advocacy in the United States (2009). Fujimura's artwork is shaped by his Christianity in profound and evident ways. For example, in his *Walking on Water* collection, he depicts the victims of the March 11, 2011, tsunami in Japan and anticipates the day in which there will be no more death or destruction. Or, in *The Four Gospels Frontispieces*, he commemorates the four hundredth anniversary of the King James Bible through five major illustrated leafs, eighty-nine chapter heading letters, and neatly hand-painted pages. All the images were completed in the traditional Japanese style Nihonga. Shaped by his Christian faith and informed by Japanese and American culture, Fujimura's creations are kingdom-minded gifts to the East and the West.

Another example is the renaissance of Christian philosophy taking place in American universities. Among the leaders of this movement is Alvin Plantinga, whose story is especially instructive. Plantinga started teaching philosophy in the late 1950s, an era in which there were very few openly Christian philosophers. Yet Plantinga worked with a small cadre of Christian philosophers to give birth to a revival in Christian philosophy. Over lunch at a restaurant in Chicago, Plantinga, together with Nicholas Wolterstorff, Ronald Nash, William Alston, and a few others, determined to start an organization of Christian philosophers. Out of this lunch meeting the Society of Christian Philosophers (SCP) and the journal *Faith and Philosophy* were born.

Today the SCP has more than a thousand members, while the journal is one of the premier journals of philosophy in Europe and North America. More significant still is the widespread recognition that recent English-language philosophy has been shaped pervasively by the work of these Christian philosophers. In fact, atheist philosopher Quentin Smith penned an editorial in his journal *Philo*, lamenting that

> the secularization of mainstream academia began to quickly unravel upon the publication of Plantinga's influential book on realist theism, *God and Other Minds*, in 1967. It became apparent to the philosophical profession that this book displayed that realist theists were not outmatched by naturalists in terms of the most valued standards of analytic philosophy: conceptual precision, rigor of argumentation, technical erudition, and an in-depth defense of an original worldview.[52]

Thus, through his vocation as a philosopher, Plantinga and his circle found some success in reversing the negative effects of the antithesis in the world of higher education.

Called to the church. Hand in hand with our calling to a workplace is our calling to a church. Just as the Genesis account shows a divine rhythm of work and rest, so there is also a human rhythm of work and rest. We work for six days, after which is a day of rest. In the new covenant this day of rest appears at the beginning of the workweek, launching us afresh and anew into our worldly mission. "For Kuyper," Peter Heslam writes, "Calvinism represented a kind of centrifugal force that moved outwards in ever-widening circles—from its initial influence in the sphere of religion—to encompass the whole of human existence."[53] While modernists wish to separate religion from culture, science, or philosophy, and while sectarian Christians may be indifferent toward those same things, we wish to argue that religion's influence necessarily pervades our cultural lives. Art, science, politics, and education are a function of culture, and at the center of culture is (ir)religion.

In *Called to Holy Worldliness*, Mouw concludes by calling attention to Mark's Gospel and its account of Jesus calming the wind and the waves. As Mark tells it, "And they were filled with great awe and said to one another, 'Who then is this, that even the wind and the sea obey him?'" (Mk 4:41). "We are surprised," Mouw writes,

[52]Quentin Smith, "The Metaphilosophy of Naturalism," *Philo* 4, no. 2 (2001): 195-215.

[53]Peter Heslam, *Creating a Christian Worldview: Abraham Kuyper's Lectures on Calvinism* (Grand Rapids, MI: Eerdmans, 1998), 113.

> by the wonders of the kingdom of Jesus. We must in turn be sources of surprise to the unbelieving world. We should be thinking and speaking and acting in ways that invite the disciples' question in forms appropriate for our day: Who then is this? Who are these people who attend to broken lives and bodies, who reconcile enemies, who promote justice and love mercy, who sanctify business dealings and overturn racial and cultural barriers? By whose power do they act?[54]

Interacting with Tillich, Mouw wonders whether Christ might wish to silence some of us for a while so that we might reflect on the magnitude of his salvation. In so reflecting, perhaps we could stop preaching a reductionist gospel that minimizes Christ's redemption and reduces his lordship to certain few aspects of life. Christ's lordship is as broad as creation, and his redemptive mission is likewise cosmic.

Conclusion

Kuyper and Bavinck always remind us that creation is all about God's glory. "Not for our sake did he create the world. He created all things for his own sake, so that the majesty of the glory of his eternal Being would be reflected in it, to the praise of his name."[55] Built into the creation is the potential and the intention for development in which culture is central. Kuyper evocatively asserts,

> The glory of the human race was enclosed like a pearl in its shell, like the grain of wheat that sprouts from the stalk as the head of grain. So what was visible and manifest did not correspond to *all* that God's plan had ordained. Only when the human race would have budded, would have blossomed, would have ripened and stood in its full strength, only then would heaven and earth be able to glorify God for the excellence of this his work. God saw in Paradise that it was *very good*, because he saw the head of grain within the seed of wheat, but the creature saw as yet nothing but Adam and Eve, undoubtedly glorious in form and majestic in appearance, who nevertheless did not yet manifest anything but the closed flower bud and the first sprouting that did not betray even a hint of the treasures God had embedded in the human race.[56]

Cultural development is thus not extrinsic to creation but at its heart. Nothing less than God's glory is at stake in cultural development, as well as human and nonhuman flourishing.

---

[54]Richard J. Mouw, *Called to Holy Worldliness* (Philadelphia: Fortress, 1980), 142.

[55]Kuyper, *Common Grace*, I/2:276.

[56]Ibid., I/2:276-77.

CREATIO CONTINUA

PROVIDENCE AND HISTORY

The Old Testament is distinctive in its presentation of the historical process. . . . It is the steady unfolding of God's one increasing purpose. . . . The Old Testament writers had a philosophy of history long before Herodotus, who among secular historians is rightly hailed as the father of history.

F. F. Bruce

What Paul Ricoeur has termed "the death of the God of providence" is a fact of Christian existence as well as of that of Western culture at large.

Charles M. Wood

Perhaps, now, clearer than before, we understand that Christ has the key to Divine Providence.

G. C. Berkouwer

As we have noted in chapter five, *creatio ex nihilo* and *creatio continua* should be distinguished. God's resting on the seventh day implies completion and separates off God's continued involvement *with* his creation from the initial act *of* creation. As Bavinck explains, "God's resting only indicates that he stopped producing new kinds of things (Eccles. 1:9-10); that the work of creation, in the true and narrow sense as producing things out of nothing (*productio rerum ex nihilo*), was over; and that he delighted in this completed work with divine pleasure. . . . Creation now passes into preservation."[1]

Having said this, the distinction between creation and providence is far from absolute and should in no way be conceived in a deist fashion. Bavinck

---

[1]Herman Bavinck, *Reformed Dogmatics*, ed. John Bolt, trans. J. Vriend (Grand Rapids, MI: Baker Academic, 2003–2008), 2:592.

says that so strong is the distinction between creation and providence that Genesis 1:1–2:3 compares it to the contrast between work and rest. At the same time, so strong is the continuity between creation and providence that the latter is described at points in the Bible as "creation" (Ps 104:30; 148:5; Is 45:7; Amos 4:13). Thus, Bavinck rightly asserts, "Preservation itself, after all, is also a divine work, no less great and glorious than creation."[2]

> John 5:1-18 provides a fascinating reflection on this relationship. Because Jesus heals a man on the Sabbath, the Jews start persecuting him because they see him as breaking the Sabbath law. "But Jesus answered them, '*My Father is still working*, and I also am working'" (Jn 5:17). Controversy over Jesus' healing on the Sabbath is common in the Synoptic Gospels, but the reason given here is unique, equating Jesus directly with God, as his opponents clearly understood.
>
> The assertion that God rested on the seventh day caused difficulties for thoughtful exegetes, but by the time John's Gospel was written, "there was a current exegesis of God's Sabbath rest sufficient to support the argument of the evangelist. God is essentially and unchangeably creative."[a] God's resting is anthropomorphic language and signifies inter alia his cessation from his initial act of creating. Bruner writes, "Since people were born and died on Sabbaths and since the world was sustained on Sabbaths as well, it was believed that, of course, *God* worked and did not rest on Sabbaths. But only God could do this unceasing work. When Jesus claims that *he* can [and probably must] work on the Sabbath as well, he seems, indeed, to be making a claim to assuming deity."[b] What commentators tend to ignore is just what this continual work of God consists of. It is, of course, the work of *providence*.
>
> [a]C. K. Barrett, *The Gospel According to St. John: An Introduction with Commentary and Notes on the Greek Text*, 2nd ed. (Philadelphia: Westminster John Knox, 1978), 256.
> [b]Frederick Dale Bruner, *The Gospel of John: A Commentary* (Grand Rapids, MI: Eerdmans, 2012), 310.

God is lovingly sovereign over his creation and remains deeply involved in it. All of this comes under the doctrine of providence.

Providence in Scripture

The word *providence* is derived from philosophy.[3] Laertius asserts that Plato was the first to use *pronoia* in this sense. The Apocrypha uses the word

[2]Ibid.

[3]An important source for this topic is Mark Elliott, *Providence: A Biblical, Historical, and Theological Account* (Grand Rapids: Baker Academic, 2020). It is wonderful to see Elliott's extensive engagement with Scripture, which is precisely the kind of theology we seek to promote in this book. Unfortunately, Elliott's work was published as ours was going to print, and thus we have been unable to engage with it in any substantial way.

(Wis 14:3; 17:2; 3 Macc 4:21; 5:30; 4 Macc 9:24; 13:19; 17:22) alongside related vocabulary. The church fathers appropriated "providence"(Greek: *pronoia*) to refer to God's governing and care of his creation as depicted in Scripture.[4]

Barth asserts that the appropriation of "providence" in this way is derived from Genesis 22:14, 8, an extraordinary text for the origins of this word.[5] Abraham calls the place of the intended sacrifice of Isaac *Yahweh Yireh* (Yahweh will see/provide), which the Vulgate translates as *Deus providebit*. In context this verse alerts us to the fact that "providence" means far more than foreknowledge. "To see" in Genesis 22 means "to see about, to care for, to provide." Barth thus defines providence as "the superior dealings of the Creator with His creation, the wisdom, omnipotence and goodness with which He maintains and governs in time this distinct reality according to the counsel of His own will."[6]

Scripture does not itself use the abstract language of providence but depicts its essence again and again, primarily but by no means exclusively, in its historical narratives. When, for example, Joseph reveals himself to his brothers, he tells them,

> And now do not be distressed, or angry with yourselves, because you sold me here; for God sent me before you to preserve life. . . . God sent me before you to preserve for you a remnant on earth, and to keep alive for you many survivors. So it was not you who sent me here, but God; he has made me a father to Pharaoh, and lord of all his house and ruler over all the land of Egypt. (Gen 45:5, 7-8)

These verses are remarkable when one thinks of Joseph's story.[7] But they are also remarkable in their juxtaposition of human action and responsibility—"you sold me here"—with divine rule. In his development of a philosophy of history,

---

[4]See Benjamin Wirt Farley, *The Providence of God* (Grand Rapids, MI: Revell, 1988), for a useful historical overview of the development of this doctrine. See also Francesca Aran Murphy and Philip G. Ziegler, eds., *The Providence of God: Deus Habet Consilium* (London: T&T Clark, 2009), 7-128.

[5]Barth, *CD* III/3, 3.

[6]Barth, *CD* III/3, 3.

[7]Especially since the literary turn in biblical studies in the 1970s, creative, literary readings of the Joseph story have proliferated. See the commentaries for the secondary literature and sources such as Eric I. Lowenthal, *The Joseph Narrative in Genesis* (Jersey City, NJ: KTAV, 1973); E. D. McGuire, "The Joseph Story: A Tale of Son and Father," in *Images of Man and God: Old Testament Short Stories in Literary Focus*, ed. Burke O. Long (Sheffield: Almond Press, 1981), 9-25; Raymond de Hoop, *Genesis Forty-Nine in Its Literary and Historical Context* (Leiden: Brill, 1999); Maren Niehoff, *The Figure of Joseph in Post-Biblical Jewish Literature* (Leiden: Brill, 1992); Ron Pirson, *The Lord of the Dreams: A Semantic and Literary Analysis of Genesis 37–50* (London: Black, 2002); Hillel I. Millgram, *The Joseph Paradox: A Radical Reading of Genesis 37–50* (Jefferson, NC: McFarland, 2012).

Augustine followed such biblical data in rejecting determinism and fortune or chance.[8] He rightly argued that God is the guarantee of true human freedom and responsibility. There is a mysterious or paradoxical aspect to the relationship between God's sovereignty and human responsibility, and it is characteristic of Scripture to hold them together, as the author of Genesis does here.

The Old Testament's depiction of God's providence is not uniform, but it is always present. In 1 and 2 Kings God's word through the prophets guides the history of his people, whereas in Esther any reference to God is noticeably absent, although Esther 4:14 is pregnant with a sense of God's providence: "Who knows? Perhaps you have come to royal dignity for just such a time as this." Jonah has to discover that fleeing from Jerusalem does not mean escaping from Yahweh, and in the Jonah narrative God's sovereignty and intimate involvement with the life of his prophet is revealed.[9] But the Old Testament is quite clear that God is sovereign over all nations, indeed the whole creation, and not just over Israel. Benjamin Wirt Farley observes that "the sovereignty of God is simply indispensable to a doctrine of providence."[10] The table of the nations in Genesis 10 develops out of the creation narrative and, with its positioning of Israel at the center, evokes God's rule over all nations of the earth. In Amos 9:7, remarkably, God declares that the Philistines and the Arameans also experienced an exodus in which he brought them up just as he did Israel from the land of Egypt.

In Jesus' public ministry his deity is concealed, but in his miracles, especially those relating to nature, such as the stilling of the stormy sea, we catch glimpses of his sovereignty over the creation alluded to in his preferred title "Son of Man" (cf. Dan 7). In the Matthean Great Commission, the veil is removed and Jesus declares, "All authority in heaven and on earth has been given to me" (Mt 28:18). Likewise, the significance of the ascension is that the risen Jesus assumes the place of royal authority over history. However, it is perhaps in his death and resurrection that the early Christian most clearly witnessed God's providence. In Acts 2, Peter says of Jesus that "this man, handed over to you according to the definite plan and foreknowledge of God, you crucified and killed by the hands of those outside the law. But God raised

[8]Cf. Gerald Bonner, *Freedom and Necessity: St. Augustine's Teaching on Divine Power and Human Freedom* (Washington, DC: Catholic University of America Press, 2007).

[9]On Jonah, see Craig G. Bartholomew and Heath A. Thomas, *The Minor Prophets: A Theological Introduction* (Downers Grove, IL: IVP Academic, forthcoming).

[10]Farley, *Providence of God*, 234.

him up" (Acts 2:23-24). As with the Joseph narrative, human responsibility and divine sovereignty are held together.

Providence and the Doctrine of Creation

Fergusson suggests that "one reason why providence has suffered some neglect may be its standard textbook location as a subdivision of the doctrine of creation."[11] He proposes that we can avoid this downsizing of the doctrine of providence by spreading it across the articles of faith. In our view all doctrines are perichoretic in this respect, and the way to avoid a reductive theology of providence is to recover robust doctrines of creation and redemption. In chapters two and three we saw again and again how the church's witness has suffered in the absence of a biblical doctrine of creation. We agree, by contrast, with Barth that providence is rightly situated under the doctrine of creation. God's sustaining, accompanying, and ruling his creation is rooted *in* and flows *from* his act *of* creation.[12]

As with creation, belief in providence is *a doctrine of faith*.[13] Our age is most certainly not the first to find providence unbelievable and unpalatable.[14] Indeed, such struggles are embedded in Scripture (see Ps 88; Lamentations; etc.). Job and Ecclesiastes stand out as different—Job more existential, Ecclesiastes more intellectual, nevertheless equally agonizing—but monumental struggles to find firm ground in what we call providence. Both books bear witness to the desperate challenge it can be to find one's way amid the morass of life back to firm footing in trust in God. Thus it is imperative that we ground belief in providence in faith, lest we succumb to "the death of the God of providence," in Ricoeur's provocative words.[15]

Although history, viewed through the lens of providence, provides multiple evocative and wonderful examples, providence simply cannot be read off the pages of history. For all our advances, the twentieth century was one of the

---

[11]David Fergusson, *The Providence of God: A Polyphonic Approach* (Cambridge: Cambridge University Press, 2018), 9. For engagements with this work see various responses, including one by Craig Bartholomew, and then Fergusson's response to them at *Sapientia*, https://henrycenter.tiu.edu/?post_type=post&s=providence.

[12]Some material in this and the following sections was also published in an adapted form in Craig G. Bartholomew, *The God Who Acts in History: The Significance of Sinai* (Grand Rapids, MI: Eerdmans, 2020).

[13]Webster, "Theology of Providence," 163-65, is eloquent in this respect.

[14]See Elliott, *Providence*, chap. 1.

[15]For a useful analysis of how providence lingers even with the rejection of God, see Vernon White, *Purpose and Providence: Taking Soundings in Western Thought, Literature and Theology* (London: T&T Clark, 2015).

most brutal: World War I, the Great Depression, Stalin, World War II, the nuclear race, environmental devastation and climate change, all leaving modernity shattered and torn apart by the start of the twenty-first century. And, as we complete this book, we are amid the coronavirus pandemic with thousands dying each day. As the Brazilian theologian Leonardo Boff rightly notes, "There is a suffering humanity whose way of the cross has as many stations as that of the Lord when he suffered among us in Palestine."[16] Boff is equally clear that it is not only humanity but the entire creation that groans in these stations of the cross. George Steiner evokes the pathos of our journey in history at the end of his classic, *Real Presences*: "But ours is the long day's journey of the Saturday. Between suffering, aloneness, unutterable waste on the one hand and the dream of liberation, of rebirth on the other."[17]

We *believe* in providence because of God's revelation, preeminently in Christ, and not necessarily because we are able to trace the lines of his workings in our lives and in history, important as this is. Berkouwer observes that "though the rule of God goes uncomprehended by us, His paths are lighted up in various ways by the Scriptures."[18] It is only as we eat and drink Christ that we will rest in God's providence: "It is in the supper—in the holy memory provoked by the broken bread and the poured out wine, in the participation in the body and blood of Christ—that the congregation is called back from murmuring to thanksgiving, from doubt to certainty, and from rebellion to doxology."[19]

Astonishingly, it is at the foot of the cross with all its horror that we find the most secure place for rooting ourselves in providence. It is in the cross that we find the best and the worst of history: terrible suffering, betrayal, torture, deceit, abandonment, agony, and at the same time supreme love, unutterable compassion, humanity, sacrifice, redemption, glory. At Pentecost, when he was called on to explain the outpouring of the Spirit, Peter seized on Joel 2:28-32 as the hermeneutical key to explain how the day of the Lord was breaking in through the outpouring of the Spirit. He moves from the quotation from Joel (Acts 2:17-21) directly to "Jesus of Nazareth" and asserts that "this man, handed over to you according to the definite plan and foreknowledge

[16]Leonardo Boff, *Passion of Christ, Passion of the World*, trans. R. R. Barr, 2nd ed. (Maryknoll, NY: Orbis Books, 2001), ix.

[17]George Steiner, *Real Presences* (Chicago: University of Chicago Press, 1989), 232.

[18]C. G. Berkouwer, *The Providence of God*, Studies in Dogmatics (Grand Rapids, MI: Eerdmans, 1952), 90.

[19]Ibid., 274.

of God, you crucified and killed by the hands of those outside the law" (Acts 2:23). No attempt is made to play down the free actions of those who catalyzed the unjust accusations and death sentence handed down to Jesus. And yet, precisely amid this horror of injustice and agony, in which Peter played his own part of betrayal, Peter affirms the sovereign action of God working out his plans for his world. The biblical teaching on providence is vast and varied, as we will see, but undoubtedly this is the best place to stand from which to see it and to embrace it.[20] Providence is a doctrine of faith in *this* God who was at work in the life, death, and resurrection of his Son. Barth is thus right to note a christological deficit in (some of) the older Reformed doctrines of providence: "Unfortunately the connexion between the belief in providence and belief in Christ had not been worked out and demonstrated theologically by the Reformers themselves."[21]

Calvin deals with providence at the end of book one of his *Institutes*. He notes the importance of providence for a doctrine of creation; without it "we do not yet properly grasp what it means to say: 'God is Creator.' "[22] God is not just creator but also governor and preserver, and this not in a mechanical way "but also in that he sustains, nourishes, and cares for, everything he has made, even to the least sparrow."[23] As we would expect, Calvin has a strong emphasis on the sovereignty of God: nothing happens without God's counsel. "From this we declare that not only heaven and earth and the inanimate creatures, but also the plans and intentions of men, are so governed by his providence that they are borne by it straight to their appointed end."[24] Providence sometimes "works through an intermediary, sometimes without an intermediary, sometimes contrary to every intermediary."[25] Calvin affirms the profound mystery of providence; mostly it is hidden in God.

Calvin's doctrine of providence, helpful as it is, is not deeply christological and trinitarian.[26] Kuyper, Bavinck, and Berkouwer do, however, relate

[20]See Elliott, *Providence*.

[21]Barth, *CD* III/3, 32. Walter Campbell Campbell-Jack ("Grace Without Christ? The Doctrine of Common Grace in Dutch-American Neo-Calvinism" [PhD diss., University of Edinburgh, 1992]) similarly critiques Kuyper's view of common grace for not grounding itself in the incarnation, thereby leading to tensions between common and special grace.

[22]John Calvin, *Institutes* 1.16.1 (Battles), 197.

[23]Calvin, *Institutes* 1.16.1 (Battles), 197-98.

[24]Calvin, *Institutes* 1.16.8 (Battles), 207.

[25]Calvin, *Institutes* 1.17.1 (Battles), 210.

[26]For an assessment of Barth's critique of Calvin, see Sung-Sup Kim, *Deus Providebit: Calvin, Schleiermacher, and Barth on the Providence of God* (Minneapolis: Fortress, 2014), 25-85. Cf. J. Todd Billings, *Calvin, Participation, and the Gift: The Activity of Believers in Union with Christ* (Oxford: Oxford University Press, 2007).

providence specifically to Christ and to the doctrine of the Trinity, as the quote from Berkouwer at the outset of this chapter indicates. Bavinck begins his chapter on creation and providence with the Trinity and develops a trinitarian and Christocentric view.[27] What stands out nowadays as a distinctive and vital insight of Kuyper and Bavinck is that "Scripture, which is the word of God, and which from beginning to end takes God's part, declares plainly and powerfully and loudly that God does not exist for the world but that the whole world and all its creatures exist for God, for His sake and for His glory."[28] If in the past the doctrine of providence was in danger of being focused too narrowly on our salvation, much modern theology is in danger of being inadequately focused on the glory of God. This was not a mistake Kuyper and Bavinck made.

There is certainly a need for a more christological doctrine of providence. If, in Christ, God has "made known to us the mystery of his will . . . as a plan for the fullness of time, to gather up all things in him, things in heaven and things on earth" (Eph 1:9-10)—the great patristic theme of recapitulation—then clearly any unpacking of God's purposes with his creation will be centered on Christology, the doctrine of the Trinity, and the divine economy as it has been far more fully disclosed by and in Christ.

We find this, for example, in John Webster and Ian McFarland.[29] The difference within the Trinity blocks attempts to reduce creation or providence to brute will. In fact, on the contrary, *ex nihilo* "affirms the ontological grounding of creatures in the inexhaustible richness of God's own life."[30] McFarland identifies God's omnipotence with his eternal begetting of the Son, in the first instance.[31] This does not reduce God's power, but it helpfully aligns it with God's radically other-person centeredness. It also reminds us that the power God gifts humans with is real, albeit creaturely: "*God is supremely powerful as the one who bestows power*."[32] In the creation "the fullness of divine being is dispersed among many creatures, each of which reflects only a splintered fragment of the whole."[33] God brings creatures into existence so that they can use their power to the full "in order to enter as far as they are

[27]Herman Bavinck, *Our Reasonable Faith* (Grand Rapids, MI: Eerdmans, 1956), 162-83.
[28]Ibid., 168; cf. Bartholomew, *Contours of the Kuyperian Tradition*.
[29]Webster, "Theology of Providence"; Ian A. McFarland, *From Nothing: A Theology of Creation* (Louisville, KY: Westminster John Knox, 2014).
[30]McFarland, *From Nothing*, 90.
[31]Ibid., 95.
[32]Ibid., 97; emphasis original.
[33]Ibid., 97.

able into fellowship with God."[34] *Creatio ex nihilo* alerts us to the fact that everything exists only insofar as God holds it in existence, and we should not conceive of the incarnation as God inserting himself into the creation from outside: "creation from nothing implies that God is *already* maximally 'inside' the world."[35]

McFarland acknowledges that affirming that in the beginning there was nothing but God, that nothing is created apart from God, and that nothing in the creation limits God easily evokes traditional views of God's self-sufficiency, omnicausality, and sovereignty.

> Read within the specifically Christological framework suggested by the opening verse of John's Gospel, however, these forbidding sounding attributes acquire a rather different spin: *Nothing but God* points to the fact that divine self-sufficiency takes the form of love that is realized in the mutual communion of the Father with the Son in the power of the Spirit. *Nothing apart from God* proposes a vision of divine omnicausality as the extension outside of God of the sharing of being that constitutes God's own triune life. *Nothing limits God* means that divine sovereignty is perfected in God's making the life of a creature to be God's own, as a means of ensuring creation's flourishing. . . . The point of creation from nothing is . . . to affirm God's . . . total and unrestricted dedication to them [creatures].[36]

It is preeminently at the cross that the stations of the cross that litter history and our world today are illumined and, without necessarily being explained—indeed, many, many remain shrouded in mystery—are cast in what Wendell Berry so evocatively calls "difficult hope."[37]

Providence and Covenant/Kingdom

By using Joel as the key to explain Pentecost to those amazed at what was happening, Peter identifies the pouring out of the Spirit as the inauguration of the day of the Lord. Pentecost is thus much "thicker" than the birth of the church, although it is certainly that; it is the beginning of the new creation. Peter exquisitely weaves creation, new creation, salvation, and providence together.

This raises the issue of the relationship between Pentecost and salvation history and God's providence. Barth is intensely aware of this issue, and early

[34]Ibid., 98.
[35]Ibid., 102.
[36]Ibid., 106.
[37]Wendell Berry, *What Are People For?* (New York: North Point, 1990), 58-63.

on in his discussion of providence he insightfully discerns that "we have to make at this point a decision of great importance with far-reaching consequence."[38] Barth is right in this regard to reject a theology of two orders or kingdoms:

> We have not to reckon with a parallelism of the two sequences, but a positive connexion between them. The particular decision of God concerning His elect and His government of all things, their love for God and their existence in the totality of things, are obviously not to be regarded apart but in conjunction, in material co-ordination. But if the One who has foreordained them heirs works all things, and if all things work together for good to those who love God, Christians can accept the occurrence of their creaturely history, certainly in faith alone, yet not in a blind faith, but in a faith which is objectively grounded, in a seeing faith, in the faith that there is here not merely a factual but a materially positive and inner connexion, so that even in their creaturely being they are *wholly in the kingdom of Christ and not another kingdom.*[39]

Another way into this issue is to ask questions such as, "What is the purpose of creation?" and "What is the purpose of covenant, of the kingdom, and of salvation?" Implicitly Barth has already answered such questions in his understanding of creation as the external basis of covenant, and covenant as the internal aspect of creation. *The* foundational covenantal text is Genesis 1. In the same way that covenant is all about God's purposes for his creation, and then his retrieval of those purposes through Israel, so too creation establishes God's kingdom, and the Christ event is about the recovery of God's reign over his entire creation, guiding it toward the telos he always envisaged for it. "In the covenant of grace it is a matter of the reconciliation of the world with God, of the redemption of man, of the hushing of the sighing of all creation, of the revelation of the glory of God."[40] Calvin evocatively describes the creation as *theatrum gloriae Dei*, and nowhere is the glory of God more clearly seen than in the face of Jesus, casting its light over the entire creation. As Barth points out,

> The faithfulness of God is that He co-ordinates creaturely occurrence under His lordship with the occurrence of the covenant, grace and salvation, that He subordinates the former to the latter and makes it serve it, that He integrates it with the coming of His kingdom in which the whole of the reality distinct from

[38]Barth, *CD* III/3, 39.
[39]Barth, *CD* III/3, 39-40; emphasis added.
[40]Barth, *CD* III/3, 45.

> Himself has its meaning and historical substance, that He causes it to co-operate in this happening.[41]

If one danger is to separate salvation history from history, another is to collapse them into each other. Clearly most of Scripture attends to the thin line of God's journey with an ancient Near Eastern nation, Israel; climaxes in the Christ event; and continues on into the period of mission as the news of Christ is spread throughout the world. In terms of history, this is, of course, a narrow focus. However, as we have seen again and again, this thin line never loses sight of the fact that Yahweh is Yahweh Elohim, that the God who has come to us in Jesus is the creator God, and that his purposes in Jesus relate integrally to his purposes for the entire creation.

The events of the Bible occur in history. But they teach us this: "That world history in its totality is the history in which God executes His will of grace must thus be taken to mean that in its totality it belongs to this special history; that its lines can have no other starting-point or goal than the one divine will of grace; that they must converge on this thin line and finally run in its direction."[42] This is manifest in the vocations of Israel, Jesus, and the church. Exodus 19:5-6 articulates Israel's vocation in a nugget. She is to be a "priestly kingdom and a holy nation." Like a priest she is to so live as to manifest the presence of God to the surrounding nations. Why? Because "the whole earth is mine." We know from John's Gospel that Jesus is the light of the world, and as they are formed in his image the disciples are called to be salt and light and to disciple the nations. Such theology is grounded in the belief that the God at work in Israel, Jesus, and the church is the creator God, and that his salvation purposes relate integrally to his purposes for his entire creation.

This means that if we want to understand God's ways with God's world, we need to attend closely to the thin line of salvation. Take Israel, for example. In the Old Testament Yahweh establishes his ancient Near Eastern people in the land, in covenant with himself. They have a distinct national, historical, and geographical identity with God living in their midst so that, as one author notes, God now has an address on earth! Israel is historically particular. But it is designed by God precisely as such to be a paradigm for the nations, and in its constitution and God's journey with it we find vital clues to God's ways with his world—that is, to his providence.

---

[41]Barth, *CD* III/3, 40-41.

[42]Barth, *CD* III/3, 36.

Below we will explore God's providence in terms of his sustaining the creation in existence (*preserving*), his active involvement with the creation in its history (*accompanying*), and his sovereignty over the creation (*ruling*).[43] In theology and philosophy, countless positions have been taken on God's providence,[44] and we will refer to these through the course of our discussion, but with two caveats. First, providence in particular is a doctrine in which reason can only wade where faith can swim. As with the doctrine of creation itself, we are again and again amid mystery and the limits of our creatureliness. Second, our main goal is to set forth a constructive theology of providence rooted in creation and to explore positively what this might mean, contra Barth, for a Christian philosophy of history and Christian practice of historiography.

Providence as Preservation (*Conservatio*)

In the Old Testament we find a rich witness to the fact that God sustains the creation in existence. Isaiah 40:12-31, for example, provides fruitful evidence of God's act of preservation (cf. 1 Chron 29:10-13; Neh 9:6; Ps 60; 36; 37; 104). Providence is envisioned as a natural, seamless extension of creation. In Isaiah 40:12, for example, God is the one who "marked off the heavens with a span"; in verse 22 he "stretches out the heavens like a curtain, and spreads them like a tent to live in." In verse 23 this same one brings princes to naught. Verse 12 speaks of God's initial act of creation, whereas verse 22 speaks of his sustaining the creation in existence. Similarly, in verse 26 the author holds creation and preservation closely together. We are exhorted to gaze at the hosts of heaven and ask, Who created them? God is metaphorically pictured as bringing them out, numbering them, and calling them by name. Verse 26 (creation) is preceded by a reference to the transience and fragility of princes and the rulers of the earth (history). As Brevard Childs says, "The only possible rival to God's incomparability—now named 'the Holy One'—lies in the astral powers so widely respected in the ancient Near East. The heavenly bodies move in complete dependency upon God and respond in concert to his sovereign will."[45]

---

[43]Cf. Barth, *CD* III/3. It seems that this threefold framework (*conservatio*, *concursus*, and *gubernatio*) was first introduced by the German Lutheran theologian Johann Friedrich König (1619–1664) in his *Theologia positiva acromatica* (Rostock, 1664), ed. and trans. Andreas Stegmann (Tübingen: Mohr Siebeck, 2006).

[44]See White, *Purpose and Providence*, 71-140; Fergusson, *Providence of God*, 43-296.

[45]Brevard S. Childs, *Isaiah: A Commentary* (Louisville, KY: Westminster John Knox, 2001), 310.

As noted above, Barth rightly redirects Reformed doctrines of providence along christological lines. Hebrews 1:1-4 is a central text in this respect. Hebrews 1:3 says of Christ that *he* "sustains all things by his powerful word." Speech and words are central themes in Hebrews, and "his powerful word" refers intertextually back to Genesis 1 and God's creation by divine fiat. "The Son sustains the world by the same word through which it was created (compare 11:3)."[46] Not only is creation brought into being by God's word, but it is borne along by his (Christ's) powerful word. Romans 11:36 concludes Paul's profound exposition of "the gospel of God" on this exquisite note: "For from him and to him and through him are all things. To him be the glory forever. Amen." The gospel reveals Christ not only as the one who sustains the universe in existence but also as the very reason for its being sustained—namely, for the glory of God.

Isaiah 40:22 pictures God sitting *above* the circle of the earth. This spatial metaphor—above—points to God being separate from his creation, and his creation being separate from him.[47] However, the creation's "separateness" is a contingent and dependent one, whereas God's is absolute. God, we might say, is self-sustaining, whereas the creation would cease to exist without being sustained by God. As Berkouwer says, "The confession sees all things as being indebted for their existence to the preserving act of God; let God cease to act and the universe would cease to exist. With this concept of sustenance the confession at once opposes every claimant to absoluteness in this world—gods and idols, and any who would autonomously and sovereignly pretend to a self-sufficient existence."[48] If anything this dependence is enhanced after the fall, as a result of which lethal potentials are released into the creation and history. Creation, salvation, and history are inseparably intertwined, and thus Barth is right to assert, "For this history to take place the creature must have space and time and permanence. Because God wills the history He creates and gives it these things, and thus preserves the creature."[49]

---

[46]Gareth L. Cockerill, *The Epistle to the Hebrews*, NICNT (Grand Rapids, MI: Eerdmans, 2012), 95. Cockerill (ibid., 85, 95) translates this phrase in Heb 1:3 as "the one who bears all to its intended end by the word of his power" and notes that it means more than sustaining in existence, but certainly not less.

[47]On the importance of transcendence for the doctrine of providence, see White, *Purpose and Providence*, 125-39. White defends a strong view of God's transcendence as "absolute otherness." In our view, Gunton's "weaker" view of transcendence, rooted in creation, is the more biblical view; see Colin Gunton, *Act and Being: Towards a Doctrine of the Divine Attributes* (Grand Rapids, MI: Eerdmans, 2002).

[48]G. C. Berkouwer, *The Providence of God*, Studies in Dogmatics (Grand Rapids, MI: Eerdmans, 1952), 50.

[49]Barth, *CD* III/3, 80.

As with creation, preservation is God's free act, but whereas in creation God acts directly, in preservation "there is need of a free but obviously not of a direct or immediate activity on the part of God."[50] Preservation is about God holding the creation in existence alongside himself and in a temporal sequence in which it can continue. Precisely how God does this is mysterious; Barth uses the word *inconceivable*.[51] God is unlimited, whereas he sustains creation *as creation* and within its creaturely *limits*. For the creature, such limits are the path to genuine freedom, built as they are into the creation and prescribed by God. Berkouwer notes,

> But even with a theoretical recognition of the dependency of all creaturely reality, it is possible in practice surreptitiously to make the creature self-existent. At bottom all deifying of the creature is the consequence of substance theories which invest the creature with self-existence. The incomprehensible act of sustaining renders idle all talk of outright independence.[52]

Berkouwer connects this with Herman Dooyeweerd's aversion to the concept of substance in metaphysics. Doubtless there are ways to define *substance* that avoid notions of independence, but it is surprising how tenacious the view of a substance as that which is independent persists in philosophy. God's preserving and sustaining makes vacuous any view of autonomous independence.

Providence as Accompanying (*Concursus*)

The present participle φέρων in Hebrews 1:3 means more than "sustains." It can also mean "lead, bear along, carry, guide." Preservation is thus not merely a static or deistic activity. Cockerill observes, "The immediate context suggests that the Son accomplishes God's ultimate purposes by making purification for sins and by his subsequent session. The broader context would add his second coming."[53] Thus, even as we attend to God's sustaining the creation in existence, we become aware of his *accompanying* his creation in its journey through history. And, as we will see in the following section, as he sustains and accompanies it, he also *guides it* to its destination. Barth speaks of the creature's "preservation in activity."[54]

---

[50]Barth, *CD* III/3, 64.

[51]Barth, *CD* III/3, 67.

[52]G. C. Berkouwer, *The Providence of God*, Studies in Dogmatics (Grand Rapids, MI: Eerdmans, 2000), 51.

[53]Cockerill, *Hebrews*, 95.

[54]Barth, *CD* III/3, 90.

> The activity of the creature takes place in its co-existence with God. . . . It is therefore accompanied and surrounded by God's own activity. . . . The history of the covenant of grace accompanies the act of the creature from first to last. . . . It is accompanied by the divine wisdom and omnipotence in their specific form of fatherliness. . . . Its own activity stands under the controlling sign of the activity of this companion.[55]

Now, God does not accompany his creation as a friend might accompany us on a journey. He accompanies it, as we will see below, as the Sovereign. "God rules in and over a world of freedom."[56] God never rules as a malevolent tyrant; rather, in his profound grace and condescension he preserves and recognizes the *relative* autonomy and *relative* freedom of the creature. "We even dare and indeed have to make the dangerous assertion that He co-operates with the creature, meaning that as He Himself works He allows the creature to work. Just as He Himself is active in His freedom, the creature can also be active in its freedom."[57] In theological terms we refer here to God's immanent involvement with his creation.

How God does this is where controversy arises. In all its dimensions providence is an article of faith, but where providence as preservation is relatively straightforward, when it comes to providence as accompanying and ruling, theologians and philosophers have developed a range of different and conflicting views. As Bavinck notes, "The difficulty for the mind to maintain both creation and preservation always arises from the fact that by creation God's creatures have received their own unique existence, which is distinct from God's being, and that that existence may and can never even for a moment be viewed as an existence of and by itself, independent from God."[58] Berkhof says, "The real problematic of preservation does not concern nature but history. God preserves the world with and in spite of his rebellious partner."[59]

Within the philosophical and theological tradition, the word for God's working with his creation is *concurrence*. Primary and secondary causality is distinguished in order to navigate away from the dangers of both pantheism and deism. For Bavinck, this distinction is a major achievement of the Christian tradition[60]

[55]Barth, *CD* III/3, 92.
[56]Barth, *CD* III/3, 93.
[57]Barth, *CD* III/3, 92.
[58]Bavinck, *Reformed Dogmatics*, 2:608.
[59]Hendrikus Berkhof, *The Christian Faith: An Introduction to the Study of Faith*, trans. S. Woudstra (Grand Rapids, MI: Eerdmans, 1979), 214.
[60]Cf. Fergusson, *Providence of God*, 302.

because it affirms secondary causes as real and not imaginary, but always and only as subordinate to God as primary cause:

> The constant teaching of the Christian church, nevertheless, has been that the two causes, though they are totally dependent on the primary cause, are at the same time also true and essential causes. It is he who posits it and makes it move into action (*praecursus*) and who further accompanies it in its working and leads it to its effect (*concursus*). . . . Hence, the primary cause and the secondary cause remain distinct. The former does not destroy the latter but on the contrary confers reality on it, and the second exists solely as a result of the first. Neither are the secondary causes merely instruments, organs, inanimate automata, but they are genuine causes with a nature, vitality, spontaneity, manner of working, and law of their own.[61]

Not surprisingly, given his caution toward philosophy, Barth is far more reticent than Bavinck in this area.[62] He recognizes the good use to which theologians have put this distinction,[63] but argues that they have not taken the relationship between creation and grace, covenant and world history, adequately into account. Their view thus lacked specifically Christian content. Barth identifies five criteria that need to be in place if causality[64] is to be used for providence appropriately:

1. "Cause" must not be understood as automatically effective. Bavinck similarly notes that causality must not be understood mechanically.[65]
2. We must avoid thinking that when it comes to God and the creature we are dealing with two "things" that can be analyzed as such.

---

[61]Bavinck, *Reformed Dogmatics*, 2:614.

[62]Barth, *CD* III/3, 94-107.

[63]Katherine Sonderegger argues that "a proper doctrine of creation . . . will resist the root notion of cause altogether" ("The Doctrine of Providence," in Murphy and Ziegler, *Providence of God*, 150). Webster ("Theology of Providence," 161) notes that the doctrine of providence cannot do without the language of causality, but the borrowing should be ad hoc, with the doctrinal substance doing the "real work." On secondary causality, see ibid., 171.

[64]The literature on causality is immense. See, e.g., William J. Courtenay, *Covenant and Causality in Medieval Thought: Studies in Philosophy, Theology, and Economic Practice* (London: Variorium Reprints, 1984); J. A. van Ruler, *The Crisis of Causality: Voetius and Descartes on God, Nature, and Change* (Leiden: Brill, 1995); Jordan J. Ballor, *Covenant, Causality, and Law: A Study in the Theology of Wolfgang Musculus* (Göttingen: Vandenhoeck & Reprecht, 2012); John Peterson, *Aquinas: A New Introduction* (Lanham, MD: University Press of America, 2008); Nicholas Jolley, *Causality and Mind: Essays on Early Modern Philosophy* (Oxford: Oxford University Press, 2013); Keith Allen and Tom Stoneham, eds., *Causation and Modern Philosophy* (New York: Routledge, 2011); William Leonard Harper and Ralf Meerbote, eds., *Kant on Causality, Freedom, and Objectivity* (Minneapolis: University of Minnesota Press, 1984).

[65]Bavinck, *Reformed Dogmatics*, 2:610.

3. Cause must not be understood as a master concept to which God and the creature are subject. Causation could be understood analogically, but Barth is ever wary of playing down the radical dissimilarity between God and the creature.
4. Causal language should not be used to turn theology into philosophy.
5. *Concursus* must relate the first article of the creed to the second. "His *causare* consists, and consists only, in the fact that He bends their activity to the execution of His own will which is His will of grace, subordinating their operations to the specific operation which constitutes the history of the covenant of grace."[66]

We can ignore point four. We do not share Barth's aversion to (Christian) philosophy, although we do recognize the danger of uncritically appropriating philosophical concepts into a theology of providence. Barth is surely right that a concept of causality cannot simply be applied to God. God is uniquely other, and we need to avoid mechanical, reductionistic concepts of causality. At its best, however, the tradition is sensitive to these dangers. Bavinck, for example, writes,

> A mechanical connection is only one mode in which a number of things in the world relate to each other. Just as creatures received a nature of their own in the creation and differ among themselves, so there is also difference in the laws in conformity with which they function and in the relation in which they stand to each other.
>
> These laws and relations differ in every sphere: the physical and the psychological, the intellectual and the ethical, the family and society, science and art, the kingdoms of earth and the kingdom of heaven. It is the providence of God that, interlocking with creation, maintains and brings to full development all these distinct natures, forces, and ordinances. In providence God respects and develops—and does not nullify—the things he called into being in creation.[67]

Bavinck here draws on the Kuyperian doctrine of sphere sovereignty to provide a nuanced account of causality. We conclude that, carefully nuanced, the notion of primary and secondary causality remains a useful heuristic for unpacking to some extent the way in which God accompanies his creation.

But what of God's *preceding* (*praecurrit*) the creature—what of his foreknowledge? Acts 2:23 uses the noun "foreknowledge" (προγνώσει) in reference to Jesus' crucifixion. As with causality, God's foreknowledge focuses

[66]Barth, *CD* III/3, 105.

[67]Bavinck, *Reformed Dogmatics*, 2:610.

the issue of human freedom. A popular solution is to deny God's omniscience (Cicero, Marcion), but omniscience is so evident in Scripture that orthodox theologians have pursued alternative ways to try to resolve this issue.[68] Bavinck divides views along the lines of Origen and Augustine.[69] For Origen, events "do not happen because they were known, but they were known because they were going to happen."[70] Augustine seeks to maintain both divine foreknowledge and human freedom but argues that if God knows something in advance, it is certain to happen: "Thus our wills have only as much power as God has willed and foreknown; God, whose foreknowledge is infallible, has foreknown the strength of our wills and their achievements, and it is for that reason that their future strength is completely determined and their future achievements utterly assured."[71]

In general scholasticism sided with Augustine, but the Jesuits introduced a different view in "middle knowledge." In his governing of creation God made possible many outcomes, and he knows in advance what he will do, however these possibilities are fulfilled by humans. This theory was put forward by the Molinists and the congruists; it procured wide acceptance among Roman Catholics and recently has been defended by Thomas Flint.[72]

The complexity of these issues should not be underestimated. In our view Scripture comes down on the side of the stronger Augustinian perspective, but such a view should always be held with a sense of the "impenetrable mystery" of providence.[73] We return again to Acts 2 and the crucifixion of Jesus. Berkhof insightfully writes,

> For we derive this certainty from his history with us, in the center of which stands the cross. The cross is the climax of our resistance and hostility toward God and therefore the nadir of God-forsakenness. Here free and guilty man seems to have the final and only say. Yet this God-forsakenness is enclosed by an unfathomable presence of God whereby the God-forsakenness becomes the way leading to a new and reconciled communion between him and man. Since this happened we know that even the greatest horrors do not happen apart from

[68]Steven C. Roy, *How Much Does God Foreknow? A Comprehensive Biblical Study* (Downers Grove, IL: IVP Academic, 2006).

[69]Bavinck, *Reformed Dogmatics,* 2:197-203.

[70]Origen, *Homilies on Genesis* 1.14. Quoted in Bavinck, *Reformed Dogmatics* 2:197.

[71]Augustine, *The City of God* (Bettenson), 5.9, p. 194.

[72]Thomas P. Flint, *Divine Providence: The Molinist Account,* Cornell Studies in the Philosophy of Religion (Ithaca, NY: Cornell University Press, 1998).

[73]Emil Brunner, *Dogmatics,* vol. 2, *The Christian Doctrine of Creation and Redemption,* trans. Olive Wyon (Philadelphia: Westminster Press, 1952), 175.

> God. He does not want them, but they cannot thwart his purpose and must ultimately serve it.[74]

In relation to God's foreknowledge, Acts 2 speaks of God's "*definite plan* and foreknowledge," indicating that precisely at this moment of supreme rebellion and horror God's will is being executed perfectly.

Providence as Ruling (*Gubernatio*)

Psalm 93:1 begins, "The Lord is king, he is robed in majesty; / the Lord is robed, he is girded with strength." This is a common emphasis in the Psalms, and as we have seen God's kingship is inseparable from his being the creator of everything. God creates the world with a dynamism and telos in view, and he rules over it to guide it to this goal. The gospel is not in any way alien to this telos. It is in many ways an unexpected explosion of good news, but it fits with and brings to perfect fulfillment God's other-person centeredness in creation, in stark contrast with ancient Near Eastern creation accounts. God's kingship, holiness, and love are not antithetical but complementary. God alone rules, and he directs history toward himself and his glory.

In the Old Testament, as has often been noted, covenant is grounded in ancient Near Eastern treaty analogies, and thus evocative of God as the conquering king. In the Synoptic Gospels, the kingdom of God/heaven is the dominant theme, with the King incarnate in our midst. "Thus in the Old and New Testaments, and in the movement from the one to the other, we see the King of Israel treading always one path."[75] In contrast with Jewish eschatology, the eschatology of the New Testament opens up between the coming of the king and the final consummation of the kingdom. As Ellis points out,

> The *two-fold* consummation of judgment and deliverance that characterized the teaching of apocalyptic Judaism becomes, in the teaching of Jesus and his apostles, a *two-stage* consummation. As "deliverance" the kingdom of God that Judaism expected at the end of this age is regarded as already present within this age in the person and work of Jesus the Messiah. As "judgment" (and final deliverance) the kingdom awaits the second, glorious appearing of the Messiah.[76]

It is to this line of salvation history that we must attend if we are to comprehend God's rule. "The King of Israel is the King of the world."[77] Our concept of God

---

[74]Berkhof, *Christian Faith*, 218.
[75]Barth, *CD* III/3, 181.
[76]Earle Ellis, *History and Interpretation in New Testament Perspective* (Atlanta: SBL, 2001), 113.
[77]Barth, *CD* III/3, 176.

as sovereign ruler will, or should, depend on our view of his journey with Israel culminating in Christ. Barth observes that "if we cannot apprehend and affirm the idea of the divine world-governance, then quite concretely this means that we stand in a negative relationship to these events which took place at definite periods and in definite places, to this reality, and to this concrete Scripture."[78] If we do affirm God's rule then, as Barth notes, "We have to look at world events in general outwards from the particular events attested in the Bible, from God's activity in the covenant of grace which He instituted and executed in Israel and in the community of Jesus Christ."[79] He rightly stresses that we "cannot make it [this history] into a private history."[80] Thus, there is in fact no such thing as secular history:

> For the very same reason that we are not allowed to make the history of the covenant a private history, we are also forbidden to make universal history private over against it. If we did . . . we should be denying the public nature and claim of what did occur, and does and will occur, in the history of the covenant and salvation to and from and in Jesus Christ—in the greatest particularity, to be sure, yet not apart from but at the very centre of creaturely occurrence.[81]

God's rule is a wonderful thing, and Abraham Kuyper was rightly vocal in opposing a diluted concept of providence purely as maintenance. "Imagine," says Kuyper, "that creation were a lifeless metal or granite structure! One can conceive of a granite mountain ridge, or of metal, gold, or silver structures preserved from decay. But then there would be only a dead structure lying in eternal stillness, and Providence would mean only that creation had been preserved in existence." Kuyper insists, like Barth, that God is the living God, the fountain of life, and that creation is alive. God sustains a world that changes and develops. Thus, God's preserving, accompanying, and ruling are not three separate activities. One cannot think of God's preserving and accompanying without bringing the rule of God into the equation.[82]

As noted above, we find McFarland's explication of creation christologically very helpful. However, an element we find missing is God's holiness and the related theme of his judgment. God's wrath is part of God's rule, as both Testaments confirm again and again. This reverts to a theme that Kuyper and Bavinck never relinquish—namely, that the goal of creation is Christ and

[78]Barth, *CD* III/3, 177.
[79]Barth, *CD* III/3, 183.
[80]Barth, *CD* III/3, 183.
[81]Barth, *CD* III, 3, 184.
[82]Kuyper quoted in Berkouwer, *Providence of God*, 67-68.

God's glory, and not ours. Ironically, but quite wonderfully, it is within such a framework as Christ increases and we decrease that we attain full humanity and flourishing.

God's rule and the theme of the kingdom of God alert us also to the fact that God has a goal in mind for his creation. The goal of redemption is not a return to Eden but a renewal of creation in the new heavens and the new earth, that end that is no end but a true beginning.[83] God never abandons his creation but leads it toward the goal he always intended for it. We should be wary of a secularized philosophy of progress, or what has been called a Whig interpretation of history, in which we are the goal of progress. "Nevertheless, it remains central to God's will for human beings that earthly growth and eschatological glorification take place."[84]

However, McFarland is understandably wary of the problem of *meliorism*, the view that creation naturally progresses to higher states. His difficulties here arise from science and Scripture.[85] He argues that generally Scripture envisages that God's purposes will be vindicated through sudden and unexpected reversals. Here we find Kuyper's doctrine of common grace insightful, so that even amid creaturely rebellion, God continues to lead his creation forward. As we have seen in previous chapters, Genesis 1–12 is important here. The development of agriculture, music, poetry, and technology, and of the nations with their different languages in Genesis 10, are normative developments of the potentials built into the creation, what Westermann calls "civilization." Of course, Genesis 10 is immediately followed by Genesis 11 with the Tower of Babel, alerting us to just how strongly humans can misdirect progress. Nevertheless, Revelation provides us with a picture of the treasures of the nations being carried into the new Jerusalem.

A Practical Doctrine

Encompassed as it is with mystery, the doctrine of God's providence is nevertheless immensely practical. A negative way to see this is to attend to the alternatives. Genevieve Lloyd tracks the secularization of providence in her book *Providence Lost*, showing how providence continues to shadow secularization and to influence how we think about life. She says, "I argue that the formation of the controlling, autonomous self of modernity—which we now

---

[83]Robert Louis Wilken, *The Spirit of Early Christian Thought: Seeking the Face of God* (New Haven, CT: Yale University Press, 2003), 63.

[84]McFarland, *From Nothing*, 135.

[85]Ibid., 153-55.

so readily take for granted—was conceptually dependent on changing ideas of providence."[86] She traces providence through Greek thought, Augustine, Descartes, Spinoza, Leibniz, Kant, Hegel, Derrida, and Bernard Williams.

What is telling are her concluding comments. She invokes Samuel Beckett's *Waiting for Godot* and *The Unnamable*:

> In the concluding lines of *The Unnamable*, Beckett shows us not only the tenuous struggles of an individual consciousness, but also the struggle of the contemporary collective mind, which has outlived the conceptual configurations that once gave form to its contents and discontents. All that remains open to it is the inexorable sense of futurity, which is also a sense of necessity: "In the silence you don't know, you must go on, I can't go on, I'll go on."[87]

Providence has its mysteries, to be sure, but it is very hard to see how such emptiness is an attractive alternative, or practical as we seek to live amidst the stations of the cross.

Barth rightly, by comparison, notes that the creator precedes every step of the way of the creature in his living sovereignty, so that all the creature has to do is *to follow*.

> And in the belief in providence this does not have the character of idle speculation, just as God's providence is not the idle onlooking of a divine spectator, but takes practical shape in the fact that the creature which enjoys this recognition may always and in every respect place itself under the guidance of its Creator, recognize its higher right, and give it its gratitude and praise.[88]

Providence reminds us that in every aspect of life it is ultimately with the trinitarian God that we have to do. Not surprisingly, therefore, providence features high in the Christian tradition of *spirituality*. We could provide numerous examples in this respect, but the works of Jean-Pierre de Caussade are particularly notable. His general principles are set out in his *Abandonment to Divine Providence*, and his *Letters on Abandonment to Divine Providence* provide a rich resource for application of these principles. In a letter to Sister Elizabeth Bourcier de Monthureux, written in 1732, de Caussade writes, for example,

> Madame and very dear Sister: You do well to give yourself up entirely and almost solely to the excellent practice of an absolute abandonment to the will of God. In this lies for you all perfection, this is the straight path leading most

[86]Genevieve Lloyd, *Providence Lost* (Cambridge, MA: Harvard University Press, 2008), 6.
[87]Ibid., 331.
[88]Barth, *CD* III/3, 14.

> quickly and surely to a profound and unchangeable peace; it is also a secure safeguard to preserve this peace in the depths of the soul even in the midst of the most violent storms.[89]

If providence is fundamental to the *via contemplativa*, it is no less so to the *via activa*. Kuyper saw this with crystal clarity:

> If God is sovereign, then his lordship *must* extend over *all* of life, and it cannot be restricted to the walls of the church or within the Christian orbit. The non-Christian world has not been handed over to Satan, nor surrendered to fallen humanity, nor consigned to fate. God's sovereignty is great and all-dominating in the life of that unbaptized world as well. Therefore Christ's church on earth and God's child cannot simply retreat from this life. If the believer's God is at work in this world, then in this world the believer's hand must take hold of the plow, and the name of the Lord must be glorified in that activity as well.[90]

The relationship between the *via contemplativa* and the *via activa* is a contested one. Here again the doctrine of providence is illuminating. In providence we have to do with God, and thus the *via contemplativa* is nonnegotiable. But the God we contemplate is the one who preserves, accompanies, and rules over his entire creation, and we cannot ignore his call to be his coworkers, a call that extends from Genesis 1 via the fall, reaches a crescendo in Christ, and extends to the new heavens and the new earth. Insofar as our work is authentically Christian, it will survive into the new heavens and new earth, but history is not dependent for attaining its goal on our efforts. God chooses to use them as he sees fit, and thus in our *via activa* we can rest in his providence and work steadily *within* our creaturely limits.

Providence in View?

To what extent can we discern God's ways in his world? At the end of his long discussion of providence, Barth identifies four signs and witnesses in history to God's providence. We focus on one of these—namely, the history of the Bible.[91]

---

[89]Jean-Pierre de Caussade, *Abandonment to Divine Providence*, trans. E. J. Strickland (Woodstock, ON: Devoted Publishing, 2017), 68.

[90]Abraham Kuyper, *Common Grace*, ed. Jordan J. Ballor and Stephen J. Grabill, trans. Nelson D. Kloosterman and Ed M. van der Maas, vol. I/1 (Grand Rapids, MI: Christian's Library Press, 2013), 23.

[91]The others are the history of the church, the history of the Jews, the limitation of human life. We are all between birth and death and thus a sign of creaturely limits.

Here Barth is thinking of the origin and transmission of the Bible and its history of exegesis. As regards the origin and transmission of the Bible, this is a timely word for today, in which what Emmaneul Tov has called *post-modern textual criticism* is not uncommon.[92] Barth notes that much depends on the perspective from which one views the origins of the Bible and the process of canonization. *If* we accept the witness of Scripture, then it is remarkable to see that "its authors were objectively true, reliable and trustworthy witnesses."[93]

Barth is insightful at this point, and his comments could be further developed. As with the *Pax Romana*, so too the Septuagint was of great missional import. Although it was initially produced for the Jews, at the same time it made the Old Testament available to the Greek-speaking Gentile world.[94] "The Septuagint had thus, in the providence of God, a great and honourable part to play in preparing the world for the Gospel."[95] "'Greek Judaism,' it has been said, 'with the Septuagint had ploughed the furrows for the gospel seed in the Western world,' but it was the Christian preachers who sowed the seed."[96] To a large extent the Septuagint became the Bible of the early church and meant that ready at hand was a Greek theological vocabulary that did not need to be invented from scratch: "the New Testament writers often use Septuagint terms or phrases that were not in common usage in the first century (e.g., *pasa sarx*, 'all flesh,' in Luke 3:6)."[97] As regards the history of the exegesis of the Bible, Barth anticipates the emphasis on reception history today and notes that despite all the aberrations "we shall always see in that history a history of their [the texts'] own self-exegesis."[98]

Even with these signs Barth is cautious and speaks of traces, noting that such witnesses function from within the perspective of faith. Barth is understandably coy about identifying God's footsteps in his world, living as he did in the shadow of World War II and the Holocaust.

---

[92]Emmanuel Tov, "Post-Modern Textual Criticism?," in *Greek Scripture and the Rabbis*, ed. Timothy Michael Law and Alison Salvesen (Leuven: Peeters, 2012), 19-38.

[93]Barth, *CD* III/3, 201.

[94]F. F. Bruce, *The Books and the Parchments: How We Got Our English Bible*, 2nd ed. (London: Pickering and Inglis, 1963), 161.

[95]Ibid., 162.

[96]F. F. Bruce, *The Book of the Acts*, NICNT (Grand Rapids, MI: Eerdmans, 1988), 49.

[97]Karen H. Jobes and Moisés Silva, *Invitation to the Septuagint*, 2nd ed. (Carlisle, UK: Paternoster, 2000, 2015), 23.

[98]Barth, *CD* III/3, 202.

Creational Law

In Barth's approach, however, we discern a contradiction. He develops a thick Reformed doctrine of providence, insists on its practicality, but is adamantly opposed to this being developed into a worldview or a philosophy of history. Partially this is related to his ambivalence about identifying *the laws of creation*. Barth rightly notes that God is not subject to creation law as are creatures.[99] Dooyeweerd similarly makes this point. For Barth, the laws we know are human attempts to witness to the fact that there are ontic laws and an order for creation. He likens such laws to arrows pointing toward real order.[100] Everything takes place within the context of God's rule and creation order.

> But we will acknowledge this the more seriously and proclaim it the more effectively, the more scrupulously we cease trying to equate even one of the laws known to us, even the law which we perceive with what we imagine to be the greatest clarity and certainty, with the order and form or constancy and faithfulness which rule in that causal nexus, with the rule to which all occurrence within it is subject.[101]

Similarly, Berkhof says that discussions of providence often include a discussion of *creation ordinances* such as the family, the state, labor, and society. He notes that he has omitted such a discussion because "the patterns of state, family, etc. are subject to so much change that in the framework of a systematic theology little that is worthwhile can be said about them."[102]

We find it remarkable that Berkhof could find little worthwhile to say about family, the state, work, and so on within the context of providence. Creation order is dynamic but insists that its God-given order *holds for the creation*. And while we should certainly be hesitant about affirming particular scientific laws as exact articulations of God's order for creation, not least since the work of Thomas Kuhn, within *Scripture* we have revealed for us many fundamental aspects of his order as well as firm indications that the whole of creation is subject to his order.

Take the first commandment, for example. Presumably Barth and Berkhof would acknowledge that it is an absolute law for the creature. As the Ten Commandments make clear, it has implications far more comprehensive than for worship/the cultus. Attempts to live without or in opposition to God are antinormative and will have deleterious consequences. Similarly, Scripture is clear

---

[99]Barth, *CD* III/3, 126.
[100]Barth, *CD* III/3, 127.
[101]Barth, *CD* III/3, 128.
[102]Berkhof, *Christian Faith*, 219.

that the male-female gender distinction is creational and normative. As we have seen, Barth himself is insightful in this respect in his discussion of the *imago Dei*. With this distinction goes marriage of a man and a woman and resultant family life as normative. This is God's order for human life, and disregard for it will have consequences. And so we could continue. Suffice it to note that there is much to be gained in developing a deep theology of creation order so that we gain insight into *God's* order for his creation and the order to which he remains faithful—how could he do otherwise?—as he accompanies and guides his creation toward its telos.

Indeed, one wonders what examples Barth has in mind when he asserts that we must allow that God "can *ruthlessly ignore* the laws known to us, that is, our own perception of the ontic laws of creaturely occurrence. Even then God does not act as a god of disorder, but as the God of His own order." Certainly, God could ruthlessly ignore our own misconception of his order, but surely he cannot ignore his order for creation, major parts of which he has revealed to us. Barth is right to remind us that it is God with whom we have to do directly, but God is the creator God, and we should not expect his personal dealings with us to operate outside—how could they?—or in contradiction to *his* order for *his* creation. Spykman provides an eloquent expression of this view:

> This network of structures and functions, governed by creational law, manifests his [God's] loving care *for all creatures. Every creature*, each in its own unique way, is subject to his constant yet dynamic ecosystem of creational laws. Compliance with it is not an odious burden. For it was not imposed by some alien force. The creation order is evidence of the caring hand of the Creator reaching out to secure the well-being of his creatures, of a Father extending a universe full of blessings to his children. Willing obedience to this life-enveloping, love-impelling, shalom-enhancing framework of law and order brings with it freedom, righteousness, and joy. It enables us to become all we are meant to be.[103]

Perhaps Barth has miracles in mind when he speaks of God ignoring the laws of creation as we perceive them. If by *our* perception Barth imagines the view that the universe is a closed system in which God cannot intervene, this is certainly true. The designation of the creator God as Yahweh Elohim in Genesis 2–3, however, alerts us clearly to the fact that God is and will remain

[103]Gordon J. Spykman, *Reformational Theology: A New Paradigm for Doing Dogmatics* (Grand Rapids, MI: Eerdmans, 1992), 178.

deeply involved with his creation; this is what theologians call his "immanence," and Barth his "accompanying." There is no sense here of God somehow *intervening* from outside the creation, since he has no need. Augustine evocatively notes that God is more within us than we are within ourselves, and the same is true of creation. The creation is his, and he holds it in existence. Apart from deism, which Scripture clearly rules out, it remains common among Christians to think of creation as governed by natural law and that in this context we occasionally experience divine intrusions into this law, intrusions that we commonly call "miracles." Spykman argues that we should reject many of the common categories used to distinguish miracles from ordinary history, including the following:[104]

- The distinction between natural versus supernatural, since everything in creation is natural in the sense of possessing its own creaturely nature, and supernatural in the sense of being constantly subject to God's sustaining, his law and his governance.
- The distinction between normal and abnormal, which assumes that in miracles God departs from his order for creation.
- The distinction between God's superintendence of history and miracles by appealing to Aristotle's distinction between primary and secondary logical causes.
- Those views that see miracles as unexplainable but regard most daily events as transparent.

Regarding the fourth point Herman Hoeksema perceptively observes,

> It is true that we cannot understand how the Lord can multiply the few loaves of bread in His divine hands, so that a veritable multitude can be fed thereby. But no more does it lie within the limits of my conception how a seed can fall to the earth and die, in order to bring forth fruit a hundred fold. . . . Miracle causes us to stand amazed. . . . But the cause of this . . . must much rather be found in this, that we become accustomed to the daily works of God's omnipresent power that we usually pay no attention to them. In the miracles God certainly performs something special which exactly through its special

[104]Ibid., 294-95. Spykman also rejects the distinction between mediate and immediate acts of God because in his view God deals with his creatures through "the mediating power of his Word." He thus disagrees with Calvin that God's providence is "the determinative principle of all things in such a way that sometimes it works through an intermediary, sometimes without an intermediary, sometimes contrary to every intermediary" (*Institutes* [Battles] 1.17.1). Spykman's view is not uncommon among Reformational thinkers, but we disagree with him on this because such a view ontologizes God's "Word."

> character draws the attention. Nevertheless, neither in the so-called supernatural, nor in the immediate character, nor in the incomprehensible character of a wonder can the proper idea of a miracle be found.[105]

Spykman thus asserts that miracles are not abnormal happenings but reaffirmations of creation order! "Miracles are signs and wonders of God's intended shalom, now shattered, but restored in Christ. . . . They represent manifestations of the future kingdom within present reality."[106]

On the whole we agree with Spykman, but with a few caveats. While it is true that since God holds creation in existence he cannot be said to violate his creation order—which includes his immanence—there is something unusual and exceptional about miracles. Of course, miracles vary. The miracles associated with the exodus have analogues in "natural" occurrences, but even if this reading is correct, the occurrence of the plagues at that time and in that order is unusual, indeed remarkable, and would have been as disturbing to an Egyptian as to an Israelite. Healing of bodies is common among medical practitioners, but immediate healing is not. Resurrection from the dead is entirely contrary to our daily experience. Daily events retain a great deal of mystery, and we need to recover a sense of wonder at "the ordinary," but even were we to do so, we would still rightly be surprised at an immediate healing or a resurrection from the dead. We need a category for such miracles in which God acts in such a way that his activity is deliberately hard to miss. Calvin's language of God's acting through an intermediary or sometimes without an intermediary attempts to get at this, and some such distinction needs to be retained. God is always active in his creation, but in miracles there is a directness and a surprising nature that calls attention to itself and thereby redirects us to the creator God.

Philosophy of History

Barth provides us with a powerful restatement of the Reformed view of providence, but what is the historian to do with it? Should she affirm it in her church life while practicing history according to the rules of the academy—whatever those are—as James Turner proposes in his dialogue with Mark Noll, asserting that "faith gives no *epistemological* edge" when it comes to

---

[105]Herman Hoeksema, *Reformed Dogmatics* (Grand Rapids, MI: Reformed Free Publishing Association, 1966), 242-43. Quoted by Spykman, *Reformational Theology*, 295-96.

[106]Spykman, *Reformational Theology*, 296.

historiography?[107] Or should the Christian historian take all Barth's insights and put them to work in the discipline of history, as Noll and others suggest?

Although in practice this will be challenging, in our opinion it is clear that we shackle ourselves unhelpfully if we refuse God's revelation when we come to write history, bearing in mind Barth's exhortation that we should understand universal history from the perspective of the thin line of salvation history. Historically, and today, a considerable amount of work has been done on Christian historiography and philosophy of history, and we see no reason to withdraw the leaven of the gospel from these—or any other—disciplines.

However, it should be noted that Barth's view is not uncommon even among Christian historians. Christian historian John Fea affirms belief in God's providence but argues, "Providence is a theological idea that is directly related to the character and behavior of God. History, however, is a discipline that seeks to explain the character and behavior of humans as they live through time. . . . Providence is part of the theologian's toolbox, and not the historian's."[108] We could quibble about Fea's definition of providence, but even taking it as presented, we surely should be interested in the relationship between the character and behavior of God as it relates to the character and behavior of humans as they live through time. It is hard to see how one could confess a belief in providence and then confine it to the theologian's toolbox.

Of course, providence has often been abused by historians. But abuse does not invalidate correct use. In our view, what is need is a nuanced philosophy of history rooted in the biblical doctrine of providence, which, as Barth so rightly insists, is rooted in creation. We live amidst "providence lost,"[109] a tragedy that needs to be overturned. Gordon Graham is one of few who recognize the potential of a providential philosophy of history today. He notes the "almost universal assumption amongst professional historians and philosophers that philosophical history is an invalid enterprise," but he observes that in practice it is hard—we would say impossible—to avoid.[110] Sacred, metaphysical grand narrative, speculative history, and universal

---

[107]Mark Noll and James Turner, *The Future of Christian Learning: An Evangelical and Catholic Dialogue*, ed. Thomas A. Howard (Grand Rapids, MI: Brazos, 2008), 106.

[108]John Fea, *Why Study History? Reflecting on the Importance of the Past* (Grand Rapids, MI: Baker Academic, 2013), 68.

[109]Lloyd, *Providence Lost.* For a perceptive engagement with Lloyd, see White, *Purpose and Providence*, 20-25.

[110]Gordon Graham, *The Shape of the Past: A Philosophical Approach to History* (New York: Oxford University Press, 1997), 7.

history all contend against scientific history that "the past has a shape."[111] Gordon Graham identifies five possible kinds of philosophy of history: progressivism, decline, collapse, recurrence, and providence. He argues that "the originating conception of sacred history, the perception of providential purpose, has more strengths than is now generally accepted."[112] Graham concludes that the only viable candidates are progress and providence.[113] These two are not necessarily antithetical; it depends on what the telos of human history is thought to be. Graham ends his work as follows: "Moreover, if what I began by calling philosophical history is intelligible, and if it begins and ends in ideas of value and significance, it is most likely to succeed if it draws upon the source or sources in which human beings have, albeit dimly, repeatedly and continuously thought that the greatest significance and value lie."[114]

Graham's work is, in a sense, an apology for a providential philosophy of history. What we need is a corpus of examples of such work. A reason many historians are justifiably wary of a providential approach is that their view of providence is rooted in neither creation nor the cross, and thus they think of a providential historiography as the attempt to identify events in which God *intervened* from outside the creation. As we have shown, this is an unbiblical view of providence; far more is to be gained for historiography by taking creation order seriously and thus the implications for understanding the history of God's faithfulness to his creation and his order for it.

[111]Ibid.

[112]Ibid., 9.

[113]Ibid., 213.

[114]Ibid., 222.

CREATION, CHRIST, THE SPIRIT, AND THE NEW CREATION

The judgment by fire . . . will . . . take place [at] the end of the Millennium when the present earth and heaven are destroyed and a new heaven and a new earth created.

LEWIS SPERRY CHAFER

All that is true, honorable, just, pure, pleasing, and commendable in the whole of creation, in heaven and on earth, is gathered up in the future city of God—renewed, re-created, boosted to its highest glory.

HERMAN BAVINCK

Although the glory of God will break into our fallen world, it will not annihilate the world but only break off its present structure of death, because it aims to transform the cosmos rather than to confirm its ontological nothingness.

J. CHRISTEN BEKER

IT IS HARD to overestimate the importance of the telos or goal of creation. Certainly within evangelicalism much cultural engagement has been derailed by the view that the materiality of creation is of secondary importance because it will all pass away. What, after all, is the value of furniture making or acting or town planning, of writing books or spending years honing one's voice as a singer or developing expertise with a musical instrument, if at the end all such pursuits get consigned to the garbage bin of history? In this chapter we explore the question of God's intentions with his creation and their implications for theology and life today.

Eschatological salvation is *for* creational existence rather than a salvific escape *from* it. As the scene in Revelation 21–22 unfolds, one notices that the original creation resonates throughout the new creation and that the original has been heightened and enhanced. Nowhere is this more clear that the elimination of sin *and* the elimination of the *potential* for its return. We argue that God brings creation to this climactic vision through a restorative, purifying redemption in which God redeems the universe that we now inhabit. God is not creating *ex nihilo* again but rather rebuilding the world from its current ruins. In this vision of the new creation, we find spiritual and physical blessing for all nations in a land where we will continue to fulfill the cultural mandate from creation without the hindrance of sin. In other words, we will enjoy perfect communion with God, the saints, and the rest of creation with no fear of breaking this communion ever again. In this communion, we also find a proleptic ethic for the church in our time, an ethic that signals to the world its own creational future.

A Creational Future in Christ, by the Spirit

Theologically, the leading of creation toward its destiny and its perfection is particularly associated with the work of the Spirit. Colin Gunton speaks of "the Spirit's distinctive form of action as the perfecting cause of the creation."[1] We saw in chapter four how the Spirit hovers over the unformed creation in anticipation of its differentiation. The same Spirit anoints Jesus for his ministry of inaugurating the new creation, and the same Spirit is poured out at Pentecost. Theologically, we should thus not restrict the doctrine of sanctification to the individual believer but "resituate it according to the present system of theology in which the Spirit brings creation to its eschatological fulfillment by communicating the redemption that is in Christ the Son."[2]

The salvation offered by Christ Jesus is one that involves the body as well as the soul, the physical realm as well as the spiritual. It is a salvation *for* creational existence rather than a salvific escape *from* it. Instead of liberating us from creation, by his Spirit Christ will liberate creation from its bondage to sin, so that his people are liberated to live together with him in a renewed and restored creation. As Jean-Louis Chrétien perceptively observes, "We are not

[1]Colin E. Gunton, *The One, the Three and the Many: God, Creation and the Culture of Modernity* (Cambridge: Cambridge University Press, 1993), 208; cf. Abraham Kuyper, *The Work of the Holy Spirit*, trans. H. De Vries (Grand Rapids, MI: Eerdmans, 1900), 18-21.

[2]Paul R. Hinlicky, *Beloved Community: Critical Dogmatics After Christendom* (Grand Rapids, MI: Eerdmans, 2015), 341-42.

exiled in the world because it is the world, as the Gnostics think. We are exiled in the world when the world is submitted to a corruption for which we ourselves are responsible, having built a prison that we can no longer unmake."[3]

So it must be stated, first of all, that the biblical language regarding the new heaven and earth, such as we find in Revelation 21–22, portrays a material world rather than some sort of spiritualized one. Such language refers back to Genesis 1–2, where the Spirit hovered over the unformed creation and where we are told that God created the heavens and the earth and declared that they were "good" and "very good."

That Revelation would refer back to the creation account in the context of portraying Christ as the King of the new creation is not surprising, since Jesus is portrayed as the sovereign over creation. Creation and new creation are unified under Christ's lordship, and they find real and abiding continuity, in the very physical and material nature of their existence. "The world," Bavinck writes, "according to [the teaching of Scripture], consists of heaven and earth; humans consist of soul and body; and the kingdom of God, accordingly, has a hidden spiritual dimension and an external, visible side. . . . The kingdom of God is fully realized only when it is visibly extended over the earth as well."[4] The heavenly Jerusalem, which served as the model for the earthly city, will come down to earth as a fully material reality (Rev 3:12; 21–22).

Revelation 21–22

Revelation 21–22 is central to any treatment of creation and eschatology, as it both embodies the essence of prior biblical teaching on this topic and furthers that teaching by developing and enhancing it.[5] In the book of Revelation (Rev 21:1-4) we encounter "a new heaven and a new earth . . . [and] the holy city, the new Jerusalem, coming down out of heaven from God, prepared as a bride adorned for her husband," so that God's home is among human beings, and pain and death are erased. Little wonder that the church, and the Spirit as the perfecter of creation, cry, "Come" (Rev 22:17). This evocative vision of a new heavens and earth cleansed of sin and its consequences unveils God's intention for his creation. It is the biblical storyline come full circle,

[3]Jean-Louis Chrétien, *Under the Gaze of the Bible*, trans. John Marson Dunaway (New York: Fordham University Press, 2015), 82.

[4]Herman Bavinck, *Reformed Dogmatics*, ed. John Bolt, trans. J. Vriend (Grand Rapids, MI: Baker Academic, 2003–2008), 4:718.

[5]We are grateful to Grant Taylor for the exegetical and archival research he undertook in order to help us expound this passage and its reception.

having moved from creation to new creation. As with the doctrine of creation, this eschatology is held by faith; it cannot be verified scientifically or predicted on the basis of past history. Although the vista is in some ways imprecise, it is nonetheless a revelation of great significance.

Such a discussion naturally raises the question of whether or how the Spirit could "perfect" creation prior to sin, and how that relates to the Spirit's work in leading the present fallen creation into the new creation. What type of perfection could creation possibly require prior to the fall and subsequent to God's pronouncement that his creation is "very good" (Gen 1:31)? If God rested from his creative work on the seventh day, in what way is the Holy Spirit's ongoing work in creation to perfect it? With Gunton, we concur that Genesis 1:31 is best read with a trinitarian hermeneutic in which the Father completes his *ex nihilo* work of origination through the Son, who provides creation its form.[a] Thus, the creative act is complete, and yet creation is not yet fully realized. Here Augustine helps by articulating God's ordering of creation according to the tripartite work of bestowing "measure, number, and weight."[b] While the Father, from whom all things proceed, gives creation its boundaries of existence ("measure"), and the Son gives all things their essential form ("number"), the Spirit provides "weight" to all things, that which draws things toward their proper place in creation in relation to God. The Spirit's work is therefore ongoing and teleological, giving life so that creation may change and develop and become ordered according to the Son's plan. That such a work precedes the fall anchors for us the fact that the Spirit's work of perfecting transcends God's work of redemption. God's work with his created order is not finally complete merely when sin has been dealt with in his work of redemption. Rather, the Spirit's work in creation is only complete in the attainment of God's eschatological vision—namely, a renewed creation with a new Jerusalem at its center, in which all is rightly ordered before the face of God.

[a]Colin E. Gunton, "The Spirit Moved over the Face of the Waters: The Holy Spirit and the Created Order," *IJST* 4, no. 2 (2002): 191-92.

[b]Augustine, *On Genesis: A Refutation of the Manichees, Unfinished Literal Commentary on Genesis, the Literal Meaning of Genesis*, ed. John E. Rotelle, trans. Edmund Hill (Hyde Park, NY: New City Press, 2005), 56, 246; cf. Scott A. Dunham, *The Trinity and Creation in Augustine: An Ecological Analysis* (Albany: State University of New York Press, 2009), 92-99.

The new heavens and the new earth (Rev 21:1-8). At the beginning of our passage, we are told, "Then I saw a new heaven and a new earth; for the first heaven and the first earth had passed away, and the sea was no more" (Rev 21:1). There is debate about what is meant by the fact that the old heaven and earth have "passed away" and have been replaced by a "new" heaven and earth. The debate consists of two main views, one in which the old creation is completely destroyed in order to make way for the new, and the other in which the old creation is renewed and restored such that it is now a "new" heaven and earth. As we will argue below, we believe this passage portrays a restoration, rather than an obliteration, of the old heaven and earth.

Osborne notes that one can find annihilative views in early passages such as 1 Enoch 72:1; 83:3-4; 91:16, and can find restorationist views in early passages such as Jubilees 1:29; 4:26; 23:18; 1 Enoch 44:4-5; 2 Baruch 32:2-6; 57:1-3. He argues that 2 Peter 3:13 and Revelation 20:11; 21:1 follow the first tradition above, because we are told that the old heaven and earth "passed away" (ἀπῆλθαν).[a] He notes Jesus' saying in Mark 3:13 as a possible antecedent. Aune has the same view as Osborne and cites 1 Enoch 96:16 as a parallel, indicating either dependence or a common apocalyptic tradition.[b] He also cites Isaiah 51:6; 66:15-16, which he argues imply at least partial destruction of the world by fire. In contrast to Osborne and Aune, Bauckham considers the restoration view more likely.[c] Beale views the portrayal as literal rather than symbolic and considers the use of Isaiah 65 as key to the section, with Isaiah probably referring to the renewal of the creation. However, Beale argues that "renewal does not mean that there will be no literal destruction of the old cosmos, just as the renewed resurrection body does not exclude a similar destruction of the old." He cites allusions to Isaiah 65:16-17 in 2 Corinthians 5:14-17 and Colossians 1:15-18 as support.[d]

[a]Grant R. Osborne, *Revelation*, Baker Exegetical Commentary on the New Testament (Grand Rapids, MI: Baker Academic, 2002), 730.
[b]David E. Aune, *Revelation 17–22*, WBC 52c (Waco, TX: Word, 1997), 1117.
[c]Richard Bauckham, *The Theology of the Book of Revelation* (Cambridge: Cambridge University Press, 1993), 141.
[d]G. K. Beale, *The Book of Revelation: A Commentary on the Greek Text*, NIGTC (Grand Rapids, MI: Eerdmans, 1999), 1040.

Next, we are told "the sea was no more." The sea in this passage symbolizes the forces of chaos and evil that threaten to derail the creation. Revelation's vision of a new heaven and earth is one in which there will be no more evil and no threat of evil.

> By describing the new creation in terms that echo the first, John highlights what is different about the new creation. He suggests that the cosmic sea, the waters of which could be set loose during this age to bring destruction and from which beasts and evil powers might arise, will no longer pose any threat in the renewed cosmos. Never again will creation be called upon to destroy the destroyers of the earth for all judgment will be past and salvation finally and definitively accomplished.[6]

[6]Jonathan Moo, "The Sea That Is No More: Rev 21:1 and the Function of Sea Imagery in the Apocalypse of John," *Novum Testamentum* 51, no. 2 (2009): 166-67.

Taking full account of "the sea" as a symbol, we suggest that already in Revelation 21:1 we have a restorative rather than an annihilationist view of re-creation in view. As is typical of Hebrew poetry, there is clearly parallelism at work in this verse. If annihilationism is in view, it is hard to see why the author would need to indicate that there would be no more sea. Typical of parallelism, this last sentence in Revelation 21:1 intensifies and further explains what has gone before, pointing to the fact that the newness will consist in the absence of any threat and evil.

In Revelation 21:2 we read, "And I saw the holy city, the new Jerusalem, coming down out of heaven from God, prepared as a bride adorned for her husband." Here John's language about the holy city recalls the Old Testament prophets' promises concerning Jerusalem and Zion. Commentators are divided on whether the "new Jerusalem" language refers to a place or a people, and those who interpret it as a place disagree on whether the new Jerusalem is a component part of the new creation or whether it is in fact coextensive or synonymous with the new creation.

In our view, the new Jerusalem as a metaphor evokes both place and people, just as does the symbol "Jerusalem." The new Jerusalem descends from heaven, signifying God's gracious, covenantal movement toward his people. G. K. Beale notes of Revelation 21:3 that it contrasts God's Old Testament presence with his new creation presence: "In Rev. 21:3 the divine presence is not limited by the physical boundaries of an Israelite temple, since not only all believing Israelites but even 'all' peoples experience God's intimate tabernacling presence."[7] With its images of tears and death, Revelation 21:4 refers back to Genesis 2–3 and alerts us to the new creation as uncorrupted by sin and its consequences.

Revelation 21:5-8 contains a speech from God, who is seated on his throne in heaven. Revelation 21:5 is repeated verbatim in Revelation 22:6 and alludes to Isaiah 43:19, in which God declares, "Behold, I am doing a new thing" (ESV).[8] Heaven is God's created abode, and there is no indication here that his making all things new involves the destruction of heaven as well as the earth. What is in view is the renewal of the creation.

Along the way, as John describes the new Jerusalem and contrasts it with its whoring counterpart, he depicts it, as Bauckham demonstrates, in terms

[7]G. K. Beale, *The Book of Revelation: A Commentary on the Greek Text*, NIGTC (Grand Rapids, MI: Eerdmans, 1999), 1047.

[8]David E. Aune, *Revelation 17–22*, WBC 52c (Waco, TX: Word, 1997), 1125; Beale, *Book of Revelation*, 1052.

of place, people, and presence. The new Jerusalem is, first of all, a *place*.[9] It is a temple in that it is the place where God is immediately present to his people. It is a holy city in that it is the place where heaven and earth meet, where God rules his people in his land, finally fulfilling God's intentions for his people to form a God-centered community. It is also a paradise, being both a return to the idyllic state of the garden of Eden and a "going beyond" Eden. Beyond Eden, it is a place that reflects God's cultural intentions, being no longer a garden but a city, and it is a place where there is no more possibility of sin and no more threat of sin's consequences.

> Beale understands the "new Jerusalem" language as referring to God's new people.[a] He writes, "The image of the city is probably figurative, representing the fellowship of God with his people in an actual new creation, though some see the new cosmos as merely an ethically renovated old earth." He notes that the language comes from Isaiah 52:1, which also contains a marriage metaphor.[b] Aune argues for a literal interpretation in which the new Jerusalem is a place rather than a people. Following Schüssler Fiorenza, he argues, "(1) Rev 21:2 *compares* the city to a bride; the city cannot be that bride. (2) Rev 21:7 mentions that the saints will inherit the city; they cannot be the city. (3) The city is described as a *place* where the saints dwell (21:24–26)."[c]
>
> [a]G. K. Beale, *The Book of Revelation: A Commentary on the Greek Text*, NIGTC (Grand Rapids, MI: Eerdmans, 1999), 1043-45.
> [b]Ibid., 1044.
> [c]David E. Aune, *Revelation 17–22*, WBC 52c (Waco, TX: Word, 1997), 1122.

The new Jerusalem (Rev 21:9–22:5). The remainder of John's vision of the new creation centers on the holy city Jerusalem, articulating in some detail its appearance, dimensions, and internal features. Following Richard Bauckham, we interpret this passage in the broader context of Revelation's portrayal of two great cities—Babylon and the new Jerusalem—which contrast with each other and which are opposed to each other. Babylon (which most likely symbolizes Rome and its empire) is depicted as a great whore, while the Holy City is shown to be pure.

The new Jerusalem is, second, a *people* among whom God dwells. It is a city of divine *presence*, full of the Spirit. Indeed, the most truly "new" aspect of the new creation is the immediate presence of God.[10] Before

[9]Richard Bauckham, *The Theology of the Book of Revelation* (Cambridge: Cambridge University Press, 1993), 132.
[10]Ibid., 140.

Revelation 21, God's presence had been confined to the heavenly throne, but now his presence fills creation and is the source of new life in that creation. Bauckham writes,

> Creation thus has a moral and religious goal—its dedication to God fulfilled in God's holy presence—and also an aesthetic goal—its beauty fulfilled in reflecting the divine glory. The latter is just as theocentric as the former. The new creation, like the old, will have its own God-given beauty, but will be even more beautiful through its evident reflection of God's own splendour. Similarly, the nations and kings will enjoy their own glory—all the goods of human culture—the more through dedicating it to God's glory. He will be "all in all" (1 Cor. 15:28), not through the negation of creation, but through the immediacy of his presence to all things.[11]

Bauckham lists nine points of contrast between Babylon and Jerusalem:[a]

1. The chaste bride, the wife of the Lamb (21:2, 9)
   v. the harlot with whom the kings of the earth fornicate (17:2)
2. Her splendour is the glory of God (21:11-12)
   v. Babylon's splendour from exploiting her empire (17:4; 18:12-13, 16)
3. The nations walk by her light, which is the glory of God (21:24)
   v. Babylon's corruption and deception of the nations (17:2; 18:3, 23; 19:2)
4. The kings of the earth bring their glory into her
   (i.e. their worship and submission to God: 21:24)
   v. Babylon's rule over the kings of the earth (17:18)
5. They bring the glory and honour of the nations into her (i.e. the glory to God: 21:26)
   v. Babylon's luxurious wealth extorted from all the world (18:12-17)
6. Uncleanness, abomination and falsehood are excluded (21:27)
   v. Babylon's ambitions, impurities, and deceptions (17:4, 5; 18:23)
7. The water of life and the tree of life for the healing of the nations (21:6; 22:1-2)
   v. Babylon's wine which makes the nations drunk (14:8; 17:2; 18:3)
8. Life and healing (22:1-2)
   v. the blood of slaughter (17:6; 18:24)
9. God's people are called to enter the New Jerusalem (22:14)
   v. God's people are called to come out of Babylon (18:4)

[a]Richard Bauckham, *The Theology of the Book of Revelation* (Cambridge: Cambridge University Press, 1993), 131-32.

[11]Ibid., 141.

Old Testament Intimations of a Creational Future

The creational nature of the eternal state, as depicted in Revelation 21–22, should not come as a surprise. From the very beginning, Scripture has affirmed God's creation as "good" and "very good" and has portrayed humanity in bodily and creational terms. William Dumbrell shows how Israel's earliest reflections on redemption are premised on a creational theology.[12] Exodus 15:1-18 contains allusions to various creation myths in order to show the particularity of Yahweh's salvation. Dumbrell argues that Israel always had a doctrine of creation and that it undergirds their doctrine of redemption. He writes, "Ex 15:1-18 presupposes behind the doctrine of redemption a well-endorsed theology of creation. The hymn implicitly argues that a doctrine of creation is theologically prior to any presentation of the place and purposes of redemption."[13] Indeed, even in the earliest chapters of Genesis, and throughout Exodus and the Pentateuch, God's redemptive activity is always depicted as taking place on a creational stage and undergirded by a theology of creation.

Paul House argues that the book of Isaiah is based on a cycle of visions, each of which culminates in a vision of the restored creation in the language of Zion.[14] So the whole book speaks to creation's restoration. In a more focused manner, Isaiah 40–66 teaches redemption in terms of new creation and further teaches that this redemption is comprehensive, reaching across all of the created order. Isaiah's address in Isaiah 40:12-26 contains a hymn praising Yahweh as the unique and incomparable creator, with the upshot being that the history of salvation is in fact a continuation of creation. In Isaiah 51:1-8 Israel is told to trust in Yahweh, who will fulfill his promises and comfort Zion, and then in Isaiah 51:9-11 Israel is reminded that Yahweh intervenes in history, that he accomplished the exodus for Israel, and that he will give them a second exodus to Zion. This second exodus to Zion is one marked by joy and gladness, features that Isaiah 65:17-25 says belongs to the new creation. "Yahweh redeems," writes Dumbrell, "because he has first created. Divine activity within history presupposes divine control over and responsibility for the course of history. This activity within creation presupposed a role as creator."[15] Indeed, it is Yahweh's redemptive work in creation that shows his authority over creation, revealing him as the creator.

---

[12]William J. Dumbrell, *The End of the Beginning: Revelation 21–22 and the Old Testament* (Eugene, OR: Wipf & Stock, 2001).

[13]Ibid., 170.

[14]Paul House, *Isaiah*, vol. 1, *Chapters 1–27* (Fearn, UK: Mentor, 2019).

[15]Dumbrell, *End of the Beginning*, 184.

When we move to Isaiah 65:17, we are plainly taught a total redemption in terms of new creation and redemption, which Isaiah 56–66 had contemplated but not as explicitly. Indeed, Isaiah 65 presents for us a future kingdom that is physical and material, one in which God's embodied people can live, rather than some sort of ethereal never-never land fit for disembodied spirits. It is a new heaven and earth with buildings and vineyards, as well as work and fellowship, and without negative emotions such as pain (v. 19). God's people will build houses and live in them, plant vineyards and eat fruit (vv. 21-22). Their work will not be frustrating or meaningless (v. 22), and their children will be blessings who do not cause sorrow (v. 23). In Isaiah 66:22 we read similarly about a new heaven and earth.

These Old Testament passages progressively reveal to us God's plan for a creational redemption and prepare us for the New Testament teaching that more explicitly describes that redemption (Rom 8:19-23; Eph 1:10; Col 1:15-20; Rev 21–22). "Biblical theology," Dumbrell writes,

> commences from the creational base provided by the initial chapters of Genesis. It moves between the poles of creation and new creation as the two great movements in history. The heavy alliance of redemption with creation underscores the OT view of redemption as an act of new creation, principally understood in terms of the Israel of the OT. Creation assumed as a basic framework is common to all strands of literature.[16]

Restoration and Renewal

The new heaven and earth is *this* universe, restored and renewed, led to perfection by the Spirit. This is why the apostle Peter, in his sermon at Solomon's Portico, referred to "the time of universal restoration" that God announced long ago through his holy prophets (Acts 3:21). God's good creation has been misdirected by sin, and his redemptive activity therefore redirects it toward the good ends he originally intended. In *Creation Regained*, Al Wolters notes that most of the Bible's basic words for salvation imply a return of some sort to the original condition.[17] To be redeemed is to be "bought free" from bondage so that we can enjoy the freedom we once enjoyed. To be reconciled is to become friends again with someone from whom we have been at enmity or with whom we have been alienated. To be renewed (Rom 12:2) is to be

---

[16]Ibid., 189.

[17]Albert M. Wolters, *Creation Regained: Biblical Basics for a Reformational Worldview*, 2nd ed. (Grand Rapids, MI: Eerdmans, 2005), 69-73.

brought back to a former newness. To be saved is to be made healthy or secure after having been sick or insecure. To be regenerated is to return to life after having been dead. Wolters writes,

> Acknowledging this scriptural emphasis, theologians have sometimes spoken of salvation as "re-creation"—not to imply that God scraps his earlier creation and in Jesus Christ makes a new one, but rather to suggest that he hangs on to his fallen original creation and *salvages* it. He refuses to abandon the work of his hands—in fact he sacrifices his own Son to save his original project. Humankind, which has botched its original mandate and the whole creation along with it, is given another chance in Christ; we are reinstated as God's managers on earth. The original creation is to be restored.[18]

Indeed, God's redemption is redirective in that it restores creation to the state God intended before sin corrupted and redirected it, and leads it forward by his Spirit to the goal he always intended for it.

> Herman Bavinck articulated this restoration of creation in terms of Aristotelian categories of "substance" and "accidents."[a] The "substance" of the old heavens and earth will remain present in the new heavens and earth, although the "accidents" will disintegrate. Theologians such as G. C. Berkouwer and Al Wolters have rejected these Scholastic categories and defended the restoration view on other grounds.[b] We find Wolters's categories of structure and direction more helpful than Bavinck's language of substance and accidents. The new heavens and earth remain structurally continuous with the old heavens and earth, even though directionally they are discontinuous.
>
> [a]Herman Bavinck, *Reformed Dogmatics*, ed. John Bolt, trans. J. Vriend (Grand Rapids, MI: Baker Academic, 2003–2008), 4:716-20.
>
> [b]G. C. Berkouwer, *The Return of Christ*, Studies in Dogmatics (Grand Rapids, MI: Eerdmans, 1972), 219-25; Albert M. Wolters, *Creation Regained: Biblical Basics for a Reformational Worldview*, 2nd ed. (Grand Rapids, MI: Eerdmans, 2005), 69-86.

The restoration view opposes several other views. It speaks obviously against those who view the cosmos as eternal, as a world that has existed forever and will exist in its present form forever. It speaks further against any view that reduces the restored cosmos to a mere repristination, a return to the Edenic state. Finally, it speaks against Christian interpretations that argue that the old creation will be annihilated in order to make room for an (ontologically) new creation. Because this sort of annihilative or destructive view has been prevalent at certain points in Christian history and has been dominant

[18]Ibid., 70-71.

especially among certain streams of recent evangelical thought, we will address it more extensively in the section that follows.

A Purifying Fire

Throughout Christian history there have been theologians who believed that God will destroy the world substantially and replace it with a new world. Among Reformation-era theologians, Theodore Beza was a proponent, and in the post-Reformation era the primary proponents have been certain Lutherans and most dispensationalists. Concerning the Lutherans, G. C. Berkouwer notes that seventeenth-century Lutheran theologians bought into the annihilative theory almost wholesale and cites Eduard Böhl and Johannes A. Quenstedt as examples.[19] Additionally, he notes that the twentieth-century Lutheran theologian Paul Althaus argued that the long tradition of restoration and renewal (including proponents such as Irenaeus, Augustine, Aquinas, most medieval theologians, all contemporary Catholic theologians, and many Reformed theologians) is a forced metaphysical concept that is not biblical and that undermines the seriousness of death. In regard to the dispensationalists, examples of annihilative eschatology abound. Dwight Pentecost, a prominent twentieth-century dispensational eschatologist, wrote about "the dissolution of the present heaven and earth at the end of the millennium," while another prominent dispensational theologian, Lewis Sperry Chafer, concluded, "The judgment by fire . . . will . . . take place [at] the end of the Millennium when the present earth and heaven are destroyed and a new heaven and a new earth created."[20]

Biblical foundations for the restoration view. In rejecting the annihilative view, we must first point out that certain passages might appear to predict a destruction of this present creation. Certain passages in the Old Testament appear to be saying the world will be destroyed. Psalm 102 serves as a representative example. In Psalm 102:25-26 the psalmist writes,

> Long ago you laid the foundation of the earth,
>   and the heavens are the work of your hands.
> They will perish, but you endure;
>   they will all wear out like a garment.
>   You change them like clothing, and they pass away.

---

[19]G. C. Berkouwer, *The Return of Christ*, Studies in Dogmatics (Grand Rapids, MI: Eerdmans, 1972), 219-20.

[20]J. Dwight Pentecost, *Things to Come: A Study in Biblical Eschatology* (Grand Rapids, MI: Zondervan, 1958), 561; Lewis Sperry Chafer, *Major Bible Themes: 52 Vital Doctrines of the Scripture Simplified and Explained*, ed. John F. Walvoord, rev. ed. (Grand Rapids, MI: Zondervan, 1974), 334.

However, as Bavinck notes, the Hebrew word for "create" (*bârâ'*), which is used in relation to the new heaven and earth, does not always mean creation *ex nihilo* but often means the bringing forth of new from old (Is 41:20; 43:7; 54:16; 57:18).

Certain New Testament passages similarly might appear to be saying that the world will be annihilated. We are told that it will pass away (Rev 21:1), perish and wear out (Heb 1:11), dissolve and be burned with fire (2 Pet 3:10), and be changed (Heb 1:12). Bavinck notes that these expressions are not referring to a destruction of substance, any more than the Noahic flood account of the world being "destroyed by water" was referring to substantial destruction. Instead of talking about destruction or annihilation, therefore, we prefer to talk about renewal and restoration because these terms resonate with what the Bible teaches about redemption.

Second, we note that perhaps the most prominent passage used by proponents of annihilative eschatology—2 Peter 3:10—does not in fact support such a view. The King James Version renders 2 Peter 3:10, "But the day of the Lord will come as a thief in the night; in the which the heavens shall pass away with a great noise, and the elements shall melt with fervent heat, the earth also and the works that are therein shall be burned up." This passage often is interpreted to be speaking about an annihilative fire that will dissolve and destroy the present creation. Various commentators and theologians have argued, however, that the passage does not in fact teach annihilation of the cosmos.

Edward Adams writes that 2 Peter 3:10 "is the text that most ostensibly expresses the expectation of the catastrophic end of the cosmos."[a] He goes on to argue that the "loud noise" referred to in the text is to be understood as the sound of the conflagration, while the "dissolving" or "melting" refers to the annihilation of the physical elements of which earthly things are made. D. C. Allison makes a similar argument.[b]

[a]Edward Adams, *The Stars Will Fall From Heaven: Cosmic Catastrophe in the New Testament and Its World* (Edinburgh: T&T Clark, 2007), 200.

[b]D. C. Allison, "Jesus and the Victory of the Apocalyptic," in *Jesus and the Restoration of Israel: A Critical Assessment of N. T. Wright's Jesus and the Victory of God*, ed. Carey C. Newman (Downers Grove, IL: InterVarsity Press, 1999), 139-40.

Wolters argues that the best rendering of 2 Peter 3:10 is that the earth will be "purified" rather than "burned up."[a] Wolters begins by noting that the Textus Receptus has the verb *katakaēsetai*, which the KJV translates as "shall be burned up." However, after Codex Sinaiticus and Codex Vaticanus were discovered (fourth-century documents), this reading was rejected. Both of these documents have the verb *heurethēsetai* (instead of *katakaēsetai*), which is best translated "will be found."

But does this later reading make sense? Bruce Metzger concludes that it does not. What could it mean for the earth to be "found" in relation to fiery heat?[b] Wolters notes that one solution is to say that *heurethēsetai* is a corruption of an even earlier original. In this case, one solves the problem by reverting back to a translation along the lines of the KJV. Others translate it as "laid bare," "exposed," or "judged."

But Wolters argues that the author of 2 Peter is comparing the coming judgment to a refiner's fire in which the world will emerge purified. Second Peter actually refers to three "worlds," a world before the flood, a present world that exists after the flood, and a future world after the aforementioned fire. Wolters notes that the first world was "destroyed" by water, but that destruction did not cause the world to vanish. Similarly, this present world will not vanish. "Just as the second world is the first one washed clean by water, so the third world will be the second one even more radically purged by fire."[c] Wolters argues that Peter probably was alluding to Malachi 3:2-4, in which God refines Israel like a "refiner's fire" and like "fuller's soap" so that Israel will emerge purified and pleasing to the Lord, but Peter goes beyond Malachi by referring not merely to the cleansing of Israel but to the cleansing of the entire cosmos.

Wolters also treats 2 Peter 3:10's use of the verb *heurethēsetai* in its canonical context by comparing it to the passive use of *heuriskō* in 1 Peter 1:7, which is used again in an eschatological context and which refers to a purifying fire. Next, he appeals to two patristic texts, *Epistle of Barnabas* and *Second Epistle of Clement*, which seem to allude to 2 Peter 3:10 and which support his reading. He concludes,

> It seems clear that the reading *heurethēsetai* in 2 Pet 3:10 is not only the best-attested text, indirectly supported by two second-century patristic allusions, but also yields excellent sense in its context. Textual criticism seems in this case to have read into Peter's text features of a Gnostic worldview which looked on the present created order as expendable in the overall scheme of things. The text of 2 Pet 3:10, on our interpretation, lends no support to this perspective, but stresses instead the permanence of the created earth, despite the coming judgment.[d]

We agree with Wolters in rejecting any annihilative views drawn from 2 Peter 3:10 but arrive at our conclusion somewhat differently.

---

[a]Albert M. Wolters, "Worldview and Textual Criticism in 2 Peter 3:10," *Westminster Theological Journal* 49, no. 2 (1987): 405-13.

[b]Bruce M. Metzger, *A Textual Commentary on the Greek New Testament: A Companion Volume to the United Bible Societies' Greek New Testament*, 3rd ed. (London: United Bible Societies, 1971), 706.

[c]Wolters, "Worldview," 408.

[d]Ibid., 412-13.

There is a broad exegetical consensus that *heurethēsetai* is best translated "will be found/disclosed" rather than "will be burned." In 2 Peter 3:7 the "fire" spoken of is a symbol for judgment and the destruction of the wicked (cf.

Zech 12:6; Is 33:11; Mal 4:1). God had promised never again to "destroy" the world by water, and so he is "destroying" it by fire. However, the fire will not destroy the entire creation but rather will destroy the godless and thus destroy the misdirection of God's good creation that has attended the godless since the sin of the first couple. Peter Davids writes, "Our author is not against the creation since that is something that God has made. He does believe that it needs to be purified, but this purification is principally a purification of the human evil that has polluted it."[21]

Further, 2 Peter 3:10 does say that the heavens will pass away and the elements will be dissolved. But this passage's central motif is judgment, and 3:10 is an apocalyptic evocation of the day of the Lord in which God strips the heavens away, as it were, so that he will pass through them. Nothing will stand between the Lord God and his creation. On this day, all of creation will find itself truly present *coram Deo*. "The point," Davids writes, "is the uncovering and exposing and thus the purifying of the earth."[22] So the issue of the translation of *heurethēsetai* is not the primary question in the passage. Even if it is translated "will be burned" in the sense of being destroyed instead of being translated "will be found/disclosed," the more central issue is the nature of the event itself. The earth could be "burned" in the sense of being annihilated, or it could be "burned" in the sense of a purifying fire. We conclude that the earth will be found or disclosed in the sense that God will purify it from evil and the consequences of evil. We agree with N. T. Wright concerning this passage when he concludes,

> The writer wishes to stress continuity within discontinuity, a continuity in which the new world, and the new people who are to inhabit it, emerge tested, tried and purified from the crucible of suffering. If something like this is plausible . . . then the worldview we find is not that of the dualist who hopes for creation to be abolished, but of one who [continues] to believe in the goodness of creation.[23]

Instead of supporting an annihilative view, 2 Peter affirms the purification and restoration of God's good creation.[24]

Third, we note that other passages of Scripture teach clearly that this universe will be saved. In Romans 8:19-23, Paul describes creation—including

---

[21]Peter H. Davids, *The Letters of 2 Peter and Jude*, PNTC (Grand Rapids, MI: Eerdmans, 2006), 274.
[22]Ibid., 287.
[23]N. T. Wright, *The Resurrection of the Son of God* (Minneapolis: Fortress, 2003), 463.
[24]For a more extensive treatment of this passage, see Craig G. Bartholomew, *Where Mortals Dwell: A Christian View of Place for Today* (Grand Rapids, MI: Baker Academic, 2011), 152-56.

believers who have "the first fruits of the Spirit"—as longing for redemption, as groaning under the weight of sin and yearning to be set free from that bondage. Wright says of the Spirit as the down payment of what lies ahead, "The Spirit is a gift from God's future, the gift which guarantees that future."[25]

The salvation Paul describes is cosmic and emancipatory and supports a restorative eschatology rather than an annihilative one. Similarly, in Ephesians 1:10, Paul declares that in "the fullness of time," all things will be gathered up in Christ, including "things in heaven and things on earth." And again, in the Colossians Christ-hymn, we learn that Christ not only created all things in heaven and on earth, including both the visible and invisible aspects of creation (Col 1:16), and not only does he presently hold together all of those things (Col 1:17), but one day he will reconcile all of those things to himself (Col 1:20). So these passages and others set forth clearly a restorative eschatology so that passages that are less clear, such as the ones listed above, can be interpreted in their light.

Fourth, our Lord's resurrection by the Spirit (Rom 1:4) serves as a preview of our own resurrection and of a future cosmic resurrection. Just as his resurrection is the "first fruits" of a future resurrection of our own bodies (1 Cor 15:20-28), so it is also a preview of the Lord Christ's future resurrection of the cosmos. N. T. Wright writes, "God will do for the whole cosmos, in the end, what he did for Jesus at Easter. . . . God will do this through Jesus himself; the ascended Jesus, remember, is the ruler within the new creation as it bursts in upon the old. And God will do it through the presence of the risen and ascended Jesus when he comes to heal, to save, and also to judge."[26] Indeed, it is traditionally held that the risen Christ retains his human body now in the heavenly realm. We are surely not to think that this too will be annihilated.

Fifth, if God annihilates the cosmos, Satan has gained a great victory, and the perfecting work of the Spirit has come to naught. As we have mentioned several times already in this volume, Satan does not have the power to corrupt God's creation in its structures, the power to make it ontologically bad. No, Satan has only the power to misdirect God's good creation as a parasite on God's good work. Thus, in the eschaton there is no need for God to annihilate the creation; it remains his good creation and has been sustained as such and led to perfection by his Spirit. In fact, for God to annihilate his

---

[25]Ibid., 146.

[26]N. T. Wright, *Simply Jesus: A New Vision of Who He Was, What He Did, and Why He Matters* (New York: HarperOne, 2011), 202.

good creation would be to concede to the Evil One a great victory. N. T. Wright rightly asserts,

> And if God's good creation—of the world, of life as we know it, of our glorious and remarkable bodies, brains, and bloodstreams—really is good, and if God wants to reaffirm that goodness in a wonderful act of new creation at the last, then to see the death of the body and the escape of the soul as salvation is not simply slightly off course, in need of a few subtle alterations and modifications. It is totally and utterly wrong. It is colluding with death. It is conniving at death's destruction of God's good, image-bearing human creatures while consoling ourselves with the (essentially non-Christian and non-Jewish) thought that the really important bit of ourselves is saved from this wicked, nasty body and this sad, dark world of space, time, and matter![27]

Thus, a restorative eschatology makes the most sense of the biblical testimony, is able to make sense of passages that might seem to speak against it, and renders coherent the biblical teaching on Christ's resurrection, the inability of Satan to make bad what God has made good, and the perfecting work of the Spirit.[28] Attention to individual passages is vital, as we hope our argument above demonstrates. At the same time, the cumulative weight of Scripture, and not least a robust doctrine of creation, is essential.

Jürgen Moltmann. Moltmann writes, "The goal of this history of creation is not a return to the paradisal primordial condition. . . . The new creation of heaven and earth in the kingdom of glory surpasses everything that can be told about creation in the beginning."[29] For Moltmann, the new heavens and earth will be far better than the old creation because God and the world will indwell each other perichoretically.[30] By way of contrast with the restoration view, he writes, "If the new creation is to be an imperishable and eternal creation, it must be new not only over against the world of sin and death, but over against the first, temporal creation too. The substantial conditions of creaturely existence itself must be changed."[31] So, for Moltmann, the new heavens and earth will be new in a substantial manner.

---

[27]N. T. Wright, *Surprised by Hope: Rethinking Heaven, the Resurrection, and the Mission of the Church* (New York: HarperOne, 2008), 194.

[28]Anthony A. Hoekema, *The Bible and the Future* (Grand Rapids, MI: Eerdmans, 1979), 281-87.

[29]Jürgen Moltmann, *God in Creation: A New Theology of Creation and the Spirit of God* (Minneapolis: Fortress, 1993), 207.

[30]On this point, see Richard Bauckham's exposition of Moltmann's thought, in "Eschatology in the Coming of God," in *God Will Be All in All: The Eschatology of Jürgen Moltmann*, ed. Richard Bauckham (Minneapolis: Fortress, 2001), 10-16.

[31]Jürgen Moltmann, *The Coming of God: Christian Eschatology* (Minneapolis: Fortress, 1996), 272.

We agree with Moltmann in his rejection of the repristination view but disagree with his rejection of the restoration view and for allowing the new creation to "overwhelm" the old creation. Petr Macek writes,

> Does not Moltmann's *creatio nova*, interpreted as a *novum ex nihilo*, rather than "restoration," presuppose total and active *annihilatio mundi* and not only *annihilatio nihil*? Or, to put it differently, does not the necessity of "new creation" undercut the goodness of *creatio originalis* and does it not in this sense fail to account for the biblical distinction between "creation" and "fall"?[32]

Indeed, in our view Moltmann's vision undercuts the biblical account of creation's goodness and of the future restoration.

Karl Barth. Eberhard Busch notes that Barth sounds like an annihilationist when he emphasizes the fact that the kingdom introduces something new to the world, something that renews it totally.[33] Barth writes about how the consummated kingdom of God has "drawn near" as "the greatest, the only true and definitive break in the world and its history. . . . [It is the] destruction . . . of all the so-called 'given factors,' all the supposed natural orders, all the historical forces, which with the claim of absolute validity and worth have obtruded themselves as authorities."[34] And yet in other passages Barth marks out his view as one that is not annihilative. He writes that God remains "bound to this world by his Word" and that "God will not allow the cosmos to be definitively bewitched and demonized or His creation totally destroyed, nor will He permit the realization of [this] dark possibility."[35]

When Barth's entire corpus is taken into account, Busch argues, Barth turns out to be a restorationist:

> Barth offers a nuanced view of this concept of "new creation." It cannot mean that a better or totally different second creation will replace the first, so that in the process the first creation is destroyed. That would mean that God had not made the first creation a good one, that it was indeed a bad reality, and that would mean that the new creation could be achieved only by a negation of the created reality made by God as good. Its newness can refer only to the destruction that threatens creation, the removal of which has been God's

[32]Petr Macek, "The Doctrine of Creation in the Messianic Theology of Jürgen Moltmann," *Communio Viatorum* 49, no. 2 (2007): 180.

[33]Eberhard Busch, *The Great Passion: An Introduction to Karl Barth's Theology*, ed. Darrell L. Guder and Judith J. Guder, trans. Geoffrey W. Bromiley (Grand Rapids, MI: Eerdmans, 2004), 280-81.

[34]Barth, *CD* IV/2, 543.

[35]Barth, *CD* III/1, 109.

> intention from the very beginning, and not only after that destruction surfaced within creation.[36]

Barth's view is one in which the old world, which has been corrupted and wounded by sin, will be healed and renewed by God.

The neo-Calvinist tradition. More than Moltmann, Barth, and the dispensationalists, however, it is the Dutch neo-Calvinist tradition that has the most invested in this discussion. Bavinck is worth quoting in summary:

> [This present world] will be cleansed of sin and re-created, reborn, renewed, made whole. While the kingdom of God is first planted spiritually in human hearts, the future blessedness is not to be spiritualized. Biblical hope, rooted in incarnation and resurrection, is creational, this-worldly, visible, physical, bodily hope. The rebirth of human beings is completed in the glorious rebirth of all creation, the new Jerusalem, whose architect and builder is God himself.[37]

> All that is true, honorable, just, pure, pleasing, and commendable in the whole of creation, in heaven and on earth, is gathered up in the future city of God—renewed, re-created, boosted to its highest glory.[38]

Indeed, salvation does not save anything less than all of creation. Its scope is cosmic and could only be wrought through the Spirit by the One to whom all authority has been given, in heaven and on earth.

Reconciling all things to himself—a summary of the restorative view. To summarize the argument so far, the self-revealing God promises one day to install a "new" heaven and earth, one that contains a new Jerusalem, and one that is devoid of sin and suffering. This restoration is universal and is accomplished by, and centers on, Christ Jesus. Colossians 1:15-20 is perhaps the clearest articulation of the Christocentric and universal nature of Christ's cosmic redemption. But so, too, is Ephesians 1:8-10 a central text: "With all wisdom and insight he has made known to us the mystery of his will, according to his good pleasure that he set forth in Christ, as a plan for the fullness of time, to gather up all things in him, things in heaven and things on earth." Why is Christ able to do these things? Because he is the "image" of the invisible God, the dwelling place of God's "fullness." In other words, because Christ is in fact God, and because he created all things and is master

[36]Busch, *Great Passion*, 281.
[37]Bavinck, *Reformed Dogmatics*, 4:715.
[38]Ibid., 4:720.

over them, and because his atonement was cosmic in scope, he has and will in fact reconcile "all things" to himself. König writes,

> The most profound link between creation and consummation lies in Jesus Christ himself, who is the beginning and the end, the first and the last, the Creator and the Consummator. In his own person he unites creation and consummation. In him they are not two events infinitely separated from each other in time, but a single reality bound together in him, the living Lord, by whose power creation proceeds to consummation and consummation comes forth from creation. All is created by him, and by him all is renewed.[39]

Not only protology but also eschatology centers on Christ.

The Blessings of the Redeemed from Every Tribe and Language and People and Nation

Just as Christ will resurrect the cosmos, so he will resurrect the believers among the nations. The promise of Revelation 5:9-10 is that Christ's atonement has ransomed believers from among every tribe and language and people and nation (v. 9), believers who will reign with God on the new creation (v. 10). This harks back to the Table of the Nations in Genesis 10 and fulfills this vision for normative development of the creation.

Spiritual and physical blessing. The biblical way of speaking of humanity's future as a "new creation" is to speak of the resurrection of the dead (1 Cor 15:12-28). Jesus' resurrection and ours are directly connected. Paul makes the strongest of connections between Christ's resurrection and humankind's future resurrection, even going so far as to say that if there were not a future resurrection, it would prove that Christ himself had not risen (1 Cor 15:12-22). Our resurrected bodies will be both continuous and discontinuous with our present bodies, in that God raises our present bodies but does so in a way that leaves them purged of sin and its consequences.

God's reaffirmation and restoration of creation includes a heightening and enhancing of his original creation. Might our glorified bodies include such heightened or enhanced powers? Jonathan Edwards speculates along these lines when he writes,

> How ravishing are the proportions of the reflexions of rays of light, and the proportion of the vibrations of the air! And without doubt God can contrive

[39]Adrio König, *The Eclipse of Christ in Eschatology: Toward a Christ-Centered Approach* (Grand Rapids, MI: Eerdmans, 1989), 62-63.

> matter so that there shall be other sort of proportions that may be quite of a different kind, and may raise another sort of pleasure in the sense, and in a manner to us now inconceivable, and that shall be vastly more ravishing and exquisite. And in all probability the abode of the saints after the resurrection will be so contrived by God that there shall be external beauties and harmonies altogether of another kind from what we perceive here, and probably those beauties will appear chiefly in the bodies of the man Christ Jesus and of the saints.[40]

We think that Edwards is correct when he speculates that the renewed heaven and earth might very well include "proportions," dimensions, and enhancements that are not now available to us.

Possessing and progressing. The eternal state is one in which God's people experience God's blessings. But will we experience those blessings comprehensively and immediately or gradually and progressively? Schleiermacher poses the question when he writes, "The state of believers after their full reinstatement in life may be conceived under two forms, either as a sudden and unvarying possession of the highest, or as a gradual ascent to the highest."[41] What is agreed on is that the eternal state is one in which we dwell in the immediate presence of God, knowing him with an immediacy with which we are now unacquainted.

Schleiermacher sees only two possibilities. Under the first possibility, the eternal state is viewed as a "sudden and unvarying possession of the highest." Schleiermacher has in mind with this first possibility the traditional Roman Catholic teaching of *visio Dei*. Under the second possibility, the eternal state is viewed as a "gradual ascent to the highest," and he has in mind the view that the eternal state is the progressive development of the Christian life as led by believers already. Schleiermacher rejected the first option but never was comfortable with the second option either because it seems to allow for imperfection and therefore dissatisfaction in the presence of God.

Following Hendrikus Berkhof, we think Schleiermacher was right to reject the first option and to remain uncomfortable with the second, but we think the biblical portrayal suggests a third way that can be viewed as a hybrid of the two options. "Could it be," Berkhof writes, "that for the human race as a whole there might be an almost endless moving toward the goal of our life, a

---

[40]Jonathan Edwards, *The Works of Jonathan Edwards*, ed. Sereno E. Dwight and Edward Hickman (Carlisle, PA: Banner of Truth Trust, 1974), 2:618.

[41]Friedrich Schleiermacher, *The Christian Faith*, ed. H. R. Mackintosh and James S. Stewart (Berkeley, CA: The Apocryphile Press, 2011), 717.

progressing in which we are called and being qualified to meet constantly new challenges and to overcome? Who can tell?"[42]

In this scenario, we can imagine that, in Berkhof's words, we will both *possess* and *progress*. We will possess a relationship with God in which we will see him, understand him, and know him. As Bavinck puts it, we will know him "directly, immediately, unambiguously, and purely."[43] And yet we suggest that this sort of possession is not at odds with progression. For if, in the eternal state, we are possessed both by body and soul, and if, as we have reason to believe, we image God as whole persons in possession of spiritual, moral, rational, creative, volitional, relational, and physical capacities, it makes sense that we will be using those capacities to image God in ways uninhibited by postlapsarian and preconsummation conditions.

God's creational design for humanity involved having dominion over God's good creation by developing its hidden potentials, thereby developing our own potential as worshipers. This divine design continued even after the fall, and it seems that this trajectory will continue even into the consummated kingdom, that we will rule with Christ in part by continuing to develop creation's hidden potentials, thereby multiplying our worship with a profusion of creative variations.

Jonathan Edwards had something like this in mind when he articulated his doctrine of "eternal increase":

> The glorified spirits shall grow in holiness and happiness in eternity. . . . Their knowledge will increase to eternity; and if their knowledge, their holiness; for as they increase in the knowledge of God, and of the works of God, the more they will see of his excellency, and the more they see of his excellency . . . the more they will love him, and the more they love God, the more delight and happiness will they have in him.[44]

We agree with Edwards's conclusion that the saints likely will increase in their knowledge of God. Additionally, we would argue that this relational development will be paralleled by a development in our other capacities and even a continued cultural development of creation's hidden potentials. The eternal state may very well be one that is very good and that is perfect in the sense that it will not be marred by sin or its consequences (and will exist without even the possibility of

[42]Hendrikus Berkhof, *The Christian Faith: An Introduction to the Study of Faith,* trans. S. Woudstra (Grand Rapids, MI: Eerdmans, 1979), 545.

[43]Bavinck, *Reformed Dogmatics*, 4:722.

[44]Edwards, *Works of Jonathan Edwards*, 2:618.

sin), but not yet perfected in the sense that God intends for his imagers to continue to develop its hidden potential and continue to teach his image bearers about him.

Cultural continuity and discontinuity. But will the cultural developments of this present life remain in the consummated kingdom? If indeed God intended all along for humanity to bring out the creation's hidden potentials as a way of spreading his glory across the face of the earth, will he in fact redeem the work of our hands in spite of the fact that our hands are tainted? Berkhof argues,

> What is certain is that one day the relation between this entire cultural development and eternity will be disclosed and shown to be meaningful. But we are not able to look beyond the great leap. It is wonderful enough to know that all the true, the good, and the beautiful we receive and achieve in our cultural development is a distant foretaste of the fullness of life and the world which God has in store for us.[45]

Richard Mouw attends to Isaiah 60, in which Isaiah portrays an eternal state that possesses both a cultural continuity and a discontinuity with present conditions.[46] The prophet lists many cultural items that will be in the Holy City, items such as lumber from Lebanon, ships from Tarshish, and beautiful crafts. What is interesting, however, is that in Isaiah 2 the prophet had declared that the ships of Tarshish are "proud and lofty" and that God is against them. Similarly, in Psalm 48 the psalmist declares that the Lord will "shatter" the ships of Tarshish. The question, therefore, as Mouw poses it, is why the biblical testimony has the ships of Tarshish being shattered because they are proud and lofty, and then at the same time has them making an appearance in the Holy City. The same question arises in relation to the trees of Lebanon, which Isaiah 10:34 portrays as being cut down by the Lord but Isaiah 60:13 has adorning the Holy City.

Mouw's solution is to say that the ships perish functionally rather than ontologically. In other words, his view of human culture is analogous to his restorationist view of the heavens and earth. As the Lord sees fit, he may strip cultural objects—such as the ships of Tarshish—of the sinful and idolatrous uses and associations for which they are now known and restore them for use on the new heavens and earth. Mouw avers that the ships of Tarshish were idolatrous in that their makers viewed them—rather than God—as their

---

[45]Berkhof, *Christian Faith*, 543.

[46]Richard J. Mouw, *When the Kings Come Marching In: Isaiah and the New Jerusalem*, rev. ed. (Grand Rapids, MI: Eerdmans, 2002).

source of security, and that God therefore must purify them of that idolatrous function before delivering them to his new creation. Mouw writes,

> Whenever God's people are tempted to look for security from a source other than God's protecting Spirit—or whenever they are inclined to "supplement" the power of God with military or technological means—they are condemned by the prophets. . . . God's present attitude, then, toward these instruments of culture is an ambivalent one. As tools of human rebellion and objects of idolatrous trust, he hates them. . . . But he hates them because of their present uses. And his hatred will lead him to transform them into proper instruments of service.[47]

Mouw's distinction between ontology and function is akin to the distinction between structure and direction that we have employed throughout this book.

In the end, Mouw argues, God will fill the renewed earth with purified human culture. Why is God so concerned with gathering the wealth of the nations? Because everything in the earth is his (Ps 24:1). He created humanity to fill the earth and subdue it (Gen 1:28), and commanded us to till it and bring out its hidden potential. In Proverbs 8:30-31 Wisdom personified speaks of being

> daily his [Yahweh's] delight,
> rejoicing before him always,
> rejoicing in his inhabited world
> and delighting in the human race.

The normative development of the creation in all its myriad ways delights God, and thus it is no surprise that such developments will find their way into the new heaven and the new earth.

Mouw goes on to note Isaiah's portrayal of the Holy City as one to which foreign kings will be drawn (Is 60:3) and in which those kings will minister to God's people (Is 60:10), will proceed into the city (Is 60:11), and will provide milk from their breasts that God's people will suck (Is 60:16). Mouw argues that the kings are present for a cameo appearance of sorts, in which they represent their nations and the cultural contributions of those nations.

Communion with God and the saints. At the center of God's redemptive purpose is the redemption of humanity, of man and woman made in the image and likeness of God. Our communion with God and the saints will include action and activity in the renewed creation, just as it does in the

---

[47]Ibid., 31-32.

present creation. Scripture does not offer much detail, but it does reveal that we will praise God (Rev 4:11; 5:8-10) and serve him continually (Rev 22:3), and will live as prophets, priests, and kings (Rev 1:6; 5:10; 22:5). Bavinck writes, "While we may not be able to form a clear picture of the activity of the blessed, Scripture does teach that the prophetic, priestly, and royal office, which was humanity's original possession, is fully restored in them by Christ. . . . That activity, however, coincides with resting and enjoying."[48]

Mouw's reading of Isaiah 60 is clearly connected to Revelation 21:23-26, which has a strong precedence in Christian tradition and scholarship. Both passages envision a cosmos lit not by celestial light but by the light of God's presence (Is 60:19-20; Rev 21:23-24); both see the Gentile nations streaming to Jerusalem (Is 60:3; Rev 21:24); the city gates will perpetually remain open (Is 60:11; Rev 21:25); and most importantly for this discussion, some form of wealth from the nations will be brought into the city as tribute to Yahweh (Is 60:11; Rev 21:26). Gilchrest argues that these elements demonstrate that Isaiah 60 is the closest parallel to the Revelation 21 passage and that the Johannine author no doubt used this text as inspiration for his own.[a] The greatest discrepancy between the two passages, at least as pertains to our discussion of Mouw's argument, has to do with whether the "glory and honor of the nations" of Revelation 21:26 is synonymous with the various forms of material wealth described in Isaiah 60.

Most interpreters see John as spiritualizing the vision of Isaiah, so that "glory and honor" are in fact representative of converted Gentiles and their offerings of praise.[b] Cruise has the best argument for this interpretation, for despite the parallels between the two passages, important discontinuity should be stressed.[c] Whereas the kings of Isaiah 60 are brought by coercion to Zion and the whole scene is steeped in a mood of fear, Revelation 21 is set in a time when the enemies of Yahweh are already dealt with (Rev 19–20), and "the ideas of tribute and servitude" do not fit with the scene of celebration at the arrival of the new Jerusalem. For Cruise, there can be no "relationship of victor and vanquished" as posited by Isaiah, and therefore John's use of Isaiah demonstrates a broadening of the prophetic vision in such a way that the "wealth of the nations," which in the Isaiah text clearly indicates material wealth, does not correspond to the "glory and honor" brought in John's vision.[d] Rather, John's vision refers most likely to the God's multiethnic people, drawn from all the nations (Rev 7:9), arriving in the restored Zion.

Despite this potential discontinuity, however, we believe along with several others that there is compelling evidence to see John's text as encompassing *both* spiritual and material realities.[e] Mathewson argues that δόξα can in fact mean both glory and

[48]Bavinck, *Reformed Dogmatics*, 4:729.

wealth, and that wealth fits best with the parallel passage of Revelation 18:16-19, which depicts the material wealth brought into Babylon in its hubris.[f] Christensen provides an extended treatment of this same notion, concluding that δόξα should be seen as a possession or attribute of τὰ ἔθνη (Rev 21:26), that it should be taken to imply cultural elements that distinguish the various groups included in John's vision of "the nations."[g] Finally, Christensen argues that when the kings "bring" (φέρουσιν) the glory of their nations into the new Jerusalem, the action is not the attribution of glory to God (i.e., "to give glory") but rather something similar to what the magi do in Matthew 2:11, presenting (προσφέρω) treasures to Jesus.[h] If material wealth representative of the unique identities of the nations is in mind in this passage, what more could be in view than the fact that cultural artifacts of the present age will find a home in the new creation?

---

[a]Eric J. Gilchrest, *Revelation 21–22 in Light of Jewish and Greco-Roman Utopianism*, Biblical Interpretation 118 (Leiden: Brill, 2013).

[b]Richard Bauckham, *The Climax of Prophecy: Studies on the Book of Revelation* (Edinburgh: T&T Clark, 1993), 315-16; G. K. Beale, *The Book of Revelation: A Commentary on the Greek Text*, NIGTC (Grand Rapids, MI: Eerdmans, 1999), 1095; J. A. du Rand, "The Imagery of the Heavenly Jerusalem (Revelation 21:9–22:5)," *Neotestamentica* 22, no. 1 (1988): 78; Robert H. Mounce, *The Book of Revelation*, rev. ed., NICNT (Grand Rapids, MI: Eerdmans, 1998), 397.

[c]Charles E. Cruise, "The 'Wealth of the Nations': A Study in the Intertextuality of Isaiah 60:5, 11," *JETS* 58, no. 2 (2015): 283-97.

[d]Ibid., 297.

[e]David E. Aune, *Revelation 17–22*, WBC 52c (Waco, TX: Word, 1997), 1173; Eric Christensen, "The Glory of the Nations: Ethnic Culture and Identity in Biblical Perspective" (PhD diss., Fuller Theological Seminary, 2011), 100; Gilchrest, *Revelation 21–22*, 220; David Mathewson, *A New Heaven and a New Earth: The Meaning and Function of the Old Testament in Revelation 21.1–22.5*, Journal for the Study of the New Testament Supplement Series 238 (London: Sheffield Academic Press, 2003), 168.

[f]Mathewson, *New Heaven*, 168.

[g]Christensen, "Glory of the Nations," 27-100; cf. Gilchrest, *Revelation 21–22*, 220.

[h]Christensen, "Glory of the Nations," 5-6.

A Proleptic Ethic for a Resurrection Community

A restorative Christian eschatology demands an ethic that signifies the comprehensive and redirective nature of the inbreaking kingdom. Already the cosmos is praising God in anticipation, even if we have not yet taken our cue to join it. Barth writes,

> All God's works . . . take part in the movement of God's self-glorification and the communication of his glory. . . . They are expressions of infinite exultation in the depth of his divine being. . . . This is their secret that will one day come out and be revealed. . . . The angels do it . . . but even the smallest creatures do it too. They do it along with us or without us. They do it also against us to shame us and instruct us. They do it because they cannot help doing it. . . . And when man accepts again his destiny in Jesus Christ in the promise and faith of the future revelation of his participation in God's glory as it is already given Him

> here and now, he is only like a late-comer slipping shamefacedly into creation's choir in heaven and earth, which has never ceased its praise, but merely suffered and sighed, as it still does, that in inconceivable folly and ingratitude its living centre man does not hear its voice . . . or rather hears it in a completely perverted way, and refuses to co-operate in the jubilation which surrounds him.[49]

Indeed, even the rocks and trees cry out in praise and in anticipation of the consummation of God's kingdom.

Creation longs for redemption. This sort of praise cannot be adequately explained by other eschatologies. A restorative eschatology explains why the rocks and trees cry out: they were created by God, are sustained in existence by the Spirit, and will one day be liberated from the bondage under which they now groan. A restorative eschatology additionally motivates us to work with the Spirit to bring all of life under submission to Christ by redirecting all our social and cultural activities toward him. Rather than embracing asceticism, we embrace the challenge of entering into the spheres of culture in order to shape them toward Christ. When Paul tells the Colossians to set their minds on the things above (Col 3:2), he is saying that the best way to do that is to take part in God's mission in this world, the very same world that Christ will one day reconcile to himself (Col 1:20). In light of that great reconciliation of all things, we have been entrusted with the ministry of reconciliation on his behalf (2 Cor 5:18). So we enter into social and cultural activity in this world as a way of obeying Christ and bearing witness to the gospel, and as a preview of the coming kingdom in which all things will be shaped by him and for him.

Disciple making. Similarly, a restorative eschatology takes seriously the responsibility to make disciples of the nations, that great missional work of the Spirit. The church's proclamation of Christ should be a proclamation of that lordship, calling the nations to come under his lordship. "This, after all, is part of the answer to the prayer that God's kingdom will come on earth as in heaven," writes N. T. Wright: "If we pray that prayer, we shouldn't be surprised if we are called upon to help bring about God's answer to it."[50]

On the basis of this indicative (his universal lordship), the Lord Christ gives an imperative: the people of God must make disciples of the nations, baptizing them in the name of the triune God and teaching them to observe

---

[49]Barth, *CD* II/1, 647-48.

[50]N. T. Wright, *Simply Jesus: A New Vision of Who He Was, What He Did, and Why He Matters* (New York: HarperOne, 2011), 207.

all his commands (Mt 28:19-20). And the testimony of Scripture as a whole resonates with Matthew's teaching about Jesus' life and teachings in portraying the godly life as one that involves both word and deed. Michael Goheen writes,

> [Jesus'] life vividly portrayed life in the kingdom: an "Abba relationship" with the Father; a life empowered by the Spirit; a deep and rich prayer life with a cry for the kingdom at its heart; a comprehensive obedience to the Father; a demanding call to justice, righteousness, joy, love, and forgiveness; an identification with the poor and marginalized; and a willingness to challenge in suffering love the idols and powers of culture.[51]

Jesus formed a community, the church, to embody and participate in his own kingdom mission, a mission that is accomplished in word and deed and that is extended to all the nations.

Creation's redemption as eucatastrophe. In an essay on fairy tales, J. R. R. Tolkien charts the difference between *dyscatastrophe* (stories ending in the triumph of sorrow) and *eucatastrophe* (stories ending in triumph out of defeat) and concludes by asking, "Which is actually the more true?" In short, because of the resurrection, it is the latter. There is such a thing as a deeply happy ending, even for a fallen world like ours, filled with pain and sorrow. To borrow a phrase from *The Lord of the Rings*, "Everything sad becomes untrue." Jesus' resurrection has not abolished happy endings; it has established them. Grace triumphs. Tolkien writes, "It does not deny the existence of *dyscatastrophe*, of sorrow and failure: the possibility of these is necessary to the joy of deliverance; it denies (in the face of much evidence, if you will) universal final defeat and in so far is *evangelium*, giving a fleeting glimpse of Joy, Joy beyond the walls of the world, poignant as grief."[52]

Conclusion

The biblical teaching about the new creation is humbling, breathtaking, exhilarating. For us it deepens in an almost painful way the fact that "although we have not seen him, we love him; and even though we do not see him now, we believe in him and rejoice with an indescribable and glorious joy" (1 Pet 1:8; adapted). At the end of times, the Lord will return, gaining a final and decisive victory over the Evil One by liberating creation from its bondage, by

[51]Michael W. Goheen, *A Light to the Nations: The Missional Church and the Biblical Story* (Grand Rapids, MI: Baker Academic, 2011), 118.

[52]J. R. R. Tolkien, *The Tolkien Reader* (New York: Ballantine, 1966), 68.

reconciling "all things" to himself (Col 1:20). This reconciliation takes the form of a renewed and restored creation, a new creation, one marked by the immediate presence of God and lighted by the Lord Christ himself. Isaiah had prophesied of this moment when he declared that light would come to the Holy City (Is 60:1), but Revelation specifies that the light is in fact the glory of Christ himself (Rev 21:23).

This Christ, to whom all authority on heaven and earth has been given, now stands at the center of the new creation, illuminating it with his radiant glory. This radiant light does not illumine some sort of ethereal new creation, devoid of physical reality or dissonant with the familiar contours of God's original creation. No, the new creation will follow the familiar contours of the old. Robert Jenson writes,

> The material of New Jerusalem's walls and streets, of the divine human community's *place*, will be jasper, sapphire, agate, emerald, onyx, carnelian, chrysolite, beryl, topaz, chrysoprase, jacinth, amethyst, pearls, and "gold, transparent as glass." [Rev 21:18-21] We are to take this information with the desperate seriousness that transcends the registering of prose. After all, will there be no jewelers or goldsmiths in the Kingdom? And will the achievement of their lives provide no matter for eternal interpretation by Jesus' love? That feast of "rich food . . . of well-aged wines strained clear," [Is 25:6] will it have no taste? Will there be no cooks or vintners in the Kingdom? Or even connoisseurs?[53]

Indeed, the new creation is a comprehensive restoration of God's original creation. But this restoration is not a mere repristination, a "going back" to Eden. In this restoration, God's grace infuses his creation, directing it toward Christ, not only healing what had been corrupted by sin, and not only redirecting what had been misdirected, but also heightening and enhancing it. The garden is now a city, led to perfection by the Spirit, reflecting the development wrought by God's image bearers, and the Lord is now immediately present to his new creation, reflecting his desire for heaven and earth to one day be present to each other.

[53]Robert W. Jenson, *Systematic Theology*, vol. 2, *The Works of God* (Oxford: Oxford University Press, 2001), 351.

CREATION AND . . .

CAVEATS ON THE IMPLICATIONS OF THE DOCTRINE OF CREATION

Oh, no single piece of our mental world is to be hermetically sealed off from the rest, and there is not a square inch in the whole domain of human existence over which Christ, who is Sovereign over all, *does not cry: "Mine!"*

Abraham Kuyper

The doctrine of creation is foundational and comprehensive. There is not an area of life it leaves untouched. In this final chapter we explore *some* of the many "creation and . . ." aspects that this doctrine opens up.

Creation and Philosophy

One of the sacred cows in the academy today is the autonomy of philosophy. Few are willing to challenge it, although we noted in chapter three how the French Catholic phenomenologists are wonderfully blurring the boundaries between philosophy and theology. Postmodernism is, however, no exception. Jacques Derrida problematized *logocentrism* but saw no alternative to it, so that one ends up sawing away at the branch one sits on—undoubtedly a very uncomfortable position, but nevertheless one that is indicative of the refusal to abandon human autonomy. Hans-Georg Gadamer similarly asserted at the Capri discussion of philosophy of religion that no matter to what extent we recognize the urgency of religion, there can be no return to the doctrines of the church.[1]

How, one might ask, does the world as creation shape our view of reason and thus of philosophy? Reason itself is a complex entity, and Peter Angeles's first reference defines reason as follows: "1. The Intellect. The capacity to

[1]Hans-Georg Gadamer, "Dialogues in Capri," in *Religion*, ed. Jacques Derrida and Gianni Vattimo, Cultural Memory in the Present (Cambridge: Polity, 1998), 207.

abstract, comprehend, relate, reflect, notice similarities and differences, etc."[2] If we work with this definition, how does the doctrine of creation relate to reason? In a myriad of ways.

First, take the issue of capacity. Alvin Plantinga's argument against evolutionary naturalism is well known.[3] Essentially it argues that if we believe in a naturalistic form of evolution, we have no basis to trust or expect that our rational capacities have evolved in order to provide true knowledge of the world. Rather, they would have evolved in order for us to survive, and there is no reason that a capacity to know the world truly should form part of that process. By comparison, the doctrine of creation and of humans in the *imago Dei* alerts us to the fact that we fit within the design of the universe and are created with the capacities for wisdom and knowledge—that is, to know the world as it is within human limits.

Second, take the issue of abstraction, which is utterly central to the practice of philosophy. Much modern philosophy is suspicious of lived experience and seeks a royal route to truth in abstraction. Leon Kass rightly notes that in modernity "science deliberately broke with ordinary human experience and gained knowledge through the mathematization of nature."[4] The problem with this is that we are embodied creatures and all abstraction emerges from lived experience, and its test is whether or not it deepens our lived experience. "Abstraction" derives from the Latin *ab* and *trahere*, meaning "to draw away from," and thus refers to "that which is regarded apart from reference to any particular object or event and which represents symbolically, conceptually, or imaginatively something not directly or concretely perceivable in experience. Examples: the abstraction (abstract concept) of redness, justice, humanity."[5] Lived experience is inescapable, and as John Polkinghorne says, for example, "Fundamental physics is abstracted from the complexity of actual experience and if the way in which this is done does not accommodate so basic a feature of human experience as the present moment, so much the worse for physics, one could say."[6]

As is well known, the history of philosophy is littered with controversy about the nature and even the very existence of universals: Do they, for

[2]Peter A. Angeles, ed., *A Dictionary of Philosophy* (San Francisco: Harper & Row, 1981), 238.

[3]See James K. Beilby, *Naturalism Defeated? Essays on Plantinga's Evolutionary Argument Against Naturalism* (Ithaca, NY: Cornell University Press, 2002).

[4]Leon R. Kass, *The Hungry Soul: Eating and the Perfecting of Our Nature* (New York: Maxwell Macmillan International, 1994), 4.

[5]Angeles, *Dictionary of Philosophy*, 2.

[6]John Polkinghorne, "The Nature of Time," in *On Space and Time*, ed. Shahn Majid (Cambridge: Cambridge University Press, 2008), 280.

example, exist independent of the mind (Aristotle), or are they constructed by the mind (conceptualism)? Are they real (nominalism)? Do they mirror reality (realism; creative antirealism)? We discussed in chapter three the different views about the origins of universals. As we argued in chapter one, the doctrine of creation implies a belief in some version of *realism*, what we are content to call a critical realism. Although we are cautious of positioning universals in the mind of God as do Augustine and Gijsbert van den Brink, the doctrine of creation does alert us to an extraordinary, intelligent (omniscient) God as the originator of our world, so that in principle the possibility is there of thinking God's thoughts after him. From this perspective one can see universals as real and not as creations of the human mind, although our attempts to articulate them are always, of course, human attempts to conceptualize the laws governing the creation.

Third, take the elements of comprehending, relating, reflecting, noticing similarities and differences, and so on. Abstraction itself always emerges from some view of the whole from which one abstracts, and this view of the whole enters strongly into any human attempts to relate, reflect, and identify similarities and differences. Many different philosophical dimensions enter in at this point: the nature of the knowing subject, the multifaceted nature of that which is to be known (subject-object relation), the place to stand (thetical point) from which we can gain a true perspective on the world or part thereof, and so on. A perennial attempt of philosophers has been to absolutize one aspect of the creation and to use it to understand the rest. The result is always a version of *reductionism* in which central aspects of the creation are marginalized and overwhelmed by this one aspect. The doctrine of creation stands as a bulwark against such reductionism. It does so in two ways.

First, it does so with its evocation of the contingency, the dependency of the creation. By the very nature of creation, God creates the space for the created order to have its own real identity in relation to God, and thus it is always tempting to imagine that the creation is fully understandable apart from God. But such attempts are what Scripture describes as folly. Wisdom, by comparison, begins with the fear of the Lord. As Gerhard von Rad has observed, Old Testament wisdom contains the poignant epistemological insight that if one goes wrong at the starting point the enterprise of knowledge is irrevocably skewed.[7] One needs to start with the fear of the Lord and to build on this foundation. At the heart of such "fear" is the recognition that we

[7]Gerhard von Rad, *Wisdom in Israel*, trans. J. D. Martin (Nashville: Abingdon, 1972).

are creatures and not the creator and that true wisdom and knowledge will only emerge from such a vantage point. The creation is not autonomous, and neither is true knowledge of it. For humans there is always a starting point from which one seeks to understand the world; if it is not the creator God, it will be some part of the creation, and this inevitably leads to reductionism, with serious and unhelpful consequences.

Second, it does so with its reminder that the creation was made "good" but that this goodness has been shattered by sin and rebellion. Already in Genesis 2 the great temptation is articulated in terms of the tree of *the knowledge* of good and evil. As Abraham Kuyper notes,[8] there is thus a real sense in which the present state of the creation is abnormal, and a central question is how we understand this abnormality and whether it affects our capacities to know, reflect, and understand. The doctrine of creation alerts us to the fact that God's order for creation impinges on all of reality, so that all humans are capable of knowing about it. We experience this on a daily basis and in the fact that non-Christians often exceed Christians in their knowledge. However, it is especially as humans move toward articulation of the relatedness of elements in the creation that one's sense of the whole exerts a profound effect.

In terms of theological epistemology, the most profound contemporary example is that of Oliver O'Donovan.[9] Creation is central to his ethics, and he develops from Galatians a heuristic of resurrection as the reaffirmation of creation. He advocates an epistemology that operates between Barth and Brunner.[10] With Brunner he acknowledges an order to creation, but with Barth he asserts we can only know the creation truly (i.e., in its relationality) in Christ. Apart from Christ, we know, but in a distorted fashion.

Bavinck similarly asserts, "Revelation, while having its centre in the Person of Christ, in its periphery extends to the uttermost ends of creation. It does not stand isolated in nature and history, does not resemble an island in the ocean, nor a drop of oil upon water. With the whole of humanity, with the family and society, with science and art it is intimately connected."[11] The world rests on revelation; indeed, the foundations of creation and redemption are the same. "The Logos who became flesh is the same by whom

---

[8]Cf. Bartholomew, *Contours of the Kuyperian Tradition*, 243-50.

[9]Oliver O'Donovan, *Resurrection and Moral Order: An Outline for Evangelical Ethics* (Leicester, UK: Apollos, 1986), 76-100.

[10]Ibid., 86-87, 90-91.

[11]Herman Bavinck, *The Philosophy of Revelation* (Grand Rapids: Baker, 1909), 27.

all things were made. The first-born from the dead is also the first-born of every creature."[12] Creation and redemption, nature and grace, go hand in hand. Yes, we can know the creation truly to a great extent, but only insofar as we are amidst that grace that restores nature.

There is, of course, much debate in theology about the noetic effects of sin, not least between Catholics and Protestants. The Catholic historian James Turner remarkably asserts, "Faith gives no *epistemological edge*."[13] A poignant insight in this respect is that of Abraham Kuyper. Referring to Ephesians 4:17-18, Kuyper develops the theme of *the darkening of the understanding*. He argues that the structure of logic is not impaired by sin but over against sin stands *love*, and love is indispensable for true knowledge:

> But, taken as a whole, standing over against the cosmos as its object, our mind feels itself isolated; the object lies outside of it, and the bond of love is wanting by which to enter into and learn to understand it. This fatal effect of sin must naturally find its deeper reason in the fact that the life harmony between us and the object has been disturbed. What once existed organically exists now consequently as foreign to each other, and this *estrangement* from the object of our knowledge is the greatest obstacle in the way to our knowledge of it.[14]

In conclusion it should be noted that, contra the mature Barth, the doctrine of creation endorses the project of philosophy and especially of Christian philosophy.[15] Barth articulated different views of philosophy in the course of his career, but in his *Church Dogmatics* he is averse to ever allowing the Christian faith to come to philosophical expression. We saw this, for example, in chapter nine with philosophy of history. L. Kalsbeek, by contrast, defines philosophy in the Reformational tradition, quoting K. J. Popma to the effect that philosophy is meant to "discern the structure of creation and to describe systematically, that is, in logical order, what is subject to that structure."[16] A cursory review will reveal that there are nearly as many definitions of philosophy as there are philosophers. That one word, *creation*, sets Kalsbeek's definition apart and transforms philosophy from an autonomous quest into

---

[12]Ibid.

[13]Mark Noll and James Turner, *The Future of Christian Learning: An Evangelical and Catholic Dialogue*, ed. Thomas A. Howard (Grand Rapids, MI: Brazos, 2008), 106.

[14]Abraham Kuyper, *Principles of Sacred Theology*, trans. J. Hendrik De Vries (Grand Rapids, MI: Baker, 1980), 111.

[15]Craig G. Bartholomew and Michael W. Goheen, *Christian Philosophy: A Systematic and Narrative Introduction* (Grand Rapids, MI: Baker Academic, 2013).

[16]L. Kalsbeek, *Contours of a Christian Philosophy: An Introduction to Herman Dooyeweerd's Thought* (Toronto: Wedge Publishing Foundation, 1975), 35.

an exhilarating, wondrous, loving exploration of the overarching structures of God's creation. In the process, all the insights of non-Christian philosophers can be appreciated and appropriated within the grand perspective of a world full of God.

Creation and the Table

Good food with good company is one of the great pleasures of life, as Ecclesiastes recognizes. Food is also essential for animate life, but the food chain in the West is one of the most damaged parts of our culture. J. H. Bavinck observes

> how often partaking of food is mentioned in the Gospels. . . . *Eating is a sacrament: it indicates our affinity to the earth, and by eating we confess our unity with the earth.* When Christ on several occasions after his resurrection ate meals in the company of his disciples, it is a clear indication that he still belonged to this world, that he maintained connection to this world and that he embraced it.[17]

If we take *sacrament* in its common meaning as "a means of grace," then this is certainly true. Kass rightly points out, "Compared to wisdom eating may be a humble subject, but it is no trivial matter. It is the first and most urgent activity of all animal and human life: We are only because we eat."[18] And that we eat, and have food to eat, is a gift, a grace. The emphasis on food as a gift appears first in Genesis 1:29-30, God's final statement before he declares everything "very good" (Gen 1:31). Intriguingly, the plants and fruit are given first to humankind as food *and then* also to animals and birds. As Kass notes, "Animal need is met by the (at least partial) hospitality of the world. . . . The world's original receptivity, in a sense re-enacted for every new organism that sees the light of day, is itself unexplained, a given—and, to all that lives, an unmerited gift."[19] Wirzba observes that, theologically, eating and food are "best understood in terms of God's own Trinitarian life of gift and sacrifice, hospitality and communion, care and celebration."[20]

---

[17]Johan H. Bavinck, *Between the Beginning and the End: A Radical Kingdom Vision*, trans. Bert Hielema (Grand Rapids, MI: Eerdmans, 2014), 122-23; emphasis added.

[18]Kass, *Hungry Soul*, 2.

[19]Ibid., 46-47.

[20]Norman Wirzba, *Food and Faith: A Theology of Eating* (New York: Cambridge University Press, 2011), xi. Eating and death are not as closely linked, in our view, as Wirzba (ibid., 110) suggests: "Eating is the daily reminder of creaturely mortality." That might be true post-fall, but it is certainly not true pre-fall.

Ellen Davis draws our attention to the focus on plants, and in particular seeds, in Genesis 1:1–2:3.[21] Days one and two establish the base rhythm of the opening salvo of the Bible, and then in this dense narrative on day three (Gen 1:9-13) the language slows down to emphasize "vegetation," "plants yielding seed," "fruit trees of every kind . . . that bear fruit with the seed in it." Unusually in Genesis 1, this language is repeated in the fulfillment of God's command. Davis notes that with its emphasis on the variety and fruitfulness of plants Genesis 1 evokes the land of Israel, which, in terms of its genetic heritage, "is one of the nutritional centers of the whole earth, both for human beings and for animals."[22] "The single factor that most effectively conduced first to food storage and then to the invention of cultivation was the very thing that Genesis 1 celebrates: seed—specifically, readily harvestable, nutritious seed."[23] In the Hebrew "plants yielding seed" reads literally "plants seeding seed." The emphasis on seeds celebrates the fruitfulness of the earth as experienced by the Israelites. This language of plants "seeding seed" occurs again in Genesis 1:29, making the fruitfulness of the earth and thus food a central theme of Genesis 1:1–2:3.

Indeed, it is intriguing how central food is to Scripture. The catastrophe of Genesis 3 revolves around food, and so too does the messianic banquet embodied in the Lord's Supper.[24] In both these cases food is richly symbolic, but it can be so only because Scripture takes food seriously and literally as part of God's good creation. Food shares in the contingency and giftedness of the creation, as is evident in the Lord's Prayer: "Give us today our daily bread." Food is a gift of our "Father in heaven."

The verses in Genesis 1 discussed above also alert us to the fact that humans and animals are portrayed as *vegetarian*. It is only in Genesis 9:3 that humans are also given "every moving thing that lives" as food, with the proviso that the blood of animals is not to be eaten. This appears to be an accommodation to sin, but still the emphasis on food as a gift (cf. Gen 9:3, "I give you everything") is to the fore.

If Genesis 1 provides support for vegetarianism, it also leads us deeply into issues of origins and of anthropology.[25] We cannot pursue such issues here;

[21]Ellen F. Davis, *Scripture, Culture, and Agriculture: An Agrarian Reading of the Bible* (New York: Cambridge University Press, 2009), 48-53.

[22]Ibid., 49.

[23]Ibid., 50.

[24]On the Eucharist and food, see Wirzba, *Food and Faith*, 123-78.

[25]On theology and vegetarianism, see Stephen H. Webb, *Good Eating*, The Christian Practice of Everyday Life (Grand Rapids, MI: Brazos, 2001); David Grumett and Rachel Muers, *Theology on*

suffice it to note that among anthropologists there is disagreement as to whether humans were originally vegetarian.[26] Writing on Genesis 1, Kass does note that "keeping to this diet would disturb almost not at all the order of creation."[27] The giving of all animals as food to Noah changes in Leviticus with certain types of animals forbidden as food. In the New Testament, Jesus has important things to say about cleanness and uncleanness, and in Acts 10 the dietary laws of Israel are revoked through Peter's dream (cf. Acts 15), but intriguingly not with a return to Genesis 1 but with a return to what was permitted to Noah. It remains an open question as to whether humans will be vegetarians in the new heavens and the new earth.[28] In our view they will, as shalom is secured for all the creation.

There is far more about food in the Bible than we can pursue here. In *Scripture, Culture, and Agriculture*, Davis opens a fertile dialogue with the new agrarians, and Wendell Berry in particular, a dialogue that illumines many largely unexplored aspects of the Old Testament.[29] She reads the manna in Exodus, for example, as inculcating among the Israelites a very different approach to *eating* compared to the industrial food economy of the Egyptians; she examines the theme of inheritance in Deuteronomy for its insights on land ownership; and she finds in Song of Songs the resources for an integrated vision of urban and rural life. Indeed, Davis's book is peppered with fresh insights as she rereads Old Testament texts from an agrarian perspective. It is intriguing and instructive to see how Davis's close readings regularly foreground creation and God's good order for creation as fundamental to land care and food. Indeed, it is because the *creator* God is at work in *Israel* that precisely in their particularity *Israel's* Scriptures provide a vision for the world that is explosively relevant today.

Old Testament Wisdom literature also contains a great deal about food. In the so-called *carpe diem* passages in Ecclesiastes, for example, eating is central.

---

the Menu: Asceticism, Meat, and Christian Diet (New York: Routledge, 2010); Grumett and Muers, eds., *Eating and Believing: Interdisciplinary Perspectives on Vegetarianism and Theology* (London: T&T Clark, 2008).

[26]Cf. Kass, *Hungry Soul*, 84-85.

[27]Ibid., 206.

[28]Cf. Wirzba, *Food and Faith*, 211-34, on "Eating in Heaven?" In our view (cf. chap. 10) it is far better and more biblical to see the telos of creation as the new heavens *and earth* rather than as "heaven." This implies that we will eat, as does the resurrected Jesus, but possibly not meat, although the resurrected Jesus ate fish.

[29]Cf. Nathan MacDonald, *Not Bread Alone: The Uses of Food in the Old Testament* (Oxford: Oxford University Press, 2008); *What Did the Ancient Israelites Eat? Diet in Biblical Times* (Grand Rapids, MI: Eerdmans, 2008).

If the minority opinion is correct[30] and Qohelet does resolve his crisis of meaning by the end of his journey, then retrospectively all the areas he explored are viewed as meaningful through the starting point and lens of fearing God as creator. The *carpe diem* passages are not the voice of despairing hedonism but the voice of a believing Israelite who cannot deny the goodness of creation, including eating and feasting. The tension in Ecclesiastes is between this view and the (Greek) view of meaning based entirely on reason, experience, and observation, with its constant ending in *hăbēl hăbālîm* ("enigma of enigmas" [Bartholomew's translation]). Resolution allows the believing view to triumph without detracting from the brokenness of the creation. In the process viticulture, gardening, cultivation, farming, feasting, eating, and drinking are all affirmed.

Proverbs and Job also have an important contribution to make toward a theology of food, also grounded in the doctrine of creation. In Proverbs wisdom is embodied climactically in the Proverbs 31 valiant woman who "brings her food from far away," "provides food for her household," and engages in viticulture. We have elsewhere noted the importance of the divine speeches in Job for a theology of creation. Suffice it here to note their emphasis on Yahweh making the ground "put forth grass" (Job 38:27) and of his provision of food for the animals (Job 38:39-41).

Davis has an excellent chapter on Leviticus, titled "A Wholesome Materiality: Reading Leviticus," in which she focuses on Leviticus 19 in particular.[31] Another important element in Leviticus, which Davis and others have attended to, is the dietary laws.[32] Many have tried to penetrate the logic behind these laws, but none entirely successfully, and in our view Kass is right to note that the human person, standing upright, "stands tallest when he freely bows his head," so that "the dietary laws, like the Creation they memorialize and the world we inhabit, will never be wholly transparent to reason."[33]

Nevertheless, biblical and anthropological studies have helped us grasp elements of the function of these unusual laws. The theology of separating/dividing occurs in Genesis 1 and in Leviticus 11, thereby grounding the dietary laws in creation order. In Kass's language they embody a sanctified or holy

[30]Cf. Craig G. Bartholomew, *Ecclesiastes*, Baker Commentary on the Old Testament Wisdom and Psalms (Grand Rapids, MI: Baker Academic, 2009).

[31]Davis, *Scripture, Culture, and Agriculture*, 80-100.

[32]See, e.g., ibid., 94-100; Mary Douglas, *Leviticus as Literature* (Oxford: Oxford University Press, 1999); Gordon J. Wenham, *The Book of Leviticus*, NICOT (Grand Rapids, MI: Eerdmans, 1979); Kass, *Hungry Soul*, 195-225; Wirzba, *Food and Faith*, 116-23.

[33]Kass, *Hungry Soul*, 224-25.

view of eating and thereby manifest a true worldview.[34] Such a worldview is rooted in creation order; acknowledges the problematic nature of eating, which requires restraint;[35] and celebrates the ultimate source of food—namely, God. They thus "commemorate the Creation and the Creator and beckon us towards holiness."[36]

Kass makes the perceptive point that the expulsion from the garden involves a move from eating fruit and plants to *bread* (Gen 3:19).[37] Such development in agriculture is normative but also affected by the fall and sin.[38] Bread is a common theme in the New Testament and takes us back to where we started this section, with Jesus' habit of sharing meals and providing them. The nature miracles, such as feeding large crowds, reveal much about the identity of Jesus; like the God of Genesis 1, he has the power and goodness to provide the gift of food.

The issue of food became a problem in the church in Corinth and is one of the issues Paul addresses in 1 Corinthians 10. The New Testament data on food, much of which we cannot attend to here, must be read against the background of the Old Testament, a background that enables us to really hear Paul when he exhorts us in 1 Corinthians 10:31, "So, whether *you eat or drink*, or whatever you do, do everything for the glory of God." The way in which we handle food, how we eat and drink, manifests our worldview, and nothing less than the glory of God is at stake in this respect. Humans are called to live in and develop the creation such that God's glory is enhanced, and that includes the food chain, as should be clear from our discussion above. Kass provides a beautiful example of this in terms of hospitality offered to strangers (cf. Gen 18:1-8): "In their acts of generosity hosts imitate and improve on the hospitality—albeit only partial—of nature, which 'provides' us with food and not because we merit it."[39]

Alas, this is an area in which the church is overwhelmingly found wanting.[40] Christians remain largely unaware of the importance of these issues and thus tend to support the abusive practices that are so pervasive in our industrial economies. As Wendell Berry notes, "Christian organizations, to this day,

---

[34]Ibid., 196.

[35]Wirzba (*Food and Faith*, 1) notes that "death is eating's steadfast accomplice."

[36]Kass, *Hungry Soul*, 198.

[37]Ibid., 211. On bread, see ibid., 120-25; Wirzba, *Food and Faith*, 12-18.

[38]Cf. Craig G. Bartholomew, *Where Mortals Dwell: A Christian View of Place for Today* (Grand Rapids, MI: Baker Academic, 2011).

[39]Kass, *Hungry Soul*, 100-107, here 106.

[40]Cf. Wirzba, *Food and Faith*, 1-34, 71-109.

remain largely indifferent to the rape and plunder of the world and of its traditional cultures. . . . The certified Christian seems just as likely as anyone else to join the military-industrial conspiracy to murder Creation."[41] Berry rightly asserts that our destruction of nature is "the most horrid blasphemy."[42] He notes that such practices are not biblical and says, "Our predicament now, I believe, requires us to learn to read and understand the Bible in the light of the present fact of Creation."[43] He asserts that, biblically speaking, "we are holy creatures living among other holy creatures in a world that is holy," and poignantly asks, "How can modern Christianity have so solemnly folded its hands while so much of the work of God was and is being destroyed?"[44] A major answer is the eclipse of creation in far too much Christian thought and practice. Few authors have alerted us to our present predicament in relation to food production and eating as has Wendell Berry.[45] However, the literature on the abuse of land, animals, plants, and food is extensive and, rightly, profoundly disturbing.

Whereas eating is an agricultural act, we have become mere consumers, what Berry calls "the industrial eater." This specialization of the act of eating has a vested interest in concealing from us the production process. As Berry notes, "It would not do for the consumer to know that the hamburger she is eating came from a steer who spent much of his life standing deep in his own excrement in a feedlot, helping to pollute the local streams, or that the calf that yielded the veal cutlet on her plate spent its life in a box in which it did not have room to turn around."[46] Far from such consumption being liberating, it enslaves us. An urgent need is a politics of food that involves our freedom and that of the animals we eat; an aesthetics of food; an ethics of food; and, we would add, a theology of food.

Berry is, however, no killjoy; he is concerned to help us recover "the pleasures of eating":[47] "Like industrial sex, industrial eating has become a degraded, poor, and paltry thing."[48] He pleads for an extensive pleasure of eating: "Eating with the fullest pleasure—pleasure, that is, that does not

[41]Wendell Berry, *Sex, Economy, Freedom and Community: Eight Essays* (New York: Pantheon, 1993), 94.
[42]Ibid., 98.
[43]Ibid., 94-95.
[44]Ibid., 99.
[45]See his many works, including *What Are People For?* (New York: North Point, 1990); *Bringing It to the Table: On Farming and Food* (Berkeley, CA: Counterpoint, 2009).
[46]Berry, *Bringing It to the Table*, 230.
[47]Berry, *What Are People For?*, 145-52.
[48]Ibid., 147.

depend on ignorance—is perhaps the profoundest enactment of our connection with the world. In this pleasure we experience and celebrate our dependence and our gratitude, for we are living with mystery, from creatures we did not make and powers we cannot comprehend."[49] The challenge of corporate food production often feels so overwhelming as to be totally disempowering. Berry, however, proposes multiple things we can do to start to glorify God in what and how we eat, actions such as preparing our own food and learning about food production and the food economy.[50]

J. H. Bavinck reminds us that "the church must stand in that world as a vital force. She may never—not even for a moment—abandon the world to its own devices. Rather, she must see the entire world as the territory where God intends to build his kingdom."[51] Similarly, Bonhoeffer asserts that this is what we do to the world that inflicts so much suffering on us: "we call it back to God, we give it hope, we lay our hands on it and say: may God's blessing come upon you, may God renew you; be blessed world created by God, you who belong to your Creator and Redeemer."[52] One way to do this is to recover practices of eating and drinking informed by a robust doctrine of creation.[53]

Creation and Time

Time and place are two fundamental constituents of life. Jean-Yves Lacoste perceptively observes, "If it is true that we cannot know who we are without asking where we are, it is just as true . . . that we cannot shed light on ourselves without interpreting the time that is the horizon of our being, and without interpreting our relation to time."[54] For both place and time, the doctrine of creation is central if they are to be understood. Craig has discussed the role of creation in a theology and philosophy of place in his *Where Mortals Dwell*, and thus we will attend here to "when" mortals dwell. John Polkinghorne notes the difficulties of thinking about time: "There are certainly subtleties

---

[49]Ibid., 152.

[50]Berry, *Bringing It to the Table*, 232.

[51]Bavinck, *Beginning and the End*, 124.

[52]Dietrich Bonhoeffer, *Conspiracy and Imprisonment: 1940–1945*, ed. Lisa E. Dahill and Mark S. Brocker, Dietrich Bonhoeffer Works 16 (Minneapolis: Augsburg Fortress, 2004), 632.

[53]There is a growing number of examples of good practice. One is Joel Salatin's Polyface Farm. See Michael Pollan, *The Omnivore's Dilemma: A Natural History of Four Meals* (New York: Penguin, 2006); Joel Salatin, *Folks, This Ain't Normal: A Farmer's Advice for Happier Hens, Healthier People, and a Better World* (New York: Center Street, 2011).

[54]Jean-Yves Lacoste, *Experience and the Absolute: Disputed Questions in the Humanity of Man*, trans. Mark Raftery-Skehan (New York: Fordham University Press, 2004), 82.

about the nature of space, which go beyond the expectations of everyday thought, but they are nothing like as perplexing as those we encounter when we attempt to think about the nature of time."[55] Augustine says in his *Confessions* that he knows what time is until he is asked to explain it![56] However, as Paul Ricoeur notes in his classic *Time and Narrative*, "A constant thesis of this book will be that speculation on time is an inconclusive rumination to which *narrative activity* alone can respond."[57]

Genesis 1 is fundamental in this respect, and as we noted in chapter four, Genesis 1:1–2:3 *is narrative*. Time comes to the fore immediately with the first word in the Hebrew—namely, בְּרֵאשִׁית, "in the beginning." However, this is a mysterious temporal expression since it ushers in the existence of time itself, as is evident from Genesis 1:5, the creation of the first day. The rhythm of days that structures this opening narrative of the Bible alerts us to the fact that time, like place, is *created*, contra Newton, for example, who argued that time is absolute and eternal.[58] Genesis 1 establishes the day and the week as constituent elements of time but also refers to the lights in the sky for *signs and seasons*. In the Exodus version of the Decalogue the Sabbath commandment connects a rhythm of work and rest to God's working and resting in Genesis 1:1–2:3. In this way, from the outset time is presented as fundamentally *good*, a vital constituent in the creation.

In the twentieth century much was made of the comparison between Greek time as cyclical and Hebrew/biblical time as linear. Critical engagement with this view has rightly nuanced it.[59] Genesis 1 alerts us to the cyclical nature of time: days, weeks, and seasons. At the same time Genesis, with its groundbreaking opening in verse 1 and its *toledoth* "generations/history of" literary structure, alerts us to the overarching linearity of time, or what we more precisely call history.

In this way it is precisely a narrative biblical theology of the Bible that helps us develop a biblical view of time and history. The genres apart from narrative

---

[55]Polkinghorne, "Nature of Time," 278.

[56]Augustine, *Confessions* 11, 15. On Augustine and time, see Paul Ricoeur, *Time and Narrative*, trans. Kathleen McLaughlin and David Pellauer, vol. 1 (Chicago: University of Chicago Press, 1984), chap. 1.

[57]Ricoeur, *Time and Narrative*, 1:6; emphasis added.

[58]Isaac Newton, *The Mathematical Principles of Natural Philosophy*, trans. Andrew Motte (New York: Daniel Adee, 1846), 77; Robert Rynasiewicz, "Newton's Views on Space, Time, and Motion," The Stanford Encyclopedia of Philosophy (Summer 2014 Edition), ed. Edward N. Zalta, https://plato.stanford.edu/entries/newton-stm/.

[59]Cf. Arnaldo Momigliano, *Essays in Ancient and Modern Historiography* (Chicago: University of Chicago Press, 1977), 179-204.

in the Old Testament are canonically all connected into the grand story it tells, beginning with Genesis 1:1, so that narrative holds the key to a biblical perspective on time. R. A. Herrera writes,

> The foundational charter of the philosophy of history is found in one biblical verse: "God, at the beginning of time, created heaven and earth." . . . This text, as traditionally interpreted, shattered the pagan conception of an eternal universe parceled out in an infinity of cycles. . . . The doctrine of creation entailing linear time opened a vast horizon of novel events that took history beyond the limits of the ancient chroniclers. Even Herodotus . . . was imprisoned in a circle.[60]

This implication of Genesis 1:1 is even clearer when the whole of Scripture is taken into account, especially the eschatology of the New Testament. Biblically, time is both cyclical and linear. In Ecclesiastes, Qohelet struggles with both of these aspects of time in relation to the meaningfulness of life. In his poem in Ecclesiastes 1 he cynically observes the cyclical nature of life, whereas in the major poem on time in Ecclesiastes 3 he affirms the positive role of time but then goes on to note that God has placed "eternity" in our hearts but that we cannot know the broader metanarrative we need in order to live meaningfully.[61] Qohelet had only the intimations of the grand story of Scripture, but we have the fuller revelation in Christ, and this provides the grand story within which it is possible to live and to discern what is fitting and wise in time.[62]

O'Donovan notes that "world and self are co-present only in the moment of time which is open to us for action." He says of the "young man," "Time lies before him as his way through the world lies before him; time and world are co-involved, so that as he approaches the one he approaches the other. Time lies behind him too, but of that he need say nothing, since what interests him is how to begin. Time before him is not determined, as time behind him is determined."[63] In his reflection on *present time* O'Donovan asserts, "The opening of the present is to the future, but not equally to the whole of the future but to the future immediately before us, the next moment into which we may venture our living and acting, the moment which presents itself as a possibility. . . . The only time of *practical* immediacy is this future moment

---

[60] R. A. Herrera, *Reasons for Our Rhymes: An Inquiry into the Philosophy of History* (Grand Rapids, MI: Eerdmans, 2001), 13.

[61] Craig G. Bartholomew, *Ecclesiastes*, Baker Commentary on the Old Testament Wisdom and Psalms (Grand Rapids, MI: Baker Academic, 2009).

[62] See Bartholomew and Goheen, *Drama of Scripture*.

[63] Oliver O'Donovan, *Self, World and Time*, vol. 1, *Ethics as Theology* (Grand Rapids, MI: Eerdmans, 2013), 15.

offered to present wakefulness."[64] O'Donovan poses the question of how the absolute future of the kingdom influences the present, and rightly notes that it draws near and thereby introduces *hope* to deliberation. This, of course, was the very thing that Qohelet struggled so hard to find.

One of the major theological reflections on time is that of Barth.[65] He observes that time "is the form of our existence. To be man is to live in time."[66] In terms reminiscent of Ecclesiastes, Barth acknowledges that time can confront us as a monstrous enigma.[67] Time is a "given"; it is part of our *creaturely* condition. But for Barth it becomes a monstrous enigma as a result of our alienation from God and thus from ourselves. For Barth, we can only come to terms with time when we recognize God as creator: "What emerges . . . is that man is not God, but a needy creature of God. . . . To say 'man' or 'time' is first and basically, even if unwillingly and unwittingly, to say 'God.' For God is for man as He has time for him. It is God who gives him his time. . . . Time as the form of human existence is always in itself and as such a silent but persistent song of praise to God."[68] The key to time is, for Barth, "the will and act of God."[69] Above all we find this in Christ, who, through his resurrection from the dead, breaks open the grave and reveals definitively that death is not the end.

Barth, like O'Donovan, discusses time as present, past, and future. The loss entailed in "the past" can be profoundly disturbing, and two unhelpful ways of responding to this are by seeking to re-create it in memory[70] or by relegating it to oblivion. For Barth, the problem of the past is only resolved in relation to God. Of the past he says, "Because God was then, its reality and fullness cannot be taken away by the fact that it has gone."[71] And so it is with the future: "We can count on the fact that the will and act of God are the meaning and ground not only of our being in time generally but also of our being in the future."[72]

---

[64]Ibid., 15-16.

[65]Barth, *CD* III/2, §47. Titled "Man in His Time," this section is over two hundred pages long.

[66]Barth, *CD* III/2, 521.

[67]Barth, *CD* III/2, 515.

[68]Barth, *CD* III/2, 525.

[69]Barth, *CD* III/2, 527. The indispensability of relating time to God as Creator is underscored in Barth's emphatic statement, "We understood time and our being in time as real by considering it as the form of human existence willed and created by God. We thus purged the concept of time from all the abstractions by which it is inevitably confused and darkened when the divine will and action are left out of account and time is not understood as His creation" (*CD* III/2, 551).

[70]Barth defines memory in this context as "an attempt to restore to the past the duration and extension which it obviously does not have any longer" (*CD* III/2, 534).

[71]Barth, *CD* III/2, 537.

[72]Barth, *CD* III/2, 545.

The importance of understanding history as the move from creation through fall to redemption and re-creation enables us to see the terror in the recovery of the doctrine of eternal recurrence and of the historicism we find in postmodernism. "The Eternal Recurrence is hardly a panacea. It is a 'terrifying vision' which moves in the opposite direction and serves only to consolidate the power of time."[73] Furthermore, as Brian Ingraffia demonstrates, Nietzsche's critique rests on an incorrect understanding of Christianity's view of time and history.[74]

Nietzsche's doctrine of eternal recurrence is closely related to *historicism*, the view that all is afloat in time and change without any all-embracing creation order. As Herrera notes, eternal recurrence, Nietzsche's "mightiest thought,"[75] attempts to deny Being and to deify Becoming: "The Eternal Recurrence is a serious attempt to authenticate, and perhaps even deify, Becoming. Following in the steps of Heraclitus, Nietzsche proposed that Being, presumed to exist behind the mask of Becoming, is merely an illusion."[76]

Historicism means that everything is adrift and that there are no sure guides to how to live or how to know what is fitting at any particular time. As O'Donovan notes in relation to marriage,

> A historicist account . . . must argue that this "natural good" is not given transhistorically in nature at all, but is the product of cultural development peculiar to a certain time and place. . . . By making marriage an item of cultural history in this way, historicism necessarily raises a question about it. . . . Historicism makes all created goods appear putatively outmoded. So that if there are currents of dissatisfaction evident in a society's practice of marriage, such as might be indicated by a high divorce rate or a prominent homosexual culture, they will be treated with great seriousness as signs of the evolution for which the institution is destined.[77]

In our view Scripture portrays God as outside time and certainly not as subject to it in the ways that creatures are. At the same time Scripture rejects any form of deism and depicts God as immanently involved in his creation, accompanying it as it unfolds and ruling over it. In terms of God's

---

[73]Herrera, *Reasons for Our Rhymes*, 172. On Nietzsche's philosophy of history, see ibid., chap. 11.

[74]Brian D. Ingraffia, *Postmodern Theory and Biblical Theology: Vanquishing God's Shadow* (Cambridge: Cambridge University Press, 1995), 19-100.

[75]Karl Jaspers, *Nietzsche: An Introduction to the Understanding of His Philosophical Activity*, trans. Charles F. Wallraff and Frederick J. Schmitz (Baltimore and London: Johns Hopkins University Press, 1965), 357-58.

[76]Herrera, *Reasons for Our Rhymes*, 145.

[77]O'Donovan, *Resurrection and Moral Order*, 69-70.

omniscience, we reject the view that even God does not know the future, while retaining a real emphasis on human responsibility and creaturely freedom to act.

Creation and Science

Much modern discussion about creation revolves around the controversy between Christianity and science, and in particular between creation and evolution. In our theology of creation, we have deliberately *not* allowed current debates to set our agenda, lest we skew a comprehensive theology of creation from the outset. Nevertheless, as Pannenberg says, "If theologians want to conceive of God as the creator of the real world, they cannot possibly bypass the scientific description of that world."[78]

In our opening chapter we observed that the doctrine of creation commits one to some form of critical *realism*. This has important consequences for science. Creation teaches us that the world has a discernable shape and that humans as image bearers are equipped by the Creator to explore the creation and to discover truth about it—in other words, to practice science. Here again we remind readers of Alvin Plantinga's argument against evolutionary naturalism. Human analytical capacities and language fit with the grain of the universe so that Christianity carries with it an immense openness to science and its benefits. As Wolters notes,

> An implication of the revelation of God in creation is that the creation order is *knowable*. That is also the significance of the *call* of Wisdom to all—she appeals to everyone to pay attention and learn from her, for insight and understanding are genuinely available to them if they heed her. This fundamental knowability of the creation order is the basis of all human understanding, both in science and everyday life.[79]

There is more to the emergence of modern science than the Christian tradition, but, as has often been noted, the Christian worldview played a fundamental part in its emergence. C. S. Lewis pointed out: "Men became scientific because they expected Law in Nature, and they expected Law in Nature because they believed in a Legislator."[80] Science requires belief in a world that is knowable and in the human capacity to know it. Both these

---

[78]Wolfhart Pannenberg, *Systematic Theology*, trans. Geoffrey W. Bromiley (Grand Rapids, MI: Eerdmans, 1994), 2:33.

[79]Albert Wolters, *Creation Regained: Biblical Basics for a Reformational Worldview*, 2nd ed. (Grand Rapids, MI: Eerdmans, 2005), 33.

[80]C. S. Lewis, *Miracles* (Glasgow: Geoffrey Bles, 1947), 140.

beliefs are provided in the West by the Christian tradition. Take time, for example, discussed above. The doctrine of creation alerts us to the fact that time is real and, contra Kant, not something that the human mind imposes on the matrix of experience. Thus time, with all its mystery, is real and "out there" to be explored and analyzed by humans.

The reference to the call of wisdom and to Job 28 above, however, also move the focus back onto a *critical* realism. The Old Testament is adamant that wisdom and knowledge must begin with and find their foundation on the fear of Yahweh. The starting point is not the journey, so that Newbigin is right to speak of Christ as "the clue to all that is."[81] The clue needs to be pursued, but nevertheless it is *the* clue, and we will skew our acquisition of knowledge if we ignore this clue.

This connects us back into our opening discussion of creation and philosophy. Just as the autonomy of philosophy is widely taken for granted today, so too is the *autonomy of science*, but less so than used to be the case. Alan Chalmers asserts,

> Modern developments in the philosophy of science have pinpointed and stressed deep-seated difficulties associated with the idea that science rests on a sure foundation acquired through observation and experiment and with the idea that there is some kind of inference procedure that enables us to derive scientific theories from such a base in a reliable way. *There is just no method that enables scientific theories to be proven true or even probably true.*[82]

Correlating the results of science with theology without taking close account of the metaphysics involved simply will not do lest we end up synthesizing alternative and contradictory worldviews. Awareness of the vital role of philosophy *in* science also foregrounds the question of religion in science.

In our view we need to take seriously that poignant insight of biblical wisdom that knowledge is shaped by one's starting point and the starting point is irretrievably religious, in one way or another. Indeed, it was the sort of insight that we find in Old Testament wisdom that led Abraham Kuyper to speak of two types of science, believing and unbelieving. Kuyper uses "science" in the European sense of *Wissenschaft*, but, allowing for our narrower use, his points remain valid. For Kuyper, God "created us as logical beings in order

---

[81]Lesslie Newbigin, *The Light Has Come: An Exposition of the Fourth Gospel* (Grand Rapids, MI: Eerdmans, 1982), 1-11.

[82]Alan F. Chalmers, *What Is This Thing Called Science? An Assessment of the Nature and Status of Science and Its Methods*, 2nd ed. (Milton Keynes, UK: Open University Press, 1982), xvi; emphasis added.

that we should trace his Λογος, investigate it, publish it, personally wonder at it, and fill others with wonder. This too proclaims the glory of his name."[83] Scholarship requires *humility*: "Genius of genuine gold, as Fichte put it so beautifully, does not know its own beauty. Real talent has the fragrance of a flower without being aware of it."[84] It also requires *faith*: "And scholars, far from being able to do without that faith, must begin by being rich in that faith if they are ever able to feel their heart stir with the holy impulse that drives them to engage in true scholarship."[85] Kuyper appeals for scholarship done out of prayer and before the face of God. He is keenly alert to the secularization that scholarship was undergoing in his day, but stresses that even this "derailed science brings gain" and rightly argues that secularization is no excuse for Christians to abandon the world of scholarship.

An honest acknowledgment of differing worldviews in relation to science and creation is found in E. O. Wilson's moving *The Creation: An Appeal to Save the Earth*. The entire book is set within the context of a letter, an appeal to a Southern Baptist pastor. Indeed, the book as a whole is an appeal for Christians and other believers to work with secular scientists such as Wilson in preserving and caring for the "creation," which is under threat from many sides. This is an appeal, we suggest, that Kuyper, were he alive today, would have responded to with full seriousness. Wilson notes the power of religion and science today and argues that "if religion and science could be united on the common ground of biological conservation, the problem would soon be solved."[86] He confesses, "Dear Pastor, what I fear most is the pervasive combination of religious and secular ideology of a kind that sees little or no harm in the destruction of the Creation."[87] Few things would enable Christians to see the importance of such cooperation as the recovery of a robust doctrine of creation, the aim of this book.

Kuyper acknowledges the delight in seeking for knowledge but is clear that the aim is *to find*, and to find *truth*. Kuyper unashamedly acknowledges the Reformed common starting point of the Vrije Universiteit (Free University): "We inhabit the Reformed house bequeathed to us by our forebears and that is where we carry on our lives. If that is called unscientific,

[83]Abraham Kuyper, *Scholarship: Two Convocation Addresses on University Life*, trans. Harry van Dyke (Grand Rapids, MI: Christian's Library Press, 2014), 8.

[84]Ibid., 11.

[85]Ibid., 12-13.

[86]Edward O. Wilson, *The Creation: An Appeal to Save Life on Earth* (New York: Norton, 2006), 5.

[87]Ibid., 82.

then notice how those who label us with that stigma factually do the same thing, only on less solid grounds."[88] Kuyper is right to stress the fact that he openly acknowledges this, whereas in mainstream scholarship to this day the worldview informing it is often unacknowledged or unconscious. Carl Sagan, for example, begins his bestseller *Cosmos* with this bald statement: "The Cosmos is all that is or ever was or ever will be."[89] Like Alvin Plantinga, Kuyper finds it absurd that we would do scholarship without the truth revealed to us, if indeed we really believe it to be the truth. He advises us to stop seeking if God reveals to us what we were seeking: "To continue searching when someone else brings you what you are looking for is contrary to everything that is reasonable, and what is unreasonable should not be called scientific."[90] The questions and answers Kuyper has in mind here are the basic worldview questions such as the nature of prime reality, what is wrong with the world, who rules this world, and so on.

In terms of the construction of theories that are integral to science, Kuyper's insights have been developed for our day by philosophers such as Nicholas Wolterstorff and Roy Clouser.[91] In different ways both authors demonstrate that religious beliefs shape theory construction and that Christians should engage their beliefs fully in the scientific process.

What form might this take in practice? With his incisive mind and lucid style, Alvin Plantinga has made several penetrating forays into the thorny issue of the relationship between Christianity and science, and in particular with evolution.[92] In his "When Faith and Reason Clash: Evolution and the Bible," Plantinga takes note of historical approaches to the antagonism between faith and reason and concludes, "We must do our best to apprehend both the teachings of Scripture and the deliverances of reason; in either case we will have much more warrant for some apparent teachings than for others."[93] In the medieval era, controversy centered around astronomy; today

[88]Kuyper, *Scholarship*, 35.

[89]Carl Sagan, *Cosmos* (New York: Ballantine Books, 1980), 1.

[90]Kuyper, *Scholarship*, 36.

[91]Nicholas Wolterstorff, *Reason Within the Bounds of Religion*, 2nd ed. (Grand Rapids, MI: Eerdmans, 1984), and Roy Clouser, *The Myth of Religious Neutrality: An Essay on the Hidden Role of Religious Beliefs in Theories* (Notre Dame, IN: University of Notre Dame Press, 1991).

[92]Plantinga has made several forays into this debate. Most recently, see his "Science and Religion: Why Does the Debate Continue?," in *The Religion and Science Debate*, ed. Harold W. Attridge (New Haven: Yale University Press, 2009), 93-123; *Where the Conflict Really Lies: Science, Religion, and Naturalism* (New York: Oxford University Press, 2011).

[93]Alvin Plantinga, *When Faith and Reason Clash: Evolution and the Bible* (Ancaster, ON: Redeemer University College, 1991), 14. Also published in *Christian Scholar's Review* 21, no. 1 (1991): 8-32.

the battleground is biology. We are all familiar with the polarization that science-faith discussions generate, and a vital contribution of Plantinga's is the nuance he brings to such debate. For example, when it comes to evolution, Plantinga helpfully points out that some elements in the Christian view of creation—and in evolutionary theory—are more probable or clearly true than are others. In descending order of clarity:

- As we have seen in this volume, it is most clear that God created the heavens and the earth, so that everything depends for its existence on him.
- Next clearest is that there was a first couple whose rebellion against God had catastrophic consequences.
- Far less clear is that the earth is young, whereas, in Plantinga's opinion, an old earth has strong scientific support, making it probable.

A tendency in modernity is to see science as the royal route to truth about everything. However, as Plantinga notes, "Science is one thing; the claim that it is enough is a wholly different thing. It is not part of science to make that claim."[94] Plantinga is keenly attentive to the broader matrix within which scientific theories such as evolution function, and he rightly observes that the theory of evolution as it is often articulated is not religiously neutral.[95] He identifies three contemporary Western approaches to reality: (1) perennial naturalism, for which nature is all there is with humans as a part of nature; (2) Enlightenment humanism/subjectivism/antirealism, whose creative antirealism he traces back to Immanuel Kant and which sees humans and not God as the authors of the structures of our world; and (3) Christian theism. All three are *religious* views, and there is a lot at stake in terms of which view we embrace: "This is a battle for men's souls." Indeed, the religious dimension at work in these views enables us to understand why the debates are so often acerbic; especially in the academy the theory of evolution has become "an idol of the contemporary tribe"[96] through which we understand ourselves and our world. As Dawkins notes, it is evolution that enables one to be a fulfilled atheist.[97]

Plantinga articulates five or six theses that constitute the grand evolutionary story:[98]

---

[94]Plantinga, "Science and Religion," 102.

[95]Plantinga, "When Faith and Reason Clash," 16.

[96]Ibid., 17.

[97]Ibid., 17-18.

[98]In "Science and Religion," 104-5, he adds the thesis of "Descent with Modification."

1. The ancient-earth thesis, which claims that the earth is billions of years old.
2. The progress thesis, according to which life has progressed from relatively simple to relatively complex forms.
3. The common-ancestry thesis, according to which life originated at only one place on earth; all subsequent life descends from these original living creatures.
4. Darwinism, according to which the mechanism of evolution is natural selection operating through random genetic mutation.
5. The naturalistic-origins thesis, according to which life developed from nonliving matter without any guidance from God.

The nuance in Plantinga's evaluation of these theses—the scientific evidence for them varies—is admirable. The evidence for the first is very strong; that for the second less so; while the fifth is, in the main, "mere arrogant bluster."[99]

Stephen Jay Gould provides three arguments in support of the fourth thesis: (1) observational evidence; (2) homologies (common ancestry explains why a rat runs, a bat flies, a porpoise swims, and we type at our laptops, all with structures of the same bones); and (3) the fossil record.[100] Of the first, Plantinga acknowledges that there is persuasive evidence for microevolution; a more complex issue is whether or not we can expand this to macroevolution. The problem with fossils is that they show few transitional forms. The argument from homologies is suggestive but far from conclusive. Universal common descent is possible but not certain. Plantinga refers to the mammalian eye in this respect:

> And here is the problem: how does the lens, e.g., get developed by the proposed means—e.g., random genetic variation and natural selection—when at the same time there has to be development of the optic nerve, the relevant muscles, the retina, the rods and cones, and many other delicate and complicated structures, all of which have to be adjusted to each other in such a way that they can work together? . . . Imagine starting with a population of animals without eyes, and trace through the space in question all the paths that lead from this form to forms with eyes.[101]

To explain such a process through random mutation, a high number of variables is required, and we don't know what they are. Biologically we cannot even be sure whether such development is possible.

---

[99]Plantinga, "When Faith and Reason Clash," 20.
[100]Stephen Jay Gould, *Ontogeny and Phylogeny* (Cambridge, MA: Belknap, 1977).
[101]Plantinga, "Faith and Reason," 25.

The assurance with which evolution is embraced and assumed nowadays is an exaggeration. A problem is that for a nontheist it appears to be the only viable theory. Certainly, from a *naturalistic* perspective evolution will be more probable than the alternatives. But, as Plantinga has so ably demonstrated, a naturalistic perspective is far from unproblematic. Plantinga has developed the compelling argument that accepting both metaphysical naturalism—only natural objects, kinds, and properties are real—*and* evolution is self-defeating.[102] If natural selection governs an unguided process of evolution, then there is no reason why our cognitive abilities should be reliable when it comes to knowing the world.

In his "Science and Religion: Why the Debate Continues," Plantinga makes the question of the guidance of evolution definitive: "This confusion between Darwinism and unguided Darwinism is a crucial cause of the continuing debate. Darwinism, the scientific theory, is compatible with theism and theistic religion; unguided Darwinism, a consequence of naturalism, is incompatible with theism but is not entailed by scientific theory. It is instead a metaphysical or theological add-on."[103] If the nontheist only has one game in town, an advantage of the theist is that there are several options when it comes to origins. The Christian knows that God is the creator but has flexibility in terms of how God brought about this creation. Plantinga is rightly cautious of the semideistic approach some Christians embrace in their acceptance of theistic evolution:

> It is important to remember, however, that the Lord has not merely left the Cosmos to develop according to an initial creation and an initial set of physical laws. According to Scripture he has often intervened in the workings of his cosmos. . . . Towering above all, there is the unthinkable gift of salvation for humankind by way of the life, death, and resurrection of Jesus Christ, his son. . . . There is therefore no initial edge to the idea that he would be more likely to have created life in all its variety in the broadly deistic way.[104]

The idea that God created humankind and many plants and animals separately and specially is more probable than the common ancestry view.

Given, therefore, that one's knowledge is always shaped by one's starting point, that the starting point is necessarily religious, and that Christian Scripture is revelatory of God's work in the world, it should therefore be

---

[102]Alvin Plantinga, *Warranted Christian Belief* (New York: Oxford University Press, 2000).
[103]Plantinga, "Science and Religion," 116.
[104]Plantinga, "Faith and Reason," 22.

unsurprising that scientific theories that reject that revelation will be flawed. Consider Darwin's claims that the totality of life is the product of evolution and that natural selection is the engine for it. These claims, taken together within the context of Darwin's metanarrative, are diametrically opposed to the biblical teaching that God created the world directly, designed and normed it, and guides and governs it. Thus, it is unsurprising that the scientific community increasingly rejects Darwinism and Neo-Darwinism on account of the failure of any scientist ever to observe "natural selection" producing anything new or complex;[105] the failure of the fossil record to reflect Darwin's predictions;[106] the lack of a successful materialistic theory for the origin of life;[107] the fact that consciousness cannot be reduced to merely physical phenomena;[108] and recent studies demonstrating the irreducible complexity[109] and self-regulative and auto-corrective capabilities of living cells.[110] Although Darwin is right that there is such a thing as biological change over time, that birds' beaks can adapt, or that viruses can mutate, it is a wild overreach to conclude that such evolution could evolve a monkey into a man or could do so randomly through such a process as natural selection. Thus, we agree that "there is *some* empirical support for the notion of *some* variation of species in natural history, but there is little or no support for the Darwinian model which claims to provide an all-encompassing naturalistic explanation."[111] The best of emerging science agrees with the historical and biblical teaching that God created the world from nothing, designed it, and guides and governs it through natural processes.

How then should Christian intellectuals contribute to this debate? More than anything, we need to do sophisticated cultural analysis and theistic science. Modern science is not religiously neutral, and we need to test the spirits of our age no matter how prestigious or acclaimed are those spirits. In addition to such cultural analysis, we need answers to the question of origins

---

[105]Michael Behe, *Darwin Devolves: The New Science About DNA That Challenges Evolution* (San Francisco: HarperOne, 2019).

[106]Stephen Jay Gould, "Is a New and General Theory of Evolution Emerging?," *Paleobiology* 6, no. 1 (1980): 119-30.

[107]Paul Davies, *The Fifth Miracle: The Search for the Origin and Meaning of Life* (New York: Simon & Schuster, 1999), 123-33.

[108]Thomas Nagel, *Mind and Cosmos: Why the Materialist Neo-Darwinian Conception of Nature Is Almost Certainly False* (New York: Oxford University Press, 2012).

[109]Michael Behe, *Darwin's Black Box: The Biochemical Challenge to Evolution*, 2nd ed. (New York: Free Press, 2006).

[110]James A. Shapiro, *Evolution: A View from the 21st Century* (Upper Saddle River, NJ: FT Press, 2011).

[111]Kenneth D. Keathley and Mark F. Rooker, *40 Questions About Creation and Evolution* (Grand Rapids: Kregel, 2014), 375.

from the perspective of *all* we know, with our faith fully engaged. Such work, says Plantinga, "is worthy of the very best we can muster; it demands powerful, patient, unstinting and tireless effort but its rewards match its demands; it is exciting, absorbing and crucially important. Most of all, however, it needs to be done. I therefore commend it to you."[112] In our view there is a great need for such work among Christians today, rigorous work done from a Christian vantage point, taking into full account contemporary discoveries and contributing to the broader scientific community.

Creation and the Self

The West, as we argued in chapter eight, is in the midst of a historically unprecedented attempt to sever society and culture from its roots in Christianity. As sociology Philip Rieff describes it, many of the West's cultural power brokers wish to sever "social order" from "sacred order."[113] Indeed, although all civilizations historically have recognized that sacred order shapes culture and that culture, in turn, shapes society, many of the West's elite cultural brokers have conspired to sever social order from its traditional religious and moral ordering, leaving social order to float on its own. The consequences of this desacralization, Rieff avers, are disastrous. Bereft of a transcendent religious and moral ordering, cultural institutions and products become "deathworks"; instead of bringing life and vitality to society, they bring death and decay.

Moreover, as philosopher Charles Taylor argues in *A Secular Age*, this move toward desacralization brings with it existential consequences, for Christian and non-Christian alike. As Westerners have learned to manage life from within the "immanent frame," historic Christianity—and especially the Christian ethic—has become increasingly implausible and even unimaginable.[114] Whereas all societies heretofore have justified their moral codes with reference to a transcendent source, the modern West is left with self-authorized morality.[115] Thus, in public debate about matters of social and political import, Western citizens cannot articulate why "the other" should submit to their moral code. Taylor refers to this as the "extraordinary inarticulacy of modern

---

[112]Plantinga, "Faith and Reason," 31.

[113]Philip Rieff, *My Life Among the Deathworks: Illustrations of the Aesthetics of Authority*, ed. Kenneth S. Piver, Sacred Order/Social Order 1 (Charlottesville: University of Virginia Press, 2006), 1-44.

[114]Charles Taylor, *A Secular Age* (Cambridge, MA: Belknap Press, 2007), 83.

[115]Ibid., 580-89.

culture," and it leaves Westerners in a situation in which all we can do is decry and deride one another.[116]

In our opinion, there are few examples more illustrative of the West's desacralization—and its attendant moral disorientation and polarization—than the emerging ideologies of transgenderism and transhumanism. Seeking to re-create the self, both of these ideologies arise from within the immanent frame, flout creation order, and seek a salvation independent of God. Moreover, both phenomena are socially and politically polarizing, with transgenderism especially playing a central role in American public policy debates.

Transgenderism, as an ideology, holds that a person can be born into the body of the wrong sex and can be transformed into the other sex through gender reassignment surgery and/or hormone therapy. Such a transition is not only possible, transgender ideologues argue, but morally laudable. Thus, in terms of public policy, it is argued that the government should ensure access to public bathrooms that match the trans person's self-authorized gender identity, mandatory instruction about the biological possibility and moral plausibility of undergoing gender reassignment, government assistance in gender reassignment surgery and therapy, and laws punishing citizens who "misgender" a trans person.

In response to transgender ideology, we must first recognize the difference between gender dysphoria and transgender ideology. Gender dysphoria is the psychological stress that occurs when a person experiences a conflict between their biological sex and the gender with which they identify. But a person who suffers from gender dysphoria does not necessarily identify as transgender, as "transgender" refers to the desire to act on the dysphoria by switching genders or otherwise modifying or expanding gender identity.

Having distinguished dysphoria from ideology, we must recognize transgenderism as deeply incoherent. As Ryan T. Anderson details, it is a gnostic denigration of the material body that nonetheless insists that a trans person must transform his or her body in order to be whole; it says gender is an artificial construct even while relating authentic gender identity to certain stereotypical activities and characteristics; it is radically individualist and subjective in arguing that people can re-create themselves but espouses a radically authoritarian social agenda that would force others to conform to transgender dogma.[117]

---

[116]Charles Taylor, *The Malaise of Modernity* (Toronto: House of Anansi, 1991), 18.

[117]Ryan T. Anderson, *When Harry Became Sally: Responding to the Transgender Moment* (New York: Encounter Books, 2018), 45-48.

Furthermore, we must recognize transgenderism as being opposed to historic and biblical Christianity. Indeed, the Bible's first significant teaching about humankind is that God created us in his image and likeness as male and female (Gen 1:27). His creation of humanity is the culmination of his creative acts, with the distinction between male and female being essential to his design. The differences are intended by God and thus are not malleable or interchangeable. Finally, we must recognize that, as with any contested question, God is the ultimate authority; attempts to supersede his intentions for a person's gender are not only immoral but futile. A person should not, and indeed cannot, change his or her gender. Attempts to nullify or suppress God's intentions will inevitably be met not only with individual frustration and failure but also social and cultural breakdown. Individual frustration and failure can be seen, as reported by genital reconstructive surgeon Miroslav Djordjevic,[118] in the high rates of gender reversal surgeries for transgendered persons who want their genitalia back, or in the high instance of crippling depression and even suicide among transgendered persons.[119] Social, cultural, and political breakdown can be seen, for example, in contentious debates about a male-identifying-as-female person's entrance into a female locker room or competition in a female athletic competition, or in attempts to coerce citizens to understand, remember, and correctly ascribe to transgendered persons an array of newly created pronouns (e.g., ze, sie, hir, co, ev, xe, thon, they). As with any idolatrous ideology that gains ascendance, no sphere of culture will be left untouched by the advance of transgenderism.

Thus, in relation to a person suffering from gender dysphoria, the Christian calling is to love them. Such love involves recognizing that person's God-given dignity, empathizing with them, having compassion on them, and patiently entering into their lives to care for them over the long haul.[120] But love also involves telling the truth, refusing to send signals to a gender dysphoric person that God approves of them living with a gender identity different from the one he gave them at birth. An "art restoration" view, therefore, is needed. A person suffering from gender dysphoria is God's handiwork, his work of art,

---

[118]Lizette Borreli, "Transgender Surgery: Regret Rates Highest in Male-to-Female Reassignment Operations," *Newsweek*, October 3, 2017, www.newsweek.com/transgender-women-transgender-men-sex-change-sex-reassignment-surgery-676777.

[119]Lawrence S. Mayer and Paul R. McHugh, "Sexuality and Gender: Findings from the Biological, Physical, and Social Sciences," *New Atlantis* 50 (Fall 2016): 10-116.

[120]Andrew Walker, *God and the Transgender Debate* (London: The Good Book Company, 2017), 93-106.

and our counsel to that person should be restorative, rather than annihilative, of God's design. Moreover, in relation to transgender ideology, the Christian calling is to engage it compassionately and critically, not only politically but in every sphere of culture. As Anderson urges, we need networks of clinicians who can provide therapy in line with God's design; we need scholars and physicians who will inform the public about the deleterious effects of gender transitions; we need lawyers and politicians who understand what is at stake and who have the courage to act; we need citizens who work to speak intelligently and persuasively on the issue.[121] Indeed, as Johns Hopkins psychiatrist Paul McHugh declares, "Gird up your loins if you would confront this matter. Hell hath no fury like a vested interest masquerading as a moral principle."[122]

Like transgenderism, transhumanism seeks to re-create the self but is focused on augmenting human intelligence and strength, and on increasing humanity's length of life and breadth of experience, by technological means. In *The Transhumanist Reader*, Max More summarizes transhumanism as a philosophy that emphasizes, and is optimistic about, perpetual self-transformation and self-progress through the use of intelligent technology, an open society, personal autonomy, and rational thought.[123] Similarly, Jacob Shatzer writes, "If we had to boil transhumanism down to two features, they would be an optimism regarding the possibility of radically altering human nature via technology and belief in a fundamental right of an individual to use technologies for that purpose."[124] Closely related is posthumanism. Posthumanism argues that humans are evolving toward a new stage of existence facilitated by our interaction with, and augmentation by, technology. Transhumanism aims to achieve that next level by developing the necessary theoretical and methodological pathways. Transhumanists envision a number of pathways toward self-expansion and self-transformation, including immersion in virtual reality, creation of hybronauts (merged human/technological beings), cloning of minds, and the implanting of computer chips in human brains.

In response to the transhumanism agenda, we wish to note that aspects of it subvert God's design and thus are opposed to historic, biblical Christianity. Foremost, transhumanism's demand for morphological freedom undermines

---

[121] Anderson, *When Harry Became Sally*, 205-13.

[122] Paul McHugh, "Transgenderism: A Pathogenic Meme," Public Discourse, June 10, 2015, www.thepublicdiscourse.com/2015/06/15145/.

[123] Max More, "Philosophy of Transhumanism," in *The Transhumanist Reader: Classical and Contemporary Essays on the Science, Technology, and Philosophy of the Human Future* (Malden, MA: Wiley-Blackwell, 2013), 4-5.

[124] Jacob Shatzer, *Transhumanism and the Image of God* (Downers Grove, IL: IVP Academic, 2019), 53.

the biblical teachings that humanity is created in the image and likeness of God and that we are more than our bodies.[125] The doctrine of the *imago Dei* means that we are not self-determining beings, and, coupled with God's promises, it means that our hope is not found in self-transformation. Furthermore, transhumanism's tendency to treat the mind as a mere physical brain undermines Christian teaching that the mind is more than a mere organ for information reception and analysis.

Furthermore, a not yet fully comprehensible array of negative consequences await the implementation of the transhumanist project. The drive to overcome limitations is limitless, and thus the transhumanist ideals of self-progress and self-transformation, combined with its demand for morphological freedom, bespeak a future of endless re-creation of the self. The transhumanist project cannot know, and thus has not yet developed, the sort of moral and technological safeguards that would be necessary to prevent augmentations and artificial intelligence from gaining the ability, on their own and apart from human supervision, to further extend the augmentation and artificial intelligence technology such that artificial technology and human-technology hybrids might tyrannize the human race.[126] Thus, although transhumanism is not yet at the forefront of public policy debate, we must put in the hard work to build a comprehensive evaluation of the transhumanist agenda toward the end of informing and influencing public discourse and debate to conform with God's creational and redemptive intentions.

Creation and Human Dignity

Biblical teaching on human dignity is rooted in the doctrine of creation. By creating man and woman in his image and likeness (Gen 1:26-28), God bestowed on all humanity a great dignity and a great humility. Our great dignity is that we are somehow *like* God, while our great humility is that we are *not* God. Thus, we cannot play God by lording it over other image bearers, by enslaving them, killing them, sexually abusing them, degrading them verbally, lying about them, and suchlike. Indeed, such abuse of human dignity is clearly ruled out not only by the biblical teaching on our creation in his image and likeness but also by the myriad ethical passages in the Bible, propounding in great detail the ways in which we should respect and even love our fellow man and woman.

---

[125]Ibid., 64-66.
[126]Ibid., 85.

And yet all around us, even and especially in nations influenced by the Christian faith, we experience the encroachment of a culture of death and degradation. This culture of death and degradation is, of course, as old as Cain's murder of his brother. The voice of Abel's blood crying from the ground was soon joined by millions of others, crying out from the battle grounds and lynching ropes and concentration camps and sex markets of past and present.

Moreover, among the many historical assaults on human dignity, we wish to focus on an egregious contemporary assault forged in the furnace of scientism and classical liberalism. As political scientist David T. Koyzis has shown, classical political liberalism is an idolatrous political arrangement that "offers a false salvation rooted in a fundamentally religious assertion of human autonomy against external authority."[127] Moreover, as political philosopher Pierre Manent argues, our inordinate love for personal autonomy is paired with an inordinate regard for science in the public domain. "*Our societies are organized for and by science and liberty.* This is a *fact* and is, I believe, the main tenet of our present world."[128] Together, these twin idolatries foster a humanity that arrogates to itself the great authority of being "*the sovereign author, in fact and by right, of the human world.* He is and ought to be its author."[129] Indeed, democratic liberalism in its late stages of development has determined to organize the world as it wishes instead of as God designed.

Nowhere is this more evident than in the legalization of abortion-on-demand in the United States. In the aftermath of *Roe v. Wade* (1973), Americans have drawn on modern technology and their claim to moral autonomy to shed the innocent blood of more than sixty million babies, a death toll higher than that of the twentieth century's world wars combined. As Harvard law professor Mary Ann Glendon has written, "There is growing awareness that the moral ecology of the country has suffered something like an environmental disaster, and that we are faced with a very complicated cleanup operation."[130] Not only does an unborn human being in the womb have far less legal protection than an endangered species of bird, and not only does

[127]David T. Koyzis, *Political Visions and Illusions: A Survey and Christian Critique of Contemporary Political Ideologies*, 2nd ed. (Downers Grove, IL: IVP Academic, 2019), 62.

[128]Pierre Manent, *A World Beyond Politics? A Defense of the Nation-State* (Princeton, NJ: Princeton University Press, 2006), 1.

[129]Ibid., 3.

[130]Mary Ann Glendon, "The Women of Roe v. Wade," *First Things* 134 (June 2003): 20.

the unborn baby suffer great pain during the abortive procedure, but all of society suffers in the process. The existence of abortion mills harms women by further enabling men to be sexual predators evading any responsibility for their predation; harms families by communicating that it is acceptable to use lethal violence when confronted with an inconvenience; harms America's claim to be a law-governed society by communicating that there is an entire class of human beings—unborn beings—who have no guarantee of justice or equality; and numbs society's collective conscience via the linguistic deception involved in referring to the unborn being as the "products of conception." To add insult to injury, the Supreme Court, in order to justify the legalization of abortion, treats the unborn being as the "personalty" (a legal term referring to moveable property) of the mother. Indeed, in one of the greatest and most tragic ironies in Western history, many Americans expressed remorse in the 1960s for its founding sin of treating black Americans as chattel property, only to turn around in the 1970s and classify unborn Americans as chattel property.

In response to the culture of death fostered by legalized abortion, we reaffirm humanity's creation in the image and likeness of God. Even in the case of an unwanted pregnancy, fathers and mothers must recognize that their unborn progeny is endowed with the great *dignity* of being created in God's image. And the parents must also exhibit the *humility* involved in recognizing that they—the parents—are *not* God and thus do not have the right to take innocent life. Moreover, we reaffirm God's promises in the gospel:

> The gospel speaks a healing word to the millions of men and women who have abortion as part of *their* story. To women who have walked through abortion, the gospel tells of a Son who died to liberate us from residual guilt. To men who approved of or pressured others into an abortion, the gospel tells of a Father who, rather than crushing us when we deserved it, allowed his heart to be crushed as he extended his arms of love to us. And to doctors whose hands have been employed in abortive procedures, the gospel introduces a Great Physician who offers eternal life, even for those who have caused temporal death.[131]

Thus, in recognition of humanity's creation in the image of God, and out of love for God and neighbor, it is incumbent on the Christian community to strive in word and deed to counteract the culture of death so that every being—unborn or born—will be protected by law and welcomed in life.

---

[131]Bruce Riley Ashford, *Letters to an American Christian* (Nashville: B&H, 2018), 83.

Conclusion

Apart from the doctrine of God, there is no doctrine as comprehensive as the doctrine of creation, and we could expand this chapter exponentially to deal with a great range of subjects. In conclusion we return to where we began, with Erich Auerbach's discussion of the temptation and betrayal of Peter.[132] Approaching the world as creation changes everything, and that includes our experience of everyday life. A major service of this doctrine is to open our eyes to see that in which we are already immersed, so that even as our eyes turn outward they will turn upward with an overwhelming sense of the glory of God and of the glory to come. The doctrine of creation is ultimately one of profound hope. Creation groans amidst the stations of the cross; indeed, "this suffering of creation can only be unveiled to the gaze of faith itself and could never be established by a physical consideration."[133] As Jean-Louis Chrétien says, "God's daylight is brighter and more ample than the candle of our hope. But we must nevertheless hold this candle straight and firm, which is the act of patience and perseverance."[134] We will often find ourselves living the long nights of Holy Saturday, as indeed we have done finalizing this book during the coronavirus pandemic, but always with the assurance that Resurrection Sunday follows, when creation shall find its goal in Christ:

> The kingdom of the world has become the kingdom of our Lord
> and of his Messiah,
> and he will reign for ever and ever. (Rev 11:15)

Veni, Creator Spiritus!

[132]Auerbach, *Mimesis*, 24-76.

[133]Jean-Louis Chrétien, *Under the Gaze of the Bible*, trans. John Marson Dunaway (New York: Fordham University Press, 2015), 82.

[134]Ibid., 84.

APPENDIX

CONTOURS OF MISSIONAL NEO-CALVINISM

MICHAEL GOHEEN AND CRAIG BARTHOLOMEW

1. We begin with Jesus the Lord Christ, and this focus opens up into a full trinitarian faith.
2. Christ is rendered to us truly in Scripture, which is fully trustworthy as God's Word.
3. Christ stands at the center of the biblical story, and the good news he proclaims is about the kingdom as the goal of history—God is restoring his rule over the whole of human life and all of creation.
4. Since Christ has revealed and accomplished the end of history, the Scriptures have a storied shape, and as such they tell the true story of the whole world.
5. A central theme in the biblical story is God's election of a people to embody the kingdom, to be a preview of the goal of history, and thus to bear witness to Christ's rule over all of life in life, deed, and word—this constitutes mission.
6. The comprehensive gospel of the kingdom has been narrowed and consigned to a very minor, private place within the dominant Western humanist worldview, and this calls for a conscious articulation of a biblical worldview in relation to the cultural worldview to enable the church to recover the public truth and all-embracing scope of the good news.
7. The good news is a message concerning the restoration of the creation, including human life, from sin, and thus a biblical worldview insists on a comprehensive and integrated understanding of creation, fall, and restoration as the most basic categories of the biblical story.
8. The fundamental backdrop of God's drama of restoration is creation, and thus we embrace a rich doctrine of creation, including its good and dynamic creation order and humanity's place within it.

9. God's order for creation unfolds in history, and thus we affirm the historical development or differentiation of creation.
10. The implication of the fall is that the power of sin and evil now radically twists every part of creation, individual and communal human life, and cultural development. While the structures of society remain good, the distorting power of sin means they have been radically misdirected.
11. The Bible tells the story of restoration centered and accomplished in the death and resurrection of Jesus the Christ, which is the recovery of God's originally good purposes for the whole of his creation and all of human life.
12. The outpouring of the Spirit brings a foretaste of God's renewing power into history.
13. The church is the community that is gathered to Christ in repentance and faith for the forgiveness of sins, based on the substitutionary work of Jesus on the cross, and so have begun to taste that comprehensive salvation with the call to make known Christ's forgiveness and renewing power in life, word, and deed across the whole spectrum of human life.
14. The local congregation plays a central role in God's story as that place where God's renewing power is at work to form and nurture a faithful kingdom community.
15. Since God's restorative power is at work in the creation by the Spirit, and since the forces of evil remain powerfully at work in the creation, we recognize an ultimate religious conflict for the whole of human life that will often lead to suffering. The church is called to side with the kingdom of God and participate in God's redemptive mission—the *missio Dei*—as witnesses to his victory. But since we await the final victory, there is no room for triumphalism.
16. The mission of God's people must be rooted in a communal life centered in the gospel, and also in a vibrant spirituality of worship, prayer, and thanksgiving.
17. God is at work leading his creation to its destiny of a new heavens and a new earth, and only then will the kingdom finally come. Then the whole of human life and the creation will be restored and renewed from sin and its consequences.

BIBLIOGRAPHY

Adams, Edward. *The Stars Will Fall from Heaven: Cosmic Catastrophe in the New Testament and Its World*. Edinburgh: T&T Clark, 2007.

Adams, Nicholas. *Habermas and Theology*. Cambridge: Cambridge University Press, 2006.

Allen, Keith, and Tom Stoneham. *Causation and Modern Philosophy*. New York: Routledge, 2011.

Allen, Leslie C. *Psalms 101–150*. 2nd ed. WBC 21. Waco, TX: Word, 1983.

Allison, D. C. "Jesus and the Victory of the Apocalyptic." In *Jesus and the Restoration of Israel: A Critical Assessment of N. T. Wright's Jesus and the Victory of God*, edited by Carey C. Newman, 126-41. Downers Grove, IL: InterVarsity Press, 1999.

Althaus, Paul. *Die Letzten Dinge: Lehrbuch der Eschatologie*. 7th ed. Gütersloh: Bertelsmann, 1957.

———. *The Theology of Martin Luther*. Philadelphia: Fortress, 1966.

Altmann, Peter. *Festive Meals in Ancient Israel: Deuteronomy's Identity Politics in Their Ancient Near Eastern Context*. Beihefte zur Zeitschrift für die alttestamentliche Wissenschaft 424. New York: de Gruyter, 2011.

Anatolios, Khaled. *Athanasius: The Coherence of His Thought*. New York: Routledge, 1998.

Anderson, Clifford Blake. "Jesus and the 'Christian Worldview': A Comparative Analysis of Abraham Kuyper and Karl Barth." *Cultural Encounters* 2, no. 2 (2006): 61-80.

Anderson, Gary A. "*Creatio ex nihilo* and the Bible." In Anderson and Bockmuehl, *Creation* ex nihilo, 15-35.

Anderson, Gary A., and Markus Bockmuehl, eds. *Creation* ex nihilo*: Origins, Development, Contemporary Challenges*. Notre Dame, IN: University of Notre Dame Press, 2018.

Anderson, Ryan T. *When Harry Became Sally: Responding to the Transgender Moment*. New York: Encounter Books, 2018.

Angeles, Peter A., ed. *A Dictionary of Philosophy*. San Francisco: Harper & Row, 1981.

Aquinas, Thomas. *Commentary on the Gospel of John*. Translated by Fabian R. Larcher and James A. Weisheipl. Washington, DC: Catholic University of America Press, 2010.

———. *Summa Contra Gentiles: Book Three: Providence*. Translated by Vernon J. Bourke. South Bend, IN: University of Notre Dame Press, 1975.

———. *Summa Contra Gentiles: Book Four: Salvation*. Translated by Charles J. O'Neil. South Bend, IN: University of Notre Dame Press, 1989.

———. *Summa Theologiae*. Translated by the Fathers of the English Dominican Province. Allen, TX: Christian Classics, 1981.

———. *Summa Theologica*. Vol. 1/1. Translated by the Fathers of the English Dominican Province. New York: Cosimo Classics, 2013.

———. *Super Boethium De Trinitate*. London: Aeterna Press, 2015.

Arand, Charles P. "Luther on the Creed." *Lutheran Quarterly* 20 (2006): 1-25.

Aristotle. *Physics*. Edited by David Bostock. Translated by Robin Waterfield. Oxford: Oxford University Press, 2008.

Aron, Raymond. *The Opium of the Intellectuals*. New York: Routledge, 2001.

Ashford, Bruce Riley. *Every Square Inch: An Introduction to Cultural Engagement for Christians*. Bellingham, WA: Lexham, 2015.

———. *Letters to an American Christian*. Nashville: B&H, 2018.

———. "Tayloring Christian Politics in Our Secular Age." *Themelios* 42, no. 3 (2017): 446-51.

———. "A Theological Sickness unto Death: Philip Rieff's Prophetic Analysis of Our Secular Age." *Themelios* 43, no. 1 (2018): 34-44.

———. "Wittgenstein's Theologians: A Survey of Ludwig Wittgenstein's Impact on Theology." *JETS* 50, no. 2 (2007): 357-75.

Ashwin-Siejkowski, Piotr. *The Apostles' Creed: And Its Early Christian Context*. New York: Continuum, 2009.

Assmann, Jan. *Of God and Gods: Egypt, Israel, and the Rise of Monotheism*. Madison: University of Wisconsin Press, 2008.

———. *The Price of Monotheism*. Stanford, CA: Stanford University Press, 2009.

Athanasius. *Athanasius: Select Works and Letters*. In vol. 4 of *Nicene and Post-Nicene Fathers*, series 2, edited by Philip Schaff. New York: Cosimo Classics, 2007.

———. *On the Incarnation*. Translated by John Behr. Yonkers, NY: St. Vladimir's Seminary Press, 2011.

Audet, J. P. "La Revanche de Prométhée Ou Le Drame de La Religion et de La Culture." *Revue Biblique* 73 (1966): 5-29.

Auerbach, Erich. *Mimesis: The Representation of Reality in Western Literature*. 50th anniversary ed. Princeton, NJ: Princeton University Press, 2003.

Augustine. *The City of God*. Translated by Marcus Dods. New York: The Modern Library, 1950.

———. *City of God*. Translated by Gerald G. Walsh. Edited by Vernon J. Bourke. Garden City, NY: Image Books, 1958.

———. *City of God*. Translated by Henry Bettenson. London: Penguin, 1972.

———. *The Confession and Letters of St. Augustine, With a Sketch of His Life and Work*. Translated by Philip Schaff. Grand Rapids, MI: Eerdmans, 2001.

———. *Confessions*. Translated by R. S. Pine-Coffin. New York: Penguin, 1961.

———. *The Enchiridion on Faith, Hope, and Love*. Translated by Henry Paolucci. South Bend, IN: Regnery, 1961.

———. *On Genesis*. Translated by Edmund Hill. Edited by John E. Rotelle. Hyde Park, NY: New City Press, 2002.

———. *On the Trinity*. In vol. 3 of *The Nicene and Post-Nicene Fathers*, series 1, edited by Philip Schaff. Buffalo, NY: Christian Literature, 1887. Revised and edited for New Advent by Kevin Knight. www.newadvent.org/fathers/130104.htm.

Aune, David E. *Revelation 17–22*. WBC 52c. Waco, TX: Word, 1997.

Ballard, Robert D., and Will Hively. *The Eternal Darkness: A Personal History of Deep-Sea Exploration*. Princeton, NJ: Princeton University Press, 2002.

Ballor, Jordan J. *Covenant, Causality, and Law: A Study in the Theology of Wolfgang Musculus*. Göttingen: Vandenhoeck & Reprecht, 2012.

Balthasar, Hans Urs von. *Cosmic Liturgy: The Universe According to Maximus the Confessor*. San Francisco: Ignatius, 2003.

———. "The Fathers, the Scholastics, and Ourselves." Translated by Edward T. Oakes. *Communio* 24 (1997): 347-96.

———. *The Glory of the Lord: A Theological Aesthetics*. Vol. 3, *Studies in Theological Style: Lay Styles*. Edinburgh: T&T Clark, 1986.

Barr, James. *The Garden of Eden and the Hope of Immortality*. Minneapolis: Fortress, 1993.

Barrett, C. K. *A Commentary on the First Epistle to the Corinthians*. 7th ed. London: Black, 1983.

———. *The Gospel According to St. John: An Introduction with Commentary and Notes on the Greek Text*. 2nd ed. Philadelphia: Westminster John Knox, 1978.

Barth, Karl. *Church Dogmatics*. Edited by G. W. Bromiley and T. F. Torrance. Translated by G. W. Bromiley et al. 4 vols. Edinburgh: T&T Clark, 1958.

———. *Dogmatics in Outline*. Translated by G. T. Thomson. London: SCM Press, 1966.

———. *The Theology of Schleiermacher: Lectures at Göttingen, Winter Semester of 1923–24*. Translated by Dietrich Ritschl. Edinburgh: T&T Clark, 1982.

Barth, Karl, and Emil Brunner. *Natural Theology: Comprising "Nature and Grace" by Emil Brunner and the Reply "No!" by Karl Barth*. Translated by Peter Fraenkel. 1946. Eugene, OR: Wipf & Stock, 2002.

Bartholomew, Craig G. *Contours of the Kuyperian Tradition: A Systematic Introduction*. Downers Grove, IL: IVP Academic, 2017.

———. *Ecclesiastes*. Baker Commentary on the Old Testament Wisdom and Psalms. Grand Rapids, MI: Baker Academic, 2009.

———. "Genesis 1:2 and the Doctrine of Creation." In *Acts of Interpretation: Scripture, Theology, and Culture*, edited by Stephen A. Cummins and Jens Zimmerman, 83-99. Grand Rapids, MI: Eerdmans, 2018.

———. *The God Who Acts in History: The Significance of Sinai*. Grand Rapids, MI: Eerdmans, 2020.

———. *Introducing Biblical Hermeneutics: A Comprehensive Framework for Hearing God in Scripture*. Grand Rapids, MI: Baker Academic, 2015.

———. *Where Mortals Dwell: A Christian View of Place for Today*. Grand Rapids, MI: Baker Academic, 2011.

Bartholomew, Craig G., and Michael W. Goheen. *Christian Philosophy: A Systematic and Narrative Introduction*. Grand Rapids, MI: Baker Academic, 2013.

———. *The Drama of Scripture: Finding Our Place in the Biblical Story*. 2nd ed. Grand Rapids: Baker Academic, 2014.

Bartholomew, Craig G., and Ryan P. O'Dowd. *Old Testament Wisdom Literature: A Theological Introduction*. Downers Grove, IL: IVP Academic, 2011.

Bartholomew, Craig G., and Heath A. Thomas, eds. *A Manifesto for Theological Interpretation*. Grand Rapids, MI: Baker Academic, 2016.

———. *The Minor Prophets: A Theological Introduction*. Downers Grove, IL: IVP Academic, forthcoming.

Basil. *Letters and Select Works*. Vol. 8 of *Nicene and Post-Nicene Fathers*, series 2, edited by Philip Schaff and Henry Wace. New York: Cosimo Classics, 1895.

Bates, Matthew W. *The Birth of the Trinity: Jesus, God, and Spirit in New Testament and Early Christian Interpretations of the Old Testament*. Oxford: Oxford University Press, 2015.

Batto, Bernard F. *In the Beginning: Essays on Creation Motifs in the Ancient Near East and the Bible*. Winona Lake, IN: Eisenbrauns, 2013.

Bauckham, Richard. *Climax of Prophecy: Studies on the Book of Revelation*. Edinburgh: T&T Clark, 1993.

———. "Eschatology in the Coming of God." In *God Will Be All in All: The Eschatology of Jürgen Moltmann*, edited by Richard Bauckham, 1-34. Edinburgh: T&T Clark, 1999.

———. *Jude-2 Peter*. WBC 50. Dallas: Word, 1983.

———. "Monotheism and Christology in the Gospel of John." In *Contours of Christology in the New Testament*, edited by Richard N. Longenecker, 148-66. Grand Rapids, MI: Eerdmans, 2005.

———. *The Theology of Jürgen Moltmann*. Edinburgh: T&T Clark, 1995.

———. *The Theology of the Book of Revelation*. Cambridge: Cambridge University Press, 1993.

Bavel, Tarsicius van. "The Creator and the Integrity of Creation in the Fathers of the Church Especially in Saint Augustine." *Augustinian Studies* 21 (1990): 1-33.

Bavinck, Herman. "The Catholicity of Christianity and the Church." Translated by John Bolt. *CTJ* 27 (1992): 220-51.

———. *De Algemeene Genade*. Kampen: Zalsman, 1894.

———. *De Katholiciteit van Christendom En Kerk*. Kampen: Zalsman, 1888.

———. *The Doctrine of God*. Translated by William Hendriksen. Carlisle, PA: Banner of Truth Trust, 1977.

———. *In the Beginning: Foundations of Creation Theology*. Translated by John Vriend. Edited by John Bolt. Grand Rapids, MI: Baker, 1999.

———. *Our Reasonable Faith*. Grand Rapids, MI: Eerdmans, 1956.

———. *The Philosophy of Revelation*. Grand Rapids: Baker, 1909.

———. *Reformed Dogmatics*. Translated by J. Vriend. Edited by John Bolt. 4 vols. Grand Rapids, MI: Baker Academic, 2003–2008.

———. "Voorrede." In *Ongeloof En Révolutie: Eene Reeks van Historische Voorlezingen*, by G. Groen van Prinsterer. Kampen: J. H. Bos, 1904.

Bavinck, Johan H. *Between the Beginning and the End: A Radical Kingdom Vision*. Translated by Bert Hielema. Grand Rapids, MI: Eerdmans, 2014.

Bayer, Oswald. *A Contemporary in Dissent: Johann Georg Hamann as Radical Enlightener*. Grand Rapids, MI: Eerdmans, 2012.

———. *Freedom in Response: Lutheran Ethics; Sources and Controversies*. Translated by Jeffrey F. Cayzer. Oxford: Oxford University Press, 2007.

Beale, G. K. *The Book of Revelation: A Commentary on the Greek Text*. NIGTC. Grand Rapids, MI: Eerdmans, 1999.

———. *The Temple and the Church's Mission: A Biblical Theology of the Dwelling Place of God*. New Studies in Biblical Theology. Downers Grove, IL: InterVarsity Press, 2004.

Beauchamp, Paul. *Création et Séparation: Étude Exégétique du Chapitre Premier de La Genèse*. Paris: Desclée, 1969.

Becker, G. *Documents of Modern Literary Realism*. 2nd ed. Edited by George J. Becker. Princeton, NJ: Princeton University Press, 1967.

Begbie, Jeremy. "Creation, Christ, and Culture in Dutch Neo-Calvinism." In *Christ in Our Place: The Humanity of God in Christ for the Reconciliation of the World; Essays Presented to Professor James Torrance*, edited by Trevor A. Hart and Daniel P. Thimell, 113-32. Allison Park, PA: Pickwick, 1989.

Behe, Michael. *Darwin Devolves: The New Science About DNA That Challenges Evolution*. San Francisco: HarperOne, 2019.

———. *Darwin's Black Box: The Biochemical Challenge to Evolution*. 2nd ed. New York: Free Press, 2006.

Beilby, James K., ed. *Naturalism Defeated? Essays on Plantinga's Evolutionary Argument Against Naturalism*. Ithaca, NY: Cornell University Press, 2002.

Beiser, Frederick. *The Fate of Reason: German Philosophy from Kant to Fichte*. Cambridge, MA: Harvard University Press, 1993.

Beker, J. Christen. *Paul's Apocalyptic Theology: The Triumph of God in Life and Thought*. Philadelphia: Fortress, 1980.

Bellah, Robert N. "God and King." In *God, Truth, and Witness: Engaging Stanley Hauerwas*, edited by Reinhard Hutter and C. Rosalee Velloso da Silva, 224-35. Grand Rapids, MI: Brazos, 2005.

Bellinger, Charles K. "The Crowd Is Untruth: A Comparison of Kierkegaard and Girard." *Contagion* 3 (1996): 103-19.

Benjamin, D. C. "Stories of Adam and Eve." In *Problems in Biblical Theology: Essays in Honor of Rolf Knierim*, edited by Henry T. C. Sun, 38-58. Grand Rapids, MI: Eerdmans, 1997.

Berger, Peter L., ed. *The Desecularization of the World: The Resurgence of Religion in World Politics*. Grand Rapids, MI: Eerdmans, 1999.

———. *Far Glory: The Quest For Faith in an Age of Credulity*. New York: Anchor, 1993.

———. *A Rumor of Angels*. New York: Doubleday, 1969.

———. *The Sacred Canopy: Elements of a Sociological Theory of Religion*. New York: Knopf Doubleday, 1990.

Berger, Peter L., and Samuel Huntington, eds. *Many Globalizations: Cultural Diversity in the Contemporary World*. Oxford: Oxford University Press, 2002.

Berger, Peter L., and Thomas Luckmann. *The Social Construction of Reality: A Treatise in the Sociology of Knowledge*. New York: Knopf Doubleday, 1967.

Bergmann, Sigurd. *Creation Set Free: The Spirit as Liberator of Nature*. Translated by D. Stott. Grand Rapids, MI: Eerdmans, 2006.

Berkhof, Hendrikus. *Christ and the Powers*. Scottsdale, PA: Herald Press, 1977.

———. *The Christian Faith: An Introduction to the Study of Faith*. Translated by S. Woudstra. Grand Rapids, MI: Eerdmans, 1979.

Berkouwer, G. C. *Man: The Image of God*. Studies in Dogmatics. Grand Rapids: Eerdmans, 1962.

———. *The Providence of God*. Studies in Dogmatics. Grand Rapids, MI: Eerdmans, 1952.

———. *The Return of Christ*. Studies in Dogmatics. Grand Rapids, MI: Eerdmans, 1972.

———. *The Triumph of Grace in the Theology of Karl Barth: An Introduction and Critical Appraisal*. Translated by Harry R. Boer. Grand Rapids: Eerdmans, 1956.

Berman, Joshua A. *Inconsistency in the Torah: Ancient Literary Convention and the Limits of Source Criticism*. Oxford: Oxford University Press, 2017.

Berry, R. J. "The Research Scientist's Psalm 1." *Science and Christian Belief* 20, no. 2 (2008): 147-61. www.scienceandchristianbelief.org/serve_pdf_free.php?filename=SCB+20-2+Berry.pdf.

Berry, Wendell. *Bringing It to the Table: On Farming and Food*. Berkeley, CA: Counterpoint, 2009.

———. *The Gift of Good Land: Further Essays, Cultural and Agricultural*. San Francisco: North Point, 1986.

———. *Sex, Economy, Freedom and Community: Eight Essays*. New York: Pantheon, 1993.

———. *The Unsettling of America: Culture and Agriculture*. 3rd ed. San Francisco: Sierra Club Books, 1996.

———. *What Are People For?* New York: North Point, 1990.

———. *What Matters? Economics for a Renewed Commonwealth*. Berkeley, CA: Counterpoint, 2011.

Betz, John R. *After Enlightenment: The Post-Secular Vision of J. G. Hamann*. Oxford: Wiley-Blackwell, 2012.

Billings, J. Todd. *Calvin, Participation, and the Gift: The Activity of Believers in Union with Christ*. Oxford: Oxford University Press, 2007.

Birkhead, Tim. *The Wisdom of Birds: An Illustrated History of Ornithology*. Vancouver, BC: Greystone, 2009.

Blocher, Henri. *In the Beginning: The Opening Chapters of Genesis*. Translated by David G. Preston. Leicester, UK: Inter-Varsity Press, 1984.

Bloom, Allan. *The Closing of the American Mind: How Higher Education Has Failed Democracy and Impoverished the Souls of Today's Students*. New York: Simon & Schuster, 1987.

Blowers, Paul M. *Drama of the Divine Economy: Creator and Creation in Early Christian Theology and Piety*. Oxford: Oxford University Press, 2012.

———. *Maximus the Confessor: Jesus Christ and the Transfiguration of the World*. Oxford: Oxford University Press, 2016.

———. "Unfinished Creative Business: Maximus the Confessor, Evolutionary Theodicy, and Human Stewardship in Creation." In Meconi, *On Earth as It Is in Heaven*, 174-90.

Boersma, Hans. *Heavenly Participation: The Weaving of a Sacramental Tapestry*. Grand Rapids, MI: Eerdmans, 2011.

Boff, Leonardo. *Passion of Christ, Passion of the World*. 2nd ed. Translated by R. R. Barr. Maryknoll, NY: Orbis Books, 2001.

Böhl, Eduard. *Dogmatik: Darstellung der Christlichen Glaubenslehre auf Reformirt-Kirchlicher Grundlage*. Amersterdam: Von Scheffer, 1887.

Bonhoeffer, Dietrich. *Conspiracy and Imprisonment: 1940–1945*. Edited by Lisa E. Dahill and Mark S. Brocker. Dietrich Bonhoeffer Works 16. Minneapolis: Augsburg Fortress, 2004.

———. *Creation and Fall: A Theological Exposition of Genesis 1–3*. Translated by Douglas S. Bax. Edited by John W. De Gruchy. Dietrich Bonhoeffer Works 3. Minneapolis: Fortress, 1997.

———. *Ethics*. Translated by Eberhard Bethge. London: SCM Press, 1955.

———. *Letters and Papers from Prison*. Translated by Reginald Horace Fuller. Edited by Eberhard Bethge and Frank Clarke. 3rd ed. New York: Macmillan, 1972.

Bonner, Gerald. *Freedom and Necessity: St. Augustine's Teaching on Divine Power and Human Freedom*. Washington, DC: Catholic University of America Press, 2007.

Borreli, Lizette. "Transgender Surgery: Regret Rates Highest in Male-to-Female Reassignment Operations." *Newsweek*, October 3, 2017. www.newsweek.com/transgender-women-transgender-men-sex-change-sex-reassignment-surgery-676777.

Bouma-Prediger, Steven. *For the Beauty of the Earth: A Christian Vision for Creation Care*. 2nd ed. Grand Rapids, MI: Baker Academic, 2010.

Bouteneff, Peter C. *Beginnings: Ancient Christian Readings of the Creation Narratives*. Grand Rapids, MI: Baker Academic, 2008.

Boyce, James P. *Abstract of Systematic Theology*. Cape Coral, FL: Founders, 2006.

Braiterman, Zachary. *(God) After Auschwitz: Tradition and Change in Post-Holocaust Jewish Thought*. Princeton, NJ: Princeton University Press, 1998.

Bratt, James D. *Abraham Kuyper: Modern Calvinist, Christian Democrat*. Library of Religious Biography. Grand Rapids, MI: Eerdmans, 2013.

Bratton, Susan Power. "The Precautionary Principle and the Book of Proverbs: Towards an Ethic of Ecological Prudence in Ocean Management." *Worldviews* 7, no. 3 (2003): 252-73.

Brink, Gijsbert van den. *Almighty God: A Study of the Doctrine of Divine Omnipotence*. Kampen: Peeters, 1993.

Brink, Gijsbert van den, and Marcel Sarot, eds. *Understanding the Attributes of God*. New York: Lang, 1999.

Broad, William J. *The Universe Below: Discovering the Secrets of the Deep Sea*. Illustrations by Dimitry Schidlovsky. New York: Simon & Schuster, 1997.

Bromiley, Geoffrey W. *Introduction to the Theology of Karl Barth*. Edinburgh: T&T Clark, 2001.

Bronner, Leah. *The Stories of Elijah and Elisha*. Leiden: Brill, 1968.

Bruce, F. F. *The Acts of the Apostles: The Greek Text with Introduction and Commentary*. Grand Rapids, MI: Eerdmans, 1990.

———. *The Book of the Acts*. NICNT. Grand Rapids, MI: Eerdmans, 1988.

———. *The Books and the Parchments: How We Got Our English Bible*. 2nd ed. London: Pickering and Inglis, 1963.

———. *The Epistle to the Hebrews*. Rev. ed. NICNT. Grand Rapids, MI: Eerdmans, 1990.

Brueggemann, Walter. *Genesis*. Interpretation. Atlanta: Westminster John Knox, 1982.

Bruford, Walter Horace. *Culture and Society in Classical Weimar, 1775–1806*. Cambridge: Cambridge University Press, 1962.

Bruner, Frederick Dale. *The Gospel of John: A Commentary*. Grand Rapids, MI: Eerdmans, 2012.

Brunner, Emil. *The Christian Doctrine of Creation and Redemption*. Vol. 1 of *Dogmatics*. Translated by Olive Wyon. Philadelphia: Westminster, 1952.

———. *The Christian Doctrine of God*. Vol. 2 of *Dogmatics*. Translated by Olive Wyon. Philadelphia: Westminster Press, 1950.

———. *Eternal Hope*. Philadelphia: Westminster, 1954.

Brütsch, Charles. *Die Offenbarung Jesu Christi: Zürcher Bibelkommentare*. Zurich: Zwingli, 1970.

Buechner, Frederick. *Speak What We Feel (Not What We Ought to Say): Reflections on Literature and Faith*. New York: HarperOne, 2001.

Bultmann, Rudolf. *Jesus Christ and Mythology*. New York: Charles Scribner's Sons, 1958.

Burrell, David B. *Faith and Freedom: An Interfaith Perspective*. Malden, MA: Blackwell, 2004.

Burrell, David B., Carlo Cogliati, Janet Martin Soskice, and William R. Stoeger, eds. *Creation and the God of Abraham*. Cambridge: Cambridge University Press, 2010.

Busch, Eberhard. *The Great Passion: An Introduction to Karl Barth's Theology*. Translated by Geoffrey W. Bromiley. Edited by Darrell L. Guder and Judith J. Guder. Grand Rapids, MI: Eerdmans, 2004.

Calvin, John. *Institutes of the Christian Religion*. Translated by Ford Lewis Battles. Edited by John T. McNeill. Philadelphia: Westminster Press, 1960.

———. *Institutes of the Christian Religion*. Translated by Henry Beveridge. Peabody, MA: Hendrickson, 2008.

Campbell-Jack, Walter. "Grace Without Christ? The Doctrine of Common Grace in Dutch-American Neo-Calvinism." PhD diss., University of Edinburgh, 1992.

Canlis, Julie. *Calvin's Ladder: A Spiritual Theology of Ascent and Ascension*. Grand Rapids, MI: Eerdmans, 2010.

Caputo, John D. *The Weakness of God: A Theology of the Event*. Bloomington: Indiana University Press, 2006.

Carroll, John. *The Wreck of Western Culture: Humanism Revisited*. 2nd ed. Wilmington, DE: ISI Books, 2008.

Carson, D. A. *Christ and Culture Revisted*. Grand Rapids, MI: Eerdmans, 2008.

Carter, Craig A. *Rethinking Christ and Culture: A Post-Christendom Perspective*. Grand Rapids, MI: Brazos, 2006.

Case-Winters, Anna. *God's Power: Traditional Understandings and Contemporary Challenges*. Louisville, KY: Westminster John Knox, 1990.

Casey, Edward S. *Getting Back into Place: Toward a Renewed Understanding of the Place-World*. Bloomington: Indiana University Press, 1993.

Cassuto, Umberto. *A Commentary on the Book of Genesis*. Part 1, *From Adam to Noah (Genesis I–VI)*. Translated by Israel Abrahams. Jerusalem: Magnes, 1978.

Caussade, Jean-Pierre de. *Abandonment to Divine Providence*. Translated by E. J. Strickland. Woodstock, ON: Devoted Publishing, 2017.

Chafer, Lewis Sperry. *Major Bible Themes: 52 Vital Doctrines of the Scripture Simplified and Explained*. Rev. ed. Edited by John F. Walvoord. Grand Rapids, MI: Zondervan, 1974.

Chalmers, Alan F. *What Is This Thing Called Science? An Assessment of the Nature and Status of Science and Its Methods*. 2nd ed. Milton Keynes, UK: Open University Press, 1982.

Chang, Curtis. *Engaging Unbelief: A Captivating Strategy from Augustine and Aquinas*. Downers Grove, IL: InterVarsity Press, 2000.

Chaplin, Jonathan. "Rejecting Neutrality, Respecting Diversity: From 'Liberal Pluralism' to 'Christian Pluralism.'" *Christian Scholar's Review* 35, no. 2 (Winter 2006): 143-75.

Charles, J. Daryl, ed. *Reading Genesis 1–2: An Evangelical Conversation*. Peabody, MA: Hendrickson, 2013.

Charles, R. H. *A Critical and Exegetical Commentary on the Revelation of St. John*. Edinburgh: T&T Clark, 2001.

Chenu, Marie-Dominique. *Nature, Man, and Society in the Twelfth Century: Essays on New Theological Perspectives in the Latin West*. Edited by Jerome Taylor and Lester K. Little. Chicago: University of Chicago Press, 1968.

Childs, Brevard S. *Introduction to the Old Testament as Scripture*. Minneapolis: Fortress, 1979.

———. *Isaiah: A Commentary*. Louisville, KY: Westminster John Knox, 2001.

———. *Myth and Reality in the Old Testament*. Studies in Biblical Theology 27. London: SCM Press, 1960.

Chrétien, Jean-Louis. *The Ark of Speech*. Translated by Andrew Brown. New York: Routledge, 2004.

———. *Under the Gaze of the Bible*. Translated by John Marson Dunaway. New York: Fordham University Press, 2015.

Christensen, Eric. "The Glory of the Nations: Ethnic Culture and Identity in Biblical Perspective." PhD diss., Fuller Theological Seminary, 2011.

Chrupcała, Lesław D. *The Kingdom of God: A Bibliography of 20th Century Research*. Jerusalem: Franciscan Printing Press, 2007.

Cicero. *On Life and Death*. Translated by John Davie. Oxford: Oxford University Press, 2017.

Clark, David K. *To Know and Love God: Method for Theology*. Wheaton, IL: Crossway, 2003.

Clark, Mary T. Introduction to *An Aquinas Reader*, rev. ed., edited by Mary T. Clark, 1-29. New York: Fordham University Press, 2000.

Clarke, William Newton. *The Christian Doctrine of God*. Edinburgh: T&T Clark, 1912.

Clines, David J. A. *Job 1–20*. WBC 17. Dallas: Word, 1989.

Clouser, Roy. *The Myth of Religious Neutrality: An Essay on the Hidden Role of Religious Beliefs in Theories*. Notre Dame, IN: University of Notre Dame Press, 1991.

———. "Religious Language: A New Look at an Old Problem." In *Rationality in the Calvinian Tradition*, edited by Hendrik Hart, 395-401. Lanham, MD: University Press of America, 1983.

Cobb, John B., and David Ray Griffin. *Process Theology: An Introductory Exposition*. Philadelphia: Westminster Press, 1976.

Cockerill, Gareth L. *The Epistle to the Hebrews*. NICNT. Grand Rapids, MI: Eerdmans, 2012.

Collins, C. John. *Genesis 1–4: A Linguistic, Literary, and Theological Commentary*. Phillipsburg, NJ: Presbyterian and Reformed, 2006.

Collins, John J. *Jewish Wisdom in the Hellenistic Age*. 3rd ed. Louisville, KY: Westminster John Knox, 2011.

Conee, Earl. "The Possibility of Power Beyond Possibility." *Philosophical Perspectives* 5 (1991): 447-73.

Courtenay, William J. *Covenant and Causality in Medieval Thought: Studies in Philosophy, Theology, and Economic Practice*. London: Variorium Reprints, 1984.

Cousteau, Jacques Yves. *The Living Sea*. New York: Harper & Row, 1963.

Cousteau, Jacques, and Susan Schiefelbein. *The Human, the Orchid, and the Octopus: Exploring and Conserving Our Natural World*. New York: Bloomsbury, 2007.

Cox, Dermot. "The Desire for Oblivion in Job 3." *Studii Biblici Franciscani Liber Annus* 23 (1973): 37-49.

Cranfield, C. E. B. *A Critical and Exegetical Commentary on the Epistle to the Romans*. Vol. 1, *Introduction and Commentary on Romans I–VIII*. International Critical Commentary. London: T&T Clark, 1975.

———. *The Gospel According to St. Mark: An Introduction and Commentary*. Cambridge Greek Testament Commentaries. Cambridge: Cambridge University Press, 1959.

Crisp, Oliver. "Karl Barth on Creation." In *Karl Barth and Evangelical Theology: Convergences and Divergences*, edited by Sung Wook Chung, 77-95. Grand Rapids, MI: Baker Academic, 2006.

Crouzel, Henri. *Origen*. Translated by A. S. Worral. San Francisco: Harper & Row, 1989.

Cruise, Charles E. *Christ and Time: The Primitive Christian Conception of Time and History*. 3rd ed. Translated by Floyd V. Filson. London: SCM Press, 1962.

———. "The 'Wealth of the Nations': A Study in the Intertextuality of Isaiah 60:5, 11." *JETS* 58, no. 2 (2015): 283-97.

Daley, Brian E. *The Hope of the Early Church: A Handbook of Patristic Eschatology*. Grand Rapids, MI: Baker Academic, 2002.

Dauphinais, Michael, and Matthew Levering, eds. *Wisdom and Holiness, Science and Scholarship: Essays in Honor of Matthew L. Lamb*. Naples, FL: Sapientia, 2007.

Davids, Peter H. *The Letters of 2 Peter and Jude*. PNTC. Grand Rapids, MI: Eerdmans, 2006.

Davidson, Donald. *Inquiries into Truth and Interpretation*. Oxford: Oxford University Press, 1984.

Davies, Brian. *Aquinas*. New York: Continuum, 2002.

———. *Thomas Aquinas on God and Evil*. Oxford: Oxford University Press, 2011.

Davies, J. G. *He Ascended into Heaven: A Study in the History of Doctrine*. London: Lutterworth, 1958.

Davies, Oliver. *The Creativity of God: World, Eucharist, and Reason*. Cambridge: Cambridge University Press, 2004.

Davies, Paul. *The Fifth Miracle: The Search for the Origin and Meaning of Life*. New York: Simon & Schuster, 1999.

Davis, Ellen F. *Scripture, Culture, and Agriculture: An Agrarian Reading of the Bible*. New York: Cambridge University Press, 2009.

Davis, Stephen T., ed. *Encountering Evil: Live Options in Theodicy*. Louisville, KY: John Knox Press, 1981.

———. "Free Will and Evil." In Davis, *Encountering Evil*, 69-82.

Day, John N. *God's Conflict with the Dragon and the Sea: Echoes of a Canaanite Myth in the Old Testament*. Cambridge: Cambridge University Press, 1985.

Day, Peggy L. *An Adversary in Heaven: Śāṭān in the Hebrew Bible*. Harvard Semitic Monographs 43. Atlanta: Scholars Press, 1988.

DeFranza, Megan K. *Sex Difference in Christian Theology*. Grand Rapids, MI: Eerdmans, 2015.

Del Noce, Augusto. *The Crisis of Modernity*. Montreal: McGill-Queen's University Press, 2014.

Delitzsch, Franz. *A New Commentary on Genesis*. Vol. 1. Translated by Sophia Taylor. Eugene, OR: Wipf & Stock, 2001.

Derrida, Jacques. *Of Grammatology*. Translated by Gayatri Chakravorty Spivak. Baltimore: Johns Hopkins University Press, 1998.

Descartes, René. "Meditations." In *Readings in Modern Philosophy*, vol. 1, *Descartes, Spinoza, Leibniz and Associated Texts*, edited by Roger Ariew and Eric Watkins, 22-55. Indianapolis: Hackett, 2000.

———. *Meditations on First Philosophy: With Selections from the Objections and Replies*. Cambridge: Cambridge University Press, 1986.

DeWitt, Calvin B. *Song of a Scientist: The Harmony of God-Soaked Creation*. Grand Rapids, MI: Square Inch, 2012.

Dodaro, Robert. *Christ and the Just Society in the Thought of Augustine*. Cambridge: Cambridge University Press, 2004.

Dooyeweerd, Herman. *In the Twilight of Western Thought: Studies in the Pretended Autonomy of Philosophical Thought*. Nutley, NJ: Craig Press, 1975.

———. *A New Critique of Theoretical Thought*. Translated by William S. Young and H. De Jongste. Vol. 3–4, *The Structures of Individuality of Temporal Reality*. Collected Works of Herman Dooyeweerd. Jordan Station, ON: Paideia, 1984.

———. *Roots of Western Culture: Pagan, Secular, and Christian Options*. Translated by John Kraay. Collected Works, series B, vol. 15. Ancaster, ON: Paideia, 2012.

Doran, Robert. "Literary History and the Sublime in Erich Auerbach's 'Mimesis.'" *New Literary History* 38, no. 2 (2007): 353-69.

Dorner, Isaak August. *Divine Immutability*. Fortress Texts in Modern Theology. Minneapolis: Augsburg Fortress, 1994.

Douglas, Mary. *Leviticus as Literature*. Oxford: Oxford University Press, 1999.

———. *Purity and Danger: An Analysis of Concepts of Pollution and Taboo*. London: Routledge, 1996.

Duhem, Pierre. *Le Système du Monde: Histoire des Doctrines Cosmologiques de Platon à Copernic*. Paris: Hermann Press, 1913–1959.

Dumbrell, William J. *Creation and Covenant: An Old Testament Covenant Theology*. 2nd ed. Milton Keynes, UK: Paternoster, 2013.

———. *The End of the Beginning: Revelation 21–22 and the Old Testament*. Eugene, OR: Wipf & Stock, 2001.

Dunham, Scott A. *The Trinity and Creation in Augustine: An Ecological Analysis*. Albany: State University of New York Press, 2009.

Dunn, James D G. *Romans 1–8*. WBC 38a. Grand Rapids: Zondervan, 1988.

Dupré, Louis. *Passage to Modernity: An Essay in the Hermeneutics of Nature and Culture*. New Haven, CT: Yale University Press, 1993.

Dyrness, William A. *Reformed Theology and Visual Culture: The Protestant Imagination from Calvin to Edwards*. Cambridge: Cambridge University Press, 2004.

Edwards, Jonathan. *The Works of Jonathan Edwards*. Vol. 2. Edited by Sereno E. Dwight and Edward Hickman. Carlisle, PA: Banner of Truth Trust, 1974.

Eliade, Mircea. *The Myth of the Eternal Return*. Princeton, NJ: Princeton University Press, 2005.

Elliott, Mark. *Providence: A Biblical, Historical, and Theological Account*. Grand Rapids, MI: Baker Academic, 2020.

Ellis, Earle. *History and Interpretation in New Testament Perspective*. Atlanta: Society of Biblical Literature, 2001.

Erhardt, Arnold. *The Framework of the New Testament Stories*. Cambridge, MA: Harvard University Press, 1964.

Evans, Donald. *The Logic of Self-Involvement*. London: SCM Press, 1963.

Fagan, Brian. *The Intimate Bond: How Amimals Shaped Human History*. London: Bloomsbury, 2016.

Falque, Emmanuel. *God, the Flesh, and the Other: From Irenaeus to Duns Scotus*. Translated by William C. Hackett. Evanston, IL: Northwestern University Press, 2015.

———. *The Metamorphosis of Finitude: An Essay on Birth and Resurrection*. Translated by George Hughes. New York: Fordham University Press, 2012.

Fantino, Jacques, and Raymond Berriot. *L' Homme, Image de Dieu, Chez Saint Irénée de Lyon*. Paris: Cerf, 1986.

Farley, Benjamin Wirt. *The Providence of God*. Grand Rapids, MI: Revell, 1988.

Farrow, Douglas. *Ascension and Ecclesia: On the Significance of the Doctrine of the Ascension for Ecclesiology and Christian Cosmology*. Grand Rapids, MI: Eerdmans, 1999.

———. "St. Irenaeus of Lyons: The Church and the West." *Pro Ecclesia* 4, no. 3 (1995): 333-55.

Fea, John. *Why Study History? Reflecting on the Importance of the Past*. Grand Rapids, MI: Baker Academic, 2013.

Fergusson, David. *The Providence of God: A Polyphonic Approach*. Current Issues in Theology. Cambridge: Cambridge University Press, 2018.

Feuillet, A. *Johannine Studies*. New York: Alba House, 1964.

Fiedorowicz, H. "General Introduction." In Augustine, *On Genesis*, by Augustine, trans. Edmund Hill, ed. John E. Rotelle, 13-22. Hyde Park, NY: New City Press, 2002.

Finger, Thomas N. *A Contemporary Anabaptist Theology: Biblical, Historical, Constructive*. Downers Grove, IL: InterVarsity Press, 2004.

Fishbane, Michael A. *Biblical Interpretation in Ancient Israel*. New York: Oxford University Press, 1985.

———. "Jeremiah 4:23-6 and Job 3:3-13: A Recovered Use of the Creation Pattern." *Vetus Testamentum* 21, no. 2 (1971): 151-67.

Fleming, John V. *The Dark Side of the Enlightenment: Wizards, Alchemists, and Spiritual Seekers in the Age of Reason*. New York: Norton, 2013.

Flint, Thomas P. *Divine Providence: The Molinist Account*. Cornell Studies in the Philosophy of Religion. Ithaca, NY: Cornell University Press, 1998.

Frame, John M. *Systematic Theology: An Introduction to Christian Belief*. Phillipsburg, NJ: P&R, 2013.

Frankfort, Henri, and H. A. Frankfort. Conclusion to *The Intellectual Adventure of Ancient Man: An Essay on Speculative Thought in the Ancient Near East*, by Henri Frankfort, H. A. Frankfort, John A. Wilson, Thorkild Jacobsen, and William A. Irwin. Chicago: University of Chicago Press, 1946.

Friedmann, Robert. *The Theology of Anabaptism: An Interpretation*. Eugene, OR: Wipf & Stock, 1998.

Gadamer, Hans-Georg. *The Beginning of Philosophy*. Translated by Rod Coltman. New York: Continuum International, 2000.

———. "Dialogues in Capri." In *Religion*, edited by Jacques Derrida and Gianni Vattimo, 200-211. Cultural Memory in the Present. Cambridge: Polity, 1998.

Geach, P. T. *Providence and Evil: The Stanton Lectures 1971–2*. New York: Cambridge University Press, 1977.

Geertz, Clifford. *The Interpretation of Cultures: Selected Essays*. New York: Basic Books, 1973.

Gentry, Peter J., and Stephen J. Wellum. *Kingdom Through Covenant: A Biblical-Theological Understanding of the Covenants*. Wheaton, IL: Crossway, 2012.

George, Charles H., and Katherine George. *The Protestant Mind of the English Reformation, 1570–1640*. Princeton, NJ: Princeton University Press, 1961.

Gilchrest, Eric J. *Revelation 21–22 in Light of Jewish and Greco-Roman Utopianism*. Biblical Interpretation 118. Leiden: Brill, 2013.

Gilson, Etienne. *The Christian Philosophy of St. Thomas Aquinas*. Notre Dame, IN: University of Notre Dame Press, 1956.

Glacken, Clarence J. *Traces on the Rhodian Shore: Nature and Culture in Western Thought from Ancient Times to the End of the Eighteenth Century*. Berkeley: University of California Press, 1963.

Gleason, Randall C. "Angels and the Eschatology of Heb 1–2." *New Testament Studies* 49, no. 1 (2003): 90-107.

Glendon, Mary Ann. "The Women of Roe v. Wade." *First Things* 134 (June 2003): 19-23.

Goheen, Michael W. *Introducing Christian Mission Today: Scripture, History and Issues*. Downers Grove, IL: IVP Academic, 2014.

———. *A Light to the Nations: The Missional Church and the Biblical Story*. Grand Rapids, MI: Baker Academic, 2011.

Goheen, Michael W., and Craig G. Bartholomew. *Living at the Crossroads: An Introduction to Christian Worldview*. Grand Rapids, MI: Baker Academic, 2008.

Gordon, Robert P. "The Ethics of Eden: Truth-Telling in Genesis 2–3." In *Ethical and Unethical in the Old Testament: God and Humans in Dialogue*, edited by Katherine Dell, 11-33. London: T&T Clark, 2010.

Goudzwaard, Bob, and Craig G. Bartholomew. *Beyond the Modern Age: An Archeology of Contemporary Culture*. Downers Grove, IL: IVP Academic, 2017.

Gould, Stephen Jay. "Is a New and General Theory of Evolution Emerging?" *Paleobiology* 6, no. 1 (1980): 119-30.

———. *Ontogeny and Phylogeny*. Cambridge, MA: Belknap, 1977.

Gow, M. D. "Fall." In *Dictionary of the Old Testament: Pentateuch*, edited by T. Desmond Alexander and David W. Baker, 285-91. Downers Grove, IL: InterVarsity Press, 2003.

Graham, Christopher A. *The Church as Paradise and the Way Therein: Early Christian Appropriation of Genesis 3:22-24*. Leiden: Brill, 2017.

Graham, Gordon. *The Shape of the Past: A Philosophical Approach to History*. New York: Oxford University Press, 1997.

Gray, John. *The Immortalization Commission: Science and the Strange Quest to Cheat Death*. Toronto: Anchor Canada, 2012.

Green, Bradley G. *Colin Gunton and the Failure of Augustine: The Theology of Colin Gunton in Light of Augustine*. Eugene, OR: Pickwick, 2011.

Green, Miranda. *Celtic Art: Symbol and Imagery*. New York: Sterling, 1996.

Greenberg, Paul. *Four Fish: The Future of the Last Wild Food*. New York: Penguin, 2010.

Gribbin, Mary, and John R. Gribbin. *Flower Hunters*. Oxford: Oxford University Press, 2008.

Griffin, David Ray. "Creation Out of Nothing, Creation Out of Chaos, and the Problem of Evil." In Davis, *Encountering Evil*, 101-24.

Grillmeier, Alois. *Christ in Christian Tradition: From the Apostolic Age to Chalcedon (451)*. London: Mowbray, 1965.

Grudem, Wayne A. *Systematic Theology: An Introduction to Biblical Doctrine*. Grand Rapids, MI: Zondervan, 2000.

Grumett, David, and Rachel Muers, eds. *Eating and Believing: Interdisciplinary Perspectives on Vegetarianism and Theology*. London: T&T Clark, 2008.

———. *Theology on the Menu: Asceticism, Meat, and Christian Diet*. New York: Routledge, 2010.

Guardini, Romano. *The End of the Modern World*. Wilmington, DE: ISI Books, 1998.

Gunton, Colin E. *Act and Being: Towards a Doctrine of the Divine Attributes*. Grand Rapids, MI: Eerdmans, 2002.

———. *Christ and Creation: The Didsbury Lectures*. Eugene, OR: Wipf & Stock, 2005.

———. *The One, the Three and the Many: God, Creation and the Culture of Modernity*. Cambridge: Cambridge University Press, 1993.

———. "The Spirit Moved over the Face of the Waters: The Holy Spirit and the Created Order." *IJST* 4, no. 2 (2002): 190-204.

———. *The Triune Creator: A Historical and Systematic Study*. Grand Rapids, MI: Eerdmans, 1998.

Guthrie, Donald. *New Testament Theology*. Downers Grove, IL: InterVarsity Press, 1981.

Gwynne, Paul. *Special Divine Action: Key Issues in Contemporary Debate*. Rome: Gregorian & Biblical Press, 1996.

Hagopian, David G. *The Genesis Debate: Three Views on the Days of Creation*. Mission Viejo, CA: Crux Press, 2001.

Hahn, Scott. *Angels and Saints: A Biblical Guide to Friendship with God's Holy Ones*. New York: Image Books, 2014.

Ham, Ken. "Young Earth Creationism," in *Four Views on Creation, Evolution, and Intelligent Design*, edited by J. B. Stump and Stanley N. Gundry, 17-48. Grand Rapids: Zondervan Academic, 2017.

Hamann, Johann Georg. *Londoner Schriften*. Edited by Oswald Bayer and Bernd Weissenborn. Munich: Beck, 1993.

Hamilton, Victor P. *Book of Genesis: Chapters 1–17*. NICOT. Grand Rapids, MI: Eerdmans, 1990.

Hammarskjöld, Dag. *Markings*. Translated by Leif Sjoberg and W. H. Auden. New York: Knopf, 1966.

Hardwood, Dix. *Love for Animals and How It Developed in Great Britain (1928)*. Edited by Rod Preece and David Fraser. Lewiston, NY: Edwin Mellen Press, 2003.

Hardy, Edward R., ed. *Christology of the Later Fathers*. Louisville, KY: Westminster John Knox, 1954.

Harper, William Leonard, and Ralf Meerbote, eds. *Kant on Causality, Freedom, and Objectivity*. Minneapolis: University of Minnesota Press, 1984.

Harrison, Glynn. *A Better Story: God, Sex, and Human Flourishing*. London: Inter-Varsity Press, 2017.

Harrison, R. K. "Garden." In *International Standard Bible Encyclopedia*, edited by Geoffrey W. Bromiley, 2:399-400. Grand Rapids, MI: Eerdmans, 1995.

Hart, D. G. *A Secular Faith: Why Christianity Favors the Separation of Church and State*. New York: Ivan R. Dee, 2006.

Hart, David Bentley. *The Experience of God: Being, Consciousness, Bliss*. New Haven, CT: Yale University Press, 2013.

Hart-Davis, Duff. *Audubon's Elephant: The Story of John James Audubon's Epic Struggle to Publish the "Birds of America."* London: Orion, 2003.

Hartshorne, Charles. *Omnipotence and Other Theological Mistakes*. Albany: State University of New York Press, 1984.

Hasel, Gerhard. *Old Testament Theology: Basic Issues in the Current Debate*. 4th ed. Grand Rapids, MI: Eerdmans, 1991.

———. "The Polemic Nature of the Genesis Cosmology." *Evangelical Quarterly* 46 (1974): 81-102.

———. "The Significance of the Cosmology in Gen 1 in Relation to Ancient Near Eastern Parallels." *Andrews University Seminary Studies* 10 (1972): 1-120.

Hauerwas, Stanley. *After Christendom? How the Church Is to Behave If Freedom, Justice, and a Christian Nation Are Bad Ideas*. Nashville: Abingdon, 1991.

———. *Christian Existence Today: Essays on Church, World, and Living in Between*. Durham, NC: Labyrinth, 1988.

———. *The Hauerwas Reader*. Edited by John Berkman and Michael G. Cartwright. Durham, NC: Duke University Press, 2001.

———. *Naming the Silences: God, Medicine, and Suffering*. Grand Rapids, MI: Eerdmans, 1990.

Hauerwas, Stanley, Richard Bondi, and David B. Burrell. *Truthfulness and Tragedy: Further Investigations in Christian Ethics*. Notre Dame, IN: University of Notre Dame Press, 1977.

Hays, Richard B. *The Moral Vision of the New Testament: A Contemporary Introduction to New Testament Ethics*. San Francisco: HarperCollins, 1996.

Hazony, Yoram. *The Philosophy of Hebrew Scripture*. Cambridge: Cambridge University Press, 2012.

Healy, Nicholas J. "Henri de Lubac on Nature and Grace: A Note on Some Recent Contributions to the Debate." *Communio* 35 (2008): 535-64.

Heine, Ronald E. *Classical Christian Doctrine: Introducing the Essentials of the Ancient Faith*. Grand Rapids, MI: Baker Academic, 2013.

Henry, Michel. *I Am the Truth: Toward a Philosophy of Christianity*. Translated by Susan Emanuel. Cultural Memory in the Present. Stanford, CA: Stanford University Press, 2003.

———. *Incarnation: A Philosophy of Flesh*. Translated by Karl Hefty. Evanston, IL: Northwestern University Press, 2015.

———. *Words of Christ*. Translated by Christina M. Gschwandtner. Interventions. Grand Rapids, MI: Eerdmans, 2012.

Herrera, R. A. *Reasons for Our Rhymes: An Inquiry into the Philosophy of History*. Grand Rapids, MI: Eerdmans, 2001.

Herriot, Trevor. *Grass, Sky, Song: Promise and Peril in the World of Grassland Birds*. Toronto: HarperCollins Canada, 2012.

Hertz, J. H., ed. *The Soncino Edition of the Pentateuch and Haftorahs*. 2nd ed. London: Soncino Press, 1967.

Heschel, Abraham J. *God in Search of Man: A Philosophy of Judaism*. New York: Farrar, Straus and Giroux, 1955.

Heslam, Peter. *Creating a Christian Worldview: Abraham Kuyper's Lectures on Calvinism*. Grand Rapids, MI: Eerdmans, 1998.

Hick, John. *Evil and the God of Love*. San Francisco: Harper & Row, 1977.

———. "An Irenaean Theodicy." In Davis, *Encountering Evil*, 39-52.

Hiebert, Paul G. *Anthropological Insights for Missionaries*. Grand Rapids, MI: Baker, 1985.

———. *Cultural Anthropology*. 2nd ed. Grand Rapids, MI: Baker, 1983.

Hiebert, Paul G., R. Daniel Shaw, and Tite Tiénou. *Understanding Folk Religion: A Christian Response to Popular Beliefs and Practices*. Grand Rapids, MI: Baker, 1999.

Hiebert, Theodore. *The Yahwist's Landscape: Nature and Religion in Early Israel*. New York: Oxford University Press, 1996.

Hildebrand, Stephen M. *Basil of Caesarea*. Grand Rapids, MI: Baker Academic, 2014.

Hillel, Daniel. *The Natural History of the Bible: An Environmental Exploration of the Hebrew Bible*. New York: Columbia University Press, 2006.

Hinlicky, Paul R. *Beloved Community: Critical Dogmatics After Christendom*. Grand Rapids, MI: Eerdmans, 2015.

Hoekema, Anthony A. *The Bible and the Future*. Grand Rapids, MI: Eerdmans, 1979.

Hoeksema, Herman. *Reformed Dogmatics*. Grand Rapids, MI: Reformed Free Publishing Association, 1966.

Holmes, Christopher R. J. *Revisiting the Doctrine of the Divine Attributes: In Dialogue with Karl Barth, Eberhard Jüngel, and Wolf Krötke*. Issues in Systematic Theology. New York: Lang, 2007.

Hoop, Raymond de. *Genesis Forty-Nine in Its Literary and Historical Context*. Leiden: Brill, 1999.

Hopkins, Gerard Manley. *The Major Works, Including All the Poems and Selected Prose*. Oxford: Oxford University Press, 1986, 2002.

Horton, Michael. *The Christian Faith: A Systematic Theology for Pilgrims on the Way*. Grand Rapids, MI: Zondervan, 2011.

———. "Let the Earth Bring Forth . . ." In *Sanctification: Explorations in Theology and Practice*, edited by Kelly Kapic, 127-49. Downers Grove, IL: IVP Academic, 2014.

———. "The Time Between: Redefining the 'Secular' in Contemporary Debate." In *After Modernity? Secularity, Globalization, and the Re-enchantment of the World*, edited by James K. A. Smith, 45-66. Waco, TX: Baylor University Press, 2008.

Houlihan, Patrick F. *The Birds of Ancient Egypt*. Cairo: American University in Cairo Press, 1988.

House, Paul. *Isaiah*. Vol. 1, *Chapters 1–27*. Fearn, UK: Mentor, 2019.

Houtman, Cornelis. *Der Himmel im Alten Testament: Israels Weltbild und Weltanschauung*. Oudtestamentische studiën 30. Leiden: Brill, 1993.

Howell, Kenneth J. *God's Two Books: Copernican Cosmology and Biblical Interpretation in Early Modern Science*. Notre Dame, IN: University of Notre Dame Press, 2002.

Hudson, Hud. *The Fall and Hypertime*. Oxford: Oxford University Press, 2014.

Hume, David. *Dialogues Concerning Natural Religion*. London: Penguin Classics, 1990.

Hütter, Reinhard. "Desiderium Naturale Visionis Dei—Est Autem Duplex Hominis Beatitude Sive Felicitas: Some Observations About Lawrence Feingold's and John Milbank's Recent Interventions in the Debate over the Natural Desire to See God." *Nova et Vetera* 5 (2007): 81-131.

Huttinga, Wolter. *Participation and Communicability: Herman Bavinck and John Milbank on the Relation Between God and the World*. Amsterdam: Buijten & Schipperheijn, 2014.

Hutton, James. *Theory of the Earth; or an Investigation of the Laws Observable in the Composition, Dissolution, and Restoration of Land upon the Globe*. Whitefish, MT: Kessinger, 2008.

Huxley, J. *Bird Watching and Bird Behaviour*. London: Chatto and Windus, 1934.

Inge, William R. *The Platonic Tradition in English Religious Thought*. 1926. Whitefish, MT: Kessinger, 2003.

Ingraffia, Brian D. *Postmodern Theory and Biblical Theology: Vanquishing God's Shadow*. Cambridge: Cambridge University Press, 1995.

Irenaeus. *Against Heresies*. In *Ante-Nicene Fathers: The Writings of the Fathers Down to A.D. 325*, edited by Alexander Roberts, James Donaldson, A. Cleveland Coxe, and Allan Menzies, 4. Peabody, MA: Hendrickson, 1994.

———. *Irenaeus's Demonstration of the Apostolic Preaching: A Theological Commentary and Translation*. Translated by Iain M. MacKenzie and J. Armitage Robinson. Burlington, VT: Ashgate, 2002.

Irons, Lee, and Meredith G. Kline. "The Framework View." In Hagopian, *Genesis Debate*, 217-56.

Irwin, Terence. *Classical Thought*. Oxford: Oxford University Press, 1989.

Israel, Jonathan I. *Radical Enlightenment: Philosophy and the Making of Modernity 1650–1750*. Oxford: Oxford University Press, 2001.

Jacob, Edmond. *Theology of the Old Testament*. New York: Harper & Row, 1958.

Janicaud, Dominique, et al. *Phenomenology and the "Theological Turn": The French Debate*. New York: Fordham University Press, 2001.

Janzen, J. Gerald. *Job*. Interpretation. Louisville, KY: Westminster John Knox, 1985.

Jaspers, Karl. *Nietzsche: An Introduction to the Understanding of His Philosophical Activity*. Translated by Chrales F. Wallraff and Frederick J. Schmitz. Baltimore: Johns Hopkins University Press, 1965.

Jenni, Ernst, and Claus Westermann. *Theologisches Handwörterbuch zum Alten Testament*. 2nd ed. Munich: Kaiser, 1972.

Jenson, Robert W. *The Knowledge of Things Hoped For: The Sense of Theological Discourse*. Oxford: Oxford University Press, 1969.

———. *Systematic Theology*. Vol. 2, *The Works of God*. Oxford: Oxford University Press, 2001.

Jerome. *Select Letters of St. Jerome*. Translated by F. A. Wright. Cambridge, MA: Harvard University Press, 1933.

Jobes, Karen H., and Moisés Silva. *Invitation to the Septuagint*. 2nd ed. Carlisle, PA: Paternoster, 2015.

Johansen, T. K. *Plato's Natural Philosophy: A Study of the Timaeus-Critias*. Cambridge: Cambridge University Press, 2004.

John Paul II. *On Human Work*. Washington, DC: U.S. Catholic Conference Office for Publishing and Promotion Services, 1981.

Johnson, A. F. "Revelation." In *The Expositor's Bible Commentary*, ed. Frank E. Gaebelein, 12:399-603. Grand Rapids, MI: Zondervan, 1981.

Johnson, Edward. "Wonder-Working Providence of Sions Savior in New England (c. 1650)." In *The Puritans in America: A Narrative Anthology*, edited by Alan Heimert and Andrew Delbanco, 112-16. Cambridge, MA: Harvard University Press, 1985.

Johnson, Elizabeth A., and Michael W. Klemens, eds. *Nature in Fragments: The Legacy of Sprawl*. New Directions in Biodiversity Conservation. New York: Columbia University Press, 2005.

Johnson, Luke Timothy. *The Creed: What Christians Believe and Why It Matters*. New York: Doubleday, 2005.

Johnson, Marcus Peter. *One with Christ: An Evangelical Theology of Salvation*. Wheaton, IL: Crossway, 2013.

Jolley, Nicholas. *Causality and Mind: Essays on Early Modern Philosophy*. Oxford: Oxford University Press, 2013.

Jonas, Hans. *The Gnostic Religion: The Message of the Alien God and the Beginnings of Christianity*. Boston: Beacon, 1958.

Jones, David A. *Angels: A Very Short Introduction*. Oxford: Oxford University Press, 2011.

Jorgensen, Larry M., and Samuel Newlands. *New Essays on Leibniz's Theodicy*. Oxford: Oxford University Press, 2014.

Kalsbeek, L. *Contours of a Christian Philosophy: An Introduction to Herman Dooyeweerd's Thought*. Toronto: Wedge Publishing Foundation, 1975.

Kant, Immanel. *Critique of Pure Reason*. Translated by Norman Kemp Smith. New York: Modern Library, 1958.

Käsemann, Ernst. *Das wandernde Gottesvolk: Eine Untersuchung zum Hebräerbrief.* 4th ed. Forschungen zur Religion und Literatur des Alten und Neuen Testaments 37. Göttingen: Vandenhoeck & Ruprecht, 1961.

Kass, Leon R. *The Beginning of Wisdom: Reading Genesis.* New York: Free Press, 2003.

———. *The Hungry Soul: Eating and the Perfecting of Our Nature.* New York: Maxwell Macmillan International, 1994.

Kaufman, Gordon D. *In the Beginning . . . Creativity.* Minneapolis: Augsburg Fortress, 2004.

Kaufmann, Yehezkel. *The Religion of Israel: From Its Beginnings to the Babylonian Exile.* Translated and abridged by Moshe Greenberg. Chicago: University of Chicago Press, 1960.

Kavka, Martin, Zachary Braiterman, and Michael Novak. *The Cambridge History of Jewish Philosophy.* Vol. 2, *The Modern Era.* Cambridge: Cambridge University Press, 2012.

Keathley, Kenneth D., and Mark F. Rooker. *40 Questions About Creation and Evolution.* Grand Rapids, MI: Kregel, 2014.

Keating, James F., and Thomas Joseph White, eds. *Divine Impassibility and the Mystery of Human Suffering.* Grand Rapids, MI: Eerdmans, 2009.

Keel, Othmar. *The Symbolism of the Biblical World: Ancient Near Eastern Iconography and the Book of Psalms.* Translated by Timothy J. Hallett. Winona Lake, IN: Eisenbrauns, 1997.

Keel, Othmar, and Silvia Schroer. *Creation: Biblical Theologies in the Context of the Ancient Near East.* Translated by Peter T. Daniels. Winona Lake, IN: Eisenbrauns, 2015.

Kelly, J. N. D. *Early Christian Creeds.* 3rd ed. 1972. Reprint, London: Routledge, 2014.

Kelsey, David H. *Eccentric Existence: A Theological Anthropology.* Vol. 1. Louisville, KY: Westminster John Knox, 2009.

Kenny, Anthony. *The Five Ways: St. Thomas Aquinas' Proofs of God's Existence.* Studies of Ethics and Philosophy of Religion 5. London: Routledge, 2003.

———. *A New History of Western Philosophy.* Oxford: Clarendon, 2004.

Kereszty, R. A. *Wedding Feast of the Lamb: Eucharistic Theology from a Historical, Biblical, and Systematic Perspective.* Chicago: Hillenbrand, 2004.

Kerr, Fergus. *Theology After Wittgenstein.* 2nd ed. London: SPCK, 1997.

Kierkegaard, Søren. *Fear and Trembling.* Edited by C. Stephen Evans and Sylvia Walsh. Cambridge: Cambridge University Press, 2006.

Kim, Sung-Sup. *Deus Providebit: Calvin, Schleiermacher, and Barth on the Providence of God.* Minneapolis: Fortress, 2014.

King, Karen L. *What Is Gnosticism?* Cambridge, MA: Belknap Press, 2003.

Kinzig, Wolfram, ed. *Faith in Formulae: A Collection of Early Christian Creeds and Creed-Related Texts.* 4 vols. Oxford: Oxford University Press, 2017.

Klapwijk, Jacob. *Purpose in the Living World? Creation and Emergent Evolution.* Cambridge: Cambridge University Press, 2008.

Klein, Naomi. *This Changes Everything: Capitalism vs. the Climate.* New York: Simon & Schuster, 2014.

Kloos, Carola. *YHWH's Combat with the Sea: A Canaanite Tradition in the Religion of Ancient Israel.* Amsterdam: Brill, 1986.

Knierim, Rolf P. *The Task of Old Testament Theology: Substance, Method, and Cases.* Grand Rapids, MI: Eerdmans, 1995.

König, Adrio. *The Eclipse of Christ in Eschatology: Toward a Christ-Centered Approach.* Grand Rapids, MI: Eerdmans, 1989.

———. *Here Am I! A Christian Reflection on God.* Grand Rapids, MI: Eerdmans, 1982.

König, Johann F. *Theologia positiva acromatica.* Edited and translated by Andreas Stegmann. Tübingen: Mohr Siebeck, 2006.

Köstenberger, Andreas J. *A Theology of John's Gospel and Letters.* Grand Rapids, MI: Zondervan, 2009.

Koyzis, David T. *Political Visions and Illusions: A Survey and Christian Critique of Contemporary Political Ideologies.* 2nd ed. Downers Grove, IL: IVP Academic, 2019.

Kraemer, Hendrik. *The Christian Message in a Non-Christian World.* London: Harper and Brothers, 1938.

Kreeft, Peter J. *Angels (and Demons): What Do We Really Know About Them?* San Francisco: Ignatius, 1995.

Kroner, Richard. *Kant's Weltanschauung.* Charleston, SC: Nabu Press, 2011.

Kuyper, Abraham. "Common Grace." In *Abraham Kuyper: A Centennial Reader*, edited by James D. Bratt, 165-201. Grand Rapids, MI: Eerdmans, 1998.

———. *Common Grace.* Edited by Jordan J. Ballor and Stephen J. Grabill. Translated by Nelson D. Kloosterman and Ed M. van der Maas. Vol. I/1. Grand Rapids, MI: Christian's Library Press, 2013.

———. *Common Grace.* Edited by Jordan J. Ballor and Stephen J. Grabill. Translated by Nelson D. Kloosterman and Ed M. van der Maas. Vol. I/2. Grand Rapids, MI: Christian's Library Press, 2014.

———. *Common Grace.* Edited by Jordan J. Ballor and Stephen J. Grabill. Translated by Nelson D. Kloosterman and Ed M. van der Maas. Vol. I/3. Grand Rapids, MI: Christian's Library Press, 2014.

———. *De Engelen Gods.* Kampen: Kok, 1923.

———. *Dictaten Dogmatiek van Dr. A. Kuyper.* Vol. 2, *Locus de Sacra Scriptura, Creatione, Creaturis.* Grand Rapids, MI: J. B. Hulst, n.d.

———. *Lectures on Calvinism.* Grand Rapids, MI: Eerdmans, 1931.

———. "Maranatha." In *Abraham Kuyper: A Centennial Reader*, edited by James D. Bratt, 205-29. Grand Rapids, MI: Eerdmans, 1998.

———. *Our Program: A Christian Political Manifesto.* Translated by Harry van Dyke. Bellingham, WA: Lexham Press, 2015.

———. *Principles of Sacred Theology.* Grand Rapids, MI: Eerdmans, 1954.

———. *Principles of Sacred Theology.* Translated by J. Hendrik De Vries. Grand Rapids, MI: Baker, 1980.

———. *Scholarship: Two Convocation Addresses on University Life.* Translated by Harry van Dyke. Grand Rapids, MI: Christian's Library Press, 2014.

———. "Sphere Sovereignty." In *Abraham Kuyper: A Centennial Reader*, edited by James D. Bratt, 463-90. Grand Rapids, MI: Eerdmans, 1998.

———. "Uniformity: The Curse of Modern Life." In *Abraham Kuyper: A Centennial Reader*, edited by James D. Bratt, 19-44. Grand Rapids, MI: Eerdmans, 1998.

———. *The Work of the Holy Spirit*. Translated by H. De Vries. Grand Rapids, MI: Eerdmans, 1900.

LaCocque, André, and Paul Ricoeur. *Thinking Biblically: Exegetical and Hermeneutical Studies*. Translated by David Pellauer. Chicago: University of Chicago Press, 1998.

Lacoste, Jean-Yves. *Experience and the Absolute: Disputed Questions in the Humanity of Man*. Translated by Mark Raftery-Skehan. New York: Fordham University Press, 2004.

Laing, John D. "Middle Knowledge." Internet Encyclopedia of Philosophy. Accessed March 10, 2020. www.iep.utm.edu/middlekn/.

Lane, William L. *The Gospel According to Mark*. 2nd ed. NICNT. Grand Rapids, MI: Eerdmans, 1974.

———. *Hebrews 1–8*. WBC 47a. Dallas: Word, 1991.

———. *Hebrews 9–13*. WBC 47b. Dallas: Word, 1991.

Lash, Nicholas. *Believing Three Ways in One God: A Reading of the Apostles' Creed*. Notre Dame, IN: University of Notre Dame Press, 1993.

Lathrop, G. W. *Holy Ground: A Liturgical Cosmology*. Minneapolis: Fortress, 2003.

Leisher, Craig, Pieter van Beukering, and Lea M. Scherl. *Nature's Investment Bank: How Marine Protected Areas Contribute to Poverty Reduction*. Arlington, VA: The Nature Conservancy, 2007. www.nature.org/media/science/mpa_report.pdf.

Leithart, Peter J. *Athanasius*. Grand Rapids, MI: Baker Academic, 2011.

Levenson, Jon D. *Creation and the Persistence of Evil: The Jewish Drama of Divine Omnipotence*. San Francisco: Harper & Row, 1985.

Levering, Matthew. *The Theology of Augustine: An Introductory Guide to His Most Important Works*. Grand Rapids, MI: Baker Academic, 2013.

Lewis, C. S. *Mere Christianity*. San Francisco: HarperCollins, 2001.

———. *Miracles: A Preliminary Study*. Glasgow: Geoffrey Bles, 1947.

Lewis, Gordon R., and Bruce A. Demarest. *Integrative Theology*. 3 vols. Grand Rapids, MI: Zondervan, 1987–1994.

L'Hour, J. *Genèse 1–2, 4a: Commentaire par Jean L'Hour*. Ètudies Bibliques, Nouvelle série, 71. Leuven: Peeters, 2016.

———. *Génesis 1–11: Los pasos de la humanidad sobre la tierra*. Cuaderno bíblico 161. Estella, Spain: Editorial Verbo Divino, 2013.

———. "Yahweh Elohim." *Revue Biblique* 81 (1974): 524-56.

Lieu, Judith M. *Marcion and the Making of a Heretic: God and Scripture in the Second Century*. Cambridge: Cambridge University Press, 2015.

Lindbeck, George A. "Re-Viewing Vatican II: An Interview with George A. Lindbeck." *First Things* 48 (December 1994): 44-50.

Lloyd, Genevieve. *Providence Lost*. Cambridge, MA: Harvard University Press, 2008.

Long, D. Stephen. *Theology and Culture: A Guide to the Discussion*. Cambridge: James Clarke, 2008.

Lopez, Barry. *Arctic Dreams: Imagination and Desire in a Northern Landscape*. New York: Bantam Books, 2013.

Lopez, Barry, and Debra Gwartney. *Home Ground: Language for an American Landscape*. San Antonio: Trinity University Press, 2006.

Lovejoy, Arthur O. *The Great Chain of Being: A Study of the History of an Idea*. 1936. Cambridge, MA: Harvard University Press, 1964.

Lowenthal, Eric I. *The Joseph Narrative in Genesis*. Jersey City, NJ: KTAV, 1973.

Lubac, Henri de. *A Brief Catechesis on Nature and Grace*. San Francisco: Ignatius, 1984.

———. *The Mystery of the Supernatural*. New York: Crossroad, 1998.

———. *Surnaturel, Études Historiques*. Edited by Michele Sales. Paris: Desclée, 1991.

Luther, Martin. *Luther's Works*. Vol. 26. Translated by Walter A. Hansen. Edited by Jaroslav Pelikan. St. Louis: Concordia, 1963.

———. *The Table Talk of Martin Luther*. Translated by W. Hazlitt. Philadelphia: The Lutheran Publication Society, 2004.

Luyster, Robert. "Wind and Water: Cosmogonic Symbolism in the Old Testament." In Morales, *Cult and Cosmos*, 228-48.

Lyons, Lawrence Francis. *Material and Formal Causality in the Philosophy of Aristotle and St. Thomas*. Whitefish, MT: Literary Licensing, 2013.

MacDonald, Nathan. "Israel and the Old Testament Story in Irenaeus' Presentation of the Rule of Faith", *Journal of Theological Interpretation* 3 (2009): 267–84.

———. *Not Bread Alone: The Uses of Food in the Old Testament*. Oxford: Oxford University Press, 2008.

———. *What Did the Ancient Israelites Eat? Diet in Biblical Times*. Grand Rapids, MI: Eerdmans, 2008.

MacDonald, Nathan, Kathy Ehrensperger, and Luzia Sutter Rehmann, eds. *Decisive Meals: Table Politics in Biblical Literature*. London: T&T Clark, 2012.

Macek, Petr. "The Doctrine of Creation in the Messianic Theology of Jürgen Moltmann." *Communio Viatorum* 49, no. 2 (2007): 150-84.

Machamer, Peter K., and Gereon Wolters. *Thinking About Causes: From Greek Philosophy to Modern Physics*. Pittsburgh: University of Pittsburgh Press, 2007.

MacKenzie, Iain. *Irenaeus's Demonstration of the Apostolic Preaching: A Theological Commentary and Translation*. Burlington, VT: Ashgate, 2002.

Mackie, J. L. "Evil and Omnipotence." *Mind* 64 (1955): 200-212. Reprinted in *Philosophy of Religion*, edited by B. Mitchell, 92-104. London: Oxford University Press, 1971.

Majid, Shahn, ed. *On Space and Time*. New York: Cambridge University Press, 2008.

Malinowski, Bronislaw. *A Scientific Theory of Culture and Other Essays*. Oxford: Oxford University Press, 1960.

Manent, Pierre. *A World Beyond Politics? A Defense of the Nation-State*. Princeton, NJ: Princeton University Press, 2006.

Mangina, Joseph L. *Karl Barth: Theologian of Christian Witness*. Louisville, KY: Westminster John Knox, 2004.

Mascall, E. L. *The Christian Universe*. New York: Morehouse-Barlow, 1966.

Mathewson, David. *A New Heaven and a New Earth: The Meaning and Function of the Old Testament in Revelation 21.1–22.5*. Journal for the Study of the New Testament Supplement Series 238. London: Sheffield Academic Press, 2003.

Maximus the Confessor. *Ambigua*. In *Patrologia Graeca*, edited by Jacques Paul Migne and Theodor Hopfner, 91. Paris: Migne, 1865.

May, Gerhard. *Creatio Ex Nihilo: The Doctrine of "Creation Out of Nothing" in Early Christian Thought*. Translated by A. S. Worrall. London: T&T Clark, 1994.

May, Herbert G. "Some Cosmic Connotations of Mayim Rabbîm, 'Many Waters.'" In Morales, *Cult and Cosmos*, 248-58.

Mayer, Lawrence S., and Paul R. McHugh. "Sexuality and Gender: Findings from the Biological, Physical, and Social Sciences." *New Atlantis* 50 (Fall 2016): 10-116.

Mays, James Luther. *The Lord Reigns: A Theological Handbook to the Psalms*. Louisville, KY: Westminster John Knox, 1994.

———. *Psalms*. Interpretation. Louisville, KY: Westminster John Knox, 2011.

McBride, Jennifer M. *The Church for the World: A Theology of Public Witness*. New York: Oxford University Press, 2012.

McCann, Clinton J., Jr. *A Theological Introduction to the Book of Psalms: The Psalms as Torah*. Nashville: Abingdon, 1993.

McClendon, James W., Jr., and Brad J. Kallenberg. "Ludwig Wittgenstein: A Christian in Philosophy." *Scottish Journal of Theology* 51, no. 2 (1998): 131-61.

McConville, J. Gordon. *Being Human in God's World: An Old Testament Theology of Humanity*. Grand Rapids, MI: Baker Academic, 2016.

McDonough, Sean M. *Christ as Creator: Origins of a New Testament Doctrine*. Oxford: Oxford University Press, 2009.

McDowell, Catherine L. *The Image of God in the Garden of Eden*. Siphrut 15. Winona Lake, IN: Eisenbrauns, 2015.

McEntyre, Marilyn Chandler. *Caring for Words in a Culture of Lies*. Grand Rapids, MI: Eerdmans, 2009.

McFarland, Ian A., ed. *Creation and Humanity: The Sources of Christian Theology*. Louisville, KY: Westminster John Knox, 2009.

———. *The Divine Image: Envisioning the Invisible God*. Minneapolis: Fortress, 2005.

———. *From Nothing: A Theology of Creation*. Louisville, KY: Westminster John Knox, 2014.

McGowan, Andrew. "Providence and Common Grace." In Murphy and Ziegler, *Providence of God*, 109-29.

McGrath, Alister. *Christian Theology: An Introduction*. 5th ed. Oxford: Wiley-Blackwell, 2011.

———. *The Genesis of Doctrine*. Grand Rapids, MI: Eerdmans, 1997.

McGrath, Alister, and Joanna Collicutt McGrath. *The Dawkins Delusion? Atheist Fundamentalism and the Denial of the Divine*. London: SPCK, 2007.

McGuinness, Brian. *Wittgenstein, a Life: Young Ludwig, 1889–1921*. Berkeley: University of California Press, 1988.

McGuire, E. D. "The Joseph Story: A Tale of Son and Father." In *Images of Man and God: Old Testament Short Stories in Literary Focus*, edited by Burke O. Long, 9-26. Sheffield: Almond Press, 1981.

McHugh, Paul. "Transgenderism: A Pathogenic Meme." Public Discourse. June 10, 2015. www.thepublicdiscourse.com/2015/06/15145/.

McMullin, Ernan. "Creation *ex nihilo*: Early History." In Burrell et al., *Creation and the God of Abraham*, 11-23.

Meconi, David Vincent, ed. *On Earth as It Is in Heaven: Cultivating a Contemporary Theology of Creation*. Catholic Theological Formation Series. Grand Rapids, MI: Eerdmans, 2016.

Megaw, Ruth, and Vincent Megaw. *Celtic Art: From Its Beginnings to the Book of Kells*. London: Thames and Hudson, 1991.

Meister, Chad, and James K. Dew Jr., eds. *God and Evil: The Case for God in a World Filled with Pain*. Downers Grove, IL: InterVarsity Press, 2013.

Melanchthon, Philip, and J. A. O. Preus. *The Chief Theological Topics: Loci Praecipui Theologici 1559*. 2nd ed. St. Louis: Concordia, 2011.

Menuge, Angus J. L., ed. *Christ and Culture in Dialogue: Constructive Themes and Practical Applications*. St. Louis: Concordia Academic Press, 1999.

Mettinger, Tryggve N. D. *The Eden Narrative: A Literary and Religio-historical Study of Genesis 2–3*. Winona Lake, IN: Eisenbrauns, 2007.

Metzger, Bruce M. *A Textual Commentary on the Greek New Testament: A Companion Volume to the United Bible Societies' Greek New Testament*. 3rd ed. London: United Bible Societies, 1971.

Michalson, Gordon E. *Fallen Freedom: Kant on Radical Evil and Moral Regeneration*. Cambridge: Cambridge University Press, 1990.

———. *Kant and the Problem of God*. Malden, MA: Blackwell, 1999.

Milbank, John. "Knowledge: The Theological Critique of Philosophy in Hamann and Jacobi." In Milbank, Pickstock, and Ward, *Radical Orthodoxy*, 21-37.

———. "The Programme of Radical Orthodoxy." In *Radical Orthodoxy? A Catholic Enquiry*, edited by Laurence Paul Hemming. Burlington, VT: Ashgate, 2000.

———. *Theology and Social Theory: Beyond Secular Reason*. Malden, MA: Blackwell, 1993.

Milbank, John, Catherine Pickstock, and Graham Ward, eds. *Radical Orthodoxy: A New Theology*. New York: Routledge, 1999.

Miller, Patrick D. *Interpreting the Psalms*. Philadelphia: Augsburg Fortress, 1986.

———. *The Religion of Ancient Israel*. Louisville, KY: Westminster John Knox, 2000.

———. "Rethinking the First Article of the Creed." *Theology Today* 61, no. 4 (2005): 499-508.

Millgram, Hillel I. *The Joseph Paradox: A Radical Reading of Genesis 37–50*. Jefferson, NC: McFarland, 2012.

Moberly, R. W. L. *The Theology of the Book of Genesis*. Old Testament Theology. Cambridge: Cambridge University Press, 2009.

Moltmann, Jürgen. *The Coming of God: Christian Eschatology*. Minneapolis: Fortress, 1996.

———. *God in Creation: A New Theology of Creation and the Spirit of God*. Minneapolis: Fortress, 1993.

Momigliano, Arnaldo. *Essays in Ancient and Modern Historiography*. Chicago: University of Chicago Press, 1977.

Monk, Ray. *Ludwig Wittgenstein: The Duty of Genius*. New York: Free Press, 1990.

Moo, Jonathan. "The Sea That Is No More: Rev 21:1 and the Function of Sea Imagery in the Apocalypse of John." *Novum Testamentum* 51. no. 2 (2009): 148-67.

Moor, Johannes Cornelis de. *The Rise of Yahwism: The Roots of Israelite Monotheism*. Leuven: Leuven University Press, 1997.

Moore, Russell D. "Personal and Cosmic Eschatology." In *A Theology for the Church*, edited by Daniel L. Akin, David P. Nelson, and Peter R. Schemm, 671-722. Nashville: B&H Academic, 2007.

Moore, T. M. *Consider the Lilies: A Plea for Creational Theology*. Phillipsburg, NJ: P&R, 2005.

Morales, L. M., ed. *Cult and Cosmos: Tilting Toward a Temple-Centered Theology*. Leuven: Peeters, 2014.

More, Max. "Philosophy of Transhumanism." In *The Transhumanist Reader: Classical and Contemporary Essays on the Science, Technology, and Philosophy of the Human Future*, 3-17. Malden, MA: Wiley-Blackwell, 2013.

Moss, Jean Dietz. *Novelties in the Heavens: Rhetoric and Science in the Copernican Controversy*. 2nd ed. Chicago: University of Chicago Press, 1993.

Mounce, Robert H. *The Book of Revelation*. Rev. ed. NICNT. Grand Rapids, MI: Eerdmans, 1998.

Mouw, Richard J. *Abraham Kuyper: A Short and Personal Introduction*. Grand Rapids, MI: Eerdmans, 2011.

———. *Called to Holy Worldliness*. Philadelphia: Fortress, 1980.

———. *He Shines in All That's Fair: Culture and Common Grace; The 2000 Stob Lectures*. Grand Rapids, MI: Eerdmans, 2001.

———. "Some Reflections on Sphere Sovereignty." In *Religion, Pluralism, and Public Life: Abraham Kuyper's Legacy for the Twenty-First Century*, edited by Luis E. Lugo. Grand Rapids, MI: Eerdmans, 2000.

———. *When the Kings Come Marching In: Isaiah and the New Jerusalem*. Rev. ed. Grand Rapids, MI: Eerdmans, 2002.

Mouw, Richard J., and Sander Griffioen. *Pluralisms and Horizons: An Essay in Christian Public Philosophy*. Grand Rapids, MI: Eerdmans, 1993.

Murphy, Francesca Aran, and Philip G. Ziegler, eds. *The Providence of God: Deus Habet Consilium*. London: T&T Clark, 2009.

Mynott, Jeremy. *Birdscapes: Birds in Our Imagination and Experience*. Princeton, NJ: Princeton University Press, 2009.

Nagel, Thomas. *Mind and Cosmos: Why the Materialist Neo-Darwinian Conception of Nature Is Almost Certainly False*. New York: Oxford University Press, 2012.

Nash, Ronald H. *The Light of the Mind: St. Augustine's Theory of Knowledge*. Lima, OH: Academic Renewal Press, 2003.

Newbigin, Lesslie. *The Gospel in a Pluralist Society*. Grand Rapids, MI: Eerdmans, 1989.

———. *The Light Has Come: An Exposition of the Fourth Gospel*. Grand Rapids, MI: Eerdmans, 1982.

———. *Truth to Tell: The Gospel as Public Truth*. London: SPCK, 1991.

Newman, John Henry. *Essay on the Development of Christian Doctrine*. 6th ed. Notre Dame, IN: University of Notre Dame Press, 1989.

Newsom, Carol A. "Common Ground: An Ecological Reading of Genesis 2–3." In *The Earth Story in Genesis*, edited by Norman C. Habel and Shirley Wurst, 60-72. Sheffield: Sheffield Academic Press, 2000.

Newton, Isaac. *The Mathematical Principles of Natural Philosophy*. Translated by Andrew Motte. New York: Daniel Adee, 1846.

Niebuhr, H. Richard. *Christ and Culture*. 50th anniversary ed. San Francisco: Harper & Row, 2001.

Niehoff, Maren. *The Figure of Joseph in Post-Biblical Jewish Literature*. Leiden: Brill, 1992.

Nietzsche, Friedrich W. *The Gay Science*. Translated by W. A. Kaufmann. New York: Vintage Books, 1974.

Noll, Mark, and James Turner. *The Future of Christian Learning: An Evangelical and Catholic Dialogue*. Edited by Thomas A. Howard. Grand Rapids, MI: Brazos, 2008.

Noordzij, Arie. *God's Word en der Eeuwen Getuigenis: Het Oude Testament in het Licht der Oostersche Opgravingen*. Kampen: University of Utrecht, 1924.

Norris, Richard A. *God and World in Early Christian Theology*. New York: Seabury, 1965.

Nuttall, A. D. "Auerbach's Mimesis." *Essays in Criticism* 54, no. 1 (2004): 60-74.

Oakley, Francis. *Omnipotence and Promise: The Legacy of the Scholastic Distinction of Powers*. Toronto: Pontificial Institute of Mediaeval Studies, 2002.

Oakley, Kenneth Page. *Man the Tool-Maker*. London: Printed by Order of the Trustees of the British Museum, 1949.

O'Brien, Peter T. *The Letter to the Ephesians*. PNTC. Grand Rapids, MI: Eerdmans, 1999.

———. *The Letter to the Hebrews*. PNTC. Grand Rapids, MI: Eerdmans, 2010.

———. "Principalities and Powers and Their Relationship to the Structures." *Reformed Theological Review* 40 (1981): 1-10.

Och, Bernard. "Creation and Redemption: Towards a Theology of Creation." In Morales, *Cult and Cosmos*, 318-30.

Oden, Thomas C. *The Living God*. Vol. 1 of *Systematic Theology*. New York: HarperCollins, 1987.

O'Donovan, Oliver. *Resurrection and Moral Order: An Outline for Evangelical Ethics*. Leicester, UK: Apollos, 1986.

———. *Self, World and Time*. Vol. 1, *Ethics as Theology*. Grand Rapids, MI: Eerdmans, 2013.

Oestigaard, Terje. *Water, Christianity, and the Rise of Capitalism*. London: I. B. Tauris, 2013.

O'Neill, Colman E. *Sacramental Realism: A General Theory of the Sacraments*. Princeton, NJ: Scepter, 1998.

Ong, Walter. *Orality and Literacy*. 2nd ed. New York: Routledge, 2002.

Origen. *Against Celsus*. In *Ante-Nicene Fathers: The Writings of the Fathers Down to A.D. 325*, edited by Alexander Roberts, James Donaldson, A. Cleveland Coxe, and Allan Menzies, 4. Peabody, MA: Hendrickson, 1994.

———. *Contra Celsum*. Documenta Catholica Omnia. 2006. www.documentacatholicaomnia.eu/03d/0185-0254,_Origenes,_Contra_Celsus,_EN.pdf.

———. *Discourses*. In *Ante-Nicene Fathers: The Writings of the Fathers Down to A.D. 325*, edited by Alexander Roberts, James Donaldson, A. Cleveland Coxe, and Allan Menzies, 4. Peabody, MA: Hendrickson, 1994.

———. *Homily XXVII on Numbers*. In *Origen: An Exhortation to Martyrdom, Prayer, and Selected Works*, translated by Rowan A. Greer. New York: Paulist Press, 1979.

Orr, James. *The Christian View of God as Centering in the Incarnation*. Edinburgh: A. Elliot, 1893.

Osborn, Eric. *Irenaeus of Lyons*. Cambridge: Cambridge University Press, 2001.

———. *Tertullian: First Theologian of the West*. Cambridge: Cambridge University Press, 1997.

Osborne, Grant R. *Revelation*. Baker Exegetical Commentary on the New Testament. Grand Rapids, MI: Baker Academic, 2002.

O'Toole, J. *The Philosophy of Creation in the Writings of St. Augustine*. Washington, DC: Catholic University of America Press, 1944.

Ouellet, Marc. *Divine Likeness: Towards a Trinitarian Anthropology of the Family*. Translated by Philip Milligan and Linda M. Cicone. Grand Rapids, MI: Eerdmans, 2006.

Pannenberg, Wolfhart. *Basic Questions in Theology: Collected Essays*. Translated by George H. Kehm. Minneapolis: Fortress, 1971.

———. *Systematic Theology*. Translated by Geoffrey W. Bromiley. Vol. 2. Grand Rapids, MI: Eerdmans, 1994.

Parante, Pascal P. *The Angels: The Catholic Teaching on the Angels*. Rockford, IL: Tan Books, 1994.

Pattison, George. *Kierkegaard and the Theology of the Nineteenth Century: The Paradox and the "Point of Contact."* Cambridge: Cambridge University Press, 2012.

Peck, M. Scott. *People of the Lie: The Hope for Healing Human Evil*. London: Random House, 1983.

Pelikan, Jaroslav. *The Christian Tradition: A History of the Development of Doctrine*. 5 vols. Chicago: University of Chicago Press, 1975–1989.

———. *Credo: Historical and Theological Guide to Creeds and Confessions of Faith in the Christian Tradition*. New Haven, CT: Yale University Press, 2003.

Pentecost, J. Dwight. *Things to Come: A Study in Biblical Eschatology*. Grand Rapids, MI: Zondervan, 1958.

Peppard, Christiana Z. *Just Water: Theology, Ethics, and the Global Water Crisis*. Maryknoll, NY: Orbis Books, 2014.

Perdue, Leo G. "Job's Assault on Creation." *Hebrew Annual Review* 10 (1987): 295-315.

———. *Wisdom Literature: A Theological History*. Louisville, KY: Westminster John Knox, 2007.

Peskett, Howard, and Vinoth Ramachandra. *The Message of Mission: The Glory of Christ in All Time and Space*. Downers Grove, IL: InterVarsity Press, 2003.

Peterson, Eugene. *Leap over a Wall: Earthly Spirituality for Everyday Christians*. New York: HarperCollins, 1997.

Peterson, John. *Aquinas: A New Introduction*. Lanham, MD: University Press of America, 2008.

Phelps, Norm. *The Longest Stuggle: Animal Advocacy from Pythagoras to PETA*. New York: Lantern Books, 2007.

Philo. *On the Creation of the Cosmos According to Moses*. Translated by David T. Runia. Boston: Brill, 2001.

Pirson, Ron. *The Lord of the Dreams: A Semantic and Literary Analysis of Genesis 37–50*. London: Black, 2002.

Pitre, Brant. "The Lord's Prayer and the New Exodus." *Letter and Spirit* 2 (2006): 69-96.

Placher, William C., ed. *Callings: Twenty Centuries of Chrisian Wisdom on Vocation*. Grand Rapids, MI: Eerdmans, 2005.

Plantinga, Alvin. "The Free Will Defense." In *The Analytic Theist: An Alvin Plantinga Reader*, edited by J. F. Sennett, 22-49. Grand Rapids, MI: Eerdmans, 1998.

———. "Reply to the Basingers on Divine Omnipotence." *Process Studies* 11 (1981): 28.

———. "Science and Religion: Why Does the Debate Continue?" In *Science and Religion: Why Does the Debate Continue?*, edited by Harold W. Attridge, 99-123. New Haven, CT: Yale University Press, 2009.

———. *Warranted Christian Belief*. New York: Oxford University Press, 2000.

———. *When Faith and Reason Clash: Evolution and the Bible*. Ancaster, ON: Redeemer University College, 1991.

———. *Where the Conflict Really Lies: Science, Religion, and Naturalism*. New York: Oxford University Press, 2011.

Plantinga, Cornelius, Jr. *Engaging God's World: A Christian Vision of Faith, Learning, and Living*. Grand Rapids, MI: Eerdmans, 2002.

———. *Not the Way It's Supposed to Be: A Breviary of Sin*. Grand Rapids, MI: Eerdmans, 1996.

Plato. *Plato's Timaeus: Translation, Glossary, Appendices and Introductory Essay*. Translated by Peter Kalkavage. Newburyport, MA: Focus, 2001.

Polkinghorne, John. "The Nature of Time." In *On Space and Time*, edited by Shahn Majid, 278-83. Cambridge: Cambridge University Press, 2008.

Pollan, Michael. *The Omnivore's Dilemma: A Natural History of Four Meals*. New York: Penguin, 2006.

Prenter, Regin. *Spiritus Creator: Luther's Concept of the Holy Spirit*. Philadelphia: Muhlenberg, 1953.

Pretor-Pinney, Gavin. *The Cloudspotter's Guide: The Science, History, and Culture of Clouds*. London: Hodder and Stoughton, 2006.

Pritchard, James B., ed. *The Ancient Near East: An Anthology of Texts and Pictures*. Princeton, NJ: Princeton University Press, 2011.

Rad, Gerhard von. *Genesis: A Commentary*. Old Testament Library. Philadelphia: Westminster John Knox, 1972.

———. *God at Work in Israel*. Translated by John H. Marks. Nashville: Abingdon, 1980.

———. *Old Testament Theology*. Vol. 1, *The Theology of Israel's Historical Traditions*. Translated by D. M. G. Stalker. Edinburgh: Oliver and Boyd, 1962.

———. *Wisdom in Israel*. Translated by J. D. Martin. Nashville: Abingdon, 1972.

Ramm, Bernard. *The Christian View of Science and Scripture*. Grand Rapids, MI: Eerdmans, 1954.

Rand, J. A. du. "The Imagery of the Heavenly Jerusalem (Revelation 21:9–22:5)." *Neotestamentica* 22, no. 1 (1988): 65-86.

Rashdall, Hastings. *Doctrine and Development: University Sermons*. London: Methuen, 1898.

Reno, Russell R. *Genesis*. Grand Rapids, MI: Baker Academic, 2010.

Reymond, Philippe. *Eau, Sa Vie et Sa Signification Dans l'Ancien Testament*. Leiden: Brill, 1958.

Richardson, Alan. *The Miracle Stories of the Gospels*. New York: Harper & Brothers, 1941.

Ricoeur, Paul. *Figuring the Sacred: Religion, Narrative and the Imagination*. Edited by Mark I. Wallace. Minneapolis: Augsburg Fortress, 1959.

———. *Time and Narrative*. Vol. 1. Translated by Kathleen McLaughlin and David Pellauer. Chicago: University of Chicago Press, 1984.

———. *Time and Narrative*. Vol 2. Translated by Kathleen McLaughlin and David Pellauer. Chicago: University of Chicago Press, 1985.

———. *Time and Narrative*. Vol. 3. Translated by Kathleen McLaughlin and David Pellauer. Chicago: University of Chicago Press, 1988.

Ridderbos, N. H. *Is There a Conflict Between Genesis 1 and Natural Science?* Grand Rapids, MI: Eerdmans, 1957.

Rieff, Philip. *The Crisis of the Officer Class: The Decline of the Tragic Sensibility*. Edited by Alan Woolfolk. Sacred Order/Social Order 2. Charlottesville: University of Virginia Press, 2007.

———. *Freud: The Mind of the Moralist*. 3rd ed. Chicago: University of Chicago Press, 1979.

———. *The Jew of Culture: Freud, Moses, and Modernity*. Edited by Arnold M. Eisen and Gideon Lewis-Kraus. Sacred Order/Social Order 3. Charlottesville: University of Virginia Press, 2008.

———. *My Life Among the Deathworks: Illustrations of the Aesthetics of Authority*. Edited by Kenneth S. Piver. Sacred Order/Social Order 1. Charlottesville: University of Virginia Press, 2006.

Rivera, Joseph. *The Contemplative Self After Michel Henry: A Phenomenological Theology*. Notre Dame, IN: University of Notre Dame Press, 2015.

Robbins, Vernon K. "Precreation Discourse and the Nicene Creed: Christianity Finds Its Voice in the Roman Empire." *Religion and Theology* 18, no. 3-4 (2011): 334-50.

Roberts, A., J. Donaldson, and A. C. Coxe, eds. *The Ante-Nicene Fathers: The Writings of the Fathers Down to A.D. 325*. Vol. 1, *The Apostolic Fathers with Justin Martyr and Irenaeus*. Buffalo, NY: Cosimo Classics, 2007.

Roberts, Callum. *The Ocean of Life: The Fate of Man and the Sea*. New York: Viking Penguin, 2012.

Robertson, O. Palmer. *The Christ of the Covenants*. Phillipsburg, NJ: P&R, 1980.

Robinette, Brian D. "The Difference Nothing Makes: Creation Ex Nihilo, Resurrection, and Divine Gratuity." *Theological Studies* 72 (2011): 525-57.

Rogerson, J. W. *A Theology of the Old Testament: Cultural Memory, Communication and Being Human*. London: SPCK, 2009.

Rose, Tim. *Kierkegaard's Christocentric Theology*. Burlington, VT: Ashgate, 2001.

Rosen, Jonathan. *The Life of the Skies: Birding at the Edge of Nature*. New York: Farrar, Straus and Giroux, 2008.

Rosman, Abraham, and Paula G. Rubel. *The Tapestry of Culture: An Introduction to Cultural Anthropology*. 8th ed. Boston: McGraw-Hill, 2004.

Ross, Allen P. *Creation and Blessing: A Guide to the Study and Exposition of the Book of Genesis*. Grand Rapids, MI: Baker Academic, 1998.

Roth, John K. "A Theodicy of Protest." In Davis, *Encountering Evil*, 7-22.

Routledge, Robin. *Old Testament Theology: A Thematic Approach*. Downers Grove, IL: IVP Academic, 2008.

Roy, Steven C. *How Much Does God Foreknow? A Comprehensive Biblical Study*. Downers Grove, IL: IVP Academic, 2006.

Ruler, J. A. van. *The Crisis of Causality: Voetius and Descartes on God, Nature, and Change*. Leiden: Brill, 1995.

Runner, H. Evan. *The Relation of the Bible to Learning*. Jordan Station, ON: Paideia, 1982.

Rupp, James E. *The Sea Motif in the Old Testament*. Dallas: Dallas Theological Seminary, 1966.

Ruse, Michael. *Science and Spirituality: Making Room for Faith in the Age of Science*. Cambridge: Cambridge University Press, 2010.

Ryken, Leland. *Redeeming the Time: A Christian Approach to Work and Leisure*. Grand Rapids, MI: Baker, 1995.

Rynasiewicz, Robert. "Newton's Views on Space, Time, and Motion." In *The Stanford Encyclopedia of Philosophy.* Summer 2014 ed. Edited by Edward N. Zalta. https://plato.stanford.edu/entries/newton-stm/.

Sacks, Jonathan. *Faith in the Future.* London: Darton, Longman & Todd, 1995.

Sagan, Carl. *Cosmos.* New York: Ballantine Books, 1980.

Salatin, Joel. *Folks, This Ain't Normal: A Farmer's Advice for Happier Hens, Healthier People, and a Better World.* New York: Center Street, 2011.

Samuelson, Norbert M. *Judaism and the Doctrine of Creation.* Cambridge: Cambridge University Press, 1994.

Sanneh, Lamin O. *Disciples of All Nations: Pillars of World Christianity.* Oxford: Oxford University Press, 2008.

———. *Whose Religion Is Christianity? The Gospel Beyond the West.* Grand Rapids, MI: Eerdmans, 2003.

Santmire, H. Paul. *Brother Earth: Nature, God and Ecology in Time of Crisis.* New York: Nelson, 1976.

———. *Ritualizing Nature: Renewing Christian Liturgy in a Time of Crisis.* Minneapolis: Fortress, 2008.

———. *The Travail of Nature: The Ambiguous Ecological Promise of Christian Theology.* Philadelphia: Fortress, 1985.

Sarna, Nahum M. *The JPS Torah Commentary: Genesis.* New York: Jewish Publication Society, 1989.

Savran, George. "Beastly Speech: Balaam's Ass and the Garden of Eden." *JSOT* 64 (1994): 33-55.

Schilder, Klaus. *Christ and Culture.* Translated by William Helder and Albert H. Oosterhoff. Hamilton, ON: Lucerna, 2016.

Schleiermacher, Friedrich. *The Christian Faith.* Edited by H. R. Mackintosh and J. S. Stewart. Edinburgh: T&T Clark, 1989.

Schmemann, Alexander. *The Eucharist: Sacrament of the Kingdom.* Crestwood, NY: St. Vladimir's Seminary Press, 2003.

———. *For the Life of the World: Sacraments and Orthodoxy.* 2nd ed. Crestwood, NY: St. Vladimir's Seminary Press, 1973.

———. *The Journals of Father Alexander Schmemann, 1973–1983.* Crestwood, NY: St. Vladimir's Seminary Press, 2000.

Schmid, Hans Heinrich. "Jahweglaube Und Altorientalisches Weltordungensgedanken." In *Altorientalische Welt in der alttestamentlichen Theologie.* Zurich: Theologischer Verlag, 1974.

———. *Gerechtigkeit als Weltordnung.* Beitraega zur Historischen Theologie 40. Tübingen: J. C. B. Mohr, 1968.

Schreiter, Robert John. *Constructing Local Theologies.* Maryknoll, NY: Orbis Books, 1985.

———. *The New Catholicity: Theology Between the Global and Local.* Maryknoll, NY: Orbis Books, 1997.

Schumacher, E. F. *A Guide for the Perplexed*. New York: Harper Colophon, 1977.

Schwartz, Richard H. *Judaism and Vegetarianism*. New York: Lantern Books, 2001.

Schweitzer, Albert. *J. S. Bach*. Translated by Ernest Newman. Vol 1. New York: Dover, 1966.

Schwöbel, Christoph. "Divine Agency and Providence," *Modern Theology* 3 (1987): 225-44.

———. *God: Action and Revelation*. Kampen: Kok Pharos, 1992.

———. "Radical Monotheism and the Trinity." *Neue Zeitschrift für Systematische Theologie und Religionsphilosophie* 43, no. 1 (January 2001): 54-74.

Scully, Matthew. *Dominion: The Power of Man, the Suffering of Animals, and the Call to Mercy*. New York: St. Martin's Griffin, 2003.

Scurlock, Joann. "*Chaoskampf* Lost—*Chaoskampf* Regained: The Gunkel Hypothesis Revisited." In Scurlock and Beal, *Creation and Chaos*, 257-68.

Scurlock, Joann, and Richard H. Beal, eds. 2013. *Creation and Chaos: A Reconsideration of Hermann Gunkel's* Chaoskampf *Hypothesis*. Winona Lake, IN: Eisenbrauns.

Seow, Choon-Leong. *Ecclesiastes*. Anchor Bible. New Haven, CT: Yale University Press, 2007.

Shahar, Galili. "Auerbach's Scars: Judaism and the Question of Literature." *Jewish Quarterly Review* 101, no. 4 (2011): 604-30.

Shakespeare, Steven. *Radical Orthodoxy: A Critical Introduction*. London: SPCK, 2007.

Shapiro, James A. *Evolution: A View from the 21st Century*. Upper Saddle River, NJ: FT Press, 2011.

Shatzer, Jacob. *Transhumanism and the Image of God*. Downers Grove, IL: IVP Academic, 2019.

Shevelow, Kathryn. *For the Love of Animals: The Rise of the Animal Protection Movement*. New York: Holt, 2009.

Shults, LeRon F. *Reforming the Doctrine of God*. Grand Rapids, MI: Eerdmans, 2005.

Sibbes, Richard. "King David's Epitaph." In *The Complete Works of Richard Sibbes*, edited by Alexander Balloch Grosart, 6:487-516. Edinburgh: Nichol, 1863.

Simor, Suzanna B. "Faith Made Visible: Paintings of Apostle's Creed in Medieval Bohemia." *Kosmas* 25, no. 2 (2012): 1.

Skillen, James W. "From Covenant of Grace to Equitable Public Pluralism: The Dutch Calvinist Contribution." *CTJ* 31, no. 1 (1996): 67-96.

Sluka, R. D. *Hope for the Ocean: Marine Biodiversity, Poverty Alleviation and Blessing the Nations*. Cambridge: Grove Books, 2012.

Smit, M. C. *Toward a Christian Conception of History*. Edited by Harry Van Dyke and Herbert Donald Morton. Lanham, MD: University Press of America, 2002.

Smith, Christopher R. "Chiliasm and Recapitulation in the Theology of Ireneus [sic]." *Vigiliae Christianae* 48, no. 4 (1994): 313-31.

Smith, Gary V. *Isaiah 40–66*. New American Commentary 15B. Nashville: B&H, 2009.

Smith, James K. A. *Introducing Radical Orthodoxy: Mapping a Post-Secular Theology*. Grand Rapids, MI: Baker Academic, 2004.

———. "Reforming Public Theology: Two Kingdoms, or Two Cities?" *CTJ* 47 (2012): 122-37.

———. "Thinking Biblically About Culture: D. A. Carson's Christ and Culture Revisited." *Reformed Journal* 1 (February 2009).

Smith, Mark S. *The Early History of God: Yahweh and the Other Deities in Ancient Israel.* 2nd ed. Grand Rapids, MI: Eerdmans, 2002.

———. *The Memoirs of God.* Minneapolis: Fortress, 2004.

———. *The Origins of Biblical Monotheism: Israel's Polytheistic Background and the Ugaritic Texts.* New York: Oxford University Press, 2001.

Smith, Quentin. "The Metaphilosophy of Naturalism." *Philo* 4, no. 2 (2001): 195-215.

Snodgrass, Klyne R. *Stories with Intent: A Comprehensive Guide to the Parables of Jesus.* Grand Rapids, MI: Eerdmans, 2008.

Solzhenitsyn, Aleksandr. *The Gulag Archipelago: An Experiment in Literary Investigation.* New York: Harper Perennial, 2007.

Sommer, Brian D. *Revelation and Authority: Sinai in Jewish Scripture and Tradition.* New Haven, CT: Yale University Press, 2015.

Sonderegger, Katherine. "The Doctrine of Providence." In Murphy and Ziegler, *Providence of God*, 144-57.

Sontag, Frederick. "Anthropodicy and the Return of God." In Davis, *Encountering Evil*, 137-51.

Southgate, Christopher. *The Groaning of Creation: God, Evolution, and the Problem of Evil.* Edited by Rachel Muers and David Grummet. Louisville, KY: Westminster John Knox, 2008.

Speiser, E. A., ed. *Genesis.* 3rd ed. New York: Bantam Doubleday Dell, 1981.

Spence, Henry D. M. *The Complete Pulpit Commentary: Psalms to Song of Songs.* Harrington, DE: Delmarva, 2013.

Spencer, Nick, and Robert White. *Christianity, Climate Change and Sustainable Living.* London: SPCK, 2007.

Spicq, Ceslas. *L'Épître aux Hébreux.* Vol. 2. Etudes Bibliques. Paris: Gabalda, 1952.

Spykman, Gordon J. *Reformational Theology: A New Paradigm for Doing Dogmatics.* Grand Rapids, MI: Eerdmans, 1992.

———. "Sphere Sovereignty in John Calvin and the Calvinist Tradition." In *Exploring the Heritage of John Calvin*, edited by David E. Holwerda, 163-208. Grand Rapids, MI: Baker, 1976.

Srokosz, Meric, and Rebecca S. Watson. *Blue Planet, Blue God: The Bible and the Sea.* Norwich, UK: SCM Press, 2017.

Stanley, Jon. "Restoration and Renewal: The Nature of Grace in the Theology of Herman Bavinck." In *Revelation and Common Grace*, edited by John R. Bowlin. The Kuyper Center Review 2. Grand Rapids, MI: Eerdmans, 2011.

Stark, Rodney. *For the Glory of God: How Monotheism Led to Reformations, Science, Witch-Hunts, and the End of Slavery.* Princeton, NJ: Princeton University Press, 2003.

———. *One True God: Historical Consequences of Monotheism.* Princeton, NJ: Princeton University Press, 2001.

———. *The Victory of Reason: How Christianity Led to Freedom, Capitalism, and Western Success*. New York: Random House, 2007.

Steenberg, M. C. *Irenaeus on Creation: The Cosmic Christ and the Saga of Redemption*. Supplements to Vigiliae Christianae. Boston: Brill, 2008.

Stegner, Wallace. *Wolf Willow: A History, a Story, and a Memory of the Last Plains Frontier*. New York: Penguin Putnam, 1990.

Steiner, George. *Grammars of Creation*. New Haven, CT: Yale University Press, 2002.

———. *Nostalgia for the Absolute (Massey Lectures)*. Toronto: Canadian Broadcasting Corporation, 1974.

———. *Real Presences*. Chicago: University of Chicago Press, 1989.

Stock, Brian. *Literary Realism in the Later Ancient Period: The Legacy of Eric Auerbach*. Stanford, CA: Stanford University Press, 1996.

Stordalen, T. *Echoes of Eden: Genesis 2–3 and Symbolism of the Eden Garden in Biblical Hebrew Literature*. Contributions to Biblical Exegesis and Theology 25. Leuven: Peeters, 2000.

Stuart, Tristram. *Waste: Uncovering the Global Food Scandal*. New York: Norton, 2009.

Swinburne, Richard. *The Christian God*. Oxford: Clarendon Press, 1994.

———. *Is There a God?* New York: Oxford University Press, 1996.

Tanner, Kathryn. "Creation and Providence," In *The Cambridge Companion to Karl Barth*, edited by John Webster, 111-26. Cambridge: Cambridge University Press, 2000.

———. *God and Creation in Christian Theology*. Minneapolis: Fortress, 1988.

———. *Theories of Culture: A New Agenda for Theology*. Minneapolis: Fortress, 1997.

Taylor, Charles. *The Malaise of Modernity*. Toronto: House of Anansi, 1991.

———. *A Secular Age*. Cambridge, MA: Belknap Press, 2007.

———. *Sources of the Self: The Making of the Modern Identity*. Cambridge: Cambridge University Press, 1989.

Tertullian. *The Apology*. In *Ante-Nicene Fathers*, edited by Alexander Roberts and James Donaldson, vol. 3, *Latin Christianity: Its Founder, Tertullian*, edited by A. C. Coxe, translated by S. Thelwall. Buffalo, NY: Christian Literature Company, 1885.

———. *The Five Books Against Marcion*. In *Ante-Nicene Fathers*, edited by Alexander Roberts and James Donaldson, vol. 3, *Latin Christianity: Its Founder, Tertullian*, edited by A. C. Coxe, translated by S. Thelwall. Buffalo, NY: Christian Literature Company, 1885.

Thiselton, Anthony C. *New Horizons in Hermeneutics*. Grand Rapids, MI: Zondervan, 1992.

Thomas, Keith. *Man and the Natural World: Changing Attitudes in England, 1500–1800*. Oxford: Oxford University Press, 1983.

Tjørhom, Ola. *Embodied Faith: Reflections on a Materialist Spirituality*. Grand Rapids, MI: Eerdmans, 2009.

Tolkien, J. R. R. *The Tolkien Reader*. New York: Ballantine, 1966.

Toon, Peter. *The Development of Doctrine in the Church*. Grand Rapids, MI: Eerdmans, 1979.

Toorn, Karel van der, Bob Becking, and Pieter W. van der Horst, eds. *Dictionary of Deities and Demons in the Bible*. 2nd ed. Grand Rapids, MI: Eerdmans, 1999.

Torrance, Thomas F. *Christian Theology and Scientific Culture*. Eugene, OR: Wipf & Stock, 1998.

Toulim, S. E., and J. Goodfield. *The Discovery of Time*. Chicago: University of Chicago Press, 1965.

Tov, Emmanuel. "Post-Modern Textual Criticism?" In *Greek Scripture and the Rabbis*, ed. Timothy Michael Law and Alison Salvesen, 19-38. Leuven: Peeters, 2012.

Tsumura, Toshio. "Symbolism of the Sea in the Old Testament." MTh thesis, Asbury Theological Seminary, 1969.

Tuplin, Christopher. *Achaemenid Studies*. Stuttgart: Steiner, 1996.

Turner, Nigel. *A Grammar of New Testament Greek*. Vol. 3, *Syntax*. Edinburgh: T&T Clark, 1963.

Tzamalikos, Panayiotis. *Origen: Philosophy of History and Eschatology*. Leiden: Brill, 2007.

Van Dyke, Harry. "Groen van Prinsterer: Godfather of Bavinck and Kuyper." *CTJ* 47, no. 1 (2012): 72-97.

———. *Groen van Prinsterer's Lectures on Unbelief and Revolution*. Jordan Station, ON: Wedge Publishing Foundation, 1989.

Van Till, Howard J. *The Fourth Day*. Grand Rapids, MI: Eerdmans, 1989.

Van Till, Howard J., Robert E. Snow, John H. Stek, and Davis A. Young. *Portraits of Creation: Biblical and Scientific Perspectives on the World's Formation*. Grand Rapids, MI: Eerdmans, 1990.

Vanderburg, Willem H. *Our War on Ourselves: Rethinking Science, Technology, and Economic Growth*. Toronto: University of Toronto Press, 2012.

VanDrunen, David. *Natural Law and the Two Kingdoms: A Study in the Development of Reformed Social Thought*. Grand Rapids, MI: Eerdmans, 2010.

Vanhoozer, Kevin. *Remythologizing Theology: Divine Action, Passion, and Authorship*. Cambridge: Cambridge University Press, 2010.

Vaughan, C. R. *The Gifts of the Holy Spirit: To Unbelievers and Believers*. Carlisle, PA: Banner of Truth Trust, 1975.

Veenhof, Jan. *Nature and Grace in Herman Bavinck*. Translated by Albert M. Wolters. Sioux Center, IA: Dordt College Press, 2006.

Veith, Gene Edward, Jr. "Two Kingdoms Under One King: Towards a Lutheran Approach to Culture," in *Christ and Culture in Dialogue*, edited by Angus J. L. Menuge, 129-44. St. Louis: Concordia Academic Press, 1999.

Veldhuis, N. *Religion, Literature, and Scholarship: The Sumerian Composition Nanše and the Birds*. Leiden: Brill/Styx, 2004.

Verheij, A. J. C. "Paradise Retried: On Qohelet 2:4-6." *JSOT* 50 (1991): 113-15.

Voegelin, Eric. *Science, Politics, and Gnosticism*. Translated by William J. Fitzpatrick. Washington, DC: Regnery, 1968, 1997.

Walker, Andrew. *God and the Transgender Debate*. London: The Good Book Company, 2017.

Walsh, Jerome T. "Genesis 2:4b–3:24: A Synchronic Approach." *Journal of Biblical Literature* 96, no. 2 (1977): 161-77.

Waltke, Bruce K., with Charles Yu. *An Old Testament Theology: An Exegetical, Canonical, and Thematic Approach*. Grand Rapids, MI: Zondervan, 2007.

Ward, Graham. "Barth, Modernity and Postmodernity." In *The Cambridge Companion to Karl Barth*, ed. John Webster, 274-95. Cambridge: Cambridge University Press, 2000.

Watkins, Peter, and Jonathan Stockland. *Winged Wonders: A Celebration of Birds in Human History*. New York: Blue Bridge, 2007.

Webb, Stephen H. *Good Eating*. The Christian Practice of Everyday Life. Grand Rapids, MI: Brazos, 2001.

Webber, Robert E. *The Church in the World: Opposition, Tension, or Transformation?* Grand Rapids, MI: Zondervan, 1986.

Webster, John. "On the Theology of Providence." In Murphy and Ziegler, *Providence of God*, 158-78.

Weil, Simone. *Gateway to God*. Edited by David Raper. London: Fontana, 1974.

Weinandy, Thomas G. *Athanasius: A Theological Introduction*. Burlington, VT: Ashgate, 2007.

Wenham, Gordon J. *The Book of Leviticus*. NICOT. Grand Rapids, MI: Eerdmans, 1979.

———. "Genesis." In *New Bible Commentary*, 4th ed., edited by G. J. Wenham, J. A. Motyer, D. A. Carson, and R. T. France. Downers Grove, IL: IVP Academic, 1994.

———. *Genesis 1–15*. WBC 1. Waco, TX: Word, 1987.

———. "Sanctuary Symbolism in the Garden of Eden Story." In Morales, *Cult and Cosmos*, 161-66.

Westermann, Claus. *Creation*. Philadelphia: Fortress, 1974.

———. *Genesis 1–11: A Commentary*. Translated by John J. Scullion. Minneapolis: Augsburg, 1984.

Westra, Liuwe. *The Apostles' Creed; Origin, History and Some Early Commentaries*. Research on the Inheritance of Early and Medieval Christianity 43. Turnhout: Brepols, 2002.

White, Ellen. *Yahweh's Council: Its Structure and Membership*. Forschungen Zum Alten Testament 2/65. Tübingen: Mohr Siebeck, 2014.

White, Gilbert F. *The Illustrated Natural History of Selborne*. London: Thames and Hudson, 1981.

———. *The Natural History and Antiquities of Selborne*. Menston, UK: Scolar Press, 1970.

White, Nicholas P. *Plato on Knowledge and Reality*. Indianapolis: Hackett, 1976.

White, Vernon. *Purpose and Providence: Taking Soundings in Western Thought, Literature and Theology*. London: T&T Clark, 2015.

Whitehead, Alfred North. *Process and Reality: An Essay in Cosmology*. Corrected ed. Edited by David Ray Griffin and Donald W. Sherburne. New York: Free Press, 1978.

Wiggins, Steve A. *Weathering the Psalms: A Meterological Survey*. Eugene, OR: Cascade Books, 2014.

Wiles, Maurice F. *What Is Theology?* Oxford: Oxford University Press, 1986.

Wilken, Robert Louis. "The Beauty of Centipedes and Toads." In Meconi, *On Earth as It Is in Heaven*, 17-26.

———. *The Spirit of Early Christian Thought: Seeking the Face of God*. New Haven, CT: Yale University Press, 2003.

Williams, Michael D. "Systematic Theology as a Biblical Discipline." in *All for Jesus: A Celebration of the 50th Anniversary of Covenant Theological Seminary*, edited by Robert A. Peterson and Sean Michael Lucas, 167-96. Fearn, UK: Mentor, 2006.

Williams, Raymond. *Keywords: A Vocabulary of Culture and Society*. Oxford: Oxford University Press, 1976.

Williams, Rowan. "'Good For Nothing'? Augustine on Creation." *Augustinian Studies* 25 (1994): 9-24.

Wilson, Edward O. *The Creation: An Appeal to Save Life on Earth*. New York: Norton, 2006.

Wingren, Gustaf. *Man and the Incarnation: A Study in the Biblical Theology of Irenaeus*. Translated by R. MacKenzie. Eugene, OR: Wipf & Stock, 1959.

Wink, Walter. *Naming the Powers: The Language of Power in the New Testament*. Philadelphia: Fortress, 1984.

———. *Unmasking the Powers: The Invisible Forces That Determine Human Existence*. Philadelphia: Fortress, 1986.

Wirzba, Norman. *Food and Faith: A Theology of Eating*. New York: Cambridge University Press, 2011.

Wittgenstein, Ludwig. *Philosophical Investigations*. 2nd ed. Translated by G. E. M. Anscombe. Oxford: Blackwell, 1997.

———. *Wittgenstein's Lectures, Cambridge 1932–1935*. Edited by Alice Ambrose. Oxford: Blackwell, 1979.

Wolters, Albert M. "Creation and the 'Powers': A Dialogue with Lesslie Newbigin." *Trinity Journal for Theology and Ministry* 4 (2010): 85-98.

———. *Creation Regained: Biblical Basics for a Reformational Worldview*. 2nd ed. Grand Rapids, MI: Eerdmans, 2005.

———. "Worldview and Textual Criticism in 2 Peter 3:10." *Westminster Theological Journal* 49, no. 2 (1987): 405-13.

Wolterstorff, Nicholas. *Art in Action*. Grand Rapids, MI: Eerdmans, 1980.

———. *Reason Within the Bounds of Religion*. 2nd ed. Grand Rapids, MI: Eerdmans, 1984.

———. *Until Justice and Peace Embrace*. Grand Rapids, MI: Eerdmans, 1983.

Wood, Charles M. *The Question of Providence*. Louisville, KY: Westminster John Knox, 2008.

Wood, Donald. "Maker of Heaven and Earth." *IJST* 14, no. 4 (2012): 381-95.

Woodhead, Linda, Paul Heelas, and David Martin, eds. *Peter Berger and the Study of Religion*. London: Routledge, 2001.

Wright, G. Ernest. *God Who Acts: Biblical Theology as Recital.* London: SCM Press, 1952.

Wright, N. T. "The Lord's Prayer as a Paradigm for Christian Prayer." In *Into God's Presence: Prayer in the New Testament*, edited by Richard N. Longenecker, 132-54. Grand Rapids, MI: Eerdmans, 2001.

———. *The New Testament and the People of God.* Minneapolis: Fortress, 1992.

———. *Paul for Everyone: Romans, Part One.* Louisville, KY: Westminster John Knox, 2015.

———. *The Resurrection of the Son of God.* Minneapolis: Fortress, 2003.

———. *Simply Jesus: A New Vision of Who He Was, What He Did, and Why He Matters.* New York: HarperOne, 2011.

———. *Surprised by Hope: Rethinking Heaven, the Resurrection, and the Mission of the Church.* New York: HarperOne, 2008.

Yoder, John Howard. *The Politics of Jesus.* 2nd ed. Grand Rapids, MI: Eerdmans, 1994.

———. "Trinity Versus Theodicy: Hebraic Realism and the Temptation to Judge God." In *The Trinity and Theodicy: The Trinitarian Theology of von Balthasar and the Problem of Evil.* Farnham, UK: Ashgate, 2013.

Young, Davis A., and Ralph F. Stearley. *The Bible, Rocks and Time: Geological Evidence for the Age of the Earth.* Downers Grove, IL: IVP Academic, 2008.

Zahrnt, Heinz. *The Question of God: Protestant Theology in the Twentieth Century.* New York: Harcourt, Brace & World, 1969.

Zakowitch, Yair. "Reflection Story—Another Dimension of the Evaluation of Characters in Biblical Narrative." *Tarbit* 54, no. 2 (1985): 165-76 (in Hebrew).

Zhiming, Yuan, and Chen Shangyu. *Lao Tzu and the Bible.* Bloomington, IN: Authorhouse, 2010.

Zimmerli, Walther. *Old Testament Theology in Outline.* Edinburgh: T&T Clark, 1978.

Zobel, H. K. "Seba'ot." In *Theological Dictionary of the Old Testament*, translated by Douglas W. Stott, edited by G. Johannes Botterweck, Helmer Ringgren, and Heinz-Josef Fabry, 12:215-32. Grand Rapids, MI: Eerdmans, 2003.

Zondervan, Antonius A. W. *Sociology and the Sacred: An Introduction to Philip Rieff's Theory of Culture.* Toronto: University of Toronto Press, 2005.

Zvi, Ehud Ben, and Christoph Levin, eds. *Thinking of Water in the Early Second Temple Period.* Berlin: de Gruyter, 2014.

Zylstra, Bernard. Preface to *The Relation of the Bible to Learning*, by H. Evan Runner, 9-34. Jordan Station, ON: Paideia, 1982.

NAME INDEX

SUBJECT INDEX

SCRIPTURE INDEX